T5-AXM-988

SERMONS

AUGUSTINIAN HERITAGE INSTITUTE

THE WORKS OF SAINT AUGUSTINE
A Translation for the 21st Century

Part III — Sermons
Volume 11: Newly Discovered Sermons

The English translation of the works of Saint Augustine has been made possible with contributions from the following:

Order of Saint Augustine

> Province of Saint Thomas of Villanova (East)
> Province of Our Mother of Good Counsel (Midwest)
> Province of Saint Augustine (California)
> Province of Saint Joseph (Canada)
> Vice Province of Our Mother of Good Counsel
> Province of Our Mother of Good Counsel (Ireland)
> Province of Saint John Stone (England and Scotland)
> Province of Our Mother of Good Counsel (Australia)
> The Augustinians of the Assumption (North America)
> The Sisters of Saint Thomas of Villanova

Order of Augustinian Recollects

> Province of Saint Augustine

Mr. and Mrs. James C. Crouse
Mr. and Mrs. Paul Henkels
Mr. and Mrs. Francis E. McGill, Jr.
Mr. and Mrs. Mariano J. Rotelle

THE WORKS OF SAINT AUGUSTINE

A Translation for the 21st Century

SERMONS

III/11
Newly Discovered Sermons

translation and notes

Edmund Hill, O.P.

editor

John E. Rotelle, O.S.A.

New City Press

Hyde Park, New York

Published in the United States by New City Press
202 Cardinal Rd., Hyde Park, New York 12538
©1997 Augustinian Heritage Institute

Library of Congress Cataloging-in-Publication Data:

Augustine, Saint, Bishop of Hippo.
    The works of Saint Augustine.

    "Augustinian Heritage Institute"
    Includes bibliographical references and indexes.
    Contents: — pt. 3, v. 11. Newly Discovered Sermons.—pt. 3, v. 1. Sermons on the Old
Testament, 1-19. — pt. 3, v. 2. Sermons on the Old Testament, 20-50 — [et al.] — pt. 3,
v. 10 Sermons on various subjects, 341-400.
    1. Theology — Early church, ca. 30-600.   I. Hill,
Edmund. II. Rotelle, John E.   III. Augustinian
Heritage Institute.   IV. Title.
BR65.A5E53 1990   270.2   89-28878
ISBN 1-56548-055-4 (series)
ISBN 1-56548-103-8 (pt. 3, v. 11)

The original Latin text for the majority of these sermons can be found in *Augustin D'Hippone,
Vingt-six Sermons au Peuple à Afrique Retrouvés à Mayence, édités et commentés par François
Dolbeau*, Collection des Études Augustiniennes, Série Antiquité-147 (Institut d'Études
Augustiniennes, Paris: 1966) 756 pages.

Nihil Obstat: John E. Rotelle, O.S.A., S.T.L.
Censor Deputatus
Imprimatur: + Patrick Sheridan, D.D.,
Vicar General
Archdiocese of New York, June 2, 1997

Printed in the United States

CONTENTS

How can we repay God for all his benefits?—48; How to be truthful, when every man is a liar—49; Repay the Lord by taking the cup of salvation—49; Returning Christ's hospitality by sharing his sufferings—50; Do not claim more credit than you are worth—51; If you fix your eye on him, he will nowhere appear—52

God's providence often denied, because bad people do well in life, and good people badly—55; God's providence to be seen first in the order that governs our natural constitution—56; The providence detectable in the order of nature must also govern the lives and behavior of human beings—58; Scripture's assertion of divine providence—59; If human reason naturally prefers order to disorder, how much more must the divine Wisdom?—60; For believers, Christ himself is the surest proof of a loving and caring divine providence—61

Two meanings of "confession"—64; Punish yourself, to avoid being punished by God—65; Praise God for your good works, blame yourself for your bad ones—66

He continues reflecting on Ps 4—69; Peace is the reward of good works and of patience—70; The true peace we seek is not to be found here—70; The light of God's features stamped on us is the image of God in the soul—71; The highest good is to be found in the heart, not in the world outside—72; Contrast between "the many" and "the single one"—72; The meaning of dwelling singly in hope—73; We must love God freely, for nothing—74; God, the good of all goods—74

We too must ask the question about the great commandment—77; A compendium of the whole law—77; A problem—78; We begin by considering love of neighbor—79; Merely natural love not enough—79; Love of neighbor presupposes love of self; true love of self presupposes love of God—80; We want those we love to enjoy what we love; the example of sports fans—81; Finding God means finding oneself; the prodigal son—82; Two commandments necessary; but by fulfilling either, you fulfil the other also—83; It's faith that obtains love, through God's mercy, not our own merits—84

Mercy first, judgment next—87; "Believe in the gospel" said to unbelievers—87; "Repent" also said to catechumens and some of the faithful—88; The temptation to put it off till tomorrow—89; The charge that God's promise of forgiveness is an encouragement to sin—90; The dangers of misplaced hope—91; The danger of despair—92; Nothing more to be said; something to be done—92

Christ's miracles are, so to say, visible words—95; Unless you repent, you shall all likewise perish—96; The meaning of the numbers in the whole passage—98; The whole human race exhorted to repent—99

Augustine preaching extempore on a passage of the gospel which he had not chosen himself; the comparison of the flood with the day of judgment—102; An urgent appeal for conversion of life; the two ways—103; So many reasons for following the way pointed out by Christ—104; Get a passage on board the ark, or get built into its very structure—106; The difficulties of the passage need to be explained—107; The camel through the eye of a needle—107; Christ himself is the camel going through the needle's eye—108; The rich can be saved, the poor can be damned—109; What the rich must do to enter the kingdom—110; Other difficulties of the passage dealt with—111; Grumbling about the hard times; blaming Christ—112; The human race one huge invalid; Christ the doctor—113

The work of God is to believe in the one whom he has sent—118; The difference between believing in someone and believing someone—119; Why, then, the commandments?—120; Believing in Christ means loving him in a unique way—122; To love like that, we need to be converted by God—122; To receive God's grace, we must know our weakness—123; The difference between my own justice and that which is by faith—124; The full meaning of turning to God—126

Church discipline does not allow catechumens to be buried in the same ground as the baptized faithful—131; Catechumens should be in a hurry to be baptized—131; Perhaps the poor man Lazarus never had decent burial; but angels carried him to Abraham's bosom—132; Believe Christ, that his yoke is easy; and hasten to receive the sacrament of grace—132

Who will separate us from the charity of Christ?—135; Cajolery as well as savagery can separate us from Christ—136; How to secure the doors of fear and of desire—136; Threats to the flesh are the hardest to withstand, because the flesh is the very garment of the soul—137; If you disregard all these things, your freedom is secure—137; If God is for us, who is against us?—137; Have you anything to add to that?—138; An apparent conflict between two commandments—138; How a wife can support her cajolery from the law—139; Specious arguments from scripture can be answered from scripture as Christ answered the devil in the third temptation—140; The analogy of the wife's case against her in-laws—140; The case of God against the wife—141; Women martyrs too have withstood cajolery from their menfolk—142; One must hate even one's own soul—142; The limits of the claims of human affection—143

brought from Palestine by Palatinus—313; What is wrong with the heresy; it denies our need of grace—313; The Pelagians abolish the need to pray as Christ taught us—314; Asking not be led into temptation means asking to be saved from things like breaking a leg—315; Jesus prayed for Peter, that his faith might not fail—316; Pelagianism empties all blessings of any meaning—316; Our freedom of choice is implied by commands to do good; our need for grace by prayers that we may carry them out—317

INTRODUCTION

The thirty sermons of Augustine collected here have been discovered since 1989.[1] Before that date twenty-one of them were completely unknown; the other nine circulated in forms that were so truncated or reworked that the power and interest of the discourses had been diminished. Since Augustine preached four or five times a week on the average, a collection of this size amounts to a month and a half of preaching, which internal criticism makes it possible to assign, in blocks of very unequal size, to the period from 397 to 416. That is, of course, not very much when compared to the 546 sermons already inventoried or to the 76 years of the saint's life. On the other hand, some of the new texts are of a really exceptional quality that is due at once to the circumstances in which they were preached and to the manner in which they were passed on. Sixteen centuries after they were spoken, the words of Augustine remain alive and are given back to us in the freshness they have in the original copies. Despite themselves, readers of them are changed into hearers. I thank Edmund Hill for having translated these thirty sermons with the care and lively style they call for.[2]

There is no point to repeating here what Cardinal Michele Pellegrino has said so well in his general introduction on the preaching of Augustine.[3] The texts of the present volume add little to what we already know about the circumstances of place and time, the themes taken up, the audience, or, finally, Augustine's own overall conception of the ministry of the word.[4] Rather they complete our information by dealing with novel passages of the Bible (Dolbeau [D.] 6, 14, 20, 23-24) or by placing the speaker in new situations: baited by his hearers (D. 2), called upon to rule on the burial of a catechumen (D. 7), faced by a sizable group of pagans (D. 25), rejoicing at the return of a schismatic brother to orthodoxy (D. 27), recovering from an illness (D. 28), or forced, in order to scotch rumors, to denounce the heresy of Pelagius (D. 30).

Four of the new texts (D. 1 and 28-30) are "strayers" (*extravagantes*), that is, they have come down to us in isolation. The other 26 (D. 2-27) are taken from the same manuscript: a collection of sermons for the use of the Carthusians of Mainz (Mainz, Stadtbibliothek, I 9) that dates from 1470-1475.[5] The collection was based on two exemplars that have now been lost, each of them containing an old series of Augustine's sermons. The first series, according to the catalogue of a ninth century library, was vouched for at one time in a renowned abbey, Saint Nazarius in Lorsch (in the German state of Hesse)[6]; the second, present in Hippo during the lifetime of its author,[7] was known, in an incomplete form, thanks to an edition of the sixteenth century that was based on a lost manuscript of the Grande Chartreuse (in the French Alps).[8] The two collections are therefore known as the "Mainz-Lorsch" and the "Mainz-Grande Chartreuse" respectively; the two collections contain sermons D. 2, 21-27 and D. 8-20, respectively.[9] It is important, then, to distinguish two levels in the Mainz manuscript. Materially, it is a book from the humanist period, copied with the forms of writing and the punctuation used at the end of the fifteenth century; textually, it is a kind of fossil, since it combines two series of sermons that preserve, in large measure, the organization and rubrics of collections from late antiquity.

As we shall see, the newly discovered sermons have quite varied subjects, but they all have one trait in common: the fact of having been little circulated in the middle ages and having been, for this reason, protected from too many inroads of copyists. In some cases (D. 2, 6-7, 24, 27) the subject of the discourse is so specialized, so connected with a society and a period, that in practice it excluded any reuse in the middle ages. The failure of some explanations of the scriptures (D. 8-9, 20, etc.) is due no doubt to the nonliturgical character of the verses commented on. On the other hand, many sermons deal with subjects that are always relevant (D. 11: love of God and neighbor; D. 12: conjugal life; etc.), and it is difficult to explain, except by the operation of chance, why they were not circulated among educated people of the middle ages.

Of the "straying" sermons, the first, to tell the truth, hardly deserves the title of "sermon": it is made up of five fragments of an "explanation of the creed" that are taken from an anthology of the Irish grammarian and poet, Sedulius Scottus; they amount in all to about a dozen lines. Their main interest is to show that in the ninth century there was another Augustinian explanation of the creed besides the ones we possess. This text is, then, a sermon "in hope" rather than "in fact": that is, it gives us the hope, and at the same time the tool, of a future discovery. That kind of optimism is not excessive, since it was in this way that the final three sermons of the volume were identified. Numbers 28 (on bodily health), 29 (on providence), and 30 (on Pelagius) contain various fragments to be found respectively in Bartholomew of Urbino and Eugippus.[10] The process of discovery consisted essentially in moving from these fragments back to a complete copy, by taking advantage of the possibilities offered by data processing and by modern catalogues of manuscript collections.[11] Since there still exist about thirty authentic passages which we know solely through medieval documents,[12] the method I just described should again prove fruitful, provided one be aided by chance or the God of Augustine. If, then, this "translation for the twenty-first century" is to be complete, it will doubtless be necessary—in a more or less proximate future, depending on progress in research and in the study of catalogues—to take in hand a further volume of sermons.

Without being completely homogeneous, the Mainz-Lorsch and Mainz-

Grande Chartreuse collections have a kind of thematic unity that is by definition missing in the "stray" sermons. Readers will therefore find it worth their while to read through each collection, despite my numbering of the texts.[13] The Mainz-Lorsch series (D. 2-7, 21-27) reflects the pastoral situation in the African Church during the first decade of the fifth century. The situation was rather explosive, since the emperors had promulgated harsh laws against pagan cults (starting in 399) and then against the Donatist schism (starting in 405). Augustine tries to calm the minds of people, to answer the intellectual objections of educated pagans, to restore the unity of African society at the religious level, and to lead recent converts to an authentically Christian life (for example, by having them avoid banquets and shows). He stresses, among other points, that it is unjust to attribute the evils of the age to Christians; that the isolation of the Donatists is destroying their claim to be the true Church; and, finally, that the Jewish prophets had foretold the closing of the pagan temples and the destruction of idols. In one of the sermons (D. 4, no. 8) the speaker calls to mind—and this is most rare—the police investigations of pagans who still participated in forbidden cults.

The Mainz-Grande Chartreuse series (D. 8-20) is organized according to the liturgical calendar, from May to August of a year which scholars at one time thought they could pin down to 397.[14] In fact, this organization of the collection may be secondary and may mask the merging, by a librarian in Hippo, of several preaching missions in Carthage.[15] In any case, the earliest part of the series seems to go back to the beginnings of Augustine's episcopate. Most of the sermons (among the thirty translated here as in the approximately twenty already known[16]) comment on passages of the Bible. In them Augustine maintains, against Jerome, that neither Jesus nor Paul twisted the truth; he defends the dignity of marriage against criticisms from ascetic circles and proves the consistency of the scriptures, which was denied by anonymous adversaries, very probably Manichees. The conversion of pagans and the winning over of the Donatists, which constituted the pastoral horizon of the Mainz-Lorsch series, are not on the agenda here.

The variety of subjects and the observable differences between the two series show that Augustine had a great ability to renew himself and a determination to tackle the problems that were worrying his contemporaries. The speaker carries on a lively and colloquial dialogue with his listeners and takes positions in ongoing debates. In my experience as an editor, the Mainz collection, like the Wolfenbüttel homiliary of yore, contains sermons that are more anchored in the reality of the fourth and fifth centuries and closer to the spoken word than the average sermons published by the Maurists in their day. Analysis of the Mainz-Lorsch and Mainz-Grande Chartreuse collections, and especially of the nine texts previously read in a truncated[17] or a revised[18] form, sheds a new light on the transmission of ancient homilies.

In dealing with sermons, the traditional idea of authenticity should be linked henceforth to that of the integrity of texts. The line presently drawn between "authentic" and "apocryphal" is too watertight. The Maurists applied a third concept, the "doubtful sermon," which ought to be revived, since it corresponds to a well-defined phenomenon in the history of transmission. Like the columns of pagan temples in Christian buildings, the sermons of Augustine were reused by medieval preachers in new pastoral "constructions." Thus there exist blended texts, for example, Sermon 97A,[19] in which passages of Augustine rub shoulders with connecting components. To retain them among the authentic sermons would be a disservice; to place them in the category of apocrypha pure and simple would be to lose a good deal of information.

Despite the many but scattered remarks of my predecessors,[20] scholars continue to allow too little room for the activities of medieval clerics who wanted to make use of Augustine's sermons in other liturgical settings. The work of those men was sometimes crude: a blow of the chisel right in the middle of a line of thought gave them a reading of the length they wanted.[21] But their work could also be more discerning and, in the end, more tricky for modern criticism: they would carefully eliminate difficult words, technical discussions of biblical variants, and references to fifth-century events or dead controversies; that is, they would cut out everything that had become unfamiliar to a medieval audience.[22] The texts thus handled retain their Augustinian tonality and provide no toehold for a critique of authenticity, and yet if we chance to unearth their original form, we see that they have been mutilated and robbed of their originality in their smallest details. In Kunzelmann's opinion,[23] Sermons Frangipane 7 (293A) and Mai 19 (299A) contained nothing on which a discussion of chronology could be based. Their unretouched versions (D. 3-4) can be dated, with the slightest margin of error, to 407 and 405. The difference is due to the fact that the medieval author of truncated forms had eliminated, without forgetting even a single point, all of the speaker's topical allusions to his own period.

The eliminations were often drastic: there is almost a 60% difference between Dolbeau 22 and Sermon 341, a five-sixths difference between Dolbeau 23 and Sermon 374, and there are over 1500 lines in Dolbeau 26 as compared to about sixty in Sermon 198. In speaking to an African audience that loved fine language, Augustine could be verbose; moreover, as a good public speaker, he knew how periodically to revive the attention of the faithful with a question or a play on words. But a read text quickly tires its hearers, and an audience of the early middle ages needed to make an effort to understand the language of the Fathers. The cuts which medieval clerics made were, therefore, understandable; moderns must take them into account when they want to make the most of Augustine's sermons.

In dealing with any sermon the first question of historians or theologians should always be: Is the accepted text complete? In answering, they must first rely on internal criticism. Has the sermon kept its exordium, its rhetorical transitions, and its peroration? Does the speaker make allusions, is he impulsive, is he attentive to his listeners? Does he carry on a dialogue with the crowd? Negative answers to these questions are rather troubling. A second, less subjective criterion is the type of transmission. Documents provided by "ancient" collections, that is, by medieval collections of sermons that reproduce, with a minimum of alteration, collections from late antiquity, offer the best guarantees of integrity and authenticity.[24] On the other hand, sermons altered in the milieu of Caesarius of Arles or compiled for practical uses by later well-read persons, such as the *De verbis domini et apostoli*, are very likely to be mixtures of good grain and weeds. Finally, sermons scattered about in patristic homiliaries, without being connected with any known collection, provide the worst examples: it may be that by chance they are complete and authentic, but there is a very high probability of their having been mutilated, robbed of their originality, or interpolated. This criterion—the kind of transmission—is a major one, though unfortunately not decisive, since extensive deletions sometimes occurred very early, as can be seen in the truncated form of Dolbeau 22-23 that are attested as early as the beginning of the seventh century[25]; thus even the earliest collections do not provide an absolute guarantee.

Most of the sermons that follow here have been, apart from material accident, preserved in their integral form and depend on ancient series by way of a very small number of links. As a result, they abound in references to current events and are altogether remarkable monuments of oral literature. Many texts can be accurately dated because of events mentioned by the preacher (solemn entrance of Emperor Honorius into Rome; contemporary destruction of pagan statues; acquittal of Pelagius at the Council of Diospolis; and so on). Many, too, have not undergone any stylistic revision and allow us to hear the very voice of the speaker, hardly distorted by the shorthand versions of the secretaries that were then written out in full. Augustine sometimes improvises from one end of a sermon to the other, as on the Sunday when he had expected to explain Psalm 147 but was diverted by the riches of a gospel pericope (D. 5). Ordinarily, he paints a picture from the scriptures—on which he has meditated beforehand—but always while letting himself be guided by the reactions of his audience. Signs of fatigue among them lead him to shorten his trains of thought; questions springing from the throng lead him along unexpected paths; manifestations of incomprehension give rise to recapitulations or repetitions. Digressions due to occurrences during the assembly or to sudden inspirations mean that the peroration is sometimes quite unrelated to the theme announced in the exordium (see D. 10), as Augustine admitted in conversation with a friend.[26]

If one reads aloud the translations of Edmund Hill, one gets an idea of what Augustine's biographer was trying to convey when he wrote, shortly after the saint's death: "Those who read his religious writings profit by them and acknowledge [his holiness]. But I think that they profited even more who saw him in person and heard him speaking in the church."[27] As a Manichean adversary put it, Augustine was truly a kind of "god" of eloquence, as Plato had been of philosophy.[28]

NOTES

1. Details about them, as well as references to editions, are given in an appendix.

2. And also for having suggested some original conjectures in some passages that have been poorly preserved in Latin.

3. *The Works of Saint Augustine* III/1 (New York, 1990) 13-137. Apart from Pellegrino's study, the best presentation of the homiletic genre is that of Alejandro Olivar, *La predicación cristiana antigua* (Barcelona, 1991).

4. The most unexpected bit of information concerns the posture of the preacher. It used to be thought that Augustine regularly preached while sitting, as a teacher in his chair; see Olivar, 735-736. References to the preacher standing, hitherto rare, are in the majority since the publication of Dolbeau 2 (nos. 10 and 23), 5 (no. 16), 10 (no. 7), and 25 (no. 5). See: Augustin d'Hippone, *Vingt-six sermons au peuple d'Afrique* (Paris, 1996) 39, 319, and 426.

5. See F. Dolbeau, "Le sermonnaire augustinien de Mayence (Mainz, Stadtbibliothek I 9): Analyse et histoire," *Revue Bénédictine* 106 (1996) 5-52.

6. See P.-P. Verbraken, *Études critiques sur les sermons authentiques de saint Augustin* (Instrumenta patristica 12; Steenbrugge, 1976) 232-233.

7. According to Possidius, Augustine's biographer, in the *Indiculum operum sancti Augustini* (no. X[6]. 102-33); ed. A. Wilmart in *Miscellanea Agostiniana* 2 (Rome, 1931) 161-208, especially 200-202.

8. See C. Lambot, "Le catalogue de Possidius et la collection Carthusienne de sermons de saint Augustin," *Revue Bénédictine* 60 (1950) 3-7.

9. This numbering respects the organization of the book of sermons, in which the Mainz-Grande Chartreuse series is set within the Mainz-Lorsch series.

10. These scholars, who lived, the former in the fourteenth century, the latter in the sixth, compiled the most extensive anthologies of Augustine presently known.

11. See F. Dolbeau, "Un sermon inédit de saint Augustin sur la santé corporelle, partiellement cité chez Barthélemy d'Urbino," *Revue des Études Augustiniennes* 40 (1994) 279-303, especially 299-303 ("A la recherche de sermons égarés d'Augustin"); idem, "Localisation de deux fragments homilétiques reproduits par Eugippe dans son florilège augustinien," *ibid.* 41 (1995) 19-35.

12. Most of these have been inventoried by P.-P. Verbraken, "Les fragments conservés de sermons perdus de saint Augustin," *Revue Bénédictine* 84 (1974) 245-70. At that time he counted 47 entries; the discoveries made since then by Raymond Étaix and myself have lowered this number by 18. But Verbraken's numbers 1, 5-13, 24-26, 28-40, 43, 45, and 47, to which should be added Dolbeau 1 and Étaix 4 (*The Works of Saint Augustine* III/6, 101), still need to be placed in their context. In addition, to be classed as *fragmenta dubia* are the incipits and extracts of the sermons discussed in *Revue d'Histoire des Textes* 23 (1993) 144, note 4 and 155, note 7, and in *Revue des Études Augustiniennes* 40 (1994) 302.

13. This numbering, without being arbitrary (see note 9, above), has the drawback of cutting one of the collections into two parts.

14. See D. De Bruyne, "La chronologie de quelques sermons de saint Augustin," *Revue Bénédictine* 43 (1931) 185-193; C. Lambot, "Un *ieiunium quinquagesimae* en Afrique au IVe siècle and Date de quelques sermons de S. Augustin," *ibid.,* 47 (1935) 114-124; O. Perler and J.-L. Maier, *Les voyages de saint Augustin* (Paris, 1969) 215-221.

15. The work in progress of P.-M. Humbert should shed light on this difficult question.

16. Namely, sermons 101 (Wilmart 20), 60, 145, 150, 285, 266, 7, 28, 133, 89, 177, 160, 104 (Guelferbytanus 29), 293, 294, 299, 299E (Guelferbytanus 30), 302 (Guelferbytanus 25), 306.

17. Dolbeau 3-4, 15-16, 22-23, 26, 30.

18. Dolbeau 5.

19. Which was thought to be authentic, but wrongly, as a reading of Dolbeau 5 (nos. 18, 20-21) makes plainly clear; see *Vingt-six sermons*, 243, 260, 262-263.

20. See especially C. Lambot, "Sermons complètes, fragments de sermons perdus, allocution inédite de saint Augustin," *Revue Bénédictine* 51 (1939) 3-30.

21. In this way Dolbeau 3 became Frangipane 7 (in the recension preserved in manuscript Monte Cassino 12 of the eleventh century); see *Vingt-six sermons*, 482-483.

22. See *Vingt-six sermons*, 120 (on Dolbeau 16), 509-510 (D. 4), 521-523 ("Sermons incomplets, mutilés, tronqués, remaniés").

23. A. Kunzelmann, "Die Chronologie der Sermones des hl. Augustinus," *Miscellanea Agostiniana* 2 (Rome, 1931) 417-520, especially 428.

24. The same holds for items that circulated, independently of sermon collections, along with the short works of Augustine; this is the case with Dolbeau 28-30.

25. *Vingt-six sermons*, 527-531 (Sermon 341) and 580-581 (Sermon 374).

26. Possidius, *Life of Augustine* 15, 1-6.

27. *Ibid.,* 31, 9.

28. Secundinus, Letter to Augustine, 3: "I found him to be at every point a supreme orator and almost a god of every kind of eloquence."

CONCORDANCE OF NAMES
OF THE NEWLY DISCOVERED SERMONS

Since their discovery, the twenty-six new texts have been designated by a number corresponding to their place in the collection of Mainz (Germany). This numbering had always been considered provisional. For the future, the numbering corresponds to one of the systems in vogue for the published sermons since the seventeenth century, that is, the classification of the sermons according to the name of the person who found these sermons, in the case here Dolbeau (second column), or the classification according to the Maurist enumeration (third column).

In this English translation of the newly discovered sermons, until they are incorporated into their proper place in Augustine's collection of sermons, that is, within the Maurist classification, three titles, where applicable, are given for each sermon. The principal title is the Maurist classification; above that is the discoverer's classification; below that the Mainz classification.

	Dolbeau 1	Sermon 214A
Mainz 5	Dolbeau 2	Sermon 359B
Mainz 7	Dolbeau 3	Sermon 293A added text*
Mainz 9	Dolbeau 4	Sermon 299A added text
Mainz 12	Dolbeau 5	Sermon 114B
Mainz 13	Dolbeau 6	Sermon 23B
Mainz 15	Dolbeau 7	Sermon 142 added text
Mainz 21	Dolbeau 8	Sermon 29B
Mainz 24	Dolbeau 9	Sermon 28A
Mainz 27	Dolbeau 10	Sermon 162C
Mainz 40	Dolbeau 11	Sermon 90A
Mainz 41	Dolbeau 12	Sermon 354A
Mainz 42	Dolbeau 13	Sermon 159A
Mainz 44	Dolbeau 14	Sermon 352A

21

Mainz 45	Dolbeau 15	Sermon 283 added text
Mainz 46-47	Dolbeau 16	Sermon 72 added text
Mainz 48	Dolbeau 17	Sermon 110A
Mainz 50	Dolbeau 18	Sermon 306E
Mainz 51	Dolbeau 19	Sermon 130A
Mainz 52	Dolbeau 20	Sermon 14A
Mainz 54	Dolbeau 21	Sermon 159B
Mainz 55	Dolbeau 22	Sermon 341 added text
Mainz 19	Dolbeau 23	Sermon 374 added text
Mainz 60	Dolbeau 24	Sermon 360A
Mainz 61	Dolbeau 25	Sermon 360B
Mainz 62	Dolbeau 26	Sermon 198 added text
Mainz 63	Dolbeau 27	Sermon 360C
	Dolbeau 1	Sermon 20B
	Dolbeau 28	De providentia Dei
	Dolbeau 30	Sermon 348A added text

*This refers to the text already published in the Maurist or other collections which has been added to after the discovery of these sermons.

SERMONS

Dolbeau 20
SERMON 14A
Mainz 52

SERMON ON THE VERSE OF PSALM 17(18):
YOUR DISCIPLINE HAS DIRECTED ME TOWARD THE END,
AND YOUR DISCIPLINE ITSELF WILL TEACH ME

Date: 405[1]

What is the end to which we are being directed?

1. Let us turn our attention, brothers and sisters, to what we have been singing. It is where the words of the psalm come from that the proposal we should consider them comes from too.[2] With the Lord's help, let me extract something from what is written and what was just now resounding in our voices and ringing in our ears: *Your discipline has directed me toward the end, and your discipline itself will teach me* (Ps 18:35). We are inquiring, you see, toward what end we are being directed, and what the discipline is that is directing us, and in what sort of way this matter is to be taught. We want to be directed, and we are inquiring, perhaps, where we are directed to. We have heard: *toward the end*. Well, when an end is mentioned, it means a thing being either consumed or completed; an end is made of food by eating it, of a garment by weaving it. When eating food comes to an end, the food is no more; when weaving a garment comes to an end, the garment is perfected. So it is toward that sort of end that we undoubtedly seek to be directed, one which means our being perfected, not our being consumed.

2. So what is this end, and what is this discipline? The end is Christ, the discipline is the law. Listen to the apostle: *The end of the law is Christ, for the sake of justice for everyone who believes* (Rom 10:4). So this then—to state it more clearly and to explain what we have sung—this then is *your discipline has directed me toward the end*: what your law is has directed me toward the end; your law has directed me toward Christ. The Jews have the law, but it has not directed them toward the end. They came, indeed, to the end, because they saw Christ; but by stumbling over the end stone,[3] the finishing point, they were disqualified; by stumbling over Christ they collapsed and fell outside the end. I mean, they rejected him, the one they should have aimed at reaching. In any

25

case, this end turned out to be a stone of stumbling for unbelievers, a cornerstone for believers. *For you,* says the apostle Peter, *who have believed, the very stone which the builders rejected has become the cornerstone, but for those who do not believe, a stone of stumbling and a rock of scandal* (1 Pt 2:7-8).

To reach the end, believing is not enough

3. We know what, we know who the end is; what being directed toward the end is, well, we already spoke about that last Sunday.[4] Being directed toward the end means coming toward Christ, that is, believing in Christ. Do the same old things have to be repeated again and again? I mean, I'm supposed to remind you of them, not to bore you with them. Although repeating the same things to you is not irksome for me, and means being on the safe side for you. We dealt with the point, you see, with an eye on those who think it is enough to believe, and who like leading bad lives, imagining that their believing will save them, not that their leading bad lives will destroy them. So we dealt with the point that this is the difference between the faith of Christians and the faith of demons— because they too believe; they said to Christ, *We know who you are* (Mk 1:24).

They believed he was the Christ,[5] but didn't believe in Christ. So what distinguishes the person who believes he is the Christ from the one who believes in Christ? Because believing in Christ undoubtedly means believing that he is the Christ, while believing that he is the Christ does not automatically mean believing in Christ. But the Son of God laid down that the whole work of God consists in this: *This is the work of God, that you should believe in the one whom he has sent* (Jn 6:29). To what end, if not for the same one, himself? Don't go looking for any end beside him, in case by looking for an end beside him, you find yourself being consumed, not completed. What is an end, after all, but the point we wish to reach, to stop at and not to look for anything beyond it? Because if you get there, but are still looking for something, you haven't yet reached the end. So to reach the end is to reach the spot where you say, "That's enough."

God is the end, God the Trinity

4. Philip thought that the Father alone was such an end, and so he said, *Lord, show us the Father, and it is enough for us* (Jn 14:8); but the Lord showed him that God is the end, God the Trinity. Accordingly, when you say, "Christ is the end," you should not be excluding God the Father; and when you say, "God the Father is the end," you should not be excluding Christ. Philip apparently wished to exclude him, supposing that Christ was only what he could see with his eyes, so he cheerfully said, *Show us the Father, and it is enough for us.*

What do you mean, *It is enough for us?*

That's where our desire ends; we won't be seeking any further; that's where we shall find total satisfaction, where we shall say, "It's enough, I don't want anything more."

Why's that?

Because we already know you. Please show us the Father. Since we can see you, after all, and cannot see him, we aren't satisfied. We are overjoyed because we can see you; but show us him, and we'll be satisfied; we won't require anything more.

And the Lord said to him, because he is himself the end, himself the one who totally satisfies, so in order to relieve him of what he was assuming—he was assuming, you see, that he wasn't seeing the Son of God, when he was seeing the form of a servant[6]—so he said to Philip, *Have I been with you all this time, and you have not recognized me?* When you are looking for the end, and do not see what you see, well that of course is why you are looking for the end, because you can't see the end standing in front of you. *Do you not believe*, he said, *that I am in the Father and the Father is in me?* (Jn 14:9-10).

5. I too can press the same point upon you from the reading[7] which has been chanted today from the gospel: *This is the will of the Father, that whoever sees the Son and believes in him should have eternal life. And I will raise him up on the last day* (Jn 6:40). You were looking for the end; are you looking for something more than eternal life? *This is the will of the Father, that whoever sees the Son and believes in him should have eternal life. And I will raise him up on the last day.* What am I to say, my brothers and sisters? What eyes do we need for obtaining this sight? Notice, I mean, that today another definition has to be demonstrated, one similar indeed to the previous one which we have already talked about[8]: *This is the work of God, that you should believe in the one whom he has sent* (Jn 6:29). And what does he say here? *This is the will of the Father*, as though to say "This is the work of God"; whoever does the work of God, after all, does the will of God.

This is the will of the Father, that whoever sees the Son and believes in him should have eternal life. He has said two things: *This is the work of God, that you should believe in the one whom he has sent*; while here he added, *whoever sees and believes.* The Jews saw, but did not believe; they had the one condition, lacked the other; how could they attain to eternal life without the other? So if the reason those who saw did not attain was that they didn't also believe, what about us, who have believed but haven't seen, if it's those two things that earn eternal life, seeing and believing, and whoever is lacking one of them cannot attain to the reward of eternal life—what are we to do? The Jews lacked the one, we the other. They had seeing, but lacked believing; we have believing, but lack seeing. Well, as regards our having believing and lacking seeing, we have prophetically been declared blessed by the Lord himself, because when Thomas, one of the twelve, felt his scars by touching them. . . .[9]

NOTES

1. This sermon was evidently preached on the Sunday after the delivery of Sermon 130A (Mainz 51); and Dolbeau argues for a date after 404; so I put it as 405. No suggestions are made about the place where these two sermons were preached.

2. That is to say, God.

3. See Rom 9:32. The image, Augustine's, not Paul's, seems to be that of a race, in which the finishing line is marked by a stone.

4. In Sermon 130A (Mainz 51).

5. *Crediderunt Christum*. As *credere* in the sense of believing or trusting someone takes the dative case, this cannot mean "They believed Christ." So it must be construed as a kind of shorthand accusative and infinitive, with the infinitive, *esse*, understood. Whether or not Augustine was the first to develop this distinction between three ways of believing, it became a commonplace of the schools in expounding the first article of the Apostles' Creed, "I believe in God." This is thus seen to affirm more than either "I believe God" (and hence believe everything he has revealed), or "I believe that God exists," or "I believe that there is a God." How much more? Well, the faith of Christians, as Augustine calls it here, involves a wholehearted commitment to "living the faith," which of course is lacking in the faith of demons. For the whole notion of "the faith of demons" see Jas 2:19.

6. See Phil 2:7. The whole text here, according to Dolbeau, is somewhat corrupt; I follow his reconstruction of it.

7. Omitting here the phrase, *quae sequitur*, "which follows." It doesn't follow; it has already been chanted. I take the *quae sequitur* to be a kind of reflex reaction on the part of the stenographer (or of a copyist writing to dictation, or of the reader dictating to copyists) to the word *lectione*, "reading." The reading seems to have been chosen to follow on that of the previous day—or week— which was commented on in Sermon 130A.

8. Above in section 3. But there he was recapitulating what he had said in Sermon 130A, sections 2-3.

9. See Jn 20:24-29. The rest of the sermon is missing. Dolbeau thinks that the major part of it, and possibly several other whole sermons too, were missing from the text that was being copied in the Mainz Charter House.

Dolbeau 28
SERMON 20B

ON THE RESPONSE OF THE PSALM:
GIVE US HELP FROM AFFLICTION, AND VAIN IS THE SALVATION OF MAN

Date: 411[1]

Augustine is glad to be back with his congregation after a long absence
due to illness; the value of such trials

1. I cannot thank the Lord God enough, nor your graces in his presence, for these joyful congratulations, which pour out, I can see very well, from the fountain of your love for me. It is this, you see, brothers and sisters, which revives me, which consoles me: your pure and genuine love, assisting me with the Lord, who has been good enough to restore me to you and my voice to your ears. Nor should you be surprised that we suffer such things in this body. It is fitting, after all, that we should suffer; nor can what the Lord wills ever in any instance be unjust; because on the one hand we are sinners and have to be scourged; and on the other, even if we were just, we would need to be tested.

In fact, if you opt for a healthy body in which the spirit which inhabits the body is not making any progress, you are opting for something futile and vain. God, however, does not consider your mistaken option, but his own merciful intention to set you free.[2] The apostle, you see, says that *we do not know what to pray for as we ought; but the Spirit himself,* he says, *pleads on our behalf with inexpressible groanings* (Rom 8:26). Sometimes, after all, we opt for things for ourselves which God knows are against our best interests; and then he shows mercy if he doesn't listen to us; or rather, it is somehow truer to say: then he really listens to us if he appears not to do so.

How God treated Saint Paul

2. I mean to say, which of us, brothers and sisters, can claim to be the equals in merit of the apostle Paul, whose praises there is no need at all for me to sing? He is read every day, after all, so there's no point in anyone praising him. As a matter of fact, he didn't wish ever to be praised simply on his own account, considering what he said about his conversion;[3] how the Churches which were

29

in Christ from among the Jews (those, that is, who had believed in Christ) heard of it, and were astonished that he had been converted: he didn't say, "They glorified me," but *In me they glorified the Lord* (Gal 1:22-24). Again, when he had much to say about how effective he had been, *Not I*, he said, *but the grace of God with me* (1 Cor 15:10). So which of us can claim to be his equals either in humility or lovingkindness or doctrine or labors or afflictions or merits or finally in his glorious crown?

So he, then, twice pleaded with the Lord for the goad in his flesh to be removed from him, and it was not removed; and yet the Lord says to the soul that serves him well, *While you are still speaking, I will say, Lo, here I am* (Is 58:9), to grant what it was asking for. Would we have the nerve, any of us, to promise ourselves what was denied to Paul? So how can we say that God was not present, when the apostle says, *There was given me a goad in my flesh, an angel of Satan to knock me about*—to stop him getting conceited; *about which I asked the Lord three times to take it away from me, and he said to me: My grace is sufficient for you; because power is perfected in weakness* (2 Cor 12:7-9)? So wasn't he present? Didn't he say, *Lo, here I am*, when God explained why he wouldn't give what he was being asked for?

God always listens to us, even when he seems not to

3. God always listens, dearest brothers and sisters—you must be absolutely clear about this, so that you can pray with complete confidence; God listens, even when God doesn't give what we are praying for. God listens, and if ever in our ignorance we ask for heaven knows what unprofitable favor, he listens more effectively by not giving, while by giving he more effectively does not listen to some who need to be punished. This is what I'm saying: sometimes a faithful Christian asks God for something, praying in the genuinely religious manner, and doesn't receive what he is actually asking for, but does receive the benefit for the sake of which he is asking for it. Sometimes a godless man, a crooked man, a vicious man asks for something, and gets given it, because he deserves to be condemned, not to be heard.

So we have the example of the apostle Paul, that he asked for something and it wasn't given him, but he is shown that the thing for the sake of which he was asking for it was given him. Because whatever faithful Christians may ask for, they ought to ask for it for the sake of the kingdom of heaven, for the sake of eternal life, for the sake of what God has promised and is going to give us after this age; that's the reason why any who ask for anything ought to ask for it—for the sake of that perfect health which we will also have in the resurrection of the body. That, you see, is when our health will be perfect, when *death is swallowed up in victory* (1 Cor 15:44). So now, because I have mentioned the eternal health and salvation on account of which we ought to ask even for temporal benefits, when we do ask for them . . .[4] and let us take some everyday instances from this kind of doctor.

Examples from ordinary medicine

4. When a sick person asks the doctor to let him have something which he fancies at that moment—and the reason he sent for the doctor was to be restored to health through his services. The only point in sending for the doctor, after all, was in order to get better. And so it is, if he happens to fancy apples, if he fancies ice cream,[5] he prefers to ask the doctor for them rather than his servant. He could, of course, to the detriment of his recovery, ask his servant for them and conceal this from the doctor. When the master commands, the servant complies, more responsive to the snap of the master's fingers than to the requirements of the master's health. But the prudent sick man, who values good health and looks forward to its restoration, prefers to ask the doctor for what he fancies at this moment, so that if the doctor refuses, he will forgo what would give him pleasure,[6] but trust the doctor to give him back his health.

So you can see that even when the doctor does not give the sick man what he asks for, the reason he doesn't give is in order to give. The reason he does not gratify his immoderate will is to satisfy his more genuine desire for health. So by not giving to him he does in fact give, and more certainly gives what he was sent for to provide, which is health. So if he gives him this by not giving, by giving in to his importunate arm-twisting he in fact fails to give—though he will frequently give someone who is despaired of what he asks for. Sometimes, however, he will give the sick person what he asks for, so that the sharper pains that result may teach the patient some sense, teach him to trust the doctor; sometimes on the other hand, when he despairs of his recovery, doctors are in the habit of saying, "Give him now whatever he asks for; there is, after all, no hope of his recovery." So let us see if we can find examples in the scriptures to fit these three situations.

Again the example of Paul not being given, for his own good,
what he asked for

5. Someone asks, and doesn't receive what he asks for. Let us turn to the example of the apostle Paul. Because the doctor actually told him why he was not giving it to him: *Power*, he said *is perfected in weakness*. Rest assured: the fact of his not giving it to you means he wants to heal you. Leave it to the doctor; he knows what to apply, what to remove, in order to restore you to health, and that's why he does this. The apostle begs the Lord three times; he was already being heard, but he didn't think he was, and he wouldn't have thought so, unless the doctor had come along actually to tell him, *Power is perfected in weakness*, so that he himself could also confidently say now, *When I become weak, then it is that I am strong* (2 Cor 12:8-10). So we have this person asking for heaven knows what unprofitable favor and not receiving it, in order for him to receive the thing for the sake of which he was asking for the other, which was for the sake of eternal salvation.

An example of receiving what you ask for, to your own detriment,
as a warning

6. Let's now see if people ever receive something as a warning, so that they may suffer some affliction from it, and so go back to medical treatment, because they are sick. Thus the Lord said, *The doctor is not needed by the healthy, but by those who are ill* (Mk 2:17). So he came to a sick humanity, and he found people given over to their desires. Precisely to cause affliction, *God handed them over*, the apostle says, *to the desires of their hearts, to act indecently* (Rom 1:24.28). They had indecent desires, and were given the opportunity to satisfy them; thereby they fell into greater misery than ever, a prey to the pangs that all the unjust must unavoidably endure, all the wicked; pangs of fear, of lust, of error, of sorrow, of affliction, of anxiety. Never any reassurance, never any rest, never any friend to turn to.

There is no avoiding their suffering justly[7]—and they're still alive. God is waiting for them; he allows these things to prod them into seeking medical treatment, so that when they suffer the painful consequences of their lusts, they may learn what they should really ask for. Because they are the ones who are told, *Do you not know that God's patience is leading you toward repentance?* (Rom 2:4). He was giving them over to the desires of their hearts, and they were doing what they liked; and yet he was sparing them, not removing them from this life in which there is still room for repentance; and he was all the time inviting them to repent, just as he still is doing, and he will never stop doing so with the human race until the final day of judgment.

The case of the devil; granted his request because he was despaired of

7. So let us next find an instance of the one who is allowed to do what he likes because he is now despaired of; and this too from the scriptures. Can anything or anyone be more despaired of than the devil? Yet he asked God to let him have Job to be tempted, and he was not refused.[8] There are great mysteries here, great matters indeed, and worthy of careful consideration. The apostle asks for the goad in his flesh to be taken away, and is not granted his request; the devil asks for a just man to tempt, and his request is granted. But the just man's being granted to the devil for tempting did not do the just man any harm, nor the devil any good, because the former came through his trials with flying colors, and the latter suffered the torment of bitter disappointment.

God's reasons in allowing the just to be tempted and tried

8. Hold onto this firmly, brothers and sisters, what I have often told your holinesses, and don't let the worries of the world rub out from your minds what you have heard: when God either hands over the just to be tempted in order to test their mettle, or to be scourged if he wishes to correct them for their remaining sins, it is for their own good. If, however, it is to show their true worth, because people didn't know about them, this is for the good of those who get to know

about them, so that they may imitate them. Because God certainly knows his servants well, but sometimes they are not known to others, and can only be revealed to them in their true worth by undergoing various trials.

Sometimes, too, people are unknown to themselves, and quite unaware of what they may be capable of. They either think they can do more than in fact they can, and so they are shown that they can't do it yet; or else they despair of themselves, and think they cannot endure whatever it may be; and they are shown that in fact they can. When they have an immoderately good opinion of themselves, they are given a lesson in humility, and when they think they are broken reeds, they are rescued from despair.

The text of the response to the psalm, at last

9. Therefore, what we should understand in the psalm we were singing is that many[9] people ask for good health, and sometimes it is not to their advantage. They are in good health, for instance, and they abuse it in order to sin. They would be better off sick and out of circulation, than in good health and gadding about. Sometimes, on the other hand, as a result of the scourge of tribulation, when something they hadn't bargained for happens to them, they are converted to God. They will emerge more careful, more chaste, more unassuming, altogether humbler, and can then rightly sing, *Give us help from affliction, and vain is the salvation of man* (Ps 60:13). He was looking for help, and help where from? He said to the Lord, "From affliction give us help, so that by being afflicted we may be corrected, may turn back to you through being humiliated, may no more stiffen our necks against you." Because when you give us help from tribulation, we will realize that *vain is the salvation*[10] which foolish man frequently goes for, and when he gets it he doesn't use it for the joys of a quiet life, but as an opportunity for gadding about.

Often enough, for instance, a man was on the point of charging out, in a furious and quite unjustified temper, and aiming to do someone an injury who had probably done him no harm. He suddenly falls sick; what would be best for him—to charge out and commit an iniquitous assault or to be ill in bed and pray for health? It is not, you see, health from God or the salvation of God that is vain, but the health of man that is vain, which man thinks is so necessary for him, as if it were something to be highly valued. It's a false salvation, a false health, and rightly said to be "of man," if it is thought to come only from man. Because there,[11] where it doesn't add "of man" and says, *Salvation is the Lord's* (Ps 3:9), what's the meaning of *Salvation is the Lord's*? It's the Lord who gives salvation, or health, who knows what to give, when and to whom to give.

As often as people, whose salvation seems to be despaired of, ask for salvation, it is God who gives it. It continues in that psalm, *And upon your people be your blessing* (Ps 3:9), that is, have mercy as much on your people, and give them the salvation which you give to those who do not belong to your people, even the salvation which this people of yours is ignorant of. You, after all, know what to give; this people doesn't know what to receive, except when this people of yours has received it. I mean, what sort of thing is this, brothers and sisters, to help you know what you are going to receive? *What eye has not seen nor ear heard, nor has it come up into the heart of man, the things that God has prepared for those who love him* (1 Cor 2:9). What do you think it is he has prepared? Eternal salvation, of course, everlasting health, which cannot come up into our hearts, which eye cannot see, and ear cannot hear; and yet he is preparing these things for those who love him, and when we have received them, we shall see what true health is, and how vain were the things that we thought were of such value.[12]

The example of the martyrs

10. If the martyrs, after all, had opted for this health or salvation, that is, the salvation of man, and valued it highly, they wouldn't have said from the bottom of their hearts, *And the day of man I have not desired, you yourself know* (Jer 17:16 LXX).[13] So if they had opted for this salvation and valued it highly, they would have lost that other eternal variety. As it is, however, they understand the meaning of *Give us help from affliction* (Ps 60:11), and they choose rather to be carried through to everlasting salvation, than on choosing this salvation of man to find it leading to their undoing and to their giving their consent to the persecutors. The persecutor, of course, would immediately grant them salvation. There was the martyr in chains, bound and confined in prison, even wasting away by himself from his wounds;[14] had he yielded to the persecutor, he would immediately have had salvation; but *vain is the salvation of man.*

The persecutors, of course, were promising salvation, which they would give immediately. And what sort would they give? The sort the martyrs had known before those afflictions came upon them. But they were reaching out to that other sort which *eye has not seen nor ear heard, nor has it come up into the heart of man* (1 Cor 2:9). What the persecutor promises can be seen, and what he promises is unreliable, and short, and limited.[15] If that greater salvation cannot be seen, but God promises that it will certainly follow (and he cannot deceive us), let us keep ourselves under his stern discipline, and not grumble under his rod; let us willingly endure his treatment and his cure, and then we will rejoice at God's presence in perfect health, fully aware at last of what he has given us, and saying, *Where, death, is your striving? Where, death, is your sting?* (1 Cor 15:55).

Augustine excuses himself for not continuing

11.[16] I know your eagerness, brothers and sisters, but it is also necessary for you to spare my fragile state of health. No, I don't want to refuse your holinesses the ministry of my preaching, whatever it may be like, so that I may serve the Lord, who has restored me to health. However, we still have to deal gently with the more recent scar, which is not yet, perhaps, completely healed.[17] May the Lord dispose of me as he will, adapting me to the salvation of us all and the service of his holy Church.

Turning to the Lord, let us pray. May he look upon us and perfect us by his saving word, and grant us to rejoice in accord with him and live in accord with him. May he put away from us *the prudence of the flesh* (Rom 8:6); may he throw down the enemy under our feet,[18] not by our efforts, but by his holy name, in which we have been cleansed through Jesus Christ our Lord.

NOTES

1. This sermon on the text of Ps 60:11 was first published by François Dolbeau in the *Revue des Études Augustiniennes*, 40 (1994). He discovered its text in one German and two Italian manuscripts, following a clue provided by a medieval anthology of Augustine texts, the *Milleloquium veritatis Sancti Augustini* of the Augustinian friar, Bartholomew of Urbino, who died in 1350. There were two occasions in Augustine's life when he tells us he was seriously ill; the summer of 397 in Carthage, when he suffered from a painful attack of piles (Letter 38, 1), and the autumn and winter of 410-411, when he was laid low with a fever shortly after returning to Hippo Regius from the great Colloquy with the Donatists in Carthage, and retired to a villa in the countryside for a long convalescence (Letter 118, 34; 122, 1; see O. Perler, *Les Voyages de Saint Augustin*, pages 438, 454). But that earlier date was so full of preaching engagements that Augustine must have recovered fairly quickly from his painful ailment, and in any case, it would be hard to fit yet another sermon into it. However, at the end of this sermon (see note 17 below), there is an allusion to his scar, to some sort of surgery then. But as Dolbeau says, Augustine could have suffered a recurrence of this trouble later in life, and not happened to mention it in his correspondence; and as there are a number of things about this sermon, its rather rambling quality, and occasional inconsequential train of thought, that suggest an old man preaching, my own instinct is to date it much later on, about 427.

2. Bartholomew's first extract from this sermon in his *Milleloquium* runs from its opening words to this point.

3. So the two Italian manuscripts. Dolbeau follows the German one in reading *conversatione* instead of *conversione*, and refers in support to Gal 1:13. I respectfully beg to differ.

4. Here Dolbeau suggests, with reason, that there is a lacuna in the text. I suggest the missing passage went something like this: "let us compare God's treatment of us with that of a human doctor, and . . ."

5. Obviously not, not in those days! But I am freely transposing to our contemporary world whatever precisely it was that he meant by *frigida*, cold things.

6. Reading *voluptatem* with the German manuscript, rather than *voluntatem*—"what would accord with his will"—with the two Italian ones and the text printed by Dolbeau, who nonetheless thinks the former may be right.

7. Omitting with the two Italian manuscripts the words *injusti sed cum patiuntur*—"there is no avoiding the unjust suffering justly; but when they suffer, they are still alive."

8. See Jb 1:2.

9. Here the *Milleloquium* starts another short extract, which concludes with the quotation from Ps 60 a few lines further on.

10. Another extract in the *Milleloquium*, to the end of this sentence. "Salvation," *salus*, also means health, and that of course is primarily how he is taking it in this sermon. But in fact he would hardly have made the distinction.

11. In Ps 3. Dolbeau considers, surely rightly, that the text is corrupt here. It looks as if a more straightforward reference to this other psalm has dropped out.

12. If the text was corrupt earlier on, I suspect this was partly because the train of thought in

these two paragraphs is so confused; what I feel to be the rambling of an old, as well as a frail and tired man.

13. I here omit a short sentence: *Quid dicitur in psalmo?* "What does it say in the psalm?" It breaks up the line of thought, and has every appearance of having started life as a query scribbled in the margin, and later incorporated into the text.

14. There is an echo here, Dolbeau suggests, from the *Passion of Saints Felicity and Perpetua*, 3, 8.

15. Here again I omit a whole sentence, which breaks the train of thought, and is in my view very dubiously "Augustinian." It runs: "Even if the salvation of the flesh were everlasting, it would still be fleshly, still be such as eye has seen and ear heard and has come up into the heart of man."

16. From here to the end—excluding the final prayer—we have the last extract from this sermon quoted in the *Milleloquium*.

17. This allusion to recent surgery points more to his earlier illness of piles in 397 than to the fever which laid him low in 410-411. But as stated in note 1, he could have had, and I suggest did have, a recurrence of that painful malady later on in his old age.

18. See Ps 110:1; 1 Cor 15:25-27.

Dolbeau 6
SERMON 23B
Mainz 13

ON PSALM 81(82):
GOD HAS STOOD UP IN THE SYNAGOGUE OF GODS

Date: 404[1]

The Son of God became a son of man, in order that the sons of men might become sons of God

1. To what hope the Lord has called us, what we now carry about with us, what we endure, what we look forward to, is well known, I don't doubt, to your graces. We carry mortality about with us, we endure infirmity, we look forward to divinity. For God wishes not only to vivify, but also to deify us.[2] When would human infirmity ever have dared to hope for this, unless divine truth had promised it? But divine truth did promise this,[3] as we have said; and that we are going to be gods, not only did it promise this—and because it made the promise, it is of course true, because such a faithful maker of promises does not deceive, and such an omnipotent giver is not prevented from fulfilling what he has promised. Still, it was not enough for our God to promise us divinity in himself, unless he also took on our infirmity, as though to say, "Do you want to know how much I love you, how certain you ought to be that I am going to give you my divine reality? I took to myself your mortal reality."

We mustn't find it incredible, brothers and sisters, that human beings become gods, that is, that those who were human beings become gods.[4] More incredible still is what has already been bestowed on us, that one who was God should become a human being. And indeed we believe that that has already happened, while we wait for the other thing to happen in the future. The Son of God became a son of man, in order to make sons of men into sons of God. Hold on to this absolutely—I think you remember what we have already spoken about to your graces[5]—that neither is he mortal from what is his own, nor are we immortal from what is our own; not from what is his own,[6] not from the substance by which he is himself God; but in another way, yes from what is his own, because from his creation, from what he established, from what he created. For the maker of man was made man, so that man might be made a receiver of God. And now

37

we have this in faith, it has been kept for us in hope, and it will be made manifest at a definite time. Those will then rejoice who now, while it is not being manifested, have believed; but those who have refused to believe while it is not being manifested will be confounded when it is.

*A great difference between the true God
and those whom he makes into gods*

2. So a Christian mind, which is told to laugh at the gods of the nations, and knows that the one God is to be worshiped, must not be horrified and so to say frightened out of its wits, when it hears in the psalm we have just sung, *God has stood up in the synagogue of gods*. What is a synagogue? Because it is a Greek word, I presume several of you know, several do not know. A synagogue in Latin and English is called a congregation; so that is what we have sung: that *God has stood up in the congregation of gods*. Why so? *In the midst to discern the gods* (Ps 82:1). Our God, the true God, the one God, has stood up in the synagogue of gods, many of them of course, and gods not by nature but by adoption, by grace. There is a great difference between God who exists, God who is always God, true God, not only God but also deifying God; that is, if I may so put it, god-making God, God not made making gods, and gods who are made, but not by a craftsman.[7]

It is better to become gods than to claim to make gods

3. And because all who make are of course better than the ones whom they make, now see what gods the pagans worship, and what God is worshiped by all of you. You worship the God who makes you into gods; while they worship gods they make, and by making and worshiping them they lose the chance of becoming gods themselves; and by making false gods they fall away from the true one. And on those, indeed, which they make, they do not bestow the reality of being gods, but only of being called what they are not. They themselves lose the chance of being what they could be, and do not give those others the chance of being what they cannot be. People who make false gods offend the true one, and by making what cannot be gods they fail to become themselves what they can. For they, if they wish, can become gods, not of the sort which they worship, but of the sort which the one whom they worship makes.

So what do people want? To become gods, or to make gods? They indeed consider it a greater show of power if they make gods than if they become gods. But even if they could make one, it won't be a god, will it, just because it is called one? The thing you slap a divine name on will be called a god; but it will still be just wood or stone or gold, or whatever else it is. Indeed, you, O godless man, want to make a god whom you cannot make; but all you can do is fashion a caricature,[8] and slap a name on it. It will not be what you call it, but it will be what the one whom you fail to call upon has made it. For it is God who made wood, God who made stone, gold, silver; you, out of that stone which God has made, wish to make a god. You neither give it what you have made, nor take away from it what he has made.

> *The idols you make answer more truly than you do,*
> *when asked what they really are*

4. So you have not made, then, what you have made; I mean, if I ask you what you have made, you will answer, "A god"; the one you have made gives a better answer than you do. We can, you see, after a fashion interrogate even these things, which lack soul and sense indeed, so that they are not aware of their interrogators, but which still present a certain[9] appearance, an appearance by which they declare to our senses, if I may so put it, what they are. You have made, for example, a wooden god. Of course, if it's a god, it isn't wood; if it's wood, it isn't a god. And yet you reply that you have made a god; I, however, putting wooden you to one side, question the wood itself. Nor should you think that I am also made of wood, because I am questioning the wood. Why should I not question it?[10] Notice; it is not a voice interrogating a soul, but eyes a shape. My glance is interrogating the appearance and material of that piece of wood. And in case my mortal glance should perhaps be misled, my sense of touch can also interrogate it. And if you think that is not enough, a hatchet too can interrogate your god, which my God made as wood. Under all these interrogations it answers me that it is wood, this thing that you say is a god; it answers without words, but it is more to be trusted than your words.

> *Even so, you are still better than "the god" you have made*

5. You say that God lies; but you are convicted of this yourself by the very one you have made. Nor, just because you are convicted by it, does it mean that it will be better than you are. Even so, even if you are lying and it is not, if you are calling it a god and it is declaring itself to be a piece of wood, it won't be better than you are. You can feel and it cannot, you can hear and it cannot, you can see and it cannot, you can walk and it cannot; you are alive, and I can't say, "It is dead," because it has never been alive.[11] You are better than the one you have made; worship the one who is better than you, the one who made you.

It is an insult to you that you should be like the one you have made. Do you want to know what sort of thing you worship? You get indignant with anyone who abuses you by saying, "May you be like that"; and yet you yourself worship what you deprecate being, and by worshiping it you are to a certain extent turned into something like it. Not so that you become a piece of wood and cease to be a human being, but since you make your inner self into something like what you have made outwardly.[12] God, after all, made you a mind, like eyes, and you don't wish to see the truth. God made you an intelligence, like the sense of hearing, and you don't wish to understand justice. While if our inner self did not have a sense of smell, there would have been no reason for the apostle to say, *We are the good odor of Christ in every place* (2 Cor 2:15.14). If that inner self did not have a mouth, the Lord would not have said, *Blessed are those who are hungry and thirsty for justice* (Mt 5:6).

So the inner self has all the senses—God has given them—but does not wish to use them, and wishes to become like the caricature, the idol, he himself has fashioned, about which the prophet says, *They have eyes and cannot see, they have ears and cannot hear, they have nostrils and cannot smell, they have mouths and cannot speak, they have hands and cannot work,* etc. And notice how he concludes: *May all who make them become like them, and all who trust in them* (Ps 115:5-8).

"How can human beings *become like* dumb idols?"

Well, according to this likeness which we are suggesting, if the inner self becomes somehow or other insensitive, stupid, he becomes in a certain manner like an idol, and having ruined in himself the image of the one by whom he was made, he wishes to take on the image of the one which he has made. After all, why should the Lord say, *The one who has ears to hear with, let him hear* (Mt 11:15), if not because there are some people who have ears and do not hear?

God's discernment of the gods

6. So don't let your hearts be scared out of their wits because *God has stood up in the synagogue of gods, in the midst,* however, *to discern the gods.* By discerning in the midst, you see, he is uttering certain precepts; those who ignore these precepts do not wish to be what he told us we should be. And some will impute to themselves. . . .[13] Why, after all, should he discern if all are gods, if not because there are some who listen to these precepts, some who ignore them? There are those, you see, who are grateful, there are those who are ungrateful for grace, and they are discerned—but by the one who knows how to discern. None of us who are made into gods should wish to discern; let the one do it who made us. Let the maker pass judgment on his works, as he cannot be mistaken when he passes judgment.

But by giving human beings his Spirit he also enables them to pass judgment, not from themselves, not in virtue of their nature, not by any merit of theirs, but by his grace and gift. *We,* it says, *have not received the spirit of this world, but the Spirit which is from God, that we may know the things that have been bestowed on us by God. For merely animate persons do not perceive the things that are of the Spirit of God; for they are foolishness to them, and they cannot know them, since they are to be judged spiritually. But spiritual people judge all things, while they themselves are judged by no one* (1 Cor 2:12.14-15). But if we have the Spirit of God, we not only discern ourselves, but also distinguish ourselves from the caricatures that are idols.

It is a worse sacrilege to insult God's image than the image of the emperor

7. The truth in fact is, brothers and sisters, that people who do not distinguish themselves from these are to be lamented, not that those who do so are to be

praised—unless of course people are to be praised who know that there is a great difference between themselves and stones. What sort of people, though, would they be, if they thought they were the same as what stones are? And if only they could get as far as that![14] They are making themselves better than stones; but if they were like them, or if they made themselves like them—because they never will be; I mean, however much they may ape their own work, they will never kill God's work in themselves—so if they were to make themselves like stones by thinking they were like them, I don't say they would be doing themselves an injustice—after all, perhaps they make light of an injustice to themselves, and they are quite right to make light of an injustice done to people such as they are—I will say what may shake them: they are doing God an injustice, insulting God. By disparaging themselves they are committing sacrilege against the one they were made by; for it was to the image of God that man was made.[15]

If, therefore, you would be guilty of sacrilege, or rather would be said to be so by civil law, if you insulted an image of the emperor, what will you be guilty of if you insult, or do injustice to, the image of God? Which is worse? To throw a stone at the image of a man, or to make the image of God into a stone?[16] So then, let us leave these people aside as being excessively dead; because even if it is possible for them to be roused, it cannot be done by us. We should not, all the same, despair of them for that reason, that we are unable to rouse them; for *God has the power from these stones to raise up children to Abraham* (Lk 3:8).

Worshiping the gods represented by idols
only marginally better than worshiping the idols

8. But we ought also to discern or distinguish ourselves from the *numina*[17] of those stones, pieces of wood, lumps of gold and silver, because there are those who think they can defend themselves with a show of reason, when they say, "We too know that idols are empty show; but they are not what we worship." And when you ask, "So what do you worship?" they reply, "The *numina* of the idols. We do indeed do homage to what we can see, but we worship what we cannot see."[18] What are these *numina*? Let us listen to our God, saying through the prophet, *Since all the gods of the nations are demons, but it is the Lord who made the heavens* (Ps 96:5), where the demons are not fit to dwell. The prophet poured scorn on demons in one way, on idols in another. How on idols? *The idols of the nations are silver and gold.* He did not wish to say stone and wood, but what they value highly, what they consider precious, their choicest things are what he held up to scorn; *silver* indeed, and *gold*, but still *the work of the hands of men.* What, though, did man make here? Not, surely, that it should be gold; not, surely, that it should be silver? That is what God made. So what was man's contribution? That *they have eyes and cannot see* (Ps 115:4-5).

So this is what human beings did in the gods which they made—what they would not like done in themselves by the one they were made by. They made blind gods, and would not like to have been made blind by God. So what, then? Because he mentioned gold and silver, precious metals, and chose to hold up to scorn what they value highly, does that mean there is any real difference between the things he poured scorn on? Gold is certainly rather different from wood, gold is more precious than wood; but as regards having eyes and not seeing, they are on a par; disparate in usefulness or brightness, on a par in blindness.

9. So there was one sort of mockery for these idols, soulless, senseless, lifeless; another for the objects they hold in high esteem and worship through them, that is, the demons, when he says, *All the gods of the nations are demons, while it is the Lord who made the heavens.* And the apostle poured scorn on an idol in one way: *We know,* he said, *that an idol is nothing* (1 Cor 8:4), while he commanded us to beware of demons in another, saying, *What the nations sacrifice, they sacrifice to demons and not to God. I do not wish you to become the associates of demons* (1 Cor 10:20). He did not say, "I do not wish you to become the associates of idols." Perhaps, you see, that would make you afraid to be what you never could be, to be the associate of a wooden idol, in case you were both thrown together on the bonfire. Be afraid to be the associate of demons, in case you are both thrown together into the eternal fire.

For notice, brothers and sisters, what I am saying: you cannot be the associate of an idol even if you want to be; but being the associate of demons is something you will be if you want to be, won't be if you don't want to. All the associates of the devil and his angels, you see, will be told at the end, *Go into the eternal fire, which has been prepared for the devil and his angels* (Mt 25:41). I have the impression, brothers and sisters, that I am in any case discerning gods in the midst; but it's not me, it's the word of God, whether it is being preached on or being sung or being read, that's what really has the force and power to make the discernment.

Diviners and soothsayers are the agents of demons

10. But somebody will say to me from the crowd, "Perish the thought that I should seek out demons, and not rather abominate them. I abominate them utterly, and shun them and execrate them." But now those are fine words, a fine declaration. What, though, if you've got a migraine, and you go looking up a diviner? What if you have some dangerous business, and desire the services of a soothsayer? Such are the instruments of demons; why search out the instruments of those whom you abominate? If you are telling the truth, I will acknowledge it by the work. Your declaration seems unambiguous enough, before there is any temptation. Recognize the one who is talking to you; Satan, after all, will never talk to you through an idol, but through a bad man whose heart he is in possession of. *He is at work,* you see, as the apostle says, *in the sons of unbelief* (Eph 2:2).

So when you start hearing this sort of thing: "Take care of yourself, look to your own interests; there's a man you should consult; everything he tells you will be true; there's a man you should entrust your business to, should entrust your year to; he will choose the right day[19] for you to enter upon a transaction"; that's when you must see the devil speaking from the shape of a man, whom he has already seduced into his society. And if you do not wish to be the associate of demons, avoid any associate of demons. What you will be, after all, is the associate of Christ, not in equality of majesty, but in one and the same inheritance, as the apostle says: *Heirs indeed of God, but co-heirs of Christ* (Rom 8:17).

"Put up with your condition, so that you may receive your possession"

11. But how do people come to seek the society of demons? By losing endurance; *Woe, you see, to those who have lost endurance* (Sir 2:14). We all know you're in a tight spot, under enormous pressures, tossed about by infirmity, wasting away with TB, harassed by the machinations of an enemy. Suppose that's so. These things are real, they're troublesome, they crush you, weigh you down, smash you. Well, so what? Have you been called by Christ to a life of luxury? I think God would have a point if he said to you, "Suffer; you're a human being, after all, made mortal by your will, by my law." Indeed it was our very nature that first sinned,[20] and we derive from there what we are born with. Let us put up with our condition. The creator says, "I will recreate you; I created you mortal, I will recreate you immortal. Put up with your condition, so that you may receive your possession."

I think if God were speaking to man, he would have a point in saying things like this: "Bear with it, endure it; it's diseased, it's septic. Endure the doctor and his knife, let it penetrate the whole rotten sore, let everything bad concentrated there burst out." The things people suffer under human doctors! They're put in splints, they're lanced, they're cauterized,[21] for as long as this practitioner pleases who is promising uncertain health, as long as this person pleases who did not make you, as long as a man pleases treating a man—and he endures it all. It's not enough to say he endures his surgery; he begs him to go ahead with it. So don't you reckon that you are being purged when you suffer tribulation? So don't you believe the one who told you, *Gold and silver are tested in the fire, but acceptable persons in the furnace of tribulation* (Sir 2:5)? So put up with what the doctor applies to the patient, what the goldsmith applies to the gold being refined.

12. This world, you see, is like a craftsman's furnace. In a goldsmith's furnace there is both straw and gold and fire; in the same way too in this world both unbeliever and believer and temptation or trial. The unbeliever is the straw, the believer the gold, the fire is trials and temptations. These three things are in a confined space; this space, however, is confined in such a way that all three have their own properties; the fire that of burning, the straw of being consumed, the gold of being refined. So don't be surprised because you see the world full of scandals, iniquities, corruption, oppression, people blaspheming, blaming "the Christian times,"[22] because these things are coming at us thick and fast. You must not let these blasphemies and this fault-finding scare you out of your wits; it's the straw burning. Indeed they say these things with eloquent and as it were flaming words. Don't let the brilliance of the straw as it burns astonish you; a

little later on it will be ashes. It flares up, it crackles, it produces smoke. O gold, keep quiet and let yourself be refined. The straw is burning in its blasphemies; you be refined from your dross.

"Christian times" no worse than previous ones

13. "Indeed there are many evils, and many are getting more common, ever since the times began to be Christian." This, in fact, is not to be readily conceded to the ignorant. Let them read about the evils of earlier ages in their own literature; let them read about the greater wars of their ancestors; let them read about the laying waste of whole regions; let them read about the captivities of nations, alternately in succession, now this way now that, ding dong snatching the supremacy to themselves. Among the ancients too there were famines, plagues. Let them read about it if they've got the time; but if they haven't got the time to read, why have they got the time to talk so much?

However, we do admit that some things are happening more frequently; that through lack of materials and a deteriorating state of affairs, those buildings that were previously constructed with great magnificence are now falling and collapsing into ruins. The pagans are astonished that things made by the hands of men should be falling down, and want to fall down themselves, though made by the hand of God. Consider, my brothers and sisters—I can say it more freely from this place, where the Lord gives you assurance of his truth being preached; for there must be no respect of persons at all, I don't mean just of any human being, but of the world and the age itself, especially because the psalm was just now reproving such an attitude: *How long are you judging iniquity, and respecting the person of sinners?* (Ps 82:2), discerning between gods and gods; so being terrified myself, I terrify you, and being ordered to do so, I speak—think, recollect, what an extravagant waste of materials constructed the theaters and amphitheaters. Were the times better because vanities were more freely available, because the reins on filth and infamy were relaxed, because anybody was allowed to do easily what it was bad for him to enjoy? Assuredly, those are the auditoria of infamous filth. . . .[23] Observe what goes on there, and see when the times are better: when these things were being built, or when they are falling down?

14. We beg them, if they are angry with us, to read their own authors. Let them see whether their own philosophers approved of these filthy shows for them, whether they didn't pour scorn on them, didn't forbid them, didn't condemn them. Let them choose all their better authors, and first recognize in them their own vices, before they come and attack the grace of our Christ. How many things were said by those authors against the extravagant and against the wasteful, against those who pour out their money to earn themselves statues, and in order to end up in stone are prepared to end up in rags![24] Let them read these things, therefore, among their own authors; there is no need for them to wish to learn even their own literature from me, because even if they would like to, it is unfitting for me to teach it, and perhaps rather more fitting that I am forgetting it.

However, as far as I can remember, those authors did reprehend many such things as these people now eagerly practice. And because there are now no means available, no wealth, license, prosperity to help them to these vain trifles, they blame Christ, ungrateful to the master who has come upon them like boys playing bad games, and with his vigorous severity has after a fashion knocked out of their hands the mud balls and glass dice[25] with which they were injuring one another even while playing. The children cry, of course, but can, if they wish, be cured. But let these people go on as they are going, go on as has been foretold; in this way God's promise is fulfilled.

The lesson of the oil press

15. Shun the bad, lay hold of the good. The time of the oil press has come. It's as if the olive tree in its freer branches used to be shaken by different winds in previous times, which were luxuriating in the freedom to indulge in such trifles; in the olives hanging from the tree both oil and dregs are crammed in together. For these two to be separated from each other by due discrimination, pressure is required. The psalm has the superscription *For the oil presses,*[26] and its text says nothing about a vat, nothing about a press, nothing about the baskets; whatever it has to say refers to the human race. You hear the word "press"; consider what sort of thing it is a press for. And the human race is to be led, from a rather freer kind of being mixed up together, into certain crushings, certain pressures; it is time to turn the screw,[27] to place the weights. In the midst of being screwed down[28] and pressed you see extravagant luxury more rife, you see avarice more rapacious, you see lusts more unrestrained; the dregs are running through the streets. You object to these things, and you say, "Look how even greater plundering is going on in Christian times, and people are being subjected to ever more burdensome impositions." It's the dregs, black, noisome, useless, running through the public places.

Oh, if only you could have the eyes also to see the oil being filtered into the jars! You notice the great number of adulterers; why don't you notice the great number of consecrated virgins? You notice men committing fornication; why don't you notice those who by mutual consent even abstain from their wives? You notice men with great avarice, without the least shame receiving property stolen from others; why don't you notice those who give away their own with great compassion, without the least insanity? You are displeased by so many people who are rich in a bad way; take pleasure in so many who are poor in a good way, because while it is hard-hearted[29] wickedness that has made those rich, it is deliberate loving-kindness that has made these poor. Why have eyes only for the dregs, so as to find fault with the pressing, while refusing to be in the press?

Be the oil which is separated from the dregs inside, not that which is carried out by them outside. Say with a certain oil, *I have found tribulation and pain, and I have called upon the name of the Lord* (Ps 116:3-4). Say with a certain oil, *It is good for me that you have humbled me, that I may learn your justifica-*

tions (Ps 119:71). How is it that you see some people blaspheming under oppression, others giving thanks under oppression, those murky, these limpid and shining? How can this be, if not that what is sung *for the oil presses* is being fulfilled? So then, don't find fault with the one who is coming to press, because he is coming to discern; acknowledge rather the time of discernment, and you will not have a tongue given to twisting the truth.[30]

NOTES

1. Dolbeau suggests the winter of 403-404, and Carthage as the place where the sermon was preached. He groups it with 346A (Mainz 12) and 361 and 362, on the strength of an entry in Possidius' *Index* and of internal evidence. As this sermon refers back, probably to one or other of those, it seems more likely that it was preached early in 404 than late in 403. See note 5 below. Dolbeau finds the text in a somewhat perilous state, and proposes numerous emendations which I usually accept without remarking on them in the notes.

2. For the theme of deification in Augustine, see an article by G. Bonner in *The Journal of Theological Studies*, 1986.

3. The text reads "promised this only," *hoc solum*. Dolbeau emends, hesitantly, *hoc* to *non*: "did not only promise this," thus anticipating the repetition of the phrase. I emend, even more hesitantly, by keeping *hoc* and deleting *solum*.

4. This "clarification," while merely tautological in the English, is not so in the Latin. There, "that human beings become gods," being an accusative and infinitive clause, could also have been heard as "that gods become human beings"—and he does not yet want to say that.

5. Possibly in his *Expositions of the Psalms* 146(147) 11, which was also a sermon preached in Carthage the same winter. But there too he says, on the same point, "as I have already told your graces." So we cannot definitely say to which sermon he is referring; very possibly to Sermon 361.

6. Here I omit a phrase, "nor from his nature," which is redundant and looks like a marginal scribble that was commenting on "from the substance," and then was incorporated into the text—in not quite the right place!

7. Like the idols of the heathen. Simply two apparent synonyms, *deificatorem* first, and then *deificum*; of which the first looks like his own invention, while the second merits a mention in the dictionary of Messrs. Lewis & Short. He seems to regard the word as slightly suspect; was it associated, perhaps, in the Christian memory with the old pagan habit of deifying the reigning emperors? Elsewhere he will make an almost equally opaque distinction between *divinitas* and *deitas*.

8. *Simulacrum*; later on I will have to translate it as "idol" or "image."

9. Reading *quandam* instead of the text's *quidem*, "indeed"; this would easily have been substituted by a copyist whose eye was caught by the *quidem* of the previous line.

10. Reading with Dolbeau *Quidni interrogarem eum?* instead of *Quid si. . .?*: "What if I were to question it?"

11. He is forgetting that wood comes from what have been living trees!

12. A very loosely constructed sentence in the Latin also.

13. There is evidently a gap in the text here. Dolbeau suggests: "Why should he discern, if all are gods?" But one can hardly impute a question to oneself. I suspect the gap is really bigger than that. I would suggest something like: "Some will impute being gods to themselves, while others acknowledge it is a grace that they have been given."

14. That is, presumably, as far as knowing that there is a great difference between themselves and stones.

15. See Gn 1:27.

16. In 387 there had been serious rioting in Antioch, during which the imperial images were stoned, and otherwise "sacrilegiously" insulted. Although that had occurred some 16 or 17 years before this sermon was preached, news of it would have spread through all the great cities of the empire, and the memory of it would have remained fresh.

17. *Numen* is really an untranslatable word: the old Roman name for what they came to call gods, but of much wider application, meaning something like "preternatural power." Paul's list of things that could not separate him from the love of God in Christ, Rom 8:38-39, could be called *numina*, or the list of things "in heaven" in Col 1:16.

18. They are distinguishing between *adorare*, to do homage, and *colere*, to worship. It is the distinction which Orthodox Catholicism will make later on during the iconoclastic crisis of the eighth and ninth centuries, in defense of the honor paid to icons and images in Christian piety and liturgy: the distinction between *doulia* or *proskunesis*, the service or homage which it is lawful to offer the saints and their images, and *latreia*, the strict worship which may only be offered to God.

19. The text is defective here. It runs, *est qui commendet causam tuam, qui commendet arnum (annum?) tuum:. . . eliget tibi inchoandi negotii. . .:* "There is a man who can commend your business, can commend your year; he will choose. . . for you to enter upon a transaction." Dolbeau suggests possibly reading *amicum*, your friend, or *arvum*, your field, or *animum*, your spirit, for the non-word *arnum*. He fills the gap by proposing *diem eliget*, which I have translated.

In the first part of the sentence, however, I propose, and have translated, this emendation: *est cui commendes causam tuam, cui commendes annum tuum.* I have kept the *annum*, year, which Dolbeau suggests may simply have been badly written to look like *arnum*, because it just makes sense.

20. It is the teaching of Augustine that original sin is precisely a sin of nature, not a sin of the individual person; thus not a sin one commits and is therefore personally responsible for. What he says here, more literally translated, is, "Indeed it was our first nature itself that sinned," thus identifying Adam, the head of the human race, with human nature as created by God. His going on to have God say, "I created you mortal," is a little careless of him; God has already told you, two or three sentences ago, that you were made mortal by your own will (meaning the will of your representative, Adam). But the provisional immortality in which Adam was created, and which he lost by sinning, is as nothing in comparison with the recreated immortality of the resurrection.

21. All without anaesthetics, of course.

22. That is, the times more particularly after Theodosius the Great made Catholic Christianity the official religion of the empire, and the old pagan cults were declared illegal.

23. This is a lacuna indicated in the manuscript itself.

24. These were the public men who sponsored the shows at enormous expense.

25. The text reads *cellas vitreas*, glass cells. I follow Dolbeau's proposed emendation to *ocellata vitrea*. Lewis & Short defines *ocellatum* as "a small stone marked with eyes or spots, like dice."

26. Not in the Hebrew, the Greek Septuagint, or the Latin Vulgate. Just possibly, the translator of Augustine's version thought that as Pss 81(80) and 84(83) had this title—in the Septuagint—the two psalms in between ought to have it too.

27. The text reads, *innitendum triturae*, "it is time to set to, threshing." But Augustine is hardly likely to have introduced a grain harvest image into the middle of his extended olive harvest comparison. So I propose emending to *innitendum torturae*, "it is time to set to, twisting," that is turning, by something like a capstan, the huge wooden screw that pushed down the weights onto the olives in the vat. The olive press, *torcular*, is so called from the verb *torqueo*, to twist or screw, from which *tortura* is also derived. Dolbeau regards the text as suspect, and wonders if *innitendum* should not be read as *immitendum*, giving the sense, "it is time for the human race to be put into the *tritura*, the threshing"; but that keeps the improbable mixing of images.

28. Again emending *trituras* to *torturas*, which would here carry definite connotations of torture.

29. Reading *dura iniquitas* instead of the text's *dira iniquitas*.

30. *Linguam supplantationis.* The second word, meaning literally "tripping up," is rather oddly associated with the first. I looked for a biblical allusion to account for it, but could not find one. Lewis & Short gives "deceit" as its meaning in two texts of the Vulgate; but that seems rather weak, and not exactly to the point here.

Dolbeau 9
SERMON 28A
Mainz 24

SERMON OF BLESSED AUGUSTINE ON THE VERSE OF THE PSALM
I MYSELF SAID IN MY PANIC EVERY MAN A LIAR
AND ON THE READING FROM SOLOMON FROM WHERE HE SAYS
IF YOU HAVE TAKEN YOUR SEAT AT THE TABLE OF A GREAT MAN
TO THE PLACE WHERE HE SAID *HE GOES TO THE HOUSE OF HIS CHIEF*

Date: 397[1]

How can we repay God for all his benefits?

1. The apostle says, *But having the same spirit of faith, according to what is written: "I believed; for which reason I spoke, " we too believe; for which reason we also speak* (2 Cor 4:13; Ps 116:10). If you want to speak when you don't believe, you are wanting to pour out from a jug you haven't filled. It has to be filled, for you to pour out. But it must be poured out for others in such a way that you are not left empty yourself. That's why the Lord, when promising believers an abundance of his Holy Spirit, said, *It will become in him a fountain of water leaping up to eternal life* (Jn 4:14). It's in the nature of fountains, you see, to pour out their water without getting empty. And if God grants us this, what shall we pay back to the Lord for all the things he has paid back to us?

And so the one who was speaking in the psalm as we heard, being full of the grace of God, and thinking about God's generous gift to him, looked around to see what he could give back in return, and didn't find any ready answer he could make. So he hesitated in his search, and said, *What shall I pay back to the Lord for all the things he has paid back to me?* (Ps 116:12). He didn't pay me, you see, but he paid me back, because what I deserved for the bad things I had done was bad things, and he paid me back good things for bad things. "What can I," he is saying, "pay the Lord—if, of course, I can pay the Lord back anything, since it says to him in another psalm, *I said to the Lord: you indeed are my God, because you have no need of my goods* (Ps 16:2)? So if the reason you are the Lord is that you have no need of my goods, *what shall I pay back to the Lord?*" And yet in his own opinion he had found something to pay back: *The cup of salvation shall I receive*, he said, *and I will call upon the name of the Lord* (Ps 116:13). This is paying back, is it? Surely, it's just receiving once again.

48

2. He had said earlier on, however, *I myself said in my panic, Every man a liar* (Ps 116:11). In so saying, though, he seems to have presented people—but only those who don't understand properly and don't pay careful attention—not so much with a confession of sin as with a pretext for it. *Every man a liar*, said scripture. You can now say, "I will tell lies without a qualm, because *every man a liar*. So you see I'm not a man unless I'm a liar." You've had your relief from qualms; now take a dose of anxiety: *You will destroy all who utter lies* (Ps 5:7). So come back again anxiously and make further inquiries, because he didn't say "without a qualm," but *in my panic*. And so I could say to you, "He said it in panic, said it shaking in his shoes, he didn't know what he was saying, he said it in a disturbed state of mind." I could say this, if Paul the apostle hadn't confirmed the assertion, when he says,[2] *God alone is truthful, but every man a liar, as it is written* (Rom 3:4).

So if God is truthful, and he alone is truthful, while *every man a liar*, how will man ever be truthful, unless he approaches the one who is not a liar? In any case, men are told, *You were once darkness* (Eph 5:8). There you have *every man a liar*. God on the other hand is told, *With you is the fountain of life, and in your light we shall see light* (Ps 36:9). And because God alone is truthful, *since God is light, and there is no darkness in him* (1 Jn 1:5), men are darkness, God is light; man a liar, God truthful. When will man ever be truthful? *Approach him and be enlightened* (Ps 34:5). So this is what scripture wished to demonstrate, that every human being, absolutely every single one, as regards being merely human, is a liar. It is precisely, you see, from what is our own that every one of us is a liar. Nor are we able,[3] from what is our own, to be anything but liars—not that we cannot ever be truthful, but that we will never be truthful from what is our own.

Therefore, in order to be truthful, *I believed; for which reason I spoke* (Ps 116:10). Take away believing: *every man a liar*. When you pull away, after all, from God's truth, you will remain in your own falsehood, because *the one who speaks falsehood speaks from what is his own*[4] (Jn 8:44). So then, if you have now become truthful, learn where you have got this from, or on this very point you will again be a liar. Yes, you see, truthful man, when you say, "I am truthful from what is my own," you are in those very words being a liar. So if you really are truthful, it's because you have been filled, because you have begun to participate in truth. You were empty, but you have been filled with truth from the heavenly fountain; that's why you will be able to say, *What shall I pay back to the Lord for all the things he has paid back to me?* (Ps 116:12). *I said in my panic*, and what I said was true, *Every man a liar* (Ps 116:11). But God pays me back, not punishment for lying, but good for evil, and by justifying the godless[5] he turns me from being a liar into a truthful person.

3. So then, *What shall I pay back to the Lord? The cup of salvation shall I receive, and I will call upon the name of the Lord* (Ps 116:12-13). *The cup of*

salvation shall I receive; the cup of Christ shall I receive. He, after all, is the salvation of God. I mean, it was about him that old Simeon said, *Now you are releasing your servant, Lord, in peace, since my eyes have seen your salvation* (Lk 2:29-30). So you then, if you are asking *What shall I pay back to the Lord?* for all the things he has paid back to you, receive *the cup of salvation.*

What cup?

The cup of salvation.

What salvation?

Christ. And which cup of Christ our salvation can it be, but the one he mentioned in his answer to the pair who had their sights set on the lofty heights and were ignoring the lowly depths: *Can you drink the cup which I am going to drink* (Mt 20:22)? Receive this cup, if you wish to pay the Lord back for all the things he has paid back to you. *For just as Christ laid down his life for us, so we too ought to lay down our lives for the brethren* (1 Jn 3:16). That is what paying him back means, accepting the cup of salvation.

But what are you afraid of, what do you dread in that sort of cup? He himself will be at your side to support you, just as he went ahead to set you an example. I mean, just look at this man who is inquiring what he can pay back, and who in his very inquiry,[6] it seems, finds this cup, as though to say, "I have found what I can pay back; *the cup of salvation shall I receive*"; and being capable of drinking it, he boldly said, *and I will call upon the name of the Lord* (Ps 116:13). Accordingly when you are trying to pay back, you haven't in fact paid back what you have received, but have just received something more in addition. You have received once the grace to believe, and a second time the grace to drink the cup of salvation. So it is by him that all things have been given us; through him we have what we are, if we are anything good.

Returning Christ's hospitality by sharing his sufferings

4. So it is too that the reading which came before the psalm seems to suggest something of the same sort to us, provided we are capable of grasping the will of the one making the suggestion. He says, you see, *If you have taken your seat to dine at the table of a great man, observe shrewdly what is being set before you, and stretch out your hand, knowing that it will be your duty to prepare the same sort of food yourself* (Prv 23:1-2 LXX). If you have taken your seat at the table of a great man, you are being told to observe shrewdly what is being set before you; then you are next told to stretch out your hand, *knowing that it will be your duty to prepare the same sort of food yourself.* Is there any man greater than Christ? Take your seat to dine at his table: be humble as you approach his altar; sitting down, you see, is a mark of humility.[7] So then, *observe shrewdly what is being set before you.* What you are receiving is the very host who has invited you. You have taken your seat at the table of your shepherd;[8] what you find there, you see, is the death of your host.

Those who take their seats at this table know what I am saying;[9] it isn't a trifling matter; the one who invited you is explaining himself to you. So then, *observe shrewdly what is being set before you, and stretch out your hand, knowing that it will be your duty to provide the same sort of food yourself.* What this means I told you a moment ago: *For just as Christ laid down his life for us, so we too ought to lay down our lives for the brethren* (1 Jn 3:16). This is the table of that great man; this is the dinner you have come to, if you have taken your seat in a humble frame of mind; or rather this is the dinner at which you have taken your seat, if you have come in a humble frame of mind. Notice what has been prepared for you: *Christ laid down his life for us.* This is what you are receiving, there you are, that's what you stretch out your hand to, *knowing that it will be your duty to prepare the same sort of food yourself.* So then, say what comes next: *So we too ought to lay down our lives for the brethren.*

So you're receiving the cup of salvation and calling upon the name of the Lord. You have received a precious death, you see; that's why you have drained the cup. What comes next? *Precious in the sight of the Lord is the death of his saints* (Ps 116:15). There you have how you eat such food, how you prepare such food.

Do not claim more credit than you are worth

5. But what's this that follows in the same reading? Let's attend to it and see; let's get to the bottom of it, if we can. *But if you are greedier*, he says, *do not set your heart on his banquets; for these things have a false life* (Prv 23:3). I see; the door's shut. And where's the knocker?[10] Let's all knock together, so that it may be opened to us. He's a great man, it's a great man's table; you're seated at it, you have humbled yourself before it, stretching out your hand, knowing what sort of things it is your duty to prepare: to suffer for the name of the Lord who suffered for you. But *if you are greedier*, he says, *do not set your heart on his banquets.* What's the meaning of *If you are greedier*? Do you really want to know what *If you are greedier* means? If you give yourself more than you eat.[11]

As I knock for all I'm worth in these obscure depths, this is what occurs to me at the moment, what he has been pleased to grant me; this for the moment is what he has opened the door upon. Look, it's a great man's table, it's the table of Christ, loaded with the grace of the Lord's passion. Take your seat at it; don't approach it in pride. *Stretch out your hand*; don't let the tongue hold forth, and the work keep quiet. That, you see, is what stretching out your hand means. Don't let there be words which are not solidly backed by deeds, faith which is not backed by works. *Stretch out your hand, knowing that you must prepare the same sort of things.* What with, you wretched pauper? From your own resources? Woe to you, if that's what you think! You will produce nothing, will have nothing. So, *if you are greedier*—giving yourself more than you are—*do not set your heart on his victuals.* Because if you give yourself more than you eat and still set your heart on his victuals, notice what follows: *for these things have a deceitful life.*[12]

6. *These things*, he says, *have a deceitful life.* What things have a deceitful

life? Your being greedier, giving yourself more, attributing more to yourself than you know you are worth, that's the deceitful life, that's hypocrisy, that's boastfulness, not obedience. It's a totally deceitful life. *For whoever thinks he is anything, when he is nothing, is deceiving himself* (Gal 6:3). Will you really pay back such a great man as that from your own means? Taking fare like that from such a great man as that, will you really prepare the same sort of things from your own resources? What loathsome greed, what a deceitful life! Finally, after he says *For these things have a deceitful life*, meaning if you give yourself more than you are, and are greedier in this way, and fail to perceive the grace when you approach the table of grace, notice what he adds, and the kind of advice he gives you. What is it you were saying, after all? "I'll pay back from my own resources, I'll give a return from my own means, I will prepare a meal from my own means, and I will prepare the same sort of meal as this rich man has provided."

Notice what follows: *Do not stretch yourself against the rich man, since you are poor* (Prv 23:4). Advice most salutary, if there's anyone to listen to it, if you hear it as a poor person, if you don't consider yourself rich in what is your own, if you don't stretch yourself against the rich man. By stretching yourself out, you see, you are more likely to be inflated than filled. You're saying all the time, "From what is mine, from what is mine"; against whom are you saying it? *For what do you have that you have not received* (1 Cor 4:7)? He is full, you are just inflated. *Do not stretch yourself against the rich man, since you are poor.* That is the deceitful life; you are remaining in the condition you stated in your panic: *Every man a liar* (Ps 116:11). *Do not stretch yourself against the rich man, since you are poor*; not against God, since you are merely human; not against the Just One, since you are a sinner; not against the one who had no sin,[13] being yourself a human being who cannot live without sin. *"Do not stretch yourself against the rich man, since you are poor; but restrain yourself in your thoughts* (Prv 23:4). Take your own measure; do not go outside yourself and mock me, but enter into yourself and observe the real you."

If you fix your eye on him, he will nowhere appear

7. For *if you fix your eye*, he says, *on him, he will nowhere appear. For he has prepared wings for himself like an eagle's, and he is going away to the house of his chief* (Prv 23:5). Who is this mighty man, whose table you were approaching, from whom you were receiving a meal and arranging to pay back the same sort of meal, apparently, from your own resources? Yes, you're stretching yourself, a pauper, against a rich man, and not rather restraining yourself in your thoughts, so that he may recognize you as needing assistance, and not find you deserving damnation. Who is this great man, whom you are seeking, it seems, to provide for from your own resources, and to provide for in the same style as he has in fact provided for you? Who is he—do you want to know? *If you fix your eye on him, he will nowhere appear.* What is this? He terrified us when he said, *he will nowhere appear.* But when will he nowhere appear? When you fix

your eye on him, this squinting eye, with which you can't see straight, with which you can't understand rightly; if you fix this eye on him, *he will nowhere appear.* He will remain hidden, you see, he won't show himself; you won't grasp him, won't understand him. Acknowledge yourself as being less than he is, in order to be able to understand him as greater than you.

It can also be understood in this way: *If you fix your eye on him,* a human eye, seeking him as a mere man, *he will nowhere appear,* because he is not a mere man. *He will nowhere appear;* seek him in the east, seek him in the west, seek him among the patriarchs, seek him among the prophets, seek him among the apostles, he will nowhere appear to you; he is not, after all, only a man, but the God man. Accordingly, *if you fix your eye on him,* that is, a merely human eye, not the divinely given spirit, *he will nowhere appear.* If you seek him just as a man, you won't find him; if you seek the one who has been providing for you just as a man, you won't find him; *he will nowhere appear.*

8. *For he has prepared wings for himself like an eagle's* (Prv 23:5). Yes, he did this; he prepared himself wings like an eagle's—he was taken up, he flew away, since it was about him that scripture said, *His life shall be taken up from the earth*[14] (Is 53:8). *And he will go away to the house of his chief* (Prv 23:5). He has returned to the Father; you, on the other hand, have remained among men. He, who made you, has gone beyond you. Yes, you don't think much of him, because he was also made, a creature for your sake. If you want to pay him back, accept from him the means to do it with. That's what poor people do, when they receive invitations from their rich patrons, and wish to invite them back in return; they beg from them something they can decently offer them.

The Father begot him equal to himself, begot him coeternal with himself, begot him of one and the same substance as himself; but for your sake he made him less, and became his chief, so that his Son could say about him, his Only-begotten, coeternal with him, equal to him: *The Father is greater than I* (Jn 14:28). What did he beget, do you want to know? Ask him, and listen to the answer: *I and the Father are one* (Jn 10:30). If you want to know what he was made for your sake, ask him, and listen to the answer: *Since the Father is greater than I.* Acknowledge his justice, cherish obedience, beware of pride; praise his power, admire his patience, obtain grace from him.

NOTES

1. This is one of the series of sermons preached in the early summer of 397 at Carthage, according to Dom Lambot. He places it between 24 May, which was Pentecost that year, and the feast of John the Baptist on 24 June. In Possidius' *Index* and in the Mainz collection, from which Dolbeau has published it, it follows immediately on Sermons 7 and 28.

A fragment of it quoted by Bede has already appeared in Volume III/2 as Sermon 28A. That, together with the footnote guessing that it was preached after 411, should now give way to this complete sermon. The heading is that of the Mainz collection; the texts are respectively Ps 116:11 and Prv 23:1-5.

2. This is where Bede begins to select the two extracts that constitute the fragment 28A. They are confined to this section 2 of the complete sermon.

3. So Bede in his quotation. But between this sentence and the previous one, this text inserts a clause which cannot possibly have been spoken by Augustine, but which must represent the marginal comment of a misguided copyist, whose bad theology was that of what one may call a coarse Platonist. With the previous sentence, here given more literally, it runs: "Man is not a liar except from what is his own; that is, from the body which consists of earthy matter. For the soul is divine, and with it he is truthful, not a liar. Nor is he able. . ."

4. John is here talking about the devil, not about Everyman.

5. See Rom 4:5.

6. Reading *in ipsa inquisitione* instead of the text's *in ipsa retributione*. This latter could easily have been substituted by a copyist, who had just written to dictation the word *retribuat*.

7. Not in our European culture; but it was in Israel: see, for example, 2 Sm 7:18, where David "went in and sat before the Lord"; and it still is in African culture, where one sits in the presence of a chief or superior. But in these cultures, of course, one is sitting on the ground, not on a chair.

8. *Pastoris tui.* But *pastor* comes from *pascere*, to feed. The shepherd feeds his flock; he is the feeder; and this connotation is very strong here, but impossible to convey in English.

9. And so, almost certainly, did the catechumens, who had not yet taken their seats at the Lord's table. But they were not supposed to know!

10. *Et ubi pulsatio?* Literally, "And where's the knocking?" But I am guessing that *pulsatio* may also have meant something to knock with; also guessing that doors in the late Roman Empire were equipped with door-knockers!

11. He is punning on the word *es* in the scripture quotation, if you are greedier: in Latin *si avidior es.* As well as meaning "you are"; it is also the second person singular of the verb *edo* and so can mean "you eat."

12. The passage is being quoted with several free variations. This supports Dolbeau's suggestion that Augustine was preaching in a church where the version in the lectionary differed from what he was used to in Hippo Regius. Perhaps, too, the various churches in Carthage, where he was preaching almost continuously this summer of 397, did not all have one identical version of the scriptures.

13. See 2 Cor 5:21; 1 Pt 2:22.

14. A singularly inapt application of the text!

Dolbeau 29

SERMON

ON GOD'S PROVIDENCE

Date: 408[1]

God's providence often denied, because bad people do well in life,
and good people badly

1. The reading from the apostle which you heard just now, brothers and
sisters, where the blessed apostle Paul says, *But is this what you suppose, O man,*
who judge those that do such things and do them yourself, that you will escape
the judgment of God? (Rom 2:3), and the rest that follows on the same point,
this reading is being used by the Lord to suggest to me that I should discuss,
insofar as he himself helps me to do so, that providence of his, that forethought[2]
which he is good enough to bestow on caring for our human affairs. A great
many people, you see, deny there is such a thing, when they observe how many
and how great and important are the things that occur in this life and in the affairs
of mortal men and women apparently by chance and not according to any plan;
and because they themselves are unable to see any rhyme or reason in such
things, they assume that they do not come under any controlling plan of God's,
but happen purely according to the luck of the draw.

Of these many objections, there is in particular the one about which the holy
apostle is replying to human difficulties in this passage, namely that of the
people who say, "If God really took care of the life of human beings, he certainly
wouldn't allow the wicked and the impious to live"; in this way, while objecting
to the impious being allowed to go on living, they themselves utter impiety
against God.[3] Paul answers them with apostolic authority: *Is this*, he says, *what*
you suppose, O man, who judge those that do such things and do them yourself,
that you will escape the judgment of God? Or do you make light of the riches
of his kindness and patience and forbearance, unaware that God's kindness is
prompting you to repentance? But in accordance with the stubbornness of your
heart and your unrepentant heart, you are storing up for yourself wrath in the
day of wrath and of the revelation of the judgment of God, who will pay each
one back according to his works (Rom 2:3-6). So how can God take not care of
human affairs, if he is going to "pay each one back according to his works"?

2. But those who don't believe that God takes care of human affairs will

55

undoubtedly not believe the apostle's words either, nor any of the divine utterances and writings which so insistently and frequently stress this very point. So then we must find out from them precisely why they are of the opinion that God's providence or forethought is indifferent to human affairs.

"Because everything," they will say, "that is governed by providence has to be well ordered and duly arranged. What though," they go on, "could show less signs of order and be in a greater mess than human affairs, where bad people frequently enjoy such outstanding prosperity and success that in addition to everything else they exercise power over good people, while the good on the contrary are ground down with misfortune, and forced into subjection to the bad?"

So if this is why they deny there is such a thing as God's providence, they ought to admit that it is his providence at work, when we see good people eminent in wealth, honors, authority, while by their enforcement of law and order bad people are kept in check. In this case, after all, the ordering of human affairs is certainly shown to be beautifully all that it should be.

"Not so," they reply; "because if this were always and uniformly the case, then we would indeed admit that human affairs are in perfect order. And again, if we observed that all bad people are doing very well, while all the good are the slaves of the bad, beset with grief and pain of all sorts, deprived of all resources, even in this case we would be impressed by the consistency of a kind of order, and be prompted to believe that the bad are enjoying such visible well-being because they have been deprived of that much better and more stable well-being that is invisible in the heart and mind; while the reason the good do not enjoy this outward variety is that they receive within themselves a much more worthwhile blessing, and that their joy, which is now kindled by the hope of immortality, will be fully realized when all their toil and trouble is over and done with. Now, however," they go on to say, "since in this life some of the best people do better than the worst and some of the worst do better than the best in a mixed up, higgledy-piggledy fashion, this very inconsistency reveals a total absence of order, proves that God takes no care at all of human affairs."

God's providence to be seen first in the order that governs
our natural constitution

3. Our reply to this is to urge them—provided, of course, they can listen patiently to anything that goes against their preconceived ideas—to urge them before anything else to nurse back their sickly understanding to health, with that piety which alone can render them fit to investigate the plans of God through the help given their unskillful powers by his Spirit; and to agree that they have already come under God's care simply in order to be human beings. Having thus made a kind of step, let them climb up to higher levels, where to the best of their ability they may understand that what sort of people we ought to be is also the business of the God whose business it was that we should be at all.

I mean, if it is their observation of human affairs as disordered and messy that drives them to deny that they are controlled by divine providence, they should at least begin by not leaving the human himself out of account, not throw it aside and trample on it and proceed on their way, not be in a hurry after passing over themselves to make rash judgments about other things. Instead they should linger over themselves a little while, and not scorn to take a somewhat more careful look at themselves, and see what a thorough and painstaking natural order is to be found there, even in the midst of the thorough mess and mire of their vices.

4. The first thing to demonstrate the beauty of a wonderfully ordered arrangement is that human beings consist of soul and body, and direct the movements of the visible subordinate element through the more important invisible one; that is to say, with the natural ruler, the soul, in command, and the natural servant, the flesh, in subjection to it. What else but order is brilliantly illustrated in the soul itself, where the highest value is put on the faculty of reason, given the superiority of its nature, and so it presides over the soul's other parts? Nobody, after all, is so given over to self-indulgence that he would have any doubt about what his answer should be, if he were asked whether it is better for him to be swept along by his thoughtless appetites, or to be governed by reason and deliberation. Thus even those whose careless lives follow no rational pattern will still answer which of these is the better, the very question obliging them to do so even if it doesn't lead them to mend their ways. So we see that not even in people who cling to their perverse habits does order lose its voice, since it is nature itself that censures vice.

5. The body too, in itself—who could ever exhaustively describe the wonderful order in which its different parts are arranged and held together in its total structure? Who could ever sufficiently sing the praises of the head, placed centrally upon the shoulders,[4] and being more signally honored than the other parts, carried by the rest of the body as its vehicle? In it the notable senses are seated distinctly in their proper places, keeping watch and ward as from a higher lookout over the body's health, and like alert and attentive assistants announcing to the mind inside what is happening outside or what is being brought in from outside, whether it's nice or nasty, while the mind inside in its kind of inner sanctum appraises and assesses it all.[5]

The eyes, I mean, are on duty to announce shapes and colors, the ears to announce sounds and words, the nostrils smells, the jaws flavors; while touch, though spread as a general sense throughout the whole body, also takes its lead from the head. Next come the hands, placed under the head, good equipment for doing necessary work, bringing in useful things, warding off threats; then the chest and belly are fixed to the backbone behind them, like a pair of boxes in which to keep safely enclosed the vital organs, because these are endangered by external contact. Finally the feet are put under the rest for carrying them all and for moving them around from place to place.

6. But now, who would not be delighted to observe, and so come to admire, the craftsman in his work more and more, how attention has been paid not only to health and utility, but also to dignity and decorum? Organs and limbs in pairs

balance each other, like the eyes, the ears, the cheekbones,[6] shoulderblades, hands, sides, feet, finally the very fingers and toes on hands and feet. On this side and that the members of each pair correspond to one another with due and acknowledged equality; and to show quite clearly that the body's beauty as well as its integrity was taken into account, even the male breast that is never going to give suck is adorned with the symmetry of twin nipples.[7]

Those parts, however, of which only one was created, have been centered down the middle—otherwise, if they were placed on one side, the other would be cheated of its due honor; thus the head and the neck, and in the head itself the nose and mouth, the navel in the belly and the other parts lower down which, just as God providently decided to make them, so man would have been able publicly to speak of them and praise them, if he hadn't made them private and shameful by sinning. Finally, would anyone willingly pass over in silence the fact, when it came to mind, that the creator has concealed the inner parts of the body beneath a covering of skin, because while they are arranged in a marvelously rational way, they are more decently thought of than exposed to view? The intellect, you see, marvels when they come to mind, but the sight shudders when they are laid bare; so to insure both their utility and their dignity, providential provision was made for them to be concealed, and for minds to be properly exercised in studying them in such a way as to avoid the eyes being offended in having to see them.

*The providence detectable in the order of nature
must also govern the lives and behavior of human beings*

7. This setting up of a rational animal, this arrangement of soul ruling and flesh serving, of mind and spirit, of head and body and unseen[8] natural parts, of knowledge and action; intelligence, sense, and movement, the reservoir of memory, the lessons of knowledge, the decisions of the will, the use and adornment of the body's limbs and organs, and everything by which human beings are human—whom could it have as its author but God? Or just because, except for the rational mind, except too for the body's upright posture by which human beings are admonished to lift their hearts up also to heaven, the same orderly arrangement is to be found as well in the souls and bodies of beasts, is that a reason for denying men and women? On the contrary, it's a good reason for acknowledging even more firmly that one and the same God is the creator of man and beast alike.

After all, there wouldn't have been any kind of life anywhere at all, unless it had been made by life that was itself not made. Nor would such a manifest order be apparent in the generation of the tiniest and least of living mites, or even of the seeds, roots, trunks, branches, leaves, flowers, fruits of countless trees and herbs, from nature's secret stores,[9] unless he were creating it whose magnificent and, if one may so put it, omnificent[10] Wisdom, containing in itself the unchangeable and invisible ideas of changeable and visible things, like artifacts in the art of the artesan or craftsman, *reaches*, as it says, *reaches from end to end mightily, and arranges all things sweetly* (Wis 8:1).

Given all this, given too that in everything that goes on in the earth what goes on among human beings takes pride of place, just as human beings themselves do, it is surely the last word in absurdity to deny in great matters that divine provision and forethought which we admire in small ones—unless of course we are to understand that the one who takes so much trouble in making and decreeing the definite number of totally insignificant hairs[11] leaves the lives of men and women free from any judgment! Let us therefore please have no hesitation in believing that what seems to be messy and disordered in human affairs is governed, not by no plan at all, but rather by an altogether loftier one, and by a more all-embracing divine order that can be grasped by our human littleness.

8. Hence we must above all believe what religion proclaims, that there is going to be a manifest final judgment, because we now see successes and disasters allotted indiscriminately to good and bad people alike without any appearance of judgment; though seeing that God's providence is so prominent in trifling matters, his justice could not possibly allow these major matters to drift aimlessly around in every direction, without any judgment being passed on them. But what could be of greater moment, not only in this human but also in the angelic world, than that the bad should be punished with well-deserved woes, while the good enjoy blessedness and bliss?

So when at present things seem to go well with a bad man, it is a hidden punishment, an unreal kind of success,[12] while when a good man is doing badly, it does not mean he is being refused a reward for his religious manner of life, but that his religion is being refined by patience[13] to earn greater rewards. Again, that sometimes even in this life a bad man does badly means either that he is being corrected, or that he is being afflicted for his sins, while when things go well with a good man, this is not the fixed and sure reward of that heavenly home country, but some sort of relief on this dangerous journey toward it. If irreligious unbelief were to give itself to these and similar reflections, it would not deny that divine providence is directing and ordering human affairs, nor would it hold out in its darkened and death-dealing vigor against the light and life of wisdom.[14]

Scripture's assertion of divine providence

9. You though, my dearest brothers and sisters, who have already come to believe in Christ, must not harness yourselves up with unbelievers,[15] by assuming that God does not care how human beings live, seeing that he takes care that not only human beings but also cattle, fish, birds should have the means to live. I mean, we mustn't take what the apostle says about God not caring about oxen as letting us assume that animals being born and fed doesn't come under God's providence, seeing that the Lord Jesus uses the clearest examples of this sort in order to chide and stir up people's faith, telling them to see the birds in the sky and how he feeds them, and how he clothes the grass of the field, and from that to trust him not to neglect the feeding and clothing of his own servants.[16] But

the reason the apostle said, *For God does not care about oxen* (1 Cor 9:9), was to stop us thinking that the text, *You shall not muzzle the mouth of the ox that is threshing* (Dt 25:4), just refers to oxen, and not in fact to people. So God was not concerned in holy scripture to give people commandments on how they should treat their animals; but this does not mean he has no concern for nature, providing for all kinds of animals to be born and to be nourished on appropriate foods.

If human reason naturally prefers order to disorder,
how much more must the divine Wisdom?

10. But as for the silly fools and unbelievers who maintain that God has no concern for human affairs, because they can't find any order in the way good things and bad happen to people, let us send them off to observe the miracles of nature. After all, how can they believe the divine scriptures are true, when they don't believe they are divine? So then, let the unbelieving person attend to something which he cannot say was instituted by men, and not deny that the God who taught the bee to arrange its honey cells in such marvelous order does not put order into human affairs. Who, indeed, gave this person the good taste to dislike disorder in things and take delight in things that are well-ordered? Doesn't he find this in the very nature of his own soul, which he didn't make for himself? Why, after all, on failing to perceive any order in human affairs, does he refuse to believe that God is in control of human affairs, if not because he knows instinctively by nature that order is to be preferred to disorder? So then, is a man capable of judging that orderliness rather than a chaotic mess is proper to divine works, and does God have no properly ordered judgment to make of all human beings, though he has created a sense for order in every single one of them?

He does, he certainly does; let it not be doubted by religious piety, even if it is not understood by human infirmity. In the same sort of way, we admire the work of smiths and carpenters which we can inspect, but we are amazed at that of machine designers and operators, and unless their workings were openly demonstrated, we would wonder at their being able to do the impossible.[17] So why do we make such a rash judgment about the judgments of God, and rush in to deny any order in the divine work, where we can't see it, praising the provident provision made by the creator in the leaves of trees and assuming it isn't there in the affairs of men? Why don't we rather believe that a hidden and inscrutable order runs through human affairs, which we are incapable of either comprehending because it is so vast, or of inspecting because it is so thoroughly concealed? But manifest evidence of order in things established by God, from which less evident systems of order may be inferred, is there to strike even the eyes of the irreligious.

11. As for us, however, besides these obvious signs of order to be perceived in heaven and earth, we have in faith the surest possible indication to prove to us that human affairs fall under God's care, such that it would be unlawful for us not just to deny this, but even to doubt it: namely our Lord Jesus Christ himself, *who though he was in the form of God, did not reckon it robbery to be equal to God, but emptied himself, taking the form of a slave, being made in the likeness of men; and being found in condition as a man, he humbled himself, becoming obedient to the death, death indeed on a cross* (Phil 2:6-8).

How then can man not fall under God's care, man on whose account God's Son became man? How can God not care for the life of human beings, for whose sake God's Son endured death? How can he not make orderly dispositions for the morals even of bad people, though he does not cause them, when it was at the hands of bad men that Christ suffered what would avail to establish the morals of the good? How can he fail to make provident use even of the sins of the disloyal, when it was through them that his loyal blood[18] was shed for the forgiveness of sins? How will he fail to visit retribution on the unfaithful, seeing that he delivers the faithful precisely in order to spare them such retribution? How will he fail to bestow on the faithful the reward of their fidelity, having endured for their sake the shame even of the cross? How will the good and bad things fail to be eternal which he will award when he judges, seeing that he taught us to despise both the good and bad things of time when he was judged? It is not only, therefore, the fact that God has a care for human affairs, but how much he cares, which we are given the surest possible proof of by the manifest reality of Christ's birth, by the patient endurance of his death, by the power of his resurrection.

12. In the establishment and regulation of other things also, to be sure, his providence is to be seen without a shadow of doubt, not a single leaf falling, not a single seed sprouting unprovided for by him; but nowhere is it shown so clearly how much he loves man as when he made into a man the one through whom he made man,[19] and when he was willing for life to die so that the one who had thrown life away might live, and when he made the one through whom he is going to give the reward into the very model of the reward itself, this *great sacrament of piety which was manifested in the flesh, was justified in the spirit, appeared to the angels, was proclaimed to the nations, believed on in the world, taken up in glory* (1 Tm 3:16). From the very origins of the human race it was foretold through the Spirit of God that this would happen until it actually did,[20] and still these unbelievers reply—*they speak iniquity* (Ps 94:4)—that human affairs do not come under the care of God.

We, however, attribute it to God's gift, not to our own merits that *while we were by nature children of wrath like the rest* (Eph 2:3)—by nature, of course, as it was vitiated later by its own iniquity[21]—we were made into children of mercy, being set apart from the rest, not by nature, not by the law, but by grace. So let us not then look down on the unbelievers for the false things they say about God's providence, but let us work hard so that they may hear the truth, let us pray hard that they may believe it.

NOTES

1. François Dolbeau, who published this sermon in *Revue des Études Augustiniennes* (1995) 41, argues for a date more generally between 399 and 410; but tentatively, from evidence in the text, and the relationship of this sermon with other works contained in the same manuscript at Mantua, he places it more precisely in 408 or 409. He came across the complete text of the sermon in the municipal library of that city in 1995. The manuscript comes from the Benedictine Abbey of Polirone, and was copied in the early twelfth century. Only extracts of the sermon were known previously in an anthology of Augustinian texts made by a certain Eugippius about a hundred years after Augustine's death.

2. There is just the word *providentia* in the Latin. But "providence" in English has become almost exclusively a theological word, and it is necessary to bring out its natural connection with such more general or secular synonyms as "foresight" and "forethought."

3. For the same objection to divine providence, see Sermons 17, 4; 18, 1 (III, 1); and 311, 12 (III, 9).

4. Literally, "placed between the shoulders," *humeris interpositum*; this calls to mind one of the monsters in Sir John Mandeville's *Travels*, which had its head precisely between its shoulders, in the middle of its chest. Given the enormous authority of Augustine in the middle ages, could this monster possibly derive from this rather careless phrase of his here?

5. For this notion see Sermons 154, 12 (III, 5); 223A, 4 (III, 6); 288, 3 (III, 8); 159B, 6 (III, 11).

6. *Jugalia*, a very rare word in this sense; Dolbeau thinks Augustine meant the cheeks by it, rather than the cheekbones, and suggests that it may lie behind the French *joues*. But while I do not question this etymological suggestion of his, I prefer to translate "cheekbones," since Augustine goes on immediately to mention *scapulae*, "shoulder blades," though this word too could be used in the broader sense of "shoulders."

7. For this point, and for what he goes on to say about the private parts and the intestines, see also Sermons 110, 1 (III, 4); 243, 3.6 (III, 7), and *City of God*, XXII, 24, 4.

8. The manuscript has an abbreviation here, *inv.que*. Dolbeau fills it out to *invisibilisque*, giving the sense "and of the invisible nature," which would in Augustine's normal usage refer to the soul. But I am suggesting filling the abbreviation out to *invisaeque*, literally "of the unseen nature," and taking the reference to be to the hidden parts of the body he has just been talking about at the end of section 6. This would fit the immediate context of this long sentence rather better.

9. He had in mind the spontaneous generation of the smallest insects and living organisms from decaying matter; the almost universally accepted "scientific theory" in the ancient world.

10. *Omnifica*, a word he appears to invent; a step beyond the *magnifica* that precedes it. The current English "magnificent" doesn't quite get the force of this word, which in the Latin means exactly what it says, "doing great things"; but I had to use it, in order to be able to go along with Augustine in inventing "omnificent." Dolbeau says this word does occur occasionally in medieval Latin; but it is not given in Du Cange's *Glossary*. For Augustine's theory of the ideas of things in the Word of God, his Christianization, so to say, of Plato's theory of ideas, see *The Trinity*, VI, 10, 11; also his work on *The Literal Meaning of Genesis* almost throughout, where he develops his notion of *rationes seminales*, these ideas sown, as it were, like seed in creation, on the day it was made (Gn 2:4), and then germinating stage by stage during the six days of Genesis 1.

11. See Mt 10:30.

12. See Sermon 301, 8 (III, 8).

13. Emending to *patientia pietas augetur* the text's *patientia pietatis augetur*: "the patience of his religion is being refined (literally, increased). . . ." The whole drift of the sentence, it seems to me, requires "religion" to be the subect of this part of the sentence.

14. An oblique allusion here, I think, to Jn 1:4-5—"In it (the Word) was life, and the life was the light of men; and the light shines in the darkness, and the darkness did not comprehend/overpower it."

15. See 2 Cor 6:14. His turning now to professed Christians indicates that he was preaching to a very mixed audience; nearly all his arguments so far have been addressed to pagans. Almost all his congregations would be thus mixed, but particularly so in cities like Carthage, or his own Hippo Regius. See Sermon 69, 3 (III, 3).

16. See Mt 6:25-32.

17. He is alluding no doubt to the contrivances for producing a *deus ex machina* in the theaters; and Dolbeau suggests that there is also an allusion to similar contrivances in pagan temples, designed to fill the devout pagan worshipers with awe. Augustine refers to such *mechanemata* in *The City of God*, XII, 6, 1-2.

18. His expression is *pius sanguis* in contrast to the *peccata impiorum*. Here in particular one feels the lack of good English words for the Latin *pius, pietas*. The primary meaning is that quality, that virtue, which binds families together, which good parents display toward their children, and children reciprocate in their way toward their parents—a loving, dutiful concern. That is why the pelican, which was mythically supposed to feed its young on its own blood, was called a pious bird; and hence why Saint Thomas Aquinas, in his hymn in honor of Corpus Christi, addresses Christ as *Pie Pelicane, Jesu Domine*; and why the pelican, thus feeding its young, figures in the coats of arms of the colleges of Corpus Christi at both Oxford and Cambridge in England. It is also featured on the coat of arms of Saint Thomas of Villanova, O.S.A, Archbishop of Valencia, Spain.

19. That is, the Word, through whom all things were made, Jn 1:3. In the next phrase I emend to *mori voluit vitam* the text's *mori voluit vita*, which makes *vita* the subject: "and life was willing to die." But the whole run of the section really requires God to be the subject throughout. For the expression "as the model of the reward" see also Sermon 196, 3 (III, 6).

20. See Sermon 379, 2 (III, 10). The text "from the very origins" which he would have had in mind would almost certainly have been Gn 3:15.

21. Reading *utique natura, sicuti est postea sua iniquitate vitiata*, instead of the text's *non utique natura. . .*; "not of course by nature as it was vitiated later by its own iniquity." But Augustine certainly interpreted this "by nature" in the text of Ephesians as fallen nature, not as nature in the creative design of God. I suspect the *non* slipped in purely by a copyist's error, his eye caught by the same word shortly before, or by the two words *non natura* shortly afterward.

Dolbeau 8
SERMON 29B
Mainz 21

SERMON OF BLESSED AUGUSTINE THE BISHOP PREACHED
AT THE VIGIL OF PENTECOST ON THE VERSE OF THE PSALM
CONFESS TO THE LORD SINCE HE IS GOOD, ETC.

Date: 397[1]

Two meanings of "confession"

1. The divine utterance is encouraging us, and saying, *Confess to the Lord, since he is good* (Ps 118:1). *Confess,* it says, *to the Lord.* And as though you asked for a reason, it adds, *since he is good.* The guilty need not fear the judge's severity; the goodness of the one who is hearing your case can reassure you as you are confessing your guilt. If you confess to a man taking cognizance of your case, you die;[2] if you don't confess to God who has precognizance of your case, you die. When a man hears your case, he is waiting to learn what your case is from your confession. God, on the other hand, is judging you even while you are just thinking of doing something wrong. So confess, then, in order to win God over to your side. If you deny you did it, after all, the fact that you did cannot be concealed. When God advises you to confess, he is not expecting you to despise him,[3] but to humble yourself.

Confession, though, in the holy scriptures, is regularly talked of, and meant to be understood, in two ways: one is a matter of your self-punishment, the other a matter of praising God. What I mean by your self-punishment is when you repent. Whenever you repent, you see, you are punishing yourself, in order not to be punished by the Lord.[4] So first of all let me prove that "confession" is talked of in two ways—that is, that beside the confession of sins there is also that of God's praises; and then go on next to sow in your ears whatever the Lord may grant me about each kind of confession.

2. Confession of sins is familiar to us all and well known, and there's no need to prove it, simply to advise it. We should rather be inquiring how we can prove that there is such a thing as confession in praise of God. Indeed, people are so used to the idea of confession with regard to their own sins, that every time, practically, that they hear from the reader's mouth, "Confess," straightaway

64

there is a beating of breasts, and a murmuring sound of stirred-up consciences. This happens almost every time; it isn't, however, every time that it is confession of sins being referred to. Sometimes, you see, it is also the confession of praise, as scripture says in some place or other: *Confess to the Lord, and this is what you shall say in confession; that all the works of the Lord are very good* (Sir 39:15-16). When you hear *This is what you shall say in confession; that all the works of the Lord are very good*, it is obvious that this means the confession of God's praises, not of your iniquities. You're confessing, I mean, all the Lord's good works, not your own bad ones.

Here's another text for you, about which there can likewise be no doubt. The Lord Jesus, of course, did not have any sin at all, and yet he says in the gospel, *I confess to you, Father, Lord of heaven and earth.* Then follows the praise: *because you have hidden these things from the wise and the experienced. Yes, Father, because such was your good pleasure* (Lk 10:21). This is the confession of a man praising God, not accusing himself. So then, since those who confess are either accusing themselves or praising God, reflect for a while on the value of each kind of confession.

Punish yourself, to avoid being punished by God

3. Those who accuse themselves of being bad are displeased with themselves. Insofar as bad people are displeased with themselves, they are already beginning to be good, because good people are not pleased with bad ones. This is the first step in attaching our hearts to the law of God, that what he punishes you should punish too, and what displeases him should also displease you; now you're beginning with God to hate sin; you in fact are beginning with him to hate yourself, so that he may begin to love you.

Sin, you see, simply cannot go unpunished. You don't want him to punish; see you punish yourself.[5] The fact is, sin cannot be left unpunished; either you punish it, and he releases you, or you pretend you didn't do it, and he punishes you. I mean, why was that tax collector justified rather than that Pharisee? How else did he deserve to be spared, but by not sparing himself? He was casting his eyes down to the ground, and lifting up his heart;[6] he was beating his breast and curing his conscience. Why say more? *He went down justified, rather than that Pharisee.* If you ask for the reason, *because whoever exalts himself will be humbled, and whoever humbles himself will be exalted* (Lk 18:10-14).

4. You're going to come before the judge; be your own judge. Get in before him in passing judgment, and you will find him ordering your release. What do I mean by "Get in before him"? See that you punish yourself before he punishes you. You have certainly read, after all, *Let us get in before his face in confession* (Ps 95:2). There are two verbs which are evidently opposites to one another: to look at and to overlook.[7] You want him to overlook your sins; take a good look at them yourself. Notice what the repentant accuser of himself says in the psalm: *Turn away your face.* But what from? He doesn't say "from me," because in another place he says *Do not turn your face away from me* (Ps 27:9). So what

does he say from? *Turn away your face from my sins* (Ps 51:9). On what grounds does he want God to turn his face away, not from himself but from his sins, so that by not seeing them he may see him? On what grounds? Take note and imitate. He says in the same psalm, you see, *Since I myself am taking a look at my iniquity.* So you, then, overlook it. *And my sin*, he goes on, *is always before me* (Ps 51:3). He put his finger on those who place other people's sins before themselves, and their own behind them; other people's before themselves, which they then find fault with and chew to pieces; their own behind them, which they then defend—and go on carrying.

5. So it's because those who place their own sins behind them both refuse to see themselves, and pretend they didn't do what they should be looking at, that the Lord threatens the sinner with the words, *These things you have done, and I have kept quiet.* What does *I have kept quiet* mean? I haven't avenged myself, I haven't punished, I haven't thrown you into gehenna. You did it, and you're still alive; and you've done it again, because you have mocked me for sparing you. *You had an iniquitous suspicion, that I will be like you* (Ps 50:21). You thought I am like you, as though I too would take pleasure in iniquity, just as you do. So see what an advantage you would gain, if your iniquity displeased you; from there on you begin to be like God, instead of perversely wanting God to be like you. Just notice, I mean, how perverse you are; God made you to his likeness,[8] and you want to bring God down to your likeness. So then, *These things you have done, and I have kept quiet,* that is, "I have not avenged myself." *You had an iniquitous suspicion, that I will be like you.*

All bad people, iniquitous, reprobates, blasphemers, and scoundrels say this sort of thing: "Really, if the things we do were displeasing to God, we wouldn't be alive."

What's this, "If these things displeased God, we wouldn't be alive"? Is that what you're saying? So these things please God, then? *You had an iniquitous suspicion*; these things don't please God, God will not be like you. Instead, straighten yourself out, and then it's you who will be like God. But you don't want to; you place yourself behind yourself. You don't do what is written, *and my sin is always before me* (Ps 51:3). Listen to what follows: *I will accuse you and set you before your face* (Ps 50:21). What you, he is saying, don't want, I for my part am doing; I'm placing you before yourself, I'm punishing you with yourself.

So do it yourself, then, if you don't want him to do it. Place yourself before yourself, and say without a qualm, *Since I myself acknowledge my iniquity, and my sin is always over against me* (Ps 51:3). Don't let it be before you, because it is before me; *turn away your face* (Ps 51:9) from what I am not turning mine; overlook it, because I am taking a good look at it. So then, don't be afraid you will die; confess, in order not to die.

Praise God for your good works, blame yourself for your bad ones

6. Take a look now at the confession of praise. Because you displeased yourself in the confession of sin, God will please you in the confession of praise.

Let that displease you which you have made of yourself in yourself, let him please you who made you. Sin, you see, is your work, God's work is you. God hates your work in his work. So turn back to him, confess to him, and by accusing yourself and praising him, you will be straightened out. Warped, perverse people, you see, do the opposite: praise themselves, accuse God. Take a look, and if you recognize this attitude in yourself, put it right, because even if you are no longer what I am going to say, you were so once.

It's the habit of warped, perverse people. When blasphemers do something good, they want to be praised for it themselves; when they do something bad, they want to blame God. "Ungrateful," says the proud, conceited spirit, "you're just ungrateful, God. I've done this and that for you, and conferred this and that benefit upon you." There, from cheeks like the drum of a brass band, comes the booming "I, I"! On the other hand, if a sin comes to light, if some theft, some adultery, something of that sort, as soon as you start being accused of it in the presence of the leader, you say, "It's my evil fate"; or if you don't mention fate, "Would I have done it, if God hadn't wanted me to?" Whether you blame God directly, or in a roundabout way through fate—since in talking of fate you are blaming the stars, and the stars are God's work—in one way or another you are willing to find fault with God, to defend yourself. Put it right and set at the bottom what you were putting on top; lift up to the top what you had placed at the bottom. You have sinned; blame yourself. You have done some good; praise God.

7. In your sin, make the voice of the psalm your own: *I myself said, Lord, have mercy on me; heal my soul because I have sinned against you* (Ps 41:4). This is where you must say "I"; It's where you say *I have sinned against you*, that you must say "I." Why remove yourself from the place in which the only thing God will find is yourself? Pay attention, and learn. *I*, he says, *myself said, Lord, I* myself *have sinned against you.* "I said myself." Remember that "I myself said," not fate, not luck, not you, not finally the devil himself, because unless I had been willing, I wouldn't have consented. Because it isn't right to blame the devil and excuse oneself. God, you see, gave instructions for pardon to be given to those who confess; you, though, haven't done anything wrong;[9] it isn't forgiven you, because you haven't done it. You are begging for pardon; confess your fault, or you will discover the penalty.

The devil himself, in fact, wants you to be angry with him; he's absolutely delighted when he's blamed, so long as he's depriving you of confession. So then, when you sin, say, "I," say "It's me doing it." But when you do some good, say what the apostle said, *It is not I who live, but the grace of God with me.*[10] You will be straightened out by confessing your own sins and God's praises; your bad works, his good ones. And you are confessing *to the Lord, because he is good*; and when you confess, he has mercy on you not just, as in this transitory life, for a time, *since his mercy is everlasting* (Ps 118:1).

Turning to the Lord, etc.

NOTES

1. To be precise, according to the calculations of Dom Lambot, on 23 May 397—one of a whole series of sermons preached at Carthage throughout that summer.

2. There were so many capital offenses in Roman law! And a conviction was only considered to be really valid, really possible, if the accused confessed—so a confession had to be extracted under torture.

3. *Non expectat contemptionem suam*—an odd thing to say. He is not, I suppose, expecting you to despise him for his goodness and mildness in forgiving you.

4. There is at least a verbal assonance in the Latin between *punitio* and *paenitentia*.

5. For exactly the same approach, see Sermons 19 (III, 1) and 20, 2 (III, 2).

6. As in the preface at Mass.

7. In the Latin *agnoscere* and *ignoscere*, which more strictly mean "to acknowledge" and "to pardon."

8. See Gn 1:26.

9. Because you are blaming the devil, not yourself. The change of person from "you" to "I" and back is rather confusing. But it wouldn't have confused Augustine's audience, since he would be vividly acting the roles in the pulpit.

10. He is rather carelessly mixing up two texts here: Gal 2:20, *It is not I who live, but Christ who is living in me*; and 1 Cor 15:10, *Not I, though*, (who have worked harder than them all) *but the grace of God with me*. Or else, what is more likely perhaps, it was the stenographer or a copyist who added *vivo*, "who live," to the *Non ego*, "Not I," either unthinkingly, because the text was running in his head, or somewhat foolishly.

SERMON 72

ON THE WORDS OF THE GOSPEL OF MATTHEW 12:33
EITHER MAKE THE TREE GOOD AND ITS FRUIT GOOD

Date: 397[1]

He continues reflecting on Ps 4

8. [Mutilated Text]

                                                               ast
                                                                on

                                                           lready
                                                      For there is
                                                              now
                                                         ing sent.
                                                       m in faith,
                                                            if he
                                                           ity in
                                                         re later
                                                    For in this way
                                                      them peace
                                                    gives *peace*[2]

upon peace (Is 57:19)? To those who keep peace here in charity, he will also give peace; he will give them peace in immortality; not to those who say, *"Peace, peace,"and there is no peace* (Jer 6:14; 8:11). So then, *Seek peace and follow it* (Ps 34:14). So it's in this way that in this psalm[3] *he has magnified his Holy One.* The reason we can be sure there is someone who listens to our case is that we have someone who is prepared to intercede for us. That's why, after saying *The Lord has magnified his Holy One*, he added, *the Lord will listen to me when I cry out to him* (Ps 4:4). Now, you see, I have an advocate there, *who is seated at the right hand of God and is interceding for us* (Rom 8:34).

9. But to the extent of giving full and perfect peace, he has only listened to those who draw back from evil and do good—and drawing back from evil amounts to being angry with oneself, being sorry on one's bed, while doing good is equivalent to sacrificing a sacrifice of justice, and seeking peace is the same as hoping in the Lord.[4] So that's why after saying *Sacrifice a sacrifice of justice,* he added, *and hope in the Lord* (Ps 4:6). You have already been angry with yourself, already been sorry, already drawn back from evil, already, still in hope, offered the sacrifice of justice in doing good works. There is one thing you do not yet have, in case you should perhaps start saying, "I have now done everything, and still received nothing"; there remains, for you to perform, the work of patience. For indeed, *tribulation produces patience, patience passes the test, passing the test gives hope, while hope does not disappoint* (Rom 5:3-5).

Don't worry, you won't be disappointed; hope in him. Right now it is still, so to say, night; you cannot see God yet, or hold in your hand what he has promised you, but during this night do what the psalm says: *In the day of my tribulation I sought the Lord with my hands at night in your presence, and I was not disappointed* (Ps 77:2). *In the day of my tribulation*; count the whole of this life as the day of tribulation, and say, *I sought the Lord with my hands,* not with my eyes; after all, it's still night. Seek with your hands, deserve well of him with your works, do good deeds and say that in this night you have sought the Lord with your hands. What follows is what also follows for you: *and I was not disappointed.* I sought at night, I sought by groping, and still I found. This is what *I sought with my hands* means; I sought diligently and with good works.

But in what way did I seek with my own hands? *In his presence,* because of that saying, *Do not perform your justice in the presence of men* (Mt 6:1); not to avoid their eyes, but in order not to go fishing for praise for yourself. Because if you avoid the eyes of the onlookers when you do good deeds, what about that other saying, *Let your works shine upon men, so that they may see your good deeds?* But notice what comes next: *and glorify your Father who is in heaven* (Mt 5:16)—so that the one who made you good may be glorified in you. You were quite capable, you see, of making yourself bad, you aren't capable of making yourself good. You were capable of wounding yourself, you are not capable of curing yourself. So when you do any good works, do them with the intention of God being glorified in you, because when you *sacrifice the sacrifice of justice*—that's the good works—it continues, that you should *hope in the Lord* (Ps 4:5).

10. "And what am I to hope for? How long have I got to go on hoping?" Don't fix your hopes here, what you seek does not come from this earth. You want to be in bliss, I know; who doesn't, after all? You're looking for a good thing, but you're not looking for it in its own proper region. It's as if you heard that gold is a good thing, and only to be found under the ground, and you grabbed

a shovel and started digging in your house. Asked what you're looking for, you answer, "Gold." But the other person, who knows where gold is really to be found, will answer you, "You're looking for a good thing, but not in the place you ought to be looking." You're seeking bliss, you want to be full of joy, you want to be sated with good things, so that you don't suffer the least want, and lack absolutely nothing; it's a great thing, but not to be found here.[5]

Let me tell you how to get there. What am I to say, though, but what I have said already? *Be angry with yourself, be sorry on your bed,* change your ways. *Sacrifice a sacrifice of justice, and hope in the Lord* (Ps 4:5-6). It is in him that you shall have what you seek; when you reach him, you will have it there, because you will have him, and about him it is said, *Lord, show us the Father, and it is enough for us* (Jn 14:8).

11. In fact, what comes next here too? After saying *Be angry*[6] and be sorry—that is, repent of having been so bad—*sacrifice a sacrifice of justice*—be fervent in good works—he added, *Hope in the Lord,* and then, *Many are saying, "Who can show us good things?"* There you are, they have felt sorry. "On my bed I realized how bad I am. I was angry with myself. I was a thief, I was a landgrabber, I was this, that and the other. I was angry with myself, I was sorry on my bed, I changed my ways. Now I perform good works. When I see people hungry, I offer them bread; when I see them naked, I clothe them; when I see strangers, I welcome them; when I see people quarrelling, I reconcile them; when I see them oppressed by debt,[7] I redeem them; when I see them sick, I visit them; when I see them dead, I bury them. Where is the good thing that I have been promised? I have now mended my ways, now changed my way of life; now that I have straightened myself out from bad actions, I do good instead; where are the things I have been promised?" *Many are saying*—if only there were just a few who were saying it!—*many are saying.* What are many saying? *"Who can show us good things?"*—"Where is what I have been promised? I invest my gold and I can see no return. I can see what I invest; I can't see the return I'm promised." It's night time; go on seeking. You won't lack hands, and you won't be disappointed. *Many are saying, "Who can show us good things?"*

The light of God's features stamped on us is the image of God in the soul

12. What was this man going to say to those who were saying to him "Who can show us good things?" And what is *the* good thing? *The light of your features has been stamped upon us, Lord* (Ps 4:7), so that we may be your coinage, packed away in your treasury. *The light of your features has been stamped upon us, Lord.* This is Christ's money; the features of our sovereign have been stamped upon us. This was the coin that Christ was looking for, like a tax collector, when they were trying to catch him out over the tribute, and showing him a coin, and answering that it had Caesar's image on it, and he said, *Pay back to Caesar what is Caesar's, and to God what is God's* (Mk 12:14-17).

Caesar looks for his image in your gold, and will God not look for his image in your soul? There you are, those are your good things. Why are many still

saying, *"Who can show us good things?" How far, you thick heads?* (Ps 4:6.2).
You are all looking for good things, so that you can be afraid of more things
when you get them.[8] You are all looking for transitory goods, looking for the
good things of time, looking for things which may say goodbye to you while
you live, or which you will say goodbye to when you die. So, *how far, you thick
heads? Why do you love what is vain and seek what is false?* (Ps 4:3) Do you
want me to show you the good? Have it, and you will know it; it can be had in
the heart, it cannot be shown to the eyes.

The highest good is to be found in the heart, not in the world outside

13. Anyway, notice what comes after *The light of your features has been
stamped upon us, Lord; you have put,* he says, *rejoicing in my heart* (Ps 4:6-7).
In my heart, not in my strongroom, not in my treasure chest, but *in my heart.*
Notice how *the light of your features has been stamped upon us, Lord.* I mean,
he also acquires gold, and puts it in his chest; his heart rejoices, but about what
is vain, not about what is true. Do you want to see how fondly you rejoice, if
you rejoice like that, and imagine that what is false is true? You have this treasure
chest quite full; you leave your house; wherever you turn, you are rejoicing,
because your chest is full. Somebody else had a treasure chest full, and lost what
he had to a thief. He doesn't know it, he's still rejoicing. He doesn't know it's
all vanished, he's still rejoicing. How could anything that was not in you really
be yours? Look, it's already vanishing, and you are still rejoicing. You are
nourishing empty hopes. How can this be, if not because *you are seeking what
is vain?* Why? What's the point, what's the use? Look, you've lost it, even if
you did love what you've lost. And how you have perished yourself!

So come back, then, to the highest good, so that you may be able to say, "*The
light of your features has been stamped upon us, Lord. We have been turned
into your coinage; gather us into your treasure chests, and we are paying
Caesar's tribute; ourselves to you, to Caesar what you have given us, to you
what you have made, yes, to you who made us. You have put rejoicing in my
heart;* that's where what gives me joy is to be found; it's an inner good, it's
packed away in an inner treasure chest." This is something you cannot lose
against your will; this is where the one who made you is to be found, delighted
with his temple, because you were sorry on your bed.

Contrast between "the many" and "the single one"

14. Anyway, after saying, *The light of your features has been stamped in us,
Lord; you have put rejoicing in my heart,* he took another look at those many
who were saying *"Who can show us good things?"* and he went on to say, *From
the time of their corn, wine and oil they were multiplied* (Ps 4:8)—their corn,
their wine, their oil. These were the things they set their minds on, and the earthly
things they desired. And when it was going well with them, and they had their
fill of these earthly things—they were multiplied—*they called the people happy*

which has these things. You, though, what do you say? *Happy the people for which the Lord is its God* (Ps 144:15). That's because *the light of your features has been stamped in us, Lord*. They, however, multiplied from the time of their corn, wine and oil, are drawing back from me; people who love such things shouldn't say to me, *Who can show us good things?* There is something I can show, but there isn't anybody I can show it to. So, *from the time of their corn, wine and oil they were multiplied.*

15. What about you? *In peace, in the selfsame*. What does *in the selfsame* mean? What doesn't change, what isn't variable, what isn't time-bound, what isn't now like this, now like that. *In the selfsame I will fall asleep* (Ps 4:8). It's hard to explain what I feel about what he said here[9]: *I will fall asleep in the selfsame. I will fall asleep in peace; in the selfsame I will fall asleep*. When you're asleep, you are having a kind of holiday from the senses. So why, for your life of bliss, seek shapes and colors outside yourself with your eyes, songs and sweet tunes with your ears, a variety of flavors with your sense of taste, a variety of pleasures with your sense of touch? It's no such good as that which can make you good, no such good as that about which you said, *Who will show us good things?*[10] Inside, in the image of God, is the good from which is formed this good *which eye has not seen nor ear heard* (1 Cor 2:9). So that's why you should fall asleep, should remove yourself from *the lust of the eyes* (1 Jn 2:16), should stop discussing things with the senses of the flesh, so that your Lord may say to you, *Enter into the joy of your Lord* (Mt 25:21.23). So then, *in peace, in the selfsame I will fall asleep and take my rest* (Ps 4:8).

The meaning of dwelling singly in hope

16. How does one get there? *Since you, Lord, have made me dwell singly in hope* (Ps 4:8). What was said earlier on, *Hope in the Lord* (Ps 4:6), was said when iniquity had already been drained off, the sacrifice of justice already been offered. *Hope in the Lord*, all of you; but *singly in hope you have made me dwell*.[11] What's the meaning of *singly*? Not like *the many who say, "Who will show us good things,"* desiring many things, and distracted by different pleasures—this one seeking one thing, that one another, not all seeking the one thing necessary. This one wants to derive good from the ills of that other; he cannot get richer, unless the other one ends up destitute. This big fish cannot be satisfied unless that smaller fish is gobbled up. Those who seek such good things are not seeking good things, because they are seeking non-good things.

So what you will receive *singly* is what the godless do not receive. O you single man—the whole body of Christ. O you single man—the body whose head is Christ—dwell singly in hope, don't seek the good things of the heathen. *For these are all the things that the heathen seek. Seek first the justice and kingdom of God*—this is the stamp of the features of God. Seek it in yourself, and if there's need of them, *all these things shall be set before you* (Mt 6:32-33). He feeds the robber, and is he going to abandon you? *The Lord's is the earth and its fullness* (Ps 24:1).

We must love God freely, for nothing

17. Don't you go drawing back from your God; love your God. You're always saying to him, "Give me this and give me that"; say to him sometimes, "Give me yourself." If you love him, love him for nothing, don't be a shameless soul. You wouldn't be pleased with your wife, if she loved your gold, if the reason she loved you was that you had given her gold, given her a fine dress, given her a splendid villa, given her a special slave, given her a handsome eunuch; because if these were the things she loved about you, she wouldn't be loving *you*. Don't rejoice in such love as that; an adulterer, very often, can give more. You want your wife to love you for nothing, and you in turn want to sell your faith to God? "Because I believe in you," you say to your God, "give me gold." Aren't you ashamed? "Because I believe," you say, "give me gold."

You've put your faith up for auction; notice its price. That's not what it's worth, it isn't to be valued in gold or silver, that's not what your faith is worth. It has a huge price tag; God himself is its price. Love him, and love him freely, for nothing. You see, if you love him on account of something else, you aren't loving him at all. You mustn't want him for the sake of anything else, but whatever else you want you must love for his sake, so that everything else may be referred to love of him, not so that he may be referred to other loves, but that he may be preferred to other loves. Love him, love him freely, for nothing. It was on this point that that great athlete had that great adversary catch him by the throat and say, *Does Job worship God for nothing?* (Jb 1:9).

God, the good of all goods

18. So then, if you want the good when you say, *Who can show us good things?* it's God himself, who made you good and who can make you better, he himself that is the good, made so by no other good, but good for himself by the good that he is himself. I mean, for you to be good, some other good happens to you, while for him to be good no other good happens to him. He, you see, is good for himself by himself. It was to commend this great good that the Lord said, *Why question me about the good? No one is good but the one God* (Mt 19:17; Lk 18:19). Aren't there any other goods? Isn't it written, *God made all things very good* (Gn 1:31)? But all these things are good through God. God, though, is not good through these things, nor is he good through other goods which he has;[12] but he is the good of all goods. There you have what sort of good he is; ask, *Why do you still love what is vain and seek what is false?* (Ps 4:2). There you have what is really good; seek the good of goods.

You're seeking wealth; it isn't single. Pay attention: *Singly in hope you have made me dwell* (Ps 4:8). Why isn't it single? Both good and bad people have it. You're seeking health of body; both good and bad people have it, both human beings and animals, it isn't single. You're seeking honors; bad people too acquire them; they aren't single. That is single which only the good will have. Here God gives good things to the good and the bad, he also gives[13] bad things to both the good and the bad; to these as a punishment, to those as useful training.

They are bad things common to both good and bad. The single bad thing is the bad eternal fire; the single good thing is the good eternal God.

Whatever else there is in creation, God also gives it to his enemies. Earth and heaven—they make use of the lights of heaven, of the fruits of the earth, of health of body, of the honors of the world; his enemies make use of all this. They are creatures; he gives them what he has created. Himself, who did the creating, he is keeping for you, but only if you love him freely, for nothing. The time will come, you see, when he gives himself to you, and says to the godless, *Let the godless man be taken away, lest he should see the glory of God* (Is 26:10, LXX). So, brothers and sisters, let us love God freely, for nothing, let us do good, put up with evil, hope in him, so that some time or other, when he has paid himself back to us, we may find satisfaction in him alone, who lives and reigns through immortal ages. Amen.[14]

NOTES

1. Mainz 46 and 47 provide almost the full text of Sermon 72, with a conclusion to it, hitherto unknown, sections 8 to 18. It is only these concluding sections that are given here. For the date see Sermon 72 (III/3).

2. Some unknown Philistine, cutting out an illuminated initial, has left the first fourteen lines of section 8 in this condition. The Latin text (?) reads:

trema
on

iam
Est enim
nunc
ttitur
m in fide
ipse si
tate in
us postea
Sic enim
eis pacem
dat pacem

3. Psalm 4; the responsorial psalm they had been singing, which he started commenting on in section 6.

4. He is fitting Ps 34:14, already quoted, to Ps 4:4-5.

5. See Sermons 231, 5; 297, 9; *The Trinity* XIII, 6-12.

6. Adding *irascimini* to the text, on a suggestion of Dolbeau's. The text simply has "After saying *and be sorry.*" Dolbeau's actual emendation is simply to eliminate the "and"; but I prefer to follow his other suggestion.

7. I have added "by debt," since in the context that is what "oppressed" must signify.

8. It is a commonplace with Augustine that possession of wealth is inescapably accompanied by anxiety, by dread of losing it.

9. In the *Confessions* IX, 8-11 (chapter 4), he has a long meditation on Ps 4, which filled his

thoughts just after his conversion, when he had resigned his chair of rhetoric and was spending a few months in retreat at the villa of Cassiciacum, before being baptized at Easter in Milan. It evidently moved him profoundly. This sermon was probably preached about the time he was writing the *Confessions*.

10. No longer "the many" saying this. He varies the text of the psalm here and elsewhere. Here he says "Who shall show. . .," *Quis ostendet*; hitherto it has been in the present tense, *Quis ostendit*, "Who can show. . ." There have been other slight variations too. This indicates that the version imprinted on his heart from Cassiciacum some ten years or so previously differed slightly from the version just sung in the Carthaginian church he was preaching in.

11. I think the contrast he is making is between the plural of the earlier injunction, *Sperate*, and the singular of the present statement. But it is hard to be certain.

12. Reading *quae habet* instead of the text's *quae habent*, "which they have"—which hardly makes sense. But it may be just a misprint.

13. Omitting *bona* from the text—"he also gives good and bad things to both the good and the bad." It is clearly redundant here.

14. These concluding words from "who lives. . . Amen" are not Augustine's, so Dolbeau assures us.

Dolbeau 11
SERMON 90A
Mainz 40

SERMON OF SAINT AUGUSTINE, BISHOP, ON THE LOVE OF GOD AND NEIGHBOR

Date: 397[1]

We too must ask the question about the great commandment

1. In this reading of the gospel which has just been chanted, it's as though we ourselves could see the Lord with the eyes, not of the flesh but of faith—which is far more salutary. So let us make our own the desire of the man who asked him what the great commandment was in the law. You see, the man who was actually asking the question was seeing him with the eyes, not of faith but of the flesh, and that's why he was testing him rather than making a genuine inquiry. Let us, though, ask the question as believers, in order as questioners to find the truth; let us too say, "Lord, *which is the great commandment in the law?*" (Mt 22:36). Let us say it, however, not craftily out to test him, but sincerely out to learn from him.[2] He gives us the same answer now, after all, as he gave that man then; he, if he didn't believe, was asking the question for our benefit, not his own; while if he did come to believe, how much more should the answer convey to the listener now, if it could convert the tricky questioner then!

A compendium of the whole law

2. The first thing, certainly, we should look at is how it is that this man inquired about one commandment, wishing to know which was the great one, not which was the only one, but which was the great one, while the Lord replied that there are not one, but two commandments. Perhaps the man, you see, when he heard which the great one was, would have gone on to look for more to follow; but the Lord, to prevent several more being looked for after the great one, added just one second one to follow, to fulfill what had been prophesied so long before: *For the Lord will make a word that shortens and completes upon the earth* (Is 10:23 LXX). Now it happens; it is fulfilled by this law of love.

The law, after all, contains many commandments; it's like an endless forest, sprouting commandments on every page. And who could fulfill what nobody could possibly keep in mind? But the Lord Christ is full of mercy; and just as he showed us his greatness in the shortened form of a human body, so too he enclosed the length and breadth of the law in a short precept. In the shortened form of that body we have the whole Son of God; in the short form of these commandments we hold the whole law of God. Mercy has put a stop to laziness; don't think any more about how long it will take you to learn them, but rather about how to carry out what you have learned in a trice.

3. *You shall love,* he says, *the Lord your God with your whole heart and with your whole soul and with your whole mind. This is the first and great commandment. But the second,* he says, *is like this one: you shall love your neighbor as yourself. On these two commandments depend the whole law, and the prophets* (Mt 22:37-40). Why were you stretching and straining through all the spreading branches? Hold onto these roots, and the whole tree is in your hands. The Lord, as we can see, stated this very briefly; I, however, am obliged to say much more about these two commandments.

Or perhaps I'm not obliged to, and what we have heard from the Lord is sufficient? Of course it's sufficient, but not for everybody. You see, the greater people's minds, the more what is briefly said suffices them. Great minds look for brief statements; but smaller minds, understanding less, want it spelled out at length. I'm afraid of boring the first sort to death, I don't want to overload the weakness of the others. And yet if I keep quiet, those who are slower on the uptake will have grounds for complaint. And so those who already understand must bear with me, so that those who don't yet understand may get to grips with me.

A problem

4. What better, what shorter thing could you be told, O man, than that you should *love the Lord God with your whole heart and with your whole soul and with your whole mind* (Mt 22:37)? Do it, and be assured of eternal life and of a blissful life. Love with your whole heart and whole soul and whole mind, love your God; and what will be left over to love yourself with? I mean, if you love the Lord your God with whole heart, whole soul, whole mind, what do you leave yourself that you can love yourself with?[3] But if you're left with nothing to love yourself with, how, in line with the second precept, *shall you love your neighbor as yourself* (Mt 22:39)? There's one problem for you; listen to it carefully: The Lord said, as we noticed when the reading was being chanted, *On these two commandments depend the whole law, and the prophets* (Mt 22:40).

On top of that, though, the apostle Paul says, if you noticed while his letter too was being read, that the law is fulfilled by the person who loves his neighbor, without adding the first and great commandment, that everyone should love God with whole heart, soul and mind. I mean, this is how he puts it: *For, "you shall not commit adultery, you shall not commit murder, you shall not covet," and any other commandment there may be, is summed up in this saying, "You shall love your neighbor as yourself." Love of neighbor works no evil, while charity is the fullness of the law* (Rom 13:9-10). This one says, *Whoever loves neighbor has fulfilled the law* (Rom 13:8). And if he had just mentioned three commandments, *You shall not commit adultery, you shall not commit murder, you shall not covet*, we would suppose that these three precepts alone were contained in the love of neighbor. But when he went on to add *and any other commandment there may be*, he included everything in love of neighbor. What's left over here for the love of God?

When you hear, *Love God with whole heart, whole soul, whole mind*, there seems to be no room for love of neighbor. Again, when you hear, "This and that and the other, *and any other commandment there may be, are summed up in this saying, You shall love your neighbor as yourself*, nothing seems to be left for the love of God. So how is it that the Lord said, not "on one," but *on these two commandments depend the whole law, and the prophets*?

We begin by considering love of neighbor

5. So then, to explain briefly what I proposed, as best I can with the Lord's help, let's rather begin with love of neighbor. We are human beings, after all,[4] mortal, ignorant, not yet made the equals of the angels,[5] far removed indeed from their imperishable company; and this very dissimilarity means that God is far away from us, although his mercy brings him near us. So who are we, and what are our powers of thought, that we should dare to tackle the Lord?[6] We've all got neighbors; reach out now to your neighbor, in order to love God with whole heart, whole soul, whole mind. O man, *if you do not love the brother whom you can see, how will you be able to love the God whom you cannot see?* (1 Jn 4:20). Yes, you recognize the words borrowed from the talk of the apostle John. So it gives us a rule to follow: let us start from our neighbor, in order to arrive at God.

Merely natural love not enough

6. But someone will say to me, "I do love my neighbor,[7] and not in words but in actions." Prove it. "I do love my neighbor," he says. What's so great about that? Can't you see how mutual love holds sway among irrational animals, how birds long to be with birds of their own kind, and how they loathe being alone? Can't you see how, when animals have shared the same stable, they like to follow each other on a journey, and take it very ill when one is separated from the other? So what's so great about what you're doing, if as a human being you want to be with another human being? It's still no different from the animals in your stable. I don't know whether that's the sort of love that God requires of us.

Perhaps you'll say, "I do love my neighbor; after all. I love my son, and as myself." That's easy enough too. Tigers love their cubs. After all, none of these animals would reproduce, unless one were loved by another. Go beyond the things that have been put in your power; none of them was made according to the image of God. Man God did make according to his image, that he might have *power over the fish of the sea and the birds of the air and all creeping things that creep upon the earth* (Gn 1:26-28). Notice what you have under you, and by what love of his image you yourself have been very differently conformed to the creator.

So finally, how can you prove that you love your son? That son of yours, I repeat, how can you prove that you love him? Because you were keeping an inheritance for him that he cannot possess together with you? He doesn't hold it with you, after all, but will succeed to it when you are deceased. Don't you remember that your father before you passed away in possession of that inheritance? And if it's an ancient inheritance, your grandfather also passed away in possession of it; all of them passing away, none of them abiding. So as one doomed to die you are leaving it to one doomed to die,[8] or rather it is truer to say that you don't know for whom you are accumulating it all—and you boast that you love your son!

Love of neighbor presupposes love of self;
true love of self presupposes love of God

7. *They will tell their children*, it says, *to put their hope in God* (Ps 78:6-7). If that's how you love him, then you really do love him. If you love him in any other way, then you don't love him, because you don't even love yourself. What is it, after all, that you heard? *You shall love your neighbor as yourself* (Mt 22:39). This is the rule I'm laying down, or rather not laying down, but acknowledging. I mean, I both observe for myself and then remind you that it has been laid down for all of us. This is the rule: *You shall love your neighbor as yourself.* I am not now saying, "Child, wife, friend next door, people you know in your street, you shall love as yourself."[9] You answer, no doubt, "I do love them." The first thing I want to know is whether you love yourself. The whole gist of the commandment lies here, the whole question turns on this point; after all, you can't love your neighbor as yourself, if you don't yet love yourself.

"Well, is there anyone," you say, "who doesn't love himself?" I for my part would like to find out who does love himself. You see, I don't pay any attention to the mistaken ideas of creatures, but to what is taught by the creator. The one who made us has a better knowledge of us, so let's listen to him. So you were saying, then, "I do love myself"; and if I asked you to prove it, you would reply, "When I'm hungry I feed my body, because I love myself. I don't want to be worn out with toil, because I love myself. I don't want to be trapped in poverty, because I love myself. I don't want to be laid low with a fever, because I love myself. I don't want to feel pain, because I love myself."

Do you want to hear what the one who made you has to say? Just see how well you are really loving yourself—whether you don't love iniquity. *For whoever loves iniquity hates his own soul* (Ps 11:5). I'm not questioning you, you must question yourself. If you want to thrive on another person's misfortunes, if you want things to go badly with someone else so that they may go well with you, then assuredly if that's the sort of wishes you have, if that's what you want, you are loving iniquity, hating your own soul. So then, if you hate your own soul, I'm not entrusting your neighbor to you, for you to love him as yourself. Am I to entrust another person to you, just so that I then have to go seeking two of you? Having lost yourself, are you going to keep me safe? So first of all love yourself, in order to know how to love your neighbor as yourself.

We want those we love to enjoy what we love;
the example of sports fans

8. How you are to love yourself—are you expecting to hear that from me? Let's rather listen to the one who made both you and me. Here's how you are to love yourself; pay attention to the great commandment, in order to love yourself. After all, you cannot but wish to draw the person you love to what you yourself love. And you love iniquity; that's what you are going to bring the person whom you love as yourself.

We have countless human interests, whether good or bad, before our eyes to illustrate this. You have a favorite charioteer; you urge all the people you love to watch him with you, to love him with you, to cheer him on with you, to go crazy about him with you. If they don't love him, you revile them, you call them idiots—like yourself.

Again, you want the person you love to have as much as you have, even if you don't want to give him half of what you have. You see, you don't want him to grow rich at your expense, you don't want his good to be to the detriment of your good. Why is this? Because you reckon gold to be a good thing, the reason you consider yourself a great guy is that you possess gold; you want him to increase, not yourself to decrease.[10]

Why love something which you diminish by giving it away?[11] In all these instances you are loving iniquity, hating your own soul. When you wish to have no qualms at all about bringing along with you the neighbor whom you love as yourself, bring him along to that capital good which is not diminished by any number of shareholders; the good which belongs in its entirety to each and every one, however many more come to possess it. Unless you love such a good as that, how will you ever love your neighbor like yourself?

9. What is this good? You have it in the first and great commandment: *You shall love the Lord your God with your whole heart, with your whole soul and with your whole mind* (Mt 22:37). You see, it's when you begin to love God, only then that you love yourself. Don't be nervous; however much you love God, you won't be going too far. For loving God, the sky's the limit, which means there's no limit. So love with whole heart, with whole soul, with whole mind. What more have you got, after all, to love your God with, than your whole self? So don't be afraid that by leaving yourself nothing to love yourself with, you may perish. You won't perish, because by loving God with your whole self, you will be in a place where you can't perish. Rather, if you lower your love down from there to yourself, you won't be in him, but in yourself; so that's when

you will perish, because you will be in a place of perishing. If you don't want
to perish, take your place in one who cannot perish.

The force, the vehemence, the ardor of love has this effect. Let's just note it
in these vile and squalid interests we have mentioned. The doting fans of a
charioteer are totally absorbed in the spectacle; they don't exist except in the
fellow they are gazing at. Such a fan is utterly unaware of himself, has no idea
where he is. Accordingly, someone less interested in that sport who is standing
next to him and sees him so excited will say, "He's miles away." You too, if
possible, be miles away from yourself when you are in God. If you stay in your
own company, you are entrusting yourself to yourself, you're going to lose
yourself, you're not a suitable person to look after yourself.

Finding God means finding oneself; the prodigal son

10. Call to mind how he went off and got lost, the one that said to the father
who was looking after him, *Give me the sum that concerns me* (Lk 15:12). Look
how he went off, look how he squandered the lot, look how he fed swine, look
how he was afflicted with penury. His preferring his own company took him a
long way away from his father. You see, in preferring his own company he didn't
even remain in his own company. If you fall away from your God, you very
soon fall away from yourself too, and turn your back even on yourself. That's
why such people are told, *Come back, transgressors, to the heart*[12] (Is 46:8),
come back to yourselves, so that you may be able to come back to the one who
made you. So it was with this young man, when he began to be in want, having
forsaken his father, being forsaken now by himself; what does it say about him?
And returning to himself, he said. "Returning to himself"; you can see that he
had even turned his back on himself.

Very good, my son, you've straightened yourself out, you've come back to
yourself. Don't stay in yourself, in case you lose yourself again. This too is
something he realized when he had taken the first step in correcting himself. As
soon as he had returned to himself, you see, he was determined not to stay in
himself, because *returning to himself, he said: I will arise and go to my father*
(Lk 15:17-18). He made a good return to himself, he understood he should be
up there where he had tumbled down from. . .[13] for him to be, or rather where
he didn't deserve to be.

11. If that is what you love, what you really set your heart on,[14] then I will
entrust your neighbor to you, because I can see where you are aiming at and
wending your way to. You will lead him there, nor can you lead one whom you
love as yourself anywhere else; you are now, after all, also loving yourself. Lead
your neighbor there too, drag him along, carry him off, *be urgent with him in
season, out of season*[15] (2 Tm 4:2).

If it were the day for the games, you there, so keen on some bullfighter,[16] you
would be up all night, ready at the crack of dawn to hurry off to the bullring the
moment the gates opened. And when they did, and your neighbor was still fast
asleep, and preferring, no doubt, to go on sleeping, you would wake him up,

giving him no peace; you would hurry the lazy fellow up, you would like, if possible, to snatch him from his bed and dump him in the bullring. And he would not find you a nuisance once he had shaken off his sleep; I mean, as soon as he was wide awake, he would go along happily, and thank you for having left him no peace. And then, maybe, once you had carried him off to the bullring, where you were both rushing off to in such a hurry, your favorite champion would be beaten, and you would go home crestfallen.

Love God, with all you've got; *with your whole heart and with your whole soul and with your whole mind* (Mt 22:37). In this way, in this way alone will you love yourself. In this way alone can you love your neighbor as yourself. You carry him off, you see, to the one about whom you can never be ashamed.

Two commandments necessary; but by fulfilling either,
you fulfill the other also

12. So then it was necessary for those two commandments to be put before us, because if you love your neighbor, you don't love him unless you first love God. When you love God, after all, you don't love iniquity, and so you don't hate your own soul by loving iniquity. So if you don't love iniquity, you love equity, or justice, and that's where you love God. You shouldn't be looking for him, so to say, with your eyes; look for him with your mind, love him, hold him dear, rather, in your heart. Don't set something before yourself that is not God, or you will start loving a non-God, start loving some empty figment of your imagination.

You see, it was to save us from being led astray by our imaginations in that way, and concocting a god for ourselves to suit our materialistic cravings, and fashioning whatever we felt like, that scripture drew us away from such ideas by saying, *God is charity* (1 Jn 4:16). So then, if you love, love what you love with, and you are loving God. Didn't you hear? If[17] you love, love too the very thing you love with, and you are loving God. What you love with, you see, *is charity.* You love with charity; love charity, and you have loved God, since *God is charity, and whoever abides in charity abides in God.*

So two commandments had to be set before us; I mean, one should have been enough: *You shall love your neighbor as yourself.* But to prevent you going wrong in loving your neighbor, because you were going wrong in loving yourself, the Lord wished to give the love you love yourself with a kind of mold in the love of God. And only then did he entrust your neighbor to you, to love as yourself.

13. So now, if you like, the apostle's one commandment can also be enough for you. You have now understood two, and just one is enough. Because before you understood two, one was not enough. You see, you're beginning to love yourself badly, and so it's badly that you love the person whom you love as yourself. Nor in fact should one say "You're loving badly," but "You're not loving at all." So then, *You shall not commit adultery, you shall not commit murder, you shall not covet*—he's calling you back where it is all concentrated,

back to yourself. After all, it could be the fear of punishment, not the love of justice, that is holding you back from adultery. *You shall not commit murder*; you're quite capable of wanting to kill, but you dread the penalty. There will be no murder on your hands, but in your heart you will be found guilty. I mean, you want to kill a man, but you're afraid to; you want to kill, you don't yet love not killing. Let your real action take place inside you, take place where the one who can reward you can see you. That's where you must fight, where you must win. That, after all, is where you have the spectator that counts.

So then, *You shall not commit adultery, you shall not commit murder, you shall not covet, and any other commandment there may be, are summed up in this saying: You shall love your neighbor as yourself* (Rom 13:9). You shall also love God.[18] You can't have this without that; this second one follows the first. Give me the first, and it pulls the second after it. You can't have the second without the first. So then, carry out just one of them, you there cudgeling your brains over two. You can't carry out one except in two. Because the second is called "second" from the Latin *sequendo*, "following."[19] So it follows. *Love your neighbor as yourself*; that's enough for me. Won't you also be able to think about God? So how can you begin to love yourself? *Love of neighbor works no evil. Now the fullness of the law is charity* (Rom 13:10). But where is charity to be found? In the love of God and love of neighbor. Choose whichever love you like. You choose love of neighbor; it won't be genuine unless God is also loved. You choose love of God; it won't be genuine unless neighbor is also tacitly included.

It's faith that obtains love, through God's mercy, not our own merits

14. But you don't yet have any love; groan and sigh, believe, ask for it, obtain it. What you are told to do, what the law commands, faith obtains. And if you already have what it obtains for you, *Well, what do you have that you have not received?* (1 Cor 4:7). If you don't have it yet, ask for it in order to receive it. What we are asking for is charity; if we don't have it yet, let us ask for it, in order not to remain empty. How, after all, shall we ever get it from ourselves, who being evil have deserved nothing good?[20] We shall get it from the one to whom our souls say, *Bless the Lord, my soul, and never forget all his benefits, who is gracious to all your iniquities*. This happens in baptism. But if this were all that happened, what would we be left like? It continues, however, *Who heals all your ills*. When our ills, you see, are healed, we won't feel loathing for our bread. So see what comes next, once our ills are healed: *Who redeems your life from decay*. This now happens in the resurrection of the dead. And what follows the redemption of our life from decay? *Who crowns you*. For your own merits, perhaps? Pay attention to what follows: *Who crowns you with compassion and mercy* (Ps 103:2-4). *For judgment without mercy on the one who has shown no mercy* (Jas 2:13).

So with our sins forgiven, our ills healed, our life redeemed from decay, our crowns bestowed on us by his mercy, what shall we be doing, what shall we have? *Who satisfies with good things* (Ps 103:5), not bad things. You were greedy; you weren't satisfied with gold, because being greedy you can't be satisfied with gold. Be just, and you will be satisfied with God. There's absolutely nothing, in fact, that can satisfy you, except God; nothing is enough for you, except God. *Show us the Father, and it is enough for us* (Jn 14:8). So let us love the works of mercy, while our ills are being healed, so that when our ills have been healed, *our desires* (Ps 103:5) may be sharpened; being healed may they be sharpened, being sharpened may they be satisfied, so that there will be judgment on us, but with mercy.

It's tiresome, after all, that it should be without mercy.[21] It's difficult for him not to find something in you that calls for punishment. You are now rather pleased with yourself; well, he knows something which escapes you, he finds in you what you were hiding, or perhaps what you didn't even know about. So let us be fervent in works of mercy, and in this time of dearth of temporal goods[22] let us love our neighbors, so that we may deserve to experience judgment with mercy.

NOTES

1. Lambot dates it more precisely to early July 397, and has it preached in Carthage, his reason being its position in Possidius' *Index*. Dolbeau considers that there is no substantial internal evidence from the sermon itself either to confirm or to counter the precision of this opinion but that a few tiny details, to be noted in due course, do support its having been preached in Augustine's early years as a bishop, and in the summer.

2. *Non temptantis astu, sed discentis affectu.* This contrast between *astus* and *affectus*, craftiness and feeling, is certainly no rhetorical commonplace with Augustine. But he employs it in his Letter 40 to Jerome, which was written, so it is generally agreed, in 397. This is one detail that in Dolbeau's judgment confirms that date for the sermon.

3. I have transposed this sentence from its place in the Latin text immediately after "a blissful life." It really does not fit there, while it fits perfectly here.

4. Reading *Homines enim sumus* instead of the text's *Homines etiam sumus*, "We are also human beings."

5. See Mt 22:30; Lk 20:36.

6. *Dominum conicere audeamus. Conicere*, literally "throw together," *con-jacere*, usually means throwing words or ideas together, and so guessing, speculating, arguing, making precise conjectures. But here, with "the Lord" as direct object, it seems a more basic sense is called for, rather like "trying a throw with the Lord"—metaphorically, of course. It is, in any case, rather hard to see how this rhetorical question really fits in here. Discussing the commandment to love God scarcely amounts either to speculating about him, or arguing with him, or tackling him.

7. Reading *Diligo proximum* instead of the text's *Diligo Deum et proximum*, "I do love God and neighbor." But loving God is not at issue here yet, as he has just been at pains to point out; nor does it feature in the section that starts here. I take *Deum et* to be the insertion of a distracted stenographer or copyist, or of a copyist who was not very bright.

8. Reading *Relinquis ergo mortali moriturus* instead of the text's . . . *mortalia moriturus* "As one doomed to die, you are leaving mortal things." He goes on to allude to Ps 39:6.

9. This sentence seems entirely superfluous, quite unrelated to the point he is making about loving oneself. I was tempted to omit it; but it is impossible to see how it can have got into the text if Augustine hadn't actually said it. There were too many thoughts buzzing in his head at the same time—a not unusual condition with him!

10. See Jn 3:30. For the whole of this section see also Sermons 28, 4 (III, 2); 90, 6 (III, 3); 128, 5 (III, 3); 306B, 4 (III, 4) 5 (III, 9).

11. Reading *quod dando minuas* instead of the text's *quod damno minuas*, which is rather difficult to construe, but which could be translated as "by loss of which you are diminished." But as he goes on to emphasize about the true good (God), that it is not diminished, however many possess it together, I think my emendation is called for.

12. This is quoted according to Jerome's new translation (the Vulgate) direct from the Hebrew. The same quotation occurs in the *Confessions* IV, 12, 18, which was also written in 397. And this is another detail which Dolbeau thinks supports that early date.

13. Dolbeau hesitantly conjectures a lacuna in the text here, with very good reason, surely, and no need for hesitancy. After *unde ruit* it carries on *ipsum esse* etc. I would conjecture that what dropped out was something like *ubi decebat*: "where it was proper that he should be."

14. On being with the Father.

15. The text just has *insta opportune*; but in the context I cannot see Augustine failing to complete the quotation and adding *importune*. So I have added it too, assuming that either a stenographer or a copyist left it out inadvertently—the easiest thing in the world to do.

16. *Venatoris*; a professional fighter of wild animals in the arena; bullfighters are the nearest modern equivalent. In the "christianized" Roman Empire such shows would have replaced the older gladiatorial combats to the death, and the throwing of condemned criminals, such as Christians, to the lions and other beasts in the amphitheaters. See Sermon 198, 3, note 7.

17. Before this sentence, after "hear?" the Latin inserts the text from Ps 11:5, *For whoever loves iniquity hates his own soul.* This does not fit the context at all. How then can it have got into the text? I would postulate a somewhat critical reader of the sermon, who inserted it in the margin as an objection to the preacher's argument: "Didn't you hear this too?" he is saying. And then later on some copyist inserts this marginal comment into the text.

18. Reading *Diliges et Deum* instead of the text's *Diligis et Deum*, "You also love God."

19. The same point about the word "second" is made in *The Trinity* XIII, 17, but with reference to quite a different topic.

20. See Lk 11:13.

21. A splendid understatement—surely uttered with tongue in cheek and a completely straight face!

22. As the summer was very frequently a time of dearth, when the granaries were almost exhausted, and the new harvest not yet gathered, this final detail, Dolbeau suggests, supports the dating of the sermon to the midsummer of 397.

Dolbeau 14
SERMON 94A
Mainz 44

SERMON OF SAINT AUGUSTINE ON THE WORDS OF THE GOSPEL
THE TIMES ARE FULFILLED AND THE KINGDOM OF GOD HAS DRAWN NEAR:
REPENT AND BELIEVE IN THE GOSPEL

Date:397[1]

Mercy first, judgment next

1. The Lord Jesus, who laid the foundations of the holy gospel, desired, by a kind of law of mercy, that nobody should perish, seeing that he came precisely in order to save what had perished. So he cried out in a kind of congress or parliament of the human race, as we heard just now: *Since the times are fulfilled and the kingdom of God has drawn near, repent and believe in the gospel* (Mk 1:15). It is the one who laid the foundations of the world that uttered these words, and the world has heard them. Let it be done, what he said when he came to bring relief to the world, lest he condemn us for making light of his words when he comes to judge the world. Let it be done, while the world is still echoing to these words of mercy, before he comes to set up the tribunal of justice. The psalmist said to him, *Mercy and judgment I will sing to you, O Lord* (Ps 101:1), and he himself has kept to this order in his intervention; he came first to make an advance payment of mercy, he is going to come again to pass judgment. It didn't only say "judgment," you see, but *mercy and judgment I will sing to you, O Lord.*

What greater mercy could be desired, begged, demanded, than that God should not spare his own Son, but should hand him over for us all, so that with him he might bestow on us all things?[2] What greater mercy than to come and die, not for the just, but for the godless?[3] What greater mercy than to come, and not condemn those who deserve to be condemned, but to set free those who do not deserve to be set free?

"Believe in the gospel" said to unbelievers

2. But we mustn't make light of this mercy, my brothers and sisters. *Merciful and compassionate is the Lord*; go on, add *long-suffering*; go on again; *and very*

87

merciful. Be alarmed by what follows; *and true* (Ps 86:15). God preserve us from making light of God the merciful, and so experiencing God the true! So what need is there for us to cry out? Let us rather listen to him crying out: "Since the times are fulfilled." *The fullness of the times*, you see, as the apostle says, *has come*, and in the fullness of the times *God sent his Son, made of a woman, made under the law, to redeem those who were under the law, that we might receive sonship by adoption* (Gal 4:4-5). It was to impress this fullness of the times upon us that the Lord said, "The times are fulfilled"; the one whom few expected, but many found, has come. So, "the times are fulfilled; repent." How long ago it is that this cry was uttered, and if only it were heeded sometimes! *Since the times are fulfilled and the kingdom of God has drawn near, repent and believe in the gospel* (Mk 1:15).

Renounce and be converted; that's the meaning of "repent and believe in the gospel." Renounce your dead works, believe in the living God. What's the use of believing without good works? It's not, indeed, the merit of good works that brought you to faith; but faith begins, so that good works may follow.[4] That's what the holy Church is told in the Song of Songs: *Come, my bride; you will come and pass through from the beginning of faith[5]* (Sg 4:8). But can you believe God unless you have first renounced the devil?[6] Therefore, in order to renounce him, *repent*; in order to be saved, *believe*.

3. This was said to the Jews, it was said to the idolatrous Gentiles. Does it still have to be said to Christians? Does it still have to be said to Christians every day, who can read that *the times are fulfilled*; still have to be said to Christians that *the kingdom of heaven has drawn near*; still have to be said to Christians: *Repent and believe in the gospel* (Mk 1:15)? Obviously, the person whom I tell, "Believe in the gospel," is not yet a Christian. There is no one, I take it, listening to me in this congregation, who does not yet believe in the gospel. There are many listening to me who have not yet taken their place among the faithful by baptism, and are still catechumens; not yet born, but already conceived. But when or how would they have been conceived in the womb of mother Church, if they had not been signed with some sacrament of faith?[7]

There are also many listening to me who have been baptized, and who ignore the grace of God in themselves,[8] because they love to go on sinning. And what am I to say to these: *The times are fulfilled*?

They reply, "We know."

The kingdom of God has drawn near?

They reply, "We heard that years ago."

Believe in the gospel?[9]

"We believed it years ago."

So what am I to say? Since I'm talking to people who love to go on sinning, who ignore the grace of the redeemer in them, what am I to say? *Repent*. I will say it loud and clear, even if they don't let me say, *The times are fulfilled*, since they know it; or *the kingdom of God has drawn near,* because they know this too; what's put last, *believe in the gospel,* they won't let me say that either, because they have already believed. Well, they can certainly hear *Repent,* because they haven't yet done so.

So let's talk about this to the catechumens and the careless ones among the faithful. Let those who take their religion seriously[10] also listen, because they cannot be lacking among the members of Christ. I hope they won't think I'm being unnecessarily wordy, not if they have any charity; it's a business we all share in; they are surely very willing that I should speak to those whose correction they desire as much as I do.

4. So let those listen to me, not as I say, *The times are fulfilled, the kingdom of heaven has drawn near, believe in the gospel,* but as I say, *Repent* (Mk 1:15).

A catechumen can answer me, "Why say *Repent* to us? First let me become one of the faithful, and perhaps I shall live a good life, and I won't have to be a penitent."

My answer to that is, "In order to join the faithful, *repent.* Those who come to baptism, after all, come by way of repentance. I mean, unless they condemn their old way of life by repenting, they won't come to the new life by being enrolled among the *competentes.*"[11] I haven't been excessively daring in saying this, or taken anything on myself that is not in accord with God's scriptures. Let the catechumens listen to the Acts of the Apostles. When the apostles were speaking to the crowds, filled with the Holy Spirit, the crowds were amazed because they were speaking in all languages, and so they listened to the word of God from the apostles all the more attentively. All of them, being people of different languages, *were pricked in their consciences,* and because they were Jews, they repented of having crucified Christ; and being worried about their salvation, and fearing certain damnation for such a monstrous deed, they said to the apostles, *What shall we do, brothers? And the apostles said, Repent, and be baptized, each one of you, in the name of the Lord Jesus Christ* (Acts 2:37-38).

You have heard how while still not baptized they were instructed to come to baptism by way of repentance. So I too will say the same thing to the catechumens. I have reminded them of the scriptural evidence, you see, in case they should think I am being impertinent in wanting to include them among the penitents before they are counted among the faithful.[12]

The temptation to put it off till tomorrow

5. As for those, now, who are among the faithful and living bad lives, they can hardly think it's impertinent of me to say *Repent* to them. So now I'll say to both sorts, "Change your way of life, in case you lose your life. Condemn past sins, fear the evil things that are going to come, hope for the good things."[13] The bad man should begin by not contradicting himself[14] in hoping for good things, while not being good himself. You're hoping for the good; be what you hope for. First listen to the orders he gives, and then require him to keep the promises he makes. God has put himself in your debt, not by borrowing from

you, but by making you promises. *For who has known the mind of the Lord, or who has been his counselor, or who first gave to him, and will be repaid?* (Rom 11:34-35) What has he received from you, seeing that he has given you everything? So he has been so kind as to make himself a debtor, because he has made promises, and to make himself a debtor of such a kind that he also makes out a bond. This bond is the gospel, is scripture, in which God has put himself in your debt, as I said, not by borrowing from you but by making you promises.

So listen: *Repent, believe in the gospel* (Mk 1:15). Listen to the orders, and then demand payment of the bond.

"Tomorrow," he says.

You see, he can't find any answer to give me, set face to face with himself, and not now a pleasing sight in his own eyes. So how much less in the infinitely purer eyes of God? So now he is not in the least pleased with himself and his bad behavior:

"Tomorrow," he says, "I will mend my ways; don't push me, let me carry on today. What's the hurry? I will mend my ways tomorrow. Why press me about today?"

Because today is not standing still for you.

Every argument with them is about putting things off, because they say, "Let today pass, like yesterday. Tomorrow I will straighten myself out, I'll change, I'll mend my ways, I will carry out the orders given; I'll repent." Which means, it's all about putting the matter off.

"Tomorrow isn't far off."

But see whether you don't want tomorrow to be like today, just as you want today to be like yesterday. Although I could say, Why tomorrow and not today, seeing that you don't know what's going to happen to you tomorrow? But fine, let's allow you that. Don't make tomorrow like today.

"Well," he says, "what if I do? Haven't I got the assurance of the Spirit: *On whatever day the wicked and godless man is converted, I will forget all his injustices?*[15] That's what was said, and said by God."

I admit it; it was written by God. How well you remember God's bond! You keep hold of what's owing to you, you forget what you owe.

The charge that God's promise of forgiveness
is an encouragement to sin

6. Godless people hear this—people ignorant of the law, cut off from the grace of God, unworthy of God's mercy;[16] they hear that it's said in our scriptures, *On whatever day the wicked and godless man is converted, I will forget all his injustices*, and they say to us, "It's your lot that make people sin, because you promise them total immmunity the moment they're converted."

Well, can we have the audacity not to promise what God has promised?

"It's not a good law," they say, "which produces an abundance of sinners."

I would like to know whether those who say this don't consider themselves to be sinners. They're even angry with God for waiting for them, the very people

God is waiting for. Suppose God hadn't made this promise, drawing sinners to repentance by his patience? If he hadn't made this promise, wouldn't more people have become sinners out of despair?

Would your graces please pay careful attention for a moment or two? Can anyone be found who is not a sinner? The weakness of the flesh, the feebleness of age, narrowness of outlook, timidity of mind, nature ignorant of so many things—into how many sins are the careless and the negligent precipitated by all this? However many may seem to be sinless, can anyone really be found who cannot be convicted of being a sinner? Take away this mercy, take away this promise of pardon, take away any haven of forbearance in this cruel, turbulent sea of iniquities, let there be nowhere for the storm-tossed to find shelter; won't they, out of desperation, pile sin upon sin, and say to themselves, "I'm already a sinner, there is no mercy for sinners, there's nothing but damnation in store for me; why not do whatever I like, why not satisfy my lusts, why not at least carry out whatever gives me pleasure here and now, since I'm bound to lose this life and not find any other after it?"

That's the kind of desperation gladiators exhibit, which has even given rise to the proverb, "Back off from the beaten man."[17] The beaten man, you see, is looking for a way to die, nor does he hesitate to commit a foul, because he has no hope of being spared. Such desperadoes give the freest possible rein to their lusts, are carried by them anywhere they can get to, love to be allowed to do whatever they please; so they perish out of despair.

But you, now, don't you go perishing out of hope. There are two siren voices, each opposed to the other, but both dangerous, which lure people to destruction; but still God has not treated either voice lightly; he has provided a remedy for both this one and that one. What are these two voices? "Why shouldn't I sin, why shouldn't I do whatever I want? When I get converted, everything is forgiven me." People like that perish out of hope. The other voice comes from the opposite direction, certainly, but is equally dangerous: "Why shouldn't I do whatever I want, since no mercy is coming my way, no forgiveness will be given me? I'll do whatever I want." They perish out of despair.

The dangers of misplaced hope

7. Which of them shall I put in the dock first: perverse hope or unbelieving despair? Why perish for hoping, why perish for despairing? Let those who want to perish for hoping listen to a thing or two: *Go back, transgressors, to your heart*[18] (Is 46:8); listen to God saying to you, because you keep on saying, "Tomorrow, tomorrow," *Do not delay being converted to the Lord*—I'm speaking to you, there, getting ready to be converted to the Lord, but putting it off; I'm speaking to you, on whose account I'm afraid of hope being your undoing; listen not to me, but to the one from whom you hope so much, and from whom your hoping too much may be your undoing: *Do not delay being converted to the Lord, nor put it off from day to day. For suddenly his wrath will come, and in the time of vengeance he will destroy you* (Sir 5:7).

Where now is what you were saying: "I'll put it off till tomorrow, and tomorrow till the day after tomorrow, because God has promised me forgiveness, saying, *On whatever day the sinner is converted* (Ez 18:21)—I mean, he didn't say: If he's converted today, but *On whatever day he's converted*"?

God answers you: I promised you forgiveness; I didn't promise you tomorrow.

Or perhaps you want to link up and join together two promises, one made by God, and one made by an astrologer? God, you see, has promised forgiveness, an astrologer, perhaps, has promised you a tomorrow. Consider, wretched fellow: the astrologer gets it wrong, and God condemns you. How many have been suddenly snatched away, and not given time either to make amends to God or bring a charge against the astrologers!

The danger of despair

8. Now let those who were likely to perish by despairing listen to their own words: "I have already committed so much evil that I cannot hope for forgiveness. All that's left to me is to follow through with my lusts, glut myself on pleasure, so that at least here and now I may have the refreshment which I am not going to get there."

You too, now listen to the voice of God, not your own: "Desperate soul, start hoping again. Listen to what Paul has to say: *For this reason I obtained mercy—I who persecuted the Church of God—that Christ Jesus might display in me all his long-suffering, to show the form to the very ones who were going to trust him for eternal life* (1 Tm 1:16). So there you have the form; don't despair; listen to the bond which was quoted a short while ago by a person who was hoping in a bad way, and let those who are despairing put themselves right by that. What was it you were hearing? How was he re-assuring himself, while putting it off from day to day? "God, yes God said to me, *On whatever day the wicked and godless person is converted, I will forget all his iniquities* (Ez 18:21-22)." Read and believe. You were sitting on the river bank, or you were carrying a noose around in your despair, you were eager to do away with yourself, perhaps; having nothing to live on, you wanted to die. Come back; you do have something to live on: here is God's bread: *I do not desire the death of the godless, so much as that he may turn back and live* (Ez 18:32).

Nothing more to be said; something to be done

9. So, brothers and sisters, we have no grounds for complaining about God, The perverse have no reason to be displeased with him, though it's only the perverse who can be displeased with him. What is right and straight doesn't please the perverse, what is crooked cannot be fitted neatly into what is straight. I mean, there's nothing more, really, to be said. You were saying, "Look at the immunity the Christians grant people! They make sin flourish." I've explained how more people would perish through despair if no haven of forgiveness were

offered the storm-tossed soul. So God hasn't abandoned either sort, neither those who hope in the wrong way nor those who despair in the wrong way. For the sake of those who despair in the wrong way he has provided the haven of forgiveness; for those who hope in the wrong way, he has left the day of death uncertain.

There is nothing to be said, but there is something to be done. So let them ask me, "What are we to do?" those who have been moved by the word of truth. Let them say, not out loud, but to themselves, "So what are we to do?" So what am I to reply, if not what we have heard: *Repent*? What more can I say? *Repent*. You're a catechumen; repent and you will be renewed. You're a bad, baptized person, not badly baptized; repent and you will be healed. I for my part[19] cannot conceive what you could say to this; you for your part know what you can do.

NOTES

1. This is the first of a group of sermons, their text deriving from an early collection (probably indeed from one in Augustine's own library), which were preached, it is generally agreed, in Carthage in the summer of 397; this one, according to Dom Lambert, a few days after 17 July. Dolbeau has composed the heading from the one given in Mainz 44 and the one given by Possidius in his *Index*, modifying it slightly to be consistent with the text of Mk 1:15, which the preacher is clearly using. Some sermons dealing with similar themes are Sermons 20, 39 (III, 2), 72, 82 (III, 3), 254 (III, 7), 334 (III, 9).

2. See Rom 8:32.

3. See Rom 5:1-7.

4. From: So, "the times are fulfilled; repent," to this point is quoted by Bede in his commentary on Mark.

5. "The beginning of faith" is the Septuagint translation of "the peak of Amarna." It is a key expression for Augustine's theology; another of those creative mistranslations, like "Unless you believe, you shall not understand" of Is 7:9. In his *The Trinity*, before he attempts to explore the mystery, he spends the whole of Book I establishing the beginning of faith, the *initium fidei*, from scripture.

6. In the rite of enrollment as catechumens.

7. The rite just mentioned probably included a marking on the forehead with the sign of the cross.

8. As they love to go on sinning, they are clearly not, as we would put it nowadays, in a state of grace. But what they still have in them, what he here means by the grace of God in them, is the sacramental character, the sheer fact of having been baptized and marked as belonging to Christ.

9. This is not in the text. I am suggesting that Augustine most probably said it, and a stenographer, lagging slightly behind, omitted it by mistake.

10. The *diligentes*, one word in the Latin, contrasted with the *negligentes* of the previous sentence.

11. The Latin just says, "They won't come to the new life *competendo*," balancing their renunciation of the old life *paenitendo*. But he is referring, presumably, to the formal request for baptism made at the beginning of Lent by those catechumens who were considered ready for it. If the request was granted, they were enrolled as *competentes*, "seekers."

12. "The penitent," the *paenitentes*, were the very visible category of the faithful who were being required to do public penance, and who were set apart in a kind of "penitents' corner" or "sin bin."

13. That is, hell and heaven respectively.

14. Reading *sibi non contradicat* instead of the text's *sibi non contradicit*, "begins by not contradicting himself."

15. Not an exact quotation of any text—it is the godless man quoting, after all! But see Ez 18:21-22; also Jer 31:34.

16. Here he means the pagans, not the bad Christians he has just been talking to.

17. *Retro a saucio.* The beaten or disabled gladiator is going to get the thumbs-down sign anyway. I suppose the English proverbial equivalent would be "May as well be hanged for a sheep as for a lamb." The source of the proverb is unknown. But Cicero in his speech against Catiline, II, 11, 24, has this to say: *Gladiatori illi confecto et saucio consules imperatoresque vestros opponite.* The mortally wounded and beaten gladiator is Catiline, against whom the Romans, *Quirites*, are being ironically urged to muster their consuls and commanders-in-chief.

18. Augustine evidently thinks this is part of the quotation he is about to make from Ecclesiasticus—or perhaps his text of that book incorporated the verse from Isaiah. See the article by S. Del'eani in the *Revue des Études Augustiniennes* 38 (1992), entitled, *Un emprunt d'Augustin à l'écriture: "Redite, praevaricatores, ad cor" Isaie 46, 8b).*

19. Here I follow Dolbeau in emending the text's *Ergo*, "So," to *Ego*. A few lines higher up I prefer to keep *Ergo*, where he emends to *Ego*.

Dolbeau 17
SERMON 110A
Mainz 48

SERMON ON THE WOMAN WHO WAS BENT DOUBLE FOR EIGHTEEN YEARS, AND
ON THE MEN UPON WHOM THE TOWER FELL

Date: 397[1]

Christ's miracles are, so to say, visible words

1. I have often reminded your graces, and indeed that has been my teaching as entrusted to me, modest though my abilities are, by the Lord, that the miracles performed by our Lord Jesus Christ in the holy gospel are not only *mighty works* (Acts 2:11)—what else, after all, could they be, all the more wonderful for being the works of God?—but are also, so to say, visible words, reminding us to try to understand as well what they signify. If we don't understand this, then they can only delight us by the sheer wonder of them, and lift our hearts up in praise of God. In fact, it's rather like somebody illiterate just marveling at a scribe as he watches him at work, and admiring his beautiful writing, delighted by the beauty of the letters, though ignorant of their meaning; he doesn't get the sense, but admires the script. But someone who knows how to read derives the full benefit from what he sees. In the same way, when we hear what miracles the Lord performed, even if we don't understand what they mean, like illiterate people just gazing at these letters, so to say, we are amazed at the work he does, even if we are ignorant of what he wishes to signify.

What could be more wonderful than this deed?[2] A woman had been in the grip of her infirmity, bent double for eighteen years, and in a single instant at a word from the Lord she was straightened up, and her malady of years and years yielded to his order, because it recognized its master. He loosed the bonds of the entangler, he performed the work of the creator.[3] She had been bent double and was straightened up, she had been tied up and was released, and this at a word, because the Word who did it[4]—*and all things were done through him* (Jn 1:3)—had come *to seek what was lost* (Lk 19:10). Yes, let us indeed be amazed, let us admire, let us love the doer and the deed. But after marveling at the script, let us inquire a little more attentively into the meaning of this writing.

95

Unless you repent, you shall all likewise perish

2. Now in the same place in the gospel, in the same context, it is related[5] how the tower of Siloam fell upon eighteen men and they died; and it was for eighteen years that this woman had suffered her infirmity, and then had been straightened up. Each story is to be found there, told consecutively. Also in the middle of this composition[6] we have what the Lord says about that tree, which he came to and found without fruit, now the third year running. When he gave orders for it to be cut down, the sharecropper[7] pleaded: he would dig round it and put in some dung, and if it bore fruit, fine; if not, let him come and cut it out. This bit about the tree was spoken as a parable, not as something done miraculously.[8]

That other bit, though, about the men whom the tower fell on, was not told by the Lord as a parable, nor was any point being made by a miracle; men were crushed by the building's collapse. It could have been assumed to have been simply an accident, happening by chance, except for even the godless realizing that not even a sparrow falls down independently of the creator's will.[9] What prompted the Lord, though, spontaneously to recall those eighteen men crushed by the collapse of the tower was his being told of some men being slaughtered by Herod[10] as a ghastly example, so that he mixed their blood with their sacrifices. People were horrified by this, and so they told him about it. And the Lord said, *Do you imagine that because this happened to them they were sinners more than other people? Amen, I tell you, unless you repent, you shall all likewise perish.* Then of his own accord he added the next bit, and to remind them of it said, *Or those eighteen men on whom the tower fell in Siloam and they died; do you imagine that they were debtors more than other men*—that is, sinners? *Amen I tell you that unless you repent, you shall all likewise perish* (Lk 13:1-5). Then he speaks about that fig tree, and now straightens up the woman.

Please, now, please, come to the aid of my weakness with your close attention; first of all I rather think we ought not to be careless and casual in inquiring what this may mean.

3. *Amen*, he says, *I tell you; unless you repent you shall all likewise perish.* In what way *likewise*? Like those, of course, *whose blood Herod mingled with their sacrifices.* Again, *unless you repent, you shall all likewise perish.* In what way *likewise*? Like those *upon whom the tower fell.* Well, since they died in very different ways, those with whose sacrifices their blood was mingled in one way, those whom the collapse of the tower crushed in another, how will they all die likewise, unless they repent? Those who are going to die in that way aren't going to die in this way, and those who are going to in this way won't of course die in that way; and yet they deserve to die likewise, in the same way. The divine scriptures cannot lie, the mouth of Truth[11] cannot utter a lie. Obviously, if we understand it, it's true.

All bad, iniquitous people, all incorrigible, criminal miscreants, lovers of the world, lewd and worthless fellows, unless they repent, die *likewise*. In what way *likewise*? In the same way as both those ones and these ones. Not in a bodily and visible way, and that's why *likewise*. Because if it means in a bodily way, they can't die in both ways. If, however, *we compare spiritual things with spiritual* (1 Cor 2:13), and from bodily comparisons take certain signs as pointing to intelligible things,[12] then they all do die likewise. All the unjust, you see, ask for bad things from God, and the things they think are good for them are in fact bad, because they think of them in a bad way. What sort of way? With thoughts prompted by bad desires, by the activity of *flesh and blood*, by the activity, that is, of *the perishable which will not gain possession of the kingdom of God* (1 Cor 15:50). So then their sacrifices, that is their prayers, are mingled with their blood, because they make their petitions in accordance with *flesh and blood*.

There is a passage of scripture which points this out and censures it, where it says, *You ask and do not receive, because you ask in a bad way, in order to satisfy your lusts* (Jas 4:3). You, then, are performing your sacrifice; let it be mingled with your blood; yours, after all, is the wisdom of the flesh, and it is in accordance with your fleshly wisdom that you petition God. You, after all, are of flesh and blood; you want to bring God down to your flesh, in the way that you ought to be lifting up your heart to God; nor are you paying any attention to what the apostle says to you: *If you have risen with Christ, seek the things that are above, where Christ is, seated at the right hand of God; have a taste for the things that are above, not for the things that are on earth* (Col 3:1-2); otherwise your prayers, issuing from flesh and blood, will bring on you the same sort of punishment as befell those whose blood a wrathful king mingled with their sacrifices. Sever your sacrifice from your blood, say to your God: *I will pay you my vows which my lips have uttered* (Ps 66:13-14). *For the spiritual person distinguishes between all things; for he himself is judged by no one* (1 Cor 2:15). By distinguishing between all things, he avoids mixing his sacrifice with his blood.

4. So how do those who fail to repent die *likewise* in the way that those men died upon whom the tower of Siloam fell? Siloam means "Sent."[13] Who is the one sent, but our Lord? The tower in Siloam, the cross of Christ. So if you aren't mortified, fixed to his cross with the bad desires of flesh and blood, the Crucified falls upon you. Why do sign yourself with the cross? If you don't act the cross, you don't in fact sign yourself with it. Recognize Christ crucified, recognize him suffering, recognize him praying for his enemies, recognize him loving those at whose hands he endured such things and longing to cure them.

If you do recognize him, repent, and if ever you entertained bad wishes, see to it that you have good ones from now on. Blot out the fault, in order not to fear the penalty. But if you don't do this, will Christ profit you at all? *Whoever eats unworthily is eating and drinking judgment upon himself* (1 Cor 11:29). If he eats and drinks judgment upon himself by eating unworthily, what else is happening but the tower falling on him? *For you shall all likewise perish*, he said—and it's true—*unless you repent* (Lk 13:5) of your evil deeds. But of course if you do, then you get straightened up and you will be like that woman.[14] But of course if you do, then you receive the dirt of repentance, like a pile of dung, not unfruitfully round your roots, and so avoid being cut down.[15]

5. It remains to inquire about the number, why eighteen men and eighteen years, and how they fit in with the three years of that tree. The solution to this problem was pointed out to us by that ruler of the synagogue, who was angry because the Lord Jesus cured that doubled-up woman. You see, he said to the crowds, *There are six days, after all, on which one ought to work; come then and get cured, not on the day of the sabbath.* He is convicted indeed of being a brute from the example of a brute: *Hypocrites,* Jesus said, *does not each one of you untie his beast on the day of the sabbath, and lead it to water?* (Lk 13:14-15). No more suitable way of convicting him, since he was being *like horse and mule, having no understanding* (Ps 32:9). And yet to his own way of thinking he was speaking from scripture when he said, *There are six days on which one ought to work* (Gn 1:3-31). Yes, certainly from scripture; but he was mixing the sacrifice with blood, because he was taking what was said spiritually in a fleshly kind of way.

Let us, however, take from him our cue for understanding, and let us too recall that in six days God constructed everything we can see, *heaven and earth and everything that is in them* (Ps 146:6); while *on the seventh day God rested* (Gn 2:2). And all those six days have an evening, because *heaven and earth shall pass away* (Mk 13:31); but that seventh day of rest has no evening, because when we too come to rest after our good works, our rest will be without end. So we find that all things were made in six days; what he signified by the number six was time. Accordingly, if the number six means time for you, take a look at the three years of that tree, because there we have the three periods of time signified: the first period before the law, the second under the law, the third, in which we are now, of course under grace. So any who haven't put themselves right even in this time must expect the axe, not pax.[16]

That tree, though, at least in the third period, was to be given the chance of being put right, and changed from unfruitfulness to fruitfulness, in order to heed the words of the one who was baptizing for repentance: *Produce fruits worthy of repentance* (Lk 3:8). So that being the case, and time being signified by the number six, there can be no doubt that those eighteen men who were crushed by the tower hadn't put themselves right in any of those three periods of time;[17] because if six signifies time, three times six is eighteen.

6. As for that woman, she is straightened up in the period of grace in those eighteen years, as if it were she who had said, *They bowed my soul down* (Ps 57:6). That soul, you see, is bowed down which is pressed down by earthly cares,[18] that soul is bowed down which is overloaded with desire for things,[19] that soul is bowed down which falsely claims that it has lifted up its heart to the Lord.[20] After all, if you have lifted up your heart, you aren't bent double. If you're always looking for earthly things, if you're longing for earthly prosperity, if you don't think there's any profit in the worship of God unless earthly prosperity comes your way in abundance, then you are bent double; your heart is not with the Lord.

Now this penalty comes from the domination of the devil. The whole human race was held bent double under the devil, the whole human race was weighed down by earthly lusts; then one came with the promise of the kingdom of heaven. There is another life, there is the society of the angels, there is a home country where no violence, no enemy is to be feared; there is a home country walled round by the will of God, encircled *with the shield of God's good will* (Ps 5:13), where no foe is allowed in, no friend ever perishes; there is a home country where nobody leaves dependents behind, nobody is succeeded by heirs. That country is called Jerusalem, Jerusalem means "vision of peace." Straighten yourself up from your doubled-up posture, don't have a taste for the earth. *You have risen with Christ* (Col 3:1), he is in heaven; stretch up toward him, and you won't be bent double.

The whole human race exhorted to repent

7. But you didn't do this, O evil-minded human race; you didn't do this before the law, you didn't do this under the law; do it now under grace. Bent double for eighteen years is how you were found by the one who came upright, came to be crucified on your account, to release you from the devil's chains. The creditor's IOU held you bent double. The devil, you see, had tied up his debtors, and after a fashion shackled them in irons. The one came who was not a debtor of his, he paid what he did not owe, and cancelled our bill.[21] What was the bill we owed cancelled with? The blood of the Just One.[22] Why, after all, could the managing director of death hold mankind to the liability of death? He held us, clearly, like his own tree, on terms of sin; he had defeated us and held us, defeated us and so owned us. He had a right to hold us, having deceived us by his evil inducements.[23]

The other came, offering good inducements, having nothing evil about him, born of a virgin, not carrying the hereditary infection of sin, but clothed with the penalty of death, having *the likeness of the flesh of sin* (Rom 8:3), in order to liberate us from the flesh of sin. Listen to him, about to go to his passion and saying, *Behold, the prince of the world is coming, and in me he will find nothing.* Not like the world in you, not like it in the whole human race; *in me he will find nothing.* So if he won't find anything in you, why are you going to die? What comes next? After saying, *in me he will find nothing,* as though he were asked, "So why are you going to die?," he said, *But that all may know that I am doing the will of my Father, arise, let us go from here* (Jn 14:30-31).

He rises and goes to his passion, to fullfil the will of his Father, like Siloam, the one sent, not because he owed anything, but to pay up for the other debtors, as though it were about him that it was said in prophecy, *What I had not grabbed I then paid back* (Ps 69:4). So he alone was undeserving of death. We, however, are all deserving of it, because we have all of us together contracted the liability to die. He contracted no liability to die, and yet he accepted death on our behalf. So he paid what he did not owe, he liberated the debtors, he cancelled the ancient bill, he drew up a new set of papers. What need is there for us any more to settle accounts with the old papers? He has burnt them with the fire of the Holy Spirit.

8. Recognize your Redeemer, don't pile up any further debts. But on account of certain daily matters, which even if minor are still sins, he has given us a daily remedy. Say it from your faith, say it from your heart, say it from your good will: *Forgive us our debts.*[24] Add, though, not only by saying it but by doing it too, *As we too forgive our debtors* (Mt 6:12). So God, whose debtor you are, wanted you to have a debtor. Your debtor is the one who does you wrong, who puts pressure on you unjustly, who wrongfully takes something belonging to you. He's your debtor, he owes you a penalty. Do you want to make sure he's your debtor? Take a look at the law:[25] *An eye for an eye, a tooth for a tooth*, etc. (Ex 21:24; Lv 24:20; Mt 5:38). The law laid down the rule, "Be done by as you did." On the other hand, when the gospel says, *I, though, say to you: love your enemies* (Mt 5:44), it is not contradicting the law, the misunderstanding of those who fancy that the mildness of the gospel is contrary to the harshness of the law. It's not like that. The law simply indicates what you are owed. The gospel wouldn't be able to make you a forgiver, if the law hadn't shown you what you are owed by your debtor.

NOTES

1. See Sermon 94A (Mainz 44), note 1, and Sermon 72 (Mainz 46-47), note 1, for the date of this series. Our sermon here concludes it, and was preached, Dolbeau suggests, on the Sunday after the feast of Saint Lawrence, 10 August, that year. His evidence for this comes from the *Index* of Possidius, from which the title of this sermon is also taken. Sermon 110, on the same topic, appears to have been preached some thirteen years later.

2. The cure of the woman bent double (Lk 13:10-17), which had doubtless concluded the gospel reading. This, however, had probably begun at Lk 13:1, with the Galileans slaughtered by Pilate and the eighteen men on whom the tower in Siloam fell, since he goes on to refer to them in the next section, and they form, indeed, an integral element of the sermon.

3. This is very much Augustine the rhetorician at work here; he goes so far, it seems, as to invent a word, *implicatoris*, the entangler, simply to get a rhyming contrast with *creatoris*, the creator. The sermon is full of such touches, so that taken by itself it could be dated even earlier, to about 394, before he was even ordained bishop. But its links with the sermons mentioned in note 1 tie it to the same year as these.

4. *Quia qui fecit verbum*: literally, "because the one who did/made the word." But the interjection that follows obliges us to treat *verbum* here as *Verbum*. Now Augustine cannot possibly have talked about anyone, not even God the Father, making the Word. So I take the *qui fecit* to be a relative clause whose antecedent is *Verbum*; this involves some bad grammar, indeed, *qui* being masculine and *Verbum* neuter; but with Christ and the *creator* of the previous sentence in his mind, this is a slip he could easily have made—especially with the relative clause preceding the antecedent. An alternative solution would be to eliminate the interjected quotation of Jn 1:3 as the marginal comment of a later reader that then found its way into the text. The whole clause would then be translated, "because the one who produced the word had come to seek what was lost."

5. Omitting *ubi* from the text: "where it is related."

6. It is indeed a very careful composition on Luke's part, running from 13:1 to 13:21; the whole held together by the numbers which Augustine concentrated on. In the first half we have two events, which include the number 18, followed by a parable which includes the number 3; in the second

half we have one event, which includes the number 18, followed by two short parables, which include the number 3. In inquiring into the significance of the numbers, Augustine is much closer to the mind of Luke than are those modern exegetes who scorn such "arithmological tomfoolery." Augustine sees it as a careful piece of literary "weaving," using the words *contextio, contextus, contextim.*

7. *Colonus,* a word that hardly fits the context of this parable. But see Sermon 72, note 8 (III, 3).

8. An allusion, no doubt, to Jesus cursing the barren fig tree (Mk 11:13-14. 20-21), an incident which Luke omits from his gospel, presumably preferring this more innocuous parable—and perhaps hinting at the "parabolic" nature of that incident in Mark.

9. See Mt 10:29.

10. This is not the only place where Augustine attributes the massacre to Herod instead of to Pilate; he also does it in his *Commentary on the Sermon on the Mount,* II, 8, 28. It looks as if it was in the African text of Luke which he was using.

11. That is, Christ; see Jn 14:6.

12. By "intelligible things" he means the same as spiritual things; he is still, this early in his career, reading Paul through Neoplatonist spectacles.

13. See Jn 9:7, where the reference is to the pool, not the tower, of Siloam.

14. See Lk 13:13.

15. See Lk 13:8-9. The dirt of repentance is on the one hand the sins repented; but on the other hand it is also, possibly, the whole somewhat "squalid business"—for the penitent—of the ancient discipline of public penance.

16. *Securim, non securitatem.* See Sermon 72, note 6 (III, 3).

17. That is, clearly, they represent or symbolize those who had not repented in any of the three periods of time, because of course the eighteen unfortunates had not lived through all three.

18. Mankind before the law.

19. Israel under the law.

20. Christians under grace, but not responding to grace.

21. See Col 2:14.

22. See Acts 3:14, 7:52-53; Jas 5:6. For similar treatment of the same theme see Sermon 242A, 3 (III, 7).

23. See Gn 3:1-7.

24. Reading *debita* instead of the text's *peccata.* I think Augustine must have said *debita*: first, it was in his version of the prayer—see Sermons 56-59 on the Lord's prayer; secondly, we have *debitoribus nostris* in the next phrase; thirdly, a copyist could have inadvertently substituted *peccata,* because it had just occurred in the first sentence of this section.

25. Reading *Intuere legem* instead of the text's *Intuere, lege*—"Take a look, read."

Dolbeau

SERMON 114B

Mainz 12

SERMON OF SAINT AUGUSTINE ON THE PASSAGE IN THE GOSPEL
WHERE THE COMING OF THE LORD ON THE LAST DAY IS DESCRIBED

Date: 403[1]

*Augustine preaching extempore on a passsage of the gospel which he had
not chosen himself; the comparison of the flood with the day of judgment*

1. The reading from the gospel which we have just heard, dearly beloved,
was not arranged by me, as usually happens. But all the same, thanks to the good
management of the Lord, who controls all our activities, it fits extremely well
with this psalm on which I had decided to speak to your graces.[2] The Lord, you
see, was talking about his second coming and the end of the age, and he had
already mentioned the many terrible things which must necessarily affect human
affairs as the end draws near. Then he turned on those who wish to live securely
in the region of no security, and scared the wits out of them, saying that the
coming of the Son of man to that judgment—to be dreaded by all, but still also
to be desired by the loving and pious faithful—so in saying that his coming was
going to be like what it had been in the days of Noah, he put the fear of God
into every heart that has any faith in it.

For, he said, *just as in the days of Noah they were eating and drinking,
marrying husbands and wives, buying and selling, when the ark was being built
by Noah, and the flood came and destroyed them all* (Lk 17:20-27; Gn 6:11–
7:23). They were all enjoying, you see, a spurious and pernicious sense of
security, amusing themselves with every secular pastime you could think of,
until Noah entered the ark, and the flood found them stripped and without any
resources. So by saying these things again now, he scared the daylights out of
every living soul. But we have time to wake up; it is not yet the day of judgment,
not yet the flood. Beams of wood that cannot rot[3] are still being cut from the
forest, the ark is still being built.

2. If the people of those times, after all, were fools, and deservedly perished
for their mindless indifference, for not saying to themselves, "There must be
some reason for this servant of God, a just man acceptable to God, and wise,

102

putting so much energy and labor into building such a huge ark; he wouldn't be doing it unless he knew of some disaster hanging over the world; the building of this ark is a sort of herald, crying out, Be converted to God. "⁴ If they had let such thoughts as that pass through their minds, they would have changed their way of life, and turning away from their wickedness and back to God, they would have made up to him for their crimes, beseeching his mercy with sighs and groans, and would not have perished.

God, after all, showed mercy in Nineveh, so he would hardly be cruel to the whole human race if it had turned back to him. *Three days, and Nineveh shall be overthrown* (Jon 3:10), said Jonah, because of their excessive sins. What a short time three days is! Yet with so little time left them they didn't despair of God's mercy; they believed that even three days of lamentation and tears would be enough to win his indulgence. So if three days was time enough for such a great city to soften God's heart toward them, wouldn't the people of that other time without a shadow of doubt have escaped that destruction unharmed, by softening God's heart toward them, if they had used the hundred years in which the ark was being built⁵ as time for changing their ways and appeasing God by offering him the sacrifice of a broken and a contrite heart?⁶ So the three days of the Ninevites is a standing rebuke to the hundred years of ark building.

But there is another here now, greater than Noah;⁷ notice the length of time, just notice, in which he is building this ark. I think, brothers and sisters, that if the years were counted up from when Christ began to design and put together the structure of this ark—that is, of the Church—by felling beams of wood that cannot rot from the forests of the nations, they will be found to be more than a hundred, even more than two hundred or three hundred.⁸ And here we are, with so many years having passed, and it's still being put together, Noah is still crying out, the structure itself is still crying out. The only thing that will ever destroy people is infidelity. Let them change their ways; let them believe God when he makes such tremendous promises, utters such tremendous threats, and in no way at all practices any deceit.

An urgent appeal for conversion of life; the two ways

3. It would take a long time to say much more about this, and because of the pressure of time and our common frailty, we must hurry on to discuss this psalm.⁹ But I would like someone, any of you, to tell me very briefly why you don't change your evil ways and make them into good ones. What can you lose by it? If you believe, do it, because it will all come true. If you still have doubts, do it, in case it may come true. For those who believe, it is as sure as can be; for those who have doubts, it is uncertain. I can count up so many things from the beginning of the world to the present day, which have happened exactly according to the scriptures, so that we can read absolutely nothing in the scriptures which we don't already see fulfilled, for the most part. Very few things remain to be fulfilled; are they the only ones that are falsely foretold? Will the few things that remain turn out to be false?

4. Brothers and sisters, what's so difficult about it? The action I'm asking of

you calls for no more than average strength of character.[10] Count up all the many past things that have come true, and believe the few that remain. For example, you're traveling by a short cut, and you had intended to go a better way. Someone told you, anyone, absolutely anyone, that that way was infested by highwaymen. That way, which you were told is infested by highwaymen, is level, it's easy, it's pleasant, it's welcoming, it's delightful; but someone, heaven knows who, told you that it's infested by highwaymen, and so effectively barred by them that you either cannot get through, or can only do so with extreme difficulty and danger. There's another way; it involves maximum toil, difficulty, harsh terrain, narrow defiles; not only are there no delights to be found along it, but scarcely any appropriate humanity is shown on it.[11] Doesn't your heart tell you straightaway, wishing as you do to gain a few extra days of this life, a life you can see ahead is going to finish some time or other: "We had better go this way; even if it means toil and difficulty and doing without things, even if means wearing ourselves out, or our beasts, all the same it's better to go this way"?

Why is it better?

Because it's safer.

But now somebody may want to direct you along that other delightful road, and so he says to you, "Were you really so quick to believe the person who told you this way is infested by highwaymen?" If you know the person is trustworthy—and perhaps you knew at least that he had never previously deceived you—how will you answer? "It's out of the question that that man should deceive me; I know the man, I've had experience of him as a serious person, I've had many dealings with him. He has always told me the truth, never lied to me."

You, though, knew he was that sort of man; let's suppose someone else, who didn't know him. Wouldn't this person too say, "I don't indeed know the man, and I can't say whether he tells the truth or not; maybe he's telling the truth, maybe he's lying. Still, because of this doubt, in case what he says is true, why should I not rather endure this toilsome short-cut, than follow the delightful road with its dangers?"

So many reasons for following the way pointed out by Christ

5.[12] Come now, my brothers and sisters, we're Christians; we all want to make the journey; even if we don't want to, we're still making it. Nobody is permitted to stay here, all who come into this life are forced by the turning wheel of time to pass on. There's no place for sluggards; walk, or you will be dragged along. As we were making our way along and found ourselves at a kind of fork in the road, we were met by a certain man—not a man in fact, but God who is man for the sake of men. He said to us, "Don't go this way; this route certainly looks easy and smooth and delightful, well trodden by many and broad; but this road in the end leads to doom. Since you aren't permitted to stop and live here, nor is it in your best interests, you have to keep on going; but go this other way. You will be proceeding through a number of difficult places, but no sooner are the difficulties over and done with than you will come to a vast field of joys, and you will have avoided those traps and ambushes which nobody can avoid who chooses to proceed along that way."

That's what this person said—I think we all know who he was, if we have a shred of faith. Or would you agree to examining this person's credibility? Let us call to mind past events and times, and the Old Testament scriptures. Isn't this man the Word of God? Didn't this Word later on *become flesh and dwell among us* (Jn 1:14)? But before he became flesh and dwelt among us, didn't he speak through the patriarchs and the prophets? Let's see what they proclaimed to the human race.

6. God spoke, by his Word, of course, to Abraham, and told him first of all that[13] there would be a stock sprung from Abraham, an old man, and Sarah, an old and barren woman. This was believed, and it happened. Next he was told that this stock, that is to say the people born thus according to the flesh, would be slaves in Egypt, and for how long; it happened. That it was to be delivered from that captivity; delivered it was. That it was going to receive the promised land; it duly received it.[14] Many things were said through the prophets; and Abraham himself was told, not only that he should bear in mind that future people, but *in your seed*, he said, *shall all the nations be blessed* (Gn 22:18; 12:3).

Things in the near future were foretold, things in the far distant future. Those in the near future happened; those in the far distant future are being enacted now. The Word of God spoke through the prophets that that nation was going to sin, and was to be handed over into the hands of its enemies, because it had offended the Lord; it all happened.[15] That it was going to go into captivity in Babylon; this too happened. That Christ the king was going to come from it; Christ too came, Christ was born; because he had himself foretold his own future coming, Christ too came. It was declared that the Jews would crucify him; crucify him they did. It was foretold that he would rise again and was to be glorified; it happened—he rose again, he ascended into heaven.[16]

It was foretold that the whole earth was going to believe in his name, foretold that kings were going to persecute his Church. These things happened. It was foretold that kings were going to believe in him. We now accept the faith of kings,[17] and do we have doubts about the good faith of Christ? The divisions caused by heresies were foretold; don't we see them too, and groan in the midst of the din they set up all around us? It was foretold that the nations would afflict the Church on behalf of their idols; and it happened. It was foretold that the idols themselves were to be destroyed by means of the Church and the name of Christ; this too we have seen fulfilled. Scandals in the Church itself were foretold, the tares foretold, the chaff foretold.[18] These are all things we can both observe with our eyes, and endure with all the fortitude we can muster, as bestowed on us by the Lord.

In which of these things were you ever deceived by this person who has told you, "Go along this way"? Say yourself without a qualm, if you are a believer, with all the experience you have had of this person who is speaking to you—

approve him on the facts, since it is on the facts that he was prepared to be judged—say: "He is certainly telling the truth, I take everything he says for the truth, in no instance has he ever lied. That's what I know him for, he is the Word of God. He spoke by the mouths of servants, and did not deceive us; can what he says by his own mouth prove fallacious?" While any of you to whom he is not yet known, who may still be having doubts about Christ, should also say, you too: "I will go along this way, in case it turns out to be true, what that person says, whom the whole world now believes." And for all that, it will happen exactly as he himself has foretold.[19]

Get a passage on board the ark, or get built into its very structure

7. Brothers and sisters, the many people who don't believe him have of necessity to find themselves on the last day in the same position as that majority found itself in during the days of Noah. The only ones who escaped were those who were in the ark. So fix yourselves up with that sort of accommodation; the shipwright's hands are available, Christ is still constructing the ark. Make yourselves available to him, give yourselves into his hands, get yourselves squared off together,[20] get yourselves fitted in together; don't let any of you push aside the fingers of this master craftsman. His grace knows just how to put each of you into the right place; only don't you be a timber of crooked pride, that will soon rot. That's how it's going to be; all the same, my brothers and sisters, many people treat all this as a joke.

I see that lack of time is going to prevent me explaining the psalm. You see, I don't want, having started on this passage from the gospel, not to complete it now, in the measure the Lord furnishes me with the material. So for the time being, if your graces wouldn't mind, let us defer the psalm. It needn't be put off to too distant a date—there is soon going to be what they call an exhibition;[21] well, we too have our own exhibitor, for whom we can foregather.[22] If the crowds of people from that wide road, who jeer and sneer at that trustworthy guide to the right way, are running to look at an exhibition where they are not going to receive what is on show—and anyone who did receive it would be disappointed; but still, they're running off like that, flocking like that to see things put on show which they are not going to receive themselves—how much more eagerly ought we to assemble, seeing that we are going to receive the marvels we are going to be watching! If it's from me you think you will receive them, don't come along, there could be none poorer than me; but if it's from him, from whom I too receive, then there's none richer than him, none richer than that one who became poor for our sakes.[23] Let us all receive from him, let us all rejoice in him. And if he should happen to show you what he is good enough to grant you through me, please also love the exhibitor's slave, but for the exhibitor's sake, because I too, brothers and sisters, love you in him and for his sake, because apart from him we are all of us simply nothing.

The difficulties of the passage need to be explained

8. So then, briefly[24] and with the Lord's help I will not keep quiet about what may perhaps seem rather obscure to some in the reading from the gospel. People really must fear being found like that on the last day. We really must be afraid, my brothers and sisters. We're exultant now, rejoicing, cheering.[25] I beg you: let that day find you all ready. The one who is saying these things is not lying, he has never lied; if you are still not sure about that, take care that perhaps what he says may be true.

But one of you says to me, "So it's essential that he should find his way into the hearts of the faithful." After all, by talking like this now, I am not going to make you all into the sort of people the Lord indicated: *Whoever has not taken his cross and followed me* (Mt 10:38), or make you all into the sort the Lord indicated: *If you wish to be perfect, go, sell everything you have, give to the poor, and you shall have treasure in heaven; and come, follow me* (Lk 18:22). Brothers and sisters, even so, is that road really to be feared, where the leader says, "Follow me"? I know that I am not suddenly going to make all I'm talking to, or certainly the majority of you, into that sort of people. So now, because the thunder of the gospel has been heard—provided at least that there are believing hearts to be filled with dread—because he said, *It was like that in the days of Noah; they were eating, drinking, marrying wives and husbands, buying, selling, until Noah entered into the ark, and the flood came and destroyed them all* (Lk 17:26-27), many people start saying to themselves, "We are ordered to wait for that day, and not to be found like those who were found outside the ark, and perished in that flood. Certainly the word of God frightens us out of our wits, the trumpet of the gospel scares us rigid. What are we to do, if you are not to marry a wife?"—that's what a young man will say, some youth or other. "There's to be no eating, no drinking, must there be perpetual fasting?"—many people will say that. And anyone who was hoping perhaps to buy something will say to himself, "So I'm not to buy anything now, in case I should be found in the number of those who perished?"

The camel through the eye of a needle

9. So what are we to do, if that's the case? We must cry, in the way the apostles felt sad for the whole human race, when they heard the Lord saying what perfection was: *Sell everything you have and come, follow me*, because the man who was told this went away saddened. And when he called the one from whom he was seeking advice about eternal life "good master," he seemed to be a good master only until he answered the question he was asked. He answered it, and saddened his questioner. And as he was going away sad, the Lord went on to say, *How difficult it is for a rich man to enter into the kingdom of heaven!* Difficult, but at least only difficult. But the Lord added an example, and declared that what he had said was difficult is in fact impossible. *It is easier*, he said, *for a camel to enter through the eye of a needle than for a rich man into the kingdom of heaven* (Lk 18:18-25). He practically slammed the door in the face of the rich.

"What will happen, what will happen? It's shut."

Knock, and it will be opened to you (Mt 7:7).

"How," he says, "shall we knock?"

How else, but with your hands? What does that mean, "How else, but with your hands"? How else, but with your works?

Let's see, brothers and sisters, if the Lord provided even the rich with room for such works. Let me say this from the scriptures, in case I should be found to be not so much a preacher as a fawner. First of all, then, let me say what the selfsame Lord said in this very place.[26] The disciples, you see, were saddened because the Lord said this. And they were saddened, indeed, not for their own sakes, because they had themselves left everything and followed the Lord. And what did they say when they were saddened? *Who then can be saved?* (Lk 18:26).

Now here it's my turn to question the apostles: "O outstanding members of Christ, O pillars confirming the truth of his resurrection,"[27] why so, why "who then can be saved"? Has he made you despair about the rich? There are only a few rich people, the millions of the poor can be saved. What did the Lord say? *It is easier for a camel to enter through the eye of a needle than for a rich man into the kingdom of heaven.* He didn't say, did he, "It is easier for a camel to enter through the eye of a needle than for a man into the kingdom of heaven"? He said *a rich man.*

I would have been the first to say that, brothers and sisters—we wish everyone well, to be sure, because this is what we are commanded, and this is what we hope for; but still, I note in the scriptures the pile of chaff that is to be consumed by fire,[28] and I can say, "If only those who were going into the fire were as few as the rich are now!" Look here, brothers and sisters; in this whole congregation listening to all this, how many rich people are there? I didn't say this, meaning I hoped that only they would go into the fire; but as many as are going to go, and those who are going to go, if only there could be as few of them as there are of rich people in the human race! As things stand now, however, there are both many from the ranks of the rich who are going to go into the kingdom of heaven, and many from the ranks of the poor who are going to go into eternal fire. Pay attention, while I demonstrate this in a few words.

Christ himself is the camel going through the needle's eye

10. The Lord said that a camel can more easily enter through the eye of a needle than a rich man can into the kingdom of heaven. And the disciples were depressed by this and said, *Who then can be saved?* (Lk 18:26), though they could observe how many millions of poor people there are in the human race, how few rich. But so what? They shrewdly observed, not who was rich in means, but who was on fire with greed. Someone or other is called rich for the abundance of all his possessions, and it is plain to see. But this man doesn't give a thought for them all, and really possesses them as their owner, is not possessed by them; as it is written, *His hope is in the Lord his God* (Ps 146:5). He's not

arrogant, not boastful, not abusing his power to oppress the poor,[29] not grasping, not panting after other people's property, not guarding and hoarding his own like a miser; but he's truly rich toward God,[30] regarding the giver of riches as the only true riches; such a person is not only rich but also enters the kingdom of heaven.

In fact, when the disciples were shocked, the Lord said, *"What is difficult for men is easy for God* (Lk 18:27).[31] You're all upset about the difficulty, because I talked of getting a camel through the eye of a needle, and indeed this is difficult and imposible for men; for God it's the easiest thing in the world. If he wants to he can even thread that gigantic beast, which is called a camel, through the eye of a needle."* And in fact this is what he was good enough to do with himself, and the reason even a rich man can enter into the kingdom of heaven is that for his sake the camel did enter through the eye of a needle.

What's all this? Let's see if it will become clear. It's not, you see, without point that John the Baptist too, the herald of the Lord, himself had a garment of camel's hair, because he took his livery, so to say, from the judge who was coming after him, whom he was going ahead of. I certainly recognize, when a camel is mentioned, a kind of figure or type of my Lord; I recognize his bigness, and yet his humble neck; I recognize how big he is, so that nobody could have loaded him with sufferings, unless he himself had lowered himself to the ground. I see also the eye of the needle by which he, so big as he was, came in. In a needle I perceive pricking, in pricking suffering, in the needle's eye the agony of being squeezed. So then, the camel has already entered through the eye of a needle; the rich need not despair, they will follow him into the kingdom of heaven.

The rich can be saved, the poor can be damned

11. But what sort of rich people? Here, by contrast, is someone or other else, covered with rags; he hugged himself and laughed loudly when it was said that the rich won't enter into the kingdom of heaven. "I will," he said. "These rags will assure me of that. Those people who treat us badly won't enter, those who oppress us."

Certainly such people won't enter; but you too, just see whether you will enter. What if as well as being poor you are also greedy, what if you're both weighed down with want, and on fire with avarice? So if that's the sort of person you are, whoever you are that are poor, it's not that you have declined to be rich, but that you haven't been able to be. *Peace*, it says, *on earth to men of good will* (Lk 2:14). So God does not inspect your means, but your will. Consider what your heart is full of, not what your money box is empty of. So if that's what you're like, leading a bad life, with a bad will, remove yourself from the ranks of God's poor; you will not be numbered among those of whom it was said, *Blessed are the poor in spirit, since theirs is the kingdom of heaven* (Mt 5:3). Look, that's what I find the rich man to be, the one you boastfully compared yourself with, and had the gall to aspire to the kingdom of heaven; I find him to be poor in spirit, that is to say, humble, dutiful, following God's will, and if he should chance to lose any of his abundant goods, saying straightaway, *The Lord has given, the Lord has taken away; may the Lord's name be blessed* (Jb 1:21). O meek rich man, not resisting God's will, really rejoicing in that *land of the living* (Ps 27:13)! For *blessed are the meek, since they shall possess the land as their inheritance* (Mt 5:4). You, though, very possibly are a thrusting type, having nothing in your storeroom indeed, but dreaming, in your greedy fantasies, of worthless treasures. This man rather than you, this rich man will enter; against you the kingdom of heaven will be shut, because it will be shut against the grasping, against the proud and the greedy.

"But look, that widow was poor, who put two farthings in the treasury."[32]

True enough; she was poor, but Zacchaeus[33] was rich. Do you think the widow was let in, and Zacchaeus shut out? On the contrary, this is why the kingdom belongs to those who are truly free,[34] because it is given equally to both rich and poor. In that kingdom Zacchaeus will not be richer than that widow, even if here he gave much more than she did. He, after all, gave half his goods to the poor, she gave two farthings. They were ill-matched in their means, they were equals in charity.

What the rich must do to enter the kingdom

12. So the rich man enters into the kingdom of heaven. Listen to a description of the sort of person he must be; how a way is opened up for him, how he is summoned to enter. Listen, those of you who have a substantial stake in the world, listen and do something before the flood comes, listen to the apostle writing to Timothy: *Command the rich of this world* (1 Tm 6:17). And as though Timothy had been inquiring about what the Lord commanded: "Sell all you have, give to the poor, and you will have treasure in heaven; and come with me, follow the Lord";[35] the Lord had already given this precept; those who hold Christ to his promises should hold themselves to his precepts. Let whoever wishes to, do it; get cracking, set about doing what you have heard from the Lord. It's to some others that the apostle is saying—and through the apostle, the Lord: *Or do you want experience of the one who is speaking in me, Christ?* (2 Cor 13:3). So what then? *Command*, he says, *the rich of this world*, about what is the source of evil, what is to be feared in the rich, *not to be proud and have haughty ideas about themselves*[36] (1 Tm 6:17).

Let's briefly fill in the picture. It's all too easy for the rich man to say, "You bad slave!" It sounds as if he has haughty ideas about himself, and yet if he didn't say it, perhaps he would be failing to keep control of his household. Frequently, I mean to say, he controls it more by harsh and frightening words than by savage beatings. He says this, compelled to say it, no doubt, by the need to be in control of his household; don't let him say it inwardly, don't let him say it in his heart, don't let him say it in the eyes and ears of God. He mustn't think he's better, just because he's rich; let him reflect on the frailty of his flesh, once he has put off his clothes.

What can I say, brothers and sisters, what can I say? Let him consider, if he were stripped of all those exterior trappings, what sort of rich man he could be, because he's flesh and blood, because he belongs equally with his slave to that mass which derives from Adam and Eve. But as a rich man he cannot engage in such reflections; you will have difficulty in stripping him of all his trappings. Nor is it desirable that he should be stripped of them; what's desired is that he should throw them away. So it's difficult to persuade him of what he really is in himself, surrounded by all these things. Let him turn his thoughts to what he was like in his mother's womb, naked once upon a time and helpless, just like that poor man. A different lot awaited him when he was born, and the lot that awaited him will remain his here, just as he didn't bring it with him.[37] When the rich man lets his thoughts run on those lines, he is inwardly *poor in spirit* (Mt 5:3), that is, he blows pride out of his system, he takes himself down a few pegs. And if he presents a stern and frightening face to those who must be subject to his control, his heart is still humble under the eye of God, and he knows with what kind of conscience he beats his breast.

But look at what comes next, and see if this is outwardly apparent in the rich. You see, he didn't just say, *not to be proud and have haughty ideas about themselves,* and then stop. Every rich man, after all, would answer you, "God knows I don't have haughty ideas about myself; and if I happen to shout, and say something harsh, God knows my conscience, that I say that sort of thing from my need to exercise control, not because I consider myself a cut above other people, as though being richer automatically made me more important." God sees these acts inwardly. Let's see what follows. *Not to be proud and have haughty ideas about themselves,* he says, *nor to set their hopes on the uncertainty of riches.* Here too he's still at liberty to say this, and only God can observe whether he's telling the truth, whether he doesn't rely on what he possesses, or set his hopes there. It goes on, you see: *but on the living God, who bestows everything on us for our enjoyment* (1 Tm 6:17).

13. "And what next?" he says. *Let them be rich in good works.* Here he is now coming out in front even of the eyes of men, this is not something you can hide. It's either done and is openly apparent, or it is not done, and there is no way of lying about it. *Let them be rich in good works, let them give readily, let them share.* In this way humility is openly apparent; you there have something; let it be shared in common between you and the one who has nothing. *Let them share.* And to what good purpose? *Let them store up for themselves a good foundation for the future, that they may take hold of the true life* (1 Tm 6:18-19). If rich people are like that, they need have no worries; when the last day comes, they will be found in the ark, they will be built into its construction, destruction by the flood won't apply to them. They needn't be scared out of their wits, just because they are rich.

Other difficulties of the passage dealt with

And if it's a young man we're dealing with, and he cannot practice continence, he is permitted to marry a wife. So is the last day going to find him among those of whom the Lord said, *They were marrying wives* (Lk 17:27)? It won't find him like that, if it finds him such as the apostle mentions. Here you are, this is how he fastens together in the ark all those who were struck with fear.[38] The apostle says, you see, *For the rest, brothers and sisters, the time is short.* And what follows? *It remains for those who have wives to be as though they had none, and for those who are buying as though they were not, and for those who weep as though they did not, and for those who are rejoicing as though they were not, and for those who are making use of this world as though they were not using it. For the shape of this world is passing away. I wish you to be without anxiety* (1 Cor 7:29-32). Brothers and sisters, if you want to be free from worries, you shouldn't let your happiness depend on these things. And if either duty or the needs of human infirmity compel you to make use of these things, don't put your trust in them, don't stick fast in them, count them among things that are transitory and temporary. All these things, after all, are drifting along in a kind of stream of events. You can see how all those misfortunes which play such a large part in human affairs give these superfluities a constant hammering.

Grumbling about the hard times; blaming Christ

14. Brothers and sisters, every day there is grumbling against God: "The times are bad, and the times are hard."[39] It's the trifles we were talking about that are taking a beating—"bad times, hard times, grievous times"—and yet shows are still being exhibited! They are what's bad, they're what's grievous; let them get them straightened out. You say the times are hard? How much harder are *you*, failing to use the hard times to straighten yourself out! Such vain, crazy processions[40] still flourishing, people still agog for such frivolities! There's simply no end to cupidity, no pauses even to its workings. For what kind of activities, I ask you, are they hoping for prosperity, what would they be doing with the security they are looking for? Let them be given some security; we'll soon see how many ills come out into the open, how much wicked extravagance is displayed, much more than now. Security and quiet times—for the sake of theaters and pipes and flutes and clowns!

You want to make bad use of what you are looking for, that's why you don't receive it. Listen, listen to the voice of an apostle, much freer than mine is—I know, you see, how many people I will offend; think of me as being rather timid; I don't dare pick holes in the object of your affections.[41] Hear something from an apostle which you would much rather not: *You desire, and you do not have*—they're the words of an apostle; *you kill and you envy, and you cannot obtain; you go to law, fight battles, and you do not have; you ask and do not receive, because you ask wrongly, to spend it on your lusts* (Jas 4:2-3). He certainly didn't flatter anyone's vanity; the lancet struck to the quick in many rotten sores. Let us allow ourselves to be cured, brothers and sisters, let us straighten ourselves out, let us correct ourselves. The one is going to come who did come and was laughed at, and is still being laughed at because he came. He's going to come, and there'll be no place for laughing then.

My brothers and sisters, let us start going straight. Look, the times will soon get better, and lo and behold they will do so right now;[42] what are you hoping for here? Change the place, change the address: "Lift up your hearts." What are you hoping for here? The human race sprang up, it reached the stage of a kind of youth, these things flourished in the world;[43] it has turned the corner and is declining into old age; it is already to all intents and purposes decrepit. What are you hoping for here? Look for it elsewhere.[44] Are you looking for rest and quiet? You're looking for a good thing; look for it in its own proper region. There is another place where he descended from to you, another place to which he is bidding you ascend.

Don't hope for times of any sort, except the sort that can be read about in the gospel. I won't tell you what sort they are; copies of the Lord's gospels are on sale all the time, the reader reads out from them. Buy one for yourself, and just you read it when you've got the time; or rather, make sure you get the time, time better spent on this, after all, than on those frivolities. Read what sort of times are foretold until the end of the world, and believe what you read,[45] don't kid yourself. It's not because Christ has come that the times are bad; but it's because they were hard and bad that he came, in order to provide comfort and consolation.

The human race one huge invalid; Christ the doctor

15. Think carefully, my brothers and sisters; it was essential for such times to come, hard and grievous. What would we do, if such a great consoler were not around?[46] The human race was going to fall very gravely ill. Like a doctor attending one huge patient, from Adam right up to the end, that is to say, that doctor attending the whole hideously injured human race—because from the moment we were born here, from the moment we were turned out of paradise,[47] the illness of course is there but at the end it was going to get much worse, immediately preceding a return to health for some, presaging death for others. So since the whole human race was ill, that great doctor attending the invalid, who was lying in a kind of huge bed, the whole world, paid attention just like a most experienced doctor to the phases of the illness, and he observed and foresaw what the developments were going to be—after all, it was he himself who had engineered this sickness, because of his justice, as a punishment for our sin.

So during the milder phases of our illness the doctor himself first sent his assistants to inspect us, he sent the prophets. They spoke, they preached; through them he cured some and restored them to health. They foretold that in the last phase of the illness there would be a kind of severe crisis, a kind of violent agitation of this invalid, which would have to be shown to the doctor himself, and would thus require him to come in person. So this is what our doctor said: "In the last times the patient will be more severely and violently agitated than ever, and to attend to the appropriate medication it will be necessary for me to come in person at that time. I myself will restore him, I myself comfort, I myself encourage, I myself make him promises, I myself will heal him if he believes."[48]

And that's what happened. He came, he became man, a shareholder in our mortality, so that we might be able to become shareholders in his immortality. And still the patient is in the grip of this agitation. And when he's panting in his fever, with a very high temperature, he says to himself, "From the moment this doctor arrived, I have been suffering from a more severe fever than ever, I'm being tossed around ever more violently. Oh, this monstrous temperature! Why did he ever come to me? I don't think it was with a lucky foot that he entered the house." That's what they all say, those who are still gravely ill with vanity. Why are they still gravely ill with vanity? Because they refuse to accept from him the potion of serious sobriety. You can see these poor wretches being tossed about and agitated by their cares, and the various afflictions and terrors of the world, and saying, "From the moment Christ came, we have been suffering these times; from the moment Christians appeared on the scene, the world has been falling to pieces in every way." O senseless patient, it's not because the doctor has come that your illness has grown more serious; but it's because your illness was going to grow more serious that the doctor came. He foresaw that, he didn't cause it.[49] He came, though, to comfort you, and to make you really and truly better.

16. What, after all, are you being deprived of, what's being taken away from you but unnecessary superfluities? You see, you were agog for harmful things; the things you were agog for were not good for your fever. Is the doctor harsh because he snatches harmful fruits from the invalid's hands? What's he taking away from you, but the bad kind of security which you were eager to swallow, to the ruin of your insides? And this very thing that you're grumbling and groaning about is part of his treatment. If you want to be cured,[50] put up willingly with being hurt. The times simply have to be harsh. Why? To stop earthly happiness being loved. It's absolutely essential—it's the appropriate medical treatment—for this life to be troubled, so that the other life may be loved.

Look here; if people still cling to earthly things with such sluggish reluctance to let go, if they are still crazy about the theaters, what would be the case if everything was smiling on such vanities, if on no occasion were your frivolities struck from your hands? Look, the world has so much bitterness and gall mixed into it, and yet it is still sweet. Come now, my dearest brothers and sisters, I beseech you by the Lord, by his cross, by his blood, by his charity, by his lowliness, by his highness, I beseech and adjure you not to listen to all this in vain, not to assume that I'm really standing[51] in this place as if I were just putting on a show. His mercy knows, under whose eyes I tremble like this, that I am led on by the duty of love to say these things to you, and that I am driven by the dread I feel, knowing that I am going to have to give an account to the Lord himself for you all.

NOTES

1. This sermon, according to Dolbeau, forms a bloc with Sermons 361, 362 (III, 10), *Expositions of the Psalms* 147, and Sermon 23B (III, 11). They are all linked with each other, and were preached during one winter. After complex argument with the suggestions of other scholars, he concludes that they were all preached in the winter of 403-404; this sermon in December, 403, and in Carthage. It coincides in part with Sermon 346A (III, 10), which Dolbeau takes to be the work of anthologists and/or composers of lectionaries messing about, to put it frankly, with this sermon. In my notes on that sermon (which other scholars date to December 399) I give reasons for suggesting that it is in fact a composite of two or more sermons; and I have the same feelings about the text we have here.

2. Ps 147:12-20. See the discourse on this psalm, which was preached a few days later and which refers back to this sermon. The gospel passage discussed here is Lk 17:20-37.

3. The Septuagint translation of the Hebrew *gopher* wood. See Sermons 260C, 2, note 6, and 264, 5, note 27 (III, 7). It seems likely that the Septuagint confused the wood from which Noah's ark was constructed with the wood out of which the ark of the covenant was made, Ex 25:10, Dt 10:3. The ark that is still being built is of course the Church.

4. An incomplete sentence in the Latin. The apodosis to this "if" sentence is to be inferred at the end of this section.

5. Calculated from putting together Gn 5:32, Noah being 500 years old when he begat his three sons, and 7:11, his being 600 years old when the flood began.

6. See Ps 51:17.

7. See Lk 11:31-32. The ark he, Christ, is building is the Church.

8. He was probably calculating from Christ's death and resurrection, not from his birth, as the careless creator of our current Christian era, Dionysius Exiguus, or Denis the Short, was to do about 100 years after Augustine's time. So 300 years later would bring Augustine to about the year of his own death! Well clearly he wasn't dead while preaching this sermon—but allowing for the roughness of his calculation, I wonder whether we do not have here a slight indication that he was preaching this sermon in the later years of his life, after 420—an alternative to the date suggested by Dolbeau. If indeed we have here pieces from two or more sermons, there need in fact be no conflict.

9. The naughty old man! If this is really one sermon, he goes on for rather more than six times as long as he has already been speaking, and the whole will have lasted at the very least 45 minutes; and halfway through section 7, some 20 minutes later than this point, he will again advert to the pressure of time. The psalm will not in fact be discussed until another day. But again, perhaps, this is a sign that the text is a composite, put together from more than one sermon.

10. *Mediocris cordis opus desideramus.*

11. A very severe criticism of ordinary Church life! Still true, perhaps? Little interest shown in newcomers, or care taken to make them feel at home?

12. This is where Sermon 346A begins. But we have already had bits and pieces of that sermon in this one.

13. I here omit a line or so that simply overloads the text, and could represent an alternative version that got incorporated into this one; or a scribbled note in the margin. It runs, *genus ejus primo futurum esset—cum ipse cui dicebatur prae senectute jam non esset*; "that there would first of all be his stock, since he who was being told, because of old age, was not yet (the stock?)."

14. See Gn 15; 17:1-8; 18:1-15.

15. He probably has in mind the stories of Judges.

16. He would have been thinking of innumerable messianic prophecies, the most important of them, 2 Sm 7:4-17; Pss 2; 110; Is 7:14; 9:6-7; 11:1-5; 52:13—53:12; Hos 6:2; Ps 16:9-10. See also New Testament texts such as Acts 2:23-29 and 1 Cor 15:3-4.

17. The Christian Roman emperors. He is undoubtedly equivocating on the senses of *fides*, which I translate "good faith" in the second instance.

18. See Mt 13:24-30; Lk 3:17. For the prophecies about the Church, persecutions, the overthrow of idols and so on, see for example Is 42:6; 62:1-16; 46:1-2; Hos 2:21-23 read through the eyes of

1 Pt 2:10. For scandals in the Church itself, he was probably thinking of Christ's own predictions in the gospels; for example, Lk 17:1; also 1 Cor 11:19.

19. I simply cannot see how this last sentence fits in with what has just been said.

20. *Conquadramini*; he sometimes talks of the ark being constructed of squared timbers, especially, of course, when he was preaching on the feast of Saint Quadratus, bishop of Utica and, it seems, of the martyrs of the *Massa Candida*, the "White Mass," whom he encouraged to bear their witness and then followed to martyrdom three or four days later. His feast was celebrated on 21 August. See Sermons 306-306D (III, 9).

21. *Munus*; that is, a big show in the amphitheater, including chariot races and the "hunting" of wild beasts, put on at vast expense by some public official. The scholars assume that the reference is to the annual New Year games celebrated on 1 January. But I think there were other occasional *munera* besides these regular ones—for example, special games to mark the arrival of a new governor or local military commander; or something like an emperor's birthday or similar imperial occasion. There is in this sermon no precise allusion to the New Year festivities.

22. God, of course, or Christ; the shows or exhibitions he usually puts on are the feasts of the martyrs.

23. See 2 Cor 8:9.

24. Again, what a nerve!

25. Is this an allusion to the general holiday atmosphere of the *munera*, or to the warm reception his sermon was receiving from his audience?

26. Here the text continues as I have translated it; but Dolbeau here inserts, hesitantly, or by way of example, "Sell everything you have and come, follow me." I don't think this is necessary; more to the point, perhaps, would be, "It is easier for a camel . . ." etc.

27. See Gal 2:9.

28. See Lk 3:17.

29. See Jas 2:6.

30. See 1 Pt 3:4.

31. In fact what he said, in all three synoptic gospels, is, "What is impossible with men is possible with God."

32. See Mk 12:42.

33. See Lk 19:2.

34. See Jn 8:36; no class distinctions, or other such human nonsense, in the kingdom.

35. See Mk 10:21.

36. For all this section on the poor and the rich, compare Sermons 36, 2-6 (III, 2); 61, 10-11; 85, 3-5 (III, 3); and 177, 7-11 (III, 5).

37. The general meaning is clear, but the expression of it cramped and obscure. Dolbeau thinks, with justice, that there are probably lacunae in the text.

38. When they heard the gospel passage from Lk 17.

39. For this part of the sermon on "hard times," see also Sermons 311, 8 (III, 9) and 346C (III, 10).

40. *Tanta insania pomparum*. The use of the latter word, closely associated with Roman triumphs, perhaps supports my tentative suggestion that the *munera* he was concerned with in this sermon were not the annual New Year fun and games, but some special shows being put on for some special imperial, or other official, occasion.

What has cupidity, in the next sentence, got to do with these shows? First, the avid eagerness for them of the general public; secondly the avid eagerness of their promoters for political and social advancement.

41. Reading *affectum*, as suggested by Dolbeau, instead of the text's *flictum*, which means "collision," and makes no sense here.

42. He doesn't mean it, of course; he is just supposing.

43. He no doubt has in mind the "high points" of ancient Greek and Roman civilization, the Athens of Pericles and Plato, the Rome of Augustus and the Augustan poets, Virgil and Horace.

44. Reading *alias* for the text's *aliud*, "Look for something else."

45. He actually says, "Believe yourself." The assumption behind this is that you would be reading the book aloud, even if you were alone, and so you are being told to believe your own voice. Most of his audience were illiterate, of course. This exhortation to them to buy copies of the gospels and read for themselves just indicates that, as usual, he was addressing himself primarily to the better off, and thus more educated, members of his congregation.

46. The implicit thought seems to be similar to that of the *felix culpa*, the "happy sin of Adam," which brought us so great a redeemer, in the *Exultet* of the Easter Vigil.

47. See Gn 3:22-24.

48. For this whole section on the giant invalid, see Sermons 175, 1 (III, 5); 340A, 5 (III, 9).

49. But at the end of the first paragraph of this section he said that Christ had engineered the whole thing, as a kind of punishment for sin.

50. Reading *curari volens*, instead of the text's *curare volens*, "if you wish to cure"—which may, indeed, just be a misprint.

51. Standing, not sitting; so we may infer that he was not preaching in his own church of Hippo Regius, where he would preach seated on his *cathedra*, but in that of another bishop, where he would preach standing in the pulpit; in Carthage therefore, most likely. But it seems he was visibly trembling—not unnaturally after such a marathon of a sermon—if indeed it is all one sermon.

Dolbeau 19
SERMON 130A
Mainz 51

SERMON OF SAINT AUGUSTINE THE BISHOP ON THE WORDS OF THE GOSPEL,
WORK FOR THE FOOD WHICH DOES NOT PERISH,
BUT WHICH ABIDES UNTO ETERNAL LIFE

Date: 405[1]

The work of God is to believe in the one whom he has sent

1. Our Lord Jesus Christ, who called himself bread,[2] is looking for hungry people. But it is only a healthy mind, that is, the belly of the inner man, which is hungry for this bread. Here's a comparison with this visible bread. Sick people, whose illness has lost them their appetite, can praise good bread, but can't eat it. In the same way, when the inner man is ill, he is not inclined to eat this heavenly bread, being afflicted with loss of appetite, and though he may praise it, he takes no pleasure in eating it. But the Lord himself said, as we have just heard, *Work for the food which does not perish, but which abides to eternal life* (Jn 6:27), distinguishing it from this visible and bodily food, about which he says in another place, *Everything that enters the mouth goes down into the belly, and is evacuated into the privy* (Mt 15:17)—and so it perishes.

Work therefore for the food that does not perish, he said, *but which abides to eternal life*. He called this food bread, and he showed how he himself was bread. But what can working for this food mean, if not eating this food? After all, if this food is bread, it is likewise Christ. Which of us works for Christ, which of us makes Christ, but the one who does what Christ commanded? *You*, says the apostle, *are the body of Christ and its members* (1 Cor 12:27). Let us work for Christ, that is, let us work for this food.

2. Those who were listening and who questioned him were doing some good listening and questioning on our behalf. *What shall we do*, they said, *in order to work the work of God?* And with that masterpiece of brevity, *This*, he said, *is the work of God, that you should believe in the one whom he has sent* (Jn 6:28-29). That's short enough;[3] if you weigh it up, it is masterly as well. It takes no time to say, it is not so easy to perform. Someone says to me from this big crowd of people standing round, someone ups and says, "Which of us here

118

hasn't professed faith in Christ? So if we have all professed faith in Christ, we can't see what this advice has now to do with us."⁴

What does it have to do with us? Just that *this is the work of God.* You aren't wanting to do something other than the work of God, are you, and then expecting some reward from God? So why put yourself out, why busy yourself with the endless pages of scripture, and toil away running through them, to seek and find how you should do the work of God? Here you are, from your own Lord talking to you, you can have the truth in a nutshell; no need to extend yourself, no need to sweat and toil and get all steamed up. *This is the work of God, that you should believe,* he says, *in the one whom he has sent.*

So what about the warning James gives us, when he says, *You believe that God is one, do you? You do well; the demons too believe, and tremble* (Jas 2:19). Don't imagine, he is saying, that you are doing anything very great by believing that God is one: *the demons too believe, and tremble.*

But perhaps the demons haven't got the right belief about the Son of God?

Then what about what they say to him themselves, *We know who you are* (Mk 1:24)? Or perhaps they're telling a lie? They're saying they know when they don't? Here it is, more plainly, in another place: *You are the holy one of God* (Lk 4:34), they say; *You are the Son of God* (Mk 3:11), they say.

Well, when Peter said this, he heard these words from the Lord: *Blessed are you, Simon Bar-jona, because it is not flesh and blood that has revealed this to you, but my Father who is in heaven. And I in turn say to you, Simon Bar-jona, that you are Peter, and upon this rock I will build my Church* (Mt 16:17-18). Why all this? Because he had said, *You are the Christ, the Son of the living God* (Mt 16:16). That's what the demons said too, and they were told, *Hush!* (Mk 1:25).

How else can we readily explain why similar words did not receive similar praise, except by noting the total dissimilarity of hearts? So please understand, my dearest friends, with me to remind you, what it is that you read and say every day.⁵ The demons too believed that he was the Christ and that he was the Son of God. They believed he was the Christ, they did not believe in Christ.⁶ So now all my efforts in this sermon are going to be directed, insofar as I can manage it, if with the Lord's help I can manage it, to explaining what believing in Christ means.

The difference between believing in someone and believing someone

3. *This,* you see, *is the work of God, that you should believe in the one whom he has sent.* He didn't say, "that you should believe him," or "that you should believe he is the one," but "that you should believe *in* him." We have heard the utterances of the prophets; we believe them, but we don't believe *in* them. We have heard the apostles' preaching; we believe what they preach, but we don't believe *in* them. We don't believe *in* Paul, but we believe Paul. As a matter of fact, there were some people who wanted to place their hope in him and as it were to believe in him, and he rebuffed them from himself, so that they should

not believe in him, but that he together with them should believe in Christ. *Was Paul crucified for you, or were you baptized in his name* (1 Cor 1:13)? Finally, it isn't only the apostles and holy teachers, but even people like us, not to be compared with them in the slightest degree,[7] who say every day, "Believe me"; we never have the audacity to say, "Believe *in* me." "Believe me"; is there anyone who doesn't say it. "Believe *in* me"; is there anyone who does say it, or who isn't manifestly crazy if he does?

So in whom are we to believe? In the one about whom the same Paul says, *For the one who believes in him who justifies the godless, his faith is counted as justice* (Rom 4:5). So it isn't Paul who justifies the godless, because in that case you would believe in him, and your faith would be counted as justice; you would be believing in him, after all, who justifies the godless. Since you don't believe in him, you see—after all, it's not Paul, not Elijah, not any angel, but the most just of the just and the holiest of the holy,[8] about whom it is said, *That he himself might be just and the justifier of the one who is of faith* (Rom 3:26).[9] About you it can be said "that you might be just"; it is unheard of "that you might also be a justifier." What after all does being a justifier mean, but making just?[10] And who is it that makes people just? The one who came without sin. Who is the just one? The one who makes just, who was not made just here himself, but who came here already just. There you have the one in whom we are to believe, in order that we may do the work of God, because this indeed is the work of God, to believe in the one who justifies the godless.

Why, then, the commandments?

4. "So that's enough for me," someone says; "I've declared my faith in Christ; what further suggestions do you have for me? *This is the work of God*; the one who has promised the reward should not require anything else of me. I mean, the one who offers a reward tells me what I have to do, and promises what I am to receive. So he sets a limit to the work, while I am in a fever of desire for the reward. He himself says to me, "Do you want to live forever?" on the lines of the one who asked him, *What am I to do, in order to have eternal life? Do you want to live for ever? Do this, and you shall live* (Lk 10:25.28). When I ask, *What am I to do?* he gives the very short answer, *This is the work of God, that you should believe in the one whom he has sent* (Jn 6:29)."

So why did he say to that rich man,[11] *If you want to reach life, keep the commandments,* and when he said, *Which commandments?* the precepts of the law were listed: *You shall not commit adultery, you shall not kill, you shall not steal, you shall not bear false witness, honor your father and mother, and you shall love your neighbor as yourself* (Mt 19:17-19). Couldn't he have also replied, with that very short answer, to the one who says *What am I to do in order to have eternal life,* "Believe in me"? This, after all, is the work of God, that's how he defined it above, and added nothing to this requirement. *This is the work of God*—why look for any more?—*that you should believe in the one whom he has sent.* That man is given commandments, and many of them; we are told, *This is the work of God, that you should believe in the one whom he has sent.* Or perhaps the Lord dealt graciously with us,[12] while on that man he wanted to lay a burden, not to give him some relief? Perish the thought!

So let us understand, if we can—this is what I, as best I can, promised I was going to explain—what it means to believe *in* Christ, and let us do that, work at that, make daily progress in that, move forward to this from day to day, until we finally, by keeping on moving, arrive. This, after all, is what we were also promised at the outset of our faith, that we would have made some sort of beginning, and when we had completed it, nothing more would be required of us.[13] This, you see, is the work of God, nor is anything else the work of God, except that we should believe in the one whom he has sent.

5. Well now, a short while ago we made this distinction between believing him, believing that he is something, and believing in him; believing him means believing that what he says is true, believing that he is something means believing that he is himself the Christ, believing in him means loving him. Now see the difference between these three in yourself: believing that the things he says are true, believing that he is himself the Christ, loving Christ. Believing that the things he says are true is something many bad people too can manage. They believe they are true, you see, and refuse to act on them; they are laggards when it comes to working. Believing, though, that he is himself the Christ is something even the demons could do. So Peter said, *You are the Christ, the Son of the living God* (Mt 16:16) out of love; the demons said it out of fear.[14]

Now not everyone who fears loves, while everyone who loves fears. But perhaps—or rather, not perhaps but certainly—everyone who loves fears, but with a chaste fear—for *the fear of the Lord is chaste, abiding for ever and ever* (Ps 19:9)—not a servile fear, because *perfect love casts out fear* (1 Jn 4:18). It is one thing to be afraid he may come, another to be afraid he may leave you. Fear that he might come upon them was evident in those who said, *We know who you are; why have you come, before the time, to destroy us?* (Mt 8:29; Lk 4:34). Fear, on the other hand, that he might leave him was evident in the one who said, *I will be with you to the death* (Lk 22:33). So when you hear "Believe in Christ," don't imagine it's enough for you to believe Christ, that is, to believe that the things Christ says are true; don't imagine it's enough for you to believe that Christ is himself the one whom God foretold through the prophets; but believe in Christ, that is, love Christ. It is when you have fulfilled this, that nothing more will be required of you, because *love is the fullness of the law* (Rom 13:10).

When you've believed in Christ like that, so that you have that kind of ardent love for Christ, see if you won't be able to make these words your own: *Who shall separate us from the love of God?* (Rom 8:35). So don't waste time wondering how to do what Christ commands; you cannot not do it, if you love Christ. Love, and you do it. To the extent that you love, to that extent you do it; insofar as you don't do very much, you don't love very much either. Fill up the love, and you complete the work. There you are, that's how truly it was said, *This is the work of God, that you should believe in the one whom he has sent*

(Jn 6:29); that is, that by loving him you should go to him, that is, that you should be incorporated in him.

Believing in Christ means loving him in a unique way

6. You could, of course, answer me and advise me to speak more carefully: "You said that believing in Christ means loving Christ, and you said that we ought to believe in Christ, but not to believe in Paul; so does that mean we oughtn't to love Paul?" So then, just as we distinguished between believing and believing, in the same way we must make a distinction with loving. I love Paul, and I don't believe in Paul. I don't love Christ, unless I first believe in Christ. I love Paul, you see, but I don't, by loving him, go into Paul;[15] I will be with Paul, I won't be in Paul. *For what is Apollos, what is Paul? Servants through whom you have believed* (1 Cor 3:4-5). Therefore, brothers and sisters, it is necessary to believe in God; by believing and loving to go into Christ. *Believe in God,* Christ says himself, *believe also in me* (Jn 14:1). What prophet ever dared to say that, what patriarch, what apostle, what martyr, what angel? So let us believe in him, let us love him, but in the sense of being incorporated in him by loving him.

We must understand that he is our God, and that he became man for our sakes, and that it is by God having become man that he justifies us. I mean, if he were only a man, he would have to be justified with us, he wouldn't be the justifier. Now, however, the one who is our God, and for the sake of our nature became man, which he had not been, still remained what he was, in possession of his own nature,[16] so that in him we might simultaneously have both the way we were to go along[17] and the destination we were to arrive at. Let us believe in him; that is, let us love him as God, so that we may go to him by love, having withdrawn from him by neglect.[18]

To love like that, we need to be converted by God

7. If that's how it is with us, then we enjoy the bread;[19] no more loss of appetite now, no more praising the bread and shrinking from it; rather, after praising it we eat it quietly because we love it, appetite restored, illness cured. How, in any case, are we to pay him back, we who say, *How shall I recompense the Lord?* (Ps 116:12); we who say, *Bless the Lord, my soul, and do not forget all his recompenses, who is gracious to all your iniquities?* This happened when we were baptized; but what comes next is still happening: *who heals all your ills* (Ps 103:2-3). Insofar as ills are healed, to that extent the heavenly bread is enjoyed; we enjoy *the bread of life which came down from heaven* (Jn 6:51), to the extent that our ills are healed.

But who are they healed by, if not the one to whom we have been saying,[20] *Convert us, God of our healings?* You, please, convert us, because before you heal us, we have our backs turned to you, and while we praise the bread, loss of appetite prevents us from receiving it. Our backs are turned when we are ill, we are converted when we are healed. So, *convert us, God of our healings, and turn your wrath away from us* (Ps 85:4). God's wrath is what the illness actually is, you see. *Whoever believes in the Son has eternal life.* Why? Because he has worked the work of God, seeing that this is the work of God, that you should believe in the one whom he has sent. *But whoever does not believe in the Son will not have life, but the wrath of God abides upon him* (Jn 3:36); not "will come upon him," but *abides upon him.* He is abandoned, not healed.

So the one who was saying *Convert us, O God* took note of the fact that we cannot be converted except insofar as we are healed, and so he added, *of our healings.* This bread, you see, cannot be enjoyed by anyone in bad health. So it's as though he were introducing the means by which we might be converted. What does *Convert us* mean? "Heal us." Indeed it is because we are in bad health that we are not really converted to the saving, health-giving bread.[21] We praise it, but we don't enjoy it. Does anyone fail to approve, fail to say, "It's true," when I say, *Do not do to others what you do not want done to you* (Tb 4:15; Mt 7:12)? "It's true," you shout, and "Nothing truer," you cry. Eat what you praise. You want to deceive someone, you don't want to be deceived by anyone. You want to get rich on someone else's misfortune, you don't want anyone to get rich on your misfortune. Aren't you enacting a law against yourself, isn't your heart enacting a rule[22] under which you should be punished? Why don't you want it done to you? If it's good, why do you shrink from it yourself? If it's bad—what are you going to answer, what are you going to say? "I enjoy doing it," and "I enjoy doing it." "I enjoy this and I enjoy that"—they're the words of a sick man. Cry out, *Convert us, God of our healings, and turn away your wrath from us.*

To receive God's grace, we must know our weakness

8. In the very same psalm, you see, this also is said: *The Lord will give sweetness, and our earth shall yield its fruit* (Ps 85:12). *But the fruit of the Spirit is love* (Gal 5:22). Where would this fruit come from, unless the Lord gave sweetness, because *the love of God has been poured out in our hearts*—not by us, but *through the Holy Spirit who has been given to us* (Rom 5:5)? You can see how the Lord will give sweetness, so that our earth may yield its fruit. You can see how our earth, that is to say, our hearts, our souls, how our earth does not yield its fruit, unless God sends rain on it. *The earth was moved*; it was moved to bring forth, to give birth. But why was it moved? *For indeed the heavens dripped*, not from themselves, but *from the face of God* (Ps 68:8). *For what is Apollos, what is Paul? Servants of God through whom you came to believe* (1 Cor 3:5). They are God's clouds; they can't rain down unless they are filled.

So then, *the earth was moved, for indeed the heavens dripped from the face of God.* It was moved by God, because it wouldn't have been moved except by *a voluntary rain*, as it goes on in that place. After saying *The earth was moved, for indeed the heavens dripped from the face of God*, in case you should assume that this rain from heaven wasn't God's, *a voluntary rain* (Ps 68:9), he says, not one that was owed—what, after all did he owe us but punishment? So then, *a voluntary rain,* because *you have crowned us,* he says, *with the shield of your good will* (Ps 5:13); not with the splendor of our merits, but *with the shield of your good will.* So then, *setting apart, O God, a voluntary rain for your inheritance, and it grew weak.* One who brings forth also grows weak. *The earth,* you see, *was moved* in order to bring forth; nor would it bring forth, unless it first grew weak; *you, however, have perfected it* (Ps 68:9).[23]

9. What does *grew weak* mean? Did not rely on itself. What does *grew weak* mean? Hoped for everything from you. What does *grew weak* mean? *When I grow weak, then am I powerful* (2 Cor 12:10). So then, *it grew weak,* it understood that it all came from God's grace, not from its own merits, its own powers; it understood, *it grew weak,* it shed its presumptuous self-reliance in order to receive the blessing.[24] *It grew weak.* Let it not, then, be so presumptuous as to rely on itself, let it cry out, weak as it is, to the Lord, *Convert us, God of our healings* (Ps 85:4).

So it continues there, *And it grew weak; you, however, have perfected it* (Ps 68:9). Why have you perfected it? Because it grew weak itself, because it understood it couldn't be perfected by itself. That's why, because it grew weak, *you, however, have perfected it.* It's this very earth that cries out in Paul, *On account of this I begged the Lord to take it away from me* (2 Cor 12:8), namely the corrective sting in my flesh. I mean, why did he say it had been applied to him, if not for the sake of checking his own self-reliant presumption and strength? For, *lest I should be elated,* he says, *by the greatness of the revelations, there was given me a sting in my flesh, an angel of Satan to knock me about* (2 Cor 12:7). So, grow weak, then. A *voluntary rain* (Ps 68:9) was set apart for you, not one that was owed you. Cry out from your weakness that *I am not fit to be called an apostle* (1 Cor 15:9). So grow weak, in order that he may perfect you. He did say to you, after all, as you were praying, *My grace is sufficient for you; strength is made perfect in weakness* (2 Cor 12:9).

The difference between my own justice and that which is by faith

10. So it is that in the reading which we have just heard, the selfsame apostle concludes like this: *That I may be found in him.* How, *in him? Not having my own justice.* Because if it's yours, you won't be *in him.* What does *not having my own* mean? As though it were produced by me, achieved by my own powers. *Not having my own justice, which is from the law, but that which is by faith* (Phil 3:9). How *my own,* if it's *from the law?* A difficult question, but I'm already rather tired. Accordingly, if I give somewhat less than a full answer, may he complete it to whom we all belong. *And that I may be found in him, not having my own justice.* If he hadn't added, *which is from the law,* wouldn't we all have assumed that he said *not having my own justice* in the sense of justice derived from human teaching? It's the way in which the Lord Christ said in another place, *My teaching is not mine* (Jn 7:16), that is, isn't human, isn't of this

palpable nature which you can see. I mean, how can it not be his, seeing that the teaching of the Father is his Word? And who but Christ is his Word?[25]

So would people perhaps have assumed that the apostle had spoken in the same sort of way, when he said, *that I may be found in him, not having my own justice*, unless he had added, *which is from the law, but the justice which is from the faith of Jesus Christ*? Why so? And didn't Christ give the law? If you had the justice which is from the law, how would you be having your own, since you yourself didn't give yourself the law, but you received it from Christ, from the Son of God? Christ, you see, didn't only begin to be when he came from the virgin, but he was from the Father before his mother, whom he created in order to be created from her, whom[26] he made in order to be made from her. For, *Zion is mother, man said, and man was made in her. And the Most High*—the one who was made man in her—*himself was her founder* (Ps 87:5). So he himself made the one in whom he would be made. So he was there at the time of Moses, to give the law, because of course Moses came, with many generations between, from Abraham; but Christ said, *Before Abraham was, I am* (Jn 8:58). It's little enough to say *before Abraham*; before the angels, before heaven and earth, before the whole of creation. *All things*, after all, *were made through him* (Jn 1:3).[27]

11. So then, what's the meaning of, *that I may be found in him, not having my own justice*, and his adding *which is from the law*? I will tell you, if I can do it briefly; the giver of grace will complete it in your hearts. What does it mean, if not that the Jews have even the law itself in such a way that they perform the works of the law out of a fear of damnation, not out of the fire of love? That's why they were slaves, because they acted out of a slavish, servile fear. But if you begin out of love to do what is written in the law: *You shall not covet* (Rom 7:7; Ex 20:17), how do you manage it, if not because *the love of God has been poured out in your heart*, not from you yourself, but *through the Holy Spirit, who has been given you* (Rom 5:5)? Since *God is setting apart a voluntary rain for his inheritance, and it has grown weak* (Ps 68:9), he would place no hopes at all in himself.

He was told, you see, "Do this," and he did it; "Do not kill," and he didn't; "Do not commit adultery with another man's wife," and he didn't. He was told "Do it," and he did; he was told, "Love what you are doing," and *it has grown weak*. It's out of fear that you don't kill your enemy; if you were granted immunity, would you spare him? Would you do what David did, when the Lord gave his enemy into his hands in such a way that he could do to him whatever he liked?[28] He chose to spare him, chose to spare him, though he had every right to kill him with impunity. How would you spare from death the one about whom you say, "Oh, if only he would die!"

So the law, imposed on you with your servile fear, has forbidden an evil act, hasn't uprooted an evil desire. You restrain yourself from the act, but the desire to commit the act remains in you. Why does the desire to commit the act remain in you? Because there is no love of justice in you. So there is no means of restraining you further. Love, then.

What must I do, to love?

... Therefore out of love, because if you do it out of fear, you don't love.[29] It will be your justice, although it is from the law; still yours, although you do not do what the law prohibits, because it is out of fear that you don't do it, not out of love. When will it not be your justice? When it comes from the faith of Christ; because it is by believing in him that you have obtained what he commands.[30]

The full meaning of turning to God

12. Scripture notes this point in the present psalm.[31] Doesn't God say, "Be converted to me"? The scriptures are full of "Be converted to me, turn to me."[32] The illness, you see, is beginning to produce movement. No, it isn't just saying that you, who were looking toward the west, should now look to the east—that's easily done.[33] If only you also did it inwardly, because that is not easily done! You turn your body around from one point of the compass to another; turn your heart around from one love to another. God cries out, "Turn to me, be converted." The earth was afraid that if it wasn't converted it would be damned;[34] it bestirred itself, to be converted. But illness did not follow the example, the bread gave no pleasure to the sick.

"Be converted to me." Illness saw that it could not do what it was ordered to, and it cried out through the prophet, *Convert us, O God* (Ps 85:4). Faith entered the heart; it asked that what it was told to do might be done to it: *Convert us, O God.* Because *it has grown weak; you, however, have perfected it* (Ps 68:9), *so that I may be found in him, not having my own justice, which is from the law, but the justice of Christ which is from faith* (Phil 3:9). What does *from faith* mean? Because he obtained it by asking for it, as best he could under the one who commanded it. *For everyone who calls upon the name of the Lord shall be saved* (Rom 10:13). That is the justice of faith which we preach, that is *the living bread which came down from heaven* (Jn 6:51), healing us so that it might be eaten, strengthening us because it is eaten, satisfying us because it is desired, since it is about this that our soul is told that *he satisfies your desire with good things* (Ps 103:5). Etc.[35]

NOTES

1. Dolbeau suggests a date after 404; so I put 405. But see note 27 below. He gives a rather fuller title, taken from Possidius' *Index*: . " . . on the words of the gospel, *I am the bread which came down from heaven*, and, *Work for the food which does not perish*, etc." But in fact the sermon is almost exclusively on the later text.

2. See Jn 6:35.51.

3. Emending the text's *Bene est hoc* to *Breve est hoc*. The text is not strictly grammatical; but

while that in itself would be no reason for emending it, it does not either fit the context. I take it, either that a copyist (or the stenographer) misheard *breve* as *bene*, or that a copyist's eye was caught by the *Bene* with which the section begins.

4. The questioner is not criticizing what Jesus said, but questioning what Augustine has just said, that the people who questioned Jesus were asking a good question on our behalf.

5. In the opening words of the Apostles' Creed, I think.

6. For the import of this distinction see Sermon 14A (Mainz 52), note 5.

7. Literally, "not to be compared with their least footsteps"; a clumsy and hardly translatable mixing of metaphors.

8. See Dn 9:2. The Latin is *justus justorum, sanctus sanctorum*. It is only the latter phrase that is quoted from Daniel.

9. A very truncated quotation.

10. Here he gives two similar examples, which are available in Latin, but not in English: *Sicut vivificans vivum faciens, sicut salvificans salvum faciens, sic justificans justum faciens*: "Just as being a vivifier means making alive, just as being a salvifier means making safe, so being a justifier means making just."

11. In the preceding paragraph of this section Augustine has been alluding to the question which the lawyer asked Jesus in order to test him, and which led to the stating of the two commandments of charity—by the lawyer—and the parable of the good Samaritan. But now he mixes it up with the incident of the rich man questioning Jesus; or perhaps it was Luke who mixed them up; it is in his gospel exactly the same question in 10:25 as in 18:18. But Augustine proceeds to quote the latter incident in Matthew's version, with echoes from Luke's—for example, the order in which the commandments are listed.

12. The text has *vobiscum*, with you. Dolbeau suggests reading *nobiscum*, and I follow him.

13. This sentence baffles me completely. My translation plays ducks and drakes with Latin grammar—or assumes that that is what Augustine was doing. Here is the Latin text; perhaps some reader may have more success with it: *Hoc enim et initium/initio fidei nostrae polliciti sumus, ut ex parte aliqua coeperimus, et cum perfecerimus, nihil de nobis amplius exigetur*. I take the *initium fidei nostrae* to refer to our enrollment as catechumens, when we make a beginning of believing, which we will complete when we are baptized. *Initio* in the ablative/dative is Dolbeau's suggestion; the manuscript has *initium*.

14. See Lk 8:28.

15. We must remember that "believing in God or in Christ" in Latin is *credere in Deum*, etc; the preposition *in* with the accusative case, meaning literally "into." We believe into God, into Christ, in a way in which we should not dream of believing into Paul.

16. A very tangled sentence, of which the text is not in the best condition. After "however" it runs in the manuscript, *quia Deus noster est, et propter nostra homo factus est quod non erat, propter possessionem mansit quod erat*. I have emended *quia* to *qui*, in order to make the whole into a sentence, instead of leaving it as a clause hanging in the air. Dolbeau emends *nostra* to *naturam*; I combine his emendation with the text, and read *nostram naturam*.

17. See Jn 14:6.

18. A contrast, playing on words, in the Latin between *diligendo*, by loving, and *negligendo*, by neglecting.

19. He now returns to where he began the sermon in section 1.

20. In the response to the psalm which they have been reciting.

21. Simply *ad panem salutis* in the Latin. But the range of meaning of *salus*, from "health" to "salvation," has to be made explicit in English.

22. The text of this second phrase runs, *et cor tuum praescriptum est quo puniaris*; "and your heart has been prescribed by which you should be punished," which hardly makes any sense. I emend by simply omitting *est*, and then I understand *statuit*, taken over from the *statuis* of the first phrase.

23. The psalm he is really interested in is Ps 85, with which he begins this section, and which he has already introduced in section 7, as the psalm they had just been singing, or listening to. Then in order to explain how "our earth shall yield its fruit," he brings in the text from Ps 68—that most opaque of all the psalms, which is no doubt why Augustine liked it so much—about the earth being

moved. This leads him on to "the voluntary rain," and to explain "voluntary" he brings in Ps 5, with its talk of "the shield of your good will," *scuto bonae voluntatis tuae*—the verbal link in Latin between *voluntaria* and *voluntatis* being more manifest than that in English between "voluntary" and "will."

24. The blessing, we might easily have forgotten, of the "voluntary rain" dripping from the heavens, which enabled the earth, in Ps 85, to yield its fruit. The earth, of course, is identified with God's "inheritance" of Ps 68.

25. If ever there was a case of explaining the obscure by the more obscure, surely this is it! In *The Trinity*, I, 27, he deals with this text from John in the same way as here, but a little more lucidly: Jesus' doctrine is "his own in the form of God, not his own in the form of a servant." In his *Homilies on the Gospel of John* 29, 3, he explains the paradox rather more neatly: "What is more yours than yourself? And what is less yours than yourself, if what you are is someone else's?"

26. Reading *quam* instead of the text's *cum*; "when he made her in order. . ."

27. He really is rambling! Admittedly he has just said he is very tired. But his constant loss of the thread of his remarks inclines me to think that the sermon was much later than the date suggested by Dolbeau, after 404. It's the sermon of an old as well as of a tired man. I think it probable it was preached, together with its sequel, 14A (Mainz 52), during Augustine's last visit to Carthage in 419.

28. See 1 Sm 24:3-7; 26:5-12.

29. The lacuna at the beginning of the sentence perhaps hides the secret of Augustine's answer to the riddle he has set! I guess that his answer to the immediate question of his interlocutor was something like this: "Grow weak, and ask for the grace to act out of love." So he goes on, in fact, to say that the good you do out of fear is done by *your* justice, because fear is very much a property of you, and is correlated with the law, as observed by the Jews, whom you resemble in this respect. But when you do it out of love, it is not your justice, because love comes to you by grace out of faith in Christ.

30. A play on words in the Latin: *impetrasti quod imperat*.

31. Ps 85.

32. For example, Prv 1:23; Is 45:22; Jer 3:14.22; Ez 18:30, 33:11; Jl 2:12; Zec 1:3; Mal 3:7.

33. Could this be a reference to the liturgical rite, performed by catechumens when they were enrolled, of first facing the west while standing on a goatskin, or horsehair mat, and renouncing Satan, and then turning to the east to profess faith in Christ? More immediately, it could be an allusion to the movement of the congregation turning to face the east when reciting the creed. But see Dolbeau's note on "Turning to the Lord, etc.," note 35 below; he assumes it refers to what the congregation did at this formal prayer, *Conversi ad Dominum*, which concluded so many sermons.

34. See Ps 68:5.

35. Here is a translation of Francois Dolbeau's *Annexe* to his edition of these sermons. I do not include his numerous references to the works of other scholars.

"Conversi ad dominum. . ."

In the manuscripts of Augustine, a prayer beginning with the words "Conversi ad dominum" is attached as a conclusion to a number of sermons, or of *Enarrationes in psalmos*, and also circulates in isolation. It is sporadically to be found in later authors, and is transmitted in various forms, some quite elaborate, others short, or even reduced to the first words (whether followed or not by an *et cetera*). In this truncated form it concludes in *Migne* many of the sermons belonging to the Mainz-Charterhouse collection, while it remains exceptional in that of Mainz-Lorsch. Such a division goes back to an epoch when the two series were still separate, perhaps even to the different habits of the stenographers, some of whom preferred putting in a final title (Mainz-Lorsch), while others liked an abridged reference to the prayer which the preacher had in fact spoken (Mainz-Charterhouse).

This prayer faces us today with two distinct problems. Did it imply a turning of the faithful to the east? What exactly was its liturgical function? Relying on the evidence of *M*, I would like to make a tentative reply to these questions, beginning with the second.

Liturgical Function of "Conversi ad dominum. . ."

The best state of the question is provided by Paul De Clerck, in *La "prière universelle" dans les liturgies latines anciennes. Témoignages patristiques et textes liturgiques* (Münster 1977). He lists the four possible solutions: (a) a prayer after the sermon; (b) a blessing placed between the homily and the dismissal of the catechumens; (c) an introduction, or more precisely an invitation by the celebrant, to the prayer of the faithful; (d) finally an embryonic form of the universal prayer spoken by the deacon. This last solution is the original suggestion of Paul De Clerck himself; but he puts it forward with a question mark, and in fact settles for the third, which gains the votes of the majority of liturgists. If, as I think, the presence of these "Conversi ad dominum"s in *Migne* is not just a matter of chance, this formula should not be related to the dismissal of the catechumens (solution b) or to the prayer of the faithful (solutions c and d). And this for two reasons.

According to its heading, Mainz 20 (= Sermon 266), which is commenting on Ps 140, was preached during a vigil of Pentecost. In *Migne* it ends with the words "Ergo deinceps lectiones adtentius audiamus," announcing further readings. As a matter of fact, Mainz 21 is an exposition of Ps 117, which was also sung during this vigil; it has the heading, moreover, "in vigilia pentecostes." The two pieces were therefore preached during the same ceremony. Now they both end with "Conversi ad dominum etc." If these words functioned as a blessing which was the cue for the withdrawal of the catechumens, or as an invitation to the *Oratio fidelium*, they would not have been transcribed at the end of a homily (Mainz 20), which was manifestly inserted in a series of readings.

Mainz 37 corresponds both to Sermon 302 and to the *Post tractatum* Guelferbytanus 25. In a quite exceptional manner, the original editor of the collection, then the medieval copyists, have left grouped together a sermon for the feast of Saint Laurence and a short *Exhortatio post sermonem*, spoken just afterward, in which Augustine reproaches his Christians for having allowed the right of asylum to be violated. Now the formula "Conversi ad dominum etc." is to be found in *Migne* at the end of Sermon 302 and not after the *Post tractatum*. How, given these facts, can we see here anything else but the closure of the sermon (solution a)?

According to this evidence, the prayer "Conversi ad dominum" was connected organically with the sermon which it terminated. If the sermon, for any accidental reason, was separated from the dismissal of the catechumens or the *Oratio fidelium*, the formula continued to be associated with it. The sermon ended eventually by absorbing it, as we can observe in Bede: "Verum nos quia in longum duximus sermonem, iam conversi ad dominum clementiam ipsius postulemus ut et memoriam beatae Mariae congruis veneremur officiis et ad celebranda dominicae nativitatis sollemnia purioribus animis venire mereamur. . ." So then it is an illusion to see in this prayer the prototype of later liturgical forms.

Did the Faithful Actually Turn Around Toward the East?

This is a complicated question, and more is at stake in it than purely scientific inquiry. I would like to discuss it here in a serene manner, without entering into the debates that so excite archeologists and liturgists. So I will limit myself to answering it strictly, while avoiding any kinds of deduction about the arrangement of African churches, or the position of the celebrants vis-à-vis the faithful.

From an early period Christians used to pray in private facing the rising sun; this ritual orientation was astronomical, not geographical, as with the Muslims. This individual custom, it would seem, also spread to prayers in common. Now at the time of Augustine most African churches had their facades at the east end of the building. What happened when the preacher said "Conversi ad dominum"? Nobody doubts that originally these words signified "Turning toward the east." But if the faithful obeyed this injunction literally, it means that one part of the congregation then turned their backs to the altar, which was usually placed in the middle of the nave. To resolve this difficulty, liturgists have thought up several subtle solutions: the movement of the congregation was spiritual, not bodily; it was only the celebrant who physically faced east; the faithful were massed in the side-aisles, so that for them turning toward the east only involved a slight movement of the head, without their having to turn their backs on the altar in the center.

For the future, the evidence of Mainz 51 rules out any hypothesis which would deny the physical reality of the movement of the faithful. When he reached the end of his sermon, just a few moments before saying the words "Conversi ad dominum" (reduced in *Migne* to a simple etc.), Augustine wanted, by the use of an image drawn from the rite they are on the point of performing, to urge conversion upon his congregation: "Quid est enim *Convertimini ad me*? Non enim—quod facile fit—, qui adtendebas occidentem, adtendas orientem. Utinam hoc intus facias, quia non est facile! Convertis corpus ex cardine in cardinem; cor converte ex amore in amorem." The exterior gesture is easy, turning from one point of the compass to another. What is not so easy is the movement of heart, renouncing love of the world for love of heaven.

Future discussion will have to take account of this passage, which implies a bodily displacement of a certain amplitude. We showed above how the prayer "Conversi" served simply as a conclusion to the service of the word, at a moment when the altar was bare and the celebrant was still not standing at it. We have to envisage the faithful standing, and segregated according to sex. All eyes during the sermon were fixed on the preacher, that is to say, were turned to the west, since he was normally speaking from the apse. The prayer "Conversi" gave rise to a general movement of the congregation toward the east; hence Augustine's statements: "Qui adtendebas occidentem, adtendas orientem. . . . Convertis corpus ex cardine in cardinem." Usually this movement of 180 degrees preceded (by a few moments) the massed and inevitably noisy departure of the non-baptized. Only the faithful in the bays of the church between the altar and the entrance would again have to turn around for the rest of the service; those who were in the other half of the church, and who until then had had their backs to the altar rails, were facing, from the moment they were *conversi ad dominum*, both the altar and the entrance. I must say that I do not understand how such a reconstruction can present any difficulty. But over now to the liturgists and archeologists.

Dolbeau 7
SERMON 142 (Appendix)
Mainz 15

ON THE BURIAL OF CATECHUMENS

Date: 406[1]

*Church discipline does not allow catechumens to be buried
in the same ground as the baptized faithful*

1. His lordship, my father and brother[2]—because he is good enough to be so regarded—commands me to put something to your holinesses about the burial of catechumens. And indeed this is above all his responsibility; but in that charity about which I was talking to you[3] we share everything, in order that we may all have a share in Christ. It is not uncommon for grief to be a little envious, and pardonably so.[4] Who wouldn't excuse someone upset by grief and bereavement, if he happened to say something out of jealousy or envy? Still, you all ought to know, dearly beloved, what most of you and in fact almost all of you do know, that according to the Church's custom and discipline the bodies of catechumens who have died ought not to be buried among the bodies of the faithful, and that such a concession should not be granted to anyone. Otherwise it would be nothing but culpable respect of persons. I mean, why should such a concession be made to a wealthier person, and not to a poor person—if indeed there can be any comfort to the dead in it? The merits of the dead, after all, do not depend on the places their bodies are laid in, but on the dispositions of their souls. My brothers and sisters, these things too, as the faithful, you must learn to consider; it's because of the sacraments[5] that bodies cannot be laid to rest where it is not right for them to be laid.

Catechumens should be in a hurry to be baptized

2. All the same, we do mourn the passing of a catechumen from this world, and we grieve for the one over whom the question arose in the first place. And on this score I must seriously remind you, brothers and sisters, that none of you[6] should take it for granted that you are going to be alive tomorrow. Run quickly to grace,[7] change your habits; may this sad event serve you as a salutary warning.

What could have been healthier than that man, what more vigorous than that man's body? Suddenly he's dead. He was in good health, he has passed away— and if only he had just passed away, and were not truly dead![8]

Well after all, my brothers and sisters, what am I to say? Am I going to pander to human feelings, and say that catechumens too go where the faithful go? Are we to treat human grief with such kid gloves that we argue against the gospel?[9] We can't do it, my brothers and sisters. The living must hurry up and run, in order not to be really mourned when dead, and not to be really and truly dead. If people ran as fast to the sacraments of the living as they run off to the funerals of the dead, perhaps there would be no good reason to mourn anyone, because even if people were mourned, it would only be out of merely human, this-worldly feelings. People shouldn't be mourned who have improved their lot, left behind them the trials and temptations of this age, and are in dread of nothing, carefree in Christ, not having to fear the devil's hostility, or to shudder at the curses of men.[10]

Perhaps the poor man Lazarus never had a decent burial;
but angels carried him to Abraham's bosom

3. I mean, perhaps that man Lazarus, whose sores the dogs used to lick, was never buried; at least God kept quiet about his burial. All that's said about him is that when he died he was carried off to Abraham's bosom. It doesn't say that he was even buried. After all, while he was still alive, and famished, he was just ignored, so perhaps when he was dead he was just thrown out unburied. And yet he was carried off by angels to the bosom of Abraham.[11] *Now the rich man also died*, he says, *and was buried* (Lk 16:22). What good, I ask you, did even a marble tomb do his soul in hell, where he was thirsting for a drop of water from Lazarus' little finger, and didn't get it? I don't want to say any more, my brothers and sisters. I've frightened you enough, I must be careful not to increase the grief of some of our brothers and sisters, who have been badly shaken by this sad event. I mean, I would have had no right to say any of this, if I hadn't been obliged to speak to you words of urgent warning.

Believe Christ, that his yoke is easy;
and hasten to receive the sacrament of grace

4. Reflect. my brothers and sisters, on how fragile we human beings are. Hurry up and run while you're alive, in order to live; hurry up and run while you're alive, in order not really and truly to die. Christ's discipline is not something to be feared.[12] He himself cries out, *My yoke is smooth, and my burden is light*, in this very passage which we were discussing a short while ago:[13] *Learn from me, for I am gentle and humble of heart. For my yoke is smooth, and my burden is light* (Mt 11:29-30), and will you now argue against that, and say, "No, I don't yet want to be one of the faithful; I can't"? What do you mean by "I can't," if not that Christ's yoke is rough, and his burden is heavy? So is your flesh suggesting the truth to you, and Christ lying? He says "It's

smooth," and your nothingness says, "It's rough." He says "It's light," and your nothingness "It's heavy."

Believe Christ, rather, both that his yoke is smooth and that his burden is light. Don't be scared, submit to the yoke with an undaunted neck. The yoke will be all the smoother to your neck, the more trusting is the neck itself. And so then, brothers and sisters, I've said all this for two reasons: so that none of you should ask for this favor, and feel hurt if you don't obtain it; and so that each one of you, dear catechumens, while you're still alive, may beware of perishing when you're dead, and of neither your own families nor mother Church herself finding means by which they can come to your aid.

NOTES

1. This is not really a sermon, but a kind of postscript to a sermon, what was known as a *post tractatum*. From evidence in one of the two manuscripts available, Dolbeau infers that it was delivered immediately after Sermon 142. Now that, according to the evidence of these manuscripts and the old collections of sermons they point to, was either preached in 404, on the same journey back from Carthage to Hippo Regius as Sermon 159B, preached at Tignica, or else in 406, when Augustine paid a visit to the small Church of Siniti, which was about 50 miles south of Hippo Regius. The bishop there, Maximinus, had been the Donatist bishop of the neighboring town of Mutugenna (see Letter 23), and had been converted by Augustine, and now as a Catholic bishop was his good friend. See O. Perler, *Les Voyages de Saint Augustin*, 159, 161. So, given the length of Sermon 142 and the nature of this appendix, I suggest it is more likely that Augustine preached, and added his postscript, in a place he was deliberately visiting on the invitation of the local bishop, than in a Church he was just passing through on his journey home.

When I translated Sermon 142 (III, 4), entirely unaware of this *post tractatum*, I proposed, in the absence of any suggestions from the scholars, a date between 413 and 417, while also allowing on grounds of style, and in fact rather preferring, a date 10 years or so earlier. So now I would entirely revise what I said there in note 8, and propose the date 406 for that sermon too.

2. The local bishop, Maximinus according to my suggestion, who was possibly much older than Augustine. He died in, or before, 411 (Perler, *op. cit.*, 410).

3. In Sermon 142.

4. It would seem that on the death of a catechumen from a wealthy Christian family, the family were putting strong pressure on the bishop to allow the deceased burial in consecrated ground; in fact, what they probably meant was burial in the family mausoleum. Either this would have provoked jealous comments from others, who hadn't been granted, hadn't even asked for, such concessions, or else the family would feel envious of catechumens who had died after being baptized *in extremis*, or, of course, both.

5. He probably means that where the faithful were buried Mass was said for the repose of their souls; and Mass could not be offered on behalf of the unbaptized. See section 4 below, last sentence.

6. He is specifically addressing the catechumens here.

7. A name for baptism.

8. That is, were not dead both to this life and the next. He was in no doubt—and neither were any of his hearers—that the catechumen, dying unbaptized without having even expressed a desire for baptism, was lost. It is only in very recent years, the last century or two, perhaps, that ordinary Catholic catechetics and popular belief have learned to be at least more modestly agnostic in such matters.

In very different contexts the point of the absolute necessity of baptism for salvation has come up in Sermons 27, 6 (III, 2); 97A, 3-4 (III, 4); 335H, 3 (III, 9).

9. For example, against Jn 3:3.

10. See Rv 14:13.

11. See Sermons 14, 3 (III, 1); 299E, 3 (III, 8).

12. The discipline incurred, as it were, by baptism, of living an innocent, Christian, moral life. It was such fears that led so many catechumens to defer baptism indefinitely.

13. In Sermon 142, sections 10 to 12.

Dolbeau 13
SERMON 159A
Mainz 42

SERMON OF SAINT AUGUSTINE THE BISHOP ON
HONORING OR DISREGARDING PARENTS

Date: 397[1]

Who will separate us from the charity of Christ?

1. The feast days of the holy martyrs are so many exhortations to martyrdom, encouraging us to take delight in imitating what we delight in celebrating. The passage from sacred scripture which was sounding in our ears a few moments ago is also encouraging and somehow firing us with that sort of enthusiasm, with the apostle saying, *Who will separate us from the charity of Christ? Tribulation, or distress, or persecution, or hunger, or nakedness, or danger or the sword? As it is written: Since for your sake we are being put to death all day long, we have been counted as sheep for sacrifice* (Rom 8:35-36). Next follow other things which seem to bring violent separation, over which, however, the one who never separates himself from us gives us the victory, so that we don't separate ourselves from him. It is, after all, because of such distress and imminent afflictions that the faithful maker and kindly fulfiller of promises was good enough to assure us that he would be with us *until the completion of the age* (Mt 28:20).

For I am certain, the apostle continues, *that neither death nor life, neither angels nor principalities, neither things present nor things to come, neither powers nor height nor depth, nor any other creature*—I mean, he couldn't name them all—*will be able to separate us from the charity of God, which is in Christ Jesus our Lord* (Rom 8:38-39). And a little earlier he said, *If God is for us, who is against us?* (Rom 8:31), to give us the strongest possible hope of not being separated from Christ, and every confidence against all the trials and temptations of this world, because our own powers and virtues are in no way sufficient for this. The apostle, then, first briefly listed the things that seem to be savagely attacking the Christian faith, and then to forestall their separating us from the charity of Christ, he fortified us to endure them all for Christ's sake.

135

2. It's not only savagery, though, that strives to separate, but also cajolery; and so just as we have been fortified by the apostle's words against the savagery with which attempts are made to separate us from Christ, so we have been fortified by the Lord Christ himself against the cajolery with which attempts are made to seduce us. It is to be feared, you see, that while you are not separated by the cruel sword, you may well be by human[2] affection. So against those things which assail our faith with cajolery, to stop them taking by storm what they are assailing, let us listen to what the Lord has to say: *If anyone comes to me and does not hate father, mother, wife, children, brother or sister, and what is more his own soul, he cannot be my disciple. And whoever does not hoist up his cross and follow me cannot be my disciple* (Lk 14:26-27).

The Lord mentioned both things both what can lure us with pleasant enticements, and what can weigh on our spirits with horrid threats.[3] Thus against the lures of cajolery he says about human affection, *If anyone comes to me, and does not hate father and mother, wife, children,* etc., while against things that turn us away from the faith by terrifying roars, he equips and arms us with the one fortifying name of the cross. *Whoever*, he says, *does not hoist up his cross and follow me cannot be my disciple.*

3. So now let us set the martyr of Christ in the middle, betweeen threats and cajolery; there is a knocking at each door which gives entry to the heart—that of desire and that of fear. Knocking at the door of desire are father, mother, wife, children, brothers. They are all caressing, all agreeable, all full of sweetness. But not more agreeable than God, are they? Not sweeter than Christ, surely? If you don't believe me, *taste and see how sweet is the Lord* (Ps 34:8). Knocking at the door of fear are threats, fury, disgrace, and in the last resort those pains of the body, which nobody can avoid feeling just by disregarding them.

I mean, if it's money you have no regard for, you suffer losses, not pains. It's all in the mind of the person doing the disregarding; the one who deprives you of what you don't love doesn't hurt you. But then, you do love money; you fear the man who threatens you with losses, and even so it's not he that's hurting you, but you that have been torturing yourself, because you have brought pain upon yourself. *For the root of all evils is avarice; by setting their hearts on it some have wandered away from the faith, and brought many pains upon themselves* (1 Tm 6:10). He's threatening you with losses; if he doesn't find you greedy, he finds you free; you have the last laugh on him, leaving him empty-handed, because you haven't brought any pain on yourself. So too with all the other things we are taught by sound and salutary doctrine to disregard; we are advised not to love them, so that in times of trial we may find ourselves free. It is to this freedom that we are urged by that passage from the apostle, where you have, *And those who make use of this world as though they were not using it, so that they might have the use of liberty, instead of the passion of cupidity. For the fashion of this world is passing away. I would have you all free from worry* (1 Cor 7:31-32).

Threats to the flesh are the hardest to withstand,
because the flesh is the very garment of the soul

4. But there remains the feebleness of the flesh, which none of us, as long as we are living in this age, can rid ourselves of. What are you to do? When the flesh is pierced, is the mind conscious of no pain? This is the wound of feebleness, until we don the garment of deathlessness. Here, there is a really great struggle. With his will indifferent to money, God's martyr stands serenely calm against those who try to scare him with financial ruin. "Let him take what I don't love," he says; "where will I feel it?" He's threatened with exile, but it's a vain threat to one who only longs for his heavenly homeland; here below the Christian, wherever he goes, is a wanderer in a foreign land. Disgrace is threatened; he has a ready answer: *This is our boast, the testimony of a good conscience* (2 Cor 1:12). He is threatened with being stripped of his honors; but what a fleeting thing is honor! A mere mortal threatens the loss of honors, but the Lord of mere mortals promises eternal honor.

If you disregard all these things, your freedom is secure

But what about the flesh? The soul is left with its garment, and it's a garment which will only be doffed with death. Now the person, that is, the soul,[4] is under pressure from close quarters, from the feebleness of its own flesh. That's why those words of the Lord in that magnificent psalm, in which the gospel is to all intents and purposes being chanted, why they seem, or rather must be understood, to be his as he hung on the cross[5]: *They have dug my hands and my feet, they have counted up all my bones. They, however, inspected me, they divided my garments between them, and over my vesture they cast lots* (Ps 22:16-18). These are the words of one already suffering, already hanging on the cross, and yet it says there, *Do not withdraw from me, since affliction is close* (Ps 22:11). If by "close" you understand "coming soon in time," they won't be the words of the one hanging on the cross; affliction was already upon him, if he was hanging there. But why then did it say *is close*? "It is already in the flesh." Nothing is closer to the soul than the flesh, and to the soul and the flesh than that door.[6] All those other things are outside, that's why they are called externals; when the flesh is being tortured, there is a hammering on the door of the soul from the closest possible quarters.

If God is for us, who is against us?

5. These things are grievous indeed, *but in all of them we are more than victorious because of the one who loved us* (Rom 8:37). But why are we victorious in these things too? Because *if God is for us, who is against us?* (Rom

8:31). That is why the Lord thought fit to signify all the terrifying, harsh, bitter, unbearable things, all the savagery by the name of the cross. I mean, among the various kinds of death there is none more unbearable than the cross. Indeed, when the same apostle was drawing the humility of the Lord to our attention, he added this name with the most weighty emphasis; he said, you see, *He did not count it robbery to be equal to God; but he emptied himself, taking the form of a slave, being made in the likeness of men, and found in condition as a human being.* What a humiliation for the Lord, to become a human being! But don't stop listening. There you are, he has been humbled, because he was made man. What more? *He humbled himself,* says Paul, *becoming obedient to the death,* not only to a human birth, but also *to the death.*

Have you anything to add to that?

"I have," he says: "*death, though, on a cross*" (Phil 2:6-7). Gazing on this end of the Lord, the most bitter imaginable, he[7] called everything a cross that the flesh of Christians can suffer rightly for the sake of his name. Their faith, after all, suffers nothing; on the contrary it even renders sufferings bearable.

Well equipped therefore on each side, and having each door, both that of desire and that of fear, strongly barricaded, we are to desire nothing more eagerly than what God promises us, to fear nothing more dreadfully than what God threatens us with; and in this way we can fend off all cajolery and all threats.

An apparent conflict between two commandments

6. But now someone steps forward and poses us with a problem and says, "Everything is indeed to be borne for the faith of Christ, however bitter, however harsh, however savage and cruel to endure, to be borne absolutely. But what bothers me is that the one who put as the first of his commandments directed toward love of neighbor, *Honor father and mother, which is the first commandment with a promise, that it may be well with you*[8] (Eph 6:2-3). And while the apostle reminds me of this very emphatically, the Lord says to me, *If anybody comes to me and does not hate father and mother* (Lk 14:26). Which am I to listen to? Which of these am I to accept? How will I comply with the one who tells me to honor father and mother, and again tells me to hate father and mother? Isn't he one and the same person giving each commandment? Or—as some emptyheaded people think[9]—is there one God who gave the law and another who sowed the gospel, since in the law it is written *Honor father and mother* (Ex 20:12; Dt 5:16), and in the gospel *Whoever does not hate father and mother?*"

God forbid! He is himself both law-maker and gospel sower, absolutely one and the same. What you have to do is acknowledge the Lord. In order not to give contradictory commandments, he suited his commandments to different situations.[10] Because if you think the commandment by which we are told to honor father and mother, being first read in the Old Testament, is contrary to the commandment in the gospel, something of the same sort as we just now heard read in the gospel is also written in the Old Testament itself: *The one who says to father and mother, "I do not know you," and who does not acknowledge his own children, he is the one who has given thought to my covenant*[11] (Dt 33:9). How similar it is, how very much a twin statement, equal in force to the other, we cannot fail to acknowledge. So then, it is one Lord, giving each commandment, but we have to distinguish the occasions or situations.[12]

How a wife can support her cajolery from the law

7. The martyr is being fortified and prepared for his prize, and along comes his father to cajole him, and his mother to stop him winning what God is promising him, as they offer him a worthless inheritance while robbing him of an eternity of light. In this case surely you must not acknowledge them as they try to hold you back;[13] on the contrary, in this case hate your father, see it as your filial duty to hate him when he's in that frame of mind, so that he doesn't remain in that frame of mind. As with father, so with mother, so with children, so with brothers and sisters, so—and here it's a thornier problem—with wife; yes, hate even her, if she too attempts to hinder you from your purpose. Beware of Eve; she isn't in this instance your better half, but the serpent's agent.

You were foolish enough to listen to her voice the first time,[14] and you haven't even profited from the experience; but now this very same wife, to stop her husband winning the prize of martyrdom, with feminine cunning quotes to her husband the apparent authority both of the law and of the gospel. "Listen," says she, "to the commandment."

"Which commandment?"

"*What God has joined together, let not man separate* (Mk 10:9)."

Certainly listen, don't shrug it aside; but just see whether your wife is not separating you from God.

"But what he has joined together, man ought not to separate."

And ought human affection to separate man from God himself? And where will you fit in what you heard just now: *Who will separate us from the charity of Christ* (Rom 8:35)?

So in this instance have no fear; man is not separating what God has joined together, but God is separating anyone who is trying to bring separation. So don't listen to your wife when she says to you, "I'm part of you; look, you're part of me."[15] Answer, "If a part of me, a limb of mine, had gangrene, and were attempting by its gangrene to undermine the whole body, wouldn't it be amputated by the surgeon? Am I not to listen to the Lord himself, the true surgeon, when he says, *For it is better for you that one of your limbs should be lost, than that your whole body should go off into gehenna* (Mt 5:30)?" So make sure you understand the law rightly, and give that answer against one who is using the law badly.

The serpent, you see, isn't doing anything very grand, it isn't a tremendous effort he's making through Eve, when he wants to take you in by means of the law, seeing that he took the first Adam in without the law. After all, he has seen you being fed on the law, and he uses it to bait a snare for you. But you only have to say, *My eyes are always on the Lord, since he will pluck my feet from the snare* (Ps 25:15). So in this peril too, where the law is being used to tempt you, let your eyes be on the Lord, because he too was tempted by the same serpent using the law.

Specious arguments from scripture can be answered from scripture
as Christ answered the devil in the third temptation

8. When the Lord, you see, was setting us an example of how to engage in the contest and win, and allowing himself to be tempted by the devil, just as he allowed himself to be crucified by the godless, the devil said to him in the first temptation—we read of three of them—*If you are the Son of God, tell these stones to become bread*; and he answered, from the law, *Man does not live only on bread, but on every word of God* (Lk 4:3-34; Dt 8:3). Again, in the next temptation, *Prostrate yourself and worship me, and I will give you these things*, and he came back with the law: *It is written: the Lord your God shall you worship, and him alone shall you serve* (Lk 4:8; Dt 6:13). But when that crafty serpent saw he had been fended off twice in a row by means of the law, he spread his third snare from the law himself: *Throw yourself down*, he said, *from the pinnacle of the temple, if you are the Son of God.* And immediately turning to the law as a weapon, in order to fight with what he had previously been defeated by, *For it is written*, he said, *He has commanded his angels about you; they are to bear you in their hands, lest perchance you should stub your foot on a stone* (Lk 4:9-11; Ps 91:11-12). "So because the angels," he is saying, "are there to catch you, if you are the Son of God, to stop you hurting yourself, throw yourself down, and prove to us that you really are so." Just because the devil here had the nerve to put his hand to the law, did the Lord then remove his own hand from the law? Here too, from the same law he inflicted a wound on the enemy, he laid him low, he forced him to withdraw in confusion. He said, you see, *It is written, You shall not tempt the Lord your God* (Lk 4:12; Dt 6:16).

So here too then, when you see your wife trying to obstruct your way to martyrdom by quoting the law to you and saying, "*What God has joined together let man not separate* (Mk 10:9)," quote the law[16] yourself too in this instance, and say, "*Whoever comes to me, and does not hate father and mother, wife and children. . .* (Lk 14:26)."

The analogy of the wife's case against her in-laws

9. So don't be angry, wife. The one you're angry with here in this case, because he hates you, also hates his father in this case, also hates his mother. But it's little enough the wife has to put up with, because it is written, *A man shall leave father and mother, and shall stick to his wife* (Mt 19:5; Gn 2:24). If the parents, you see, were to say to their son, "If your wife is unwilling to stay

with us, you stay with us, and leave her," the wife should take over this precept and fight, she should lay down the law to her husband, and say from God's law, "On the contrary, leave them and don't leave me; I mean, I'm only quoting, *A man shall leave father and mother, and shall stick to his wife.*" You've quoted, you've understood, you've won the argument. No one can have the slightest doubt that father and mother attempting to separate their son from his wife should be left, in order for the wife not to be abandoned.

But just consider, Mrs. X, if you would deign to be faithful, and not disdain to hear the word of faith, just consider; you will have won your case on the authority of the gospel;[17] please allow yourself to lose on the same authority. Look, we've won a court order restraining your father- and mother-in-law, your husband's father and mother who bore him, who reared him, who brought him up to the age at which he could become your husband. We've put an absolute restraint on them and checked them with divine authority and said, "Stop wanting to separate your son from his wife for your own sakes, because it's better he should be separated from you than from her. If you can manage it, all live together; but if you can't, it's better that he should live with her than with you and without her."

We've successfully pleaded your case; you've won your case in this trial; allow yourself to lose in the other, because there too we are in fact pleading your case. In a word, we have loyally pleaded the case of your flesh; should we abandon the case of your eternal salvation? Learn the lesson; your husband's father and mother haven't separated you from your husband; of course you won't separate your husband from your God.

The case of God against the wife

10. Fornication is more to be feared with reference to the chastity which the soul owes God; fornication is more to be feared with reference to the chastity for which the apostle was afraid, when he said, *I have betrothed you to one husband to present you to Christ as a chaste virgin. But I am afraid that as the serpent led Eve astray with his guile, so your minds too may be corrupted from the chastity of God which is in Christ Jesus* (2 Cor 11:2-3). You can see that here too chastity is being required. Why do you, for example, not wish to be separated from your husband? In order not to be driven to fornication? But in the martyrdom of your husband there's nothing you should fear. When he has won his prize and been transferred from the human sphere to the divine, you will be a widow; if you marry, it won't be fornication. But perhaps as the wife of a martyr you'll be ashamed to marry again; so there you are—with your husband now wearing the victor's crown, your fidelity to him also can be in safe-keeping.

Don't drag your husband away from the embrace of the spiritual marriage. There too chastity is required, and much more so there because a greater kind there, much more so there because an eternal kind there. *You have destroyed everyone who goes fornicating away from you* (Ps 73:27). What else are you doing, after all, in trying to overcome your man with your cajolery, but ensuring that he won't show any manliness? No manliness in him, what a failure he will be as your man![18] He's overcome, shattered, made effeminate by your blandishments; how will he be your man, when he no longer is a man? What are you doing, after all, but trying to ensure that he yields to your cajolery, ignores God's commandments, denies Christ, sacrifices to idols? There you are, the soul whose flesh you desire is fornicating; there you are, he's hearing the words *You have destroyed everyone who goes fornicating away from you.*

But you want him to stick to you and separate himself from God; listen to what follows: *You have destroyed everyone who goes fornicating away from you; but for me it is good to stick to God* (Ps 73:27-28). Listen to your man, armed with faith, hurling against your iniquity the javelins of justice: *I am certain,* he says, *that neither death nor life, neither angel nor principality, neither height nor depth nor any other creature will be able to separate us from the charity of God, which is in Christ Jesus* (Rom 8:38-39). Doubtless you will say here, "But he didn't mention a wife in this whole list." In this whole list, you're saying, he never mentioned a wife. Artful hussy, the apostle's manliness was wide awake even against you, in adding *nor any other creature.* Or perhaps you will have the nerve to say you aren't a creature? If you are a creature, or rather because you are a creature, not even you will separate one whom no creature will separate.

Women martyrs too have withstood cajolery from their menfolk

11. We've been speaking like this, as though it were just men who are hurrying toward martyrdom and being hindered by their wives; let us also reassure the weaker sex. How many women have won the martyr's crown, and not been overcome by their menfolk cajoling them in no manly fashion! How did Perpetua become perpetually blessed . . .?[19] What made Felicity fit for such infinite felicity, but her not being terrified by momentary infelicity? So then, for women too to avoid being seduced in this matter by the cajolery of their men,[20] let them fix their minds on Perpetua, fix them on Felicity, and so take hold of perpetual felicity.

One must hate even one's own soul

12. So then, nobody must get angry in this kind of case; not father and mother, not wife, not children, not brothers and sisters. And if they are angry, it adds "hate, what is more, your own soul."[21] So in this kind of case you are quite wrong to love your wife, when you are told to hate even your own soul. *What does it profit you,* he says, *if you gain the whole world, and suffer the loss of your own soul?* (Mt 16:26). And yet you are told to hate it, in case it too should seduce you in its craving to be here, its craving always to stick to this flesh, its unwillingness to emigrate to better climes. Hate such a soul, in order not to have such a soul. What else, after all, is it whispering inside people who are being

tested by the danger of persecution, but "Deny him; stay alive; you can repent afterward"? That's the soul; it wants to perish.

Hate it, when it wants to perish. Don't allow it to perish, chastise it, scold it, educate it, call on God to assist you. You see, it's fading away from you, it's shrinking from the dangers of this life, it's with a cross-eyed faith that it contemplates eternal life. Straighten it out with some encouragement, and say, *Why are you sad, my soul, and to what purpose are you troubling me?* Perhaps it will answer you, "Because I am so feeble." So you have what comes next: *Hope in the Lord*, he will be your strength, he will be your firmness of purpose. *Hope in the Lord, since I will confess to him*; I won't deny him, because I will confess him. You however, soul, were muttering, "Deny him." *I will confess to him the saving of my countenance and my God* (Ps 42:5.11; 43:5). So let those who love their souls lose them here, in order to find them for eternal life.[22] So then, you mustn't listen to anyone whispering the contrary, neither father, nor mother, nor wife, nor children, not even to your own soul.

The limits of the claims of human affection

13. Your wife must be listened to, for fear of the marriage breaking up, as long as she isn't trying to persuade you to do something by which God would be offended.[23] The husband at the point of martyrdom is afraid his wife may be for him another Eve, and the wife at the point of martyrdom is afraid her husband may be for her another serpent. Neither of them, though, must listen to anyone trying to persuade them to any course against God. Thus far let human affection and the rights of flesh and blood[24] prevail; but the weakness of the flesh must not climb over the spiritual wall.[25] Let it be underneath, because it is underneath. Let the soul, subject to God, lead the flesh, not be seduced away from God under the leadership of the flesh;[26] that's just perverse. You there want to exercise the leadership in your own house; much more so does God in his.

Remember these things and meditate on them, imitate these things on all the feast days of the martyrs, *and the God of peace will be with you* (Phil 4:9). Turning to the Lord. . .

NOTES

1. Dolbeau argues plausibly—but the argument is too intricate to reproduce here—that the sermon was preached on 15 July 397, the feast of the Carthaginian martyr, the deacon Catulinus, and his companions. The opening sentence indeed implies that the sermon was preached on the feast day of a martyr, or martyrs; and Augustine did, it appears, not infrequently preach on such feast days without mentioning the martyrs' names, or name (see, for example, Sermons 328—335J, III, 9). But it is just a little strange that Saints Perpetua and Felicity are mentioned in this sermon, and it was not their feast day, whereas those martyrs who are being celebrated are not named or even alluded to at all.

2. He says literally, "carnal affection." But *carnalis* here does not, I think, have the loaded overtones that "carnal" invariably does in English; it just means what we usually mean by the phrase "all too human." See *The Trinity* II, 3, note 8 in this series (I, 5), where *animalis* is given the same translation.

3. I have given the sentence greater balance than it has in the Latin, which runs, literally, "both what by enticing is pleasant to lure us, and what by threatening is grievous." So Dolbeau suspects, reasonably enough, that something has dropped out after "grievous," *grave est*, and suggests something like *ut deiciat*, "to cast down."

4. This is Augustine the unqualified, unrepentant Platonist speaking—and hence, in my judgment, the comparatively young Augustine. As he grew older he was constrained by both his moral reflections and his pastoral experience to modify this Platonist stance very considerably, and to integrate the flesh, the body, into the complete human person.

5. The reference is not to the words that follow immediately, but to those of verse 11 which he will quote a little later. They alone connect with what he has just said about soul and flesh.

6. The text reads, . . . *proximius animae et carni quam porta illa*, ". . . closer to the soul and the flesh than that door." But this, surely, misses entirely the point he is making. So before *animae* I have added *animae quam caro et*. These words could easily be omitted by a copyist in a simple case of haplography.

7. Paul; Augustine is forgetting that it was Jesus in the gospel who had labeled all suffering by the name of the cross. This sentence is somewhat corrupt according to Dolbeau, but he is not sure precisely where the fault lies. In my judgment it lies in the inclusion, after "his name," of the phrase *fides perpessa fuerit*, "all that faith has suffered in his name." Dolbeau, simply to show there is something wrong, adds *etsi*, "even if," in front of *fides*, which would allow us to construe the flesh as suffering all those things in his name, but wouldn't aid the sense in any way. I see the offending phrase as a marginal scribble—perhaps in criticism of the next sentence—that has crept into the text, and so I leave it out.

8. This is an uncompleted sentence in the Latin too. Dolbeau indicates a small gap in the text after "neighbor," but also suggests, and I think rightly, that it may in fact just be a sentence that Augustine forgot to complete.

9. The Manichees.

10. Literally, "he distributed times to his commandments." At first it looks like an allusion to the time of the Old Testament, given to the law, and of the New Testament, given to the gospel. But that can scarcely suit his purpose, as he goes on to find an Old Testament parallel to the hard saying of the New Testament, and then subsequently in the sermon he confines himself to explaining this hard saying with reference to the particular situation of the martyrs.

11. The reference is to a particular incident, the Levites slaying all who had worshipped the golden calf, Ex 32:26-29.

12. Literally "the times"; see note 10 above.

13. Following a suggestion of Dolbeau's, and reading *Hic plane noli agnoscere retinentes* instead of the text's impossible . . . *agnoscere ne timetis*, the last two words not even being grammatical, let alone having any meaning. An alternative emendation could be: *Hic plane non agnoscere ne timeatis*; "In this case surely do not be afraid not to acknowledge them."

14. See Gn 3:6.

15. See Rom 12:5; 1 Cor 7:4, conflated in "the wife's" mind.

16. The text reads "the law the gospel," and Dolbeau has suggested, hesitantly but surely rightly, eliminating "the gospel." It has every appearance of being a marginal annotation, and a somewhat pedantic one, to boot, that has crept into the text.

17. The text simply reads, *superaveris et inde te patere superari*; "you will have won your case and from the same authority allow yourself to lose." The meaning is entirely clear, but I feel that something like *ex evangelio*—or *ex lege*, but here he might ring the changes—must have dropped out. It would read much better like this: *superaveris ex evangelio; et inde patere te superari*.

18. An intolerable, but no doubt effective, pun in the Latin: *In quo non erit virtus, quam male erit vir tuus!*

19. There is a gap in the text here. For these two principal martyrs of the African Church, Saints Felicity and Perpetua, and the inevitable play on their names, see Sermons 280—282 (III, 8).

20. I translate *virorum* "men," not "husbands" here, because it was Perpetua's father above all who tried to deter her from her purpose.

21. Your *anima*—which also, and particularly in this verse, means "life." But in the whole context of this sermon and of Augustine's Platonist thought world, I think I have to keep "soul."

22. See Jn 12:25; Mt 16:25; Lk 17:33.

23. Here I transfer three sentences to this note, as they seem to me to have no place at all here, and to break up the whole current of thought. They run: "In this way (!) all grades will keep their proper order; first in excellence virginity, next widowhood, in the third place the married state; none of them without its reward. Let virgins reflect on Mary, widows on Anna, married women on Susanna. All have their rewards, and from none of these grades have martyrs ever been lacking."

The last sentence, I suggest, has been added later, in a desperate attempt to fit the first two into the context of this sermon. See Sermon 391, 6 (III, 10). I think at one stage of the transmission of the text there must have been a bit of confusion on one copyist's desk, combined with some distraction of his attention.

24. I have added this last phrase, as a a kind of gloss on *carnalis affectus*, "human affection," which I feel is not quite sufficient here by itself.

25. Or perhaps, sit on top of it, like Humpty Dumpty, a position in which it is sure to have a great fall.

26. Reading *non in carnisprincipatu anima seducatur a Deo*, instead of the text's . . . *in carnis principatum*. . .; "seduced away from God to leadership over the flesh." *In* with the ablative can in Augustine's African Latin (under the Semitic influence of Punic) signify the agent or instrument.

Dolbeau 21
SERMON 159B
Mainz 54

SERMON OF THE BLESSED AUGUSTINE ON THE WORDS OF THE APOSTLE:
OH THE DEPTH OF THE RICHES OF THE WISDOM AND KNOWLEDGE OF GOD;
AND OF PSALM 60(59):
O GOD, YOU HAVE REPULSED US AND DEMOLISHED US,
YOU HAVE BEEN ANGRY AND HAVE TAKEN PITY ON US;
AND OF PSALM 119(118):
IT IS GOOD FOR ME THAT YOU HAVE HUMBLED ME, SO THAT I MAY LEARN YOUR
JUSTIFICATIONS.

Date: 404[1]

Introduction; the mystery at which Paul exclaims is that God has
locked all up under sin so that he may take pity on all

1. The readings from the word of God, which provide us with spiritual nourishment, are advising me that I should anticipate your eager expectations, and seeing that you are so hungry should set something before you straight away from the Lord's pantry, the keys of which have been entrusted to me. In the reading from the apostle, which your holinesses will recall with me, these were the words chanted to us: *Oh the depth of the riches of the wisdom and knowledge of God! How incomprehensible are his judgments, and untraceable his ways! For who has known the mind of the Lord, or who has been his counsellor, or who first gave to him and will be repaid? Since from him and through him and in him are all things, to him be glory for ever and ever, Amen* (Rom 11:33-36). Now for the apostle to cry out, *Oh the depth of the riches of the wisdom and knowlege of God,* and to say this in terror at heaven knows what unfathomable deeps, as it were, of God's judgments, he had said just before, *God has locked all up in sin, so that he might take pity on all*[2] (Rom 11:32).

So after this statement in which he says *God has locked all up under sin, so that he might take pity on all,* seeing that it is indeed a mystery of heaven knows what unfathomable deeps that human beings should first be found manifestly guilty by their own consciences, so that they might be rescued when they confessed, he cried out, *Oh the depth of the riches of the wisdom and knowledge of God!* Where precisely does the depth of the riches of God's wisdom and knowledge lie? In the fact of God's locking us all up in sin, so that he might take pity on us all. What sin? The sin of unbelief. You see, that's the word he actually used: *God has locked all up in unbelief so that he might take pity on all* (Rom 11:32). And so may the Lord our God himself be present with us, whose riches the apostle cried out in praise of, and may he be pleased to share with us a little from those hidden and profound riches, so that while I am all too well aware that it is beyond my powers to display them to you fully, I may still somehow or other say something, not indeed to display them perfectly, but to commend them to you as indeed defying full display.

The apostle, you see, appears to have failed, so to say, out of some kind of human feebleness, in displaying what he was so overjoyed at gazing upon. He saw some heaven knows what reality which no tongue might describe; he observed in his mind what he was incapable of putting into words, and he could find no means of making us intent on seeing what he saw, except by crying out and straightening up our hearts with the exclamation, *Oh the depth of the riches of the wisdom and knowledge of God!* Being thus straightened up, our hearts could be aimed straight at the one, the sight of whose riches made the apostle cry out, and not at the lips of the feeble steward who was unable to display those riches. And so this is what I will do according to my own small measure, and I will direct your hearts straight at the one to whom we all belong, and under whom as our one master we are all fellow pupils in this school, in which God's riches are to be found, in which is the very depth of those riches, and where his unsearchable judgments are and his untraceable ways,[3] because *he has locked all up in unbelief, so that he might take pity on all.*

It is part of God's kindness to humble us first

2. The one who locked us all up in unbelief seems to be angry, but the one who takes pity on us all is in a gentle mood. So the passage from the apostle agrees with the psalm, *O God, you have repulsed us and demolished us; you have been angry and taken pity on us* (Ps 60:1). Listen to him being angry and taking pity: *God has locked all up in unbelief, so that he might take pity on all* (Rom 11:32). What was the Lord our God up to, what was he meaning to do? First to be angry, to repulse, to humiliate us, and then after that to come to our aid, to call back those who had turned away from him, to listen to those who had turned back to him, to help those he had listened to, to change those he had helped, to give the crown of glory to those he had changed. Let us join up[4] other evidence to this from the scriptures.

There is the voice of a certain individual human being, toiling away on this earth, that is of Adam himself, the human race[5]—the human race, however, which was not left to itself by the second man from heaven, so that we might first of all be of the earth, earthy, and later become heavenly.[6] In that we were humbled we were earthy, in that we were just dropped we were earthy, in that we were repulsed we were earthy; but because the one who repulsed us and dropped us and humiliated us also took pity on us, that's why we became heavenly.

So let us listen to the voice of this Adam saying somewhere else, *Before I was humbled, I myself did wrong* (Ps 119:67). Groaning and sighing in his humiliation, he acknowledged his sin; to himself he attributed iniquity, justice to God. What did he say, after all? *"Before I was humbled*—that's the punishment God inflicted—*I myself,"* he said, *"did wrong."* So that God who humbled me might not seem unjust, my wrongdoing came first, my humiliation followed. So he is *the just judge* (2 Tm 4:8), is the Lord my God. I wouldn't, after all, have come to this humiliation, unless I had first done wrong. Now humiliating him sounds indeed very much like the anger of God the judge; but that in fact it stems from his mercy, you can tell by listening to the same man's voice a little later on: *It is good for me*, he says, *that you have humbled me, so that I may learn your justifications* (Ps 119:71).

Would your graces notice carefully what he is saying: *Before I was humbled, I myself did wrong.* He seems to be groaning under punishment, sighing in the stocks; to be seeking by confession in the feeble mortality of this earthly existence the help of the one he had offended by wrongdoing. That, you see, is what these words sound like: *It is good for me that you have humbled me, so that I may learn your justifications;*[7] that is, "I am not blaming you for my humiliation, my God; I myself have done what is evil, you in your turn have done what is just."

3. These words are matched by the ones we have just sung. The man, you see, who is saying, *O God, you have repulsed us and demolished us* (Ps 60:1), is the same one who is saying, *Before I was humbled, I myself did wrong* (Ps 119:67). You heard, I mean, how God repulsed him; you heard how God dropped him, cast him down, that is, from the heights to the earth. You heard this. Look for the reason why God did this: *Before I was humbled, I myself*, he says, *did wrong.* You have heard about your prior wrongdoing, and God's subsequent justice; now hear how the very justice of God which humbled you doesn't only indicate the severity of the just judge, but also the clemency of the merciful one. He says, you see, what I mentioned a moment ago, *It is good for me that you have humbled me, so that I may learn your justifications* (Ps 119:71).

So where are we, my brothers and sisters? Was God being angry when he humbled him, or taking pity? If humiliation didn't do us any good, it could be put down to God's excessive severity; though even if that were the case, we couldn't complain about his being unjust. Sinners, after all, must pay back what they owe; the proud and the iniquitous have no business to delude themselves. They should first find out what they deserve, and in this way come to recognize what quality he has shown. Can the consciences of any of us sinful human beings have the nerve to tell us that anything but punishment is our due, anything but the most just of pains and penalties? Or if severe punishment follows on a man's iniquity, can the just judge be told, "You were wrong to condemn the sinner"?

So then, let this be what we sinners tell ourselves, let this be how we acknowledge in the penalties that overtake us both our own wrongdoing and the justice of our God. In this way, you see, we shall be found worthy to discover the mercy of God in the very penalties themselves. This, my dearest brothers and sisters, none will discover but those who have first humbled themselves. And while I am going to explain this as best I can, I somehow don't think that any of you are going to understand what I am going to say, unless you have first rid yourselves of the smoke of pride, which gets in the eyes of the mind and blinds them, so that you are unable to appreciate God's mercy in the very punishment itself.

The example of good masters punishing slaves, or of parents
punishing children they love

4. But first of all take a look at this point in everyday life—that, you see, can give you a way to understanding that he[8] has not abandoned humanity in its mortal condition; take a look at something similar in the way people behave, which will show us that punishment can be inflicted by way of showing mercy, or taking pity. What shall I say? You there are disciplining your slave, and by disciplining him, of course, you are taking pity on him in the very fact of appearing to punish him—but I won't say your slave; you may perhaps be angry with a slave to the extent of hating him. Not of course that you ought to, if you are a Christian; not indeed that you ought to, if you stop to consider that you are a human being; not that you ought to, if you consider that "slave" and "master" are indeed two different names, but "man" and "man" are not two different things. You certainly oughtn't to go after your erring slave with hatred. But because people are not infrequently in the habit of doing so, let's put this comparison aside, let's substitute a son.

Nobody can help loving his children; I mean, you don't praise a man for loving his son. *For if you love those who love you, what reward will you get,* said the Lord; *do not the tax-collectors do that?* (Mt 5:46). How much more their sons, whom men beget as their successors! Nobody at all, by the law of nature itself, can hate the one he has begotten. Nor are human beings to be praised for a quality that is to be found in dumb animals. Nobody praises a man who loves his children. And it isn't only in the gentler kinds of cattle that you find this; the ferocity of lions grows gentle toward their young, tigers love their young, snakes hatch their eggs and nurture their brood. So if those creatures that seem to be savage and wild by nature do not maintain their wild and savage demeanor toward their offspring, what is so wonderful about a man loving his son?[9]

But the reason I've said this, brothers and sisters, is so that you may see that punishment can be the work of caring or kindness, from the example of children, from that kind of thing which nobody can hate.[10] So someone sees his son going the way of pride, setting himself up against his father, claiming more for himself than is proper, wanting to let his life trickle away in trifling pleasures, wanting to squander what he doesn't yet possess. And there he is, when he's behaving like this, cheerful, laughing, blithely enjoying himself. His father, though, brings him to heel with a rebuke, with punishment, with a whip; he wipes the grin off his face, reduces him to tears. He has apparently deprived him of what is good,

and brought what is evil upon him—see what he has deprived him of: enjoyment; see what he has brought on him: groans. And yet if he had left that
enjoyment unpunished, he would have been cruel; because he has reduced him
to tears, he is shown to be caring and kind.

So if a father who reduces someone to tears is shown to be caring and kind,
why can't we understand that our creator could also have done what we have
been singing: *O God, you have repulsed us and dropped us?*[11] But why should
he do this? Not, surely, for our destruction, for our ultimate ruin? Listen to what
follows: *You have been angry and taken pity on us* (Ps 60:1). Now put two verses
together, as I said, *Before I was humbled, I did wrong* (Ps 119:67); what good
does it do you to have been repulsed and dropped? *It is good for me that you
have humbled me, so that I may learn your justifications* (Ps 119:71).

The first of all sins is pride; the example of the "slave-owning slave"

5. Let us now turn our minds back to those words of the apostle: *God has
locked all up in unbelief, so that he might take pity on all* (Rom 11:32). The first
sin of man was pride; that's what we read in Genesis, that's what we find
elsewhere in scripture.[12] What do we read in Genesis? That man, created and
formed, was placed in paradise under a certain law, under a certain commandment. What the commandment which was imposed upon him showed him was
this: that he had been made great in such a way as to have one greater above
him. So God instructed man, his subject, that humility was always to be held
onto; that is, that the lowliness of man placed under God should be preserved.
Man indeed had been made according to the image of God,[13] and as it says in
another place, *Wisdom gave him strength to control all things* (Wis 10:2); all
things were under him, but over him was the one who made all things. So it was
man's duty to attend to the things that were under him in such a way that he paid
more attention to the one who was over him. In adhering, you see, to the one
above, he would be all the more secure in his possession of the things beneath
him; while on withdrawing from the one above him, he would be subjected to
the things beneath him.

As if we were to suppose three men; one man who has a slave and also has
a master, as it frequently happens that property-owning slaves[14] have slaves
themselves. Pay careful attention; he has a slave, he has a master; he's subject
to one, in command of the other; he is over his slave, under his master. The third
we have supposed is the slave of the slave, while the first is the master of the
master, and the middle the one who is both slave and master, the master of his
slave and the slave of his master. Now he is secure in the possession of his slave,
provided he doesn't offend his master. And indeed we have spoken of three
men; all are of the same kind, all consist of the same substance and nature. Not
so with this other trio, God and man and the creation beneath man. Of different
kinds, after all, and by no means of the same substance are fashioner and thing
fashioned, maker and thing made, craftsman and his work, creator and creature.

But indeed even things that have been created are generically called creatures, it is true, but they differ from each other in their natures and worth and their place in the order of things. First, you see, come spiritual things and after them material[15] ones, of the things which God fashioned, which God made. Spiritual things occupy the first place, material bodies the last. The human mind, though, is something spiritual, and it is on it that the *likeness and image of God* (Gn 1:26) has been impressed. Material bodies are all the things which we perceive to be within the grasp of the senses of the body; everybody knows them—things that can be seen, heard, smelled, tasted, touched; hard soft, hot cold, rough smooth, they are all called material, they rank lowest. Above them all are set human beings, but as regards the spirit, the mind, as regards that in them which is made *to the image and likeness of God.*

God, after all, is not circumscribed or enclosed in a material shape, so as to have a back on one side, eyes on the other, but he is a kind of light, and not such as we see with our eyes, not even if you amplify this kind we see with our eyes, extending it in imagination and making fields of light and mountains of light and trees of light, flitting through the idle fancies of your thoughts. Do you want to understand spiritual light? Look for something to understand it with.

The immaterial nature of the mind, where the image of God is located

6. Understand, I'm saying, this very light by which you understand. What have I said? You see white and black with your bodily eyes, you are given external help in this by the light of either the sun or the moon or a lamp or some little flame. If that light, what's more, were not helping from outside, in vain would you open your "lights," and there would be no point in calling them "lights."[16] Now what it is in you that must be open and sound, namely the eye; and what it is that must be brought in to help from outside, namely light; and what it is you are helped by it to see, namely colors and shapes, all this you know perfectly well and can distinguish. So much for the eyes. You hear voices, you know what you hear with. The eyes can't hear, but neither can the ears see. The eyes lack the necessary means for perceiving voices, and the ears lack the means needed for seeing colors. You, though, lack none of these means, because you see with your eyes, you hear with your ears.

So you are also aware of scents, and you know what organ you have to bring to bear in order to perceive a smell. I mean, you don't present your ear for perceiving a pleasant smell, but you stick the thing in which God created for you to smell things with. Nor, when you want to taste some sauce, do you put it in your eye or your ear; you know that that's not where the sense is which distinguishes flavors. And do you want to perceive whether something is hard or soft, or cold or hot? You know that you can perceive it by contact all over your body. You know all this. Good.

Now turn your attention to that interior something. Who is this inside, to whom all these senses report whatever it is that people sense? These, after all, are really no more than instruments, like things that have been reduced to servitude. There is I don't quite know what kind of interior sense, an emperor to whom these messengers report whatever they discover outside. But this one inside, who distinguishes between all these, is accordingly superior to them all. So then, the eye has something it can see, the ear something it can hear, the nose something it can smell, the palate something it can taste, the hand something it can touch—and does the mind have nothing it is able to observe by itself? It is indeed the mind that perceives white and black, but as reported by the eyes; yes, the mind that perceives the tuneful and the harsh in voices, but as reported by the ears; yes, the mind that perceives what is sweet smelling and evil smelling in odors, but as reported by the nose; yes, the mind that perceives sweet and bitter, but as reported by the palate; yes, the mind that perceives hard and soft, but when the hand has reported on what it has felt. So it can perceive all these things, so many and various, as reported by the body; it can't be unfit, can it, to perceive anything by itself, without any organ of the body reporting it?

So then, look for what it can and does perceive by itself, and you will discover where the image of God is located. White things and black it was perceiving through the eyes, the ears were reporting tuneful and discordant sounds; and to save running through them all again one by one, these things that are adjacent to the body were being reported by organs of the body. What is just and what is unjust—do the eyes report that? It is the mind that distinguishes the just and the unjust, and says, "This is just, this is unjust." Inquire who reported it. If justice is a color, the eyes reported it, if justice is a sound, the ears reported it; if it's a smell, the nose reported it, if a taste, the palate reported it; if it's hardness or softness, the hand reported it. If it's none of these things, who reported it, if not an inner light?

So then, this nature, this substance, which you can see surpasses the rest by a long way, and which there's no time to speak about more fully, as I would very much like to, this inner something, this divine something in us has been made *to the image and likeness of God* (Gn 1:26), is above all material things, and was made like that in order that every material creature might be subjected to it and serve it faithfully; but for all that, the mind itself is not God. I mean, if it were God, would it ever have sinned? God, you see, is unchangeable. But our mind, being created, being made, is not what God is; it is changeable. Even now we can see how it changes. It's sensible, it's silly; it remembers, it forgets; it wants something, it doesn't want it; it enjoys itself, it's miserable. Such chopping and changing doesn't occur with God, who is above the mind, and the creator of the mind.

The analogy of the slave-owning slave applied to the mind; for its
pride God has it flogged by its own slave, the body

7. But still, this whole thing I've been talking about is above the body, is under God, is under the Lord and master, is above the slave. These are the three I was talking about a little earlier on. So if three men, though they are all equally human, are related by some social arrangement of this life in such a way that one of them is lord and master only, another is slave only, while the third is both slave of the master and master of the slave, don't you think the whole creation

would be both more readily and more distinctively arranged on those lines—the nature and substance of mind placed under God, the nature of material bodies as a whole placed under mind? So as I was saying in that case, that man is secure in the possession of his slave as long as he doesn't offend his lord and master; so too this human mind, if it hadn't offended its Lord by a kind of pride in wishing to be its own independent authority, would have had the whole material world of bodies subject to it as its slave. But because it did offend its Lord through pride, the bodily creation, which had been given it as its servant, was turned into its torturer for its punishment, its torturer to requite it. It is through the body's distress, after all, that the mind is now being crucified, whereas previously it was lording it over the whole material world of bodies.

It's as if that man—here after all you can easily get a clearer illustration of the point, because this very thing that we have difficulty in understanding is part of the punishment by which we have been humiliated; so I'm giving some examples from situations we are familiar with. Set those three slaves[17] before your eyes once more, because you can hardly understand this point, though in itself it is more distinctly defined; I mean these three things are more distinct from each other, in that they are of different kinds; God, after all, is something vastly different from mind, and mind something vastly different from body. But in those other three there is a man, and a man, and a man. No difference of nature, but social status dictates their relationship. Still, because we are familiar with such situations, we can understand their relationship more easily than that of those things which are in fact more distinct from each other. So now then, understand what I'm saying.

Assume that the one in the middle—because he's a slave in such a way as also to be a master; he's a master in such a way as also to be a slave, the slave of the one above him, the master of the one beneath him; so then, assume that he has offended his master. How has he offended him? By some sort of pride. He reckoned, you see, that he too had a slave, and he had the nerve to set himself up against his master, simply on the grounds that he apparently had his own slave under his own authority. He stood up against his master, his master ordered him to be flogged by his own slave. After all, that master of the master was master of them both; I mean that slave did not have so much authority over his own slave as the master of both had over both of them. How, after all, could number three ignore that master who was nobody's slave, and refuse to flog his own master on the orders of the more powerful master of them both?

So then our God gave orders, because we had offended him, that we were to be tormented by means of our own bodies; and our bodies were made mortal, and we began to suffer pains and penalties from that very thing which had given us the nerve to behave proudly against our Lord and master. So we are now being flogged by our own slave. We are being tormented in the torments of our flesh; the Lord and master has humbled us, so that we are being beaten by a slave.

8. But why did he humble us, and have us beaten by a slave? Because we had first done wrong. *Before I was humbled, I did wrong* (Ps 119:67). So then,

strapped down there under the whip of your own slave, cry out to the Lord your God and say to him, *It is good for me that you have humbled me, so that I may learn your justifications* (Ps 119:71). Which of *your justifications*? That just as I, certainly, have a slave in my body, so you too have a slave in me. And just as I, certainly, require my body to comply with my wishes, so I ought to have complied with yours. So this is how I learned your justifications, as though my Lord and master were speaking to me from above and saying, "*You wicked servant* (Mt 18:32), at least now that you find yourself in this humiliating position, acknowledge who it is you have offended, and who it is you were subordinated to. For sure, you are being tortured by your own slave; you have a body and you want it to comply with your wishes in all matters. When you raise your hand, you want your hand to follow your instructions; when you raise your foot, you want your foot to follow your instructions. And although I wanted you to be flogged by your own slave, your slave is still at your service."

And indeed, when we wish to walk and change the place where the body is, we give orders to the feet and they comply; we give orders to the eye to see, when we wish to look at something; it doesn't contradict us, it turns in that direction, it reports back to us. We turn an ear toward sounds, it immediately reports what the sound is; we raise a hand to do some job, it doesn't resist. Insofar, you see, as the body serves us, it indicates that we are its masters, while insofar as it resists us, it indicates that we too have a master. But let's see in what ways your body does not comply with your wishes. For example, you are able to walk ten miles, you want to walk twenty; it doesn't comply. You are able to walk fifty miles, you want to go sixty; it doesn't comply. You wish to keep vigil for two nights; it complies for part of the time, for the other part it doesn't. You want to move your hand to pick something up; you do so; you make an effort to pick something else up; it doesn't comply. Add all those excruciating distresses arising from its feebleness and its perishability, impossible to count, and just remark how *the body which is perishing weighs down the soul* (Wis 9:15).

So then, insofar as it serves you, it shows that you are its lord, while insofar as it resists you, it is warning you to be a good slave to your Lord. So then, say to your Lord, *It is good for me that you have humbled me, so that I may learn your justifications*. How do you learn his justifications? So that in this way you no longer disdain to be a good slave to your Lord, just as you want your body to be a good slave to you. And now you really do begin to serve your Lord and master well—and your body doesn't yet serve you as you want it to. Yes, you now believe, who were previously an unbeliever, you follow your Lord's commandments, you are walking along the way; but justice has not yet been perfected in you; that's why there is not yet perfect obedience in your slave. There is still a little bitterness left, in case this world should grow so sweet to you, that you stop having any desire for your Lord, who made the world.[18]

Christ's humility in assuming our mortal nature

9. Cry out to him from the ends of the earth, O Church spread throughout the whole wide world; say in the psalm, *From the ends of the earth I cried out to you, when my heart was in anguish.* It's in the psalm that this is written: *You have set me high upon the rock, you have led me along, because you have become my hope* (Ps 61:2-3). Yes, God has indeed set us high upon the rock. Which rock? *Now the rock was Christ*, says the apostle (1 Cor 10:4). And how did that become our hope? Because our Lord Jesus Christ, through whom we were made,[19] is himself the Word of God, *through which all things were made* (Jn 1:3). He took flesh from the lump of our mortality, yes, and he too took to himself the death which was the penalty for sin, but didn't take the sin; instead with the merciful intention of delivering us from sin, he handed over that flesh of his to death.

It wasn't unwillingly, after all, that he was handed over; he wouldn't have been crucified unless he had handed himself over. Because as for Judas handing him over and betraying him,[20] he handed over one who so willed it. The merit of Christ's will, however, is not put down to Judas' account, but rather the merit of his own greed. When he betrayed the Lord, after all, he did not have our salvation in mind, but his own avarice and treachery.[21] I mean, the handing over was done by Judas, was done by Christ himself, was done by the Father of Christ. They all seem to have done one and the same thing. They did do one and the same thing, but they didn't do it with one and the same intention.[22] The Father handed over the Son out of compassion, the Son handed himself over out of the same compassion, Judas handed his master and teacher over out of sheer treachery. There is no apparent difference between handing over and handing over, but there's all the difference in the world between compassion and treachery.

How did the Father hand him over? Listen to the apostle: *Who did not spare his own Son, but handed him over for us all* (Rom 8:32). How did the Son hand himself over? The same apostle says about the Lord himself: *Who loved me and handed himself over for me* (Gal 2:20). So he handed over this flesh to be slain, so that you wouldn't be afraid of anything that could happen to your flesh. He showed you, in his resurrection after three days, what you ought to be hoping for at the end of this age. So he is leading you along, because he has become your hope. You are now walking toward the hope of the resurrection; but unless our head had first risen, the other members of the body would not find anything to hope for.

10. So where are we, my brothers and sisters? Although, even before the Lord suffered, the body was entirely at his service as its lord and master—he wasn't, after all so encumbered with a body by way of requital, by way of a penalty, as to be flogged by his slave as we are—still if he wished to suffer anything in his body, he suffered it because it was his will and by his own authority, not because he had to or couldn't help it; as he said himself, *I have authority to put away my soul, and I have authority to take it back again; nobody takes it from me, but I myself put it away from me* (Jn 10:18). So he had great authority indeed; and yet by his being willing to suffer in the flesh, he thereby demonstrated that you

suffer deservedly. He did not deserve to suffer, you do. But to help you endure the fact that you suffer what you deserve, he reassures you by having suffered what he in no way deserved. So endure the fact that you must suffer, until you are rid of your mortality.

So then, your kingdom is coming[23] within predetermined limits of time; he delivers the goods he has promised, because he has already delivered in himself his own resurrection. He rose again, I mean, after three days; he wanted to rise again first, and to show us what we should be hoping for at the end. We were assuming that the flesh was going to perish; that was why he didn't wish to take flesh from anywhere else than where we too had our flesh from. I mean, if he had taken it from somewhere else, we would say, "Flesh which was taken from somewhere else was able to rise again. It wasn't taken, was it, from where we have taken it from?"[24] It's true, he didn't allow his mother a man's embrace, because he was the Only Son of God;[25] because he had a Father up above, all he looked for on earth was a mother.

He is showing us that what he created isn't evil; he created male and female, he created both himself.[26] But because the man was led astray by the woman, women might have despaired of themselves had not their sex been honored through the virgin Mary. He chose to be born of a woman; it was proper that she should bear a man, that he should be born as a man. But God hadn't only created a man, he had also himself created a woman. Women might, as I said, have despaired of themselves, and said they had no share in God's mercy, because the man had been deceived by the woman. So he was prepared to be born of a woman giving birth to a man, and thus he honored the sex. He demonstrated that he was the founder of each sex, and later on the liberator of each.[27]

You see, because death was prepared for the man by the serpent through the agency of the woman, it was through the agency of women that life was announced to men; because it was women who first saw the Lord rising again, and announced it to men, to the apostles.[28] So our Lord Jesus Christ showed us in his flesh what we ought to be hoping for at the end. So he humbled us, in order that we might learn his justifications.[29]

Pride, the root cause of all our ills

11. So now at last let us return to him, humbled, having been thrown out for being proud. The whole cause, you see, of our mortality, the whole cause of our feebleness, the whole cause of all the torments, all the difficulties, all the miseries which the human race suffers in this age, is nothing but pride. You have the text of scripture saying, *The beginning of all sin is pride.* And what does it say in the same place? *The beginning of man's pride is to apostatize from God* (Sir 10:13.12). If pride strikes you as a minor evil, at least tremble at the thought of apostatizing from God. Next, if you tremble at the thought of apostatizing from God, throw out the cause of apostasy. It was pride, you see, that made man apostatize from God.

So because this is the fountainhead of all our ills, that's why we are sick in this life. It's like when an experienced doctor sees someone ailing from a variety of disorders, he doesn't attend to the immediate causes and neglect the origin of all the causes—after all, if he cures the immediate causes while leaving untouched the source of the disorders, the calamities drawn off from it will return, and while he seems to have provided a remedy for a time, he is not curing the patient deep down. No, the really experienced doctor is found to be the one who thoroughly ties up all the causes of all the disorders, and on finding the first of them from which all the rest seem to stem like branches, he cuts out the root, and the whole thicket of aches and pains is chopped down.[30] That's how our Lord Jesus Christ did all these things, and because he could see that pride was the root cause of all our disorders, he cured us with his own humility—it's why he is called "Savior,"[31] and why the one who said, *It's not the healthy who need the doctor, but those who are ill* (Mt 9:12), came to the sick, because the sick couldn't go to him; he sought those who were not seeking him, he turned to the weak and feeble, he suffered many things, he allowed himself to be slain by the blind, and used his death to heal their eyes with.

We must not be disgusted by Christ's humility, as the Manichees are

12. So don't poke fun at the humility, the lowliness of Christ. Many of the pagans, you see, do poke fun at Christ for coming in a lowly fashion—and if only it were just pagans alone!—and many of the heretics too, who call themselves Christians.[32] It disgusts them that Christ was born of a woman, it disgusts them that he was nailed to the cross and wounded, and that they were real wounds which he received, and that they were real nails which were hammered into him. It disgusts them, and they say, "He put on an act with all those things, he pretended, and didn't really endure them."

So Truth set you free with a lie? You were afflicted with falsehood, and you were healed by means of falsehood? But any who say things like that reveal what sort of magisterial teachers they are. I mean, if the Lord rose again, and presented his hands to his doubting disciple to be touched, and his scars to be felt, when the disciple said, *I will not believe, unless I put my fingers in his side* (Jn 20:25-27); he showed himself, not only to be seen with the eyes but also to be felt with the hands, while he, on feeling the scars, discovered that they expressed the truth, and so he exclaimed, *My Lord and my God*[33] (Jn 20:28).

So if Christ deceived us, you're going to be telling the truth, are you? How am I to listen to you, tell me? Do you want me to listen to you as a master?

"As a master," he says to me.

What are you telling me, what are you teaching me?

"I'm teaching you," he says, "that Christ was not born of a woman, and didn't have real flesh, and that wasn't a real death, nor were those real wounds, and if not real wounds, then neither real scars."

And I, on the contrary, have learned the Lord Jesus Christ from the gospel, and how he offered his scars to the disciple when he doubted. Of course, he could have risen again without scars, just as he was able to heal the eyes of the man born blind.[34]

"But why should he wish to bring forward the evidence of scars?"[35]

Because the evidence of the scars is medicine for the wounds of the mind.

So what are you going to teach me? That all that was false, and Christ simulated these things, and that the disciple had been taken in by a falsehood when he exclaimed, My Lord and my God? So if he, according to you, wished to heal by means of falsehood, how am I to know whether you now are telling me the truth or lying? You don't, after all, think it is a crime to lie, when you are attempting to oppose Christ to me as the author of a lie. You see, I'm going to say to you, "You're lying," and you to me, "Perish the thought! I'm not lying." Certainly you're lying. "Perish the thought that I should lie!"; that's what you're going to say to me, so that I may believe you. Because tell me you're lying, and I will want to know whether I should believe you in anything. But so that I may believe you in something, you're going to say to me, "Perish the thought that I should lie!" Why have you said, "Perish the thought that I should lie!," if not because you think it's criminal to lie when you are teaching? So you assign to Christ something you think would be criminal for you?

So away with with human deceits; just as it's written in the gospel, that's exactly how Christ came. Don't let the lowliness of Christ disgust you; that lowliness is disgusting to pride. Don't be proud, and you will not find the humble, lowly Christ disgusting.

The potion of Christ's humility is the cure for the swelling of pride

13. The apostle said, *All things are clean for the clean; while for the unclean and the unbelieving nothing is clean, but both their minds and their consciences have been defiled* (Ti 1:15). Say with a chaste mind, "A woman conceived, a virgin conceived. She conceived by faith, she conceived as a virgin, she gave birth as a virgin, she remained a virgin." Believe all that, and don't let yourself think of that womb as unclean. Because even if that flesh had been unclean, Christ on coming would have cleansed the unclean flesh, would not have been rendered unclean by its being unclean. Note the lowliness of your Lord; if it horrifies you, you are proud; lowliness does horrify the proud.

You are proud in that way to some extent;[36] force yourself not to be horrified by the potion for your swelling. When you're proud, I mean, you're swollen; you aren't big. If you're swollen, drink the potion so that the swelling of your insides may subside, and you can be restored to health. This potion has been mixed for you by the doctor, for you to drink. The doctor himself has mixed a cup for you; drink the bitter cup, if you wish to be restored to health. Can't you see that you're swollen, can't you see that your insides are not healthy? You think you're big, and you're only swollen. This isn't genuine bigness, but a disease. Do you want to be rid of the disease, do you want to be rid of the swelling? Drink the cup of humility; it has been mixed for you by the one who came to you in humility. And in case you should hesitate to drink, the doctor drinks it first, not because it was needed by the doctor, but to overcome the hesitation of the patient.

So don't despise the humility by which you are being restored to health. The fountainhead of all diseases is pride. He came to cure the fountainhead of all diseases, the one who was pleased to become the head of the Church. With the fountainhead of all diseases removed, you will be restored to health. Humble yourself, and you will be whole, and you will say without the slightest qualm, *It is good for me that you have humbled me, so that I may learn your justifications* (Ps 119:71). You lifted yourself up, you see, and you've been humbled. Humble yourself, and you are lifted up, because *God withstands the proud, but gives grace to the humble* (1 Pt 5:5). So that's why *God has locked all up in unbelief, so that he may take pity on all* (Rom 11:32).

All involved in the sin of pride, Jews as well as Gentiles

14. Humanity drew away from God, followed its own lusts,[37] let the reins go slack; in its straying and wandering around it came eventually to the worship of idols. Even the nation of the Jews, which worshiped the one God, had grown proud, grown proud and sunk into iniquity. God wished to show them that they were weak, wished to show them that they were still prostrate under the frailty of the flesh, that the covetousness which derived from the first parents still remained in them; so he gave them the law, and commandments that were just and good and holy, as the apostle says: *And so the law indeed is holy, and the commandment is just and holy and good. So did what is good*, he says, *become death for me? Perish the thought! But sin, to be shown up as sin, through what was good wrought death for me* (Rom 7:12-13). Notice how he said that the law which was given to the Jews was a good thing. He called it a good thing, because God had given it. And indeed all the things laid down in the ten commandments are good. Or is there, perhaps, something bad about *You may not steal, you may not kill, you may not commit adultery, you may not bear false witness,* etc., *you may not covet your neighbor's goods* (Ex 20:13-17)? I mean, even if you haven't taken anything, but have just coveted it, the laws in the courtroom can't touch you, but God in his judgment can and does.

So pay close attention, brothers and sisters; the law was given to the Jews, who were weak, but proud. They started making an effort to perform the just requirements of the law, and were thrown by their covetousness and greed; and they incurred liability, where previously they had been iniquitous, but not liable to the law, not transgressors. That's why the apostle says, *For where there is no law, neither is there transgression* (Rom 4:15). When a law is given, any who act against the law, even if they are only doing what they used to do, still when they used to do it without a law against it, they were sinners, they weren't transgressors; while when they do it after already receiving the law, they are not only sinners but also transgressors. So because they are not only sinners but also transgressors, what the apostle said is verified: *But law came in that wrongdoing might abound* (Rom 5:20). Why, though, did wrongdoing abound? Well, this is the same as *O God, you have repulsed us and dropped us* (Ps 60:1). He continues, however, and says, *But where wrongdoing has abounded, grace has abounded all the more* (Rom 5:20). So because wrongdoing has abounded we can rightly say, *O God, you have repulsed us and dropped us; you have been angry.* But because grace has abounded all the more, we are right to add, *and have taken pity on us* (Ps 60:1). So the Jews have no business to say, "We, though, are something." *For God has locked all up in unbelief, that he might take pity on all* (Rom 11:32).

Let us hold on to Christ's humility, until we join the angels in singing Alleluia

15. So, dearest brothers and sisters, let us get to know our life, our Lord Jesus Christ; let us hold on to the humility of our Lord Jesus Christ as the cure for our pride. Let us believe in him, let us hope for everything from the mercy of the one *who did not spare his own Son, but handed him over for us all* (Rom 8:32). And when perhaps we make a little progress in his justifications, let us not grow proud and start looking down on other people, but let us take note on the journey of justice, not of how far we have traveled, but of how far we have still to go; and everywhere en route let us sigh and groan, and go on doing so as long as we are travelers, because there will be no joy for us anywhere but in the home country, when we have been made *the equals of the angels* (Lk 20:36). *As long as we are in the body, we are traveling abroad, away from the Lord.* Why are we traveling abroad, away from the Lord? *For we are walking by faith,* he says, *not by sight* (2 Cor 5:6-7). Faith is believing what you cannot see; sight is seeing what you had previously believed. So when sight comes, that flame of charity will be all the keener, because you will be embracing as present what you were longing for in its absence; what you were believing in its absence, you will be seeing as present. And if God is sweet when he's believed in, what will he be like when he's directly beheld?

So when all these things are over and done with that are still tormenting us because of the dregs left by our sins, that's when the fullness of justice will be ours, that's when, arm in arm with the angels, we shall sing the everlasting hymn, "Alleluia."[38] We shall be praising God without ever growing tired, nor will hunger ever drive us away from that, because the only kind of body that is hungry is the one that is perishing and *weighs down the soul* (Wis 9:15). Nor shall we be thirsty, or ill, or growing old or dropping off to sleep, or feeling any kind of weariness or fatigue; but in the resurrection of the dead our flesh will be just like the bodies of the angels.[39] Don't be surprised that this flesh of ours will provide us with celestial bodies in the resurrection of the dead. Just reflect that before we came to be we were nothing, quite simply, and from there go on to believe what we shall be like when we have risen again. Let us each consider: "Before I was born, what was I, where was I, where was I hidden? All these distinct parts of the body, ears, eyes, face, breath animating the whole bulk of the body, where were they all?"

Certainly in some secret laboratory of nature, certainly where they couldn't be seen. They issued from there, God fashioned and shaped you, you who previously were not. What's so hard about God making an angel out of a human being, seeing that he made a human being out of mud?[40] What were you? And you're a human being. You're a human being, and shall you not be an angel? There's less of a gap to bridge in making an angel out of a human being than in making a human being out of what you were. He has achieved in you already the more wonderful of these two changes; isn't he going to achieve what remains to be done?

God has fulfilled most of his promises;
he will certainly fulfill the promise of resurrection

16. You simply must believe, and your faith must not waver from Christ, not waver from the gospel, not waver from his promises. You must understand that nearly all the things written have come about, only a few remain. This Church, which you can see is spread throughout the whole world—a short time ago it didn't exist. You yourselves were pagans a few years ago, now you're Christians. Your parents served demons, the temples were previously full of people offering incense; now the church is full of people praising God. How suddenly God has changed human affairs! Before all these things came about, they were there in writing and were being read; they were believed by people who didn't see them; now we see happening what our forebears could only read about. So if so many of these things have been fulfilled, are the few that are left not going to come about?[41]

Believe firmly that they are going to come about, brothers and sisters, because all these things too that have come about have done so no differently from the way they were written down and foretold before they happened. Many thousands of years ago, when Abraham was told, *In your seed shall all the nations be blessed* (Gn 22:18), it was said to just one man, *In your seed shall all the nations be blessed.*[42] He considered himself, just one man, and this seed, and his wife already an old woman and worn out with age, and he was told, not merely, "There will be seed from you"—if it were being said about only one, what could be more wonderful?—it was not enough to say to a man already worn out with age, "You will have a son"; *In your seed*, he said, *shall all the nations be blessed.* God was telling him marvelous things, telling him impossible things, but easy enough for himself. That one old man believed what he couldn't see, and it's we who do see. What he believed has been displayed to us; or rather, what has been displayed in us has been rendered to him. From the seed of Abraham, you see, came Isaac, and from Isaac Jacob, and from Jacob the people of the Jews, and from the people of the Jews David, and from the seed of David the virgin Mary, and from the virgin Mary the Lord Jesus Christ.[43] So in the seed of Abraham shall all the nations be blessed, because all the nations are blessed in Christ.[44] There you have how[45] what was promised to him has been displayed and granted to us.

So God, being almighty and faithful, granted what he promised to one man; will he not grant what he has promised to all? My brothers and sisters, may this build up your faith, may this lend vigor to your hope. He didn't cheat one man, will he be able to cheat the whole world? He granted one man a whole world full of Christians; he will grant a whole world life forever with Christ his Son.

Christ bought the whole world, not just the Donatist part

17. Hold firmly onto this, brothers and sisters, and so understand that the Church is not in a part, but in the whole. Christ bought the whole, he gave his blood for the whole, the whole wide world has Christians in it, the unity of Christ is the Church. The heretics have no cause to litigate with the Church of Christ; it's not enough for them wanting to be disinherited, they must even bring false charges against the heirs.[46] It's you who must be enticing them in unity to the whole, not they enticing you to the part. If you people follow them, you will be going off to a part; if they listen to you, they will come to the whole; they will be defeated in argument to their own advantage. Christ, you see, bought the whole while he hung on the cross, my brothers and sisters; Christ's passion was Christ's commercial transaction. That's where he bought us, where he was crucified. That, after all, is where he shed his blood, our price, right there where it had been foretold in the psalms, while still in the future.

Notice how many years before it had been foretold: *They have dug my hands and my feet, they have counted up all my bones; they, however, gazed at me and inspected me, they divided my garments among them, and over my vesture they cast lots* (Ps 22:16-18). It's scarcely possible to tell whether this is heard in the psalm or chanted in the gospel. Aren't the words read in the gospel just as they are sung in the psalm, *They have dug my hands and my feet, they have counted up all my bones?*[47] That's when Christ bought us, when all his bones were counted up; when his hands and his feet were dug with nails, that's when he bought us. That, you see, is when he shed his blood, which is our price. The psalm itself gives a clear indication of what he bought. Do you want to know? Question the psalm itself.

"What did Christ buy, hanging on the tree?"

After a few verses, you see, it says, *All the ends of the earth shall remember and be converted to the Lord, and all the families of the nations shall worship in his presence.*

"Why will they worship?"

Since his is the kingdom, and he shall lord it over the nations (Ps 22:28-29). It's as though the answer was being given to why, and to the question who this is, to whom all the ends of the earth shall be converted, and in whose presence all the families of nations shall worship; *Since his*, it says, *is the kingdom, and he shall lord it over the nations.* Why is it his? Because he's the one who bought it.

The meaning of Christ's tunic, woven from the top

18. Now the enemy who was in possession comes charging in, and that under the name of Christ. He can divide some of Christ's garments; but nobody will

divide that tunic, which *was woven from the top* (Jn 19:23). *They divided*, he says, *my garments among them, and over my vesture they cast lots* (Ps 22:18). And the evangelist says, *There was a tunic there, woven from the top, and they said to one another*, those who crucified the Lord: *Let us not divide it, but let us cast lots over it* (Jn 19:23-24). It wasn't put with the rest to be divided, that tunic was left out of the division. Why was that tunic left out of the division? Because *it was woven from the top*. Why was the garment which was *woven from the top* not suitable for division? Because it was intended as a sign. What does it mean that it is woven from the top? The same as why we are told "Lift up your hearts." And thus all who have their hearts lifted up, up to the top, cannot be divided into parts, because they will belong to that tunic which cannot be divided.

So then, my brothers and sisters, this tunic fell by lot to our Lord himself, Jesus Christ, because his lot is his inheritance.[48] And since it was his inheritance, he bought it. Those, however, who have been divided can belong to Christ's other garments, because he clothed himself with all.[49] All who believe in him, in some way or other he puts them all on. But any who are on the look-out for earthly honors, for temporal advantages, for bodily fancies, are not woven from the top, from above, because they desire worldly things.[50] So they, then, can be divided. That tunic, though, which *is woven from the top*, cannot be put in for division. Rejoice that you belong to it, you that are sprigs of the Catholic Church. Question your hearts, to see whether you are seeking from Christ the kingdom of heaven; not vanities, not temporal benefits, not bodily images, not things that give pleasure in this age and on this earth. When you've questioned yourselves, may your consciences give you the answer[51] that you "have lifted up your hearts." And if you really have lifted up your hearts, you are woven from the top, from above. If you are woven from the top, you cannot be divided.

NOTES

1. This excessively long title is that given both in the Mainz manuscript and in Possidius' *Index*. The words of the apostle are from Rom 11:33, and of the psalms are from Ps 60:1 and 119:71.

Dolbeau dates the sermon fairly confidently to February 404. According to one manuscript from the monastery of Lorsch near Mainz, it was preached at a place called Tignica, which was in the province of Proconsular Africa (Tunisia) on the southern route from Carthage to Hippo Regius, as distinct from the northerly coastal route. It was on the direct road from Carthage to Augustine's home town, Thagaste, so he would have been very familiar with it. The town (now Ain Tounga) had both a Catholic and a Donatist bishop, who were both present at the conference in Carthage in 411 (O. Perler, *Les Voyages de Saint Augustin*, 410-411).

2. There is here an "infection" of the Romans text from its parallel in Gal 3:22, *God has locked up all things under sin.* The phrase really used in Romans, as Augustine will shortly point out, is *in unbelief.* The infection very probably lay in the Tignica lectionary. Augustine had the correct word in his head, but of course had to explain the text his congregation had heard.

See Sermon 27, 7 (III, 2) for similar reflections on this text.

3. See Rom 11:33. For the theme of our all being fellow pupils under one master, one *magister*, see also Sermons 23, 1, note 5 (III, 2); 270, 1, note 3 (III, 7); and 340A, 4 (III, 9).

4. The passive infinitive, *Conjungi*; literally, "Let there be joined together," according, I suggest, to an idiom to be found, for example, in Rom 12:15. It may be more Greek than Latin, this use of the infinitive as a kind of general imperative; but the Latin versions translate the Greek literally, and so it could have become a manner of speaking characteristic of "Christian" Latin. Dolbeau, however, emends to the active imperative singular, *Conjunge*.

5. Dolbeau finds this passage very suspect, possibly from the state of the manuscript, though he doesn't say so. But if it is because of the identification of Adam with the whole human race, and the treating of the whole human race as one individual, this is fairly typical of Augustine. We have had him treating the whole human race as one gigantic invalid prostrate on the bed of the world. See Sermons 346A, 8 and 366, 2 (III, 10), where the human race, Adam, is seen as represented by the man who fell among thieves in the parable of the good Samaritan.

6. See 1 Cor 15:47-48.

7. The text here simply repeats the quotation *Before I was humbled* etc.; but I really think this must be a stenographer's or a copyist's mistake.

8. Or "it," that is, his mercy. Dolbeau suspects something wrong with the text here.

9. For this whole section see also Sermons 90A (in this volume); 349, 2: 361, 21; 385, 2 (III, 10).

10. Augustine and his hearers must have known instances of men, even of women, hating or at least intensely disliking their own children. But his unqualified statement of its impossibility would have passed unquestioned as legitimate rhetorical license.

11. His quotation from the psalm varies; he began with "and demolished us," *destruxisti nos*, although in commenting on the text he uses the phrase "dropped us," *deposuisti nos*. From now on he will stick to this latter. In his *Expositions of the Psalms*, on this verse of Ps 60, he has *destruxisti*, and comments on it: "You have demolished us in order to build us up, you have demolished us as badly built, demolished an empty building, to allow for the building of the new man." So Dolbeau suggests that *destruxisti*, "you have demolished," is the version Augustine was familiar with, the Hippo Regius version; while *deposuisti* was the version of the church of Tignica where he was preaching, and which the congregation had sung as a refrain; and so he switches by stages to that.

12. See Gn 2-3; Sir 10:12-13.

13. See Gn 1:26-27.

14. *Servi peculiosi*, slaves who have a substantial *peculium*, or savings account. It seems the formal juridical term for them was *peculiati* (Justinian's *Digest*, 19, 1; 13, 4 etc.). Dolbeau makes the interesting suggestion that this social fact of slaves being owned by other slaves (and thus being the lowest of the low) is the source of the papal title *Servus servorum Dei*. He says Augustine sometimes so describes himself, though he gives no reference, and I have been unable to find an instance. The first pope so to style himself as a matter of course was Gregory I, the Great, 200 years after Augustine; but the style is found in a bull of his predecessor John III in 570 (see old *Catholic Encyclopedia* under the entry "Servus servorum Dei"; the entry is omitted by the *New Catholic Encyclopedia*).

Notice, the word translated "master" is *dominus*, which we translate by "Lord," of course, when it refers to Christ or God. But one hardly pairs "lord" with "slave" in English.

15. *Carnalia*. But I'm sure he meant to say *corporalia*, "bodily things"—which is what I have in fact translated. *Carnalia* is too limited a word here, really only applicable to living creatures, in particular to human ones. The whole passage is a bit overloaded. He seems just to be rambling on.

16. *Lumina*; we don't in fact usually call our eyes our lights in English, though it has been done in poetry, and according to the Oxford English Dictionary is still good English slang.

17. Of course, only two of them were slaves; he's being a little careless. The only word that really fits what Augustine is doing here, it seems to me, is "bumbling."

18. See Sermon 346A, 8 (III, 10), last sentence.

19. He must, in the context, mean through whom we were made what we now are, that is, Christians.

20. The Latin *trado*, and the Greek word it translates, has this wide range of significance from betrayal to handing over ("extradition") to handing on ("tradition"), on which Augustine follows the example of Paul (see 1 Cor 11:23) in ringing all the changes.

21. See Mt 26:14-16.

22. See Sermons 52, 12, note 18 (III, 3), and 301, 5, note 12 (III, 8).

23. A novel, but surely deliberate, echo of the Lord's prayer; more obviously so in the Latin, which has the second person singular in both cases; here, *Venit regnum tuum*; in the prayer, *adveniat regnum tuum*.

24. This, surely, is where our speech properly ends. The Latin text, however, ends it where I have put the period. I thus attribute the second sentence to Augustine. One can see why some copyist or stenographer, or even editor, should have carried on "our speech" to this point; it's because he would have had in mind the uniqueness of Christ's virginal conception, which the preacher goes on, indeed, to talk about. But in fact what Augustine means here is that Christ was born of a woman (Gal 4:4), as we all are, and didn't take flesh, say, from the air or the earth, as Adam's flesh was taken at the beginning.

25. See the Apostles' Creed. See also Sermon 273, 9 (III, 8).

26. See Gn 1:27; 2:7.21-22. For the next sentence see Gn 3:1-7.

27. See Sermons 51, 3; 72A, 4 (III, 3).

28. See Mt 28:8-10; Jn 20:11-18; Lk 24:22-24.

29. See Ps 119:71.

30. See Sermon 360B, 17 (this volume).

31. The same as "Healer" in Latin; *salvator* from *salus*, "health, salvation." This long parenthesis, which begins here, comes in the Latin text after "Jesus Christ." I found it altogether too indigestible to leave it there in translation. Yet another piece of "bumbling," I fear, or stream of consciousness rambling.

32. The heretics he has in mind here are the Manichees and related Gnostic sects, from the Docetists of the second century on, who all disliked the whole idea of the incarnation.

33. See, for this theme of the reality of Christ's wounds and scars, Sermons 88, 2 (III, 3); 145A (III, 4); 242, 3 (III, 7); 362, 12; 375C, 3 (III, 10). The whole sentence is a non-sentence in the Latin too.

34. See Jn 9.

35. With some hesitation I am translating this as a question addressed to Augustine by his Manichee interlocutor. The Latin text treats it as a rhetorical question asked by Augustine. I just like to keep these pulpit conversations going as long as possible.

36. Reading *quodammodo* instead of the text's *quomodo*, "Thus, just as you are proud. . ." Dolbeau considers the whole passage to be suspect.

37. See Sir 18:30.

38. See Sermon 252, 9 (III, 7).

39. In the case of angels, made of some celestial material; in our case, transformed into it. See Sermons 126, 4; 127, 15; 130, 4 (III, 4); 360B, 21 (this volume).

40. See Gn 2:7.

41. See Sermons 38, 10 (III, 2); 346A, 2 (III, 10; 360B, 20 (this volume).

42. The text quoted is the promise repeated to Abraham after he had shown his obedient willingness to sacrifice his son Isaac. But Augustine, while seeming to realize this, since he goes on to mention Abraham reflecting on "this seed," also appears to be conflating it with the original promise of Gn 12:3.

43. See Mt 1:1-16.

44. See Gal 3:16. See also Sermons 113A, 10; 130, 3 (III, 4); 360A (this volume).

45. Reading *Ecce quomodo* instead of the text's *Ecce modo*, "There you are now."

46. A reference to the original Donatist charge that in the great persecution of 303-313 Catholic bishops had been *traditores*, had handed over the sacred scriptures to be burnt.

47. This is a passage from the psalm that is *not* in fact quoted in any of the passion narratives! Verses 7-8, "All who see me mock me," etc., and verse 18, "They divided my garments," etc., are quoted or alluded to in all the gospels, but not these verses 16-17.

48. See Ps 16:5-6. It was a commonplace interpretation of the undivided tunic that it signified the Church.

49. In becoming man, in assuming human nature, he clothed himself with all humanity, all human beings. More particularly, he put on all who call themselves Christians. One is reminded of Vatican II's Constitution on the Church, *Lumen Gentium*, chapter 1, paragraphs 14-16, on what one might call the various degrees of belonging to the people of God, and more specifically of the Council's Declaration on the Relationship of the Church to Non-Christian Religions, *Nostra Aetate*.

50. And thus are woven from the bottom, from below.

51. Reading, at Dolbeau's suggestion, *respondeat vobis conscientia vestra* instead of the text's *respondet. . .*, "your consciences give you the answer."

Dolbeau 10
SERMON 162C
Mainz 27

SERMON OF THE BLESSED AUGUSTINE
ON THE WORDS OF THE APOSTLE TO THE GALATIANS,
WHERE PAUL TAKES PETER TO TASK

Date: 397[1]

Justice and holiness can only come as graces from God

1. We know, brothers and sisters, and are confident with the certainty of charity, that you all give joyful thanks for us when you observe us conducting ourselves with justice.[2] It follows naturally, you see, that when God's holy ones see their high priests[3] living just lives, they should rejoice over their pastors, and in turn give them joy by the quality of their own lives. This is what we even now sang to the Lord our God with one voice and one heart: *May your high priests be clothed with justice, and your holy ones will exult exultantly* (Ps 132:9.16); seeing them clothed with justice, they will rejoice with genuine joy and totally sincere love, without a trace of fawning flattery. So then, in order that you may exultantly exult, we must see to it that we are clothed with justice, and set you good examples in every kind of good work.

But as you want to rejoice over us, you must pray for us. Justice, you see, has to be put on, exactly as we sang in the psalm. And who gives out this garment, but the one who brought out the first robe for the younger son, after he had strayed and gone to rack and ruin?[4] By the very fact of justice being represented as something to be put on, he indicated that we do not have it from ourselves.[5]

The faithful share with bishops the challenge of being Christians

2. *It behooves a bishop, therefore, to be irreprehensible* (1 Tm 3:2). But while it behooves a bishop to be irreprehensible, does that mean it is right for a Christian to be reprehensible? "Bishop" is a word coming from the Greek *episkopos*, which in ordinary English can be translated "superintendent" or "overseer." We are bishops, but together with you we are Christians.[6] We get our special name from overseeing, we get the name we all share in common

167

from anointing. If the anointing is something we share in common, so is the struggle, the wrestling match.[7] And why should we bishops oversee, if there is nothing good for us to see in you?

If Peter was at fault, bishops must not claim to be beyond criticism

3. . . . may be found. If that's what we wanted, if that is what we brazenly laid claim to,[8] falling flat on our faces, we would certainly be terrified by today's reading. We all heard, after all, when the apostle Paul's letter to the Galatians was being read: *When Peter came to Antioch, I withstood him to the face, because he was to blame* (Gal 2:11). Peter was to blame, and shall I brazenly have the nerve to claim that I am wholly beyond reproach? Shall I, a feeble sheep, not dread this whirlpool, when I see the ram drying out his fleece? He was strong enough to haul himself out of this whirlpool; if I, though, fall in, who will find me? So I will shun this swelling surge of water, I will not dive in, not hurl myself in, not even were I absolutely clear in my conscience that nothing could be found in me which men could take me to task for. The eyes of God are another matter, another matter altogether the eyes of the one to whom it was very truly said, *In your sight shall no one living be justified* (Ps 143:2).

And yet Peter, as we heard just now when the story was being read, was also taken to task by men. And so a truly Christian spirit should be a total stranger to this rash and brazen presumption of claiming to live such a life, that men at least can find nothing in it to take them to task for. Let a man too take me to task, if there is anything that calls for it; of course, of course he should take me to task; do so twice, if I take it badly the first time. Peter, you see, insured that he was only taken to task once, by putting up so calmly with his critic. He did not give an example, like Christ, of absolute perfection, but he did give one of total humility. He quietly accepted a rebuke from a man who did not precede him in the apostolate, but came after him.

I hope the apostle Paul will excuse me, but what he did was easy; what Peter did was difficult. We live surrounded by daily experience of this in human relationships; I've often seen a person taking someone to task, I'm not sure if I've ever seen anyone quietly putting up with being taken to task. So what Paul did was frank and straightforward enough, but what Peter did was more admirable. But I'm not sure if it's even more straightforward to notice someone else's fault than freely to admit one's own.

A misguided solution to the problem of Paul rebuking Peter:
that it was all a piece of make-believe

4. But it troubles some people that Peter is said to have been taken to task; it troubles them and they question it. They are not, however, to be dismissed out of hand, if it is not their own presumptuous conceit that troubles them, but their love of Peter. They refuse to believe that he really was taken to task; they consider this was all a pretense, a piece of make-believe put on for the eyes of

others. "One thing," they say, "was being done inwardly, another was being shown to the people." My dear man, you're reluctant to find fault with one of them, and you won't let me be reluctant to find both of them deceitful? Out of love of Peter you don't believe he was really criticized; it's because of your love for Peter that you don't believe he was taken to task; it's because of my love for Paul and for Peter that I believe he was. I refuse to believe about apostles that they could act in one way inwardly, and put on a pretense of something else for the people.

We are bishops; we are following in their footsteps to the best of our ability; I don't want us to be allowed to deceive you. If one thing is being done inwardly, some other pretense being put on for the people, won't all sanctity be something to fear? We neither wish to deceive you, nor to be deceived by you. I mean, if you think we may be deceiving you, and we think you may be deceiving us, where is the charity that believes all things? *Charity*, he says, *believes all things* (1 Cor 13:7). It is in order to be held onto that it believes, not in order to be taken in.

If this solution is accepted, the scriptures as a whole lose all credibility

5. But he answers, "What did Paul find to criticize in Peter?" What else but what he said himself, what he wrote himself? He himself composed a letter as a record, he left it to posterity to be read in the Church. What can I safely believe in the divine books, if I don't believe what is written in that letter? It's an apostolic letter, it's a canonical letter. It's a letter from Paul, who *labored more than them all; not he, though, but the grace of God with him* (1 Cor 15:10). So it's a letter from the grace of God. And if we recall who was speaking in him, it's a letter from Christ. *Or do you wish*, he says, *to have experience of the one who is speaking in me, Christ?* (2 Cor 13:3). Listen, and fear. He said "experience," not a pretense. But if you don't think that's enough, listen to his own public assertion, in which he even calls God to witness. This is how he started the tale of what he was going to point out, as though foreseeing that there would be some people who queried the truth of it: *But what I am writing to you*, he said, *see before God that I am not lying* (Gal 1:20). So then, when he calls God to witness like that, is he lying, seeing that without any calling of God to witness *the mouth that lies*, it says, *will kill*, not the body, but *the soul* (Wis 1:11)? I beg you, don't love Peter in such a way that you kill Paul. I beg you, don't let Paul be killed in the soul for Peter's sake; they were both killed together in the flesh for Christ's sake.

And yet again you question me and say, "What was it that Paul criticized in Peter?" And again I answer you, "Paul criticized in Peter what he said and wrote that he did." With God as his witness Paul tells us what he criticized in Peter; why ask me? The epistle is read to everyone; call it to mind with me: *When Peter*, he says, *came to Antioch, I withstood him to the face, because he was to blame. For before brothers came from James, he used to eat with Gentiles. But when they came, he withdrew, afraid of those who were from the circumcision;*

and the other Jews also pretended to agree with him, to the extent that even
Barnabas was won over to their pretense (Gal 2:11-13). There you are, you've
heard what Paul found to criticize in Peter. Let me explain, and with God's help
I will do this so that you may understand. I will do it, you see, not just for your
sake, but for the sake of those who are listening to both me and you.[9]

A comparison between the traditional sacraments of the Jews and the
heathen traditional rites of the Gentiles

6. The sacraments of the Jews, that is to say, circumcision, the sabbath rest,
the avoidance of certain kinds of food and the other things of that sort, were
given them from God, they were written in the law, they were ordained by God
as future sacraments for future times. These things were not like the abominable
sacrilegious rites of the Gentiles, these things were not the sacrifices of demons,
this was no kind of worship of idols. God had ordained this for his people
through Moses, the one God, the true God, the very God who said, *I am who
am* (Ex 3:14). But *after the fullness of time had come, God sent his Son, made
from a woman, made under the law*, because he too was circumcised. *From a
woman*, though, who was a virgin; since if it wasn't in fact in accordance with
Hebrew usage for a virgin too to be called a woman,[10] Eve would not at the
beginning have been fashioned as a woman.[11] So *after in the fullness of time
God had sent his Son, made of a woman*, having made the woman through him,
made under the law, having given the law through him, *in order to redeem those
who were under the law, that we might receive sonship by adoption* (Gal 4:4-5),
the shadows began to be no longer necessary with the coming of the light; but
just because they were no longer necessary, that doesn't mean that like the
sacrilegious rites of the Gentiles they were now to be condemned.

The Jew was not to be told, "Don't circumcise, because you have come to
believe in Christ," in the same way as the pagan who had become a Christian
was to be told, "Don't sacrifice to idols, because you have come to believe in
Christ." In fact, if you set these two things side by side, a sacrifice of the pagans
and a sacrament of the Jews, the first of these was never necessary, always
pernicious; while the second was at one time necessary, later on not necessary
but not yet pernicious to those from among the Jews who at that time accepted
the gospel. So while those sacraments too of the Jews were no longer necessary
after the coming of Christ, all the same the one who made them no longer
necessary had been foretold by their means, and so they were now to be
terminated with honor, not rejected and spurned with horror.

This being so, the apostle Paul, who had been particularly sent to preach the
gospel to the nations, had to take particular and deliberate[12] care to see that the
salvation of the nations was not in any way impeded by the sacraments of the
Jews. So with Christ speaking to this effect in him,[13] with God inspiring him
and revealing this to him, he decided that at that period, when the gospel was
still a novelty, none of the Jews should be forbidden for the time being the use
of these sacraments, none of the Gentiles be compelled to observe these sacra-

ments. Thus he hinted that they were like the remains of one's father so soon to decay, like bodies, no longer animated by the soul of prophecy, now ready to be conveyed with due respect and ceremony to the graveyard; and yet that because they were both unfamiliar and dead they were in no way to be laid upon Gentile shoulders.

What Paul criticized in Peter was his forcing Gentile Christians to judaize

7. So then, turn your attention to what at that time was sinful about those sacraments, for which Peter was taken to task; and assist my powers which are almost certainly less than adequate for shifting and solving this massive question, which then troubled the apostles themselves; but help me with it, I beg you. Yes, you've certainly had a great many things to listen to already; but as though you had just freshly come in, listen to what you want to hear even more, and I'll go on standing and speaking to you and feeling weak.[14] Certainly, since the problem has been practically put to you afresh, this, so it seems, is what my discourse should be about. Because now the man who was questioning me a short while ago, before I had explained as I wished, by telling the story, what it was that Paul found to criticize in Peter, has learned to be more careful, thanks to my account of the case; and this is what he now says: "If at that time on the one hand those who came from among the Jews were not required to forgo the practice of such sacraments, and on the other the Gentiles were not required to observe such sacraments, and Peter who was doing things like that was coming from the Jews, how could Paul have been right in criticizing him?"

Let me tell you, brothers and sisters, what the words of the text imply. What Paul found fault with in Peter was not that he was observing the Jewish sacraments, but that he was imposing them on those who came from the Gentiles.[15] Any Jew, you see, who at that time believed in Christ, if he wished to observe them was not forbidden to do so; and if he didn't wish to he wasn't forced to. But any from among the Gentiles who had come to believe—when would he ever wish to be circumcised, since he was told that this was not necessary for salvation? The Jews themselves, in all probability, would scarcely ever be circumcised, unless they had undergone this as babies. But what was there to compel Gentiles to observe these sacraments, over which we have said that Peter was taken to task by Paul—suppose somebody were to ask what there was to compel him to it? Were they to be grabbed against their will, tied down and circumcised? Ridiculous! So what was there to compel them to it, what can we suppose there was, but saying to them, "You people cannot be saved, unless you observe the precepts of the law, like the Jews"? Given such a condition, of course, because they were seeking salvation, and were told that they could not otherwise attain to salvation, they were being compelled to observe those sacraments unwillingly, not because they loved them, but because they desired salvation.

8. So that compromise, by which neither Jews were to be forbidden nor Gentiles to be compelled, was kept by the apostles and decreed by a council.

When this issue, you see, was agitating many people, troubling many people, a meeting was held in Jerusalem, and when all the apostles had assembled and the elders of the Church, that is, the presbyters and any preachers of the gospel and those in charge of Churches, it was enacted by common consent, under the Lord's inspiration of course, that these things were neither to be forbidden to the Jews nor forced on the Gentiles. Many will recall that this is all written in the Acts of the Apostles;[16] those who don't recall it should read it. So this was a very very moderate, very very religious, very very careful compromise. If it had been ordained that these things were to be immediately given up and rejected, in the same way as sacrifices to idols were to be, then people wouldn't believe that the one who had laid them down was the true God.

So this is what Paul criticized in Peter: not that he was himself observing these things, but that he was forcing the Gentiles to do so. How was he forcing them to? By agreeing, even though he only pretended to, with those who were saying that the Gentiles could not otherwise be saved, unless they kept the Jewish sacraments. This too is written in the Acts of the Apostles, the story's told in the same book: *There came*, it says, *to Antioch some people from James*, that is from Jerusalem, Jews, that is to say, who had already come to believe in Christ, and they started saying to the brethren who had come from the Gentiles, *You cannot otherwise be saved, unless you keep the precepts of the law* (Acts 15:1). That is certainly compelling them, saying that they cannot otherwise be saved.

Observance of the Mosaic law not necessary for salvation

9. Against this the apostle Paul campaigned with the most unflagging zeal. He moved aside this boulder of dreadful pressure, to let the unfortunate Gentiles finally rise again, as though from the tomb of Lazarus.[17] I mean, if he had been finding fault with this observance itself, and not with compulsion, he would have been finding fault with himself, because he too upheld them, and celebrated some Jewish sacraments with some Jews in the temple in Jerusalem. But he was observing them as a man coming from among the Jews, not forcing them on the Gentiles. Paul, coming from among the Jews, the preacher of the gospel to the nations, who took part in enacting the holy resolution of the apostles[18] and faithfully carried it out, showed even more by his example what the pleasure of the Holy Spirit was on this kind of issue, what he had enacted and laid down.

Because James, you see, said to him when he had already arrived in Jerusalem, "Many people are convinced that you oppose the usages of our fathers, and are a foe and enemy of the law. So what is the case? Listen to me. There are some men here who have come to undertake a purification. Be purified with them, so that all may know"—it doesn't say "so that all may think"; an act of devotion, you see, was being enjoined on him, not a piece of make-believe being suggested—"so that all," he said, "may know that you are zealous for the law and our ancestral observances."[19] Paul did this as a Jew among Jews, not however in order to be justified through these sacraments, but so as not to be thought to condemn them.

10. So he did this too. Because he also circumcised Timothy, who was born of a Jewish mother, to avoid the Jews being scandalized. He did this, with Timothy willingly agreeing, not being forced into it, to show through him too that he did not condemn these rites, but neither did he impose them on Gentiles as being necessary for salvation. But after he had circumcised Timothy with that impartiality which I have often commended to you, and which I imagine is now properly appreciated by you, some from among the Jews, who had not shed that old skin, and for that reason wanted the Gentiles to be circumcised, because they said there could be no salvation for them without those sacraments—and a heresy has arisen from this position; because even today there are some who both believe in Christ and circumcise their sons, believing, that is to say, that without these sacraments they cannot have salvation.[20] So when he had circumcised Timothy out of this dutiful impartiality, not out of necessity, some of them, as I was saying, who made salvation depend on these things, which vexed Paul and for which he took Peter to task, began to boast, in order to take in others, that Paul too held this opinion. They went round saying, "He too believes what we have been saying all along, that there can be no salvation without these sacraments. After all, if he doesn't believe this, why did he circumcise Timothy?"

When Paul heard this, Paul who had done this freely, not out of necessity, to avoid scandalizing the Jews, not to ensure Timothy's salvation, he saw that they had used it as an opportunity to preach another gospel,[21] and to spread nasty suspicions about Paul; and so he refused to circumcise Titus. But now it's clear why he wished to circumcise that one, refused to circumcise this one: that one to avoid scandalizing the Jews, this one to deny people the opportunity of spreading their wrongheaded belief.

The different cases of Timothy and Titus

11. And in this very letter of his, notice how plainly and clearly he presents the matter. *But neither was Titus,* he says, *since he was a Greek,* like Timothy,[22] *compelled to be circumcised.* And as though he were asked, "Why wasn't Titus compelled to be circumcised, since Timothy, likewise being a Greek, was compelled to be circumcised?" Why not? Do you want to hear? *Because of false brethren slyly brought in, who crept in to spy out our freedom* (Gal 2:3-4). So in the circumcising of Timothy it was not necessity at work, but freedom, while what was criticized in Peter was necessity, not freedom. *Because of false brethren,* he says, *slyly brought in, who crept in to spy out our freedom, in order to reduce us to slavery.* They would reduce us to slavery, he is saying, by turning freedom into necessity, *to whom we did not give in or submit for a single moment.* So that what? *So that the truth of the gospel might remain at your disposal* (Gal 2:4-5). What is *the truth of the gospel*? That Jews at that time were not to be forbidden, Gentiles not to be compelled; that the sacraments of the Jews were not to be condemned for the Jews nor to be imposed on the Gentiles. What is *the truth of the gospel*? That it is possible without those sacraments to attain to salvation through Christ.

This was what those people were denying, with whom Peter pretended to agree. That's why he adds, *Other Jews pretended to agree with him, to the extent that even Barnabas was brought over to their pretense. But when I saw*, he says, *that they were not marching straight in tune with the truth of the gospel* (Gal 2:13-14)—as he said in that other place, *that the truth of the gospel might remain at your disposal* (Gal 2:5). You hear truth being insisted on everywhere, and everywhere you suspect intrigue; so much everywhere, that even among the apostles. So he saw *that they were not marching straight in tune with the truth of the gospel.* Over and above this, he saw that the Gentiles were beginning to think that those sacraments were necessary for their salvation. This is not *the truth of the gospel.* These things were not any longer necessary for salvation; perhaps they had been once upon a time, when they were foretelling the Christ to come. Once upon a time a stone knife had been necessary, before the stone itself came.[23]

The difference between Paul and Peter

12. *I*, he says, *when I saw that they were not marching straight in tune with the truth of the gospel, I said to Peter in the presence of them all.* "I said to Peter," Paul to Peter, the lesser to the greater, the follower to the leader; both "I said," and "to Peter," and "in the presence of them all." Great confidence indeed, but great patience too on the other's part. Since you've gained our rapt attention, let us hear, Paul, what you said to Peter, and where. Let us understand what you did, what you had in mind, because in no case was it your intention to be a liar. *I said to Peter*, he tells us, *in the presence of them all: "If you, while being a Jew"*—what's "while being a Jew"? One who was allowed to observe these things anyhow—*"live like a Gentile and not like a Jew"*—because *before some people came from James, he used to eat with the Gentiles—"if you, while being a Jew, live like a Gentile and not like a Jew"*—he ought to have gone on and said, "how is it that you are now keeping Jewish sacraments?" That's not what he did say, but on the point on which he was to blame, from which all this trouble arose, on which he was zealous for God because he was exerting himself to remove this blockage from the gospel, on that point he said with confidence, on that point he said in the presence of them all, *"If you, while being a Jew, live like a Gentile, how is it that you are forcing the Gentiles to judaize?"* (Gal 2:12-14).

"You are forcing them," he said, "*to judaize.*" I have already said how you are forcing the Gentiles to judaize; it's by consenting to those who said that the Gentiles could not otherwise gain salvation. This was something Paul did not do, when he took the purifications on himself with some men;[24] he did not force the Gentiles to judaize when he circumcised Timothy, who was fully aware that it made no difference, because *circumcision is nothing and uncircumcision is nothing* (1 Cor 7:19). He did not force the Gentiles to judaize. And in case he should be thought of as so forcing them, he didn't circumcise Titus. Paul did not force the Gentiles to judaize. This was something he did not do himself, and

therefore he was quite right to take Peter to task for this, because he did not do it himself.

The dreadful consequences of supposing
that Paul was not telling the truth here

13. But let's suppose that he too had done this, although there is no evidence at all for this, let alone proof. I'm not saying this as what I think myself; but in accordance with certain people,[25] if I may say it for the time being, let us assume that Paul had done what Peter had done, and that Paul was finding fault with Peter for what he himself, Paul, had also done. It is easier to allow that they both needed correcting, than to let that detestable moth creep in among us, that is to say, lying or the suspicion of lying. This is like a malignant little grub, ready to gnaw away at every page of scripture. I dread the thought of its persuading us that Paul lied about something in his canonical letter, which he entrusts to the Church so widely extended by succeeding generations. I beg you all; fear this evil, let us all fear it, or later on we may all be wringing our hands in vain. It is no slight evil, this; I'm warning you, fearful myself I'm trying to put the fear of God into you. Pardon my anxiety; I have fewer chances of addressing you than you would like.

Those people who find your ears ready can whisper into them whenever they like, while I, on the other hand, only occasionally have the chance to speak to you, and only from this place. I'm not saying they are evil-minded, I don't wish to insult them; but beware of their mistaken ideas, and deal with them in such a way that they, rather, may be straightened out instead of you getting twisted up by them. You see, when they say this sort of thing to you: "Peter put on an act of doing this, Paul put on an act of rebuking him; Paul wasn't telling the truth in his letter when he wrote that Peter *was at fault* (Gal 2:11); Paul wasn't telling the truth in his letter, when he wrote that he saw *that they were not marching straight in tune with the truth of the gospel*; Paul was not telling the truth in his letter when he wrote that Peter *was forcing the Gentiles to judaize* (Gal 2:14); but it was all an act, a pretense"; what shall we be able to hold onto as true, what page of scripture will we still have that is not under suspicion of lying?

14. Look, the weight of the plainest possible authority is being brought to bear on us, mere human beings—and still they won't yield to the thunder and lightning of the truth! Where are we to turn? What are we to do, when I say to someone, maybe, "It is good to marry, but it is better not to marry, as the apostle Paul wrote,"[26] if someone who condemns marriage then says to me, "Paul most certainly did condemn marriage; but he was only pretending when he wrote this, since the truth itself could not be borne by the weak; it's because continence can only be undertaken with great hardship that he said, It is good to marry; because in fact he knew that it's bad to marry"?

How can you prove that Paul was lying when he said, *Anyone who gives a girl in marriage does well* (1 Cor 7:28)?

"How can I prove it?" he says. "Just as he was lying when he said, *When I saw that he was not marching straight in tune with the truth of the gospel*—it wasn't the case, you see, that Peter was not marching straight in tune with the truth of the gospel; like, *I said to Peter in the presence of them all: If you, while being a Jew, live like a Gentile and not like a Jew, how can you force the Gentiles to judaize?* (Gal 2:14)—Peter was not in actual fact forcing the Gentiles to judaize. So just as Paul was pretending over these matters, so too, when he saw that the excellence of virginity could not be kept up by carnal people, he said, *Whoever gives a girl in marriage does well.* He was really holding one view, pretending to hold another."

If that's how things are, where can we turn to, what oracles can we consult? That, after all, is what the divine utterances entrusted to us in the canonical scriptures ought to be for us, as they really are oracles. Is deception to be feared in the very place where truth is to be found, where truth is to be presumed? I beseech you, keep an eye out for this little moth, be on your guard against it; don't let it into the linen cupboards of your hearts. If you do let it in, unless you give the linen a good shake-out at once, you won't find anything there that is not moth-eaten.

The difference between the canonical scriptures
and any other writings of Christian authors

15. I have said what I thought had to be said with great solicitude. I have long kept hold of your love, solicitude for you has long kept its hold on me. Everything written in the holy canonical books, well, we who engage in public debates and write books write in a very different fashion; we make progress as we write, we are learning every day, engaged in research as we dictate, knocking at the door[27] as we speak. Certainly, I won't keep quiet, if I can help it, where I can be useful to the brethren both by speaking and by writing. I solemnly admonish your graces,[28] don't even think of regarding as canonical scripture any debate, or written account of a debate by anyone. In the holy writings we learn how to judge, in our own writings we are quite ready to be judged. What of course we would prefer, and this would be our choice between the two options,[29] is that in writing or speaking we should always say what is true, never go wrong.

But since this is difficult to achieve, that's why there is this other firmament of the canon, like the heaven in which are set the luminous bodies of the scriptures, a firmament as it were between waters and waters, between the peoples of angels and the peoples of men; those above, these below.[30] Let us treat scripture like scripture, like God speaking; don't let's look there for man going wrong. It is not for nothing, you see, that the canon has been established for the Church. This is the function of the Holy Spirit. So if anybody reads my book, let him pass judgment on me. If I have said something reasonable, let him follow, not me, but reason itself; if I've proved it by the clearest divine testimony, let him follow, not me, but the divine scripture.

If, on the other hand, he wishes to find fault with me for something I have said quite correctly, he is not in fact acting correctly; but still I get angrier with that kind of fan of mine who takes my book as being canonical, than with the man who finds fault in my book with things that are not in fact at fault. I implore you; although I can see that you are as keenly attentive as if you had only this moment arrived, as if you were only now beginning to hear the sermon, still I don't want to say any more, so that you may hold all the more firmly onto this last thing that I have said.

Turning to the Lord, etc.

NOTES

1. The title is as given in Possidius' *Index*. The text here adds: "Where first of all he teaches what sort of person a bishop should be." This is the title Bede gives to his extract from this sermon in his anthology of patristic texts on Paul's epistles. The Mainz manuscript is defective near the beginning, and Dolbeau takes section 2 from Bede, to fill a small portion of what was probably quite a large gap.

The sermon in the Mainz collection is one of a trio, of which the other two have already appeared in these volumes: Sermon 133, "On the words of John's gospel, 7:2-10, where Jesus had said he was not going up to the festival day, and yet went up"; and Sermon 89, "On the words in the gospel of Matthew, 21:12-19, where Jesus caused the tree to wither; and about those in Lk 24:20, where he pretended he was going on further." Thus all three are on a common theme of difficult texts, in which either Jesus himself seems to be "economical with the truth," or Paul, as interpreted by reputable Church authorities, notably Jerome, is assumed to have perpetrated a "useful lie."

On the latter point, the issue dealt with in this sermon, Augustine had a long, in some ways farcical, argument with Jerome, all conducted by letters among which the crucial ones either went astray, or were only delivered several years after being written. In the course of the correspondence Jerome got extremely cross, and in consequence rude, while Augustine remained unfailingly polite and deferential all through, but firmly insistent that Jerome was wrong. There is an excellent account of the whole episode in an old book by Hugh Pope, O.P., called *Saint Augustine of Hippo* (Sands & Co, London, l937). See his chapter, "St Augustine the letter writer," section III, "Letters that went astray" (page 209). The letters, which include those from both correspondents, are the following: from Augustine to Jerome, 28 (394-5), 40 (398), 67 (402), 71 (404-5), 73, (404-5), 82 (405), 167 (415); from Jerome to Augustine, 39 (397), 68 (402-3), 72 (403-4), 75 (404), 81 (405), 123 (410), 172 (416), 195 (418), 202 (419).

Lambot dates the sermon to May/June 397, between the feast of Pentecost on 24 May that year, and the Birth of John the Baptist, on 24 June. The three sermons were presumably preached on three consecutive days, and most likely in Carthage.

2. "We" and "us" here are all the bishops. They were gathering in Carthage for a council to be held shortly, or perhaps it had already begun.

3. God's holy ones: he actually says *sancti Dei*, God's saints, meaning the lay faithful, who are called in the old Roman canon *plebs sancta Dei*, God's holy people. The "high priests" he mentions are of course the bishops. But the word he uses, quoting from the psalm, is simply *sacerdotes*. To translate this just by "priests," however, would be misleading, as it was *not* at that time a term applied to presbyters, who are the rank of clergy we nowadays automatically mean by "priests." This word has, in fact, become misleadingly equivocal, serving to render both *presbyter* (which simply means "elder," though the English word "priest" is derived from it), and *sacerdos*, the sacred functionary "appointed to act on behalf of men in relation to God, to offer gifts and sacrifices for sins" (Heb 5:1). At that time, and still for a century or two to come, only bishops were so referred to.

4. See Lk 15:11-22. The first robe was traditionally interpreted as signifying primordial innocence.

5. Here is where the big gap in the text begins, one or more of the leaves of the manuscript having been torn out or otherwise destroyed. The next section is taken from Bede's anthology.

6. See Sermon 340, 1, note 6, a sermon preached on the anniversary of his episcopal ordination: "For you I am a bishop, with you I am a Christian. The first is the name of an office undertaken, the second the name of a grace; that one means danger, this one salvation." This is quoted in the Second Vatican Council's dogmatic constitution on the Church, *Lumen Gentium*, 32; in the chapter on the laity, curiously enough, not in that on the hierarchy, where it surely belongs.

7. An allusion to the practice of athletes, especially wrestlers, oiling their bodies before a match; this was the symbolism implied in the anointing of catechumens with oil in the rites leading up to baptism. But the chief anointing we all share, making us partakers of Christ's own anointing and thus "Christ-ians," is that received in the sacrament of confirmation, when we are anointed with chrism. It is implied, Augustine is saying, in the very name of "Christ-ian."

8. Presumably to be exempt, as bishops, from all censure or criticism coming from the people, from "God's holy ones."

9. Evidently Augustine was really talking here to a genuine "objector" in the congregation, not just having one of his typical conversations with an imaginary interlocutor. Yet at the beginning of section 7 below, it looks as if the man had put his difficulty to Augustine *before* the sermon. It is not easy to reconstruct the actual *mise en scène*.

10. But not in accordance with Latin usage for a *virgo* to be called *mulier*, any more than it would be with English usage to call a virgin a "wife"; compare the traditional contrast between "maid and wife." See Sermons 49A, note 2, and 52, 10.

11. See Gn 2:22.

12. An attempt to get the meaning of *praecipua voti cura*. I do not really understand what the *voti* signifies.

13. See 2 Cor 13:3.

14. They were all standing—except the other bishops and the bishop of Carthage himself, seated in the apse. If Augustine had been preaching in his own Church of Hippo Regius, he would have been seated on his *cathedra*. He has been speaking for four and a half columns, say between 20 minutes and half an hour; and he will go on for another six and a half, about another three quarters of an hour. But I wonder, in view of what he is just going to say about the new formulation of the difficulty, whether there wasn't perhaps a short break in the proceedings.

Was he just feeling weak, or actually feeling ill? It is a very odd little sentence: *et ego stans loquor vobis et infirmor.*

15. See Gal 2:14.

16. See Acts 15. Augustine is wrong, it would seem, in assuming that the matter at issue betwen Paul and Peter when Peter came to Antioch, as described in Galatians, was the same as the one settled when Paul and Barnabas went to Jerusalem, as described in Acts. What was settled at Jerusalem was that Gentiles were not to be obliged to be circumcised or to observe any of the "sacraments" of the law. What was at issue between Paul and Peter at Antioch was, it seems, only the dietary laws: Peter siding with those stricter Jewish Christians who would not sit at table with their Gentile brethren—and hence would not share in the eucharist with them—because they were not eating *kosher* food. This was to put pressure on them to observe all the dietary laws about clean and unclean foods, to "judaize" as Paul puts it in Gal 2:14.

He also seems to be treating as one and the same "judaizing mission" to Antioch from Jerusalem, "certain people coming from Judaea" in Acts 15:1, and "certain people coming from James" in Gal 2:12. In fact he goes on to misquote Acts 15:1 by conflating it with Gal 2:12.

17. See Jn 11:38-41.

18. At the council in Jerusalem, Acts 15.

19. He is quoting very freely and inaccurately from Acts 21:18-26, mixing in echoes from 15:13 and 28:17.

20. The heresy of the Ebionites in the first century or so after Christ. They must have been a tiny

sect in Augustine's time. He mentions them in his book on *Heresies*, written at the request of the deacon Quodvultdeus about 418.

21. See Gal 1:7.

22. Here Augustine is wrong; it was precisely because Timothy was Jewish on his mother's side that Paul was prepared to circumcise him. Titus was a Greek, a Gentile pure and simple. Nor, in fact, does Paul put the matter all that plainly and clearly; as he breaks off, characteristically, in the middle of a sentence, he leaves it in doubt as to whether in fact Titus was or was not eventually circumcised. Augustine thinks it is clear that he was not; Bishop Lightfoot in his commentary (London, reprint of 10th edition, 1896) agrees, though with less assurance, and suggests that the unfinished sentence ended, in Paul's mind, something like this: "But because of false brethren . . . those who were reputed to be something (v. 6) put pressure on us to have him circumcised"; and not, as other commentators have suggested, "But because of false brethren. . ., we did eventually circumcise him."

23. See Jos 5:2-3, where Joshua circumcises the people with stone (flint) knives; and Acts 4:11, 1 Pt 2:7, where Christ is called the stone which the builders rejected. The Latin, however, says "a rock knife," *cultellus petrinus*, and "before the rock itself came," this being an allusion, rather, to 1 Cor 10:4, Christ the spiritual rock.

24. See Acts 21:26.

25. I suppose he must have had Jerome in mind.

26. See 1 Cor 7:28.

27. See Lk 11:9.

28. I here leave out a phrase, *a me, usque ad me*, "by (from?) me, as far as me," which makes dubious sense in itself and hardly fits, even awkwardly, into the sentence. It looks to me like a marginal scribble—the reader underlining the probability that Augustine was primarily thinking of his own works—which has then been clumsily inserted in an inappropriate place.

29. Of being judged (criticized), I presume, and being always right.

30. See Gn 1:6.8.14.

SERMON 198

DISCOURSE OF AUGUSTINE THE BISHOP AGAINST THE PAGANS

Date: 404[1]

The pagan celebration of New Year

1. I would urge your graces, since I observe that you have come together here today as if it were a feast, and have gathered for this particular day in greater numbers than usual, to fix most firmly in your memories what you sang just now. Don't let it be a case of noisy tongues and dumb minds; rather, what your voices have been shouting in one another's ears, let your feelings cry out in the ears of God. This, after all, is what you were singing: *Save us, Lord our God, and gather us from among the nations, that we may confess your holy name* (Ps 106:47).

And now, if the festival of the nations which is taking place today in the joys of the world and the flesh,[2] with the din of silly and disgraceful songs, with the celebration of this false feast day[3]—if the things the Gentiles are doing today do not meet with your approval, you will be gathered from among the nations.

Three sentiments of the soul: believing, hoping, loving

2. You were certainly singing—and the sound of the divine song must still be echoing in your ears—*Save us, Lord our God, and gather us from among the nations.* Can you be gathered from among the nations without being saved, made safe and sound? So those who mix with the nations are not safe and sound, while those who are gathered from among the nations are made safe with the soundness of faith, a spiritual soundness, the soundness of the promises of God, the soundness of a good hope, the soundness of the most genuine charity.

So if you believe, hope, and love, it doesn't mean that you are immediately to be declared safe and sound and saved. It makes a difference, you see, what you believe, what you hope for, what you love. Nobody in fact can live any style of life without those three sentiments of the soul, of believing, hoping, loving. If you don't believe what the nations believe, and don't hope for what the nations

180

hope for, and don't love what the nations love, then you are gathered from among the nations. And don't let your being physically mixed up with them alarm you, when there is such a wide separation of minds. What after all could be so widely separated as that they believe demons are gods, you on the other hand believe in the God who is the true God? That they hope for the vanities of this age, you hope for eternal life? That they love the world, you love the world's architect?

So if you believe something different from them, hope for something different, love something different, you should prove it by your life, demonstrate it by your actions. Are you going to join today in the celebration of good luck presents[4] with a pagan, going to play at dice with a pagan, going to get drunk with a pagan? How in that case are you really believing something different, hoping for something different, loving something different? How can you keep your countenance as you sing *Save us, Lord our God, and gather us from among the nations*? You're segregated from the nations, after all, when you mix physically with the nations, but differ in your style of life. And you can see how wide apart this segregation sets you, if only you act accordingly to prove it.

It's like this: our Lord Jesus Christ, the Son of God, who became man for us, has already paid the price for us. And so if he has already paid the price, the reason he paid it was to redeem us, to gather us from among the nations. But if you get mixed up with the nations, it means you don't want to follow the one who redeemed you. Instead, you are mixing with them in lifestyle, actions, mind and heart by hoping for such things, believing such things, loving such things. You are being ungrateful to your Redeemer, you are not acknowledging the price paid for you, the blood of the Lamb without blemish. So in order to follow your Redeemer, who redeemed you with his blood, don't mix with the nations by the same kind of morals and actions. They give good luck presents; see to it that you *give alms* (Lk 11:41).

You see, I'm not telling you, brothers and sisters, "They give, don't you go giving"; on the contrary, give more than they do, but like people who believe something different, hope for something different, love something different. Because I'm not telling you, "They believe, don't you believe; they hope, don't you hope; they love, don't you love." Rather I'm telling you, "They believe that; as for you, believe this. They hope for that; as for you, hope for this. They love that; as for you, love this. They give that sort of thing, or to that sort of person; as for you, give this sort of thing or to this sort of person." So then, they give good luck presents; as for you, *give alms*. They entertain themselves with lascivious songs; as for you, entertain yourselves with the words of the scriptures.[5] They run off to the theater, you people to church; they are getting drunk; you see to it that you fast. If you do all this, you have genuinely sung *Save us, Lord our God, and gather us from among the nations*.

What demons, masquerading as gods, take pleasure in;
and what the martyrs and true Christians do

3. At this moment, of course, those who are happy to hear what I have been saying are standing all together with those who are not so happy to hear it; and yet the former have already been gathered from among the nations, the latter are still mixed in with the nations. I am now speaking to real Christians; if you believe what the nations, the Gentiles, believe, if you hope for what the Gentiles hope for, if you love what the Gentiles love, then by all means live as the Gentiles live. But if you believe something else, hope for something else, love something else, then live in another kind of way, and prove how vastly different your faith and hope and charity are by the vast difference of your morals.

What is it that the Gentiles believe? As I have already said, the beings they call gods have been shown to us by the apostle Paul in a different light: *For what the Gentiles sacrifice,* he says, *they sacrifice to demons and not to God. I do not wish you to become the associates of demons* (1 Cor 10:20). So their morals give pleasure to their gods. But the man who said *I do not wish you to become the associates of demons* wished us to set ourselves apart in life from those who serve demons. Now those demons take pleasure, don't they, in idle songs, they take pleasure in the trifling chatter and manifold indecencies of the theaters, in the mad frenzy of the chariot races,[6] in the cruelty of the amphitheater, in the unrelenting rivalries of those who take up quarrels and disputes, to the point of open hostilities, on behalf of pestilential persons, on behalf of a comedian, an actor, a clown, a charioteer, a hunter. When they do these things, it's as though they were offering incense to demons from their hearts. These spirits, you see, given to seduction, rejoice in the people they have seduced, and feed on the bad morals and shameful and shocking lifestyle of those they have seduced and deceived.

But now, suppose you say to a man, "You love that chariot jockey, don't you?" and he answers, "I most certainly do," because should he deny it, he can be caught out fancying him, shouting for him, quarreling for him. And suppose you add, "You dote on him, in fact," he will answer, "I definitely do." If you then say to him, "May you turn out like him, and your sons too," he will immediately take umbrage, if he is to all appearances a respectable man, and answer you, "Why are you insulting me?"

"I insulting you, when I say, 'May you turn out like him'? Aren't you, rather, insulting yourself when you dote on the sort of man you are horrified at the thought of resembling?"

You people, on the other hand, all love the martyrs. So then, just as you say to a pagan, "You love this chariot jockey, don't you?" and he unblushingly replies, "I do," now say to a Christian, "You love Cyprian, don't you?" and he answers, "I do." Then say to him, "May you turn out like him," and he will answer, "Oh, if only God would grant me that!"

How genuine this love is, how chaste, how sure of itself, especially when directed to one who has already received the victor's crown! Because love of one who is still wrestling is filled with anxiety. But all the same, they are all loved in the one who has already overcome, who is already seated at the right hand of the Father, is already not only watching them from up above as they wrestle, but also helping them as they endure and persevere, as the promoter of that contest which Paul mentions.[7]

Genuine Christian love; fear is the servant of charity

4. And so it is that many people will be wrestling today with their consciences over the words they've heard. I said, you see, "Don't give good luck presents, give to the poor." It's little enough that you should give that much, you should give even more. You don't want to give more? At least give that much.

But you say to me, "When I give good luck presents, I too receive them."

So what then? When you give to the poor, don't you receive anything? Certainly, I trust, you wouldn't be believing what the Gentiles believe; you wouldn't, I trust, be hoping for what the Gentiles hope for; you wouldn't, I trust, be loving what the Gentiles love. Look, if you say you get nothing back when you give something to the poor, you've joined the Gentile party, you've had no reason to sing *Save us, Lord our God, and gather us from among the nations* (Ps 106:47). You've forgotten what will be said to those who have given: *Come, blessed of my Father, receive the kingdom,* and what will be said to those who haven't: *Go into the everlasting fire which has been prepared for the devil and his angels* (Mt 25:34.41).

If he gave those the kingdom in such a way that he gave these nothing, but just left them alone, you still ought to have loved what he gives, and been unwilling to do yourself out of such a stupendous and inexpressible good. It's not, however, the case that he simply sends those off to the kingdom and not these; he also says to these, *Go into the everlasting fire, which has been prepared for the devil and his angels.* You are being herded by fear and love. If you don't love what you are being promised very much, fear what you are being threatened with. By being afraid of gehenna, you do what you are told to, and as long as you do it out of fear, you do it as a slave, while when you do it lovingly, you do it as a free person. Be a good slave, in order to earn your freedom. Start fearing the one you should love, and when you have begun to love him, you won't fear him anymore. You see, it's written, *There is no fear in charity, but perfect charity casts fear outside* (1 Jn 4:17-18). It's the apostle John who says this.

But if perfect charity casts fear outside, let fear first of all take possession of the breast; charity will be born there, and thus, to the extent that charity grows, fear decreases; to the extent that she expands, he diminishes;[8] when she reaches perfection, he goes out of the door. You see, *there is no fear in charity, but perfect charity casts fear outside.* If you love, you do this;[9] if you don't yet love, do it out of fear. But if you neither fear nor love, you will have no cause to sing, *Save us, Lord our God, and gather us from among the nations.* You yourselves, in that case, are still Gentiles, still the nations, *bearing the yoke with unbelievers* (2 Cor 6:14).

Do yourself for the pagans what your Lord did for you, because when the

Lord did it for you, you weren't yet a Christian. Let them hear, willy-nilly, what I'm saying, those who believe something else, hope for something else, love something else; as for us, let us say what we know. Let them do what they like, let them just realize that they don't get off scot-free with whatever they do. There is due payment, after all, not only for good deeds, but also for bad ones. Payment for bad deeds is called punishment, for good ones a prize.[10]

Try to become a little more like Christ by fasting today for the pagans

5. So what was it that your Lord did for you, before you were a Christian? He suffered for you. And what does he say in the Psalms? *But I, when they were troublesome to me, clothed myself in sacking, and I humbled my soul with fasting* (Ps 35:13). If you take it in a figurative sense, the Lord was, so to say, fasting by not taking the godless into his body. And he was hungry from that fasting when, not finding any fruit on that tree, he cursed it, and it withered away.[11] What's the meaning of *I clothed myself in sacking*? As though to say, "I concealed my power within the weakness of the flesh and presented that same mortal flesh to the eyes of my persecutors." It was in that flesh, after all, which he took on from our stale old mortality without any sin of his own, that *he was bearing our sins* (1 Pt 2:24; Is 53:4.12). And sacking, of course, refers to sins because of sackcloth being made from the hair of the goats which will be placed on the left hand side,[12] unless they have first crossed over into the Lamb.

So then, in that *form of a slave* (Phil 2:7) he committed no sin, and thus owed no debt to death; but all the same he paid back on our account what he didn't owe himself, in order to release us from our debt. He was carrying our price in that sacking. Sacking, you see, is what sacks or little bags are made from.[13] But he was carrying our huge price in the sack he clothed himself with and presented to his persecutors, whose godlessness he fasted from, thus humbling his soul. Finally, as he was hanging on the cross, the sacking was ripped open with a lance, and the price of the whole wide world flowed out. So your Lord suffered for you before you were a Christian, in order to buy you and enable you to become a Christian.

6. But what does scripture say? *Just as he laid down his life for us, so we too ought to lay down our lives for the brethren* (1 Jn 3:16). If we cannot yet suffer for the Gentiles, we can at least fast for the Gentiles. What a long way away you are from imitating your Lord! Even when you fast, how far you still are from doing that! And it would be good for you to draw a little nearer. But how you shudder at the prospect of that perfection, fearing as you do the first step up toward it, a step so close to you, and such a low one! This step is practically at ground level—I really don't know if it can be called a step—and yet you are reluctant to step up onto it.

Is it such a big deal, after all, fasting at this time of year, putting off your dinner till the evening of such a short day?[14] It's no big deal at all, not in the least difficult or demanding. Preoccupation with some business matter frequently compels you to do what you aren't prepared to offer up to God out of devotion. Because the Church of God wants you to fast, you don't want to. If you were playing in a game of chance, you would be fasting, and fasting in order not to get up from the game beaten.[15] In order to win, afraid of being beaten by a man in a matter of money, you fast; and you don't fast, afraid of being beaten by the devil in your heart. I mean to say, there's nothing easier than fasting on such short days. But no, you refuse to fast on the first of January. Test yourselves, in order to be able to rejoice over yourselves, in order that I may be able to rejoice over you. What a tiny little test this is! Still, it does reveal how Christian the heart is that beats in your breast.[16]

Fervent devotion is fanned to a greater blaze by the winds of opposition

7. You're now listening to the sermon; you're all ears, you're being stimulated by the word of God, and this very exhortation is beginning to glow in your heart.[17] I have kindled something in your spirits; I can see it, I acknowledge it. But let this flame take hold of the solid oak strength of character in you all. In a short while, you see, when the sermon's finished, you are going to leave this place and go out into the icy blasts and cold weather of the world. The world, as you know, is apparently at boiling point with its wrongheaded festivity; but the winds are cold, and one dreads the prospect of their turning Christian hearts to ice. And so, brothers and sisters, as I said, let the flame of God's word take hold of the solid oak of your characters. If it does this, those icy blasts which you will experience shortly, the moment you step outside, will fan it into a greater flame than ever and not blow it out—provided it isn't just a feeble little spark which can be blown out.

If your hearts are simply burning now like a wax taper as you shout, as you express your love of the word of God and your joy in it, you're all going to go outside in a little while, and it will be blown out by one puff of the mouth, when any of you gets asked, "Is it really true that you're going to fast today?" It'll be blown out at once, because it had only flared briefly like a wax taper. But if it is burning like *coals of fire* (Ps 18:12), however furiously the contrary blasts of wrongheaded persuasion may blow, they will only fan the blaze and stir it up to burn more fiercely than ever. Now people burn like coals when they have come to life again. When coals burn, you see, it's as though they were coming to life from the dead. Many people use this kind of expression; when they send for servants to light a fire, they say, "Bring live coals," by which they mean burning ones; so they imply that ones which have gone out are to be thought of as dead.

So if you have all come to life again with the heat of the charity of Christ, let your desire for him burn so brightly in your hearts, that no blast from those who would dissuade you from it can extinguish it. You see, I know perfectly well what you are going to have to endure when you leave here—and thank heaven that you have come together here at all. Because of course that you should assemble here during these days in greater numbers than usual doesn't displease me; on the contrary, it even gives me great pleasure.[18] It means, after all, that because those who don't share your style of life are all hurrying off to occupy themselves with a variety of empty pleasures, and so are presenting you with time off and a holiday, you have found a way of bringing about in you what is said in the psalm: *Save us, Lord our God, and gather us from among the nations* (Ps 106:47).

So you have been gathered together right now; even if you go out and mix with them in general social intercourse, without however consenting to their bad and worthless ways, you will remain gathered from among the Gentiles, wherever you may actually be. And if only it were just in the streets that you have to put up with such shameless opposition, and not also, it may be, in your own homes! The father would like to fast, the son wouldn't, or the son would like to, the father wouldn't; or the husband wants to, the wife doesn't, or she does and he doesn't. So any who don't want to fast, and don't want to precisely because they regard this as a feast day, are a contrary head wind. The others, though, should burn so brightly that not only can they not be blown out themselves, but the opposition can also catch fire from them.

Let us grieve over and pray for the pagans

8. My brothers and sisters, if you rightly understand what you are hearing, I am quite sure that you are grieving for those who are still caught up in this insanity. You are grieving over them because you too, once upon a time, were perhaps caught up in this sort of insanity; and now you are of sound mind, and you compare your sanity with their insanity, and you feel so sorry for them you want to weep. But you mustn't weep in despair, you mustn't feel *desperately* sorry for them. After all, if the result could be produced in you that you no longer love today what you used to love yesterday, it can be produced in them. And if it can be produced in them, as long as it hasn't been and you are grieving over them, you must pray for them. But in order that your prayer may be heard, fast for them and give alms, and for your part spend the day like that on behalf of those you love—it's because they don't love themselves that they spend it in their contrary activities, seeing that *whoever loves iniquity hates his own soul* (Ps 11:5)—so that some time or other they too may come to hate iniquity and love their own souls, and inwardly to grieve with you over others, and together with you may pray and fast for them.

Indeed, brothers and sisters, while other days too engage them in their frivolities, still it is above all on these feast days of theirs that their frivolity can really let itself go, and thus arouse in them a greater love of the world and of destructive pleasures.[19] I mean, when one person does this sort of thing in his own house, with the neighborhood looking on rather coldly, he doesn't go quite so crazy; but when they all do it, they set each other on fire. But I've already told you: what gets them hot leaves you cold. Love is always a kind of heat. But it makes all the difference, what is loved. When the heart is on fire for the world, God leaves it cold; so then, let the world leave it cold, and God set it on fire.

So then, when they behave like this with greater eagerness than usual and in greater numbers, just as they rouse one another to wicked misconduct against their best interests, so may they rouse you to sorrow and acts of kindness on their behalf. We must always grieve over them indeed, as long as they are pagans, as long as they pursue their futile vanities, as long as they are devoted to demons. As long as they are determined to worship what they have made, forgetful of the one by whom they were made, we must always continue to wring our hands over them. But during these special festivities of theirs they should rouse in us fresh feelings of grief. When you see them wasting themselves on frivolties of all sorts, on extravagant pleasures, on unrestrained drunkenness, on gambling and every variety of crazy folly, their fresh excesses should cause in you a fresh feeling of grief, if you are a Christian, if you are capable of compassion, because when you were not what you are now the Church had compassion on you, and that while it was still few in numbers.[20] But now that it has grown up, and in the name of Christ is widely and copiously spread abroad, aren't those to be more lamented than ever, whose hearts are still closed right until now, and who *love what is futile and seek what is false* (Ps 4:3)? Yes of course, those few who have remained cut off from the human race by heaven knows what stiff-necked, unreasonable obstinacy are surely entitled to greater compassion, because they are wasting away with a worse disease, which resists the healing power even of such a great authority.

Let us fast also for the conversion of bad Christians

9. And if only it were just the pagans that we had to wring our hands over! We would then be wringing them for practically nobody. Let Christians stop going to the theaters; the pagans will slink away from them, even if not out of a love of the truth, at least out of shame at what a small audience they constitute. Yes certainly, we have to offer up a greater sacrifice of prayers, and from a keener sorrow in the heart, that those who call themselves Christians may be found worthy of correction. So then, brothers and sisters, there is nothing impudent about fasting for them; on the contrary it is entirely opportune, when it is undertaken for those who *labor* because they wish to, who wouldn't be laboring if they didn't wish to. They are weighed down, you see, with their sins, and they pride themselves on their vile pleasures, and so they don't hear the voice that says to them, *Come to me, all you that labor and are overburdened, and I will refresh you* (Mt 11:28). They don't wish to be refreshed with the sweetness of Christ, and they imagine they can be refreshed by taking their fill of their lusts. That is not refreshment, but ruin.

And don't either, please, celebrate the feast days of Christian saints in the same way as the drunkards do, though of course you must ease off your fasting as a mark and sign of rejoicing.[21] But it's one thing to signify joy by easing off on fasting, another to thrust aside justice by overloading your hearts and drinking yourselves silly. The Lord says, Truth says, *Let not your hearts be weighed down with drugs[22] and drunkenness* (Lk 21:34). It's sheer folly, as well as being irreligious, to wish to win the favor of the martyrs by behavior, which would have stopped them attaining to the glory of martyrdom if they had not spurned it with contempt.

How sophisticated pagans compare the idolatry of the masses to the
superstitious practices of Christians

10. But perhaps you are not going to experience pagans of this sort. There are some of them, you see, who condemn[23] these ones that are given over to infamous pleasures and drunken bouts, and they say: "Just as you have bad Christians, so too we have bad pagans. I mean, consider what good pagans are like." Then they name, for instance, some wise men and philosophers of the world, as being outstanding in the excellence of their teaching. But don't let them overawe and scare you. Being big is one thing, being swollen another; I mean, something that's swollen looks as if it's big, but it isn't healthy. Listen to what the apostle has to say: *Beware of anyone leading you astray through philosophy and empty deceits, according to the tradition of men, according to the elements of this world and not according to Christ; because in him dwells bodily all the fullness of the godhead, and you have found fulfillment in him, who is the head of every principality and power* (Col 2:8-10).

You see, in order to give a learned and apparently sensible interpretation of their idols, they take refuge in *the elements of the world.*[24] You find fault with someone for worshiping an idol, and it's clear that he really does venerate the idol; the thing itself is there to convict him, and that precisely is the object of his affection, the actual idol; that's what he relies on to grant his requests. But what does the seemingly cleverer and better educated pagan say to you? "Un-educated pagans do this, so that they venerate the idol as if it were itself divine,[25] just as your people also do, those who venerate the columns in the church."[26]

Praying and singing together in church is like singing chanties
when hauling heavy weights

11. That's why I have to say, brothers and sisters: don't do things for which the pagans can jeer at us; enter the church in such a way that you don't give pagans an excuse for not wanting to enter the church. The reason we come to church anyway, you see, is for the sake of getting together as brothers and sisters; because the temple of prayer is your own heart. Clean up the place where you pray, and you will be heard. After all, if you keep the visible place clean where you say your prayers, not to please God's eyes—I mean, he sees everything just as he created everything—but so that your own eyes won't be offended and so distract your attention, how much more should you keep clean the heart where you call upon God, and with which you call upon him? Your inner room, where you are to enter and shut the door (that is, the bodily senses) as the Lord tells you,[27] you should keep bolted against bodily allurements; but brothers and sisters coming together makes for greater fervor in praying and praising God.

Suppose there was a heavy weight that had to be moved, and what they call a chanty[28] were being sung, wouldn't the mass voices of the men all singing and pulling together, to keep up the swing and rhythm of their joint effort, stir up even your feeble powers, so that you too would want to grab the rope and have the fun of sharing in that work? So that's how the meetings of the brethren sharpen charity. And everyone, if praying well, prays inwardly, as the Lord said in his answer to the Samaritan woman: *The hour is coming*, he says, *and now is when neither on this mountain nor in Jerusalem shall you worship the Father*; and a little later, *The hour is coming*, he says, *and now is when the true worshipers shall worship the Father in spirit and truth. For the Father in fact seeks such people to worship him. God is spirit, and those who worship him should worship in spirit and truth* (Jn 4:21.23-24). So if God is to be prayed to in spirit, a residence should be made ready for him; the resident will soon arrive. *We will come in to him*, he says, *I and my Father, and will take up residence with him* (Jn 14:23).

So then, come to church in order to rouse yourself to more fervent prayer, in order that the devotion of a quiet and orderly congregation may earn you a hearing with God, not because God stays in an earthly kind of courtroom to hear your case. Don't imagine that it's only within walls like this that God listens to you; he listened to the martyrs in prison. *What house*, he says, *will you build for me, or what is the place of my rest? Did not my hand make these things?* And yet he said that he had a place in anybody's loving and devoted heart. He goes on, you see: *Upon whom does my spirit rest? Upon one who is humble and quiet, and trembles at my words* (Is 66:1-2; Acts 7:49-50).

The martyrs, like good servants and sons,
hate being venerated in the place of God

12. Why have I said this? So that when we jeer at the pagans we shouldn't do things the pagans can jeer at us for. Visit the shrines of the martyrs in such a way as to remember them with devotion, and to stir your hearts, by honoring the martyrs, to feel a greater love for God, who didn't abandon the martyrs in their trials, who supported them in their struggles, who crowned them when they were victorious. In this way make yourselves worthy of having the martyrs pray for you. Otherwise the good slave gets very indignant when his master is ignored and he himself is venerated, the good slave who has also been made from a slave into a son.

You see, it's one thing to be still a slave, who is also going to be made into a son from a slave, and another to be already a son. One thing to be a slave in fear, another to be a son in charity.[29] *A great house* (2 Tm 2:20) has everything: both hired servants and slaves and sons. The hired servants are those who are looking for secular advantages in the Church, about whom the apostle says that they proclaim the gospel *not sincerely*; and yet he allows them to, when he says, *Whether for ulterior motives or whether for the truth, let Christ be proclaimed* (Phil 1:17-18). The slaves, on the other hand, are those who do what the master tells them to out of fear. They belong to the house indeed, and are more part of a great house than are the hired servants;[30] it's from the very slaves that sons are made, when they start serving out of love.

So then, as I was saying, a great house has everything. What are we to suppose the martyrs are, my brothers and sisters? Perish the thought that we should count them among the hired servants! But we can't place them either among the slaves who are not yet sons. They loved Christ, after all, and for love of him they despised not only all the pleasures of the world but also all its torments; they were drunk with the cup of his Spirit, about which it says, *Your heady cup, how noble it is!* (Ps 23:5). So the good slave, as I said, who is already to be called a son, doesn't wish himself, but his master, to be venerated. Think a little, brothers and sisters, and recall what you attend every day; what does truth teach you in church?[31] The faithful know in what style the martyrs are commemorated in the mysteries, when our wishes and prayers are addressed to God. Yes, the faithful know, and the catechumens should be in a hurry to know. Who's stopping them, after all? The door is only closed to those who keep on putting off the day; but isn't it open to any who are keen to enter?

The examples of Paul, Barnabas, and Peter

13. But let's observe, brothers and sisters, what some good slaves did while still living in this body, when they were being honored by men, and were on the point of being worshiped as gods of the nations. Because Paul and Barnabas were working miracles in Christ, because they had exceeded merely human limits, the pagans according to their wont called Barnabas Jupiter and Paul Mercury, because he was the readier talker, and they had already started to dedicate victims to them.[32] They were so horrified by this honor that they tore their clothes and tried to teach them, as best they could, who alone was to be venerated, the one by whose power they were doing these things.

Pay attention to this story, brothers and sisters, so that you may be strong and have a good defense against the pagans, even the grander ones among them. But why do I call them grander, when they are the ones in greater peril? The more learned, I mean, they think they are, the more unteachable they become. You see, they are ashamed to learn, because that would mean admitting their ignorance, and there is none of that dutiful humility in them, which was the one thing the humble God came to teach. Or is someone going to say, perhaps, "The reason Paul and Barnabas rejected with abhorrence the honor of the sacrifices that were being prepared for them was that those people made one of them out to be Jupiter, the other Mercury, whom the apostles, being religious Christians, abominated as false gods, and that's why they were indignant at being compared to demons or idols; it wasn't because they wanted God to be worshiped rather than themselves."

In that case, this is what they would have said to those who wished to sacrifice: "You're insulting us; we are much better than the demons you're identifying us with." But on the contrary, they tore their clothes in their horror, and humbly admonished the crowds that such things should not be done for them or for anybody, but that instead they should be converted from these vanities to the one God. Thus they said, *Men, what are you doing? We are human beings like you, declaring to you that you should turn back from these vain things to the one who made heaven and earth and sea and everything that is in them* (Acts

14:15; Ps 146:6). *With these and similar words, they scarcely managed to persuade them not to sacrifice to them* (Acts 14:18).

But to help you prove to the godless more effectively that it wasn't because they thought they were being insulted that they rejected those sacrifices, but in order that God alone should be so honored, since all their efforts were directed to having everyone converted to his worship, just consider the case of Peter. When people were astonished at his deed—though not in fact his, but God's—when that man who had been lame for forty years, who used to sit at the Beautiful Gate, rose again at the word of God and walked,[33] he didn't want the glory to be given to him, but to Christ, and he said, *Men of Israel, why are you astonished over this, or why do you gaze at us, as though it were by our own power or authority that we have made this man walk? The God of Abraham and the God of Isaac and the God of Jacob, the God of our fathers, has glorified his Son, whom you handed over to judgment* (Acts 3:12-13).

The example of a good angel

14. But if what men did is not enough, in wishing the glory to be given to God and not to themselves, take a look at the angels. In the Apocalypse a holy angel—because there are also crooked angels, for whom everlasting fire has been prepared, together with their chief, the devil—so an angel who had not fallen through pride but remained under God in holy humility, not lifting himself up against God in self-aggrandizement, nor saying, *I will set my throne in the North, and I will be like the Most High* (Is 14:13.14), but abiding in the South,[34] where Christ feeds his flock, and where he lies down. . .

You see, it's written, *Where you feed your flock, where you lie down in the South* (Sg 1:7). Opposite the southern region, of course, is the northern one; that's why it stands for spirits that are cold and darkened, while the South stands for those that are enlightened and fervent. So those who are good, as in the South, are fervent and shining brightly, while those who are bad, as in the North, are cold and covered with dark, dense fog. God feeds his flock and lies down in the South among the former, as it says *Where you feed your flock, where you lie down in the South*; not among the latter, whose part the devil takes when he says, *I will set my throne in the North, and I will be like the Most High*. He could only be venerated, after all, by such as would take him to be God.

So that angel who abides in the South, fervent in holiness and shining bright in wisdom, was showing some things in the Apocalypse to the apostle John. And he was overwhelmed, and fell at the angel's feet.

North and South, symbols of darkness and light, bad angels and good, pride and humility

15. Notice above all else, brothers and sisters, which angels humble people are like, and which angels proud ones. People, you see, who bring about schisms and heresies want their own names to be renowned, and the name of Christ to

sink into obscurity, and they choose thrones in the North. Nor would people forsake the Church and follow them as though they were Christ, unless their understanding were darkened and they had become strangers to the fervor of charity.[35] Which ones, on the other hand, would those people be like who keep hold of humility and choose *to be abject in the house of the Lord rather than to dwell in the tents of sinners* (Ps 84:10)?

What did Simon want, but to be admired for miracles, to exalt himself in pride? That, you see, was what drove him to imagine that the gift of the Holy Spirit could be bought with money.[36] As against such pride the apostle, abiding in the South, *fervent in spirit* (Acts 18:25), shining brightly in his good sense, says in humility, *Neither the one who plants is anything, nor the one who waters; but the one who gives the growth, God*; because he had just said, *I planted, Apollo watered, but God gave the growth*[37] (1 Cor 3:7.6). And again, *Was Paul crucified for you, or were you baptized in the name of Paul?* (1 Cor 1:13). How he utterly rejects being worshiped instead of Christ, how jealous he is for the bridegroom, and refuses to parade himself as the bridegroom to any soul bent on fornication!

So just as those saints, within their limits—because it is only after the resurrection of the body that they will be as perfect as angels—but still, just as they too, within their limits scorned the honor which people were paying them as though it were their due, because they wished him alone to be worshiped and all hearts to be converted to him alone, in whom they too made their boast as truly *good and faithful slaves* (Mt 25:21), as sons, such too are the holy angels. Because although still only human beings living in the flesh and placed in the midst of so many trials and temptations, they scorned the honor which was being conferred on them as conducive to pride, so that he alone might be honored in all things, who alone has ever been honored without any risk to the one doing the honors.[38] Where, after all, do they place themselves, so that he may be honored? How do they abase themselves? Isn't it a great thing, evidently, to plant and to water? But *neither the one who plants is anything, nor the one who waters*. How very anxious and concerned he was![39] He doesn't claim to contribute anything to the salvation of those whom he was longing to build up in Christ.

So if men still living in the flesh act like that, how much more the martyrs and the angels! The more holy, you see, their quality of life, the more they love God's glory.[40] Because we too shall be like the angels, but after the resurrection. That's what the Lord said: *They will be equal to the angels of God* (Lk 20:36).

16. So come back with me to what I had started to tell you about, and receive some salutary instruction on why you should have time only for God.[41] So that angel was showing wonderful and mystical visions in the Apocalypse to the apostle John, slave of Christ, son of mother Church and counted among the sons of God. But he was confused in one of the visions, and fell down, as I had begun to say, at the angel's feet. The angel, though, wouldn't accept a man showing him the honor which was due to God alone, and said to him, "Get up; what are you doing? *Venerate God. For I too am your fellow slave and the fellow of your brethren* (Rv 19:10; 22:9).

The falsity of the explanation given by educated pagans
for the veneration of idols

Why have I said this? Please consider carefully the chief point I'm making. We had started to deal with the apparently better educated pagans—because the less educated are the ones who do the things[42] about which these do not wish to be taken to task—so with the better educated ones, since they say to us, "You people also have your adorers of columns, and sometimes even of pictures."[43] And would to God that we didn't have them, and may the Lord grant that we don't go on having them! But all the same, this is not what the Church teaches you. I mean, which priest of theirs ever climbed into a pulpit and from there commanded the people not to adore idols, in the way that we, in Christ, publicly preach against the adoration of columns or of the stones of buildings in holy places, or even of pictures? On the contrary indeed, it was their very priests who used to turn to the idols and offer them victims for their congregations, and would still like to do so now.[44]

17. "We," they say, "don't adore images, but what is signified by the image." I ask what the images signify, I ask what the image of the sun signifies; nothing else but the sun, surely? For yes, perhaps the explanations of other images convey deeper, more hidden meanings. For the time being let's leave these, and put them on one side to come back to shortly. The image of the sun, certainly, can only signify the sun, and that of the moon the moon, and that of Tellus the earth.[45] So if they don't adore what they see in the image, but what the image signifies, why, when they have the things signified by these images so familiarly before their very eyes, do they offer adoration to their images instead of directly to them? I mean, if what is signified couldn't be seen, it would make sense to offer adoration to the sign for the thing signified. But since they can see the sun, which is signified by the image of the sun, why do they turn their backs to what is signified, and their faces to the sign it is signified by?[46]

You see, if they didn't make images for the things that can be seen, and only made them for things that can't be seen, they could deceive the less wide awake among us, and say, "Look, we worship the sun. But because we can see him, we haven't set up any image to him. It's the same with the moon and the stars; as we see them, so we worship them. We haven't made any images of them, nor do we have any. It would be silly, after all, to place a visible sign in a closed temple for a thing which can be seen and worshiped in the open sky. But when we worship Mind or Wit or Soul or Virtue or Justice—these now are all invisible—we set up their visible images, which we can see and adore, and thus venerate in our thoughts the invisible realities."

As it is, however, they can now be openly convicted of being devoted to the actual images, and not to what the images signify, seeing that they have made images even of visible objects, plain for the eyes of all to see. The sun has an image, though they would very properly be blamed by true piety and religion if they offered it adoration in the sky. What's more, they have come to such a pitch of mindless folly, that they turn their backs to the sun, and their faces to its image.

"How can you expect him to hear you, when you abandon him, and turn to some false and totally misleading image of him? It's as if you went to the house of some landowner to beg for something, and he was standing in his courtyard, while you turned your back to him and faced his portrait; and if you not only poured out your heart to a picture and not to a man, but did so in the presence of the man portrayed in the picture, wouldn't he assume you were making fun of him, or put you down as crazy, and in any case have you thrown out of his house?"

Nothing could be more like such folly than what these people do, even if the sun were rightly to be venerated. That such things, though, are not be venerated I will explain in the Lord's name, if he allows me the time and gives me the capacity.

But now what I am talking about is how these people are caught out in their very activities.

"You've built a temple to the moon, you have set up in it an image to her. The moon rises every day, there are scarcely two, or perhaps three days in a month when she cannot be seen. Venerate her, if she must be venerated, if you have come to this pitch of impropriety that you want to venerate a visible creature as a god, though manifestly the invisible creation excels it in power, and not even that, but only the creator, is to be venerated as God. But look, the things you worship are there before your eyes, whether sun or moon or stars or earth; so why go looking for their images, when they are there present for you to venerate? It can only be because human beings are devoted to what they have made with their own hands, forgetful of the one by whose hands they were made themselves."

The same point made with reference to the cult of Neptune

18. But now let's see how they explain images. "By Neptune," he says, "I do not mean Neptune's statue; but Neptune is something else which is signified by this image."

What is Neptune, then?

"The sea," he says.

That's the sum of what it means, that Neptune is the sea. But Christians worship neither that statue which you call Neptune, nor the sea which you say Neptune means.

"And what do they worship?"

The one, of course, *who made heaven and earth and sea, and all that is in them* (Acts 14:15; Ps 146:6). You, though, what do you say?

"This statue signifies the sea." And this is said, as it were, aside, in secret, whispered in your ear, so that it should be accounted a great mystery that this statue signifies the sea, so that of course any who venerate that statue should reckon they are venerating the sea.

So then, only people living inland ought to have images of Neptune, people who can't see the sea itself, so that as they don't have the reality they may have a sign or symbol to stand for the reality. But in fact now they have put up a chapel of Neptune right next to the sea, and they turn their backs to the sea when they venerate Neptune. Not even the waves of the sea crashing on the beach behind them can make its worshipers turn round to it; and what's even sillier, those who are praying would like the sea to be quiet and the statue to listen, because the sea, that is to say, has its sense of hearing not in its own salt waves but in ears made of that alien material, bronze.

And the cult of Tellus, Mother Earth

19. It's the same too with the image of Tellus. "It's not," he says, "this thing you can see that is being worshiped; but this represents the earth." That, even if he didn't say so, would be perfectly obvious. In vain does he try to state as something mysterious what is shouted at us by the very name. *Tellus*, I mean, is just another word for earth. Still, they call her Mother Earth, and it is for her that they have built a temple and made an image. Yes, yes, I understand; as with the sun, as with the moon, there's no need for him to explain. The images are called by the same name as the things they are images of, which of course we can all see, and which are totally familiar to us.

Or perhaps their also adding the word "Mother," this is something we have to learn? "She's the mother," they say, "of all growing things." Well, let her be the mother of all growing things; am I, for that reason, going to pray and make vows to the earth, and not to him who said, *Let the earth produce* everything that it has produced (Gn 1:24)? I mean, without his word, not only would it be barren, it simply wouldn't exist at all. So what is this fellow, as if he were the expounder of mysteries,[47] in his desire to turn me away from the creator and convert me to the creature, what is he trying to explain to me as a great and compelling reason for my engaging in the cult of the earth? Obviously it's quite right to tell farmers that if they don't want to endure famine they should engage in the cult, or rather cultivation, of the earth, not by praying and vowing vows to it, but just by plowing it.[48]

And of Juno; Christians do not treat their mysteries as secrets
to be concealed from the uninitiated

20. Likewise I inquire about the image of Juno; now here we do need the services of a mystagogue, an interpreter of the mystery. Juno, you see, does not indicate what she represents by her very name, like Mother Earth, or the images of sun and moon. So Juno's cult is a great secret. What is the secret, I beg you?

"This," he says, "is something only a few people know." Perhaps many have heard about it from those few, and told about it. Perhaps their literature divulges it to people to whom they don't want what they worship to be divulged—although our literature too divulges to them what we worship, but we aren't afraid of that.

Our volumes are put up for sale in public; the light never needs to blush. Let them buy them, read them, believe them; or else buy them, read them, make fun of them. Those scriptures know how to hold people guilty who read them and don't believe. A volume is hawked round for sale, but the one who is proclaimed in the volume is not up for sale. Or is he too, in fact, up for sale, because he displayed himself to the nations to be bought for whatever price anyone might afford? Zacchaeus bought him for half his estate, that widow bought him for two farthings, a hospitable pauper bought him by offering a cup of cold water.[49] And he is possessed in full ownership by all buyers; there is none he has no room for, he increases the capacity of all.

Such is the one who is proclaimed in this volume; you there, buy the volume and read it—we certainly don't blush for it. Go and hide the volumes of your sacred rites in remote caves—such is the power of human curiosity that it will track them down and publish their contents.

21. So then, what is Juno?[50] "Juno," they say, "is the air." Just now they were inviting us to worship the sea in the form of Neptune, to worship the earth in the idol of Tellus; now they're inviting us to worship the air. These are the elements of which this world consists. So the apostle Paul warns us in advance about all this in his letter: *Take care*, he says, *that nobody deceives you through philosophy and vain deceit, according to the elements of this world* (Col 2:8). He was referring, you see, to the people who give an apparently sensible explanation of idols. That's why, after saying *through philosophy*, he said in the same passage, *according to the elements of this world*, warning us to beware, not of any old worshipers of idols, but of the apparently more learned interpreters of signs.

"So," they say, "the air is Juno." They can call it what they like, a thing known to everyone; I, though, certainly won't engage in the cult of the air, because it cannot even be cultivated in the way the earth is cultivated by farmers.[51] The farmer, you see, goes to work with the earth, as I said earlier on, not by praying and paying vows to it, but by toiling away at it in order to obtain a crop. This air, however, cannot be cultivated like that, nor is it to be prayed and paid vows to. Praise the artifact, venerate, with prayers and vows, the artificer.

"To show you," they say, "that the air is Juno, that's what the Greeks call her. Her name is Hera in Greek; but if you repeat 'Hera' often enough and fast enough, it sounds like 'air.' "

We, for our part, who say that religious service is to be paid to the one creator only, do not venerate Juno for the good reason that she is an idol; we do not venerate the air[52] for the good reason that it is created.

God alone is to be worshiped—for our good, not h

22. Now what I want to know from these people is this: whether the air gets angry if I worship God alone; because God certainly gets angry if I worship the air. Although he is always at peace, and administers and governs the whole of his creation without any emotional disquiet or passion, nonetheless in some

totally inexpressible manner God does get angry. He wishes himself alone to be worshiped, and he alone can have such a wish without pride. After all, he alone is worthy of worship, and the reason he wishes to be worshiped is not to get himself into a higher position, but to get us into better shape. He, I mean, has no need of worshipers; you, though, do need him worshiped. *I said to the Lord,* says the prophet, *my God you are, because you have no need of my good things* (Ps 16:2). So if he alone can without pride demand to be worshiped, anyone else who demands this and arrogates to himself the right to be worshiped as his own personal and proper due, who is not satisfied with being venerated in the one who created him, is demanding this out of pride. And the pride of the devil is to be avoided, so that we may attain in humility to the heights of God. The devil alone, you see, wishes himself to be worshiped instead of God, because he said himself, *I will set my throne in the North, and I will be like the Most High* (Is 14:13.14).

The case of the god Vulcan

23. What, I ask you, are they going to say about the signification, for example, of Vulcan, just to mention all the elements? There are said to be four of these, you see: earth, water, air and fire; and we have already spoken about the heavens, when we were talking about sun and moon.

"Vulcan," they say, "is fire," not the ethereal fire of the region where the sun and moon and other heavenly bodies are to be found, but this fire which is to be found on earth and is accommodated to human use. "Because the reason," they also say, "why Vulcan is depicted as being lame is that the flames of this fire quiver as though they were limping."

So what, then? Since we human beings have it in our power to kindle fire and extinguish it when we like, to use it how we like, does that mean that human beings have such power over a god that anyone who blows out a lamp is extinguishing a god? I don't know which is worse: worshiping the image of Vulcan in itself, or giving such an interpretation of it. But what concern is it of ours? Very possibly, you see, they will want to give similar interpretations with reference to invisible realities; these, after all, which we've dealt with so far, are all visible. Let's come straightaway to the security and certainty of our faith, so that we may not be in any way at all corrupted by them.

The case of the god Mercury

24. "When I worship Mercury," he says, "I'm worshiping wit;[53] wit cannot be seen; it's something invisible." We too unreservedly grant that wit is something invisible, and that it is invisible in such a way, and is such a kind of reality, that it is better than heaven, than earth, than sea and all those things that can be seen. An invisible substance, that is to say, in that it is a kind of life, is better than any and every visible substance, because everything visible is a body. And certainly wit is a superior kind of reality.

However, if you were to give a thought to wit itself, which they say they worship, what has it achieved? Don't many people go astray with great wit, and perhaps chiefly those who imagine that wit is to be worshiped in the image of Mercury? So if human wit can go astray when it is not being guided by God, human wit that is sound and healthy does not wish to be venerated in God's place, but wishes him to be venerated by whom it wishes itself to be illuminated. Unless, in fact, human wit is illuminated by God shedding his light on it, it is dismally dark in its own delusions.

But what I want you to tell me is what you worship in Mercury. "Wit," you said. Wit is a kind of middle reality, because wit either turns away from the creator and so is darkened and becomes foolish, or turns toward the creator and so is enlightened and becomes wise. Now you said a kind of middle thing, when you said you worship wit.

"Yes," he says, "a middle thing, because the very name of Mercury sounds like *medium currentem*, one in the middle running." (It is said, you see, that he was called Mercury as being one in the middle, who runs.[54])

So if the reason he's worshiped is that he is a middle something, why is that one not rather worshiped who calls back to himself the wit which you put in the middle, in order to make it break with and turn away from inferior things and unite itself to him? Such is the wit of the saints, the wit of the martyrs, the wit of the angels. Because if wit is such as that angel displayed whom I mentioned, wit enlightened by God, it thrusts away from itself any human veneration, and admonishes the one who would venerate it to venerate God instead. *Venerate God*, he said, *for I too am your fellow slave, and the fellow of your brethren* (Rv 19:10; 22:9).

Should you then be worshiping the wit in the middle, about which a better wit is very critical of you? I mean, if you worship wit in the middle, enlightened wit will certainly criticize you. Why? Because enlightened wit does not desire wit to be worshiped, but the enlightener of all wit. In virtue of that enlightenment it is in fact kindly and benevolent, and desires the wit of everybody to be converted to the one by whom it knows it too has been enlightened. Or is it perhaps a foolish wit that desires to be worshiped itself? That is clearly true. So take care, when you want Mercury to be worshiped as wit, that you don't worship the devil, who has a foolish wit. Because the devil too, when he said *I will set my throne in the North, and I will be like the Most High*, was refusing to worship God and wished to be worshiped in God's stead, rising up against God. But because he withdrew, as it were, from the South to the North his wits became dark, and because dark also proud, and because proud, that's why he wishes to hoodwink you into worshiping Mercury, so that while you are worshiping Mercury, you will in fact be worshiping the devil.

The distinction between body and spirit

25. Would your holinesses please concentrate, and observe in the human field what I am saying. Concentrate your minds and understand. Everything created

is either body or spirit. The creator is simply spirit; what's created, though, as I said, is body or spirit. Concentrate now, in order to have something, as the Lord may help me to the best of my ability, to say against the pagans—not any kind, but those who consider themselves better educated, and good at explaining the meaning of images, and who are so full of themselves they fill others too with conceit, and being void of truth make a mockery of the very name of truth.

Everything created, as I said, is either body or spirit. Body, like the earth and everything that grows and breeds on it, like the sea and everything that swims or crawls in it, like the air and everything that flies in it, like the sky and everything that shines in it. All these creatures are bodies. Spirit, on the other hand, is better than body. What is created spirit? That which cannot be perceived by the senses of the body, but only by the intelligence of the mind, such as are all souls, whether irrational as in beasts or rational as in human beings,[55] whether falling behind as in the godless or making progress as in the converted, or perfect as in the angels and archangels, the thrones, dominations, principalities and powers dwelling on high.[56]

So since created things are either bodies or spirits, and there is no third category to be found, the highest bodies, than which there are no better, are the heavenly ones, in the sky. Now what goes beyond them, not in space but in natural power, is not any other body, but spirit; a kind of life, but changeable life, because created; true, unchangeable life is the creator. So changeable life, that is, created spirit, is also capable of being formed and enlightened,[57] while unchangeable life, that is, the very substance of the creator, is creative and enlightening. So the creature is formed and enlightened, while the creator forms and enlightens.

The difference between created and uncreated spirit

26. Pay attention, please, and understand. So every life that is capable of being enlightened and attaining to wisdom, when it has good will, loves God who is enlightening it, and by turning toward him it makes progress, and by clinging to him it is formed and molded to the integrity and perfection of wisdom, and in its own degree to the fullness of bliss. Such is the rational and intellectual life of angels and of human beings. So if this kind of life, when deserving of praise, loves the one who enlightens it, every such life that by culpable ill-will turns its back on the life that enlightens it is thereby darkened and becomes proud, as is the case with either a wicked angel or a wicked human being; it refuses, you see, to cling to God, but with a kind of self-absorbed disdain it wishes to be regarded as God.

It was to this kind of proud and wicked life that an archangel and his angels turned and fell; and he thereby was turned into the devil[58] and they into demons, and they were allotted a kind of space in this dark, foggy air, where they could rule over all wicked human beings. And that's why the apostle says, *According to the ruler of the power of this air, who is now at work in the sons of unbelief* (Eph 2:2). And again, when encouraging them to endure the persecutions of this age, *Our struggle*, he says, *is not against flesh and blood,* that is, against human beings, *but against the rulers and authorities and governors of the world of this darkness, against the spiritual hosts of wickedness in the heavenly places* (Eph 6:12). He said, you see, that the ruler of the power of this air was at work in the sons of unbelief, to prevent his correspondents from fixing their minds on men and assuming that their wrestling was with those at whose hands they were suffering persecution, instead of looking steadily in spirit at that enemy whom they had to overcome in Christ. That's why he went on to say, *Your struggle is not against flesh and blood, but against the rulers and authorities and governors of the world of this darkness, and against the spiritual hosts of wickedness in the heavenly places.*

Again, he didn't want it to be thought that by calling them *governors of the world* he was saying they were governors of this universal fabric which God has instituted, and so he showed what world it was he meant by adding the words *of this darkness.* And what darkness is you can easily recognize. I mean, the apostle himself said that unbelievers were signified by the name of darkness, when he was talking to believers: *For you were once upon a time darkness, but now light in the Lord* (Eph 5:8). In the same way too we have to understand that by saying *in the heavenly places* he was not referring to those sublime habitations of the holy angels, where the luminaries and stars are also located,[59] but that this lower air too is called heaven, which is why scripture talks of *the birds of heaven* (Gn 1:26).

The origin of idolatry, and of more refined forms of paganism

27. And so would your holinesses please concentrate, so that the Lord's mercy may enlighten you. I, you see, am dinning all this into your ears; he, however, is at work within, as we believe, as we hope in the mercy of him to whom we sing our praises.[60] So then, as I had begun to say, the soul that turns away from God as from the light of truth and as from the South[61] ends up in the North. Now the kingdom of the North is the kingdom of the devil, who says, *I will set my throne in the North, and I will be like the Most High* (Is 14:13-14); human hearts grow cold there, and once grown cold they cannot catch the flavor of spiritual things from that fire of divine wisdom. And so they start thinking only about bodies, to the extent of even looking for divinity in bodies, that is, in the sea, in the earth, in the air, and above all in the heavenly bodies, as in the moon or the sun or the stars. You see, the sense of sight takes first place among the senses of the body, and so whatever shines for the eyes, especially if it also occupies the highest place in the cosmos, is considered great. But if anyone suggests to them that there is something great *which eye has not seen nor ear heard, nor has it come up into the heart of man* (1 Cor 2:9), they say that there isn't anything which cannot be seen.

Such hearts, then, have grown cold; if they've grown cold, they are in the North; if they're in the North, they are under the dominion of the one who said, *I will set my throne in the North, and I will be like the Most High.* Those, on the other hand, who have in any way at all raised up their hearts, and as best they could have sharpened them with study, in order to see something which cannot be seen with the eyes of the body, and have transcended the earth they walked on—which was easy enough—and everything on the earth, transcended too the sea and anything that swims or crawls in it, transcended also the air and all birds—because it too is a bodily element—transcended the whole of that ethe-real[62] sky with all the luminaries that shine in it, or any others which are perhaps hidden from our eyes: those have seen that there is something which cannot be seen, such as mind is, such as wit, such as reason. They have also seen that even this kind of thing is subject to change, and they have sought something that is unchangeable; they have soared in thought and with the keen glance of the mind even above the spiritual creation, and have understood the creator spirit. Then, as though dazzled by the unaccustomed brightness of wisdom, they have re-turned as it were to rest in the shady darkness of their flesh; and some of them have perceived that their souls stand in need of purgation, in order to be cleansed of all fleshly lusts and so become fit to attain to that object whose ineffable light had given them a glancing wound.[63]

How the devil presented himself as a mediator to philosophers
through their pride

28. Just consider, my brothers and sisters, and take note in sorrow. They have seen that they stand in need of purgation, in order that that light, which cannot be grasped by the mind's feeble gaze, may eventually be grasped by the same gaze once it has been put into shape and strengthened. They have seen that there is a need of some medicine, and while they were looking around for such a medicine the devil immediately presented himself, because they were looking around in pride, preening themselves, as it were, on their own teachings; above all because they were able, if anyone has been, to attain such acuteness of wit and sharpness of mind, that transcending all created things, both bodily and spiritual, they came to understand that there is something which is both spiritual and unchangeable, and that from it come all these things that subsist in either a spiritual or a bodily mode. They understood that that creator is not subject to motion either in space or in time, while bodies move in space and change in time, whereas the substance of the soul, that is, of a created spirit, does not indeed move in space, but nonetheless changes in time through the variability of its feelings and thoughts. This, they realized, makes it a kind of medium in the middle, because God at the top is subject to motion neither in space nor in time, while the substance of bodies, that is, the part of creation at the bottom, is subject to motion both in space and in time. Hence that other substance is the medium in the middle, because it is not subject to motion in space, as God isn't either, while it is subject to motion in time, like bodies.

So while they were seeing the need for purgation and searching for it, that proud being the devil stepped in and accosted them as they were proudly seeking and proudly preening themselves, and presented himself as a mediator, through whom it seemed to them that their souls could be purged. He, to convince them by certain signs of his pride that he was necessary to them, and to persuade men and women that the soul which desires to attain to God can be purged by magic arts, instituted sacrilegiously sacred rites in temples, which promise purgation to the sacrilegious, because many of the images there, as scripture says,[64] were set up in order to honor men, whether absent or dead, who were held in great esteem. All of them, indeed, have been removed in the name of Christ by the laws of the state, and have ceased to be honored on official state occasions, as some of them had been treated as official magic rites. But just as previously there were also private magic rites, so too these things are still being done secretly, after their public official practice has been forbidden.

It is pride that gives the devil his chance

29. So then, that proud and wicked enemy of souls presented himself as a mediator; now listen to the apostle teaching us why he so presented himself— clearly because their pride gave him his chance. This is what he is warning us about when he says, *And do not give the devil a chance* (Eph 4:27). Now let the same apostle tell us how we may uncover their pride. And first let us just note that some of them too had attained to a knowledge of God, and yet he still wished them to be saved through Christ. You see, they had attained to a knowledge of God, but had not attained to salvation. I mean, it's one thing to attain to a knowledge of God, another to attain to salvation, when knowledge itself reaches its fullness, when the knower clings to the one known.[65]

When the apostle was speaking to some men among the Athenians as the pagans they were—and among them was to be found, so to say, the very summit of philosophy; that's where the learned and the wise of this world[66] fore-gathered—so when the apostle was speaking there, he did not present them with testimonies from the prophets, but from their own writers, and he made it quite clear that they were theirs, not ours, because even if something good can be found in that quarter, there are many bad things to be found there too; they are not like our prophets, in whose writings everything they have put there is good. And so when the apostle was speaking among the Athenians about God, *In him,* he said, *we live, we move and are, as some in your own tradition have said* [67] (Acts 17:28).

30. But what those "some" were really like, and why they were rejected, he explains in another place: *The wrath of God,*[68] he says, *is being revealed from heaven against all ungodliness.* What are we to understand by "against all ungodliness," but that of both Jews and Gentiles? But it may well be said, "Why is the wrath of God being revealed against the ungodliness of the Gentiles—because you said 'against all'? Did the Gentiles, after all, ever receive the law and become transgressors of it? The wrath of God will rightly be revealed against the Jews, to whom the law was given, and they were unwilling to keep it; but it wasn't given to the Gentiles." To meet that point, consider the matter carefully, brothers and sisters, and understand how the same apostle shows that all are

guilty, and all in need of salvation and of God's mercy.[69] *For the wrath of God is being revealed from heaven against all the ungodliness and injustice of men, of those who hold down the truth in iniquity* (Rom 1:18). Understand, brothers and sisters; notice how he didn't say, "They do not have the truth," but *They hold down the truth,* he said, *in iniquity.*

And as though you were to ask and say, "How can they have the truth, if they didn't receive the law?" he goes on: *because what is known of God is manifest among them.*

"How could what is known of God be manifest among them, if they didn't receive the law?"

He continues, and says, *For his invisible things can be descried from the creation of the world, being perceived through the things that have been made; also his everlasting power and divinity* (Rom 1:19-20); we must of course understand, *being perceived can be descried.*

"Through what can it be descried?"

Through the things that have been made.

Awareness of the work should make one seek the craftsman

31. Why, I mean to say, should one look at the works and not look for the craftsman? You look at the earth bearing fruit, you look at the sea full of its animals, you look at the air full of flying creatures, you look at the sky bright with stars; you recognize the changes of the seasons, you consider the four parts of the year, how the leaves fall from the trees and come back again, how their seeds are given their numbers, and each thing has its measurements, its weights,[70] how all things are being administered in their own ranks and order, the sky up above with total peace, the earth down below having its own proper beauty, the beauty *sui generis* of things giving way to and succeeding each other.[71] Gazing on all these things you behold them now all given life by created spirit, and you don't go looking for the craftsman of such a great work?

But you will say to me, "I can see them, I can't see him."

Because he made you one thing to see these things with, another with which he himself might be seen—for seeing these things he gave you the eyes in your head, for seeing himself he gave you a mind—you cannot therefore be allowed to say in that inane way, "I can't see him"; examine all these things with your intelligence, and you will see the one at work in them. After all, you cannot see a person's soul either; a person's soul cannot indeed be seen, but from the control of the body, when we observe it walking, working, moving all its limbs according to the proper function of each, we say, "It's alive, there's something in it which we do not see," and we are made aware of it through these things which we do see.[72] So just as from the movements and control of the body you become aware of the soul, which you cannot see, in the same way become aware of the creator from the manner in which the whole cosmos is controlled and souls themselves are regulated.

32. But it's not enough merely to be aware of this, because these people too were aware of it, and notice what the apostle says; consider the words which I had started to quote from the beginning of the passage:[73] *The wrath of God*, he says, *is being revealed from heaven against all the ungodliness and injustice of men, who hold down the truth in iniquity, because what is known of God is manifest among them; for God has manifested it to them.* And as though you were to inquire how he manifested it, *The invisible things*, he says, *from the foundation of the world can be descried, being perceived through the things that have been made; his everlasting might, also, and divinity*—that is, being perceived can be descried—*so that they are*, he says, *inexcusable* (Rom 1:18-20). Why inexcusable? You see, having said *who hold down the truth in iniquity*, he now shows how they do it. *Because knowing God*, he says —he didn't say, "Because they didn't know God"; but what did he say?—*Because knowing God, they did not glorify him as God or give thanks, but they became futile in their thinking, and their senseless minds were darkened.* For what other reason, but pride? Because just notice what follows: *For by asserting they were wise*, he says, *they became fools* (Rom 1:21-22).

They should not, you see, have arrogated to themselves what he had granted them, nor have preened themselves on what they had got from him, not from themselves. This, of course, should have been credited to him, so that in order to hold on to what they had been able to see, they might be healed by the one who had enabled them to see. Because if they had done this, they would have preserved humility, and been able to be purified and so continue to cling to that most blissful contemplation. It is to such people as that, after all, that the true and truthful physician would have revealed himself, the mediator, the over-thrower of pride, the exalter of humility.[74]

But you will say, "He had not yet been born in humility, had he?"[75]

No; but he would have revealed himself through prophecy, as he revealed himself to Abraham—because the Lord said himself, *Abraham longed to see my day, and he saw it, and rejoiced* (Jn 8:56)—as he revealed himself to the other patriarchs and prophets. They, you see, were saved by faith in his birth and passion to come, just as we are saved by faith in his already having been born and suffered. It is not surprising, though, that he revealed himself to their humility, and concealed himself from the pride of the others. But because they were infected with pride, that self-deceiving and deceitful and proud being[76] intruded himself, with ready promises that their souls could be purified by goodness knows what pride-engendered arts, and thus he made them worshipers of demons, that is, of bad angels. That's the origin of all the "sacraments" celebrated by the pagans, which they claim are effective for purifying their souls.

33. And listen to the apostle going on to say this, that it was to pay them for their pride that they received these things, because they did not honor God as

God should be honored. *Their senseless minds,*[77] he says, *were darkened. Saying that they were wise, they became fools,* now however through the agency of that false mediator who rejoices in idols, who rejoices when unclean herds are fed—the pigs, that is, which that younger son had to feed, having traveled such a long way from his father;[78] because just as *the Lord is near to those who have crushed the heart* (Ps 34:18), that is, to the humble, so the Lord is far from those who have exalted the heart, that is, the proud—*Saying that they were wise,* he says, *they became fools, and changed the glory of the imperishable God into the likeness of the image of perishable man* (Rom 1:21-23).

So now we have idols. And these to be sure are the ones of the Greeks and the other nations, which resemble human beings. But because there is no greater and more superstitious form of idolatry than that of the Egyptians—for Egypt has flooded the world with such fetishes as the apostle mentions from now on—after saying *into the likeness of the image of perishable man,* he added, *and of birds and quadrupeds and reptiles.* I ask you, brothers and sisters, have you ever seen idols in any other temples with heads of dogs or bulls, and reproductions of the rest of the irrational animal kingdom? Has anyone ever seen such things in any temple but the temple of Isis?[79] They are, after all, the idols of the Egyptians. The apostle included both sorts when he said, *into the likeness of the image of perishable man, and of birds and quadrupeds and reptiles. That is why God handed them over to the desires of their hearts, to uncleanness, so that they would treat their bodies with contumely among themselves* (Rom 1:23-24).

These evils of theirs stemmed from impiety; their head and source, after all, was pride. But the sins that follow are not only sins, they are also punishments. When he says, you see, *God handed them over,* it means it is already the penalty of some sin that they should do these things; but these punishments are still also sins. Why? Because they can still pull back from them, should they wish to. When it comes to punishment, however, it is no longer granted to turn back from it; that will be the punishment which will not anymore be called sin. In these middle stages, you see, they are both punishments and sins. The first stage, which is pride, is only a sin, not yet a punishment. The things that follow are both sins and punishments. Anyone who declines to pull back from them will come to the punishment which is not a sin anymore, but the penalty for all sins.

That pride, though, is the first sin is stated openly somewhere else: *The beginning of every sin is pride* (Sir 10:13). And how then is *avarice the root of all evils* (1 Tm 6:10)? Because to want more than God is avarice, to want more than is enough is avarice. Only God, after all, is enough for the soul, which is why Philip says, *Show us the Father, and it is enough for us* (Jn 14:8). But what could be prouder than to forsake God through overweening self-confidence? What more avaricious than not being satisfied with God? Pride, therefore, is the same thing as avarice at the origin of sins. That is why the fornicating soul, having forsaken the one true God as its lawful husband,[80] prostitutes itself to many false gods, that is, to demons, and finds no satisfaction at all.

How the Romans took over the gods of other nations,
all of them, in fact, demons

34. How many gods the Romans used to worship! First of all, having renounced the one, true and unchanging God, they started worshiping their own
as if they belonged to them. They began to do battle with other nations, and
supposing that these were defended somehow or other by their own gods, they
were at pains to seduce these other gods with certain sacrifices; and they went
on increasing the number of their gods by taking over the sacrilegious sacred
rites of nations they had either subjugated or were about to subjugate. In this
way they invited along the dog-faces and bull-faces and the shapes of creeping
things and winged creatures and all the monstrous gods of the Egyptians, and
thus, by so to say apologizing to them, they solicited their favor.

I mean, you can read in their own authors how, not long before the time of
the Lord's incarnation, the gods of the Egyptians had opposed the Roman gods.
Because just as the apostle says about the Cretans, *One of their very own*
prophets said: Cretans are always liars, evil beasts, idle bellies (Ti 1:12), so we
too can say, "One of their very own prophets said:
All kinds of monstrous gods and barking Anubis
Against Neptune and Venus, Minerva too,
Are brandishing their weapons."[81]
You see, it did not seem fitting to this poet that the dog-heads of the Egyptians
should engage the human-shaped idols of the Romans.

But it was in fact demons battling against demons, those of the Egyptians for
the Egyptians, and those of the Romans for the Romans. In order, however, that
they might all together take possession of both nations, they made it up with
each other, and all of them started being worshiped by the Romans. That, you
see, is what the apostle says: *Not that an idol is anything; but what the Gentiles*
sacrifice they sacrifice to demons and not to God. I do not wish you to become
the associates of demons (1 Cor 10:19-20)—which is what these people do,
deceiving themselves and saying: . . .[82] as though you were scornful of the idol
which the sculptor has made, because it is lifeless.

You really would be scornful of the idol, if you scorned the demon which
rejoices in the idol. So it's in vain that you interpret the image as standing for a
creature, because the creature for its part does not rejoice in any worship and
veneration coming from men—except the sinful creature which in its pride
demands an honor that is not its due, and deceitfully fills human frailty with
alarm. *God handed them over,* he says, *to the desires of their hearts, to unclean-*
ness, so that they would treat their bodies with contumely among themselves,
who transformed the truth of God into a lie, and worshiped and served the
creature rather than the creator, who is blessed for ever (Rom 1:24-25). What
is "transformed the truth of God into a lie"? *Into the likeness,* that is to say, *of*
perishable man and quadrupeds and creeping things (Rom 1:23).

The vanity of worshiping both idols and what they signify

35. And in case any of them should say, "I do not worship images, but what the images signify," he immediately added, *and worshiped and served the creature rather than the creator* (Rom 1:25). Understand this with precision, dearly beloved. Either, you see, they worship an idol or a creature. Worshiping an idol means turning the truth of God into a lie; because the sea is truth, Neptune on the other hand a lie made by man, the truth of God turned into a lie, because God made the sea, a man the image of Neptune. In the same way God also made the sun, while man by making an image of the sun turned the truth of God into a lie. But in case he should say, "I do not worship the image, but I worship the sun," let him listen to what follows: *They worshiped and served the creature rather than the creator.*

So letting go of the creator, they fell down to the level of the creature.[83] And what is more shameful still, they were not even content with that. If, after all, on letting go of God they had just worshiped what God has made, they would have deserved to be execrated. But how much more deserving of execration are those who have even let go of what God has made, to worship what artisans have made! Letting go of a creature, you go off to an idol; and put to shame over the idol, when you attempt to defend yourself you go back to the creature. Now, surely, it's high time; in order really and truly to defend yourself, go over from creature to creator.

"But I can't reach him," he says, "except through these things."

"Who is saying this?"

That learned man.

"Who is saying this?"

The one who is holding down the truth of God in a lie.

"Who is saying this?"

The one who, while he knew God, did not glorify him as God or give thanks; not that person who did not know him, but the one who did.

*Philosophers who relied on their own powers,
and those who used magic arts to reach God*

36. But of these people who hold down the truth of God in a lie there are two kinds. Some have entrusted themselves to their own virtue, have sought no helper, thinking their souls can be purified through philosophy, as though they needed no mediator. But we don't have to discuss these at present. What we are now going into action against is the sacrilegious sacred rituals of the pagans. But these people said that no sacrifices were of any use to them. They say Pythagoras was such a man.

This kind of boastfulness too should see what it is promising itself by its own powers. Whoever relies on himself is relying on man. Unhappy man, though! *Who will deliver him from the body of this death, if not the grace of God through Jesus Christ our Lord* (Rom 7:24-25), through the one and only true mediator, God and man? If he were only a man, he would not be a mediator; if he were only God, he would not be a mediator. But if he were not a mediator, he would not reconcile man to God, man who has been set so far apart through iniquity. These too, therefore, hold the truth of God in a lie, because they rely upon themselves, though *every man is a liar* (Ps 116:11), nor can anyone at all be set free except by confession of sins, when the appeaser has intervened.

These too are being seduced by that proud enemy of souls, not indeed by means of sacrilegious sacred rituals, but by making them like himself in another way, through the arrogance of human self-sufficiency, which stops them seeking again in humility the one from whom they fell away in pride. Such were all those to whom Christ did not reveal himself, even if they did not wish to be purified by any spurious sacred rituals. It is indeed a great uncleanness of the unclean soul, thinking it can purify itself all on its own. But one must not say anything rashly about those who have not worshiped any idols, nor bound themselves over to Chaldean or magical rituals, in case perhaps it has escaped our notice how the savior, without whom nobody can be saved, has revealed himself to them in some manner or other.[84]

37. But there are others who have seen and believed that there is a God with whom they must be reconciled, and have not relied presumptuously on their own powers, and so they have wanted to be purified by sacred rites. But they too have had heads swollen with vain curiosity, and being imbued with the doctrines of demons they have thought themselves a cut above others; and so they have given the devil a foothold, and have decided that they can be purified by the tricks and vain mysteries of the *powers of the air* (Eph 2:2), that is, of demons. Such are the ones the apostle had in mind when he said, *They changed the glory of the imperishable God into the likeness of perishable man and quadrupeds and creeping things* (Rom 1:23).

In fact some of them did stretch themselves, and transcending the entire creation they perceived the creator above all things; but while remaining feeble they still went on to pride themselves on this.[85] And now it is such people, or those who follow their authority, that say to us, "We can only be purified through these mediators," through powers, clearly, of this sort.

So they are looking for a mediator; why?

"Because the human mind, wrapped up in its greedy desires and weighed down by them, stands in need of purification. And unless it is purified, it takes no delight in what it sees to be unchangeable, even if to some extent and in any way this can be seen."

And here indeed they have the right idea, because without a mediator nobody can come to God.

The true mediator and the false

38. But we have to ask what a mediator is. There is, you see, a false mediator, there is a true one. The false mediator, as I have often said, is the devil. He puts himself forward, by performing certain signs and wonders, to those who seek in a bad way and want something to pride themselves on. I mean, Pharaoh's

magicians also did the same sort of things as Moses, though they couldn't do all of them,[86] because these people only do as much as the airy spirits,[87] through whom they do them, are allowed. God, on the other hand, did just as much as he pleased. Through certain signs, therefore, as I said, proud spirits put themselves forward and promise these people purification.

But the true mediator, the Lord Jesus Christ, is one,[88] and the humble men of old also acknowledged him through his revealing himself to them, and wished to be purified through him. Before he was born of Mary he revealed himself to those who were worthy, so that they might be saved through faith in him who was going to be born and to suffer, just as we are saved through faith in him who has been born and has suffered. That indeed is why he came in such humble fashion, to show that he only purifies and saves the humble.

At that time, after all, before the Word had become flesh, it was not only among the Hebrew people to the holy patriarchs and prophets that he used to reveal himself; there are also in fact examples to be found in other nations, since the humble mediator never failed any people who sought him humbly, he the only one who reconciles to the Father, who alone could most truly say, *Nobody comes to the Father except through me* (Jn 14:6). He accommodated his humility to them, so that persevering in humility they might deserve to be purified through him, the humble mediator. Was Melchizedek, after all, of the people of Israel? And yet scripture commends him as *priest of God Most High* (Gn 14:18-19), as prefiguring the mediator himself. I mean, it is by him that even Abraham is blessed. Was Job, great man that he was, and such a great wrestler with the devil that he won the bout, sitting there on the dunghill, full of maggots, defeating in his humility the one by whom proud Adam, enjoying perfect health, was defeated in paradise—was this man of the people of Israel? And yet the true mediator is understood to have been proclaimed and foretold in his words.[89]

But just as scripture[90] mentions some people like that, as much as sufficed to make the point, so it is to be confidently believed that the revelation of the mediator, through whom they could be purified, was available, even before he appeared in the flesh, to all who humbly sought a purifying mediator, without whom nobody can be purified. Nobody, though, unless purified through the mediator, can come to that which cannot be obtained except by the most purified, even if it can be glimpsed in however small a degree by a certain intelligence of soul.[91]

So then, even if some of them sought, as the apostle says, in such a way that *they could descry the invisible things of God, understanding them through the things that were made* (Rom 1:20), but in such a way too that they *held onto the truth of God in a lie* (Rom 1:18), that is, that they called themselves wise and were puffed up with pride, not worthily honoring him from whom they had received their understanding—to such as these, as I said, that proud mediator presented himself as to the proud, just as the humble one did to the humble, through certain matching suitabilities and through a certain inexpressible and wonderful justice, which abides in God's inner sanctum, and which we should respect even if we cannot see it. That proud mediator, therefore, comes to meet the proud, the humble one to meet the humble; but the reason the humble one comes to the humble is to lead them to the heights of God; the reason the proud one comes to the proud is to bar the heights of God to those who are high and mighty in themselves.

39. Notice, I mean, how the devil insinuates himself as a mediator. He isn't mortal in the flesh, but he is a sinner. The Lord, on the other hand, wished to be mortal in the flesh, but not a sinner. He shared death with human beings, not sins. Because if he had also been a sinner, he could not have been a mediator. If he had been both mortal and sinner, after all, he would have been what the rest of humanity is, and would not now have been a mediator, but in need of a mediator. Any human being you like, after all, is a sinner. The humble mediator, however, is the just God, and also mortal; just, also mortal, and not in any old way just, but just because God, mortal because man.[92]

The proud mediator, on the other hand, is unjust and immortal; I mean he doesn't experience bodily dissolution, because he was never clothed with flesh—it is in this respect that I call him immortal. True immortality, you see, belongs only to God, according to the text, *Who alone has immortality and inhabits light inaccessible* (1 Tm 6:16), according to which the only Son is also immortal, because *he and the Father are one* (Jn 10:30); but he willed to be mortal by assuming a man.[93] So the devil, unjust and in a certain way immortal, insinuated himself as a mediator for man, who is unjust, and mortal.

Two things at the bottom end of the scale, two things at the top. But for things at the bottom to be reconciled with things at the top, they need a mediator. What are the two at the bottom? Unjust, mortal. What are the two at the top? Just, immortal. So the mediator who is to purify and lead back would not, if he were both unjust and mortal, be a mediator, because he would not have one thing from the bottom and one from the top, but each of them from the bottom, both iniquity and mortality. Again, if he had immortality from the higher realms and iniquity from the lower, he would indeed have one thing from here and one from there, and thus would seem to be a mediator, but not one to lead back, because not one to purify. In having iniquity together with man, you see, he would be held worthy of punishment with him, and would only be a mediator of a kind to block the road to God. The only thing, after all, that sins have ever known how to do is to separate from God; listen to scripture saying, *Did God make his ear dull, in order not to hear? But your sins make a separation between you and God* (Is 59:1-2).

40. So sins bar the way; but mortality does not, because mortality is the punishment of sin, coming from the judgment of God. What bars the way is the

thing that deserved this punishment. What I'm saying is this: it is not what God has done to you that bars your way to God, but what you have done to yourself. The mortality of the body, you see, is what God has done to you, while sin is what you have done to yourself. And so that true and trustworthy mediator has shared with you what God has done to you by way of retribution, but he has not shared with you what you have done to yourself by way of sin. He has shared mortality with you, but not shared iniquity with you.

He was made subject to death,[94] you see, in the flesh, not however made through sin a debtor owing a death. For *he emptied himself, taking the form of a slave, being made in the likeness of men, and being found in condition as a man* (Phil 2:7). This was not said in such a way that we should conclude he had been changed, but because he wished to be manifested in a humble and servile guise, while remaining secretly Lord and God with God, the Son equal to the Father, *through whom all things were made* (Jn 1:1.3). And so having taken on mortality and shared with us the infirmity of our punishment, he purifies us from sins and sets us free from that very mortality, the reason he was found worthy to slay death by dying being that he suffered death without deserving it. This is the true and trustworthy mediator, the humble and exalted mediator, leading us back to where we had fallen from.

But that proud mediator, the self-deceiving and deceitful mediator, has iniquity in common with sinful human beings, but he does not have the mortality of the flesh. And the reason he does not undo their mortality, when he presents them with iniquity to be imitated, is that just as the iniquity of life in the beginning was what earned this death now, so the persevering iniquity of this life now is what earns eternal death. This indeed the devil will endure in common with those whom he leads astray, while not for their sake taking on the mortality which culminates in the death of the flesh. And that is why he fancies himself as a mediator: because he has one thing in common with them—that is to say, iniquity—but does not have the other—that is to say, mortality.

The proud abhor the mortality of Christ more than the iniquity of the devil

41. The reason the proud are more readily led astray by the proud mediator is that the proud are offended more by mortality than by iniquity, and that is why they are quicker to abhor mortality in Christ's humanity[95] than iniquity in the devil's pride. And so he leads them, bloated as they are with vain and false doctrines, through I don't know what sacrilegious sacred rites, promising purification in temples; and through magical consecrations and detestable secrets he lures them to astrologers, to soothsayers, to augurs, to diviners. He has the audacity to boast that he is stronger and mightier than Christ because he was not born of a woman in the flesh, not arrested, not scourged, not spattered with spittle, not crowned with thorns, not hung on a cross, not dead and buried.

These are all things that the proud deride, which the humble mediator underwent, not taking upon himself iniquity with men and women and taking upon himself humanity, in order to heal them of the tumor of pride and make them conquerors of that false mediator, when they have learned to confess their sins, and have been purified through the justice of Christ from their own injustice, and have come through lowly fellowship with his mortality to the sublime summit of immortality.

God our Father, the Church our mother

42. And so, brothers and sisters, let us spurn the malign mediator, the self-deceiving and deceitful mediator, the mediator who does not reconcile but separates more and more. Let no one promise you any kind of purification outside the Church, whether in temples or anywhere else, by means of sacrilegious sacred rites. Let nobody do so outside the unity[96] even by means of Christian sacraments, because even if the sacrament is to be found outside the unity—which we cannot deny and dare not violate—still the power and saving effect of the sacrament, making one a *fellow heir with Christ* (Rom 8:17), is only to be found in the unity and *in the bond of peace* (Eph 4:3) of the Church.[97]

Let no one turn you away from God, no one from the Church; no one from God your Father, no one from the Church your mother. We had two parents who gave birth to us for mortality, we have two who give birth to us for immortality, God and the Church. Those gave birth to heirs to succeed them, these give birth to heirs to abide with them. Why else, after all, are we born of human parents, except in order to succeed them when they are dead? But we are brought forth by our Father, God, and our mother, the Church, in such a way as to live with our parents for ever.[98] Any who go off to sacrilegious rites or magical arts, or go consulting astrologers, augurs, diviners about their life or anything to do with this life, have cut themselves off from their Father, even if they do not leave the Church. If any, though, have cut themselves off from the Church by the division of schism, even though they may seem to themselves to be holding on to the Father, they are most perniciously forsaking their mother, while those who relinquish both Christian faith and mother Church are deserting both parents. Hold on to your Father, hold on to your mother. You are a little child; stick to your mother. You are a little child; suck your mother's milk, and she will bring you, nourished on milk, to the table of the Father.

Christ the high priest, and head of the Church,
drinks from the torrent on the way

43. Your savior took flesh to himself, your mediator took flesh to himself, and by taking flesh he took the Church to himself. He was the first to make a libation, as coming from the head, of what he would offer to God, *a high priest for ever* (Heb 5:6), and *the propitiation for our sins* (1 Jn 2:2). The Word took human nature to himself, and the two became one,[99] as it is written, *They shall be two in one flesh. This is a great sacrament,* he says, *but I mean in Christ and in the Church* (Eph 5:31-32). The bridal chamber of this marriage was the womb of the virgin. *And he, like a bridegroom coming forth from his chamber, exulted*

like a giant to run the way (Ps 19:5). A giant because strong, overcoming weakness with weakness, annihilating death with death.

But he ran on the way; he did not stop on the way, in order not to become the man who was signified as having stopped on the way of sinners. For when the psalm says, *Blessed the one who has not turned aside in the counsel of the ungodly, and has not stopped on the way of sinners* (Ps 1:1), it signifies a particular man who did stop on the way of sinners. So the Lord Jesus Christ ran on the way of sinners, but Adam stopped on the way of sinners. And because he stopped, he was wounded by robbers, he fell and lay there. But the one who was traveling along this way, not stopping but running, saw him; he found him wounded, put him on his beast, and handed him over to the innkeeper,[100] because he himself was running the way in order to fulfill what had been foretold about him: *He drinks from the torrent on the way; therefore he shall lift up the head* (Ps 110:7). The torrent, you see, is this world. Waters which flow as a result of sudden storms or winter floods are called torrents—which are, of course, going to stop flowing just as quickly. That's what all these affairs of time are like—a transient torrent, soon going to cease.

Today, New Year's Day, those who are enjoying the excesses and vanities of the world don't see that they are being swept along by the rushing force of the torrent. Let them summon back, if they can, this same day last year; let them at least call back yesterday. They don't see that their enjoyments too pass like a torrent, so that they will find themselves saying later on, *These are the ones whom at one time we held in derision and in the likeness of a reproach. We, fools that we were, reckoned their life madness and their end without honor. How they are counted among the sons of God, and their lot is among the saints! So we strayed from the way of truth, and the light of justice did not shine on us, and the sun did not rise for us* (Wis 5:3-6).

Which sun? Not this visible one, surely? This one rises for them daily. It is about this one, after all, that the Lord says, *Who makes his sun rise upon the good and the bad* (Mt 5:45). There is another sun who made this one, invisible and intelligible, the sun of justice, about which it says in another place, *The sun of justice has risen for me* (Mal 4:2). This is the sun that did not rise for them. And listen to their lament: *What use to us was pride, and what did the boastfulness of riches confer upon us? All those things have passed like a shadow* (Wis 5:8-9). It has all flowed away already like that torrent; but yet that other one who was born, who suffered, was crucified, was buried, has risen again. He drinks from this torrent on the way; that is why he has lifted up the head, which is to say, himself.

How the proud aspire to outstrip Christ himself

44. He himself, you see, is *the head of the Church* (Eph 5:23), the one who has already ascended into heaven and is seated at the right hand of the Father,[101] showing us in his whole burnt offering of himself what we should also be hoping for where our flesh is concerned, because as the apostle says, *For it is by hope*

that we have been saved, and we groan in ourselves as we await adoption, the redemption of our bodies (Rom 8:24.23). We, you see, have been adopted, while he was born the only Son. The Word who was in the beginning, *God with God* (Jn 1:1), as the evangelist testifies, and equal to the Father, as the apostle Paul says,[102] still made himself lowly, to be *the one mediator of God and men, the man Christ Jesus* (1 Tm 2:5).

But all proud people aspire to be just like that evil and false mediator who bars the way to God; wherever they may be, they wish to be like their mediator. And just as you see this in human beings, so it is in angels. The one who wished to be mediator and reconciler to God, about whom we have already said much, that is, the humble and exalted mediator, the Lord Jesus Christ, took to himself the whole range of creation—the whole range of creation is in fact to be found in man; we said above, after all, that the created is either spirit or body. So he took to himself the whole of man, *accepting the form of a slave* (Phil 2:7); whatever there is in the rational mind, whatever in the soul, whatever in the flesh, he took to himself the whole of it, apart from sin. Thus in him all things are included, so that nobody should err by wandering off to look for some mere creature to mediate a seemingly cleansing purification. The reason this mediator has the whole, the reason this mediator took the whole to himself, is that only a mediating creature like this can purify from iniquities and liberate from death, a creature which does not presume to be of any avail in itself, but cleaves personally[103] to God the Word, and is coupled and mingled with it in an inexpressible manner, so that it is possible to say, *the Word became flesh* (Jn 1:14). To this end was his lowliness despised and exalted, that people should not in humility despair of themselves, nor presumptuously rely on themselves in pride.

So when proud human beings want to be worshiped,[104] and then get angry if God is preferred to them, they are imitators of that deceitful mediator. As against this, when humble, saintly human beings are honored in this way by erring people who wish to place their hopes in man, being inattentive to the divine scripture which says, *Cursed be everyone who places his hopes in man* (Jer 17:5), they grieve over them and faithfully warn them, as best they can, to hope in God, not in man, seeing that even[105] the apostle himself did not want people to place any hopes in himself, but rather in the truth he was proclaiming. What was being said through him was something better than he was, through whom it was being said, and he wanted believers to place their hopes in what was being said through him, not in him through whom it was being said. *Though even if we,* he says. That's nothing, *if we*; listen to what follows: *or an angel,* he says, *from heaven were to proclaim to you something else besides what you have received, let him be anathema* (Gal 1:8). He realized that the false mediator could *transfigure himself into an angel of light* (2 Cor 11:14), and preach something false. So then just as proud human beings want themselves to be worshiped instead of God, want to arrogate to themselves whatever they can, to have their names on everybody's lips, and if possible outstrip Christ himself in fame, so do the devil and his angels.

The Donatists put Donatus in the place of Christ

45. My brothers and sisters, I am speaking to Catholics. The Donatists put Donatus in the place of Christ. If they hear some pagan disparaging Christ, they probably put up with it more patiently than if they hear him disparaging Donatus.[106] You know what I'm talking about, and you are forced to experience this every day. They are so perverse in their love of Donatus that they put him before Christ. Not only, I mean, do they have nothing they can say, but they even know they have nothing they can say. Nothing, you see, holds them under the name of Christ but the name of Donatus; they have been seduced into accepting the name of a man against Christ. The reason they have conceived the most monstrous and . . .[107] hatred against us is that we cry out to them, "Do not place your hopes in a man, or you will be accursed."[108] They hate those who preach peace, and if they ever suffer anything for this colossal villainy of theirs—and not for Christ's sake, but for the sake of Donatus—they think they are martyrs.

And because we say to them, "Don't puff out the baptism of Christ;[109] love peace, give yourself back to the whole wide world; Christ redeemed the whole; don't reduce the buyer of the whole to a mere part," that's why they hate us, and if they get the chance kill us at the hands of the Circumcellions.[110] But because the Lord was at hand to help us, we escaped, giving thanks for the Lord's mercy, which is why we admonish and beg you to pray for us, that the Lord may always inspire us with the confidence to preach his peace, and that we may not be afraid of them, but may rather love them and rejoice that there is fulfilled in us what is written: *With those who hate peace I was peaceful; when I spoke to them, they waged war on me for nothing* (Ps 120:7). And if they cannot be cured in any other way, let them wage war on us, let them strike, let them slay, and still let them be cured.

The right way of honoring the holy angels

46. But let us get back, brothers and sisters, to what I had started to say; grief, you see, snatched me away from what I had intended. Just as there are proud human beings—they prefer themselves rather than God to be worshiped—so in the same way the proud angels prefer themselves rather than God to be worshiped. And just as there are holy human beings—they would rather God were worshiped than themselves—so in the same way all the holy angels, which we must also undoubtedly believe about the martyrs, would rather God were worshiped than they themselves. They want the one whom they honor to be honored; their choice is to be loved in him; not only do they not accept private honors from human beings, they positively reject them, which is why we also gave the example, as far as the Lord enabled us to, of that angel in the Apocalypse, who did not want himself, but God to be adored by a man.[111]

So don't be afraid, brothers and sisters, that if you worship God alone with religious service, you may offend some holy angel or some martyr. You see, if *the prudence of the flesh* (Rom 8:6) should persuade you of this, and judging from yourselves—if perhaps out of some personal arrogance or pride you take delight in being honored in yourselves for your own sake, not in God for God's sake (and if this doesn't happen, you get indignant)—you should assume that either the holy angels or the holy martyrs enjoy such obsequious veneration from men, and demand for themselves the service that is owed to God alone, you will fall the easiest of victims to the seductive lures of the pagans, and will most certainly withdraw a long way away from the Lord your God, about whom we have received such a clear commandment: *The Lord your God shall you adore, and him alone shall you serve* (Lk 4:8; Dt 6:13; 10:20).

Do you wish to be safe in honoring the holy angels and the holy martyrs? Worship him in whom alone they wish to be honored. If they are holy, you see, they get angry with you if you worship them separately, and not him alone from whom they too have received the gracious gift of their bliss. So because they are holy, you should decline, rather, to offend them by wishing, as it were, to worship them on the side, because in worshiping God, you worship everyone who cleaves to God with pious love and holy devotion. But if a being gets angry because he is not being worshiped himself with his own proper sacred rites, he can now only be that proud transgressor and false mediator, *transfiguring himself into an angel of light* (2 Cor 11:14). Now, if he has swung you aside to himself, he has blocked your way; not only can you not reach your destination through him, but rather it's a case of your being prevented through him from reaching it.

The fallacy of calling pagan gods the powers of God

47. Don't let them sell any of you their idle talk, and say, "What we worship is the powers of God, in order to reach God through them, and so we perform these sacred rites for Saturn, those for Jupiter, others for Pluto, others for Neptune, those for Mars, these for Ceres."[112] The reason, of course, why these gods don't all enjoy the same rites is that they arrogate to themselves their own personal and proper cults; which means that these are not in fact sacred, but sacrilegious rites. And in all these rites it is their prince who exults in triumph, though he delights not so much in the rites themselves as in deceiving human beings and leading them astray, such is his proud malevolence. And so you mustn't let them seduce you, when they say to you, "If you people worship the martyrs, and assume that through them you are being assisted in God's presence, how much more in the right are we to worship the powers of God, to be assisted through them in God's presence."

I mean, just pay attention to the Church's sacraments, and see if sacrifice is offered to any of the martyrs, with us presenting one sacrifice to this martyr, another to that one. On the contrary, at all their memorial shrines we offer the one sacrifice, and not to any of them either, but to the Lord of us all; and in this sacrifice we also honor the martyrs according to their status, not in themselves but in the one through whom they defeated the devil.[113] And they are mindful of us all the more lovingly, the less we are inclined to perform for them private personal rites, because they find their honor in him alone, in whom alone they find their joy. If anybody says to you, "Invoke the angel Gabriel in this way, invoke Michael in that; offer the former this little ritual, the latter this other"; don't be taken in, don't consent. And don't let him mislead you just because the names of these angels can be read in the scriptures;[114] observe rather in what role they are to be read there, whether they ever demanded from men any kind of personal religious veneration for themselves, and did not rather always wish glory to be given to the one God, whom they obey.

No good angel will demand special worship from us

48. It's not only, though, if some human being, but also if any angel, seemingly, should wish to tempt you, either through some kind of apparition or through a dream, and say, "Do this for me, celebrate this rite for me, because I am"—for example—"the angel Gabriel"; don't believe him. As for you, stick safely to worshiping the one God, who is Father and Son and Holy Spirit. If it's really an angel, he will rejoice at your worshiping like that; but if he gets angry because you haven't given him something extra, then you must now understand him to be the one about whom the apostle says that he *transfigures himself into an angel of light* (2 Cor 11:14). He wants to block your way, he is intruding himself with evil intent; he is not the mediator who reconciles, but rather the one who separates.

I mean, that angel in the Apocalypse[115] and others like him don't want themselves, but God, to be adored. They are messengers, announcing whatever message they have been given to announce; they are *attendants* (Heb 1:14), doing whatever they have been ordered to do, presenting our prayers to God, not demanding them for themselves in God's stead. The angel says to the man, *I offered your petition in the presence of the glory of God* (Tb 12:12); and yet the man wasn't pleading with the angel but with God; the attendant offered his prayer. He didn't say, did he, in the way the crooked and corrupt attendants of some authorities do, "Give me something, if you want me to take your message, if you want me to admit you to the presence"? That is not the kind of great household that our Lord runs. His servants love him, his children love him. If you want to corrupt any of them as it were on the side, in order to be admitted to their master, you will be expelled very far indeed from that great household.

If, you see, ...[116] are imitating the angelic mode of life—because it is written, *There is one soul and one heart toward God, and nobody has any private property, but all things are in common among them*, as we read in the Acts of the Apostles that there were so many thousands converted from among the Jews,[117] and that as they possessed nothing as private property, *distribution was made to each as each had need* (Acts 4:32.35); so if these people are imitating the angelic mode of life, and if any of them has a friend, or brother or father or mother or any other relative who wants to offer him something to keep privately as his own, he doesn't only spurn the offer; he also advises the well-wisher that if anything is to be offered and accepted, it must be offered to God; this, you

see, is what those people did, who laid the price of their possessions at the feet
of the apostles, and those too who were urged by the apostle to make some
offering for the poor among the saints in Jerusalem—and what he's teaching
them is that they should know they are offering to God whatever they do in this
respect.[118] So how much more will those angels, who are of course more perfect,
who serve on the heavenly staff and in the great house and the heavenly city
Jerusalem, *the mother of us all* (Gal 4:26), want nothing to be shown them as
their personal and private honor, because they rejoice in that honor, and that
honor alone, which is shown in common to God as God and to that city as to his
temple, that is, to the universal Church!

Christ our mediator, by being our priest

49. And the reason why, for the sake of the purification that is effected by a
mediator, the one who is equal to the Father wished to be the one mediator and
himself become man was so that we through a related substance (because he is
man) might attain to the supreme substance (because he is God). And the reason
he descended was because we were in the lower regions, while he ascended so
that we might not remain in the lower regions. He is the one true mediator who
cheats nobody, who even while he is equal to the Father was also willing for
our sakes to become less than he, not by losing what makes him equal, but by
taking on what makes him less.[119] He has already liberated even our flesh in his
flesh. *He dies now no more, and death will not lord it over him any further* (Rom
6:9). It is to him that our prayers come, although in the liturgy[120] of the Church
they are addressed to the Father.

He dies now no more. It is he,[121] you see, the high priest, who offers them,
having offered himself as a holocaust for us. He is the one who takes us through
to the end, confronting us on the way, not to block our way, but to direct it, not
to separate, but to reconcile us, not to put obstacles in our way, but to break up
all obstacles. He is the one and only pontiff, the one and only priest, who was
prefigured in God's priests of old. That is why they used to look for a priest
without bodily blemish ,[122] because he alone ever lived without the blemish of
sin, even in his mortal body. For what was prefigured in their bodies found its
real meaning in his life.

The reason, though, why all of us bishops[123] are called priests is that we are
the people in charge. However, it is the whole universal Church which is the
body of that one priest. To the priest belongs his body. That, after all, is why the
apostle Peter[124] says to the Church itself, *A holy people, a royal priesthood* (1
Pt 2:9).

50. In those days only one priest used to be anointed; nowadays all Christians
are anointed.[125] The king used to be anointed, the priest used to be anointed, the
rest never were. The Lord assumed each role, not just figuratively anymore, but
now in real truth, the roles of both king and priest; because that's why each role
was prefigured in King David himself *from whose seed he was made according
to the flesh* (Rom 1:3). He was a king as we know, and it's obvious. The priestly

role was also prefigured in him, when he ate of those loaves of proposition, *which it was not lawful to eat, except for the priests alone* (Mk 2:26; 1 Sm 21:6); the Lord himself recalled this in the gospel, so that those who can understand might recognize him as having been prefigured in David.[126]

Because Mary herself also traced her descent not only from the royal line, but from the priestly one as well. That it was from the royal line is obvious; that's why the apostle says, *who was made for him from the seed of David according to the flesh.* For although Joseph was called his father in the order of love,[127] still he wasn't born of his seed, as is clearly stated in the gospel.[128] So it remains that it is on Mary's account that Christ is said to be of the seed of David, because she was of the seed of David, of the royal seed, that is. But how do we also discover a priestly ancestry in Mary? It's written in the gospel that the priest Zechariah had a wife, Elizabeth, *of the daughters of Aaron* (Lk 1:5); so Elizabeth was of priestly descent—Aaron, of course, the brother of Moses, was a priest, and the whole tribe of Levi. But in the gospel the angel says to the virgin Mary, *Your cousin, Elizabeth* (Lk 1:36). So if Elizabeth, one of the daughters of Aaron the priest, was a cousin of Mary's, it cannot be doubted that Mary was of priestly as well as of royal blood.[129]

Thus it is that each role, both royal and priestly, is to be found in the Lord as regards the man whom he assumed; royal, whereby he leads us to follow him totally in his spiritual warfare, *until he puts his enemies under his feet, and the last enemy to be destroyed will be death* (1 Cor 15:25-26)—because even our king himself was tempted by our enemy, so that the mere soldier might learn the business of soldiering.[130] But he is a priest in that he offered himself as a holocaust for expiating and purging away our sins. That's why in those days two persons used to be anointed to prefigure him: the king and the priest.

All Christians, being anointed with chrism,
share in Christ's priesthood and kingship

51. That too is why there are *two fish* (Mk 6:38) with those five barley loaves. Fish, after all, is eaten as relish,[131] and relishes are as a rule seasoned with oil. So there are two fish with the five loaves, that is, with the Old Testament, of which the five books of Moses are the chief part. But with the seven loaves, which are not said to be of barley, and which now stand for the New Testament, we are told there were *a few fish* (Mk 8:7), because there had already begun to be a few Christians, that is, anointed ones, with whom the universal Church would soon be filling the whole world. The five loaves of barley, you see, which is veiled by the little skirts, so to say, of its husks, represent those things which are to be understood in a spiritual sense in the law itself, which the Lord explained in his training of the apostles. That is why in that instance twelve baskets were filled with the scraps left over.[132]

The seven loaves, on the other hand, represent the sevenfold working of the Spirit in the New Testament, as John also says in the Apocalypse. He is of course to be understood as mentioning the *seven spirits* (Rv 1:4) for the seven operations of the Spirit which Isaiah had listed before him: those *of wisdom and understanding, of counsel and courage, of knowledge and piety, and of the fear of the Lord* (Is 11:2-3). And that's why with *those scraps left over seven hampers were filled* (Mk 8:8), the number which signifies the universal Church. Thus the same apostle John also writes to seven Churches.[133] And in the letters of the apostle Paul the same number seven, not of letters but of Churches, is to be found. And there are many things in those sacramental symbols of scripture,[134] to be found with all the more pleasure, the more diligently they are looked for.

But just now I mentioned something from there about seasoning fish with oil, to show that the royal and the priestly role was signified on that occasion in the two fish, because two persons used to be anointed in those days, the king and the priest. Now the name Christ comes from chrism, that is, from anointing. But Christ's body is the Church. And that is why all Christians are anointed, in a sacrament hidden from the rest, but known to the faithful.[135] But the one and only priest is the mediator himself, the sinless head of the Church, through whom is effected the purging away of our sins.

Bishops are not mediators, as Parmenian claimed

52. Here the very painful thought occurs to me that I should remind you that Parmenian, who was once a bishop of the Donatists, had the audacity to state in one of his letters that the bishop is the mediator between the people and God.[136] You can see that they are putting themselves forward in the place of the bridegroom; they are corrupting the souls of those others with a sacrilegious adultery. This is no mean case of presumption, one that would strike me as totally incredible had I not read it. You see, if the bishop is the mediator between the people and God, it follows that we must take it there are many mediators, since there are many bishops. So then, in order to read the letter of Parmenian, let us censor the letter of the apostle Paul, where he says, *For there is one God, and one mediator of God and men, the man Christ Jesus* (1 Tm 2:5). But between whom is he the mediator, if not between God and his people? So between God and his body, because the Church is his body. Truly monstrous, therefore, is that pride which has the audacity to set up the bishop as mediator, guilty of the adulterous fallacy of claiming for itself the marriage of Christ.

Let us observe the friend of the bridegroom being jealous for the bridegroom, not putting himself forward in the place of the bridegroom. Does he say, "I have betrothed you to myself"? That man can say this, the one who calls himself a mediator between the people and God, not this one who says, *Was Paul crucified for you, or were you baptized in the name of Paul* (1 Cor 1:13); not this one who says, *For there is one God, and one mediator of God and men, the man Christ Jesus*; nor this one who says, *I have betrothed you to one husband, to present you as a chaste virgin to Christ* (2 Cor 11:2). And that's why that adulterer, *who did not have on a wedding garment* (Mt 22:11), was thrown out of the wedding feast; he was not wearing, you see, the proper garment in which to do honor to the bridegroom, but by the clothes he was wearing he sought his own honor at the bridegroom's banquet.

The priesthood of Christ, head and body, prefigured in the Old Testament

53. So, brothers and sisters, we have one mediator, who is also our head. But as for us bishops, even though it is not together with you that we are the rulers of Churches, still it is together with you, in the name of Christ, that we are members of the body of Christ. We all have one head, not many, because the body which wants to have many heads is already a monster. But we were saying about anointing that in those days only the priest was anointed and the king, while nowadays it's all Christians. From this please observe that you all belong to the body of the one priest together with us bishops, which is because we are all of us the faithful.[137] However those who are in charge of Churches are particularly called priests; this doesn't mean, all the same, that the rest of the body is not the body of the priest.

And that's why, because[138] in those ancient sacraments and symbols that one priest was being prefigured, that is, our Lord the priest Jesus Christ, the one priest alone used to enter the holy of holies, while all the people stood outside. Are you nowadays outside, while the bishops stand at the altar, and not watching inside, and hearing and attesting and receiving?[139] In those days the one priest used to enter the holy of holies once a year. The year represents the whole of time. So just once in the whole course of time our one and only priest rising from the dead, our Lord Jesus Christ, entered the true, not the figurative, holy of holies, beyond the veils of heaven, offering himself for us.[140]

He entered, and there he now is. But the people, together with us bishops, are still standing outside; we haven't yet risen *to go to meet Christ and to remain with him for ever* (1 Thes 4:17) inside, when he is going to say to the good servant, *Enter into the joy of your Lord* (Mt 25:21). So what was symbolized in those days by the one priest alone entering the holy of holies and the people standing outside is what has now been fulfilled through our Lord Jesus Christ alone entering the secret places of the heavens above, and the people still groaning and sighing outside, *saved in hope, awaiting the redemption of their bodies* (Rom 8:24.23), which is going to be achieved in the resurrection of the dead.

But all the same we do have our priest and pontiff, *interceding for us* (Heb 7:25) in the holy of holies, seated at the right hand of the Father, so that we need have no fear in the course of these wanderings of ours, provided we don't *stray from the way of truth* (Wis 5:6), provided we don't love someone else instead of him, but love one another in him, so as to see him in every single one of our brothers and sisters who is walking in his paths, in them to honor him, to support him *who was handed over on account of our transgressions, and rose again on account of our justification* (Rom 4:25), because[141] he himself speaks in his saints, as the apostle says: *Or are you seeking an experience of the one who is speaking in me, of Christ?* (2 Cor 13:3). And while he may say, *Neither the one who plants is anything, nor the one who waters, but the one who gives the growth, God* (1 Cor 3:7), because he didn't want himself, but God in him, to be loved, still he bears witness to some people with the words, *You accepted me like an angel of God, like Christ Jesus* (Gal 4:14). So in all his saints it is he that is the one to be loved, because he said, *I was hungry and you gave me to eat* (Mt 25:35). You see, he didn't say "you gave them," but *you gave me*. Such is the love of the head for his body!

54. And so because this mediator and priest has entered alone into the holy of holies, while the Church—*which is his body* (Eph 1:23)—is still, as we said, groaning and sighing outside with tearful prayers and in laborious activities, we don't find in the old books that the priest ever commended himself to the prayers of the people, because he was typifying our Lord Jesus Christ, for whom nobody prays. Who after all could be typified by the priest for whom nobody used to pray, but our Lord Jesus Christ *who intercedes for us* (Rom 8:34), and is in no need of our prayers on his behalf?

He himself was also pleased to signify this on this earth, when he was praying alone on the mountain, while his disciples were being tossed about in the boat by storms.[142] We too in the Church, as in a boat, are rolling and pitching in the storms of this age; but because he, as then on the mountain, so now in the heights of heaven, *is interceding for us*, let us cast care, not ourselves, to the winds.

The apostle John never claimed to be a mediator

55. John the apostle too says, *I am writing this to you so that you may not sin. And if anyone does sin, we have an advocate with the Father, Jesus Christ the Just One; he it is who is the propitiation for our sins* (1 Jn 2:1-2). Notice who this John is: the one who was lying on the Lord's breast, and who at that banquet drank from that breast what he would gush forth to the peoples: *In the beginning was the Word and the Word was with God, and the Word was God* (Jn 1:1). So did this John, then, ever say, "And if anyone does sin, you have me with the Father; I am praying for you"? Just notice who said what. Not only, I mean, did he not say that, but even if he had said, *And if anyone does sin,* you have *an advocate with the Father, Jesus Christ the Just One; he it is who is the propitiation for* your *sins*, he would have seemed somewhat proud and arrogant. He didn't say that. And if he didn't say that, what colossal pride it would have been for him to say, "You have me as an advocate with the Father"! What even more monstrous sacrilege it would have been for him to say, "You have me as a mediator with the Father," wishing in this way to place himself between sinners and God!

And that is what these people are neither afraid nor ashamed to say, that the bishop is a mediator between God and men. Sure, that man is a mediator, but in the party of Donatus, to block the way, not to lead the way, as Donatus himself did; he introduced his own name, you see, to close off the road to Christ. That's why they refuse to come to the Church, because Donatus has blocked the way, because - - - - - - - through a *wall which had been whitened* (Acts 23:3) (it was made of earth, after all) but not with the Christian religion. He whitewashed it in order to deceive - - - - - - - - - - - - - - - -[143] so that, coming as far as him, they might not be able to pass over to Christ, that is, to the body of Christ, which is the Church spread throughout the whole world. There you have how he made himself a mediator, in the same way as that proud angel also does, about whom we have already had much to say.

But pay attention to precisely what it is that John says: *I am writing this to you, so that you may not sin. And if anyone does sin, we have an advocate with the Father.* He wouldn't have said *we* have, unless he had known himself well and was presenting himself humbly as he really was. *And he it is,* he says, *who is the atonement for our sins.*[144] He didn't say "your," as though distancing himself from sins. If he had said that, he could have been quoted against himself from another place, where he says, *If we say that we have no sin, we are deceiving ourselves, and the truth is not in us* (1 Jn 1:8).

Do your best to avoid sin and to be fervent in good works

56. And so then, brothers and sisters, take real trouble over not sinning, exert yourselves energetically not to sin. But if anyone does sin, that one will purge our guilt who is *the atonement for our sins* (1Jn 2:2). Avoid all those evil kinds of behavior for which *God's name is blasphemed* (Rom 2:24), so that your good manner of life may redound, by gaining others, to the glory of the name of Christ. Avoid those things which above all can separate you from God's altar. As for the sins, though, which creep in every day through the habits of daily life, and never stop seeping in, as from the waves of the sea of this world, through whatever weaknesses we have, pump out the bilges with good works, to save the ship from being wrecked.[145] Let these daily wounds be healed by the daily remedies of alms, fasting, prayers.

Be fervent in good works, neither showing off to men, for your own glory, what you do,[146] nor avoiding the eyes of those who would like to imitate you, *that they may see your good works, and glorify your Father who is in heaven* (Mt 5:16). *Whatever you do* (Col 3:17), *do all things for the glory of God* (1 Cor 10:31), so that that humble and exalted one may exalt us from our humility. Our alms, you see, will reach him, who *for our sakes became poor, though he was rich* (2 Cor 8:9), in the same way as our fasting will reach him, who fasted for our sakes;[147] in the same way too our prayers will reach him, when we sincerely ask in them that *our debts may be forgiven, just as we too forgive our debtors* (Mt 6:12), just as he too forgave his debtors, as he hung on the cross, saying, *Father, forgive them, because they do not know what they are doing* (Lk 23:34).

Let that one be blessed, who gave you the ability to do whatever good you do do. Because if you attribute your good works to yourselves, and arrogate the credit to yourselves, so that you are being puffed up with pride in the very sacrifices of humility, you will be giving that false mediator his chance,[148] enabling him to intrude himself and block your way. He searches out all the entries, you see, and tries to crawl in even through the good works themselves. And if he finds people doing good and attributing to themselves what they do, and putting on airs like turkey cocks over others who don't do the same, he immediately presents himself deceitfully to be taken as a mediator.

57. But as I had started to say,[149] we don't find any priest in the old books commending himself to the prayers of the people, because they symbolized the one for whom nobody was going to pray, that is, our Lord Jesus Christ, who is the one, not symbolic but true, mediator and priest. On the other hand Paul the apostle, who knew that he belonged with all the other members to the body of the priest, does commend himself to the prayers of the Church, because *the members care for each other; and if one member is glorified, all the members rejoice with it, and if one member suffers, all the members suffer with it* (1 Cor 12:25-26). The head intercedes for all the members, the members should intercede for each other under the head. So what does the apostle say? *Praying at the same time,* he says, *for us too, that God may open for us a door of the word* (Col 4:3). And the Church prayed for Peter when Peter was in chains,[150] and its prayers were heard, just as Peter too prayed for the Church, because the members pray for each other.

These apostles don't call themselves mediators, and prayers are offered for them by those whose prayers they ask for; and those people do call themselves mediators—and if they would only remove themselves from the midst, both of them, which have been divided in pride, would be made one.[151] Far, therefore, from the hearts of Christians be what is demonstrated in the pride of heretics! As I said to your graces, that first priesthood had a kind of symbolic reference; what was then symbolized has now been realized. We do have a mediator and high priest. He has ascended into heaven, he has entered *into the inner place behind the veil,* into that true, not merely symbolic, holy of holies. The sacrament of this reality is celebrated in the Church; you are praying with us inside, to the bishop's words you reply, "Amen." That, you see, is the way the people, as it were, underwrites his words, because all of us belong to the body of the priest.[152] So don't let anybody, as the saying goes, sell you smoke;[153] we have one mediator, the Lord Jesus Christ; *it is he who is the atonement,*[154] *he the propitiation for our sins* (1 Jn 2:2); let us all hold on to him without a qualm.

58. Certainly you can see, brothers and sisters, to return now to what I was saying against the pagans,[155] how you should arm yourselves, not only so that you are not overcome by them, but also, insofar as this is within your competence, that you may convince them and gain them for salvation; and how you should pray and fast for them, that they may come to know God and honor him as he should be honored, not as the apostle says about some of them, *because while they knew God, they did not glorify him as God or give thanks, but they became futile in their thinking, and their senseless minds were darkened* (Rom 1:21), so that they went looking for a superstitious and sacrilegious defilement under the name of purification. Wishing to adhere, you see, to that thing which always is, which is always the same, abiding unchangeable, they were able to attain to it after a fashion by the acuteness of their wits, but refused to honor it

with humble hearts. So they stumbled on that false mediator who is jealous of the human soul, and strives by all available means to prevent it passing from the labors and difficulties which he is in control of to that peace where there is one more sublime than he is himself. To him pertain all the sacrilegious rites and the wickedly deceitful machinations of the astrologers, fortune-tellers, sooth-sayers, Chaldeans.[156]

Pride may see where we are meant to go; only humility can get there

59. As for you, though, my brothers and sisters, who perhaps are not able with your mind's eye to see what they have seen, and are not yet of a caliber to pass in your rational thinking beyond the universal creation, spiritual as well as bodily, and to see the unchangeable God *from whom and through whom and in whom all things were made* (Rom 11:36), don't be alarmed, don't despair, because he has himself come down to the lowest and the weakest, and made himself into the way for you.[157] What good, I mean, does it do them to see the home country from the vast distance of their pride? They can't find the way to it, because the way to those heights of the home country starts from humility. They can see the home country, as it were, from the mountain of pride, from the mountain on the other side of the valley. But nobody can go up to it without first coming down. They refuse to come down so that they can go up; that is, they refuse to be humble so that they can become Christians.

When they say to themselves, "And am I going to be what my janitress is, and not rather what Plato was, or Pythagoras?" puffing pompous inanities from heedless mouths, they are refusing to come down, so they cannot go up. Our Lord, you see, came down to us from the heights of his majestic eminence, and these people refuse to come down to him from the swollen pimple of their pride. So he, then, came down, in order *to choose the weak things of the world and confound the strong, and the foolish things of the world to confound the wise, and he chose the base-born and contemptible things of the world and the things that are not as though they were, in order to cancel out the things that are* (1 Cor 1:27-28).

The humility of the incarnation

60. Because the reason he was willing to become man was to teach humility as God who had become man, not by changing himself into a man, but by assuming a man, it would seem that nothing could be added to such humility, and yet in his human status he didn't choose the things on which human beings pride themselves. He didn't choose high-born parents, or ones of any profes-sional distinction. I mean, it was his will to be born of a woman who was betrothed to a carpenter, so that nobody might boast of the rank of his parents as against the justice of someone poor and base-born, and so become incurably conceited. At least he didn't choose a noble city in which to be born—Bethlehem has few inhabitants. It's true he himself was from the tribe of David, which came

from there; but still there were many poor and base-born people in that tribe, as in the others. And David himself, *from whose seed according to the flesh the Lord Jesus Christ came* (Rom 1:3), well, wasn't he herding sheep before he was chosen by God for the kingship?[158] You see, already in him too he had chosen the base-born things of the world to confound the high-born, and to prefigure in him what would be fulfilled through his seed. So he did also choose a humble stock from which to be born.

But someone[159] may say, perhaps, "Even if he himself was born in humble circumstances, he wanted to be able to boast about the nobility of his disciples." Well, he didn't choose kings, or senators, or philosophers, or orators; on the contrary, he chose common people, poor people, uneducated people, fishermen. Peter was a fisherman, Cyprian[160] an orator. Unless the fisherman had faithfully gone ahead, the orator would not have humbly approached. None of you should despair of yourselves because you are disregarded and treated as of no account. Only hold onto Christ, and your hope will not let you down.

Some can glimpse the home country from afar, some can't

61. Those people, you see, who as I was saying can see the home country from a long way off, and from the mountain of pride on the opposite side of the valley, scorn humility; that's why they don't stick to the way, because our way is humility. Christ showed us this way in himself. Any who deviate from this way will stumble upon a mountain of tangled and impenetrable thickets, the devil placing himself in their way, destructively and deceitfully intruding himself as a mediator through countless sacrilegious rites, through soothsayers, augurs, fortune-tellers, astrologers, magicians. People who are sold on these don't come down to the way, but wander around on a kind of wooded mountain, from which some of them lift up their eyes and see the home country, but they can't reach it, because they don't keep to the way.[161]

Those on the other hand who do now keep to the way, that is, to the true and trustworthy mediator, the mediator who leads along the way and doesn't block it, the mediator who purges away guilt and doesn't involve us in it, these persevere in walking along in the faith they hold.[162] Because some of them too can see the home country, some of them can't. But let those who can't yet see the home country not depart from the way, and they will reach exactly the same place as those who can. You see, some people have such sharp eyes that they can see things from a long way off. It does these no good to see where they are going and not know how to get there. But if they know the way, being able to see from afar the place they have to reach is not so much use to them as knowing how to get there. Those on the other hand who are not so sharp-sighted, if they walk along together with the others, are going to arrive together with them.

So then, those of you who can rise in mind beyond the whole of creation and catch a glimpse of the inexpressible light of wisdom, will see, when you see her, that she cannot be put into words, and will see that nothing that has been said on the subject is worthy of that greatness, although it may all be suitable for the little ones, who are being nurtured to hear things as they can be put into words, until they come to hear what cannot be put into words. Let those of you, on the other hand, who cannot rise above creation and glimpse the inexpressible truth, hold onto the mediator, because unless even those who can already glimpse something unchangeable hold onto him, it is surely in vain that they glimpse it. In him we have the bodily creation, which he also took to himself in the flesh; in him we also have the spiritual creation, because there is a soul there, a rational mind there; in him the very Word *through which all things were made* (Jn 1:3), because *the Word became flesh and dwelt among us* (Jn 1:14). Let us hold onto this way and not deviate from it, or else we will stumble on false mediators who promise us purification and provide us with obstacles to it.

In Christ God is as near to us as to the celestial powers

62. He alone, after all, is the mediator *in whom are hidden all the treasures of wisdom and knowledge, who is the head of every lordship and authority* (Col 2:3.10); by what we already hold he leads us on to what we ought to hold. Nothing, you see, holds human beings so fast in its grip as human affection. That is why he, being God and man, through what we already hold carries us across to what ought to be held onto.[163] Indeed, to stop human beings assuming that he is far from human nature, that Word of God *through which all things were made . . .*[164]

. . . but to be near only to the celestial or supercelestial powers; and that is why they would want these powers to be their mediators to that Word, and their cleansers; and in this way through pride and vain curiosity they would stumble on the powers of this air which trick and deceive the senses of weak humanity with all sorts of various errors, envious as they are of its passage to God, and eager to dominate those they have ensnared. That is why the Word itself through which all things were made became flesh; that is, it also coupled to itself, from man, the nature of flesh,[165] so that in this way humanity might learn that what it had assumed to be near only to celestial beings is not in fact far from its own nature either, and then, being purified through this kindred mediation might cleave to the unchangeable godhead.

That is why he was good enough to perform both earthly and heavenly miracles, to show that those beings too are subject to him, which can terrify us mortals *by false signs and prodigies* (2 Thes 2:9). He also showed that every spiritual power either fears Christ or loves Christ, so that any which fears Christ needn't be feared by a Christian, while any which loves Christ should be loved in Christ.

God is faithful, pagan rites useless

63. So then, dearest brothers and sisters, don't let people scare you on this account either, when they say that these powers of the elements have to be placated and honored with their own sacraments on account of the necessities

of life and the temporal goods that we need for our various uses, because in fact they have no power over these matters except what is allowed them from above. Recollect that that holy man Job could not even have been tested by such enormous trials, unless the tempter had received the power from the Lord God.[166] And pay attention to what the apostle says: *God is faithful, who will not allow you to be tempted beyond what you can bear, but with the temptation he will also provide a way out, so that you may be able to endure* (1 Cor 10:13).

Also pay attention to those who do rely on such things, who bind up souls of light with the sacraments of demons and magical arts;[167] observe how gratuitously they forfeit their salvation. They don't, after all, avoid suffering the same things as other people, or even suffering worse things with the torture of a bad conscience: financial losses, diseases, convictions, deaths, frequently sharing in the scourges common to the human race, frequently suffering too for their own misdeeds. Observe whether those who worship Neptune have better luck with their sea voyages than those who don't worship him; whether those who have bound themselves to the service of the temple of Tellus have richer harvests from their fields than those who have not tied themselves down to any such superstition; whether women who worship Juno give birth with slighter labor pains or less danger than Christian women who execrate her; whether those who worship Mercury are more quick-witted than those who pour scorn on such fancies, or else, because he is also said to be the god of commerce, whether those who sacrifice to him make bigger profits than those who refuse to contaminate themselves with any such sacrilege.

And in this way run the searching eye of your minds over all these temporal advantages; you will find that they are all controlled by the supreme authority of God. Christians who serve him alone and hold to his mediator, *the way* (Jn 14:6), care nothing for the deceptive enticements and terrors of such nonsense, but render honor to the most true God, whether their self-restraint is being tested by temporal prosperity, or their courage by temporal adversity, because *God is faithful, who does not allow us to be tempted beyond what we can bear, but with the temptation provides a way out, so that we may be able to endure* (1 Cor 10:13). Thus he comforts us in all circumstances, and fills us with the joy of *good hope* (Wis 12:19), until he brings us through to the place we are being led to, by the way which he has in his gracious goodness provided for our weakness.

Turning etc.

End of the treatise of Saint Augustine, delivered on the first of January against the pagans, on the false mediator the devil and the true mediator Christ.

NOTES

1. This sermon includes the fragment already published as Sermon 198, together with 197 and 198A (III, 6). Dolbeau dates it very precisely to 1 January 404. As the sermon refers to the imperial edict outlawing public pagan worship (section 16, note 44), it must be after 399, the year that edict was promulgated, and therefore at the earliest, 1 January 400. As it doesn't mention the edict of 405 imposing union on the Donatists, its latest possible date is 1 January 405. But that New Year's day was a Sunday, and the preacher in this sermon is exhorting his congregation to fast today; and that he could and would never have done on a Sunday. So now 404 is the latest possible date. Finally, a reference to an attack on Augustine by Donatist Circumcellions (section 46; see note 110) and a word for word echo of his *Letter against Parmenian* indicate that it could not have been preached before 403: hence 1 January 404 is the only possible date.

It is perhaps the longest sermon he ever preached—three hours?—and it was in fact a deliberate "filibuster," intended to keep his audience as long as possible in church, and so prevent them from rushing off to the wicked pagan jollifications which he was preaching against. Dolbeau thinks that Carthage is more likely to have been the place it was preached in than Hippo Regius; while there are some points of style and other little things that suggest Augustine was preaching to his own people, the weight of the internal evidence does tend to favor Carthage.

Some sections of this sermon have already appeared in Sermon 198, in Sermons 197 and 198A, which were taken from the anthologies of Bede and John the Deacon. The text in these sections will differ occasionally from that found in these fragments, sometimes because of differences in the Latin text, sometimes just as variations in the translation.

2. See 1 Jn 2:16.

3. Possibly celebrated, to judge from the more detailed description he is going to give, in honor of the goddess Fortuna, or Luck. But see also the next note.

4. *Strenae*, described by Sextus Pomponius, a second century lawyer, as presents "given for the sake of a good omen." Strena was also the name of the goddess who presided over the occasion. Perhaps the habit survives in the Christmas cracker, which you pull while making a wish, and in the bits and pieces hidden in the Christmas pudding; and in the giving of Christmas presents too, no doubt.

5. Here I stick to the text of the fragment, Sermon 198; this Mainz text has: "They devote themselves to earthly affairs; as for you, devote yourselves to the words of scripture"; a less effective, and less likely, antithesis.

6. Literally "of the circus," which was the racetrack. See Sermon 198, note 7 (III, 6).

7. See 1 Cor 9:24-26.

8. Charity and fear are being implicitly personified as mistress and slave, respectively feminine and masculine nouns. There is also a faint allusion to Jn 3:30: "He must increase, I must decrease."

9. That is, give to the poor.

10. The flow of ideas is anything but smooth. He is, of course, deliberately spinning things out, marking time so to say, in order to keep them in church as long as he can.

11. See Mk 11:12-14.20.

12. See Mt 25:33.

13. The Latin literally says, "From *saccus* you get the diminutive form *saccellus*," which means a purse; at least it had come to mean that in the Latin of Augustine's day. But Lewis & Short says it is a diminutive of *sacer*, sacred, and means a little chapel or sanctuary. So was Augustine also thinking here of Christ's side, from which blood flowed on the cross, as a sanctuary? Quite possibly—thereby anticipating by 1,250 years devotion to the Sacred Heart.

14. Thus fasting in the ancient Church, in Africa at least, was the same kind of mortification as the fast of Ramadan still is for Muslims—not eating, or drinking, anything until sunset.

15. Was this a common kind of superstition—fasting in order to be rewarded, so to say, by winning at the poker table, or the crap game? But it is possible, and perhaps even probable, that by fasting, at least in the context of the pagan New Year revels, he and his audience understood above

all else abstaining from alcohol—and to combine drinking with the serious business of the poker game, dice in those days, would be regarded as sheer folly, impairing the necessary concentration.

16. Rather briefer in the Latin: *Probat tamen pectus christianum.*

17. Back to the second person singular for this sentence, then immediately back again to the plural for the rest of the section. I imagine this was quite an effective rhetorical device, especially if accompanied by appropriate gestures from the preacher. But its effect, impossible to reproduce in a translation, would probably be lost anyway on readers of the written text.

18. Why on earth should it not? Because it meant that they were treating this day as a holiday, and so had closed their shops, and so forth? That seems to be the implication of what he immediately goes on to say. The whole tone of this passage, as of others, does tempt me to the conclusion that he was preaching at home in Hippo Regius to his own flock.

19. Reading *ad majorem amorem mundi et perniciei voluptatem* instead of the text's . . . *et perniciem voluptatum*. It is hard to see how they could be roused to the destructiveness of pleasures as well as to love.

20. Is he treating his congregation as though they were converts in the age of persecution, 100 years or so earlier, or is he implying that it was only after the accession of Theodosius to the Empire in 379, and the harsher laws against paganism which that event brought with it, that the Church really began to grow in numbers and embrace a majority of the population?

21. *Propter sacramentum laetitiae.* Feasting, in its place—in this context having a few glasses of wine, since as noted above, note 15, fasting seems to refer principally to abstinence from alcohol—is as sacredly significant as, in its place, is fasting.

22. See Sermon 361, 19, note 29 (III, 10); the Latin is *crapula et ebrietate*, which is literally "with drunkenness and drunkenness." That is why I introduce a kindred modern addiction. He is, of course, alluding to the custom of getting drunk at the shrines of the martyrs on their feast days, something he inveighed against at Hippo Regius from the moment of his ordination. See Letters 22 and 29.

23. Emending the text's *contemnunt*, "despise," to *condemnant.*

24. That is, they treat their idols, indeed their gods, as representations of "the elements of the world"—for example, of the sun and moon and planets, and the sea. Augustine has in mind the learned pagan "theologian" Varro. See *The City of God* VIII, 5.

25. Emending the text's *idolum tanquam idolum*, "the idol as an idol," to *idolum tanquam divinum.*

26. He returns to this practice in section 16 below. But we cannot say what "adoring the columns in the church" actually involved. Perhaps it was a custom for people to kiss the columns at the church door as they came in, seeing that he goes on to tell them how they should enter the church. I just wonder, not indeed very seriously, if they were thought of as representing the apostles, who were called pillars of the Church, Gal 2:9.

27. See Mt 6:6.

28. He uses a Greek word, probably less common than chanty: *keleuma*, the rhythmic cry or shout of the man in a galley giving the time to the rowers at their oars.

29. See Gal 4:7; see also section 4 above. In the lines that follow there are also echoes of Lk 15:19; Jn 10:12.

30. The slaves are the domestics, the hired servants the workers on the estate, it seems.

31. At the eucharist. The martyrs are commemorated as intercessors, they are not being prayed to, like God; that is the point he is making. The catechumens, being excluded from "the Mass of the faithful," are not supposed to know this yet.

32. See Acts 14:8-18; see also Sermon 273, 8 (III, 8).

33. See Acts 3:2-10; 4:22.

34. Usually, when the following text is quoted, I have translated *meridies* by "noonday"; but the context here requires "South."

35. See Eph 4:18.

36. See Acts 8:18-19.

37. This last clause is missing in the Mainz 62 text, but is given by Bede in his excerpt from this

sermon (see Sermon 197, 4). It is really required, because Augustine goes on to talk of "these saints" in the plural, and to refer to this verse of 1 Corinthians.

38. The risk of committing idolatry—or at the very least of lapsing into servility and flattery.

39. *Quomodo timuit* added from Bede's excerpt. It must surely have been in the original, since Bede would not have added anything in making his selection of extracts.

40. Omitting a final phrase, *et in illo solo habent spem suam*, "and in him alone place their hope." It is entirely out of place in the context—angels and martyrs in glory have no more to hope for. I take it as the thoughtless addition of some copyist.

41. *Quare vacatis Deo*—which I treat as if it were *quare vacetis Deo*—a very strange expression. I am not at all sure I have got its drift.

42. I have added "who do the things" to the text. As it stands, the parenthesis reads, *nam illi indoctiores sunt de quibus isti sibi praescribi nolunt*. It is problematic in several ways. First, who are the *illi* and the *isti*? The answer would really have depended on the preacher's gestures and tone of voice; lacking either aid, I take *isti* as more naturally referring to the apparently better educated pagans. So they "do not wish to be prescribed for"—to be given a prescription—which it is doubtless rather a liberty on my part to render as "be taken to task." But in any case, it doesn't make sense for this to happen to them about the *indoctiores*; hence my suggested addition, *qui faciunt ea*, or something like it.

On the other hand he could be saying that the apparently better educated are in fact less well educated than the illiterate masses. In that case these masses are unwilling to have rules made for them about, I suppose, the way in which they should regard their idols. So taking it like that, one would have to add something like *qui dicunt de idolis ea de quibus*, "who say about idols things about which" these others (with a gesture at the pagans junketing outside the church) don't want rules laid down for them.

43. The implication is that there were already icons and sacred images in Christian shrines and basilicas.

44. But were now forbidden to do so by imperial edicts.

45. *Tellus* being in fact simply a poetic word for *terra*, the earth. It was the name always used for Earth treated as a goddess.

46. The image of the sun, it should be noted, was in all probability a representation, in North Africa, of the demigod Hercules. In any case, it wouldn't have been just a kind of spherical model of the sun.

47. It is very possible that the worship of Tellus had something about it of the mystery cults, so popular in the Roman world, like the Eleusinian mysteries in Greece, dedicated to the corn goddess Demeter, whose name in all probability means Earth Mother. These mysteries were secret rites, with secret, sacred symbols, into which worshipers had to be initiated before they could fully participate and benefit.

48. Word play in the Latin: *non adorando, sed arando*. In addition he is playing on the two meanings of *colere*, to worship and to cultivate.

49. See Lk 19:8; Mk 12:42-43; 9:41.

50. This section, the first paragraph of section 21, repeats Sermon 197, 6.

51. See note 48 above.

52. Adding *aerem*, the air, on the suggestion of one scholar, to the text, which simply runs *propterea non adoramus, quia creatura est*, the unstated object being, presumably, *Junonem*. But I doubt if Augustine would have called Juno, a false pagan goddess, a creature; the air, certainly. It could easily have been inadvertently omitted, whether by stenographer or copyist, after *propterea*.

53. *Ingenium*. A word that has really no proper English equivalent. Sometimes it can mean roughly what we call genius. I think Augustine only uses it here, because it was the word conventionally employed in this context by the pagan authors he has in mind; and for the most part he equates it with intelligence. I did think of "ingenuity" as a possible translation; but on reflection decided that "wit," occasionally "wits," would be better.

54. In *The City of God* VII, 14, Augustine attributes this weird etymology to Varro, who justifies it because "speech runs as one in the middle between people," and Mercury, the messenger of the

gods, was, as we have already seen in Acts 14:12, always ready to talk. A more respectable etymology, favored by almost all other classical authors, derived the name from *merces*, Mercury being the god of trade. Augustine refers to this etymology in the last paragraph of his gigantic "filibuster," section 63 below.

55. It's worth noting that souls are not confined to human beings; in Latin obviously not, since everything animated, like animals, must be animated by an *anima*, a soul; and since this is not a body, it too must be a spirit.

56. See Col 1:16.

57. I have rather shortened the Latin, which literally runs, ." . . is also formable and enlightenable, that is, able to be formed and enlightened."

58. *Diabolus*—the Latin, retaining the Greek form, thereby retained more obviously than the English the word's proper meaning of slanderer, accuser, traducer—which makes it the very accurate translation of the Hebrew *Satan*.

59. See Gn 1:14-17.

60. A reference, presumably, to Ps 106, from which (v.47) the refrain they had been singing was taken.

61. See Sg 1:6; also section 14 above and note 34 above.

62. That is, consisting of an ultra-fine material substance, a "fifth element," a quintessence, which was given the name of "ether." Does his going on to refer to other possible constellations that were hidden from sight, *quae forte alia latent*, suggest that ancient astronomy was alive to a much vaster universe than it is usually given credit for?

63. He is thinking of some neo-Platonists, especially Porphyry. See *The City of God* X, 9; XII, 27. For the following section on how the devil offers a false purgation through his false mediation, and on the contrast of this with the purgation offered by Christ, the true mediator, see *The Trinity* IV, 13-24.

64. See Wis 14:20; also Sermon 273, 3, (III, 8), and note 6 to that sermon. The sentence here has no logical connection with what has just gone before. I get the impression that the preacher is just yielding to a "stream of consciousness," an element, no doubt of the filibuster technique. It means that these sentences lose all syntactical coherence.

65. Reading *cum inhaeret cognitor cognito* instead of the text's . . . *cognitori cognito*, untranslatable, clearly a mistake. Dolbeau suggests emending it to . . . *cognitori cognitus*, "when the one known inheres in the knower"; but I respectfully maintain my emendation is the more likely, especially as the section ends with the quotation "in him we live" etc., not "in us he lives."

66. See 1 Cor 1:20; 3:19. In this and the next section Augustine gives a peculiarly mean and ungenerous (but I regret to say not uncharacteristic) slant to Paul's modest attempt at what might be called an ecumenical spirit, to an attempted dialogue with pagan philosophy.

67. "As some have said" in fact refers to the quotation Paul goes on to make. But Augustine is not entirely mistaken; both phrases, "in him we live" etc., and "For we are his offspring," come from pagan poets, the first from Epimenides, sixth century BC, the second from Aratus, third century BC; he like Paul hailed from Cilicia.

68. From here to just over halfway through section 33 has already appeared in Sermon 197, l as a fragment culled from this sermon by Bede. For similar treatment of Rom 1:18-19 see also Sermon 241, l (III, 7).

69. See Rom 3:23.

70. See Wis 11:20, one of Augustine's favorite quotations. A thing's weight, he will say, is its love, the force carrying it to its "proper place."

71. *Cedentium succedentiumque rerum*—an Augustinian commonplace. This is a beauty *sui generis*, because it is a beauty of *movement*, like that of music or dancing, and not of unchanging form, which was for Augustine in his Platonist tradition the archetypal mode of beauty.

72. These last few lines, from "a person's soul cannot indeed be seen," are omitted by Bede in his excerpt, in Sermon 397, 1.

73. In section 30. The words, however, which he wants them to consider are the ones he hadn't yet quoted, from Rom 1:21: "Because knowing God they did not glorify him as God" etc., a few lines further on. Bede in his excerpt omits this preamble and comes straight to those words.

74. This last sentence, and the first three of the next paragraph, down to "from the pride of others," are omitted by Bede.

75. The assumption is that the persons Paul had been castigating were the ancient Greek philosophers. It is interesting that Augustine should consider the possibility of a revelation to the pagan Gentiles. It is an idea that had been more magnanimously entertained and developed by Clement of Alexandria, 200 years earlier.

76. The devil.

77. From here to "they became fools," just before the end of the paragraph, is omitted by Bede.

78. See Lk 15:13-16.

79. This sentence is omitted by Bede.

80. See Ps 73:27; see also Sermon 9, 3 (III, 1).

81. Virgil, *Aeneid*, VIII, 698-700.

82. Here Dolbeau hesitantly, but I am sure rightly, suggests there is a lacuna in the text. What they said is fairly obviously what they have already said often enough: "We don't worship the lifeless idol, but the deity which the idol represents, for example the sun, the sea, or the earth."

83. Compare Sermon 113A, 7 (III, 4).

84. A *caveat* which, while it did not figure very largely in Augustine's thinking, or that of most of his contemporaries, is playing an important part in current Catholic theological dialogue with other religions, for which a special secretariat has been set up in the Holy See.

85. *Etiam superbierunt in eo.* At first sight it seems to mean "they even took pride in him," in the creator. But I don't think Augustine would have objected to that. So I am treating *in eo* as meaning "in this thing," that is, in this achievement.

86. See Ex 7:11.22; 8:7.18.

87. So called, either because Augustine thought of them as having airy bodies, or because they inhabited this lower air—were "powers of this air" (Eph 2:2).

88. As opposed, I presume, to the many false mediators, the unclean spirits acting under the devil, who have just been mentioned. There can hardly be a reference here, I think, to the unity of person of Christ, the Word incarnate.

89. See Jb 1 & 2; and for his foretelling the true mediator, see especially 19:25.

90. Reading *scriptura* instead of the text's *mediator*—which surely found its way into the text here, either as a slip of the tongue on the preacher's part, or by a very natural mistake on the part of stenographer or copyist, the word occurring so frequently in this passage.

91. For this whole theme of true and false mediation, see *The Trinity* IV, 13-24; also *The Confessions* X, 42-43.

92. I have changed the punctuation to make better sense—indeed to make sense at all. The Latin text is punctuated thus: *Deus autem justus, etiam mortalis. Mediator humilis, justus, mortalis, et non utcumque justus, sed justus quia deus, mortalis quia homo*: "But God just, also mortal. The humble mediator, just, mortal, and not in any old way. . ."

93. We now conventionally talk of God the Son assuming human nature; and perhaps fifty years or so after Augustine preached this sermon, the expression he uses here would have smacked of Nestorianism, the error which basically made Jesus Christ into two persons; hence Nestorius' denial of the title *Theotokos*, "Mother of God," to Mary, on the grounds that she was the mother of the man only, not of the divine person. But Augustine's expression also has its orthodox value as emphasizing that Jesus Christ was, is, a particular individual human being, not a kind of two-dimensional "human nature."

94. Reading *in carne mortalis* instead of the text's *in carne mortali*, "He was made/came to be in mortal flesh."

95. As indeed all Gnostic and neo-Platonist critics of Christianity always had been. They considered the doctrine of the incarnation, especially as involving the death of the Incarnate One, as a blasphemous affront to the Deity.

96. That is, outside the *Catholica*, the Catholic Church.

97. He is here warning the unbaptized members of his audience against seeking the sacrament from the Donatists.

98. Compare Sermon 22, 10 (III, 2).

99. *Et facta sunt duo unus*; one in the masculine gender, that is, one person, in contrast to what Jesus says in Jn 10:30, *Ego et Pater unum sumus*, one in the neuter gender, that is, one thing, one nature.

100. See Lk 10:30-35.

101. See the Apostles' Creed.

102. See Phil 2:6.

103. Here Augustine does use the word *personaliter*, and he is talking almost technically of what theologians term "the hypostatic union of the two natures in the one person of Jesus Christ."

104. The reference would seem to be to the official emperor worship which had lain behind the persecution of Christians, and which was of course no longer even tolerated, let alone required, in Augustine's time under Christian Emperors.

105. This section 44 is culled by Bede, and appears in Sermon 197, 4.

106. A quite unwarrantable slur. See Sermon 197, note 15.

107. Dolbeau suspects a short lacuna here; there must indeed be something missing after the *et* in the Latin: *Propterea contra nos odium immanissimum et contraxerunt*; probably just one word, another adjective, something like *implacabile*.

108. See Jer 17:5.

109. A reference to the pre-baptismal rite of "exsufflation," in which the minister breathes on the catechumen as a gesture of blowing out the evil spirit of unbelief. As the Donatists rebaptized Catholics who joined them, with all such preparatory rites, Augustine is implying that they puff out or "exsufflate" the baptism of Christ, that is the Spirit of Christ received in baptism.

110. The circumcellions were, according to Lewis & Short, "a class of monks who without fixed abode wandered about from cell to cell." But in fact they were the Donatists' strong-arm men, probably not all monks, who wandered round the countryside (*cella* can also mean a granary, and slave quarters) terrorizing the country people. They had recently tried to ambush Augustine himself, an incident he goes on to allude to. This is one of Dolbeau's clues to the date of the sermon, since the incident probably occurred in the summer or autumn of 403, about the same time as a much more serious attack on Possidius, bishop of Calama, Augustine's biographer many years later.

111. See above, section 16.

112. So Saturn, the father of Jupiter and the other great Olympians in the Greek and Roman pantheon, would have represented, presumably, the original creative power of God, or perhaps the power of the Father in generating the Son (it is educated pagans, remember, talking to Christians, and they know at least something about Christian doctrines); Jupiter his lordship of the heavens and angels; Pluto his dominion over the underworld and the dead; Neptune his command of the sea; Mars his being "the Lord of hosts," as for example in 1 Sm 1,3, 4:4, or "a man of war," Ex 15:3; Ceres his being the one "who makes things grow," 1 Cor 3:6.

113. For this theme see Sermon 273, 7, notes 14 and 15 (III, 8); also *The City of God* VIII.27.

114. See Dan 8:16; 9:21 for Gabriel; 10:13.21; 12:1 for Michael.

115. Rv 19:10; 22:9; see section 16 above.

116. Here there is a gap in the text; not a very big one, I suspect. I would supply something like, "those who live together as servants of God imitate" . . .

117. See Acts 2:41; 4:4.

118. See Acts 4:34-35; Rom 15:26; 2 Cor 8—9. This is all a vast ramshackle non-sentence in the Latin too.

119. See Phil 2:6-7; Jn 14:28.

120. He says "in the sacraments." Yes, they are addressed to the Father, but through Jesus Christ; so he is envisaged both as receiving them together with the Father, and as presenting them to the Father.

121. This section, the end of number 49, was excerpted by John the Deacon, and has appeared in Sermon 198A, 3 (III, 6).

122. See Lv 21:17.21.

123. This seems to imply that he was preaching in the presence of several other bishops. If so that would be a probable argument in favor of Carthage as the city where this "filibuster" was preached.

Notice it is just *bishops* he mentions as being called priests (*sacerdotes*); not presbyters, whom we now think of quite simply as priests, as distinct from bishops.

In *The City of God* XX, 10, presbyters too were evidently being given the sacerdotal title. All this indicates that this was only applied to the ordained ministry, first to bishops and then to presbyters, quite late in the ecclesiastical tradition. It is never so applied in the New Testament. And we will see in due course that it was the Donatists who first drew exaggerated conclusions from it about the sacerdotal powers and dignity of ordained ministers. The Catholic Church eventually followed suit, especially from the time in the eighth and ninth centuries, when the Frankish and German Churches began to take a lead in theology.

124. The last sentence of section 49 and all of section 50 begin another substantial extract culled by John the Deacon; to be found in Sermon 198A, 1.

125. In the rite we now call confirmation, which Augustine probably thought of as one element in the whole paschal liturgy of baptism.

126. The priestly role was prefigured in David much more profoundly, less accidentally, as it were, than by this incident, if Augustine and the general exegetical tradition had only realized it. By making Jerusalem his capital, and buying the threshing-floor of Araunah the Jebusite to build the temple on (2 Sm 24:18-25), David deliberately constituted himself heir to Melchizedek, king of Salem, priest of God Most High (Gn 14:18). For 2 Sm 24:23 runs in the Hebrew text (but the scholars from the beginning have always emended it), and it is so translated in the Vulgate—perhaps Jerome appreciated its significance——All these things Araunah the king gave to the king,— Araunah the king was heir (descendant perhaps) of the priest-king Melchizedek.

So it was in the first place David himself who was acclaimed in the royal psalm, 110:4, as "priest for ever according to the order of Melchizedek." But the tradition from the letter to the Hebrews onward has so immediately applied the text to our Lord that it has overlooked its prefigurative applicability to David. Again, in 2 Sm 8:18 there is the otherwise anomalous statement, "and David's sons were priests."

127. See Lk 2:48.

128. See Mt 1:20; Lk 1:35.

129. See Sermon 51, 3 (III, 3).

130. The primary function of kings was always thought in the ancient world to be leadership in war. This was particularly the case in the Roman Empire, in which the Emperor (Basileus, King) was in effect a military dictator.

131. The little something extra taken with a meal which otherwise consisted entirely of bread; the usual poor man's dinner.

132. See and compare Sermon 130, 1 (III, 4); and for the further elaboration of the incident with seven loaves, see Sermon 95, 2 (III, 4).

133. See Rv 2—3.

134. Simply *in illis sacramentis* in the Latin. A common theme of his; unraveling the obscurities and mysteries of scripture is so much more fun than reading and hearing straightforward lessons in it.

135. See note 125 above.

136. It is interesting to note the roots in the Donatist heresy of some of the more extreme forms of contemporary, so-called "conservative," clericalism in the Catholic Church. See Augustine's *Answer to the Letter of Parmenian*, II, 8.

137. See sections 49-50 above. See also Sermon 340, 1 (III, 9), where he says, on the anniversary of his ordination as bishop, "For you I am a bishop, with you I am a Christian. The first is the name of an office undertaken, the second a name of grace; that one means danger, this one salvation"—a text quoted in Vatican II's document on the Church, *Lumen Gentium*, 32, in the chapter on the laity.

138. Most of section 53, selected by John the Deacon, has already appeared in Sermon 198A, 2.

139. The altar in those days was not in a section of the church called "the sanctuary" (a later Frankish regression to the Old Testament model), but nearer the middle of the nave, in a railed-off enclosure, with the congregation standing round on all sides of it. They "attested" to the offering

of the eucharistic sacrifice, took part in it, by their "Amen," which they may well have spoken immediately after the consecration, as well as at the end of the whole eucharistic prayer. What is now called the sanctuary was then simply called the apse, and was the place where the bishop sat with his clergy to preside over the liturgy of the word, before coming down to officiate at the altar for the "Mass of the faithful."

140. See Heb 9:24-28.

141. The last section of 53, last paragraph, by Bede, to be found in Sermon 197, 5.

142. See Mk 6:45-48.

143. The spaces indicate the letter spaces left blank in the manuscript. The key to the sense of the whole passage lies in the phrase "whitened wall" (which I have had to render "a wall that had been whitened" for syntactical reasons), which is what Paul called the high priest Ananias in Acts 23:3, for commanding him to be struck on the mouth. Paul's allusion was to Ez 13:10-15, to false prophets whitewashing ramshackle walls built by unrepentant Israel. Dolbeau refers to Augustine's *Expositions of the Psalms* 95(96), 3, and the *Expositions of the Psalms* 103(104), I, 6, where he interprets the expression as meaning "hypocrisy and pretense." On Ps 95(96) he talks about the Donatists not building in the house (in his version the title of the psalm connected it with the rebuilding of the temple after the exile), but instead erecting a whitewashed wall. Here, however, he talks of them—or him, Donatus—doing something by means of the whitewashed wall. Perhaps the first gap could be filled with the word *divisit*, because he led them astray, separated them from the Catholic Church, through a whitewashed wall.

The next phrase, *Terrenum est enim, non autem christiana religione*, is very difficult to make sense of as punctuated in the text, a sentence on its own. It cannot be this if *terrenum* qualifies *parietem* (wall), because this is a masculine noun; which means that *terrenum* cannot be the subject, neuter gender, of a sentence, but must be an accusative agreeing with *parietem* in gender. So I treat *terrenum enim* as a little parenthesis, and the ablative *christiana religione* as governed by the participle *dealbatum*.

For the second gap I tentatively suggest supplying *parvulos credentes*, and changing the following *et* into *ut*, so that the whole would read: ". . . in order to deceive the little ones who believe, so that coming as far as him, they. . ."

144. The verse quoted twice in passages so close together, and in two versions: "the propitiation" (*propitiatio*) and "the atonement" (*exoratio*) for our sins, is again a possible indication that he was preaching away from home, his Hippo Regius version (which he would almost know by heart) here differing from the local, presumably Carthaginian, version to hand in the pulpit.

145. For this image of pumping out the bilges, see also Sermons 56, 11, 58, 10, 77B, 8 (III, 3); 179A, 6 (III, 5); 278, 13 (III, 8). For the three remedies for daily wounds, see Sermon 9, 17 (III, 1).

146. See Mt 6:12. For the comparison of this verse with Mt 5:16, and the little problem they set when taken together, see Sermons 47, 13 (III, 2); 93, 14 (III, 3); 149, 14 (III, 5); 338, 3-4 (III, 9).

147. See Mt 4:2.

148. See Eph 4:27.

149. In section 54. He has the technique of the filibuster to a T!

150. See Acts 12:5. There is as far as I know no specific text recording that Peter prayed for the Church.

151. See Eph 2:14. Augustine just alludes to the verse, and doesn't actually mention the word "wall." But I think this dividing wall mentioned in the verse must have been linked in his mind to the whitewashed wall he talked about earlier on. See note 143 above.

152. See Sermons 229A, 1 (III, 6) and 272 (III, 7).

153. See Sermon 164, 10 (III, 5). The expression, one imagines, means much the same as our "throw dust in your eyes," or "pull the wool over your eyes."

154. Reading *exoratio*, which we had up above at the end of section 55, instead of the text's *oratio*. Augustine is here giving both his versions of the verse.

155. See sections 5 and the following, above; also section 30.

156. That is, magicians. Chaldeans were the magicians *par excellence*. In modern terms he might just possibly have said "Gypsies."

157. See Jn 14:6; "to the lowest and the weakest" is in the Latin *ad infimos et infirmos*. For the same thought see Sermons 20A, 4 (III, 2) and 91, 7 (III, 3). For the next sentence see *The Trinity*, IV, 20.

158. See 1 Sm 16:11.

159. The last paragraph of section 60 was culled by Bede, and has appeared in Sermon 197, 2. For the theme, see also Sermon 87, 12 (III, 3).

160. Bishop of Carthage from 248 until he was martyred in 258; the great patron saint of the African Church. See Sermon 197, note 10.

161. For this passage see also Sermon 142, 2 (III, 4); also *The Confessions* VII, 21, 27; *The City of God* X, 29.

162. A somewhat amplified rendering of *in eo quod tenent*, "in that which they hold."

163. The logic of the passage, in which we shift from what we hold to what holds us, and conclude to what we ought to hold, is impossible to follow. Of course, the filibusterer must by now have been as exhausted as his audience, and was doubtless finding it a little hard to think straight.

164. Here there is a considerable gap in the text; Dolbeau says the space is just under fifty letters. Presumably the sentence will at least continue "became man," or "shared in human nature." Then a new sentence would run something like, "But when human beings assume he is far from the world of matter, and is only near the celestial" etc.

165. In the Latin, *carnalem ex homine naturam*. If we take Augustine's rather Platonist anthropology into consideration, in which the essential man is the *animus*, the *mens*, the spirit, while the flesh, the material element, is a kind of secondary adjunct, then I think we can see that he is suggesting the Word could have become man in a purely spiritual conjunction, without also taking on the nature of flesh. If that is what is implied here, then it is a view he will modify as he grows older, and becomes, in an admirable way, more "materialist," at least more down to earth, more integrated, in his concept of human nature.

166. See Jb 1:12.

167. An allusion here, I think, to the mysterious passage in Ez 13:18-19. The phrase "souls of light" doubtless echoes "the sons of light" of Lk 16:8, the conclusion to the parable of the unjust steward.

SERMON 218

SERMON NOTES FOR GOOD FRIDAY

Date: before 420[1]

The meaning of the passion

1. The passion of our Lord and Savior Jesus Christ, by whose blood our delinquencies have been blotted out, is solemnly read, solemnly celebrated, so that our memories may be the more happily refreshed by this annual devotion, and our faith rendered more brilliantly illustrious by the faithful people assembling in great numbers. So this solemn occasion requires of me that I should deliver you a sermon, such as the Lord himself grants me, on his passion. And indeed in the things that our Lord suffered from his enemies, he was pleased to give us an example of patience, for our salvation and our guidance in the way we manage this life, so that we ourselves should not refuse to suffer anything for the truth of the gospel, if that should be his will.

The fact is, however, that not even in his mortal flesh did he suffer anything out of necessity, but everything of his own free will. And so it may rightly be assumed that by every single deed that was carried out and recorded about his passion he also wished to signify something to us.[2]

Christ carries the cross

2. And first, that when he was handed over to be crucified, he himself carried his cross;[3] by this he gave a sign of self-restraint, and by going ahead like that he showed what should be done by anyone who wishes to follow him. He also impressed this upon us by word, when he said, *Let anyone who loves me take up his cross and follow me* (Mk 8:34). You see, you take up your cross after a fashion when you control your mortality.[4]

Calvary

3. That he was crucified at the place of the skull,[5] Calvary, signified the

forgiveness of all sins through his passion, about which it says in the psalm, *My iniquities are multiplied above the hairs of my head* (Ps 40:12).[6]

The two crucified with Jesus

4. That two others were crucified with him on either side[7] indicated that some are going to suffer on his right hand, others on his left; on his right, those of whom it says *Blessed are those who suffer persecution for the sake of justice* (Mt 5:10); on his left, those of whom it is said, *If I hand over my body so that I am burned, but do not have charity, it profits me nothing* (1 Cor 13:3).

The king of the Jews

5. That a title was placed over his cross, on which was written *The king of the Jews* (Jn 19:19), showed that not even by killing him could they manage not to have him as the king who is going by his supreme authority to repay them in the most public way imaginable, according to their works. This is why we sing in the psalm, *I, however, have been established by him as king on Zion his holy mountain* (Ps 2:6).

Written in three languages

6. That the title was written in three languages, *Hebrew, Greek, and Latin* (Jn 19:20), amounted to a declaration that he was going to reign over the nations as well as the Jews. Accordingly, after saying in that psalm *I, however, have been established by him as king on Zion his holy mountain,* where he reigned, that is to say, in the Hebrew language, he added straightaway, as though in Greek and Latin, *The Lord said to me,* he said, *You are my Son, I today have begotten you; ask of me, and I will give you the nations for your inheritance, and as your possession the ends of the earth* (Ps 2:7-8).

Not that Greek and Latin are the only languages of the nations, but they are the most notable ones, Greek because of its literary classics, Latin because of the imperial power of the Romans. Although in these three languages the subjection of the totality of the nations to Christ was being indicated, it still wasn't written there "and king of the nations," but only now of the Jews, to remind us of our roots in the people there named.[8] *For the law has gone forth from Zion,* as it says, *and the word of the Lord from Jerusalem* (Is 2:3). I mean, who are the people who say in the psalm, *He has subjected peoples to us, and nations under our feet* (Ps 47:3), but those of whom the apostle says, *If the nations have shared in their spiritual goods, they ought at least to attend to their needs with material goods* (Rom 15:27)?

Do we not see, then, the nations subject to the sovereign grace of the apostles? Or should we concentrate on the broken-off branches who are called Jews today, and not rather listen to that *Israelite of the race of Abraham* (Rom 11:1),[9] admonishing the engrafted wild olive and saying, *It is not you that carry the root, but the root that carries you* (Rom 11:18)? So Christ is the king of the Jews, under whose mild yoke the nations too were passed to salvation.[10] That by this real concession they were being shown the greater mercy is made very clear by the apostle himself, where he says, *For I say that Christ was the minister of the circumcision because of God's truth, to confirm the promises made to the fathers, but that the nations glorify God over his mercy* (Rom 15:8-9). It would not have been right, after all, to take the children's bread and throw it to the dogs, unless the dogs had humbled themselves to pick up the scraps which they salvage from their masters' table and, being raised up through this very humility and made human, had earned the right of access to the table itself.[11]

King of the Jews and the Gentiles

7. That the leaders of the Jews urged Pilate not to write without qualification that he is the the king of the Jews, but that he himself said he was the king of the Jews, to which he replied, *What I have written, I have written* (Jn 19:21-22): this had Pilate representing the wild olive to be grafted on, while the leaders of the Jews represented the broken-off branches.[12] He was, you see, a man of the nations, writing for the nations their confession of faith, convicting the Jews of their denial of it, so that the Lord himself rightly said to them, *The kingdom shall be taken away from you, and given to a nation that does justice* (Mt 21:43).

That does not mean, however, that he is not the king of the Jews. The root, after all, carries the wild olive, not the wild olive the root. And although those branches were broken off for unbelief, that does not mean that God has repudiated his people, whom he foreknew; *I too*, he says, *am an Israelite* (Rom 11:2.1). And although the sons of the kingdom, who did not wish the Son of God to reign over them,[13] go off into the outer darkness, all the same *many shall come from East and West and sit down*, not with Plato and Cicero, but *with Abraham, Isaac and Jacob in the kingdom of God* (Mt 8:12.11).

Pilate, certainly, wrote *king of the Jews*, not "king of the Greeks or the Latins," although he was going to reign over the nations. And what he has written, he has written, and he didn't change it at the urging of unbelievers, as had been foretold such a long time before in the psalm: *Do not corrupt the inscription of the title.*[14] All the nations believe in the king of the Jews; he reigns over all the nations, but nonetheless as the king of the Jews. Such was the worth and potency of that root that it could change the engrafted wild olive into itself, while the wild olive could not eliminate the name of the olive.[15]

The garments divided

8. That the soldiers divided his garments into four parts and took them away[16] means they signified his sacraments destined to traverse the four corners of the world.

The tunic without seam

9. That they cast lots for his tunic alone, *woven from the top without seam* (Jn 19:23-24), rather than dividing it, demonstrated clearly enough that the visible sacraments, even though they too are the garments of Christ, can still be had by anybody, good or bad, but that sincere and genuine faith, which *works through love* (Gal 5:6) to achieve the integrity of unity—*because the love of God has been poured out in our hearts through the Holy Spirit who has been given to us* (Rom 5:5)—that this faith does not belong to anybody at all, but is given by God's hidden grace as by lot.[17] Thus to Simon who had baptism, and didn't have this, Peter could say, *You have no lot or part in this faith* (Acts 8:21).

Mary entrusted to the beloved disciple

10. That on the cross he acknowledged his mother, and entrusted her to the beloved disciple,[18] aptly indicated his human affection at the time when he was dying as a man. This hour had not yet arrived when, as he was about to turn water into wine, he had said to this same mother, *What have I to do with you, woman? My hour has not yet come* (Jn 2:4). You see, he had not received from Mary the power he had in his divinity, as he had received from Mary what was hanging on the cross.[19]

Vinegar on a sponge

11. As for his saying, *I thirst* (Jn 19:28), he was looking for faith from his own people; but because *he came to his own possessions and his own people did not receive him* (Jn 1:11), instead of the sweetness of faith they gave him the vinegar of faithlessness,[20] and that in a sponge. They are indeed comparable to a sponge, a thing not solid but swollen, not open with the straight access of confession, but hollow with the tortuous twists and turns of treachery.[21] It's true that that drink also contained hyssop,[22] which is a lowly herb, said to have an extremely strong root, with which to cling to the rock. There were some, that is to say, among this people, for whom this dark deed was kept as a means of humbling their souls by their repudiation of it later on, and their repentance. The one who accepted the hyssop with the vinegar knew who they were. After all, as the other evangelist bears witness, he even prayed for them, when he said as he was hanging on the cross, *Father, forgive them, because they do not know what they are doing* (Lk 23:34).

Death with a bowed head

12. That he said, *It is accomplished; and bowing his head he gave up the spirit* (Jn 19:30), showed how he died not by necessity but by his own power and authority, waiting until all that had been prophesied on his behalf had been accomplished—because this too had been written: *And in my thirst they gave*

me vinegar to drink (Ps 69:22), as one who had the authority to lay down his life, as he had himself testified about himself.[23]

He handed over the spirit with humility, that is, with a bowed head; he would receive it back again by rising again, with a head lifted up.[24] That this death and bowing of the head were acts of great power and authority was shown by that ancestor Jacob, when he blessed Judah, and said, *You have gone up lying down, you have slept like a lion* (Gn 49:9); by "going up" he signified the cross, by "lying down" his bowing of the head, by "sleeping" his death, by the "lion" his power and authority.

The broken legs of the two thieves

13. Now next, that the legs of those two were broken, while his were not, because he was already dead, why this happened was stated in the gospel itself.[25] It was fitting, you see, to demonstrate by this sign as well, that the true point and purpose of the Jewish passover, which contained this instruction not to break the lamb's bones[26] was to be a prophetic pre-enactment of his death.

Blood and water from the side of Jesus

14. That his side, struck by a lance, poured out blood and water on the ground[27]: without a shadow of doubt these are the sacraments by which the Church is formed, as Eve was fashioned from the side of the sleeping Adam,[28] who was *the model of the one who was to come* (Rom 5:14).

Burial

15. That Joseph and Nicodemus buried him: as some people have explained their names, Joseph means "increase," while Nicodemus, being a Greek name, many will recognize as a compound of "victory" and "people," because *nikos* means victory and *demos* means people. So who was increased by dying, if not the one who said, *If the grain of wheat does not die, it remains alone; but if it does die, it is multiplied* (Jn 12:24)? And who, even by dying, won a victory over the people of his persecutors, if not the one who by rising again will sit in judgment upon them?

NOTES

1. Sermon 218, we saw in volume III, 6, proved to be something of an ugly duckling; after an introductory paragraph, which reads very much like other sermons, we just have a series of fifteen notes on details of the passion narrative, nearly all from the fourth gospel, each beginning with the conjunction *quod*, "that." This has led certain scholars recently to question the sermon's authentic-

ity, although the Maurists expressed no doubts about it. Raymond Étaix, however, who has been collating the texts of many more manuscripts than the Maurists used, together with earlier scholars finds it thoroughly Augustinian in content, and accepts the explanation offered by Suzanne Poque for its unusual form: that it was not a sermon actually preached by Augustine, but a set of notes for a sermon. In note 1 on the sermon in volume III, 6, I suggest a slight modification of this idea: that it was not a set of notes Augustine made for a sermon he was going to preach himself, but that being unable for some reason to do so that particular year, he asked one of his priests to stand in for him, and gave him this set of notes to use, writing out a short introduction in full.

There will be a number of variations from the Maurist text; but the chief interest of this edition is that Étaix discovered a little medieval pocket lectionary in the municipal library of Vendôme, which contained the text of this sermon with a few notable additions, the biggest one being at the end of section 6.

2. Typically, he wants to go beyond the literal sense even of Christ's passion; to explore its meaning more deeply by examining the figurative significance of its details.

3. See Jn 19:16-17.

4. Mortality, signified by the cross, and experienced by us in the passions that are part and parcel of our mortal nature.

5. See Jn 19:17-18.

6. And all the hairs have been removed from a skull!

7. See Jn 19:18.

8. A nice little piece of word play here: *ut commendaretur origo seminis in proprietate nominis.*

9. I here omit a phrase which Étaix, quite rightly in my view, considers thoroughly unAugustinian: *de Saulo Paulum et ideo de parvo magnum*, "that Israelite . . . from Saul turned into Paul, and thus from little into great." In the first place it interrupts what he is saying about the relationship between Jews and Gentiles. In the second, it is playing on the meaning of the name *Paulus*, which indeed means "small," in a manner Augustine himself never did. The point he always makes is that Paul deliberately made himself little, *paulus*, which he glosses as *minimus* and *modicus*; see 1 Cor 15:9. See Sermons 77, 3 (III, 3) note 7; 168:7; 169:5 (III, 5); 315:7 (III, 9).

10. A reference to the custom the Romans had of making their defeated enemies "pass under the yoke," not to salvation but to slavery and subjection. See Mt 11:28-30.

11. See Mk 7:27-30; also Sermon 77, 11-12 (III, 3), where he also refers to Paul's metaphor of the wild olive.

12. See Rom 11:17.

13. See Lk 19:14.

14. See the titles of Pss 57 and 58 in the Greek Septuagint.

15. Augustine is anticipating the famous words of Pius XI, repudiating fascist anti-semitism: "We are all spiritually Semites."

16. See Jn 19:23. The sacraments, especially baptism and eucharist, are represented by his clothes because they bring the faithful into contact with the body of Christ.

17. In his *Homilies on the Gospel of John* 118, he gives the traditional patristic interpretation of Christ's seamless robe, as signifying the unity of the Church, woven together from the top by charity.

18. See Jn 19:26-27.

19. He is clearly right, and truly discerns the evangelist's intentions in linking the two episodes in which Jesus addresses his mother as "Woman." He makes the same rather unsatisfactory comment on the link in his *Homilies on the Gospel of John* 119, 1. Neither there nor here does he take notice of the third text to which both these allude, Gn 2:23: *She shall be called woman.* Mary is the new Eve; but in Cana Jesus addresses her precisely as his mother, whom he is about to leave in order to cleave to his wife, his bride, the Church, and so he keeps her at arm's length. Here on the cross he addresses her precisely as representing the wife of the new Adam, and as *mother of all the living* (Gn 3:20), who are represented by the beloved disciple.

20. See Ps 69:21.

21. He is forgetting that it was a Roman soldier, not "the Jews," who gave Jesus the vinegar to drink.

22. Augustine interprets John's saying "placing a sponge full of vinegar round hyssop," 19:29, as meaning that they flavored the vinegar with hyssop. And he may well be getting the evangelist's meaning correctly, because John must have known perfectly well that the reed, on which Mark says they placed the sponge (Mk 15:36), cannot be a hyssop reed, hyssop not running to reeds, but being what Augustine says it is here. So it could be that the soldier wrapped a sponge round a little bunch of hyssop, and then stuck it on a reed. John, in any case, probably introduces it here in an oblique allusion to Ex 12:22, the sprinkling of the blood of the passover lamb on the doorposts of the Israelites' houses with a bunch of hyssop.

23. See Jn 10:18.

24. See Ps 3:3.

25. See Jn 19:33.36.

26. See Ex 12:46; Num 9:12.

27. See Jn 19:34.

28. See Gn 2:21-22. The blood and water represent the sacraments of eucharist and baptism.

Dolbeau 15
SERMON 283
Mainz 45

SERMON OF SAINT AUGUSTINE ON THE BIRTHDAY OF THE HOLY MARTYRS OF MAXULA

Date: 397[1]

Against pleasure continence is needed; against pains, patience

1. Let us by all means admire the courage of the holy martyrs in their sufferings, but in such a way that we proclaim the grace of God. They themselves, after all, certainly did not wish to be praised in themselves, but in the one to whom it is said, *In the Lord shall my soul be praised*. Those who understand this are not proud; they ask shyly, they receive joyfully; they persevere, they don't lose anymore what they have received. Because they are not proud, they are gentle; and that's why, after saying *In the Lord shall my soul be praised*, he added, *Let the gentle hear and be glad* (Ps 34:2). What is feeble flesh, what is it but maggots and rottenness? Or wherever would it be, unless what we have been singing were true: *My soul will submit itself to God, since it is from him that my patience comes* (Ps 62:5)? Now the virtue the martyrs had, in order to endure all the ills inflicted on them, is called patience.

You see, there are two things by which people are either drawn or driven into sin—pleasure and pain; pleasure draws, pain drives. Against pleasures self-control is needed, against pains, patience. This, after all, is how the suggestion is put to the human mind that it should sin: sometimes it is told, "Do it, and you will get this," while sometimes it's, "Do it, or you will suffer this." A promise points the way to pleasure, a threat the way to pain. So it's in order to get some pleasure, or to avoid suffering pain, that people sin. That's why against these two tempters, of which one works through smooth promises, the other through terrible threats, God too has been good enough both to make promises and to inspire terror, promising the kingdom of heaven, terrifying with the punishments of hell.

Pleasure is sweet, but God is sweeter. Temporal pain is bad, but much worse is eternal fire. You have something to love instead of the world's loves, or rather of worthless loves;[2] you have something to fear, in place of the world's terrors.

245

The letter kills, but the Spirit gives life

2. But it's not enough to be warned, unless you also obtain assistance, which is where the uttering of threats comes in.[3] The law cries out to you against all pleasures, *You shall not lust* (Ex 20:17; Rom 7:7). You've heard it; it's a divine oracle, it's God who said it. No believer has ever doubted that it was a good commandment he gave, and a true warning. But notice what the apostle says: *The law came and sin revived* (Rom 7:9). You see, before you were told *You shall not lust*, you thought you were allowed to sin, and in fact it wasn't thought of as sin while it was not forbidden. It was because sin was forbidden that it was recognized for what it is. So once you've recognized it, you should avoid it, if you were looking for help from the law. You heard; what more do you want from the law? *You shall not lust.* The letter of the law has stuck in the gullet of your mind. You've something to struggle against, but you'll be beaten if you don't get any help. Help from where? From grace. *Love*, you see, *has been poured out in our hearts*, not through ourselves, but *through the Holy Spirit which has been given to us* (Rom 5:5). Take away this grace, remove this help; *the letter kills* (2 Cor 3:6).

The world had you in the first place as a sinner; when the law comes along without any help, it will also have you as a transgressor. So then, *the letter kills, but the Spirit gives life* (2 Cor 3:6), because *the love of God has been poured out in our hearts, through the Holy Spirit which has been given to us* (Rom 5:5). This is why the law terrifies us, to force us to beg for help. *The law*, as the apostle says himself, *is like a nursemaid* (Gal 3:24). The nursemaid doesn't instruct a child, but takes it along to the master. Once instructed and well equipped by the master, it will no longer be under the nursemaid, which means that the letter will have no further terrors for you, when you have the help of grace.

The day so soon to end, the day that has no end

3. I've said this because of the text, *You shall not lust* (Rom 7:7). This, after all, seems to be the commandment laid down against those sins which are committed through the allurements of pleasure, and the apostle reiterated it as a kind of general statement, as though this were the one and only word of the law, *You shall not lust.* Does this commandment also avail at all against fears of pain? Perhaps it does; I mean to say, he doesn't want to feel pain, he desires, he's lusting after, health. The one who's afraid to die is lusting after life. Against this distorted lust for health of body, where it's of precious little use,[4] or for bodily life, as against a death which is going to come whether you like it or not, deploy the commandment, *You shall not lust*, and say with the prophet, *And the day of men I have not lusted after, you know* (Jer 17:16).

That was the watchword of the martyrs; they didn't lust after the day of men, in case they should fail to reach the day of God. They didn't lust after the day so soon to end, in order to reach the day that has no end. What did they brush aside, what did they receive? Well of course, there's absolutely no comparison between those gains and these temporary losses. Painful work for an hour, and what you win is eternity.

4. Reflect, brothers and sisters, upon the day of the martyr;[5] it's right that we should spend some time drawing encouragement from his patience. Reflect upon the toils of soldiers in the army, of those who bear arms, upon what dangers they face, what harsh and difficult conditions they endure, in cold and heat, in hunger and thirst, wounds and death never far away. Not a day passes without its dangers, and yet they don't have the toils of a soldier before their eyes, but the leisured life of the veteran.[6] "Look," they say, "the hard work comes to an end, after a few years it will be followed by retirement; we will be in clover, our pensions will be paid, we will enjoy immunity, no civil duties will be imposed on us; after the burden of our military service, nobody is going to impose his own burden upon us."

With such a reward before their eyes, they toil away without any certainty of obtaining it. I mean, the man on military service who says, "The toil comes to an end"—how does he know he won't come to an end himself before the end of his service? Maybe too, his service at an end, no sooner does he enter on his retirement than he dies; and the one who was advised to extend his service a little longer for the sake of a more profitable retirement is not permitted to enjoy for very long the retirement which he worked so hard to attain to. Military service is attended by all these uncertainties, and yet men still undertake the undoubted hardships of service with a view to a very doubtful retirement.

Bestir yourselves, Christian hearts! Join up, be a soldier for God; with him no hard service can be in vain, with him no danger can be fruitless. By dying in battle, you see, the soldier of the world loses his reward, whereas it's precisely by dying that the soldier of Christ finds his. Finally, after the labors of a short time, one comes to enjoy rest, not for a long time, but simply without time. We come to the enjoyment of rest, you see, not in a place where time will be long, but where time will not be at all. Our maturity, after all, will be eternity, where there's neither any growing up nor growing old, and no day being added to our age, because no day is being left behind.[7] So if you were told, "Work for twenty years, in order to have a leisured retirement for forty," who would turn down a double term of leisure for a single one of work? And yet there is scarcely any veteran who is lucky enough, even if he lives to old age, to enjoy a retirement as long as his period of service.

About us, on the other hand, what has been said? And how does our commander-in-chief, who is going to pay us our eternal reward, not just a daily wage, how does he encourage us through the apostle? *For what is*, he says, *just a momentary light tribulation of ours, to a quite incredible degree is earning for us an eternal weight of glory* (2 Cor 4:17).

5. What astonishing words, brothers and sisters! How little he's made of what we suffer, how much of what we hope for! *What is*, he says, *just a momentary light tribulation of ours, to a quite incredible degree* ... "to an incredible

degree, because *eye has not seen nor ear heard nor has it come up into the heart of man, what God has prepared for those who love him* (1 Cor 2:9). So it's to the faithful that he says, *a light and momentary tribulation*; it's to the faithful that he says, *to a quite incredible degree is earning for us an eternal weight of glory* (2 Cor 4:17). "To a quite incredible degree": we are being commanded to believe what is incredible.[8] Believe what is incredible, faithful soldier, because for God nothing is impossible.[9] The "weight" he mentioned means what will give you gravity, so that you avoid levity or lightmindedness. *In a grave people*, it says, *I will praise you* (Ps 35:18). He mentioned weight, so that the gravity, the weight of love might make you firm, and the wind of trial and temptation not carry you off. Think of the threshing floor and love gravity and weight, fear lightness and levity. There's chaff there on the floor, there's grain there; each is tossed up by the winnowing fork, but each is not snatched away by the wind. One remains, thanks to its weight and gravity, the other flies away, thanks to its lightminded levity.[10]

It's the cause you suffer for that counts

6. So this is what will happen with us, when we endure every kind of adversity for the sake of faith and of justice, not, you see, for any kind of matter.[11] *Blessed*, he says, as we've just heard, *are those who have suffered persecution for the sake of justice* (Mt 5:10). With that addition he distinguished us from adulterers, from bandits, murderers, parricides, those who go in for sacrilege and witchcraft, heretics. They too, you see, suffer persecution, but not *for the sake of justice*. If you want to come through trials unscathed, take note of the distinction. Choose your cause, in order not to shrink in horror from the pain; and when you've chosen the cause, commend it to God and say to him, *Judge me, O God, and distinguish my cause from an unholy nation* (Ps 43:1).

Your cause is distinguished by the one from whom your patience comes.[12] Yes, his gift is genuine patience, because what endures pain for a bad cause is stubborn, obdurate hardness, not firm patience. Anything that has grown hard in the body, involving a loss of sensitivity, is all the more difficult to cure. All the praiseworthy virtues, you see, have their next-door neighbor vices, which can deceive the unwary; they also have their opposites. You can easily take care not to lurch into the number opposite; it's rather more difficult to avoid the neighbor. Neighboring vices, you see, have a certain semblance and shadow of the virtues. I will illustrate what I'm saying with a few examples for you to remember, and leave the rest to be understood.

Obdurate stubbornness the shadow of genuine patience

7. Look, we're talking about patience. The opposite of this virtue is impatience.[13] Patience is the endurance of evils for the sake of justice, impatience is the failure to endure evils for any cause whatever. This endurance is the contrary of non-endurance. Endurance in the form of a vice is stubborn, obdurate hard-

ness. Stubbornness, you see, imitates patience, but it isn't patience. So just see if it isn't perhaps deceiving you by being the next-door neighbor, if you aren't, perhaps, merely obdurate and stubborn while you flatter yourself on being patient. I mean, just as the person whom not even evil can force into evil is better than others, so the person whom not even evil can turn back from evil is worse than others.

Pain is an evil, iniquity is an evil. You've been promised a reward for doing iniquity, you don't consent; you've overcome the lust for rewards. You will come under pressure[14] from the other side; pains will be set before you. You overcame the tempting pleasure of rewards; now overcome also the threatened bite of pain. The one who promises you a reward in order to lead you into iniquity is after a fashion using what is good to lure you into evil. The one who threatens you with evil in order to force you into iniquity is using what is evil to push you into evil—but using a small evil to push you into a great evil. Now just brushing off the maker of promises won't make you a great man; what will certainly make you greater is not being cowed by the one who is venting his savage rage upon you. That's why I said that just as the person whom not even evil can drive into evil is better than others, so the one whom not even evil can turn back from evil is worse than others.

You've admonished a man to stop committing adultery, he has brushed aside your admonitions, he hasn't been turned back from evil by good. But if you now start threatening him with penalties, having him horsewhipped, imposing a number of vexatious restrictions on him, and if even then he doesn't put a stop to his evil behavior, how much worse he shows himself to be, someone whom not even evil has been able to turn back from evil! There you have the calamitous condition to which stubborn obduracy, patience's neighbor, is liable to reduce you. The effect of stubbornness, you see, in the hearts of the godless, is to stop them being turned back from their evil deeds, even by the threat or the infliction of painful penalties.

What you were boasting about only makes you worse.

"I endured," you'll say, "I overcame, I didn't give in, I wasn't cowed."

I would admire all this, if I could recognize patience there. But as it is, I detest the obdurate stubbornness I see.[15]

He's a bandit, he's paying the penalty for his banditries. He's being tortured, and he's not confessing what he knows in his conscience to be the truth.[16] What shall we say? "Great patience, wonderful endurance"? Let us rather say, "Detestable, obdurate stubbornness."

But if he endures this for a wicked crime, what will you there endure for the faith? With him, the refusal to confess can seem wonderful; with you, to confess will be glorious. He after all is suffering for a crime which he insists on denying, you for Christ whom you insist on confessing. Sometimes, though, you will find such a degree of obduracy that a person will both confess the evil and for the confession of that iniquity will suffer evils, simply in order not to slip away or withdraw from this evil. He's prepared to be tortured for the sake of Donatus, and he doesn't conceal this by denial, but he confesses, he's not ashamed, he boasts of his iniquity.[17] If only he would go away and hide, while he continues to be what he appears to be! You have a wound you don't want healed, and you have the nerve to lay it bare. This isn't sensitive health, but insensitive hardness and obduracy.

The difference between the spirit of the world and the Spirit of God

8. Let us love patience, let us hold on to it fast; and if we haven't got it yet, let us ask for it.[18] Our patience, you see, comes from the same one as self-control comes from; our self-control is his gift to us to arm us against pleasures, patience his gift to arm us against pains. But this psalm here which we have been singing has been teaching us that our patience, in the face of pains of course, comes from him.[19] Where can we find that our self-control too, which we need against pleasures, also comes from him? We have the plainest proof here: *And since I knew*, he says, *that nobody can be self-controlled unless God grants it; and this too was a matter of wisdom, to know whose gift this was* (Wis 8:21).

So if you have something from God, and don't know who you have it from, you won't be gifted, because you remain ungrateful. If you don't know who you get it from, you don't give thanks; by not giving thanks, you lose even what you have. *For the one who has, to him shall be given.* What is having, in the complete sense? Knowing where you have it from. *But the one who does not have*, that is, who doesn't know where he has it from, *even what he does have shall be taken away from him* (Mk 4:25). Finally, as that author says, *this too was a matter of wisdom, to know whose gift this was.*

In the same way[20] the apostle Paul also said, when he was commending the grace of God to us in the Holy Spirit: *We, however, have not received the spirit of this world, but the Spirit which is from God.* And as though he were asked, "How do you tell the difference?" he went on to add, *that we may know what things have been bestowed on us by God* (1 Cor 2:12). So the Spirit of God is a Spirit of charity, the spirit of this world a spirit of self-esteem. Those who have the spirit of this world are proud, are ungrateful to God. They have many of his gifts, but do not worship him, though they have them from him; that's why they are unhappy. Sometimes one person has greater gifts, another has lesser ones, for example intelligence, memory. These are gifts of God. You will sometimes find a person of extremely sharp wits, with astonishing, incredible powers of memory; you will find another of little intelligence and a poor memory, but endowed with both to a small degree. But the first is proud, the second humble; this one giving thanks to God for his small gifts, that one attributing the greater ones to himself. The one who gives thanks to God for small gifts is incomparably better than the one who prides himself on great ones. You see, the one who gives thanks for little things is admitted by God to great things, whereas the one who doesn't give thanks for great things loses even what he has. *For the one who . . .*[21]

NOTES

1. To be more precise, 22 July 397, this being the feast day of these martyrs in the Carthaginian calendar. The year is the one preferred by Dolbeau, following Lambot; it is inferred from the collection of sermons in which this one is found.

This is a longer version of Sermon 283, volume III, 8. There it was given by the Maurists, on the authority of Bede's extract from it in his anthology, the title of "On the birthday of the martyrs of Marseilles," *In Natali Martyrum Massilitanorum*. There is of course no reason why Bede should have heard of the Maxulitan martyrs, and I suppose to read them as "Massilitan martyrs" was as good a guess as any.

Those parts of the sermon which have already appeared in volume III, 8, are repeated.

2. He is punning on *mundus/immundus*: *pro mundi amoribus; immo pro immundis amoribus*.

3. How, will shortly become clear; but it does strike one at first sight as a rather glaring *non sequitur*. This is perhaps why the abbreviator responsible for the text in III, 8, whether Bede or someone else, skipped from here up to section 8. For this whole passage see also Sermons 145, 3 (III, 4); 153, 7 (III, 5).

4. He is thinking of the situation where you are faced with being tortured, or put to death, for the faith; in such a situation health is not a prime necessity—nor is life. The text seems to be very corrupt here; it goes on immediately, in a literal translation, "nor of bodily death, which is going to come whether you like it or not, deploy . . ." My translation requires the addition to the text after "where it is of precious little use," *ubi non est opus*, of—*aut vitae corporalis contra mortem, quae* instead of *nec mortis corporalis, quae* . . . See Sermons 77A, 4; 93, 8 (III, 3).

5. Was there just one martyr celebrated on the feast of "the Maxulitan martyrs"? The sermon did begin with a reference to "the courage of the holy martyrs"; but in the whole of it there is not a single specific reference to the particular story of their martyrdom, to their *passio*. I begin to entertain the irreverent thought that Augustine, preaching almost every day in Carthage that June and July, was told at the last minute as he was about to enter the pulpit that this was the feast of the martyrs of Maxula, and that he hadn't the slightest idea either of where Maxula was or who its martyrs were, though it seems it was a small town with its own bishop, a few miles south of Carthage—the modern town of Rades in southern Tunisia. So Dolbeau.

6. In the Roman army you signed on, not for a year or two, but for a solid 25 years. After that you could retire as a veteran, given your own piece of land and a pension.

7. For this theme see Sermon 216, 8 (III, 6).

8. I have here fairly radically rearranged the punctuation. As it stands in the text, it presents us with a wholly ungrammatical accusative as the subject of a sentence, thus: Fidelibus ergo dicit: *Juxta incredibilem modum aeternum gloriae pondus operatur nobis* levem et temporalem tribulationem. Fidelibus dicit: *Juxta incredibilem modum* jubetur quod incredibile est credere.

Treating that accusative, levem. . .tribulationem, as subject of the sentence, this would mean: So it's to the faithful that he says, *To a quite incredible degree* a light and momentary tribulation *is earning for us an eternal weight of glory*. It's to the faithful that he says, *To a quite incredible degree* one is ordered to believe what is incredible.

My translation assumes the following repunctuation:

Fidelibus ergo dicit: *Juxta incredibilem modum aeternum gloriae pondus operatur nobis*; "levem et temporalem tribulationem" fidelibus dicit. *Juxta incredibilem modum*; jubetur quod incredibile est credere.

9. See Lk 1:37; see also Sermons 247, 2 (III, 7); 289, 1 (III, 8).

10. See Lk 3:17; also Sermon 260D, 2 (III, 7).

11. Emending the text's *non enim pro quacunque requie*, "not for any kind of rest," to *non enim pro quacunque re*.

12. See Ps 62:5. For this whole theme see also Sermons 53A, 13 (III, 3); 274; 285, 7 (III, 8); 306, 2; 306A; 325, 2; 328, 4; 335G (III, 9); 359B (III, II).

13. These two words have become seriously devalued in ordinary current English use to signify

a high or low level of tolerance for petty inconveniences. We must remember that he is thinking all the time of the patient *courage* of the martyrs, the opposite of which would be the *cowardice* that refuses to endure the threatened torments—and that's what he means here by "impatience."

14. Reading *urgeberis*, following a suggestion of Dolbeau's, instead of the text's *arguebaris*, "you were being tested from the other side."

15. Here Dolbeau indicates a lacuna in the text, a kind of half sentence, which is then followed by two sentences in quotation marks: . . . *patientiam a duritia: "Noli interrogare vocem meam, sed causam meam. Causa ipsa tibi respondeat."* . . . patience from obduracy: "Don't question my words but my cause. Let the cause itself answer you."

Whatever has dropped out in the lacuna, the whole little passage simply interferes somewhat nonsensically with the current of his thought. So I am treating it as the remains of a marginal comment, referring to some passage in another of Augustine's works, perhaps a sermon or a letter, where he distinguishes between *patientia* and *duritia* by saying, *Noli. . .* What I suggest is that the first part of this long reference got scratched out, and what remained got inserted into the text. Perhaps it ran something like this: "See Sermon/Letter XX, where he says, in order to distinguish patience from obduracy, 'Don't question. . .' "

16. He is being tortured in order to extract a confession from him.

17. The iniquity of schism or heresy.

18. From section 4 of Sermon 283 (III, 8), its penultimate sentence.

19. See Ps 62:5.

20. Here section 3 in Sermon 283 (III, 8) begins. Doubtless the reading that had preceded the singing of Ps 62 had been 1 Cor 2, and perhaps Mk 4 or Mt 13.

21. Here the Mainz manuscript ends, with a whole leaf being badly torn. The text would presumably have continued as it does in Sermon 283 (III, 8). See Mk 4:25.

Dolbeau 3
SERMON 293A
Mainz 7

SERMON OF SAINT AUGUSTINE ON THE BIRTH OF SAINT JOHN THE BAPTIST,
AND ON THE VOICE AND THE WORD

Date: 407[1]

Augustine finds himself unexpectedly with this particular congregation

1. It was the Lord who decided to provide your graces today with my voice and presence, and he did this not through any arrangements of ours, but according to his own wishes. So together with you I give him thanks, and render you the service of a sermon, which is my job, in which it is right and proper for me to serve you. Your business, though, dearly beloved, is to accept with charity whatever is provided for you by any of the servants of God, and together with me to give him thanks for granting us all the privilege of spending this day together.

The superiority of John the Baptist over all other prophets

2. So what else should we talk about today, but the man whose birthday it is? So Saint John, born of a barren woman as the forerunner of the Lord who was born of a virgin, became the one to greet his Lord from the womb, the one to proclaim him after leaving the womb.[2] The barren woman was not suited to giving birth, the virgin did not have the means of giving birth; the barren woman bore the herald, the virgin the judge. But the Lord Jesus Christ, who was going to come from the virgin's womb, had sent many heralds ahead of him to mankind. All the prophets had been sent on ahead by him, but he was himself speaking in them; though he came after them, he was before them.

So considering that the Lord had sent many heralds before him, what was the extra special merit of this man, whose birthday is being brought to our notice today; what altogether superior excellence was to be found in him? I mean, even the fact that his birthday is not unknown to us, just as his Lord's birthday is not unknown to us, is a sign of some special greatness. When other prophets were born we don't know; about John we have not been allowed to remain in

253

ignorance.[3] This next point too shows his unique merit, that the others foretold the Lord and desired to see him and did not see him; even if they saw him in spirit, they saw him as coming in the future;[4] but they weren't here to see him actually present.

In fact, the Lord himself says about them to his disciples that *many prophets and just men have wished to see what you see, and have not seen it; and to hear what you hear, and have not heard it* (Mt 13:17). Wasn't it he that was sending them? But they all had the desire, if it could possibly happen, to see the Christ here in the flesh. But because they went ahead of him in death, just as they went ahead of him in birth, Christ didn't find them here, but all the same Christ did redeem them for eternal life. And as an indication of what sort of desire they all had to see the Christ here, call to mind that old man Simeon, whom the Holy Spirit had told as no small favor that he would not depart from this world until he had seen the Christ. Christ was born. He recognized him in the infant in his mother's arms, he took him, held him in his own arms, though he was himself being carried by the infant's divinity; and holding in his arms the infant, un-speaking[5] Word, he blessed God, saying, *Now, Lord, you are letting your servant go in peace, since my eyes have seen your salvation* (Lk 2:29-30). So[6] the other prophets never saw him; Simeon saw him as an infant; John recognized and greeted him newly conceived, proclaimed and saw him as a young man. So he excelled all the others.

Among those born of women, none has arisen greater than John, but the one who is less, is in the kingdom greater than he is

3. Listen also to the Lord's testimonial to him; he put himself before him, nobody else. He was extraordinarily great, surely, if there was none but Christ who could be put before him. So then this is what the Lord himself says about him: *Among those born of women, nobody has arisen greater than John the Baptist*; and to put himself before him, he went on: *but the one who is less, is in the kingdom of heaven greater than he is* (Mt 11:11).[7] He called himself both less and greater; less by birth, greater by being Lord. The Lord, you see, was born after him, but in the flesh, but from the virgin; before him, however, he *was in the beginning the Word* (Jn 1:1). It's a great matter; John in fact came after Christ, because *all things were made through him, and without him was made nothing* (Jn 1:3).[8]

So why did John come? To show the way of humility, so that human pretensions might diminish, the glory of God increase. So John came, a great one commending a great one. John came as *the measure of a man* (Rv 21:17). What does that mean, the measure of a man? No human being could be more than John; whatever was more than John must thereby be more than human. After all, if the measure of human greatness had reached its limits in John, you wouldn't now find any human being greater; and yet you have found someone greater. Confess that he's God, whom naturally you have been able to find greater than a man. John was a man, and Christ was a man; but John only a man,

Christ God and man. Insofar as he's God, he made John; insofar as he's man, he was born after John.

John came to teach the proud humility, to proclaim the way of repentance

4. And yet, just notice how this forerunner of his Lord, of one who is God and man, how much he humbles himself. This man, than whom nobody has arisen greater among those born of women, is questioned about whether he is himself the Christ. He was so great that people could make this mistake. They wondered whether he was himself the Christ, and they wondered about it seriously enough to question him. Now if he had been a son of pride, not a teacher of humility, he would not have opposed the mistake the people were making, and would not indeed have taken steps to make them think that, but would simply have accepted what they were already thinking. It would possibly have been overreaching himself, to wish to persuade people that he was the Christ; if he had tried to do so and hadn't been believed, he would have been left high and dry, both rejected and dejected, both despised among men and condemned in God's eyes. But there was no need for him to persuade people; he could already see they were thinking this about him; he could simply accept their mistake and boost his own prestige.[9]

But far be it from the faithful friend of the bridegroom to wish to be loved instead of him by the bride. He confessed that he was not what in fact he was not, in order not to lose what he was. John, after all, wasn't that bridegroom, because when he was questioned about it, this is what he said: *The one who has the bride is the bridegroom; but the friend of the bridegroom stands and listens to him, and rejoices with joy because of the bridegroom's voice* (Jn 3:29). *I indeed am baptizing you in water for repentance; but the one who is coming after me is greater than I am.* How much greater? *And I am not worthy to undo the strap of his sandal* (Jn 1:26). Consider how inferior to him he would have been, even if he had been worthy, how much he would have been debasing himself if this is what he had said: "He is greater than I am, and all I am worthy to do is to undo the strap of his sandal." He would have been calling himself worthy to stoop down to his feet. But now as it is, how exalted he proclaimed him to be when he declared himself unworthy even to touch his feet, or rather his sandals! So John came to teach the proud humility, to proclaim the way of repentance.

Christ the Word, John the voice

5. The voice came before the Word. How can the voice be before the Word? What is said about Christ? *In the beginning was the Word, and the Word was with God and the Word was God; this was in the beginning with God* (Jn 1:1-2). But in order to come to us, *the Word became flesh* (Jn 1:14), in order to dwell among us. So we've heard that Christ is the Word; let us hear that John is the voice. When he was asked, *You then, who are you?* he answered, *I am the voice of one crying in the desert* (Jn 1:22-23).

So[10] for a little while then, dearest friends, for a little while, to the extent that the Lord gives us the ability, let us deliberate upon "voice" and "word." Christ is the Word, a word that does not just make a sound and pass away; I mean, what makes a sound and passes away is a voice, not a word. So then, the Word of God, through which all things were made, that is what our Lord Jesus Christ is; *the voice of one crying in the desert*, that is what John is. Which comes first, voice or word? Let us see what a word is, and what a voice, and then we shall see which comes first.

6. What do you think a word is, brothers and sisters? Let's leave aside that Word of God; let's talk a little about our own words, and see if we can't use some comparisons as steps from the lowest level to the highest. Who can grasp, after all, the Word of God through which all things were made? So for a little while let us set aside his greatness, his inexpressible eternity and co-eternity with the Father. Let us believe what we cannot see, so that by believing we may earn the right to see. So come on then, let us deal with that Word as though with the sort of thing that is going on every day in our minds or in our ears or on our lips.

What is a word? We aren't still thinking, are we, that this is a word which is sounding in your ears? The word is that thing which you want to say. You have conceived something in your mind for you to say; that very concept has already become a word in your mind; but this word, that is what you want to say, the thing you have undertaken to express, you already know yourself, and you have already said it to yourself.[11] May that Word assist me which is the Son of God, so that I may be able to publish to your ears in a way that is fitting what he himself has seen fit to grant me to conceive in my mind.

But if it should happen that I buckle under the sheer magnitude of the task, being so feeble and so unequal to the subject that I fail to express it as it deserves, you have someone to turn to from me. May he, the Son of God himself, the Word of God, be present in your minds and achieve by conversing with you inwardly what I, as a mere man, cannot achieve outwardly in your ears. All the same, please assist my efforts by your attentiveness, and by pleading on my behalf that I may be able to say something, and on your own that you may be worthy to hear it.

7. So, that a word, as I said, is what you conceive in your mind in order to say it, let the thing you wish to say, conceived in the mind in order to be said, be called a word;[12] so when you conceive an idea of something you want to say, and this thing itself, this very thought, has become a word in your mind, you will then consider whoever it is you are talking to and wish to say this to; and if you see he is a Greek, you look for a Greek "voice" with which to give voice

to your word; if you see he is a Latin speaker, you look for a Latin "voice" with which to present the word; if you see he's a Hebrew speaker, a Hebrew "voice," if a Punic speaker, a Punic "voice"—provided you know these languages.[13] If you don't know them, though, when you see someone there in front of you who only knows a language which you don't know, you are then not at a loss for a word, but at a loss for a voice.

So that word which you had conceived in your heart was antecedent to all voices and before all voices, before the Greek, before the Latin, before the Hebrew, before the Punic; and whatever languages and voices there may be throughout the whole world, that concept was antecedent to them all, and was being carried by the pregnant soul as a fetus of the soul, and a way was being sought of how it might be brought forth, since what was already being held in the mind could not be brought forth to anyone else except by some voice. Unless that voice, though, were a specific one, how could it ever be recognized? It would have to be a specific one out of all the various languages, so that you spoke in a Greek voice to a Greek, in a Hebrew one to a Hebrew, in a Punic one to a Punic speaker. That word, however, which you had conceived before all voices, was neither Latin nor Greek nor Punic nor any such thing.

So notice what a great mystery there is here. In any case, if you kept silence completely, does that mean that the word would cease to live in your mind, and that if there were nobody to whom you could speak, what you had conceived in your mind would not remain evident to you? It would be evident, though, without any diversity of language, in simple knowledge.[14]

8. Let's say something by way of an example, to make things plainer. God is a particular thing above all that he has made—if indeed he is to be called a thing; so God is something which surpasses all that he has made, *from whom and in whom and through whom are all things* (Rom 11:36). Is all this that I have said, which is what God is, just one syllable, and all that vast power confined to one syllable? Now God was there even before I conceived this in my mind. How can I can conceive this very thing, in order to say "God"? But what is called God in English, *Deus* in Latin, what is called *Theos* in Greek, what in Punic is called *Ylim* [15]—I've spoken four languages[16]—what I conceived in my mind was nothing belonging to any of these languages. But when I wanted to bring forth, to proffer what I had conceived in my mind about God, if I found a Punic speaker, I said *Ylim*; if I found a Latin speaker, I said *Deus*; if I found a Greek, I said *Theos*; before I found any of them, what was in my mind was neither Greek nor Punic nor Latin. So what I conceived to be brought forth was a word; what I provided it with to bring it forth was a voice.

9. We have discussed voice and word: a word before all languages, a voice in some language or other. So which comes first, word or voice? With me, word comes first, because unless I conceived a word in my mind, I wouldn't provide the word with a voice to bring it forth. So a word was conceived before a voice, and provided itself with a voice as a kind of vehicle by which to come to you, not in which to be in me. I, after all, know what I am going to say, even if I don't say it. Look, before I say it, I haven't provided a voice, and the word is with me.

But in order to indicate it to you I provide it with a voice, so that when you in your turn hear the voice, the word may also be in you.

So then with me, in order for me to teach, the word comes first and the voice follows. Pay very careful attention and try to understand, with the Lord's help, because I know that I am talking about hidden matters, located in the depths of great mysteries;[17] but I am talking to faithful Christians, of whatever sort and condition,[18] who have gone ahead in faith to what I am going to say. So with me, then, the word has come first, and the word coming first has been provided with a voice. With you my voice has come first, and then you have understood the word which was in my mind.

How Christ the Word is both before and after John the voice

10. So if Christ is the Word, John the voice,[19] Christ the Word came first with God; but to us the voice came first, so that the Word might come to us. So *the Word was with God* (Jn 1:1), and there was as yet no voice, no John. I mean, can you possibly say that before there was John as the voice, there was no Word with God? He was there, but John was taken over as the voice in order that the Word might be spoken to us; and that the Word might come to us, the voice preceded it. That's why it's both true that Christ was before John in eternity, and that all the same he had not to be born first, unless John came to us before the Word as the voice.

Blessed is the Lord our God, because I have said it as best I could, and you have understood what you have been able to.[20] May he increase and multiply your understanding,[21] and may the Word who sent the voice ahead shine his light upon you.

Consequences of the Word's abiding, the voice's passing away

11. But notice, my brothers and sisters: the voice makes a sound and passes away, the Word abides. Notice what I'm saying. Here you are, what I have said is "God"; first I conceived in my mind what I would say, then this single syllable made a sound and passed away. What I conceived in my mind didn't pass away with it, surely? Again, when I said "God," it came about in your mind that you should think God. It came first in my mind for me to say it, and the thought of God was produced in your mind when you heard this one syllable. This one syllable performed its service and passed away. All the same, what I had conceived in my mind has not passed away; it was in me, and after this one syllable has been spoken it has remained in me; and the thought that was produced in your mind, when this single syllable touched your ear, has remained in your mind even after this syllable has passed away.

So then, brothers and sisters, the service of the man John was going to pass away like a voice. Rightly did he[22] also receive baptism; but John's baptism was transitory, and it was called *John's baptism* (Acts 19:3). There's the baptism of Christ and the baptism of John, but the baptism of John is transitory, as being that of the voice, while the baptism of Christ abides and abides forever, just as the Word abides.

12. And the more progress we make in God, so much the more do voices diminish, and the Word grow in us.[23] Why, indeed, do we have voices, except to help us understand something? If we enjoyed fullness of understanding, we wouldn't need voices. If we could see one another's thoughts, would we need any language to talk to each other in? So there is going to be a time when we shall see the Word as he is seen by the angels, and there will be no need of voices. After all, there will be no evangelizing to be done, when we all see the Word itself. All time-bound things will pass away, because the voice is of the flesh, is of the hay; now *the splendor of the flesh is like flowers in the hay; the hay has dried up, the flowers have fallen; but the Word of the Lord abides for ever* (Is 40:6.8). So it's because the more we make progress toward understanding the less need there will be for voices by which we are led toward understanding, that John himself said, *He must grow, while I must diminish* (Jn 3:30). As the Word grows, the voice diminishes. What do I mean, "as the Word grows"? The Word itself, after all, doesn't grow, but it's we who grow in him, we who make progress in him, we who increase in him, until we no longer find voices necessary.

This was also apparent from the very births of the Word and of the voice. The Word was born on 25 December,[24] from which point the day begins to increase; the voice was born before the Word of God, when the day begins to diminish. *He must grow, while I must diminish.* And their deaths also showed this; John was diminished by having his head cut off; Christ grew by being raised up on the cross.

Misinterpretations of the Donatists and Augustine's answer

13. And so let us celebrate the birthday of the voice in honor of the Word;[25] and let us not pay any attention to the subtleties of empty-headed people who don't understand what they're talking about;[26] don't let us be taken in by them. You see, because John had a baptism, and we find in the Acts of the Apostles that some people who only had John's baptism were baptized again—some disciples, you see, were found who had John's baptism, and Paul the apostle gave orders for them to be baptized, because they only had a transitory baptism, because they had the baptism of the voice, not yet of the Word; I mean, you look for John's baptism now and you don't find it; the voice, you see, has sounded and passed away, while the baptism of Christ abides to this day—so because the apostle Paul gave orders for those who had received John's baptism to be baptized, for the sake of the mystery itself,[27] the heretics have tried to extract an argument from this in support of rebaptism. We grieve over their error, and we rejoice over their deliverance.[28] So let's answer them briefly on this point.

14. The reason you think a person who has received the baptism of Christ ought to be rebaptized is because the apostle Paul gave orders for people who had John's baptism to be baptized, and this is how you argue: "If, after the

baptism of John, about whom the Lord said, *Among those born of women there has not arisen one greater than John the Baptist* (Mt 11:11), if after him the apostles baptized, how much more ought people to be baptized after heretics!"

I answer: You think John is being insulted, seeing that people were baptized after his baptism, if they aren't baptized after the baptism of heretics. I too grieve over the serious insult; but this is how I throw the ball back to you:[29] "If they were baptized after John's baptism, shouldn't they also be baptized after the baptism of Optatus?"[30] What do you say to me about that? Who was John?

"Among those born of women, none will arise greater than John the Baptist."

With you there is some priest who is at any rate a drunkard—I won't say a usurer, I won't say an adulterer—for the time being we stick to what is common enough and what is public knowledge; there is at least some priest or other with you who is a drunkard.

"Granted."

Why don't you rebaptize after him? If you baptize after John, who didn't drink wine,[31] shouldn't you baptize after a drunkard? At this point, certainly, he's confused and has nothing to say. So what next? Listen to the answer from me.

15. Yes, Paul gives orders for those to be baptized who had John's baptism and didn't have Christ's. After a drunkard, though, why don't you baptize? Because the baptism he gave is none other than Christ's. Let a sober man give it, let a drunkard give it, it's Christ's; it doesn't belong either to the sober man or to the drunkard. Peter gave this baptism, it's Christ's; Judas gave it, it's Christ's. You see, just because Peter gave it, it doesn't mean it's Peter's baptism. Why not?

That was called John's baptism; this, though, isn't in the same way called Peter's baptism, Paul's baptism, Judas' baptism, in those whom Peter baptized, whom Paul baptized, whom John the evangelist baptized, whom Judas baptized. No, but in those whom Peter baptized, whom Paul, John, Judas baptized, it is the baptism of Christ. In those, however, whom John's disciples baptized it was John's baptism,[32] because John had received this charge and preparatory service; voice before Word. So you, then, don't wish to baptize after a drunkard, nor I after a heretic.

16. And if by any chance you are thinking that a heretic doesn't enter the kingdom of heaven, while a drunkard does, the apostle Paul made this point absolutely clear when he said, *Now the works of the flesh are evident, which are fornications, impurities, self-indulgence, the service of idols, sorceries, grudges, quarrels, jealousies, animosities, divisions, heresies, envies, drinking bouts, orgies, and similar things; of which I forewarn you, as I have forewarned you, that those who do such things shall not gain possession of the kingdom of God* (Gal 5:19-21). He put drunks in the same list as heresies, and he concluded, *those who do such things shall not gain possession of the kingdom of God.*

Get me a heretic and a drunkard; if the heretic persists in heresy, he doesn't enter the kingdom of heaven; so too the drunkard, if he persists in drunkenness, he doesn't enter the kingdom of heaven. Now give me a lesson; both of them:

whose baptism do they give? They are both outside the kingdom of heaven, but they give a thing that pertains to the kingdom of heaven. The herald proclaims the judgment, but he doesn't set innocence free. The judge does do this, and it's he who has told the herald what to say. Sometimes a villain is the herald, and an innocent person is set free through him. The villainous herald says, "My orders are to release him," and an innocent person is set free by the agency of a villain.[33] Why? Because the herald's voice is the decision of the judge.

Now a drunkard baptizes; it's the act of a minister.[34] A heretic has baptized; it's the act of a minister. The gift of baptism is the gift of almighty God. Obviously, if he baptized in the name of Donatus, baptism would have to be repeated. But if I recognize there the baptism of Christ, if I recognize the words of the gospel,[35] if I recognize the image and brand mark[36] of my king, then even if you were a deserter and could be convicted and put to death through his mark upon you, come to the camp with the Lord's mark; you can earn a pardon, you cannot get the mark changed.

NOTES

1. This is the complete version of what has already appeared in Volume III, 8, as Sermon 293A. That abridged version had been reduced to that more manageable size by medieval copyists, producing sermons for lectionaries, for readings in the divine office. They cut out whole sections which they regarded as either merely philosophical or as of no immediate relevance to their communities, because they were full of references to the Donatist question. Dolbeau dates the sermon, convincingly enough, to 24 June 407, and locates it in Carthage, where a Council had just issued some directives about the reception of Donatist individuals and communities wishing to be reconciled with the Catholic Church.

Those sections that have already appeared in Sermon 293A (III, 8) are repeated. The translation here will occasionally differ from that one, either because there are slight changes in the Mainz manuscript, or because I am adjusting the translation, I trust for the better.

2. See Lk 1:41.76.

3. See Sermons 287, 1; 290, 2; 292, 1; 293, 1 (III, 8).

4. See Jn 8:56.

5. Just *infantem* in the Latin; but its literal meaning is "unspeaking."

6. In the text in Sermon 293A, III, 8, section 3 begins here.

7. For this unusual punctuation of this sentence, see Sermon 293A, III, 8, note 6.

8. Here the Mainz text differs fairly considerably from the previously published version in III, 8; that one does seem to be the more authentic of the two.

9. See Sermon 288, 2 (III, 8).

10. Here we leave behind the older published text of Sermon 293A (III, 8). For this whole passage, see Sermon 288, 3 (III, 8); also 119, 7 (III, 4), where, however, he has a different signification for "voice." There it is the flesh which the Word became, and which conveys the divine Word to our senses and our minds, just as my voice conveys my "mental word," my meaning, to your senses and mind.

11. An overloaded sentence; I have omitted a phrase after "what you want to say": *conceptionem in corde tuo factam*, "the concept made in your mind," which being in the accusative has no syn-

tactical place in the sentence, and looks like a puzzled marginal comment which has wriggled its way into the text.

12. As "bumbling" a sentence in the Latin as here in the English.

For this section see Sermon 288, 3 (III, 8); also 225, 3 (III, 6), where again the "voice" with which I give utterance to my mental "word" is presented as analogous to the flesh which the divine Word became, not as representing John the Baptist.

13. Augustine's use of the word "voice" here is as strained in Latin as it is in English. In Sermon 288, 3 I adapt Augustine to our contemporary world, and have him talking about a French voice (Greek), an English one (Latin), and a Welsh one (Punic), leaving Hebrew as Hebrew. See that sermon, note 11—and note 14, which will explain why I do not do the same now; if I did I would have to find out what the Welsh for "God" is! But this sermon here indicates that I was a little hard on Augustine in that note, in suggesting that he didn't know the Punic word for "God."

14. See Sermon 288 (III, 8), note 12.

15. Cognate, clearly, with the Hebrew *Elohim*.

16. He actually said "three," of course, as he didn't speak any English.

17. He is referring to the mystery of the divine Word of God, and his "voice," which has been so laboriously illustrated with this example. It is to this mystery that even simple, illiterate Christians will have gone on ahead in faith.

18. *Loquor qualiscumque*; I am treating *qualiscumque*, which at first glance seems to be a nominative, giving the meaning (wholly irrelevant to the context), "I am talking, whatever sort of person I am," as a "dialectical" dative, a form of *qualibuscumque*, in agreement with the datives that immediately follow.

19. Here we rejoin Sermon 293A (III, 8), in a curiously scrappy manner. The medieval abbreviator responsible for that text was clearly intent on reducing the illustrating example to a minimum.

20. There had, no doubt, been clapping and cries of approval to call forth this benediction; for its form, see Nm 6:24-26. It had become a regular liturgical form.

21. An echo, perhaps, of Gn 28:3, itself an echo of Gn 1:28.

22. John "received baptism," not in the sense of being baptized, but in the sense of receiving the commission to baptize. See *Homilies on the Gospel of John* 5, 4: "The baptism which John received is called the baptism of John; he alone received such a gift."

23. See Jn 3:30.

24. He says "on 8 of the Kalends of January."

25. These last short extracts from Sermon 293A (III, 8) come from the end of it, sections 5 and 6.

26. The Donatists, as will shortly be evident. For this section see Sermons 287, 4; 288, 5; 293B, 3; 293C, 2; 293D, 5 (III, 8); 380, 8 (III, 10).

27. Which mystery? The mystery of Christ, the mystery (sacrament) of baptism? A most opaque remark. The particular Donatist heretics who had used this passage in support of their practice of rebaptizing Catholics (heretics for them) were among others Petilian and Cresconius, who figure prominently in Augustine's anti-Donatist writings. The passage their argument hinged on is Acts 19:1-7.

28. Hardly the deliverance, that is, the reconciliation with the Catholic Church, of the Donatists just named in note 27, but of others, about whom the Council he had just attended had laid down certain rules. See note 1 above.

29. *Tibi replico*; not quite the same image in the Latin, but an image nevertheless, "I fold it back to you"; not just a colorless "I reply." Augustine's grieving over the insult is, of course, ironical.

30. Optatus of Thamugadi, a very violent, not to say bloodthirsty Donatist bishop of that place, who had been implicated in Gildo's rebellion in 398 or thereabouts.

31. See Lk 7:33.

32. An expansion of a "shorthand" Latin text, which Dolbeau suspects of being faulty.

33. See Sermons 44, 6, note 10 (III, 2); 74, 3 (III, 3).

34. *Ministerium est*. In the published text Dolbeau transcribed this, both times, as *mysterium est*—which would mean "it's the sacrament." In a footnote to his edition of *Nouveaux sermons*. . .

(VII), *Revue des Études Augustiniennes* 40 (1994) 143, he admits this was a mistaken transcription of a conventional abbreviation for *ministerium*.

35. See Mt 28:19.

36. *Formam et characterem*. These two words, largely as a result of Augustine's use of them, became technical terms in Latin sacramental doctrine: the "form" of a sacrament being the words spoken by the minister over the "matter"; the "character" of three sacraments being, as it were, the stamp of Christ imprinted on the recipients of them, marking them as belonging to Christ, by baptism, confirmation, and order; the scholastics will later on say that they are thus marked as sharing in Christ's priesthood. But here Augustine is using the word *forma* in quite a different sense from the one just noted; in conjunction with the word *character*, which was the brand-mark (an ancient equivalent of tattooing?) Roman soldiers were branded with on enlisting; it evidently refers to the image of the emperor on the stamp—like his image on coins. It is worth reminding ourselves, as we recall our catechism treatment of sacramental character, that it is a metaphorical use of the word, taken from this Roman military practice.

Dolbeau 4
SERMON 299A
Mainz 9

SERMON OF SAINT AUGUSTINE, PREACHED TO THE PEOPLE
ON THE BIRTHDAY OF THE HOLY APOSTLES PETER AND PAUL

Date: 404[1]

Peter and Paul suffered on the same date, not in the same year

1. I am delighted to be sharing in your joy and your gratitude, as we commemorate this holy day, which has brought us all together today for its celebration; it is of course very familiar to your ears, your minds and your actions. It is the birthday of the apostles Peter and Paul which has dawned today, not the birthday which entangled them in the world, but the one which set them free from the world. It is in virtue of human feebleness, of course, that people are born for distress, and in virtue of Christian charity that martyrs are born for a crown. And it is on account of their merits that this day has been set before us for the solemn celebration of their feast and the imitation of their holiness,[2] so that by recalling the glory of the martyrs we might love in them what those who slew them hated, and by loving their manly courage[3] we might honor their sufferings. It was by their courage that their merit was acquired, and by their sufferings that their reward was earned.

One day for two martyrs and two apostles; as far as we have gathered from the tradition of the Church, they did not suffer on one and the same day, and yet they did suffer on one and the same day. Peter was the first to suffer on this day, Paul suffered on this day later on.[4] Their merits gave equal value to their sufferings; this was brought about for them by the one who was in them, who was suffering in them, who was suffering with them, who was helping them as they fought, awarding them the crown when they won. But as I said, what has been set before us is a day for the solemn celebration of their feast, not one for the aimless or worldly expression of joy, but for fixing our eyes on their spiritual crown[5]—everyone wants to receive the crown, hardly anyone wants to fight the match; so let it be in the order in which they suffered, not in the order in which we heard the readings, that we hear about the merits of Peter from the gospel, hear about the merits of Paul from the apostle's letter.[6]

Peter's threefold confession of love atones for his threefold denial;
he is bidden to feed Christ's sheep, not his own

2. The gospel was chanted just now, just now we heard, *The Lord said to Peter, Simon Peter, do you love me? He answered, I do; and the Lord said, Feed my sheep. And again the Lord, Simon Peter, do you love me? And he said, I do, Lord. And the Lord again, Feed my sheep* (Jn 21:15-16). He questions him a third time on exactly the same point as he has questioned him on twice. He made it his business to ask him a third time; Peter was already tired of answering a third time. *Peter was grieved,* you see, so the gospel says, *because the Lord questioned him the third time, and he said, Lord, you know everything; you know that I love you. And the Lord said, Feed my sheep* (Jn 21:17). Anyone who asks a question he knows the answer to is wanting to teach something; so what did the Lord want to teach Peter by questioning him a third time on what he knew already? What else can we suppose, brothers and sisters, but the lesson that charity should eliminate weakness, and that Peter should realize he had to confess a third time out of love, having denied three times out of fear?[7]

It was Peter's merit that he fed God's sheep; he would never have won the prize of true martyrdom if he had fed his own sheep. It was not without reason that the Lord added *my sheep* three times—he wouldn't have done so, unless there were going to be people who wanted to glory in martyrdom when they fed their own sheep.[8] The apostolic soul, the Catholic soul, simple, humble, subject to God, not seeking its own glory but his, so that *whoever glories may glory in the Lord* (1 Cor 1:31), tends the sheep for the shepherd, and in the shepherd is a shepherd. The heretics feed their own sheep, but they brand the Lord's mark[9] on their own sheep, not by way of admitting the truth, but as a precautionary tactic. There are many people, you see—we all know it, the property market is full of examples—who out of fear of losing their properties register them in the names of some influential persons, so that by this act someone else may appear as the owner, someone else frighten off marauders.

So because they don't see their name made famous and glorious throughout the world, they have imposed the name of Christ upon their sheep—and would to God that the sheep had been bought, and not plundered! One bought them, the others stole them. He it was who bought them, who bought them back, redeemed them, from the devil, who gave his blood as their price; a fitting price indeed with which to buy the whole world. So then it is runaway slaves who are in possession—I won't say of their own sheep, but of ones they want to call their own; they have placed the Lord's brand-mark on their stolen stock. But the Lord, the true owner, doesn't keep quiet; he calls to the sheep with his true voice through other slaves of his, so that they may recognize the voice of the shepherd, and come back to him. Let them come back to the flock, come back with nothing to fear; we take the sheep back, but we don't deface the brand-mark.

3. A few of the brethren and sisters were very possibly surprised that in the earlier sermons I preached I said nothing about the heretics, although I am certainly very keen to win back and take in our brothers and sisters from the dead end of their error. And it has come to my ears that those pitiable and ever to be pitied people have been saying that it was dread of the circumcellions which imposed silence upon me.[10] It is indeed very true that they never stop trying to deter me by terror tactics from preaching the word of peace; but if I am to be frightened off by wolves, what answer shall I give to the one who tells us, *Feed my sheep* (Jn 21:15-17)? They thrust forward their fangs for savaging the sheep, I my tongue for healing them. I speak openly, and I don't keep quiet, and I say the same things, and I say the same things very often; let them hear what they don't want to hear, let them do what they ought to do. Yes indeed, I make a nuisance of myself to those who are unwilling to hear; but if the reason I enjoy the love of those who hear willingly is that I should go on facing danger from the unwilling, I will put my trust in the name of Christ as I persevere in preaching the word of God, with your prayers helping me along.

I am convinced, you see, that when you hear of the perils I face, of how I have to spend my time among the furious assaults of men who are no better than bandits, then you do pray for me; what makes this clear to me is our mutual love for one another. Not, of course, that I have entered into your minds; but the one who is in you makes it clear to me, because he is also in me. All I would urge upon you, though, is that when you pray for me, what you should pray for is that God should above all take care of that safety of mine which is in his eyes eternal safety, or salvation. About this safety in time, let him do what he knows is best for me and his Church. After all, we have heard from the same master, the shepherd and chief and head of shepherds, that we shouldn't *fear those who kill the body, but cannot kill the soul* (Mt 10:28).

We have also heard, in the words of the psalm, that most salutary prayer, *Do not hand me over, Lord, by my desire to the sinner* (Ps 140:8). It's bad, you see, to be handed over to the sinner by one's desire; the martyrs were handed over to sinners, the apostles whose birthday[11] we are celebrating today were handed over to sinners, but before them all the Lord of martyrs and apostles was handed over to sinners; all these were handed over to sinners, but not by their own desire. So who then are handed over to sinners by their own desire, if not those who give in to their persecutors because of any kind of worldly desire? As though, to keep on with this example we are spending our time over, if I keep silent out of desire for this life when these people make their threats and furiously brandish their clubs, their swords, their firebrands, I will be handed over to sinners by my desire, and will go on living while really dead, preserving the well-being of the flesh, while losing the soul of charity. In order, though, to go on living a good life, I must love both you, to save you from being led astray, and them, in order to gain them. They threaten, let me go on arguing with them; they rage, let me go on praying for them; they repulse me, let me go on teaching them.

4. Well, we also heard about the merits of Paul, if I may now speak too about his merits, in the order which I promised at the beginning.[12] He was speaking to his disciple, to tell him of his own approaching martyrdom, and to rid him of fear by his example: *I adjure you before God and Christ Jesus, who is going to judge the living and the dead, and by his manifesting of himself and by his kingdom*; he bound him by adjuring him like that, and then added, *preach the word; press on in season and out of season* (2 Tm 4:1-2). When I hear this, I too in my small measure am seasonable for you, unseasonable and a nuisance for them. All the same, I do not rest from publishing the word of God, from the preaching of peace, and from repeating it again and again in Christ's name, *in season, out of season*.

You are seasonable for the hungry when you offer them bread, unseasonable for the sick when you force them to eat. Food is offered the first, rammed into the second; refreshment is pleasing to the one, distasteful to the other, but loving concern neglects neither. So let us take the merits of the apostles as examples for ourselves, while as for their sufferings, let us not only not be afraid of them, but also, should it be necessary, share them.

Listen to what the same apostle has to say: *As for me, I am already being immolated* (2 Tm 4:6)—or *poured out as a libation*; some copies mention libation, some immolation; both libation and immolation are connected with sacrifice.[13] He knew that his martyrdom would be a sacrifice to God. It was not the people who slew him that offered such a sacrifice to the Father, but the high priest who had said, *Do not fear those who slay the body* (Mt 10:28). *Time presses*, says Paul, *for me to cast off*.

So what, my dear Paul, are you hoping for when you cast off? What sort of rest and quiet, you tireless worker?

Time presses, he says, *for me to cast off*.

So what have you done? What are your hopes?

I have fought the good fight, I have completed the course, I have kept the faith (2 Tm 4:6-7). In what way did he keep the faith, except by not being scared off by his persecutors from preaching the word of God *in season, out of season*? So how criminal it is of us, that when we are afraid we don't keep faith, particularly with the one who is teaching us both to love better things and to fear more dreadful things!

5. However pleasant this life may sometimes be, it isn't paradise, it's not heaven, not the kingdom of God, not the company of the angels, not the fellowship of those citizens of the Jerusalem which is above. Let the heart be raised upward, the earth of the flesh[14] be trampled on. The Lord has taught us to make light of things that pass away, to love those that are eternal. He has taught us, he has cured us, and he goes on curing us, because such is his pleasure.

He didn't find us in good health, after all, but came to us in our sickness as a doctor. The cup of suffering is bitter, but it completely cures all diseases. The cup of suffering is bitter, but the doctor drinks it first, in case the sick patient should hesitate to drink it.

So drink it, if that is his wish; his will in our regard, after all, is better than our own. He is more far-sighted than we are, knows better than we ourselves what is good for us, and knows better than we do what is happening in us. It's the same as with a patient and a doctor; the first is suffering and doesn't know what he's got; the second examines another person's ailments and makes a true diagnosis. One man asks another what's going on inside him, and looks for evidence about his insides from external symptoms.[15]

And if this is what the skill of a human doctor can do, how much more the ability and authority of the Lord! I mean, from this very day's feast I am prompted today to give you an example. Before the Lord's passion, and when the Lord was on the threshold of his passion, this Peter whose feast we are celebrating today was a sick man, and didn't know what was going on in himself; he was utterly unaware of his inner infirmity. When he took it for granted that he would die for the Lord, he was venturing more than he was capable of. The sick man took for granted that he would be ready to suffer, the doctor forecast that he would soon be denying him.[16] So why be surprised if in the case of that sickness the doctor's judgment turned out to be truer than the patient's? The fever, so to say, came to its greater climax, and he couldn't even follow the Lord's passion. So drink this cup, if you are given it by the one who knows what he is giving and to whom he is giving it. But if he doesn't want you to drink it, let him heal you some other way, provided he does heal you anyhow. Let us, though, submit ourselves without a qualm to the hands of the doctor, being absolutely sure that he is not going to prescribe anything that isn't good for us.

When God awards a crown to Paul's merits,
he is rewarding his own gifts

6. Paul, you see, was claiming as his right what he was demanding as his due. And what right did he have to it? *I have completed the course, I have fought the good fight, I have kept the faith.*

That's what you have done; what are you hoping for? *For the rest there remains for me the crown of justice, which the Lord will award me on that day, the just judge* (2 Tm 4:7-8).

The just judge will award it, but it was the merciful Father who made the person to award it to. What sort of person, after all, was Saul, later on Paul, what sort of person was it that Christ found? Wasn't he desperately and dangerously ill, with a disease inducing a kind of frenzied delirium among the Jews?[17] Wasn't it that very Saul who was present when Stephen was stoned, who looked after the coats of those who were doing the stoning, so that he might do the stoning himself in the hands of all the others?[18] Wasn't he the one who received letters from the chief priests, authorizing him to go where he could, and arrest Christians and bring them back for punishment? As he was on his way, breathing out threats and slaughter, wasn't he called, as we read, laid low by the voice from heaven, recalled by the Word to the word?[19]

So then, for him to be called by the Lord like that, what merits of his own had come first? I am not saying what had come first for him to be crowned, but what for him not to be condemned. It was the Lord who made a persecutor of the Church into a preacher of peace; he absolved him of all his sins, he gave him a post in which the sins of others would be absolved through him. All this was the gift of mercy, not the due of any merits. Listen to Paul himself, certainly not ungrateful for the grace of God, listen to him reminding us of all this and proclaiming it openly: *I who was previously*, he says, *a blasphemer and a persecutor and a hurler of insults; but I obtained mercy* (1 Tm 1:13). He didn't say here, did he, "I was awarded"? You see, if he had said, "I who was previously a blasphemer and a persecutor and a hurler of insults, but I was awarded," what should he have been awarded for such actions but damnation? But what he said was, "*I obtained mercy*; I was not awarded punishment, so that later on I might be awarded a crown."

There you are, brothers and sisters, the one who was owed punishment is owed a crown. *I was previously*, he says, *a blasphemer and a persecutor and a hurler of insults*. You can see what he deserved; what he was owed was punishment. So he is not awarded punishment; instead of punishment he obtains mercy. But having received mercy, not being ungrateful he fights the good fight, he completes the course, he keeps the faith. He made the forgiver of his sins into his debtor. *There remains for me*, he says, *the crown of justice, which the Lord will award me on that day, the just judge* (2 Tm 4:6). He doesn't say "gives," but "will award"; if he awards it, he owed it. Yes certainly, I've the nerve to say, if he awards it, he owed it.

"He surely hadn't received a loan, had he, that he should owe it?"

He owes a crown, he awards a crown; he puts himself in our debt, not by our lending him anything, but by his promising us something. You see, when he was crowning Paul's merits, he was also crowning his own gifts.

God's promises and their fulfillment

7. So what makes God a debtor, dearest brothers and sisters, is the fact that he is a maker of promises.[20] In the same way, if anyone promises us something, when we go to meet him so that he can give it, we use this word, "Award[21] me what you promised." We are making a demand on him as a debtor when we say "Award" or "Give back"; but all the same we acknowledge his kindness when we say, "Give back what you promised," not "what you borrowed." So he has made promises both to all of us and to the whole world, he has promised certain things, and these certain things are stupendous. Not to mention a vast list, he promised Christ, he promised Christ's passion, he promised Christ's blood shed for us, promised it all through his prophets, promised it through his books; he promised the Church, spread throughout the globe, promised the martyrs their

victories, promised the Church the smashing of idols, promised at the end judgment and eternal life.

To avoid running through a vast list—it is certainly difficult to count all his promises—let's just consider for the moment these that I've mentioned. He promised Christ: *Behold, a virgin shall conceive and bear a son, and you will call his name Emmanuel, which is interpreted God-with-us* (Is 7:14; Mt 1:23), and others which you know, and which it would take too long to run through.[22] He made promises about his passion, his resurrection, his glorification;[23] these all happened. He promised the martyrs they were going to face their sufferings bravely for the sake of his name, winning the day by their steadfastness.[24] The world raged; its raging was promised, not for the seed to be trampled on, but for the crop to be sown;[25] everywhere the blood of the martyrs was shed, the harvest of the Church filled the world; these things all happened.

It was also promised in the scriptures that the Church was going to reign supreme; it wasn't yet brought about in fact. The apostles were proclaiming the Church, everywhere sowing the seed.

What was foretold had not yet come about: *And all the kings of the earth shall worship him, all the nations[26] shall serve him* (Ps 72:11); it hadn't yet come about, but was being held under guarantee. God, you see, wanted human weakness to be so assured of his promises that he not only spoke them but put them in writing. For believers he spoke them, for doubters he provided a guarantee; and all the promises were contained in a kind of autograph, in holy scripture, not yet being brought actually into force. Kings too came to believe; it was there, after all, in God's own autograph: *All the kings of the earth shall worship him, all the nations shall serve him*. Now that all the nations too serve him, the Church has extended far and wide. You also have this in the autograph: *And attention will be paid also to the idols of the nations* (Wis 14:11). You have this in the autograph: *Lord God, to you the nations shall come from the uttermost bounds of the earth, and they shall say: Truly our fathers worshiped lies, idols which profited them nothing* (Jer 16:19). It was not, indeed, the idols themselves, but demons and men, that raged on account of the idols, slew the martyrs, gave them occasion to triumph over themselves; Babylon is paid back in her own coin.

Babylon repaid double by Jerusalem

8. You see, there's a certain godless city, described as consisting of a kind of conspiracy of human godlessness throughout all countries, and it is mystically called Babylon in the scriptures. Again, there is a certain city, an alien wanderer on this earth, consisting of a conspiracy of godliness, and this one is called Jerusalem. Right now both cities are mixed up together, at the end they will be sorted out and separated. And divine scripture addresses both of them in many places, and in one place it says to Jerusalem, *Repay her double what she has done, repay her* (Rv 18:6), so that Jerusalem is to pay Babylon back double. What is this double? How are we to take double being paid back to the city of Babylon? She used to kill Christians for the sake of her idols, but Christ, but our

God, she could not kill. She used to devastate the flesh of Christians; their spirit she never harmed, never got at our God. She's paid back double, both in her human inhabitants and in her gods. They, you see, used to slay men and women, our God they could not slay.

Now, however, her men and women, their unbelief having been put to death, are being welcomed into Jerusalem, her idols are being smashed. They look for their fellow citizens and can't find them; after all from being pagans they are becoming Christians. People who have stopped being what they were have in a sense been slain. In the way that Paul, who was previously Saul, does indeed live as a preacher, but has been slain as a persecutor. Previously Christians used to look for places to hide in from the rage of the pagans; now pagans look for places to hide their gods in. And when these are smashed, their defenders still won't keep quiet, but mutter on the side, if ever they dare to. . .;[27] as though indeed they can do anything but what the one who has us in his hands had promised, or indeed, when they have done such things,[28] as if they did them by their own power!

Here were Christians being arrested, confessing Christ, being put to death. Let any of these people confess Mercury, swear by Mercury; why, they only have to see a single guard at a posting stage, even when he's not in uniform,[29] and, "I didn't do it, I wasn't present, I didn't sacrifice, where did you see me?" Those holy servants of God, on the other hand—"Were you present in an assembly of Christians?"

"I was."

We read the confessions of faith made by the martyrs, we exult and rejoice at these examples. These things happened, the Lord paid up, because he had promised. They were previously being held in bond in scripture, now they were also brought out publicly. And all that I have been saying about idols has also been brought out publicly, and is still being so. And the Church, spread throughout the whole wide world, has now taken hold of practically all nations, and those that it doesn't yet hold, it will. It's growing day by day; the Christian people is increasing everywhere in the name of Christ.

Good and bad Christians; the winnowing of the threshing floor

9. There are a few among Christians who live good lives, many among Christians who live bad lives. But those few are few only in comparison with their heap of chaff; in comparison, I say with their chaff they are few. This threshing floor[30] is going to be winnowed, there will be a huge pile of chaff, but there will also appear a shining mass of saints.[31] The chaff will go into the fire, the wheat into the barn; but now, all the same, each sort is everywhere.

How can this be? Those who sowed the seed, brothers and sisters, whose memory we are celebrating today—well through these saints God has publicly exhibited what he promised to those apostles, and through those apostles what he promised to us. What did he promise to the apostles? *For the rest, there remains for me the crown of justice, which the Lord will award on that day, the just judge* (2 Tm 4:8). What did he promise to us? *In your seed shall all the nations be blessed* (Gn 22:18). How did this come about through them? *Their sound has gone forth into all the earth, and their words to the ends of the whole wide world* (Ps 19:4). What will the heretics chant against this? I imagine that they too are celebrating the birthday of the apostles today; they pretend, indeed, to celebrate this day, but they certainly daren't sing this psalm.[32]

NOTES

1. Sermon 299A, as already published (III, 8), is a fragment of this longer sermon. The entire text is included here. Dolbeau convincingly dates the sermon, from its anti-Donatist and anti-pagan polemics, to 29 June 404, if it was preached, as he thinks most likely, in Carthage; if in Hippo Regius, then it would have been in 405 or 406. I myself, while accepting his earlier date, think it is a little more likely that it was preached, not in Carthage but in Utica, on his way to or from Carthage for the Council of that year, 404. First, his opening sentence, in my view, suggests his presence in a church and with a community where he did not preach all that often. Secondly, and more to the point, I detect at the very end of the sermon a veiled allusion to the martyrs of the *Massa Candida*, the White Mass, who were martyrs of Utica. See Sermons 306, 306A, and 306B (III, 9). See note 31 below. Note in particular the opening words of 306B, which rather resemble the opening words of our sermon here.

2. See Sermon 299A (III, 8), note 2.

3. *Virtutem.* I previously rendered this as "virtues." But the Latin singular does suggest that he has in mind the basic meaning of *vir-tus* as manliness.

4. In the following year or so, is what he means.

5. *Ad spiritalem imitandam coronam*; but I don't know how you can imitate a spiritual crown. You can *imagine* one, and I think *imitor* here must have something like that meaning. The crown, we have to remind ourselves, was not a royal diadem of jewels and gold, but the laurel wreath placed on the head of the winner of an athletic event—the equivalent of the Olympic gold medal. I would almost prefer to translate *corona* as "medal" in these contexts; but the expression "a martyr's crown" is so fixed in our ecclesial vocabulary that it would look silly to talk about a martyr's medal.

6. As Dolbeau remarks, the readings were already fixed by the liturgical tradition. So in paying equal honor to each of the apostles, the preacher could either follow the order of readings and begin with Paul (first reading 2 Tm 4:1-8), or the order of their martyrdom and "seniority" and start with Peter (second reading Jn 21:15-19). Augustine usually, as here, took the second course, but in Sermon 299 he followed the first.

7. For this treatment of the passage, see also Sermons 147, 3; 147A, 1 (III, 4); 229D; 229N, 1; 229O, 2 (III, 6); 253, 1 (III, 7); 295, 4; 299, 7 (III, 8); 340A, 3 (III, 9).

8. He means the Donatists.

9. His *character*, impressed on them by their valid baptism and confirmation.

10. The circumcellions, the strong-arm roughs of the Donatists. It was in the autumn of 403 that Augustine had, by the grace of God, escaped an ambush they had laid for him. This provides Dolbeau with a date before which this sermon is unlikely to have been preached. The circumcellions were so called because they wandered round the countryside from *cella* to *cella*. These "cells" were probably not monastic cells, as Lewis & Short suggests, but either the granaries, or the "slave quarters" of the big estates.

A council of the Catholic bishops of Africa in Carthage in the early summer of 404, which specifically dealt with the Donatist question, would have provided the background for this sermon of Augustine's, and the others to which he here alludes, preached no doubt on the feast of John the Baptist, 24 June, and the days between that and the 29th. None of the surviving sermons for those days, however, seem quite to fill the bill.

11. That is, the day of their death and entry into true life.

12. See above, end of section 1.

13. Immolation was a preparatory rite in pagan Roman sacrifices, which consisted of sprinkling the head of the victim with sacred meal before it was slaughtered. Libation was a drink offering made to the gods, usually by spilling a little wine on the floor at a banquet before drinking a toast.

14. Reading *terra carnis* instead of the text's *terra carne*; let the earth be trampled on by the flesh.

15. It could be the patient asking the doctor to tell him what's wrong with him, or the doctor questioning the patient about his symptoms, or both. For this whole medical analogy see also Sermons 4, 2 (III, 1); 20A, 8 (III, 2); 80, 4; 88, 7 (III, 3); 126, 4; 137, 3 (III, 4); 286, 2; 295, 3; 296, 2 (III, 8).

16. See Lk 22:33-34. Peter boasted he would die first for Christ; when it came to the point, he couldn't even face death after Christ had died.

17. Reading *inter Judaeos*, following a suggestion of Dolbeau's, instead of the text's *in Judaeos*, against the Jews. This could possibly be the correct reading, and would presumably mean, as Dolbeau says, against the first, Jewish, disciples of Christ.

18. See Acts 7:57-59.

19. See Acts 9:1-6.

20. This sentence doesn't occur in the already published, fragmentary version of Sermon 299A (III, 8), because it was deleted by an earlier distinguished editor, Dom Morin, as "an ill-considered addition by the compiler of the book of homilies" in which that text was found. Dolbeau thinks Morin was wrong here; I myself am half inclined to think he was right.

21. We don't, of course, in English use this word, or any of the more usual translations of *reddere*, to give back, to pay back—very commonly to pay back a loan. But for obvious reasons I have to pretend that we do. See Sermons 110, 4; 113A, 5 (III, 4); 158, 2 (III, 5).

22. For example, Is 9:6, 11:2; Ps 2.

23. See Ps 22; Is 53; Hos 6:2; Ps 47.

24. See Mt 10:17-31; Mk 13:9-13; Lk 17:33; Jn 12:24-26.

25. See—I think conflated in Augustine's mind—Mt 13:4 and 5:13; then Jn 12:24 again.

26. Reading *nationes* instead of the text's *reges*, which looks like a very natural mistake by a copyist, given "all the kings," *omnes reges*, in the first phrase of the sentence.

27. This sentence and the following one seem very defective, and hardly make sense as they stand. In this gap, which I infer the existence of, my guess is that what these pagans mutter is that their gods too can work miracles. I have transferred "if ever they dare" from its place in the text the other side of the suspected gap, after "as though indeed."

28. Like the magicians of Pharaoh performing some of the same wonders as Moses did with his staff, Ex 7:11, 22; 8:7.

29. *Vel birratum.* The word probably means "clothed in a *birrus*," and this was any poncho-like garment, worn by anyone, which is why I render it as "not in uniform." You could say "in mufti" in the old-fashioned dialect of the military in British India. But later on, in early medieval and monastic Latin, according to Du Cange, it came to signify the wearing of some kind of distinctive military cloak—and so would mean "in uniform."

Seeing the guard at a posting stage, and suddenly denying all involvement in some by now forbidden pagan rite, may explain why Augustine has just referred to confessing Mercury, swearing by Mercury. Mercury, the messenger of the Olympian gods, was the guardian god of travelers, who no doubt still furtively performed some pagan rites in his honor to propitiate him.

30. See Lk 3:17. See also Sermons 223, 2 (III, 6); 252, 5; 259, 2; 260D, 2 (III, 7).

31. *Lucida massa sanctorum*; the phrase recalls the *Massa Candida* of Utica; see Sermons 306, 306A and 306B (III, 9). Quite possibly—since one would expect him here, in the middle of this image of the threshing floor, to say "a shining mass of wheat"—this may indicate that he was preaching in Utica.

32. See Sermon 271 (III, 7). The Mainz text here adds: "End of the sermon of Saint Augustine on the birthday of the apostles Peter and Paul."

Dolbeau 18
SERMON 306E
Mainz 50

SERMON OF SAINT AUGUSTINE THE BISHOP
ON THE BIRTHDAY OF THE MARTYR SAINT QUADRATUS

Date: 397[1]

The perfect justice of the martyrs means overcoming
both the allurements of pleasure and the pangs of affliction

1. The day previously announced to your graces of the solemn festival of the crowning of Quadratus has dawned today; let us celebrate it with a sermon as well as by our gathering here together. So then, we speak about the renown of the martyrs, both *with God and men* (Lk 2:52), as often as we celebrate their feast days. May our frequent celebration serve as constant exhortation, and so lead to eternal exultation.

We have been singing a psalm that certainly accords with a feast of martyrs: *Like a pile of sand*[2] *I was pushed that I might fall, and the Lord upheld me* (Ps 118:13). This is being said, you see, by the whole choir of martyrs, this body of Christ living in the world, like Lot in Sodom, living in the midst of trials and temptations, seeing many things it doesn't like, but not in the least consenting to the deeds of evil men. The human spirit, after all, is pushed into sinning in all sorts of different ways, whether by the allurements of pleasure or the pangs of affliction; and any who have overcome pleasure so as not to be lured into sinning have made great progress, but still have not yet reached perfection. The love of justice, you see, should be such that pleasure gives way to it, and it does not itself give way to pain. Any who have attained to it to that extent have reached perfection.

That's why the martyrs are believed to have been made perfect as they left this world, because they wrestled and were victorious not only against the pleasures of the world, but also against its afflictions. Finally, as the faithful know,[3] we do not pray for the martyrs in the course of the Christian sacraments. Not only, though, do we not pray for them, but we actually commend ourselves to their prayers.

274

Left to myself I would fall, but the Lord upheld me

2. Paul's letter to the Hebrews[4] asks for and requires this perfection, where it says by way of mild reproof, *For you have not yet wrestled against sin to the point of shedding your blood* (Heb 12:4). The martyrs, on the other hand, did wrestle to the point of shedding their blood. It wasn't, however, against the man persecuting them that they wrestled, but against the devil laying traps for them, and—if you want the whole truth—against their own weakness. It's within oneself, when all is said and done, that the great contest takes place, where the theater of conscience is located, and where, moreover, the chief spectator is the inspector of conscience. But if he were only the inspector of conscience, and not also the reinforcer, every contestant would lose every bout.

And as a matter of fact, in the very words we've been singing you will find the point I'm making: *Like a pile of sand I was pushed that I might fall.* So why didn't you fall? *And the Lord upheld me* (Ps 118:13). He said this as though making an admission about his weakness. "Left to myself," he is saying, "I would fall, but the Lord upheld me." So be in the Lord, stay in the Lord, and when you are being pushed by trials and temptations you don't fall, because you don't fail.[5] But if by resisting you don't fail by giving in or yielding, then by not consenting you don't fall.

The significance of the very name of Saint Quadratus

3. Let me give you an illustration from the very name of the man whose feast we are celebrating; he was called Quadratus, which means squared. When you push a squared stone over, it gives in or yields, and doesn't fall. It yields by not resisting, but it doesn't fall, in virtue of its remaining upright on every side. Being squared, after all, it's straight on every side; it's pushed over from one, it's settled on another, it can never fall.[6] Very properly too did the Lord God instruct the just man Noah of old to build the ark of squared timbers.[7] He wanted timbers used in its construction that were both immune to decay[8] and squared off—immune to decay to signify eternity, squared off to signify the way of dealing with trials and temptations.

May we too be squared off—or rather may the whole body of Christ be the Mass of the Squared One.[9] This Mass, after all, has a cornerstone, as was sung just now: *The stone which the builders rejected, this has been made into the head of the corner* (Ps 118:22; Mk 12:10). So how was he made into the head of the corner, the one rejected by the builders? By these he wants us to understand the Pharisees and scribes and teachers of the law. They rejected this stone as though it were not the real one; they said, "This is not the one; we are indeed awaiting the Christ, but we don't recognize this man."[10] By admitting that they were awaiting the Christ, they were like the builders, but by saying that they didn't recognize the one who really was the Christ, they were rejecting the cornerstone, because they themselves were not built on rock, but on sand.[11] But in case you there too should be wondering how the stone rejected by the builders was made into the head of the corner, scripture added, *This was done by the*

Lord (Ps 119:23)—rejected indeed by those builders, but made into the head of the corner by the Lord.

Walls from different directions have run together in this corner: the circumcision and the uncircumcision.[12] If you just notice where they come from, could anything be so different? If you notice where they clasp each other, could anything form such a unity? A corner indeed is made by walls coming from different directions, but clasping each other in one place *in the bond of peace* (Eph 4:3). It happened; they came from the circumcision, they came from the uncircumcision, they were joined together in the cornerstone. What the apostle said was fulfilled: *He is our peace, who has made both one* (Eph 2:14).

God has no need of his temple; his temple needs him

4. Accordingly, my dearest friends, come polished and square to the cornerstone, so that the builder may not reject you. All the same, put your trust in God for all of this; it's he that squares you off, just as it's he that cements you together. *You yourselves*, says the apostle Peter, *like living stones be built up together into a holy temple of God* (1 Pt 2:5; Eph 2:22). We should so think of God's temple here, that we also remind ourselves that God is in no need of a temple, while this temple is certainly in need of God. We must certainly not reckon that it is we who are doing God a favor, by providing him with a place to stay in. That God should dwell in you is to your advantage; by dwelling this way in you he makes you blessed, he is not made blessed himself by his dwelling place.

This shows, you see, that he is a true Lord and master, who doesn't need any slave, and all the same has a slave whom he doesn't need, but whom he takes care of. It is human weakness, surely, that needs a slave, for the slave to do work which the master is unable to, and, in doing what he can, to help the master who can't. God, after all, is almighty; he doesn't need you, though he did make you.[13] Don't imagine you are being of any use to God, just because you believe in God. I mean, if you didn't believe, you wouldn't be harming him, but yourself. This is well expressed in the psalm, where it says, *I said to the Lord: It is you that are my God, because you have no need of my good things* (Ps 16:2). That's why, Lord God, you are my true lord, because you have no need of my good things, but I of yours.

We cannot square ourselves off and straighten ourselves

5. We should none of us think ourselves capable of squaring and straightening ourselves out, as we were capable of warping and twisting ourselves, because we oughtn't to imagine we are capable of healing ourselves, even if we were capable of wounding ourselves. Darkness falls within the power of the eyes—after all, they get shut and they're in it. When you shut them, you're in darkness. So it was in your power to be in darkness by shutting your eyes; is it in your power to see when you open your eyes, if there's no light around to enable you to see? The shutting[14] of your eyes had no need of help for not seeing, while the

opening of the eyes does need help for seeing. After all, unless there's light present, whether of the sun or a lamp or the moon or any other kind of illumination, unless it's present as you open them, your eyes can see nothing even when wide open. So it's our part to receive, our part to have. But *what do you have that you have not received* (1 Cor 4:7)?

> *In the trials of life you can be a martyr
> just by being a person of good will*

6. That's the reason for the pious expression *like a pile of sand*:[15] not just "a pile of sand," but *like a pile of sand*. The body of Christ, you see, though it had been placed solid and foursquare on its feet, has been reckoned by the blind to be a pile of sand; and because it has been reckoned to be a pile of sand, that's precisely the reason why it hasn't fallen.[16] Even this, however, he didn't ascribe to his own powers, since he added, *the Lord upheld me* (Ps 118:13).

So in all these trials and temptations of the world—Sodom, you see, hasn't yet been burnt up, that other great Sodom, of course,[17] because the first one was burnt up for an example, the second is being kept for the judgment—so in all these trials and temptations of the world, let us have the daily intention of *wrestling against sin to the shedding of our blood*, (Heb 12:4), which is elsewhere expressed as *Wrestle for the truth even to the death* (Sir 4:28). "Against sin" there is the same as "for the truth" here; and "to the shedding of blood" there is the same as "to the death" here. What's required is the spirit of the martyr, because God, after all, does not delight in the shedding of blood. He has many hidden martyrs: *Peace on earth to men of good will* (Lk 2:14).[18]

> *For example, by not consenting to the use of magic spells
> to cure you of a fever*

7. Nor should we be hoping for that kind of persecution which our ancestors endured at the hands of the earthly powers that be, in order to become martyrs. The world doesn't give up, there is no let-up in the multitude of trials and temptations. Sometimes you're suffering from a fever, and you are fighting in the arena. To leave aside the different sorts of threat made by enemies and rivals, the different sorts of trial that come the way of each and every one of us, you are suffering, as I started to say, from a fever, and you are fighting in the arena. You're weak, and you're battling away, and you're winning.

I mean, what if someone comes along as you're lying there in a fever and in danger of death, and assures you that he can rid you of your fever with certain spells and charms, and these spells and charms are unlawful, diabolical, to be detested and cursed? And then the man who's trying to persuade you to this course mentions instances of people who have been cured in this way, and says to you, "When that person had this fever, I did this to him, I recited a spell over him, I purified him, I attended him, and he got better.[19] Ask him, question him, listen to him." The others also say, "It really happened, we were at death's door, and we were delivered in this manner; and you can be quite sure that if you allow that charm to be recited over you, you will be delivered in that very moment from this disease."

Won't you be a martyr if you don't agree, choosing rather to die, and not agreeing to the sacrilege? What, after all, used the unjust judge to say to the martyr in chains or on the scaffold? "Agree to sacrifice, and I will release you from this affliction." Well, that's what the devil is secretly saying to you in your fever: "Agree to this sacrilege, and I will release you from this fever."[20]

Our wrestling is against the rulers of this darkness

8. So if you don't consent, if you overcome not a man but the devil, not any old sinner like yourself, but the very prince of sinners—because *your wrestling is not against flesh and blood*, that is, against the human beings from whom you experience the vexations of either enticement or harassment, *but against the princes and powers and rulers of the world*, not of heaven and earth, but *of this darkness* (Eph 6:12), that is, of unclean and iniquitous people, so that to those set free from this state the apostle says, *You were once darkness* (Eph 5:8)—so if you don't consent, don't count yourself as not being a martyr. Your feast day is not indeed in the calendar, but your crown is ready waiting for you. It is customary to celebrate the solemn feast days of those who fought in the public arena. How many martyrs have left this world from their beds, and as conquerors over that infirmity[21] have passed to the realms above!

So you must realize that you are being tried and tested if you experience any such thing, if attempts are made to persuade you to use such means; that's when you need to have the mind and spirit of a martyr, since the one who made you is watching you, and the one who called you is helping you. That's when you should make your own those words of the holy trio,[22] *God is powerful enough to deliver* me even from this deadly fever, *but if not. . .* (Dn 3:17-18). Let your very struggle be your spellbinder, because in that case the one it is addressed to won't be a transgressor.[23] In this way, after these words, whatever pleases your Lord will happen to you. Either you will be restored to life and health, or you will be united to the angels. He will carry out what he has chosen for you; you for your part be ready for each eventuality, if you want to be foursquare, like Quadratus.[24]

Comparison of Daniel and his companions with the Maccabee brothers

9. Do you suppose, after all, that those words of the psalm which you heard just now, *Chastising, the Lord chastised me, and did not hand me over to death* (Ps 118:18), are appropriate only to Daniel, who stopped the mouths of lions? Do you suppose they are only appropriate to the three lads who handled with faith the flames in the midst of which they were walking?[25] Do you imagine that to them alone these words belong, *Chastising, the Lord chastised me, and did not hand me over to death*, because the lions didn't devour the one, and the fire

didn't burn the others? Perish the thought! You don't imagine anything of the
kind; theirs are not the only voices to be heard in these words; in them too can
be heard the voices of the Maccabee brothers.[26] The God of those, after all, was
no different from the God of these, nor was he right there with those and not
there with these, or supporting those and raging against these. He is one and the
same God, capable of delivering in either way, to show that he has absolutely
everything under his authority.

By shutting the mouths of the lions, he chastised Daniel with humiliation,
but did not hand him over to death; by cooling the flames he chastised the three
lads with humiliation,[27] but did not hand them over to death. By making the
Maccabees victorious in the fire through not surrendering to their tortures, but
instead wrestling against sin to the shedding of their blood,[28] *chastising, he
chastised them, and did not hand them over to death* (Ps 118:18). All of them,
you see, are alive to him.[29] To what death did he not hand them over, I ask? The
devil was eager to hand them over to *the second death* (Rv 20:14), to eternal,
not to transitory death. So God delivered those openly, crowned these secretly,
while neither those nor these did he hand over to death.

Various kinds of temptation to "deny Christ"

10. So as I said,[30] we ought to be ready for each eventuality. God, you see,
is powerful enough to deliver from every kind of affliction. But what we ought
to do above all is to pray that he will deliver us from affliction so that we may
be victorious over affliction, so that we may not surrender to affliction and sin.
And don't only think of yourself as a martyr if you are told "Deny Christ," and
you don't deny him. When the thought occurs to you to do something contrary
to justice, you aren't being told anything different from "Deny Christ."

Certainly John the Baptist was a great martyr when he had his head cut off,
and yet he wasn't told, "Deny Christ." He had spoken the truth to an evil king;
the king when he was enraged ordered his imprisonment, when he was enthralled ordered his execution.[31] Some dancing, you see, was done to get him
killed; the girl danced, the saint's head fell. Or rather, it was the king who fell,
by having the just man killed. No, it wasn't the one who was killed that fell, but
the one who ordered the killing. And yet he wasn't told "Deny Christ"; but
because he died for the truth, he died for Christ, who said, *I am the way, the
truth and the life* (Jn 14:6).

11. And the man who says to you, "Give some false evidence for me," isn't
saying anything different to you from "Deny Christ." I mean, if you confess Christ
with your tongue, and then give false evidence, what Paul says is happening with
you: *For they confess that they know God, though they deny him by their actions*
(Ti 1:16). You have confessed in words, denied in action. Actions after all amount
to more than words; to act and to speak is good, but to speak and not to act isn't.
So you can count yourself a martyr if you put up a fight.

"Give some false evidence for me."

I won't.

"Accept so much, and then give it."

I won't accept it.

You have overcome greed. If you also defeat fear, you have struggled against sin to the shedding of blood.

The one who didn't succeed in luring you with a reward will make every attempt to break you with threats, pointing out that he is going to treat you as an enemy, going to do you serious harm, and when he has the power is going to kill you—and perhaps he has the power already: what do you do? He isn't saying, "Deny Christ," and yet he is saying, "Act against Christ," that is against the one who said, *You shall not bear false witness* (Mk 10:19). How many temptations there are every day, not directed at everybody, as though against the whole Church, as though *the pile of sand were being pushed over* (Ps 118:13);[32] but the enemy frequently skirmishes against individual grains, often tempting them one by one. What difference does it make, whether he tempts people one by one, or brings pressure to bear on all of us together? There's never any want of one to tempt; but neither let there be any want of one to wrestle, because there will be no want of one to bestow the crown.[33]

Turning to the Lord. . .

NOTES

1. More precisely on 21 August of that year, the feast of the saint, who had been bishop of Utica, where he was martyred four days after the crowd of martyrs of his flock, known as the *Massa Candida*, the White Mass, on whom see Sermon 306 (III, 9) note 1, without however attaching too much credence to what I said there! Dolbeau does not accept the date 258/259 for their martyrdom, as it is based solely on the evidence of a legend being rehearsed by the poet Prudentius in the late fourth century, but he suggests no other date, and on the point of which persecution they suffered under, the legend may just as well have been right as wrong. As for Dolbeau's choice of 397 for the date of this sermon, it depends chiefly on the place allotted to it by Possidius in his *Index*, in a group of sermons which seem to represent Augustine's homiletic activity in and around Carthage in the summer of that year.

2. Where Augustine's Latin text got this phrase from I cannot tell; it is not in the Greek Septuagint. In the Vulgate, Jer 9:11, there is talk of making Jerusalem "into heaps of sand." Possibly that text had been used as a marginal comment on this verse of the psalm.

3. But the catechumens did not yet know by experience, since they did not stay on for the "Mass of the faithful," which he here calls "the Christian sacraments."

4. According to Mlle. de la Bonnardière, Augustine stopped attributing the letter to the Hebrews to Paul after 411, so that would give us a date at least before which this sermon must have been preached. But see Sermon 159, 1 (III, 5), which "a leading authority"—I cannot recall whether it was de la Bonnardière—dates to 418, where the Hebrews text is attributed to "the apostle," and 306B, 3 (III, 9), dated to 399, where it is not.

5. Word play: *non cadis, quia non cedis.* "Non cedis" more precisely means "you do not yield." And here we find ourselves on the verge of an incoherence which I do not know how to resolve, and which evidently worried some copyists. He continues: "But if by resisting you don't fail (yield), then by not consenting you don't fall." And in the next paragraph he goes on to give the illustration

of a foursquare block of wood, a cube, which when you push it over *cedit et non cadit*, "yields and doesn't fall." It yields by rolling over onto another side, but doesn't fall because it remains foursquare. Now back to the last sentence of this paragraph, following immediately on this note: Dolbeau has eliminated from the text the two words *si non*. I take it the manuscript text reads, as you might say, impossibly, *Si si non resistendo non cedis*. The *si non* would, I suppose, have started as the marginal comment of a copyist, who was as puzzled as I am by the incoherence, and wondered if Augustine had not said, "But if by not resisting you don't fail. . .," as the martyrs didn't resist, that is, didn't put up a fight against their executioners.

6. See the other sermons on Quadratus, 306B, C and D (III, 9); also 107A, 6 (III, 4), where there is no reference to the martyr Quadratus, but to an honest man who found a purse full of money, and didn't hang on to it, but advertised for its owner; he was a *homo quadratus*.

7. See Gn 6:14; also Sermons 306B, 3, where see note 8; 306C, 2; 335E, 1 (III, 9).

8. *Imputribilia*. This word is the Septuagint description of the wood to be used for making the other ark, the ark of the covenant, Ex 25:10. See Sermons 260C, 2 (III, 7), note 6, and 346A, 3 (III, 10), note 14, which is incorrect about the Septuagint translation of Gn 6:14. It is only in Ex 25:10 that it uses the word *asepton* (aseptic).

9. A reference to the martyrs of Utica, the White Mass, whose bishop the martyr Quadratus had been. Here of course the Squared One, the Arch-quadratus you might say, is Christ.

10. See Jn 7:40-44; 9:27-29.

11. See Mt 7:24-27.

12. For this theme see Sermons 4, 18 (III, 1); 60A, 2; 88, 10; 89, 4 (III, 3); 204, 3 (III, 6); 258, 1 (III, 7); 337, 1 (III, 9).

13. I here omit a whole sentence: *Non enim aliquid mereris quia portas Dominum, qui merebaris ut fieres a Domino*; "For you do not deserve anything because you are carrying the Lord, you who were deserving to be made by the Lord." In the first place, Augustine would never say you deserved to be made by the Lord; he points out when the subject arises that you weren't there to deserve it before he made you. One could, of course, assume that a *non* had been omitted by mistake, and read, "you who were not deserving to be made by the Lord."

But next, the real incongruity lies in the first half of the sentence, "because you are carrying the Lord." Augustine does talk about us carrying the Lord, but with reference to Jesus riding into Jerusalem on a donkey, for example in Sermon 189, 4 (III, 6), and I think elsewhere, though this is the only reference I have been able to track down. So I treat this whole sentence as a marginal comment, assuming that the copyist, or a reader, remembered this other illustration of God's grace and our need of him, and then added the second half of the sentence as a gloss, which lost its necessary negative on its way into the actual text from the margin.

14. A word Augustine may possibly have invented, *clausio*, which doesn't appear in any other ancient text before the 8th century. But it may have been common enough in the spoken language.

15. See note 2 above.

16. The line of reasoning, I confess, is totally opaque to me.

17. See Rv 11:8; Jude 6-7.

18. He assumes that his listeners will understand the point of this quotation and allusion. If they had heard Sermon 306B, (III, 9), and remembered section 5 and how it ended, they would certainly have done so. He is there saying that we can share both in the martyr's self-control, in his indifference to the allurements of pleasure, and in his patient endurance of physical suffering, and hence in his reward, simply by having "a good will." The same point is frequently made with reference to other good works, in particular to giving up everything and following Christ, or being generous to those in need. Even if you lack the means, it's the good will that counts. See for example Sermons 101, 11; 107A, 8 (III, 4); 299D, 4 (III, 8); 359A, 12 (III, 10).

19. I have emended all the verbs in this sentence from the 3rd person singular to the 1st person singular, by simply knocking of the final "t" from *fecit, incantavit, lustravit*, and *adfuit*. It makes rather better sense.

20. For this theme see also Sermons 286, 7 (III, 8); 318, 3; 328, 8; 335D, 5 (III, 9).

21. By which he doesn't mean over this illness, but over the infirmity of character tempted to resort to unlawful charms.

22. Following Dolbeau's suggestion, and instead of the meaningless *inveni* ("I have found") of the text, reading *Illum* (*trium*).

23. Like the one invoked by illicit spells and charms.

24. He simply says, "if you want to be *quadratus*"; in Latin the allusion to the saint is obvious.

25. See Dn 6:16-22; 3:25.

26. See 2 Mac 7. For this favorite comparison see also Sermons 32, 15 (III, 2); 286, 6; 301, 2 (III, 8); 343, 2 (III, 10).

27. How with humiliation? I think he has primarily in mind the humiliations of every day we are all liable to suffer, but in these particular cases it would be, I suppose, the "humiliation" of being convicted "criminals," subject to public execration and execution.

28. See Heb 12:4.

29. See Rom 6:10-11.

30. At the end of section 8.

31. See Mk 6:17-29; also Sermon 94A, 1-2.

32. I here omit a short clause, *qui putatur cumulus arenae*, "who is thought of as a pile of sand." It has no antecedent, and is something again to be treated as starting in a marginal scribble.

33. *Non deest temptator, sed non desit et luctator, quia non deerit coronator.*

Dolbeau 22
SERMON 341
Mainz 55

ON THE THREE WAYS OF UNDERSTANDING CHRIST IN SCRIPTURE:
SYMBOLIZED BY JACOB'S THREE RODS

Date: 417[1]

Introduction, using Psalm 22

1. This psalm, as all Christians know, was modeled on the person of our Lord and Savior Jesus Christ; seeing that it is written there, *They dug my hands and feet, they counted all my bones; they, however, looked me up and down, they divided up my garments between them, and over my garment they cast lots* (Ps 22:16-18). Now I don't imagine for a moment that you are unaware of the way in which the person of our Lord Jesus Christ is presented to the minds of the faithful and impressed upon them; all the same I must remind you of it, because one or two, no doubt, don't know, and many of you have forgotten what they heard, and quite a few would like confirmation of what they remember; and I rather think there are those among you who would like to hear what they are are very sure of precisely from me, because they are fans of mine.[2] A clear understanding of this point though, which to the best of my ability as sustained by the Lord I will try to impress upon your graces, is of value for understanding many obscurities in these most sacred books—that is, how Christ is talked of there.[3]

Christ to be understood in the scriptures in three ways

2. I mean, as far as I have been able to tune my mind to the holy volumes, he is named in three ways, whether he is being proclaimed in the law and the prophets, or in the letters of the apostles, or through our confidence about his deeds, which we know about from the gospel. One way is: as God and according to that divine nature which is coequal and coeternal with the Father before he assumed flesh. The next way is: how, after assuming flesh, he is now understood from our reading to be God who is at the same time man, and man who is at the same time God, according to that pre-eminence which is peculiar to him and in which he is not to be equated with other human beings, but is the mediator and

head of the Church. The third way is: when he is preached to believers and
offered for their approval to the wise as in some manner or other the whole Christ
in the fullness of the Church, that is, as head and body, according to the
completeness of a certain *perfect man* (Eph 4:13), the man in whom we are each
of us members.

Still, in the short and limited time available we cannot recall or expound all
the innumerable testimonies of the scriptures, by which these three kinds could
be established. Let us not, all the same, leave them entirely without proof. Let
me then remind you of some of the testimonies, so that the rest, which lack of
time does not permit us to recall, you can go on to note and discover in the
scriptures for yourselves.

The first way

3. So as regards the first way of putting forward our Lord Jesus Christ our
savior, the only Son of God, through whom all things were made, we have that
text that is the most noble and glorious one in the gospel according to John: *In
the beginning was the Word, and the Word was with God, and the Word was
God; this was in the beginning with God. All things were made through him,
and without him was made nothing. What was made was in him life; and the life
was the light of men, and the light shines in the darkness, and the darkness did
not comprehend it* (Jn 1:1-5). These are wonderful and amazing words, even
before they are understood; once understood they have to be wholeheartedly
embraced.

We are enabled, though, to understand them, not by human aids but by being
inspired to grasp them by the one who was good enough to inspire fishermen to
utter them.[4] This, you see, was said by that fisherman, the son of Zebedee, who
left father and boat and nets and followed God,[5] not so much forsaking his
human father, as choosing God for his father. And certainly when he gave up
his little boat and his nets, he is to be credited with having given up the whole
world. Our Lord Jesus Christ, you see, did not pay any attention to what the poor
people who followed him had given up, that is, to what they had given up in its
actual amount, but to what they had given up hankering after. Everyone, after
all, who has too little wants to have more; and so the one who gives up the
meager possessions that he used to have has in fact given up the more that he
used to hanker after.

And that's why, when that rich man had gone away saddened from the Lord,
whom as God he had called *good master* in order to get advice from him, and
whom on his giving him advice he had left as a bad master, and the disciples,
on hearing as he went away sad that it was easier for a camel to go through the
eye of a needle than for a rich man to enter the kingdom of heaven, had despaired
of their salvation, but were reassured on then hearing that the rich could enter
the kingdom of heaven through the mercy of God; that's why they went on to
say, *Look, we have left everything and followed you; so what will there be for
us? You will sit, the Lord answered, on twelve seats, judging the twelve tribes*

of Israel[6] (Mt 19:23-28). He also promised a great reward to all others who leave everything and follow him, both a great relief in the time of the promise itself and a great joy in the time of its fulfillment, because whoever for his sake has left everything he had in this world *shall receive,* he said, *in this age a hundred times as much, and in the age to come life everlasting* (Mk 10:30).

If all this were to be more thoroughly explained, it would hold us up and distract us from the matter in hand. Would your graces, though, at least note this point that is relevant to the subject we have undertaken:[7] that it was first of all poor men who gave up all their possessions and followed God and became apostles, and that they are given as much credit for leaving their few things as those are who give up great things. And what is really astonishing—a rich man heard at that time from the Lord's own mouth that he should give up everything and follow God, and he went away sad, though he heard this from the Lord's own lips, while nowadays, without seeing the Lord in the flesh, people hear this from his gospel and do what that man didn't do, and thus there is fulfilled in them, *Blessed are those who do not see, and yet believe* (Jn 20:29).

Why poor, unlettered men were chosen as apostles

4. So[8] why the Lord should first have chosen low-born men, poor, inexperienced and not at all refined, when before his eyes he had a great crowd who, while certainly few in comparison with the vast number of the poor, were still many of their kind: the rich, the high-born, the learned, the wise, whom he also took account of later on—he did not, after all, just abandon them; people of all those kinds came to the faith—well, the apostle explains the secret: *The weak things of this world he chose, in order to disconcert the strong; and the foolish things he chose, in order to disconcert the wise; and the low-born things of this world God chose, and the things that are not* (that is, they don't count), *as though they were, that the things that are might be rendered vain* (1 Cor 1:27-28). He had come, you see, to teach humility and overthrow pride; God had come in humility.

In no way would he here seek the high and mighty, when he had come so humbly himself before,[9] because he had chosen to be born of that woman who had been betrothed to a carpenter. So he did not choose important family connections, or this world's aristocracies would have taken it as justifying their pride. He did not choose a most important city at least to be born in, but he was born in Bethlehem of Judah, which is not even considered to deserve the name of a city. I mean, those who live in that place today call it a village,[10] so small it is and tiny and almost non-existent, had it not been ennobled by the birth there in days gone by of Christ the Lord.[11] So he came, not as one who would derive nobility from the place, but as one who would confer nobility on the place; and so it is with all the rest of the circumstances of our Lord Jesus Christ, which it would take far too long to run through.

So he chose the weak, the poor, the unlearned, the low-born, not because he abandoned the strong, the rich, the wise, the well-born, but if he were to choose them first, they would imagine they were chosen by right of their honors, by right of their wealth, by right of their family connections, and puffed up in this way about these things, they would not have received the healthy condition of humility, without which no one can return to that life which we would never have fallen from had it not been for pride.

So the doctor cures the disease with its contrary: a cold condition with hot aids, a hot state with cold compresses, a dry state with moist dressings, a moist condition with dry ones.[12] So if we see the art of medicine curing a patient by the application of contraries, it's not surprising if we who were sick with human pride are cured by the humility of God. And so it was safer and sounder for the Lord to gain an orator through a fisherman than a fisherman through an orator. You see, the martyr Cyprian was an orator, but before him the apostle was a fisherman. Emperors later on became Christians, but first of all fishermen preached Christ.[13]

And to such an extent did God, in choosing the weak things of the world, really disconcert the strong—he disconcerted them, though, in order to heal them, cast them down in order to raise them up—that there was presented to us in our own times what we know and cannot keep quiet about.[14] In our own times, you see, an emperor came to the city of Rome, where there's the temple of an emperor, where there's a fisherman's tomb.[15] And so that pious and Christian emperor, wishing to beg for health, for salvation from the Lord, did not proceed to the temple of a proud emperor,[16] but to the tomb of a fisherman, where he could imitate that fisherman in humility, so that he, being thus approached, might then obtain something from the Lord, which a haughty emperor would be quite unable to earn.

On the nature of the Word

5. Why did I say "And so"?[17] Because we have been reminding ourselves of that way of putting forward Christ in terms of his divinity before his taking on of flesh, a way that fills all who hear it with wonder and amazement, but is really grasped by the few who understand, when they have continued knocking to such effect that they are as it were struck by a kind of lightning flash of that everlasting and inexpressible light, when they say and reflect upon, *In the beginning was the Word, and the Word was with God, and the Word was God,* etc. (Jn 1:1). To save you from wasting your time seeking an understanding of these words from me, I told you[18] that you can only understand them when you are inspired by the one whose inspiration was the cause of an uneducated fisherman proclaiming them.

That fisherman, after all, did not come to know this simply on his own, nor was he of such genius or learning that his mind's eye could penetrate and soar above the whole of this atmosphere and all the ethereal powers,[19] and from there reach the natures of the luminaries, powers, authorities and angels, and every spiritual and superlative creature, none of which has ever fallen into any sin, but which all cleave in continuous contemplation to the unchangeable Truth, could soar beyond all this as well, and finally reach what *no eye has seen nor ear heard, nor has it come up into the heart of man* (1 Cor 2:9).

What sort of thing could the Father's Word be, how could it be a word? Was it thought, did it make a sound? Of course not. Because if it was thought, it took some time; if it made a sound, it was projected on air waves. Not so is the Word of God, but a Word that abides, and always a Word that is brought out and not broken off—or rather not even brought out, in case that should be taken to imply some sort of material extension. And however it is to be said, nobody can express it with a human tongue. The Word is piously believed to be begotten; he can express himself, the Son of God alone can utter his own self. The person, though, to whom he expresses himself, can understand that Word, but cannot express it. How did a fisherman come to see it, if not because it wished to show itself? The fisherman saw it in the same way that he drank it; where, though, did he drink it from?

Let us turn our attention to the Lord's festive supper, if by any chance we are to find where the fisherman drank this from. The disciples were all reclining at table with the Lord; John is described in the gospel as being in the habit of leaning back on the Lord's breast.[20] So what's so surprising if he was drinking from his breast what he would say about his divinity? The Lord of the feast, after all, and the Lord of those feasting would hardly allow his disciple to fill his belly at that table, and not fill his mind at his breast. He for his part, having drunk his fill, gave a good belch, and that very belch is the gospel. And so with the eyes of faith in the gospel you have seen the fisherman feasting; now listen to him belching: *In the beginning was the Word, and the Word was with God, and the Word was God. This was in the beginning with God* (Jn 1:1-2). You were a bit scornful when you heard "the Word"—words are heard all the time, after all; well, don't go on being scornful, because *the Word was God.*

"And how am I to understand him being God and Word?"[21]

May the one who gave the fisherman his fill also cause you to drink. Meanwhile, just listen to the one who's belching, believe his belching, so that you too may climb up on the ladder of faith and take your fill of lively understanding.

The Word's identity with the Son; their unity

6. "What then?" you will say. "Now I can believe that the Son of God is the Word of God."[22] The one and only Son of God: not two Words, but one Word, even if there are often two words in scripture, for example those two precepts that are concerned either with the twin kinds of love, or double retribution.[23] The Lord, you see, says some things to the godly who are placed on his right, and he says other things to the ungodly placed on his left. He doesn't say the same things to the godly as to the ungodly. Two words, or sayings, are as it were distributed by the narrator according to our capacity to grasp it, according to our merits; at this level they are distributed, at that one there is a certain . . .;[24] it's rather like, if I may make a comparison with material things—well suited, all the same, to the senses of weak creatures like us—if I may say this, it's rather

like the brightness of a fire, or a star, or the moon or the sun being simply one and the same. But if it's looked at by different eyes, by one person with sound and healthy eyes, by another with injured and bleary eyes, the light will seem pleasant and kindly to the first, harsh and apparently angry to the second. It dazzles the injured sense of sight and causes pain with what the healthy sense of sight was rejoicing in. There you are, it's pleasant, there you are, it's harsh. Is it divided in itself, different in each case? No, but it depends on the merits of those looking at it in different ways.

Please concentrate, my brothers and sisters, and come to an understanding of great things from small ones. That's how the Word of God is one, but distributes suitable words according to people's merits, saying to these, *Come, you blessed of my Father, take possession of the kingdom which has been prepared for you from the origin of the world*, while saying to those, *Go into the eternal fire which has been prepared for the devil and his angels* (Mt 25:34.41). What could be more diverse than "Come into the kingdom" and "Go into the eternal fire"? So is there diversity in the Word? No. It's one, but the merits of those who are listening to it are diverse. Listen to the prophet saying this very same thing in the psalms: *Once has God spoken; two things have I heard* (Ps 62:11). Big problem; now though, if you've understood what I've been saying, it needn't worry you. He has spoken once, and you there have heard two things? He has spoken once as regards the one and only Word; so how have you heard two things? *That yours is the power*, it goes on, *and yours, Lord, is mercy*—power therefore for punishing, mercy for setting free. Listen to what follows: *since you will pay each one back*, it says, *according to his works* (Ps 62:11-12).

The Spirit desires hearts which will love God sincerely,
and being humble will soar up to him beyond the heights of creation

7. O one and only Word, delightful Word, may he breathe his love into us! Now he breathes with the Holy Spirit; there, you see, you have the Trinity: the Father who begot, the Word which he begot, the Spirit by which charity is breathed forth, or inspired. In order that this most delightful and surpassing and inexpressible Trinity may be loved, soaring beyond the universal creation which it initiated, completed, arranged, soaring beyond it altogether, the Spirit desires the hearts of lovers. It is quite right to say he desires, because he makes us desire.[25] I mean, the Spirit is also said to rejoice, because he makes us rejoice. And of God it says, *The Lord your God is testing you, to know if you love him* (Dt 13:3). What does "to know" mean, if not "to make you know"?[26]

So he nourishes the hearts of lovers, of those who desire purely, who love freely, because they can find nothing better to love—or let them find something better, and be content with that for their reward; if they can't find something better, let them seek this.[27] So if your creator, than whom you can find nothing better, were not to give himself to you, you should rather spend your entire time bewailing the fact than go seeking something else. If your creator, than whom there is nothing better, were not to give himself to you—if he allows such words to be said about himself, though he does allow them because we are little ones, he allows them because if we wanted to say only something worthy of him, we wouldn't say anything at all. So if your creator, as I had started to say, were unwilling to give himself to you, you should spend your entire time bewailing the fact, rather than go seeking anything else.

Now though, he in fact is offering himself, and you there are looking for something else; he is asking somehow or other to be loved by one whom he is not loved by. Oh, it's you that are wretched, not he! So then, he is on the lookout for the hearts of those who love him sincerely, which in loving, filial intention may pass beyond every changeable creature—and they do so pass beyond if they are humble; it's only those who are not high and mighty that can pass beyond the heights of creation. If you wish to pass beyond every creature, and reach that something else which you have heard of from the lips of the belching fisherman, be humble, seek in a pious, filial way. You see, when you have soared beyond all changeable things, spiritual as well as material, you will come to the contemplation of that Trinity, and you will drink from the same source as he drank from. When you come to that, you will laugh at all those who misrepresent this faith—and when you have begun by laughing, you will maybe weep later on, at the way in which with their futile contentions they fill their own eyes with smoke, to prevent them seeing it.

The divine Word simultaneously with the Father and in Mary's womb

8. So, brothers and sisters, I think that's enough to have put before you. In order fully to understand it, though, knock at his door. None of you should say, thinking in materialistic fashion, "How was the Word with God and how in the virgin's womb, in order to be born?"

So did the Word itself come down in such a way, that when it was in the virgin's womb it had withdrawn from the Father?

"Well, if it didn't withdraw from the Father, how could it be here? Or perhaps half stayed with the Father, and half was in the womb? Or perhaps a large part stayed with the Father, and some small or tiny piece came down into the virgin's womb?"

Don't cut God up into pieces; let your discordant thoughts be united in him, instead of him being dissected by them; let him gather you, don't you go scattering him.[28]

"And how," you say, "am I ever going to understand? I don't get it, I can't. He's both with the Father and in the virgin's womb? Who could possibly understand this?"

But you're hearing it about *God*; it's you that are making a kind of body for yourself, with your habit of thinking in material terms. When you've made it, then of course you have now to cut it up; I mean, you can't find the whole of it everywhere. One part of the earth is here, another outside in the street; not the same part, because it's earth, because it's a body; one part's big, another small.

Water too is divided in the same way; one part is beside this beach, another beside that one, and it's not the same part here as there. Although the whole sea may seem to be extended everywhere in its places, still it doesn't have the same part of it everywhere, but one part here, one there.

Likewise with this air we breathe; there's one air in this basilica, another in that,[29] since there is one and the same air everywhere, but one part of it here in this building, another part in that; it's not the same part here as there, nor the same there as here. So too with the parts of the sky; the parts we look at when facing the east are not the same as we look at when we turn to the west. It's not possible for one and the same part to be everywhere; even though the whole seems to be everywhere by its parts, still the whole of it isn't everywhere, but one part there, one part somewhere else.

So don't go on thinking about God like that, as if he were a body. Or maybe it's only things of that sort that you can think about? I will give you an example, which may possibly help your graces to grasp the point.

The point illustrated from human speech and ideas

9. You want to divide the Word of God, and it doesn't seem credible to you that it should all be with the Father, all in the womb of the virgin Mary. I will go further than that; it is all of it wherever you like, but it didn't everywhere take on the person of a man, with whom to become one God and man. Don't divide; grab all you can. Do you want to divide the Word of God? Listen to the word of man. Certainly it seemed to you that the Word of God couldn't be both in Mary and with the Father, unless so to say distributed piecemeal, with one part of it being here, another there. When you hear a word from me, or when you hear words from me—please attend to what I'm saying;[30] you'll get a better illustration of the point, after all, from this word that is being spoken to you all together than from those words (though of course they are the same kind of thing) that you are speaking to each other. I mean you are dealing with small groups, I am dealing with big numbers; all hear what I am saying, and all hear it all.

If I were setting out food for you to feed your bodies with, you would be dividing the food among you, and one would be taking away this bit to eat, another that.[31] Even though you were all eating one and the same kind of food, still you wouldn't all be eating the same bits of it, but what was set out you would be dividing piecemeal among yourselves, according to your capacity, one person taking that part of the food, another this; the same food would reach you all, but not all the food would reach you all. Certainly, that's how it would be. Now just as that food would be set before your mouths, so too a kind of food consisting of voices and words is now being set before your ears; and yet all of it does reach you all. Or is it the case, perhaps, that while I'm speaking one of you takes one syllable for himself, another a second one? Or does one get one word, another a second word? If that's how it is, I am going to utter as many words as I see people, so that at least one word may get to each of you. And in fact that's easy; I'm speaking more words than there are people here, and all of them reach all of you. So a human word does not have to be divided up into syllables for all to hear it; and is the Word of God to be cut up into slices, in order to be everywhere? Can we suppose, brothers and sisters, that these spoken and passing words are comparable in any respect to that unchangeably abiding Word? Or have I, by saying this, been comparing them? But I just wanted to suggest to you, in any way I could, that what God provides us with in material things can help you to believe what you cannot see about spiritual words.

But now let's pass on to better things, because words are spoken and fade away. Think about spiritual things, think about justice. Someone who stays in these western regions thinking about justice; someone staying in the east thinking about justice; how is it that the first one thinks about the whole of justice, and the second one also about the whole of it? And that the first sees the whole of it and the second the whole of it? I mean, if you are seeing justice, and doing something according to it, you are doing it justly. You are seeing inwardly, acting outwardly. How can you be seeing inwardly if nothing is present to you? If however it is present to you because you are situated in this region, the other person's thinking won't reach this region. But since you, situated here, see the same thing in your mind as he does, though he is staying so far away, and the whole of it shines on you, the whole of it on him, you can see that things which are divine and immaterial are whole everywhere, and can believe that the Word is wholly in the Father, wholly in the womb. After all, you're believing this about the Word of God, who is God with God.

The second way: Christ as God and man

10. And now listen to the other proposition, the other way of proposing Christ which scripture proclaims. It says those things, you see, before the taking on of flesh. But how does scripture proclaim this way? *The Word*, it says, *became flesh, and dwelt among us* (Jn 1:14). He had said, you see, *In the beginning was the Word, and the Word was with God, and the Word was God; this was in the beginning with God; all things were made through him, and without him was made nothing* (Jn 1:1-3). But he would have declared the divinity of the Word to us in vain if he had kept quiet about the humanity of the Word. In order, I mean, for me to see that, he deals with me from this end; in order to refurbish my gaze for contemplating that, he himself comes to the aid of my weakness. By receiving from human nature the same human nature, he became man. He came with the packhorse of the flesh to the one who was lying wounded on the road,[32] in order to to give shape to our little faith and nurture it by the mystery of his incarnation, and to clear the mist away from our intellects, so that they might see what he never lost as a result of what he took on. He began to be man, you see, but did not cease to be God.

So that is the proclamation of our Lord Jesus Christ insofar as he is the mediator, insofar as he is the head of the Church; that God is man, and man is God, since John says, *And the Word became flesh and dwelt among us.*

The apostle presents us with Christ in both ways

11. Listen now to each way in that very well known passage from the apostle Paul: *Who, while he was in the form of God*, he says, *did not think it robbery to be equal to God* (Phil 2:6). That's the same as, *In the beginning was the Word, and the Word was with God, and the Word was God* (Jn 1:1). How could the apostle say, *He did not think it robbery to be equal to God*, if he isn't equal to God? But if the Father is God and Christ isn't God, how can he be equal?[33] So where that one says, *The Word was God*, this one says, *He did not think it robbery to be equal to God*; and where that one says, *The Word became flesh and dwelt among us* (Jn 1:14), this one says, *But he emptied himself, taking the form of a servant* (Phil 2:7).

Pay careful attention, please. So by his becoming man, by the fact that *the Word became flesh and dwelt among us*, he thereby *emptied himself, taking the form of a servant*. Why, in fact, did he empty himself? Not in order to lose divinity, but in order to put on humanity, appearing to human beings as what he was not before he was man. It was by appearing visibly in this way that he emptied himself, keeping back, that is to say, the majestic greatness of divinity,[34] and presenting us with the fleshly garment of humanity. So it was by the fact that *he emptied himself, taking the form of a servant*—not taking the form of God. When he was talking about the form of God, he didn't say he received it, but *While he was in the form of God*; but when it came to the form of a servant, *taking*, he said, *the form of a servant*. So it was by this that he is the mediator and head of the Church, through whom we are reconciled to God, through the mystery of his humility and passion and resurrection and ascension and of the judgment to come, so that those two things may be heard, though God has spoken only once.[35] When are two things to be heard? When he renders *to each one according to his works* (Mt 16:27).

We are not to be seduced by the cunning questions of the Arians

12. So then, hold on firmly to this, and don't be taken by surprise at the problems people raise, which creep along like a cancer, as the apostle said;[36] but guard your ears, and the virginity of your minds, as betrothed by a friend of the bridegroom to one man, to be presented *as a chaste virgin to Christ*. Virginity of the body few people have in the Church; virginity of the mind all ought to have. It is this virginity that the serpent wishes to corrupt, about which the same apostle says, *I have betrothed you to one man, to present you as a chaste virgin to Christ; and I am afraid that, just as the serpent took in Eve by his cunning, so also your senses may be corrupted away from the chastity which is in Christ* (2 Cor 11:2-3). "Your senses," he said; that is, your minds. This surely is the more suitable way of taking it. There are, I mean, also the senses of this body, of seeing, hearing, smelling, tasting, touching. It was our minds that the apostle feared might be corrupted, where the virginity of faith is to be found. So now, O soul, preserve your virginity, later on to be made fruitful by the embraces of your bridegroom. So then, hedge your ears about, as it is written, with thorns.[37]

The weaker brothers and sisters in the Church have been troubled by the problem raised by the Arians, but by the Lord's mercy the Catholic faith has triumphed. He hasn't, after all, deserted his Church; and even if it was troubled for a time, it was so that it would always continue to make supplication to him by whom alone it could be kept firmly established on solid rock.[38] And the serpent is still hissing, and doesn't keep quiet. He is trying, by promising us a kind of knowledge, to cast us out of the paradise of the Church, not permitting us to return to that paradise from which we were originally thrown out.

The serpent now falsely suggesting that the Son is less than the Father

13. Pay close attention, my brothers and sisters. What was done in that paradise is still being done in the Church. Don't let anyone seduce us out of this paradise. Let it be enough that we fell from that one; at least let us show that we've learned our lesson from experience. It's the same old serpent, who is always suggesting iniquity and impiety.[39] He sometimes promises impunity, just as he did then: *You will not die the death*, he said, because God had said, *You will die the death* (Gn 3:4; 2:17). He makes the same sort of suggestion now, that Christians should lead bad lives: "Is he really going to going to throw them all away?" God says, "I will condemn them; I will pardon those who change their ways; let them change their deeds; I will then change my threats."

So he is also the one who whispers and hisses, and says, "Look, it's written, *The Father is greater than I* (Jn 14:28), and you there call him equal to the Father?"

I accept what you say;[40] but I accept each statement, because I read each statement. Why do you, though, accept one, not want the other? Because you have in fact read each of them with me. Here we are, *The Father is greater than I*; I accept that, not from you but from the gospel; and you in your turn, please accept from the apostle that the Son is equal to the Father. Join each of them together, let each of them be harmonized, because the one who spoke through John in the gospel is the same as the one who spoke through Paul in his letter. He cannot be discordant with himself; but you for your part are unwilling to understand the harmony of the gospel, seeing that you love disputing.

"But I can prove it," you say, "from the gospel: *The Father is greater than I*."

And I too from the gospel: *I and the Father are one* (Jn 10:30).

"In what way can each be true?"

In the way the apostle teaches us. Listen: *I and the Father are one: Who, since he was in the form of God, did not think it robbery to be equal to God.* Listen: *The Father is greater than I: But he emptied himself, taking the form of a servant* (Phil 2:7).

There you are, I've shown you why he is greater; now you show me in what way he is[41] equal. After all, we read that each is the case. He is less than the Father insofar as he is the Son of man; equal to the Father insofar as he is the Son of God; because *the Word was God* (Jn 1:1). The mediator, God and man; God, equal to the Father, man, less than the Father. So he is both equal and less;

equal in the form of God, less in the form of a servant. So now you show me in what way he is both equal and less. Can he be equal in one part, less in another? So there you are; apart from the taking on of the flesh, show me how he is both equal and less. I really want to see how you are going to demonstrate it.

The notion of God consisting of parts held up to ridicule

14. Notice, all of you, the stupid impiety of having ideas according to the flesh; as it's written, *Having ideas according to the flesh is death* (Rom 8:6). I'm still setting aside the incarnation of our Lord, the only Son of God, and not yet talking about it; but as though what has already happened hadn't yet happened, I'm attending with you to *In the beginning was the Word, and the Word was with God, and the Word was God* (Jn 1:1). I'm attending with you to *Who, since he was in the form of God, did not think it robbery to be equal to God* (Phil 2:6). Precisely there, please, show me how he is less. What are you going to say? Are you going to divide God up by qualities, that is, by certain dispositions of body and soul, in which we perceive a variety of states? . . .

. . .[42] before the taking on of the flesh, before the Word became flesh and dwelt among us, show how he is less, show how he is equal. Is God one thing and another thing, so that in one part the Son can be less than he, and in another his equal? As though, if we were to say "They are bodies of a sort," you could say to me, "Equal in length but less in strength." We often come across such bodies, after all, such that they are equal in length but in strength one is less, the other greater. So are we going to think of God and his Son as such bodies? Are we really going to think like that? May God avert such thoughts from the minds of Christians! He was wholly with the Father, wholly in the flesh, wholly above the angels. But perhaps you will be thinking like this, and saying, "Both in strength and length they are equal, but they are disparate in color." Where but in bodies do you find color? There, on the other hand, is to be found the light of wisdom. Show me the color of wisdom, show me the color of justice. If these things have no color, would you be saying such things about God, if you had any color of shame?[43]

The Son cannot be equal in one attribute, less in another

15. So what are you going to say? They are equal in power, but the Son is less in sagacity? God is unjust, if he has given equal power to less sagacity. If they are equal in sagacity, but the Son is less in power, God is guilty of jealousy, for having given less power to equal sagacity. In God, though, everything that is said about him is one and the same; in God, you see, power isn't one thing and sagacity another, courage one thing and justice another, or chastity another. Whichever of these you attribute to God, it isn't to be understood as one thing and another, and none of them in any case is attributed to him worthily, because these are qualities of souls, upon which that divine light is shed somehow or other, so that it affects them with its own qualities—rather like when this visible

light rises upon material bodies. If it is removed, all bodies have one color, or one should rather say no color. But when it comes up to shine upon bodies, though in itself it is uniform, nonetheless, given the varying qualities of bodies, it sprinkles them with a variegated luster or sheen. So these qualities are dispositions of souls, which have been affected and disposed in a good way by that light which is not itself affected or disposed by anything, and formed by that light which is not itself formed by anything.

Nothing can be said worthily of God

16. And yet we say these things about God, brothers and sisters, because we cannot find anything better to say. I call God just, because in human terms I can't find anything better; in fact, he is beyond justice. It says in the scriptures, *The Lord is just, and loves deeds of justice* (Ps 11:7). But it also says there that God repents, it also says there that God doesn't know things.[44] Who wouldn't be horrified at the idea? God doesn't know things, God repents? All the same, scripture does descend to the salutary use of these terms which horrify even you, precisely in order to save you from imagining that terms you think are fine are said about God fittingly and worthily.

Thus if you were prepared to believe that God may repent of something with the feelings human beings have, and someone else who understands things better were to put you right, he would explain to you that if you find anything like that in scripture, it isn't said because God really feels the same pain as you do, when you condemn some plan or action of your own with heartfelt sorrow; but it's said because he makes some change over and above what people think, because if human beings do such a thing, they do it by repenting, if they turn back from something they were proposing to do, whereas his plans remain eternally fixed and certain; but because people were expecting him to do one thing and he does another, he is metaphorically said to repent.[45]

And thus if you ask, "So then, what can worthily be said about God?" someone may perhaps answer you and say that he is just. But another person, who understands things better than this one, may tell you that even this term is overridden by God's total excellence, and even this one is not worthy to be said of him, although it is suitably said of him according to our human capacity. So when the former tries to prove his point from the scriptures, because it is written, *The Lord is just*, this other will very properly answer him that it is stated in the same scriptures that God repents.

"Just as you don't take this according to the common way of speaking, the way human beings normally repent, so too you should likewise understand that what is meant by 'just' doesn't fit God's super-eminence, though scripture was indeed right to state this, so that the human spirit might be led gradually by all sorts of words to that which cannot be said at all. Yes, you call God just, but you must understand something beyond the justice which you are in the habit of attributing to human beings."

"But the scriptures called him just."

That's why they also called him repentant and ignorant, which you now don't want to call him. So just as you realize that those things which now horrify you were said on account of your weakness, in the same way these things which you value highly were said on account of a certain tougher weakness of yours.[46]

But any who have risen beyond even these words, and begun to think worthily of God as far as human beings are permitted to, will find a silence that is to be praised by the inexpressible voice of the heart.

The argument concluded; a rule for interpreting the scriptures

17. So then, brothers and sisters, because in God power is identical with justice (and whatever you say in him, you are saying the same thing, since in fact you are not saying anything that is worthy of him), you cannot say that the Son is equal to the Father in justice and not equal in power, or equal in power and not equal in knowledge, because if he is equal in one respect he is equal in every respect, because all the things you say in that field are one and the same, and all have the same value. So it remains that you cannot say how the Son can be equal to the Father, unless you posit some variations in the substance of God.[47] When you do posit them, Truth casts you out, and you forfeit all access to that inner sanctuary of God, where he can most perfectly be seen.[48] But since you cannot say he is equal in one part and unequal in another, because there are no parts in God, and you cannot say he is equal in one quality, less in another, because there are no qualities in God, it follows that as regards God you cannot say he is equal unless he is equal in every respect. So how can you say he is less, except because he took the form of a servant?

And so, brothers and sisters, this is what you must always bear in mind: if you accept a certain rule in the scriptures, that very light will make everything clear to you. Wherever you find the Son called equal to the Father, take it as being according to a certain essence of divinity. Wherever you find him less, take it as being according to the form of the servant he took on. On the one hand according to what is said, *I am who I am*; on the other according to what is said, *I am the God of Abraham, and the God of Isaac, and the God of Jacob* (Ex 3:14-16). In this way you will hold firmly both to what is in his nature and to what is in his mercy.[49]

My Father and your Father, my God and your God

18. But don't let it worry you that what the Lord said in the gospel and what we have sung just now in the psalm is also said in terms of this distinction. But let me explain and put it before you with clearer evidence; it was said in the gospel, *To my Father and to your Father, to my God and to your God* (Jn 20:17).[50] "To my Father and to your Father" shouldn't bother you. He is always, you see, the Father of the Son; his Son was never not begotten, he was never not his Father. But he's our Father in a different way, by doing us the kindness of adopting us. He begot him *before the daystar* (Ps 109:3), which you mustn't

take as meaning one particular star; but symbolically what ushers in the light is the daystar,[51] not that it is the light, but it is lit up by the light so that it may usher in the light. I mean, it's also said of that archangel who did not stand in the truth that he was rising like the daystar,[52] but he did not remain standing in the light itself. So every soul that is enlightened so as to shine with light is called a daystar, or light-bringer; but if it turns away from the enlightening light it becomes darkness.

That's why John the evangelist says about the Lord himself, *He was the true light*—and as though he were asked, "What does true light mean?"—*which enlightens every human being* (Jn 1:9), he says; so not "which is enlightened," but "which enlightens." But of John the Baptist he says, *He was not the light* (Jn 1:8). But what sort of light wasn't he? The sort that enlightens and is not enlightened. You see, John was a light that is enlightened, because he had received from his fullness,[53] which is why the Lord himself said, *And you people were willing to exult for a while in his light* (Jn 5:35). And to his disciples he said, *You are the light of the world* (Mt 5:14). They were enlightened, you see, in order to be light, but he was *the true light which enlightens every human being*; what is made light by being enlightened is something else. So the true light that enlightens, that's our Lord Jesus Christ, while light made so by being enlightened, that's John, that's the apostles, that's all the holy souls and most blessed spiritual intelligences,[54] who become light-bearers, daystars, by receiving light. So then, *before the daystar I begot you*, which is to say before every creature. It is to be understood as meaning before all creation, in which the foremost place is held by the spiritual and rational creation, which brings light on being enlightened.

So then, brothers and sisters, let us hold on to each of these things in our Lord Jesus Christ: that he is both equal to the Father insofar as he is God, and that he is less than the Father insofar as he is man. But as I had started to say, nobody should stumble over his saying *My Father and your Father* (Jn 20:17). He is always, you see, the Father of the only-begotten Son, and he in turn is always born, and born before the daystar, that is, before every creature which becomes light on being enlightened. And so *my Father and your Father* is quite right, because we have received our being children of God from him who *gave us the right to become children of God* (Jn 1:12). And our adoption, which the apostle mentions, is well known to your graces, about which he says, *Waiting for adoption, the redemption of our bodies* (Rom 8:23); and again, *God sent his Son, made of a woman, made under the law, to redeem those who were under the law, that we might receive sonship by adoption* (Gal 4:4-5). So he had every reason to say first *my Father*, and then *your Father*.

But what about *my God and your God* (Jn 20:17)? Well now, if you all know the rule, what are you expecting from me? *My Father* always, *my God* from the moment he becomes man. Listen to the psalm which was read: *On you have I been cast from birth, from my mother's womb it is you who are my God* (Ps 22:11). I think that that is enough said also about that way in which our Lord Jesus Christ is presented to us in the scriptures as having become our savior, the head of the Church, the mediator through whom we are reconciled with God, both God and man.

19. The third way is how the whole Christ is predicated with reference to the Church, that is as head and body. For indeed head and body form one Christ. Not that he isn't complete without the body, but that he was prepared to be complete together with us as well, though even without us he is always complete, not only insofar as he is the Word, the only-begotten Son equal to the Father, but also in the very man whom he took on, and with whom he is both God and man together. All the same, brothers and sisters, how are we his body, and he one Christ with us? Where do we find this, that head and body form one Christ, that is, the body together with its head? In Isaiah he is speaking as if in the singular, and it's one and the same person speaking; and see what is said: *As for a bridegroom he has bound a turban on my head, and as for a bride he has decked me out with ornaments* (Is 61:10). As bridegroom and bride: he calls one and the same person bridegroom with reference to the head, bride with reference to the body. There seem to be two, and there's one.

Otherwise, how are we the members of Christ, with the apostle saying as clearly as can be, *But you are the body of Christ and its members* (1 Cor 12:27)? If we are the members of Christ and all of us together are his body, then it's not only those of us who are in this place, but throughout the whole world, and not only those of us who are alive at this time, but—what shall I say?—*from Abel the just* (Mt 23:35) right up to the end of the age, as long as people beget and are begotten,[55] any of the just who make the passage through this life, all that are here now—that is, not in this place, but in this life—all that are going to be born after us, all these constitute the one body of Christ, while they are each individually members of Christ.

So if all constitute the body and are each individually members, there is of course a head, of which this is the body. *And he himself*, it says, *is the head of the body, the Church, the firstborn, himself holding the first place* (Col 1:18). And because it also says of him that *he is the head of every principality and power* (Col 2:10), this Church which is now on its pilgrimage is joined to that heavenly Church where we have the angels as *fellow citizens* (Eph 2:19), with whom we would be quite shameless in claiming equality after the resurrection of our bodies, had Truth not promised us this, saying, *They shall be equal to the angels of God* (Lk 20:36); and there is achieved one Church, *the city of the great king* (Mt 5:35), the city whose Son he was also willing to be,[56] from whose pilgrim section he took flesh as its king who makes it fruitful, in order to summon back to it whatever had strayed away from it. She, after all, is symbolically represented by Zion, of whom it is written, *Zion is mother, a man will say, and a man was made in her and the Most High himself established her* (Ps 87:5 LXX); that is, the very one who was made a man in her, since he was the most humble, is the Most High himself who established her, because *all things were made through him, and without him was made nothing* (Jn 1:3).

The trunk of a body without the head cannot be called complete, but the head wishes to be admired together with its body. And Christ is one with his body because he graciously consents to be, not because he has to be. We, after all, stand in need of the goodness of God; God has no need of our goodness. Listen to the prophet: *I said to the Lord, It is you who are my God, because you have no need of my good things* (Ps 16:2).

The three ways recapitulated

20. Thus it is then that sometimes Christ is presented in the scriptures in such a way that you are to understand him as the Word equal to the Father, sometimes in such a way that you are to understand him as the mediator, since *the Word became flesh and dwelt amongst us* (Jn 1:14), since that only-begotten Son, *through whom all things were made* (Jn 1:3), *did not consider it robbery to be equal to God, but emptied himself, taking the form of a servant, becoming obedient to the death, even death on a cross* (Phil 2:6-8).

Sometimes, though, in such a way that you are to understand the head and the body, with the apostle himself expounding as clearly as can be what was said about husband and wife in Genesis: *And they shall be two*, it says, *in one flesh* (Gn 2:24). Notice his exposition, because I don't want to give the impression of being so bold as to say something I've cobbled up for myself. *And they shall be two*, he said, *in one flesh*; and he added, *This is a great sacrament*. And in case anybody should still think that this is to be found in husband and wife according to the natural coupling of the sexes and their bodily coming together,[57] *but I mean*, he went on, *in Christ and the Church* (Eph 5:31-32). So this is how we take as referring to Christ and the Church what is said elsewhere: *They shall be two in one flesh; they are not now two, but there is one flesh* (Mt 19:5-6).[58]

Just as bridegroom and bride, so also head and body, because *the head of the woman is the man* (1 Cor 11:3). So whether I say head and body, or whether I say bridegroom and bride, you must understand the same thing. And that's why this very apostle, while he was still Saul, heard the words, *Saul, Saul, why are you persecuting me?* (Acts 9:4), since the body is joined to the head. And when as a preacher of Christ he was now suffering from others what he had done himself as a persecutor, *that I may fill up*, he said, *in my flesh what is lacking from the afflictions of Christ* (Col 1:24), thus showing that what he was suffering was part and parcel of the afflictions of Christ. This can't be understood of the head, which now in heaven is not suffering any such thing, but of the body, that is the Church, the body, which with its head is the one Christ.

As body and bride, we must live worthily of our head and bridegroom

21. So present yourselves to such a head as a body worthy of him, to such a bridegroom as a worthy bride. The head can only have a correspondingly worthy body, and such a great husband as that can only marry a correspondingly worthy wife. *To present himself*, it says, *with a glorious Church, not having stain or*

wrinkle, or any such thing (Eph 5:27).⁵⁹ This is the bride of Christ, not having stain or wrinkle. You don't want to have any stain? Do what is written: *Wash yourselves, be clean, remove the wicked schemes from your hearts* (Is 1:16). You don't want to have any wrinkle? Stretch yourself on the cross. You see, you don't only need to be washed, but also to be stretched, in order to be without stain or wrinkle, because by the washing sins are removed, while by the stretching a desire is created for the future life, which is what Christ was crucified for.⁶⁰

Listen to Paul himself, once he was washed: *Not*, he says, *because of the works of justice which we have done, but according to his own mercy he has saved us, by the washing of rebirth* (Ti 3:5). Listen to him as he is stretched: *Forgetting*, he says, *what lies behind, stretched out to what lies ahead, according to intention I follow after to the palm of God's calling from above in Christ Jesus* (Phil 3:13-14). Fittingly therefore does he, being without any stain of iniquity and without any two-faced wrinkle, as a good and loyal *friend of the bridegroom* (Jn 3:29), betroth her to him, *to present her to one husband as a chaste virgin* (2 Cor 11:2) without stain or wrinkle. It's not without reason, after all, that we are told of Isaiah making his prophecy by the fuller's road.⁶¹

Hidden meanings locked up in the "sacraments" of scripture:
the example of boys buying nuts

22. All such passages, brothers and sisters, have a kind of sacramental meaning; anything in the scriptures that sounds absurd, sounds quite unnecessary, is under lock and key, not, however, locked up and empty; it's on something full of meaning that God turns the key, but he's looking for people to knock, so that he can open.⁶² Be sure, in any case, to weigh it up. If I may give you a nice everyday example; when boys buy themselves nuts, they weigh them in the hand, and when they find they're heavy, they hold on without a qualm to what is still closed. So weigh them up, when you hear statements whose meaning is closed to you in these writings that are so holy, so illustrious, known to everyone,⁶³ spread throughout the whole wide world. From the time they were first published until the present, nothing has happened in human affairs but what was there foretold; so they have an enormous weight of authority.

Weigh its statements with this weight in mind, and suppose your soul says to you, already inclined, no doubt, to sneer at what is said, *And they shall be two in one flesh* (Gn 2:24)—it was already saying to itself, "What is all this? Was God really going to bother about how a man and a woman should couple, to the extent of saying *they shall be two in one flesh*?" Don't throw it away; you're a boy; weigh it.

"And how," you say,⁶⁴ "shall I weigh it?"

Say to yourself, "Oh sure, any kind of fool would have said this, not to mention someone who's called a man of God. Moses, who wrote this, was a man of at least average intelligence."⁶⁵ Add, because it is not without reason that these writings have become known to the whole world, and are held in honor throughout the whole world in the religion of the faithful: "He wouldn't say

They shall be two in one flesh without a reason; it must be because there's something there, I don't know what, that beggars human thought, but is somehow or other locked up. It isn't just empty."

When you say this to yourself, you are weighing it; if you've weighed it, you've found that it's heavy; you can hold onto it without a qualm. But perhaps you are such a feeble little boy that you can't break it; just go on holding it and rejoicing, aware that you're holding something full of meaning. You won't be long without someone to break it for you and give it to you to eat.

"And who," he says, "will break it for me?"

There's someone who can break it for you straightaway—let's carry on as if dealing with a little fellow; give it to a certain indulgent father, who said, *It is not to put you to shame that I am saying this, but I am warning you as my dearest children.* There you are, it's the apostle—in a definite kind of way he is a father; he's breaking open for you this thing you are carrying around locked up, which you have already weighed and felt to be heavy.

He'll break it open, never you fear, showing as he does a father's love for you, when he says, *Even if you have many tutors in Christ, but not many fathers; for in Christ Jesus it was I that begot you through the gospel* (1 Cor 4:14-15); and a mother's love, when he says, *I became a little one among you, like a nurse caressing her children* (1 Thes 2:7). The reason[66] he did not say "mother" was that sometimes mothers are either too refined[67] or have too little love for their children, and so when they give birth to them they hand them over to other women to nurse. Again, if he had merely said "caressing like a nurse," and had not added "her children," it would look as if another had borne them and he had just received them to nurse. He called himself a nurse because he was feeding them; and he added "her children," because he himself had given them birth, as he says: *My little children, with whom I am again in labor until Christ is once more formed in you* (Gal 4:19). But he gives birth in the same way as the Church brings forth, from her womb, not from her seed.

So give it to this father or mother—call him whichever you like; he won't be offended, since he wished to be each in affection, though he's neither biologically; give him to break open what you are carrying around locked up, so heavy with such great authority. It's written in the book of Genesis; it's not a light matter, there's something hiding there, locked up. Doesn't he strike you as having said something, when he said *sacrament*? I can feel it; after all, it's heavy, but it's still locked up. *But I mean*, he says, *in Christ and in the Church* (Eph 5:32). There you are, there's the food. Eat it, you that never scorned it while it was locked up. But any who scorn it while it's locked up and throw it away won't get at the edible content.

The example of Jacob's rods

23. Since I've mentioned nuts, something else occurs to me which we can indeed most suitably weave into this sermon, because we have come to be dealing with the locked-up meaning of symbolic sacraments. It was not without

point, you see, that Jacob placed three striped rods in the water trough, from which the flocks were to drink at their time of breeding; and he didn't want them to be from just one tree, but from different kinds.[68] To produce the effect he was aiming at, rods from one tree would have been sufficient, nor did there have to be just three of them, but there could have been more or fewer, provided he put striped rods in the water trough. So what can it mean that he put in three rods, and from three kinds of tree, if not that he is hinting at a mystery or sacrament, but this is locked up? As far as the Lord is pleased to give me the capacity, let me break it wide open for you.

Jacob had agreed with his father-in-law, whose sheep he was tending, that if anything was born striped among sheep or goats, it should be his, that is, it should go to his shepherd's wages. That's why he was making sure of this with the striped rods, which the ewes would see as they conceived, and from this kind of desire impressed upon them through their eyes they would give birth to striped offspring. By the variegated animals there was signified the variety of the nations. Those ewes were all of one sort, and they conceived and gave birth to variegated striped offspring. In the same way the first preachers of the gospel were all from the one nation of the Jews; but for many nations to be begotten through the gospel, they had to conceive and give birth to variegated offspring. And this is *the portion of Jacob* (Jer 10:16; Dt 32:9). In Jacob, after all, it was Christ that was being prefigured. In the person of Jacob that people, you see, was the younger, of which it was said, *And the elder shall serve the younger* (Gn 25:23). Yes, you are already recalling that I explained to your holinesses about Esau and Jacob,[69] who was told in that blessing which he extracted from his father, *All nations shall serve you* (Gn 27:29). So the variety of the nations belonged to Jacob; but unless there had been preachers from the people of the Jews, so that sheep of the one kind might conceive from that rod-doctored drink, they wouldn't have brought forth the faithful from among all the various nations.

The three rods signify the mystery of the Trinity

24. But by what means would the ewes conceive a variety of nations? This could of course be managed by the three rods. The animals, you see, were already in heat when he variegated the rods, that is, peeled the bark off in places at intervals, and placed them in the water troughs, from which as they drank the animals would derive a yearning for that variety which would appear in the colors of their offspring. But this could have been managed with any number of rods and any kinds of rods you like. The sacrament, though, pointing to the Christian people that was to be in the future, was not known to the people of the Jews, except for a few holy prophets, and a few jealous teachers of the law, to whom the Lord said, *Woe to you who hold the keys of the kingdom of heaven, and neither enter yourselves nor allow others to enter* (Lk 11:52; Mt 23:13).

These were also signified in that parable, where the tenants of the vineyard, who wouldn't pay the rent, said, *This is the heir; come, let us kill him and the inheritance will be ours* (Mk 12:7)—which they would not have said if they had not to some extent recognized Christ, though his divinity for all that, in which he is equal to the Father, escaped them: *For if they had recognized him, they would never have crucified the Lord of glory* (1 Cor 2:8). But it was not from their number that preachers were sent by the one who *chose the weak things of the world in order to disconcert the strong* (1 Cor 1:27), so that it might be said, *Where is the wise man? Where is the scribe? Where is the questioner of this age? Has not God made foolish the wisdom of this world?* (1 Cor 1:20).

Thus it was that the sacrament that was hidden from them, while being revealed to the uneducated and the simple,[70] was also indicated through the baptism of Christ to the various nations; that's why it was from three rods placed in the water that the ewes conceived variegated offspring.[71] For you see, as long as God the Father was being preached, while the incarnation of the Son was concealed, being still only prophetically foretold and understood by extremely few, a variety of nations was not being brought forth, not indeed until[72] those sheep drank from the three rods, that is, the first Israelites through whom would be born the variety of nations belonging to the lot of Jacob, that is, to the inheritance of Christ. It's about these Israelites that the apostle says, *For I too am an Israelite from the seed of Abraham of the tribe of Benjamin* (Rom 11:1); because Peter too was an Israelite, and Andrew and John and James and the other apostles and all the rest of the first preachers of Christ, about whom the apostle says that the nations are in their debt. *For if the nations*, he says, *have partaken of their spiritual things, they owe them service in material things* (Rom 15:27). So those Israelites were like beasts of one color, because they were from the one nation; they drank after a fashion from the sacrament of the Lord's incarnation, so that through the sacrament of the Lord's incarnation they might give birth in the gospel to the various nations, that is, to a variety of beasts.

The reference of the three kinds of rod to the conception and birth of Christ

25. So how then is the sacrament of the Lord's incarnation shown in the three rods?[73] What sort of rods were they? One was *a nut tree*, one was *from a plane tree*, the other *a balsam tree* (Gn 30:37). That's how it's written. And so how does faith in the Lord's incarnation stand? Let us question our faith;[74] now we believe he was born of the Holy Spirit and the virgin Mary. The child born belongs to the rod from the nut tree. Because just as with a nut one gets to the edible thing by way of the wood, so our Lord Jesus Christ would not give us our bread,[75] unless we came to his body by way of the wood of the cross. This is so clear that your quick wits got there before the words were out of my mouth, that before I could explain what I had begun to say, it was your voices that declared it. Who led you to this food, that you should understand so promptly, if not the one who hung upon the wood? After all, you wouldn't be Christians, were it not for the cross of the Lord; if you weren't Christians, you wouldn't have received this so promptly and with such pleasure.

Where does the rod of the plane tree belong? We say Christ was born of the Holy Spirit. I consider the rod of the plane tree suitably refers to the Holy Spirit, because there can be no doubt that the balsam rod which is left is to be attributed on account of its delightful odor to the undefiled integrity of Mary the virgin. For it was this, surely, that gave such delightful, sweet-smelling fragrance to the report of the Lord's nativity, that he was born of a virgin. To come to an understanding of the rod of the plane tree is harder work: how it can be shown to refer to the Holy Spirit. The Lord will be present, with the help of your prayers, and will open up for you, through my ministry and my humble service, devoted to your progress, the way in which we should take the rod of the plane tree as the Holy Spirit.

I look for what I should pick on in the plane tree, and I find no other reason for praising the plane tree than that it provides such a wide-spreading shade for people resting from the heat. Those who know what this kind of tree is will understand that what I'm saying is true. This is why people like and choose plane trees, on account of their wide-spreading shade and the deep shadow they cast, in which we can rest from the heat. Now the virgin Mary was not going to conceive a son in the heat of sexual desire, but in the coolness, so to say, of totally faithful chastity and undefiled virginity; not yearning for a man's embrace but conceiving by faith; with child as a virgin, due to give birth as a virgin, due to remain a virgin. So all this she received from the Holy Spirit. It was the Spirit himself who bestowed on her that cool relief from the heat of carnal desire, and that's why he is represented by the rod of the plane tree. I'm very much mistaken if in the gospel itself the angel doesn't speak and say to her, *The Spirit of God will come upon you, and the power of the Most High will overshadow you* (Lk 1:35).

Conclusion: fast and pray for the pagans and bad Christians
taking part in the pagan shows and games

26. So now, dearly beloved, as the Lord has willed, may he grant us[76] whatever he is pleased to do on account of our faith, not anything in consequence of our merits. As I always say, and must never stop saying, any profit there may be from the word is to be found in your good works. Wretched indeed is the soil which after receiving good rain either produces no crop or even generates thistles. Grieve with us[77] over those whose conduct we are lamenting. We regularly say that fasting is to be practiced during these festive days of the pagans, precisely as a kind of prayer to God for the pagans themselves. But what really shocks us about the miserable entertainments of the multitude is that we have to urge you, brothers and sisters, to pray with us for some of our Christian brethren, that they may sooner or later change their ways and give up this vile kind of behavior, and allow themselves to be corrected.

What is this, I ask you? How great and how lamentable an evil! He doesn't despise such trifling, such futile shows and games; what is such a Christian going to despise, what is he going to suffer for Christ's sake, when some trial and tribulation comes along? His mouth waters, and he's carried away—how the river in spate will overwhelm him![78] So don't let it be in vain, brothers and sisters, that I have told you of our grief. Those of you here today who didn't fast yesterday should grieve that you spent the other festival days of the pagans in this way, while we were feeling so sad for you, and should please have the goodness, some time or other, to relieve us of our sadness and yourselves of your vile behavior.

NOTES

1. This sermon is the full text of Sermon 341 (III, 10), and also incorporates Sermon 4A (III, 1). The text clearly had a very complex history in its transmission, fully set out by Dolbeau in his account of the discovery of the complete Mainz text, in *Revue des Études Augustiniennes* 40 (1994), "Sermons de Saint Augustin... (VII)." There are other important manuscripts containing parts of the text, besides those used by the Maurists in publishing Sermon 341. From one of the most ancient, which he calls P, and which comes from Lyons, Dolbeau concludes that it was mainly the accidental loss of a whole section of P's manuscript that accounts for the truncated form of Sermon 341 (III, 10). Another manuscript is an anthology of patristic texts from Verona, which yields the information that the sermon was preached in the Restored Basilica in Carthage, "on the day before the Ides of December," that is on 12 December. From internal evidence Dolbeau deduces that it was most likely to have been preached in 409 or 417. On his evidence, I personally prefer 417. It is from fuller fragments of the anthology of Saint Bede, from which Sermon 4A is taken, that one can infer with certainty that this pair of fragments also belongs to the complete sermon.

2. *Propter nos ipsos a nobis audire velint*—"just on my account." Dolbeau very justly infers from this remark, and from the sermon's starting straight off with the text from the psalm, that it was not preached during a Mass, but during what we would nowadays perhaps call a penitential service, held because there were pagan games going on, which were being attended by many rather "indifferent" Christians. See the final section, 26, below.

3. This last phrase may possibly be, as Dolbeau suggests without at all committing himself, a marginal comment by a reader; but it could equally be Augustine making himself clear; and this is perhaps the more likely, considering how the next paragraph begins in the Mainz text: just ." . . he is mentioned in three ways."

4. A point of theological method, I suggest, which is insufficiently appreciated and applied in the teaching of scripture in a great many seminaries and theological colleges today, even granted that here Augustine is too dismissive of human aids, *opibus humanis*. But in his *Teaching Christianity* he qualifies this extreme stance.

5. See Mk 1:19-20. For this theme of choosing obscure fishermen instead of wealthy and illustrious persons, see also Sermon 105A (III, 4), and 301A, 4 (III, 8).

6. This is as appallingly constructed a sentence in the Latin as it is in the English.

7. "The subject we have undertaken," *susceptam rem*, is presumably the same as "the matter in hand," *re proposita*, of the previous sentence; and that is the three ways of understanding Christ, from which we would be distracted if we went on discussing this particular point of giving up everything and following Christ. So how is what he goes on to say—about poor men giving up everything and following Christ—relevant to the subject of the three ways of understanding Christ, from which he has just said it would distract us? Perhaps we will find some sort of resolution of this apparent incoherence in the next section.

8. Most of the next three paragraphs appeared in Sermon 4A, taken from Bede's anthology.

9. I here change the punctuation of the text and read, . . . *qui tam humilis venerat prius, quia . . .*, instead of . . . *qui tam humilis venerat. Prius, quia. . . .* This is really Bede's punctuation, but he

reads *Primo* instead of *Prius*, and to make sense of *Prius* with this punctuation, you have to treat it as if it meant the same as *Primo*, which it doesn't.

10. He is most probably quoting Jerome's estimate of Bethlehem here, that crusty old gentleman being the most notable of Bethlehem's inhabitants at the time.

11. See Lk 2:11.

12. Four qualities associated, I am not quite certain how, with the four "humors" of ancient physiology and medicine, blood, phlegm, black bile and yellow bile.

13. For this theme see Sermons 49, 6 (III, 2); 51, 4 (III, 3); 250, 1 (III, 7); 198, 60, full text; 360B, 24 (III, 11).

14. Here I omit a whole long phrase, which it is almost impossible to construe, and which seems to be just repetitive; I think it must have started as a marginal scribble or comment: *rebus ipsis nota fide, quia infirma mundi elegit Deus, ut confunderet fortia.*

15. The allusion is most probably to the visit of Honorius to Rome in the winter of 403-404. The temple of an emperor is the mausoleum of Hadrian, specifically mentioned in *Expositions of the Psalms* 86, 8. It is now the Castel Sant'Angelo, and the tomb of the fisherman is of course Peter's tomb where Saint Peter's basilica now stands, the approach to it guarded by the Castel Sant'Angelo. See Sermons 335C, 11 (III, 9) and 381 (III, 10).

16. Reading *ad templum imperatoris superbi*, instead of the text's *ad templum imperatoris superbum*, "to the proud temple of an emperor." Hadrian was particularly to be condemned for pride, because after the second Jewish war he had Jerusalem rebuilt and renamed Aelia Capitolina— Aelia after the name of his own *gens* or family, Aelius.

17. *Quare itaque dixi?* Dolbeau thinks *itaque* here is just a strengthened *ita*, giving the sense, "Why have I spoken thus?"; and in any case he finds the place suspect. I take it as referring to the opening word of the previous sentence; in some roundabout and obscure way this incident helps to illustrate the way Christ is put forward in the scriptures as divine. Possibly the implied reasoning goes like this: mere fishermen by themselves could not have converted the world and brought emperors to beg for their intercession with Christ, so the driving force behind them must have been the divinity of Christ.

18. In section 3.

19. See Sermon 198, full text, 27 (III, 11), note 62, for the ancient concept of "ether," *aether*. See also 1 Cor 15:24, Eph 1:21, Col 1:16.

20. See Jn 13:23. Augustine rather stretches the text in saying that John was in the habit (*solere*) of leaning back on Jesus' breast. But that is perhaps the force he gives, incorrectly, to Jn 21:20, where the verb is in fact an aorist referring back to this particular occasion, not an imperfect stating a habitual action. For this theme see also Sermons 20A, 8; 34, 2 (III, 2); 119, 1; 133, 6 (III, 4); 198, full text, 55 (III, 11).

21. Literally, "How am I to understand God and Word?" But the interlocutor would not, I think, be just inquiring about the meaning of the terms.

22. Or, "that the Word of God is the Son of God."

23. See Mk 12:30-31; Mt 25:34.41. I confess I find his thought almost impossible to follow here. The writing conventions of his time did not use capital letters in the way we do, and did not therefore visibly distinguish between "Word" and "word"—the Word of God which God's Son is, and the word of God we find in scripture. I get the impression, though, that here Augustine is deliberately confusing (well, identifying) the two, suggesting that the one divine Word of God, which he has been at such pains in the last section to distinguish from words in the ordinary sense, as it were expresses itself in the word(s) of God in scripture.

24. Here Dolbeau notes a lacuna in the text: *ibi est quiddam. . . .* It's anybody's guess what to supply; the simplest would be *ibi est quiddam unum*, "at that there is a certain unity." Dolbeau wonders if *quiddam*, neuter, shouldn't be *quidam*, masculine; then the lacuna could be filled by a pair of words like *unus fons*, "a certain single source." The comparison which Augustine goes on to give is one with which he usually illustrates the unity in substance of the Son (Word) with the Father; but here he seems to be concerned just with the unity of the Word/Son in itself/himself; there aren't two or more Sons, even though there may seem at times to be two or more words/Words.

25. From "the Spirit desires . . ." I follow a suggestion of Dolbeau's in his apparatus, and read,

... *amantium corda desiderat Spiritus. Desiderat recte dicitur, quia. . .*, instead of the text's ... *amantium corda desiderat. Sed desiderat recte dicitur quia. . . .* Here the subject of the first *desiderat* must be "this . . . Trinity."

26. A favorite little rule of Augustine's exegesis.

27. The text here, according to Dolbeau, is in a rather sorry state. The whole paragraph, indeed, seems to be one in which the preacher is tying himself up in thoroughly Augustinian knots.

28. See Lk 11:23. For this whole theme see Sermons 52, 13 (III, 3); 117, 4; 119, 6; 120, 2 (III, 4); 225, 3 (III, 6); 242, 6 (III, 7); 277, 18 (III, 8).

29. Dolbeau suggests "another in that" to fill a short gap in the text here.

30. Whether the chattering in church broke out at this point, or whether it had been going on for some time, while they had been arguing with each other about "dividing up the Word," one cannot say for certain. I rather think the latter is more likely to have been the case, and that Augustine took advantage of this particular illustration to call his congregation to order.

31. For this illustration see also Sermons 28, 4; 47, 30 (III, 2); 120, 3 (III, 4).

32. See the parable of the Good Samaritan, Lk 10:30-37.

33. Here he is beginning to argue against the Arians. This indeed is mentioned in the title of the sermon according to some manuscripts. But as Dolbeau says, it doesn't at all necessarily imply that the sermon was preached after Arianism became an actual pastoral problem in Africa, with the arrival of Gothic mercenaries to reinforce the Roman troops there about 318. Arianism in one form or another had been the principal heresy of the whole fourth century.

34. Taking *divinitatem majestatis* as meaning *divinitatis majestatem*, a case of an inverted genitive. The text here varies in several details from that of Sermon 341 (III, 10).

35. See Ps 62:11; see above, section 6.

36. See 2 Tm 2:17.

37. See Sir 28:24 (Vulgate).

38. See Mt 7:25; 16:18.

39. Iniquity—bad actions; impiety—wrong faith.

40. Augustine is now addressing the Arian, I think, rather than the old serpent hissing through the Arian.

41. Here Sermon 341 (III, 10), inserts *non*; ". . . in what way he is not equal." It was of course the Arian's case that he is not equal. But what Augustine is doing here, as he makes explicit a few lines further on, is rubbing the Arian's nose in Phil 2:6, and asking him to explain it in his, the Arian's, terms—which he can't do, of course. For an *ex professo* response to the Arians, see above all *The Trinity* V.

42. I here omit a sentence and a half, which is omitted by the Mainz manuscript, M 55, but which Dolbeau includes in the text, since it occurs in other manuscripts. It is really impossible to make sense of; see Sermon 341 (III, 10), section 7, note 16. Dolbeau says he suspects a lacuna here. I could begin the paragraph here with, "So, as I had begun to say"; but as M 55 omits it, I am being loyal to that manuscript, and beginning the paragraph with a gap.

43. His argument has turned totally inconsequential! I fear he is rambling.

44. See Gn 6:7; also 18:21, which implies that God doesn't yet know what he is intending to find out.

45. One cannot say whether this truly reprehensible sentence is due to the mental fatigue of the preacher, or of the stenographer, or represents the combination of the work of two stenographers. One can in any case wholeheartedly appreciate the concern that filled the mind of the person originally responsible for the version in Sermon 341 (III, 10) in leaving it out.

46. Reading *pro aliqua infirmitate validiore* with some of the manuscripts, instead of the *pro aliqua infirmitate validiorum* of Dolbeau's slightly reconstructed text, "on account of a certain weakness of tougher minds." See Sermon 341 (III, 10), note 21.

47. Here Augustine is addressing the Arians again, whose basic premise was that the Son is less than the Father; if they also try to say that he is equal in some respects (to satisfy Phil 2:6 etc.), then they will have to posit these variations.

48. See Ps 73:17.

49. See Sermon 341 (III, 10), note 24.

50. Presumably this gospel, Jn 20:1-18, had been read at this service, perhaps before the singing of Ps 22.

51. In the Latin it's *lucifer est, quod lucem ferat*; in English we only keep "Lucifer" with the reference Augustine is just about to mention. But in Latin it clearly keeps its common meaning of the daystar or morning star which heralds the dawn.

52. A reference, almost certainly, to Is 14:12, the whole of that chapter being the source of what we could call the Lucifer legend about the fall of Satan. For while that verse does indeed begin, "How are you fallen from heaven, Lucifer, star of the morning," the whole verse reads in the Greek LXX, and hence in Augustine's Latin version, "How has he fallen from heaven, the Daystar (Lucifer) who was rising early."

53. See Jn 1:16.

54. Literally, "intellectual spirits"; perhaps I here "Thomistify" Augustine a little. For a similar treatment of this theme see Sermon 4, 6 (III, 1).

55. Following the text of Sermon 341 (III, 10). Mainz 55, given in the text here by Dolbeau, has ". . . to the end of the age, when people no longer beget or are begotten"—which hardly fits the context, and looks like a reflection scribbled by a reader in the margin.

56. The Latin could also be construed as, ". . . of the great king, whose son he was also willing to be"; and that is the most obvious way of taking it. This would mean understanding the great king as David—and it was possibly this distorted interpretation of the saying from the sermon on the mount that persuaded the early abbreviator responsible for Sermon 341 (III, 10) to omit this whole passage. But the fact that Augustine goes on immediately to discuss Ps 87, where Zion is called mother, makes my rendering obligatory.

57. An oblique criticism, perhaps, of an incipient theology, based on this text, of marriage as a sacrament? It rather looks like it. That interpretation would derogate in his view from the reference of the Genesis text to the union of Christ with the Church.

58. And is he here rather brushing aside the literal interpretation of this passage as an absolute prohibition of divorce? Again, it rather looks as if he is.

59. See Sermon 341 (III, 10), note 30, where you are referred to his *Revisions* II, 38. There he indicates that in his mature view this text is to be referred to the Church at the end of time.

60. For this treatment of the text see also Sermon 181 (III, 5), especially section 7.

61. See Is 7:3. Fullers were the people who completed the laundering process by stretching cloth out and beating it, and treating it in various ways with various concoctions—nowadays a lost art, one imagines, superseded by the iron, the ironing board, and starch.

62. See Lk 11:9-10.

63. *Universo mundo notis.* I am treating *universo mundo* here as meaning no more than the French *tout le monde.*

64. Reading *inquis* instead of the text's *inquit.* In the preceding paragraph I considerably recast the punctuation. As punctuated in the text, it would run: "and suppose your soul says to you—it was already inclined to sneer—what is said, And they shall be two in one flesh. It was already saying to itself. . ."

65. You are being told, of course, to take yourself to task in sarcastic terms.

66. This passage has already appeared as the second paragraph of Sermon 4A (III, 1).

67. *Delicatiores.* In Sermon 4A I translated this as "too fond of pleasure." That's what *delicatus* mostly means in classical Latin. But I now feel that that somewhat exaggerates his strictures on some society ladies. The most accurate translation here, perhaps, would be "too nice" in the old-fashioned, not to say obsolete meaning of that word.

68. See Gn 30:37-39.

69. See Sermon 4, 3, 26 & 30 (III, 1). I think there was probably a little outbreak of vocal acknowledgment and nodding of heads in the congregation at this point.

70. See Mt 11:25.

71. The sacrament or mystery he has in mind here is thus clearly the mystery of the Trinity. But it was not the only sacrament or mystery contained in this episode.

72. Following Dolbeau's suggestion in his apparatus, and reading *quoad factum est*, instead of the text's (beginning a new sentence) *Quod autem factum est*—which is in fact almost impossible to construe.

73. As well, that is, as the "sacrament" of the Trinity.

74. Meaning, concretely, the Apostles' Creed, that is, the African Church's version of the baptismal creed, which in those days was cast in the interrogatory mode, as we still have it in the full rite of baptism.

75. Reading *non nostrum nobis panem daret* instead of the text's *non nos portaret*. Dolbeau suggests reading either *pasceret* or *potaret* instead of *portaret*. I wonder, though, if some radical abbreviations of the longer phrase I suggest may not have been misread by a subsequent copyist as *nos portaret*.

76. Reading *praebeat* instead of the text's *praebet*, "he is granting us." The context, though, at the end of the sermon, really requires a wish, a prayer, not a plain statement.

77. Us clergy. For similar remarks on pagan festivals see Sermons 51, 1 (III, 3); 198 full text, 6-9 (III, 11).

78. See Mt 7:25.

Dolbeau 30

SERMON 348A

SERMON OF BISHOP AURELIUS AUGUSTINE AGAINST PELAGIUS

Date: 416[1]

Christ came into the world to save sinners

1. The reason for the coming and the incarnation of our Lord Jesus Christ—that he found all, when he came, to be sinners.[2] The apostle very neatly states this as the cause of his coming in this way: *It is a human[3] word*, he says, *and worthy of total acceptance, that Jesus Christ came into this world to save sinners, of whom I am the first* (1 Tm 1:15). So there was no other reason to fetch the Son of God, true God and eternal God and coeternal and equal to the Father, to fetch him down from heaven to earth in order to take flesh and to die for us, than the fact that there was no life in us. The doctor would not have come down, except to the sick; life would not have come down, except to the dead.

Today, when the apostle was read, you heard, those of you who were paying attention:[4] *So God*, he says, *commends his charity among us, in that while we were still sinners Christ died for us; much more, being justified now by his blood, shall we be saved from the wrath through him* (Rom 5:8-9). This is *the grace of God through Jesus Christ our Lord* (Rom 7:25), which first of all the prophets, then he himself by his own mouth, next the apostles after he was no longer present in the flesh, and finally the whole Church holds, acknowledges, preaches and commends, cultivates, and reveres.[5]

We cannot be saved by our own powers and merits

2. Hence the first thing your graces should know—or rather should recollect what you already know and have always heard—is that no human being can be delivered from evil and sin[6] by their own merits and powers. Man was adept enough at wounding himself, but not at healing himself,[7] just as you can easily be rid of the very life of our flesh by killing yourself; can you then revive yourself? So in order to fall we needed no assistance; or rather the reason we fell was because we dispensed with God's assistance. But in order to rise from

310

the wreck of ourselves let us beg for his assistance, so that we may not remain in our sins.

Christ died for us—you heard the apostle—not for himself but "for us," because he personally had no cause to die, in whom there was no sin. Death is the punishment of sin. I mean, Adam too would assuredly not have died if he hadn't sinned, nor would we have been born mortal from his stock. But that one man came without sin, to undo all sins; had he been bound in together with us[8] he could not have undone our bonds, nor cancelled our condemnation had he been guilty. He took flesh of the virgin, without any male lust being involved; the flesh he took was not a wound, but medicine for the wound.[9] *Christ died for us.*

The Word became flesh in order to be able to die for us

3. What more should we ask from the one who is the Christ?[10] You heard what answer, when he questioned his disciples, was given by Peter: *You are the Christ, the Son of the living God* (Mt 16:16). He is Son by nature, we by grace; he is the *only Son* (Jn 1:18), we are many, because he is born, we are adopted.[11] So while God had a one and only Son, *he did not spare*, as the apostle says, *his very own one and only Son, but gave him up for us all* (Rom 8:32). What greater medicine could the human race demand or hope for, than that the only Son should be sent, not to live with us, but to die?

In order, though, to die for us, he took flesh in which to die, because when he was God the Word with God the Father, he didn't have the wherewithal to die.[12] *In the beginning was the Word, and the Word was with God and the Word was God* (Jn 1:1). Where is the possibility of being seen and touched in the Word, where the possibility of suffering or death in God? Only the mind can see what cannot be seen. But the mind itself too, clouded over with darkness, blinded by sins—why, it's the whole man that is feeble, the whole that is sick, the whole that is wounded, I make bold to say the whole that is dead and done for[13]—how should it see the one who is everywhere present, lacking as it does the healthy inner eye with which invisible things may be seen?

We must rely on the divine doctor, not on ourselves

4. So the whole human being in us was totally lacking in health; the doctor came down to cure body and soul, because he is the savior of body and soul. If doctors, after all, can cure what they haven't created, with these medicines and herbal remedies they haven't created—so if a human doctor can cure what comes from God with what comes from God, how much more will God cure what is his own with what is his own? The doctor, though, cures one who is going to die, God cures one who is going to live forever. And the very fact that he wished to die for us was our remedy. Great indeed, brothers and sisters, is the mercy of our doctor, that he wished to provide a remedy for us not from his medicine chest, but in his blood.

Much more, it says, *being justified now*. By what means? *By his blood*, not by our own powers, not by our own merits, but *by his blood, shall we be saved from the wrath through him*, not through ourselves, but *through him* (Rom 5:9). He has tied us up to the cross; assuredly, if we want to live, let us cling to that death. If you cling to yourself, you are clinging to death; life, after all, is not be found in one who is dead. Why, being dead, do you rely on yourself? You were able to die of your own accord, you cannot come back to life of your own accord. We were able to sin by ourselves, and we are still able to, nor shall we ever not be able to.[14] Let our hope be in nothing but in God. Let us send up our sighs to him, let us rely on him; as for ourselves, let us strive with our wills to earn merit by our prayers.[15]

The new heresy of Pelagius, denying the need of grace

5. This being so, then, brothers and sisters, let me speak to you more plainly, because it's not something we should cover up; there's a new heresy lurking about and secretly spreading its tentacles far and wide. Until it broke out into the open, we tolerated it in silence as best we could, though we were always refuting the actual error.[16] But to give the people concerned a chance to correct themselves, we kept quiet about their names. Nothing, you see, would have been better, nothing we would have liked more, than that when they heard what was being preached by us according to the Church's most ancient and fundamental tradition, they would be afraid to preach their errors, and would be cured of them in private, turning to the one who cures *all that call upon his name* (Jl 2:32; Rom 10:13).

For a long time this was the course I preferred. I mean, I did write a number of things against this kind of impiety, and they came into the hands of readers; however, not all the works of the people whose ideas I had written about had yet been brought to my attention. There were some of these people here, and quite a few of them corrected their errors, over whose salvation we rejoice in the name of the Lord and in his mercy. In fact, some of these who were converted from that error have begged me insistently to publish letters too about the erroneous doctrine itself.

Pelagius absolved by the bishops of Palestine

6. Now, however, we have just heard that this very man, who is the chief author of this pernicious opinion, they were saying[17] was absolved and declared to be Catholic[18] by a synod of bishops in the East. This was because he denied that the things objected to in his teachings were his own, but seemed to have been intruded there by others; he not only denied that he held those views, but he even anathematized them. The acts of the synod have indeed not yet reached us here. However, I have been in the habit of writing to him in a friendly way as a servant of God, as he has done to me, and so last year, when my son the priest Orosius, who is a servant of God with us from Spain,[19] had gone to the

East with letters of mine, I wrote by him to the same Pelagius, not branding him in my letter as a heretic, but urging him to hear from the priest what I had commissioned him to say.

This priest, however, found the place where Pelagius was staying to be all at sixes and sevens and the brethren all at odds over his preaching;[20] he has brought me a letter from there from the holy priest Jerome, for whom I have the greatest veneration on account of his age, his sanctity and his learning, and who is well known to you all. Now this priest Jerome had already written a book against him. . . .[21] free will, which has also been brought to me. He however, as I said, was absolved by a Church synod, confessing the grace of God, which he seemed to deny and attack in his conferences.

Letters and news brought from Palestine by Palatinus

7. Later on, just a few days ago now, there came to us from those parts our fellow citizen of Hippo, the deacon Palatinus, son of Gattus. Many of you know him, even more know his name. His father[22] is present here; he is here himself, standing there among the deacons, listening to me. This man, you see, has brought me a short pamphlet by Pelagius himself in answer to the objections made to his teaching. It doesn't seem to be a part of the acts of the synodal hearing, but the defense he made and put into writing, recording perhaps how he had defended himself too at the hearing by the bishops, the record of which, as I said earlier, has not yet managed to find its way into my hands. And he instructed the deacon to give me this defense of his to read; he didn't, however, send me a covering letter. This makes me anxious that he may later on deny that he even sent me this pamphlet. So I have been reluctant to discuss any of it until we have read the official record, which can be seen to carry the authority of the Church and the bishops.

But why have I wanted to bring all this to the attention of your faithful ears?[23] Because there has been heaven knows how terrible a disturbance in Jerusalem, and the very sad event has also been reported to us, that the rioting populace is said to have burned down two monasteries in Bethlehem.[24] There would have been no need for me to mention this if I didn't know that the news has already reached some of you.[25] So it's better that you should hear the whole story from me, rather than be hurt by rumors circulating stealthily.

What is wrong with the heresy: it denies our need of grace

8. So now let me tell you briefly what's wrong with this heresy, so that you may be on your guard against it, and not conceal from me the names of anyone you may hear whispering such things privately or noising them abroad in public conferences. I'm afraid, you see, of the canker spreading when it's ignored, and of our suddenly finding many such people, so many that we could hardly restore them to health, if ever. So listen then to what's wrong with this heresy.

A few minutes ago I was talking about and commending to you *the grace of*

God through Jesus Christ our Lord (Rom 7:25); well, this is the grace which that pestiferous heresy attacks with its conferences and in its arguments.[26]

You ask how?

They say that human nature is capable of so much, we by the free decision of our will are capable of so much, that just as we became sinners by ourselves, so too we can be justified by ourselves. And since it's better being a just man than just being a man—the word "man," after all signifies a nature, the word "justice" points to happiness and blessedness; so since being a just man is better than just being a man, they say that God made man, but that man himself makes[27] himself just, so that man seems to give himself more than God gave him in the first place.

The Pelagians abolish the need to pray as Christ taught us

9. So would your graces please pay close attention; by these malignant arguments our very prayers are attacked and called in question. I mean, these people act in such a way, argue in such a way that there seems to be no point in our praying. The Lord, you see, taught us how to pray, in case in our prayers we should just make requests for material and temporal things, such as asking not to have a headache, not to die, not to have to bury our child, not to suffer financial loss, not to be put in prison by some oppressor,[28] and any other such temporal and secular concerns here below. These things they grant we may pray for; but what the Lord taught us they cancel, not that they have the face to deny it outright, but that their arguments imply its cancellation.

You see, when people say to you, "You're capable on your own of acting justly; if you want to, you can do it; you don't need any help from God for carrying out whatever it may be,[29] because there is no other grace of God except that by which he made you with free will"—so when they say things like that, they are referring to the grace of God by which we were made, a grace we have in common even with the pagans. It's not the case, after all, that we were created and they weren't, or that we have issued from the workshop of another craftsman than they. Both we and they have the one God for our author, one maker, one creator, *who makes his sun rise upon the good and the bad, and sends rain upon the just and the unjust* (Mt 5:45). That's what these people call the grace of God; they refuse to consider another kind, not by which we are human beings together with pagans, but by which we are Christians. So now that you know what grace they are denying, listen to it put even more plainly.

10. You know how the apostle Paul set before our eyes the conflict we have with the flesh, in order to live devout and just lives, and the very nature of the contest in which we are painfully engaged: how he says, *I take delight in the law of God according to the inner man. I see another law in my members fighting back against the law of my mind, and taking me captive to the law of sin*—and of death—*which is in my members.* Caught in this quandary, he cried out and said, *Wretched man that I am, who will deliver me from the body of this death?* and it's as though the answer came, *The grace of God through Jesus Christ our Lord* (Rom 7:22-25).

These people don't deny this grace,[30] but they hear that you are struggling with the flesh, and with the bad habits formed by your sins: "You're capable of winning on your own. Why are you demanding help? You can carry it through by your own strength and virtue."

The apostle though was overcome. He confessed his weakness in order to obtain health and strength. *I see*, he said, *another law in my members fighting back against the law of my mind, and taking me captive to the law of sin.* What good does it do me that as the inner man I take delight with my mind in the law of God? Look, here am I fighting, here am I being dragged along, here am I being overwhelmed, here am I being taken captive.

Just see if he wasn't looking up out of some great distress, as from the pit of an oil-press,[31] when he cried out to God. If he had said, "Who will deliver me from the body of this death, if not my own strength?" he would have seemed to be speaking rather proudly—but perhaps we could understand even this in a good sense, that he could only say it about God, to whom the psalm says, *I will love you, Lord, my strength* (Ps 18:1). So then, he didn't say, did he, "Who will deliver me, if not my nature, if not my will, if not my powers of free choice and self-sufficiency?" He didn't say that. He humbled himself, so that he might be exalted;[32] *The grace of God*, he said, *through Jesus Christ our Lord.*

Asking not to be led into temptation means asking to be saved from things like breaking a leg

11. It was on account of this grace that the Lord recommended to us what we should pray for: *Hallowed be*—well, what?—*thy name.* Is God's name not holy, then? How can it be hallowed, except in us? Now you there, if it's from your free will, if it's from the powers of your own nature that you can hallow God's name in yourself, what are you praying for, why are you begging from the supreme majesty what you have in your own power?

What else? These two petitions:[33] *Forgive us our debts, as we too forgive our debtors*, and *Do not bring us into temptation* (Mt 6:9.12-13). When they are leveled as objections to these people, how do you think they answer? I was shocked, my brothers and sisters, when I heard. I didn't, indeed, hear it with my own ears, but my holy brother and fellow bishop, our Urbanus who was a priest here and is now bishop of Sicca,[34] when he got back from Rome and there crossed swords with someone holding such opinions—or rather mentioned that he had crossed swords with him—when he was being pressed hard by the weight of the Lord's prayer.[35] He was pressing him, you see, and saying, "If it's in our power not to sin, and in our power to overcome all temptations to sin by our wills alone, why do we say to God please not to bring us into temptation?"

What do you think he replied? "We ask God," he said, "not to bring us into temptation lest we should suffer some evil over which we have no control—lest I should fall from my horse and break my leg, and a highwayman should kill me, and that sort of thing. These are things, after all, which I do not have," he said, "any control over. Because my temptations to sin I can overcome if I wish to, and it's without God's help that I can do so."

12. You can see, brothers and sisters, what a malignant heresy it is. You can see how shocked you all are. Take care you aren't caught in its coils. I know, you see, the cunning twists and turns of these godless people who have turned away from the truth, and who refuse to be convinced, because they have already fallen so deep into their opinions. Watch out, I beg you. Here you are, you see, he has found something to say: "The reason we say, *Do not bring us into temptation*, is lest something should happen to us which we have no control over, as regards the trials and temptations of our bodies."

So is that why the Lord said, *Watch and pray, lest you should enter into temptation* (Mk 14:38)? Is this what he said: "Watch and pray lest you should break a leg, or have a headache, or incur some financial loss?" That's not what he said; but what did he say? What he said to Peter: *I have prayed for you, that your faith may not fail* (Lk 22:32). *I have prayed*, says God to a man, the Lord to a servant, the master to a disciple, the doctor to a patient. *I have prayed for you*, that your what may not fail? Your what? Your hand, your leg, your eye, your tongue, by any paralysis, that is, by any enfeeblement of your limbs?[36] No; but *that your faith may not fail*. According to these people we have it entirely under our own control that our faith should not fail.

13. Why is God asked on our behalf to grant us what these people say we ought not to ask for from his eternal majesty, but which we have under our own control? Take the blessings, my brothers and sisters, the blessings we call down upon you; they empty them of meaning, make them totally pointless, eliminate them. You have heard me, I believe, my brothers and sisters, when I say, "Turning to the Lord, let us bless his name; may he grant us to persevere in his commandments, to walk in the right way of his instruction, to please him with every good work," and other such.[37] "All this," they say, "is placed absolutely under our own control." So we, then, are quite vainly desiring these things for you. Let me defend both ourselves[38] and you, or else we may find that we are pointlessly giving blessings, and you are equally pointlessly subscribing your "Amen." Your "Amen," my brothers and sisters, is your signature, is your consent, is your agreement.

In case some of them should condemn both us and you, let us defend ourselves with the help of the apostle Paul; let us see if he wished for his people the sort of things we pray for over you. Listen to what he said in some place or other. It's a very short thing I have to say. What do you say, Mr. New Heretic,[39] whoever you are, listening to me, if you are present here? What do you say? That we have it in our power not to sin, and that we can fulfill this obligation without the help of divine grace? Is that what you say?

"That's it," he says.

So we have it in our power not to sin, without any help from God?

"Certainly," he says; "our freedom of choice is quite sufficient for us for this purpose."

So what about what the apostle says, writing to the Corinthians: *We pray to God that you may do nothing evil* (2 Cor 13:7)?

You've all noticed, you've all heard, accepted, and because it's as plain as can be, you have undoubtedly all understood what the apostle prayed for. *We pray*, he said, *to God that you may do nothing evil.* "We teach you," he could have said, "not to do anything evil, we order you, we command you." And to be sure, if he had said that, he would have said something perfectly in order, because our wills do also contribute something; it's not the case, after all, that our wills do nothing, but only that they are not sufficient by themselves. However, he preferred to say, *We pray*, in order to emphasize the role of grace, so that those correspondents of his might understand that when they did not do anything evil, they were not shunning evil solely by their own will, but were fulfilling with help from God what had been ordered.

Our freedom of choice is implied by commands to do good, our need for grace by prayers that we may carry them out

14. So, brothers and sisters, when a command is given, acknowledge the will's freedom of choice; when prayer is made about what has been commanded, acknowledge the favor of grace. You find each of them in scripture, after all: both the giving of commands and the making of prayers. What is commanded is also prayed for. Notice what I'm saying. We are commanded to understand. How are we commanded to understand? *Do not be like horse and mule, which have no understanding* (Ps 32:9). You have heard it commanded; ask that you may be able to fulfill what has been commanded.

"How," you say, "am I to ask for this?"

Listen to scripture. What order are you given? *Do not be like horse and mule, which have no understanding.* Because the order has been given, you have acknowledged the role of the will. Listen to where prayer is made, so that you may acknowledge the role of grace: *Give me understanding, that I may learn your commandments* (Ps 119:73).

We are enjoined to have wisdom; I can read the place where it is so enjoined.[40]

"Where can you read it?" he says.

Listen: *You that are senseless among the people, and foolish, sometime be wise* (Ps 94:8).

Now what does he say? "You see how God commanded us to be wise; so wisdom is something in our power."

I've already said it, I've heard the commandment, I've recognized the role of the will. Listen to the prayer, so that you in your turn may be able to acknowledge the role of grace. We are dealing with the wisdom which has been enjoined upon us. Let us hear what the apostle James has to say: *If any of you lacks wisdom, let him request it from God, who gives to all lavishly* (Jas 1:5).

Self-control is enjoined upon us.

"Where is it enjoined?"

The apostle writing to Timothy: *Practice self-control* (1 Tm 5:22). It's a command, it's an order, it has to be listened to, has to be carried out. But unless God comes to our help, we get stuck. We try, indeed, to do it by will power, and the will makes some effort; it shouldn't, though, rely on its ability, unless it is assisted in its debility. Yes, certainly the command is given, *Practice self-control*. But listen to another place of scripture: *And when I perceived*, he says, *that nobody can be self-controlled unless God grants it, and this in itself belonged to wisdom, to know whose gift it is.*

"And what," you say, "did he do?"[41]

I approached the Lord and besought him (Wis 8:21).

Is there any need, my brothers and sisters, to run through many instances? Whatever we are enjoined to do, we have to pray that we may be able to fulfill it, but not in such a way that we let ourselves go, and like sick people lie flat on our backs and say, "May God rain down food on our faces," and we ourselves wish to do absolutely nothing about it; and when food has been rained down into our mouths, we say, "May God also swallow it for us."[42] We too have got to do something. We've got to be keen, we've got to try hard, and to give thanks insofar as we have been successful, to pray insofar as we have not. When you give thanks, you are taking care not to be condemned as ungrateful, while when you ask for what you do not yet have, you are taking care not to be left empty-handed, because blocked by your own incapacity.

15. So think about these things, my brothers and sisters. Anyone who approaches you and says to you, "So what shall we do? Have we no control over anything, unless God gives us everything?[43] So it's not us that God will be rewarding, but himself that he'll be crowning"—you can now see that he comes from that vein of thought. It's a vein of thought, but a poisonously vain one.[44] It's been bitten, you see, by the serpent, it isn't a healthy one. That's what Satan, after all, is busy about every day, how to get people thrown out of the Church by the poison of heretics, just as he then got them thrown out of paradise by the poison of the serpent.[45]

As for that man,[46] nobody should say he was absolved by the bishops. What was absolved was his confession, a kind of correction was absolved, because what he said before the bishops seemed to be Catholic, but the bishops who absolved him were unaware of what he has written in his books. And perhaps he really did correct his errors. We ought not, after all, to despair about the man, who possibly did decide to attach himself to the Catholic faith, and to take refuge in his[47] grace and help. Perhaps this did happen. All the same, it's not the heresy that was absolved, but the man denying the heresy.[48] But when I have read the official record, when it has come into my hands, I will have the duty of telling your graces, with the Lord's help, whatever further details I learn about this sorry business, and perhaps about his repudiating his errors.

NOTES

1. A considerable fragment of this sermon, from just after the beginning of section 11, has already appeared in this series as Sermon 348A (III, 10). The complete sermon, translated here, was found by François Dolbeau in Cesena in the Biblioteca Malatestiana, in a manuscript dating from 1453. The lord of Cesena at that time, Malatesta Novello, like so many of his contemporaries, was a keen collector of both classical and patristic texts. From what older manuscript this copy was made, coming from what monastic library, there is no telling.

Dolbeau has published the text in *Recherches Augustiniennes* 28 (1995); and he there argues in detail, from events and persons mentioned in the text, for a much more precise date: the end of May or very early June, 416. The sermon was clearly preached in Hippo Regius. The occasion for the sermon was the arrival of news from Palestine that Pelagius had been absolved by a synod of the bishops of that province, meeting at Diospolis. See note 18 below for other works of Augustine which cover the whole episode.

2. A very abrupt beginning to a sermon! One wonders if there may not still be a piece of it missing. This summary statement of the reason (*causa*) for the incarnation, together with the whole following paragraph, supports the Thomist view that if there had been no sin, God the Son would not have become man, as against the Scotist view that so marvelous a divine act of love did not depend on human sin, and that the Word would have become flesh in any case.

3. This odd reading for the Greek text's "faithful" is found in several of the old Latin versions. "Human" must be taken, I suppose, almost in the sense of "humane," indicating the humanity, the kindness of God.

4. For a similar little dig at signs of inattentiveness in the congregation see Sermon 272B, 2 (III, 7).

5. This last pair of verbs just represents the single *colit* of the Latin.

6. I have added "from evil and sin"; Augustine just said "can be delivered," *liberari*. But we require a more specific statement today in English.

7. This last phrase Dolbeau suggests should be supplied; it is not in the text. But there is just a slight indication from the punctuation of the manuscript that something may have dropped out there. For this concept, see Sermons 156, 2 (III, 5) and 306E, 5 (III, 11).

8. Dolbeau suspects the Latin text, *nobis noxius*, "liable for us, with us," of being corrupt, and suggests the true reading may be *nobis innexus*, which I have translated. The Latin as it stands, however, would make sense, especially if one emended *nobis* to *nobiscum*; but it would not have provided the contrast that is required with "our bonds," *ligatos*, as *reus* in the next phrase does with *damnatos*.

9. The wound in our nature which we call original sin, and which Augustine saw as both transmitted and exemplified by the "lust" necessarily involved, for the man, in sexual intercourse. See Sermons 294, 11; 299, 8 (III, 8).

10. Here Dolbeau indicates a gap in the text—but "hesitantly," as he says—and suggests supplying "Who are you?" But I respectfully suggest, for my part, that the text makes good sense as it stands, being taken up a few sentences further on by the question, "What greater medicine could the human race demand?"

11. See Gal 4:5; see also Sermon 183, 3 (III, 5).

12. See Sermons 80, 5 (III, 3); 265D, 7 (III, 7); 299F, 2 (III, 8).

13. A very odd construction: all this about "the whole man" is in the accusative case; so strictly, that is, grammatically speaking, it should form the object of the verb *videret* (coming soon), of which the subject is "the mind," and should also be qualified by the adjective "everywhere present." But that, to make sense, clearly means God. So this long accusative interlude I have to treat as—I do not know the correct grammatical term—a kind of exclamatory accusative, like *me hercle*.

14. I have added "not." The text runs, *potuimus et possumus, nec aliquando poterimus*; "we were able and are able, nor shall we ever be able." So I am guessing that *non* got left out by the easiest of scribal errors (we all have a natural inclination to "accentuate the positive, eliminate the negative") between *aliquando* and *poterimus*. But as Dolbeau remarks, the whole passage seems a little corrupt; or else the preacher is being rather disconnected in his thoughts; it looks in fact as if he was somewhat discombobulated.

15. This sounds like a slightly Pelagian remark! But it is presumably intended to reverse what one may call the Pelagian order of things; and see the last few sections of the sermon, 9-15, on the effect of the heresy on prayer.

16. We—the African bishops, not just Augustine personally, I think; but later on by this first person plural he clearly does mean just himself, so I there translate with first person singular.

Dolbeau notes a gap in the text here, and supplies *ut*, "in order that." Others suggest supplying *donec*, "until." I am just sticking my little oar in, and suggesting amplifying Dolbeau's suggestion to *sed ut*.

17. The Latin text is odd here, and the syntax incoherent, to say the least. Dolbeau suggests some emendations; but I am sticking to the text—on the assumption, aired in note 14, that Augustine was indeed a little discombobulated. This continues to show throughout the paragraph, but it is also a very faulty text.

18. Reading *catholicum* as Dolbeau suggests, instead of the text's *canonicum*. The synod of Palestinian bishops at Diospolis which absolved Pelagius had met in December 415. This particular episode of the whole Pelagian controversy is dealt with by Augustine in *The Acts of Pelagius* and *Letters* 146, 168, and letter 19 of the recently discovered Divjak letters.

19. Does this expression mean that Orosius was a member of his monastic community in the bishop's house in Hippo Regius? I think Augustine would certainly have liked him to become one. He had come to Africa from Spain to consult Augustine about the Priscillian heresy, and had then been referred by him to Jerome in Palestine, and there had got involved in the Pelagian affair which this sermon is all about. He did some more traveling after his return to Hippo Regius, but eventually seems to have settled there, and at Augustine's instigation later wrote a world history, to act as a kind of reference book for Augustine's *City of God*.

20. The place was principally Bethlehem, where Jerome had been residing for many years, and indeed presiding over monasteries of men and women. But Jerusalem was also in turmoil, it seems, and the scene of bad riots.

21. There is a gap in the text here. For Jerome's book see Augustine's Letter 180, 5.

22. Reading, on Dolbeau's suggestion, *pater*, instead of the text's *patri*, which would give the sense "he is present to his father," that is, just possibly, "he is staying with his father." He is mentioned in Divjak letter 19, precisely in connection with this occasion. He was probably not a deacon of the Church of Hippo Regius, but had come there to visit his father; and Jerome, it seems, had taken the opportunity to entrust him with the book he had written against Pelagius, to deliver it to Augustine. Perhaps, like Jerome, he was normally resident in Palestine. This is the only mention of his father, Gattus, whose name according to Dolbeau may be a corruption, or local variation of the widely attested African name Cattus or Cattius.

23. Literally, "to your faith," *fidei vestrae*, in the style of the more common honorifics *caritati vestrae, sanctitati vestrae*.

24. In the *Acts of Pelagius* he tells us further that a deacon was also killed, and that the monks and nuns in the monasteries, which were under Jerome's care and spiritual direction, were the victims of "a most wicked slaughter." He would surely have mentioned that here, had he already been told such further horrid details.

25. The text rather oddly reads "that some of you had already got there," *aliquos vestrum pervenisse*. Dolbeau emends the last word to *praevenisse*, giving the sense "that some of you had got there first." I am following the suggestion of his colleague Petitmengin, which Dolbeau thinks may be more correct, and reading *et ad aliquos vestrum pervenisse*.

26. Two words to translate *disputationibus suis*. Pelagius was a monk with a considerable reputation as a spiritual director, and so I think the giving of conferences to the devout was one of the chief ways in which he and his followers propagated their ideas.

27. Reading *facit* instead of the text's *fecit*, "man himself has made himself just."

28. Most usually, perhaps, by moneylenders.

29. Keeping the text's *quaevis sint*, which Dolbeau emends, but hesitantly, to *quae jussit*, "what he has commanded." I respectfully carry his hesitation a step further. In the next phrase I emend *nisi ista quae te fecit*, "except that which made you," to . . . *qua te fecit*.

30. The whole burden of Augustine's interminable struggle with Pelagianism was that they do!

All he can mean here is that they don't deny it head on in so many words, but the way they go on to engage the apostle in conversation in fact means that they do deny it.

31. Here I am giving a very concrete meaning to *quasi ex magna pressura*. I think this is required by that *quasi*.

32. See Lk 14:11, and all parallel passages.

33. From here to the end (almost) is the fragment preserved in Sermon 348A (III, 10). The text here translated will occasionally differ slightly, and so too will the translation.

34. The full name of the town was Sicca Venerea, presumably because it was dedicated to the goddess Venus, probably in honor of Julius Caesar, who claimed descent from her through his fabled ancestor Aeneas the Trojan. Urbanus had only very recently been elected bishop there. He seems to have been employed fairly frequently by the African hierarchy on diplomatic missions, both before and after becoming a bishop himself.

35. This non-sentence faithfully reflects the syntactical chaos of the original.

36. He has to explain the Greek word *paralysis*, which we don't have to do in English, and so adds *id est dissolutio*, a very close Latin rendering of the Greek. He had to allow for the large uneducated, not to say illiterate, section of his congregation, though many of the citizens of Hippo Regius, a considerable seaport, would have known Greek.

37. We have not come across this particular "Turning to the Lord" concluding prayer before. Yet another formula will be found at the end of Sermon 36 (III, 2).

38. All bishops and priests.

39. Pelagianism was a new heresy compared with the Donatism and Manichaeanism that Augustine had been combating in the earlier years of his ministry, and also compared with the Arianism he was to encounter at first hand in the last few years of his life.

40. Emending to *Qua jussum est, lego* the text's *Quia jussum est, lego*, "I can read that it is so enjoined."

41. Emending the text's *Et quid, inquit, feci?* "And what, he says, did I do?" to *Et quid, inquis, fecit?*

42. Augustine is ridiculing the simplistic view of the matter which makes grace and free will mutually exclusive alternative sources of our activity—we *either* act by free will *or* are moved by grace; if by free will, we don't need grace, if by grace we haven't got free will. This view is put forward by the simple Pelagian at the beginning of the next section. Whether Pelagius himself was quite so simplistic may be questioned. What he was originally condemned for—or rather his colleague Coelestius—in a synod at Carthage in 411, at which Augustine, apparently, was not present, was the denial of original sin and of the necessity of infant baptism.

43. This is a statement in the text. It makes better sense to treat it as a question.

44. *Jam videtis quia de illa vena venit. Vena est, sed venenum habet.*

45. See Gn 3:4-5. 23.

46. Pelagius.

47. He presumably means God, and is just being a little careless in his manner of speaking; grammatically the antecedent of *ejus*, his, her, its, is "the Catholic faith."

48. Thus far Sermon 348A (III, 10). The next sentence is only found in the complete Cesena manuscript.

SERMON 354A

SERMON OF SAINT AUGUSTINE THE BISHOP ON THE GOOD OF MARRIAGE

Date: 397[1]

Introduction: memento mori

1. The Sunday readings in the holy scriptures[2] which have just been chanted, the divine word and heavenly authority, are urging the human race to remember its mortality for this reason, that the end is coming. For all human beings, you see, that is, for each and every single person, the end is near, even if the end of the whole human race, perhaps, is a long way off. So this then, as I started to say, is what the divine word seems to be urging upon us, that we should bear our mortality in mind precisely because the end is coming. Let us reflect,[3] though, upon the life which has no end; those who bear in mind that they are mortal will be found worthy to obtain immortal life.

Questions on marriage have a reference to the last things

2. You heard the Pharisees trying to catch the Lord out by questioning him on whether it is lawful to put away one's wife for any cause whatever.[4] He answers with the truth, because he is *the truth* (Jn 14:6). They failed, you see, to make the Lord a liar by trying to catch him out; both believer and unbeliever were to learn the truth, and for the instruction of those who worship God, those who tempt God hear the truth. The reason I've said this is in case people should imagine that the Lord God might have said something at variance with the way things really are, just because those men were not questioning him sincerely, but were trying to catch him out with their question.

So what should matter to us is not what sort of people were questioning him, but what he said; not what sort of person struck the rock, but what sort of water poured out from it.[5] So married couples have something to learn from the Lord's reply; and so do those who are not yet married, or who have already formed the good intention of forgoing marriage. The time also is admonishing me to say something in connection with these words of the Lord, because, as is commonly supposed, these are the last times.[6]

322

3. What concerns us rather more here and now, calling for greater care, more serious attention and more fruitful devotion, is what the apostle says: *For the rest, brothers, the time is short. It remains that those who have wives should be as though they had none*, and so on, *and those who buy as though they were not buying, and those who rejoice as though they were not rejoicing, and those who make use of this world as though they were not making use of it. For the shape of this world is passing away. I wish you to be without anxiety.* Then he adds, *The one who is without a wife gives thought to the things of God, how he may please God; but the one who is tied by marriage gives thought to the things of the world, how he may please his wife* (1 Cor 7:29-33). A vast difference—giving thought to the things of God, and giving thought to the things of the world. There can be no comparison, where thought makes such a thorough division.

But now some married man is all on fire to make a vow of sexual abstinence; let him look to his better half,[7] let him see if she is following, and if she is, let him lead on; but if she isn't following, he mustn't put her away. Perhaps he is able to do this and she isn't, or she is able and he isn't; they[8] must understand that they are one flesh. You all heard, not just any human being, but the Lord himself of humanity, giving commands to Christians in his answer to Jews: *Have you not read*, he said, *that from the beginning God made male and female? And he said, For this reason a man shall leave father and mother and shall stick to his wife, and they shall be two in one flesh. And so they are not now two, but one flesh. What therefore*, he says, *God has joined together, let man not separate* (Mt 19:4-5).

> *Beginning of commentary on 1 Cor 7:1-11; the absolute equality of husband and wife in the matter of conjugal rights*

4. It seems to offend against modesty to discuss this matter any more thoroughly. But we mustn't think of ourselves as being so healthy that we cannot enter into the difficulties of the sick. What, after all, are we in comparison with the holiness of the apostle Paul? And yet in a spirit of fatherly humility, with salutary advice, he entered human bedrooms bringing divine medicine. And this great holiness approached the beds of married couples, looked at them lying there, did not lay aside the garment of holiness, and yet gave advice to weakness:[9] *Let the husband*, he said, *pay the debt to the wife*. It's a debt; let him pay it. *Likewise too the wife to the husband. The wife does not have authority over her own body, but the husband*. That's not surprising; the woman, after all, is subordinate to the man, and making decisions is the man's job, complying with them the woman's. However, in this matter in which both sexes come together, while in all others the woman should be the man's servant, in this matter, I'm telling you, their status is equal. So it was little enough for the apostle to say, *The woman does not have authority over her own body, but the man*—he uses the word "body" for the sex organs, to avoid obscenity. He made it quite clear, what he was really saying: *The woman does not have authority over her own body, but the man. Likewise the man does not have authority over his own body,*

but the woman (1 Cor 7:3-4). In this matter his sex is at the disposal of the wife;[10] it belongs to another; it is owed to the woman.

Husbands may not resolve on complete sexual abstinence
without their wives' agreement

5. From this it follows that a husband cannot have such a right of decision that he may say, "I am now able to abstain from sex. If you are able to, do so together with me; if you aren't, in no way shall you prevent me. I myself will do what I can." So what's all this then? Is it your wish, Mr. Man, that your better half should perish? I mean, if the weaker flesh[11] is unable to abstain, her sicklier will is liable to go fornicating, and by fornicating to be condemned. God forbid that her punishment should be your crown!

"You're wrong; it won't be, it certainly won't be like that. It won't do for you to tell me that what she will be condemned for is fornication;[12] anyway, better her alone than both of us together."

If that's what you say, it's you who are wrong. Marriage, after all, is not condemned, there's no condemnation of *what God has joined together let mere man not separate* (Mt 19:6). You there are a man; by grabbing at sexual abstinence without your partner's consent you are wanting, as a man, to separate what God has been good enough to join together.

"But it's God," he says, "who's doing the separating, because it is for God's sake that I'm doing this."

Certainly, if you can read anywhere that God said, "If you lie with your wife, I will condemn you," then do what you want, so that you won't both be condemned together. But when you hear Christ's apostle saying, *The wife does not have authority over her own body, but the husband. Likewise too the husband does not have authority over his own body, but the woman. Do not defraud one another* (1 Cor 7:4-5). . . .[13]

"Do not defraud one another" does not mean "Do not commit adultery"

6. "Defraud" is what he said: by withholding the debt, not by committing adultery. He was talking, after all, about paying debts, and obliging them to pay each other the marital rights they owed. He wouldn't, surely, have been permitting adultery with the following words, in which, after saying *Do not defraud one another*, he added, *except by agreement for a time* (1 Cor 7:5). So is adultery to be committed by agreement? If you think that the words *Do not defraud one another* refer to adultery, what's the meaning of *except by agreement*? God forbid that by agreement husband and wife should allow each other to commit adultery! Modest and patient married women are used to putting up with such things. But that's no reason for husbands not to worry; it's taken for granted they have to be tolerated now; they should take care they aren't due to be damned later on.

But it's an open and shut case, the apostle's words call for no explanation; what he was getting at in saying *do not defraud one another* was that they should not withhold from each other their conjugal debts, *except by agreement for a time, so that you may have leisure*, he goes on, *for prayer*. So you can see that the apostle laid down a certain sexual abstinence, or rather a kind of truce in the relationship, as a means of their bestirring themselves to the offering up of prayer; and then with that thoughtfulness with which such perfect health did not disdain to approach the beds of the infirm, he concluded, *and once more come together* (1 Cor 7:5).

"Once more come together" is said as a pardon, not as a command

7. When you link up "for a time, so that you may have leisure for prayer," and "again come together," is this the command you are really giving, Apostle?

"It is," he says.

And where's the decency, where's the modesty of such great holiness as yours?[14]

"But I," he says, "know the dangers of infirmity."

And to clinch the matter, he didn't keep quiet about the reason for his advice.

"Would you like to hear," he says, "why I said *Once more come together*? *In case Satan should tempt you on account of your lack of restraint*."

Then it goes on, in case he should seem to have ordered this, rather than just allowing it—permission given to infirmity, after all, is one thing, a command given to faith quite another: *But I say this*, he declares, *by way of pardon*. When I say, *Once more come together, I say it by way of pardon, not by way of a command*. I am not giving a command to chastity, but a pardon to infirmity. It isn't something to be praised, but to be excused—*by way of pardon. Because I would wish you all to be as I am; but each one has his own proper gift from God, one like this, another like that* (1 Cor 7:5-7). Hence too the Lord's words, *Whoever can take this, let him take it* (Mt 19:12).

What is implied is not that marriage is a sin, but that undue exercise of conjugal rights is

8. Here maybe someone may say, "If the apostle conceded this *by way of pardon*, and gave in to human infirmity, then marriage is sinful. To what else, after all, but sin is pardon to be conceded?" To be sure, what the apostle conceded to infirmity *by way of pardon* is, I make bold to say, a sin; but it is not here that the good of marriage lies.[15] And so, brothers and sisters, please try and make some distinctions, and help me with your careful attention, as I twist and turn in a most difficult place, and toil away for you in the presence of the Lord.

He makes a concession by way of pardon to this kind of activity; what he has in mind, of course, is the sexual relations of married couples, not of adulterers, and yet he says *by way of pardon, not by way of command* (1 Cor 7:6). "I'm excusing, not commanding."

A married man may then say, "My dear apostle, if you are excusing, I'm sinning. And so I don't want the defender of the good of marriage to bring me this kind of argument and say, 'The reason marriage is a good thing is that it keeps adultery at bay.' I want a real good, not a small evil; because if you say, 'The reason marriages should be contracted is to make sure adulteries aren't committed; because marriage is excusable, pardon can be conceded to marriage,' you are mentioning two evils, not one good and one evil, but two evils, one a small one and the other a big one."

9. But it wasn't the good of marriage that the apostle found fault with, but the evil of lack of restraint, which consists of making use of one's wife[16] beyond the necessity of begetting children. I mean, to learn why you take a wife, don't read my arguments,[17] but your own marriage lines. Read them, pay attention to them, and if you go beyond them, blush for shame. Read them, I too will listen; it's on your account that I need to. Undoubtedly this is what you read there: "for the sake of begetting children." So then, *if there is anything over and above this, it is from the evil one* (Mt 5:37).[18]

Take a look, inspect, examine yourself. If you do nothing over and above what has to be done "for the sake of begetting children," you have done nothing for which the apostle needs to excuse you. If however you do do anything over and above, what you do is bad, what you do is a sin. But still, would you like to know what sort of thing the good of marriage is? Through the good of marriage, the evil of unrestrained sexual desire is pardonable. Desire has been roused, you have been defeated, you've been dragged along—but you haven't been dragged away from your wife. The penalty for being overcome by unrestrained desire would overtake you, unless the fact of your being married interceded for you. So then, if you're married, and don't want the apostle to have to make a concession to you about anything by way of pardon, don't exceed the limits of your marriage lines.

Advice to the unmarried

10. But you haven't yet tied the knot;[19] please, don't even want to do so. I mean, the kind of man who is able not to make use of a wife "except for the sake of begetting children" is also able not to make use of one at all. He's the conqueror of lust, master of the movements of the flesh, with a firm grip on the reins of restraint; he turns that movement like a horse whichever way he wishes, he doesn't let go of the right to rein it in. So that's your condition, and you haven't yet tied the knot[20] and are not yet bound; *free of a wife, do not seek a wife.* After all, if married people are told, *The time is short; it remains that those too who have wives should be as though they did not have them* (1 Cor 7:27.29), why do you want to have one, when you are able, while still practicing restraint, not to have one?

*The difference in this matter between the time
of the Old Testament and that of the New*

11. I mean, why should a people still have to be propagated for God, so that Christ, the salvation of the nations, may come through it? When that particular

people, you see, was being propagated, even those who were well able to practice sexual abstinence were constrained to marry wives by the very obligations of kinship.[21] It was out of their duty to the kindred that the holy fathers begot children, out of their duty to the kindred that the holy mothers gave birth to children; they would have been perfectly capable also of abstaining. They served the propagation of the people; it was a duty, an obligation.

Now, a vast multitude is plainly visible, and all over the world, from which spiritual children may be selected[22] and become a people holy to Christ[23] by immortal adoption for the heavenly inheritance. Then, therefore, it was a time for embracing, now it is a time for refraining from embraces. It's what a prophet says; let us listen: *There is a time for everything; a time for embracing, a time for refraining from embraces.* "A time for embracing"—the time of the prophets; "a time for refraining from embraces"—the time of the gospel. *A time for throwing stones, a time for collecting them* (Eccl 3:5). The time for throwing stones was the time for propagating human beings. You see, *God is able from these stones to raise up children to Abraham* (Lk 3:8); why are they still being thrown? Let those that have already been thrown now be collected. The order was given for stones to be thrown: "Cursed be the man who has not raised up seed for Israel."[24] The order is given for stones to be collected: *The time is short; it remains that those who have wives should be as though they did not have them* (1 Cor 7:29). So now, *whoever can take this, let him take it* (Mt 19:12).

At that time even one who could take it did not undertake the duty of sexual abstinence; but all the same the man had the appropriate virtue. Thus they had wives for God's sake—unless of course we are to assume that if Abraham had been told to abstain, he would have dreaded the prospect, a man of such devotedly religious virtue that at the Lord's bidding he was able even to offer his own heir to be slaughtered in honor of the one from whom he had received him to be reared. So their time was different from ours.

It is better to marry than to burn

12. So nobody should make a rule out of this, nobody should reckon that the necessity for this thing has been imposed upon us. *Whoever can take this, let him take it* (Mt 19:12).[25] "But I can't," he says.

You can't?

"No, I can't."

To your aid there comes a particular authority from the apostle, to feed you on milk, to the effect that *if they cannot manage sexual abstinence, let them marry.* Let something be done, in order to obtain pardon. The function of pardon is to save you from landing in eternal punishment. Let what is lawful be done, in order for what is not lawful to be excused. He indicates this by what comes next: *I prefer them to marry, rather than to burn* (1 Cor 7:9). "I made a concession," he is saying, "to lack of restraint, because I feared something worse; I feared eternal pains, I feared what's waiting for adulterers, what's in store for them." Even the fact that married couples, overcome by desire, make use of each other more than is necessary for having children is something they can place among the things for which we say, *Forgive us our debts as we too forgive our debtors* (Mt 6:12).

Those however who can take it should take it, and should pray that they may be able to. *And since I knew*, says holy scripture, *since I knew that nobody can be self-controlled unless God grants it; and this too was a matter of wisdom, to know whose gift this was* (Wis 8:21). When you are afraid of sexual abstinence as a punishment, you fail to knock at the door of grace. Don't think of it as a punishment. When you are capable of it, it will not be irksome. The one whose rewards we are out to obtain will grant it. Knock, you will receive; ask, seek, you will find.[26] The spring is always flowing; faith mustn't be sluggish. And yet, *Whoever can take this, let him take it*; anyone who can't, *If he cannot manage sexual abstinence, let him marry.*

Paying the marriage debt can be a work of charity

13. Love one another. The man is able to, the woman is not. You are not demanding payment of the debt; pay it yourself. And insofar as you are paying what you are not also[27] demanding, you are performing a work of mercy. I have absolutely no hesitation in saying: "It's a work of mercy." You see, if you don't pay it, your partner, overcome by desire—or if you, the woman, don't pay it, your husband, overcome by desire—is going to be an adulterer. I don't want you to accord yourself this more ample honor in such a way that you are willing for him to be damned. What if you no longer demand, but only pay the debt? It's put down to your account as self-control. After all, it is not being demanded out of lust, it's being paid out of mercy. Accordingly, say to your God, "Lord, you know in me what you have given me; but I also hear what you have advised, because you have made both me and my partner, and have not wished either of us to perish."

Turning to the Lord. . .

NOTES

1. Dolbeau dates it a little more precisely to the first fortnight of July. His argument invokes the sermon's relationship, both in Possidius' *Index* and in the manuscript tradition, with other early sermons and works, notably the *Answer to Faustus*, who was a leading Manichee controversialist. It also makes use of internal evidence, which will figure in the notes as we come to it. A fragment of this sermon preserved by Bede in his anthology has already appeared as Sermon 354A in volume III, 10.

2. Dolbeau finds the opening words, *Dominicae lectiones*, suspicious. I follow a suggestion which he airs, but withdraws, of treating *Dominicae* as standing for *Dominici/ae diei*, Sunday. And I then omit the next word, *et*; if it is left in, it suggests that "the divine word and heavenly authority" are somehow distinct from the holy scriptures. I prefer to treat these as simply in apposition to

lectiones. A puzzled scribe could easily have added *et* to make what he thought, but I don't think, better sense.

3. The Latin has the verb in the 3rd person singular. It's difficult to see what the subject of it could be; "each and every single person" is too far away. So I am in effect emending *meditetur* to *meditemur*.

4. See Mt 19:3.

5. See Nm 20:8-12: Moses striking the rock in the desert, and doing it, apparently, without proper faith and trust.

6. An ironic reference, so Courcelles suggested (*Recherches Augustiniennes* 1 [1958], 177, note 149), to a Greek oracle which declared that Christianity would disappear after 365 years, that is to say, in the year 398, counting from the conventional date of our Lord's death and resurrection. But someone, somewhere, has always been saying that the end is upon us.

7. Augustine just says "his side," *latus suum*, an allusion to Eve being formed from the side, the rib, of Adam, Gn 2:21-23.

8. This is in the singular in the Latin text, *intelligat*; perhaps what Augustine actually said, thinking of the "one flesh" as the subject?

9. Reading *infirmitati* instead of the text's *infirmitatis*, "advice of weakness," to which the dative could have been, so to say, spontaneously adapted by a scribe who had just written the preceding *sanctitatis*, "of holiness." The word I translate "garment" is *habitus*, and it may be thought that either "habit" or "condition" would be a more suitable rendering. But in the somewhat crude visual context Augustine is vividly evoking, I think "garment" fits best. For this whole theme see also Sermons 332, 4 (III, 9) and 392, 5 (III, 10).

10. The text reads *Qua in re sexus ab uxore discernitur*, which means "In this matter the sex is distinguished/separated from the wife"—which means nothing! As he is talking about the wife's *authority* over the husband's body, *ab uxore* must mean "by the wife," and not "from the wife." So I emend *discernitur* to *decernitur*, literally, "is decided by the wife"; and I take *sexus* here as meaning "sexual organ," the husband's. Augustine has just said that Paul calls *sexum* by the name of *corpus* for the sake of decency; and he himself for the sake of brutal clarity is clearly casting decency to the winds.

11. See 1 Pt 3:7.

12. This is a very free, possibly impermissible translation of *Non erit ut dicas mihi quoniam fornicando damnabitur.* But the whole "conversation" is somewhat incoherent; possibly some of the text has fallen out. Augustine in his reply goes on to interpret the man's words as implying a condemnation of marriage, hence of suggesting that what his wife will be condemned for is her use of marriage. This was, roughly, the view of the Manichees.

13. He leaves the sentence unfinished—no doubt dramatically with an expressive shrug of the shoulders and spreading of the hands.

14. We must here remind ourselves that it is not Augustine who is implying that there is something indecent and immodest about all sexual activity, even between married couples; it is his interlocutor, who wants to practice perfect and permanent abstinence, even without his wife's consent.

15. For similar treatment of this matter, and use of the phrase *secundum veniam* to support this very narrow judgment on the morality of sexual intercourse in marriage, see Sermons 51, 22 (III, 3) and 351, 5 (III, 10)—in which I translated the phrase respectively "by way of permission" and "by way of license." The Vulgate, no doubt thanks to Jerome's revising hand, substitutes *secundum indulgentiam.* The fact that Augustine here talks of "the good of marriage" in the singular, as though there were only one good, that of offspring, whereas he very soon came to talk of the three goods of marriage, offspring, fidelity, sacrament, *proles, fides, sacramentum,* is seen by Dolbeau as one pointer to an early date for this sermon. It is also to be borne in mind that his view on the morality of sexual activity in marriage was much more liberal than that of most of his contemporary "Fathers," particularly than that of Saint Jerome.

16. Perhaps the Latin *uti uxore* is not quite so brutally crass as this expression in English—but it probably runs it pretty close!

17. He could be referring here to his polemical *Answer to Faustus*, the leading Manichee spokesman, but not, according to Dolbeau's calculations, to his treatise specifically devoted to marriage,

The Excellence of Marriage, published in 401, in which he first begins to develop his doctrine of the threefold good of marriage. See note 15 above.

18. A totally illegitimate application of a text about swearing!

19. Emending the text's *nondum devictus es*, "you haven't yet been utterly defeated," to *nondum devinctus es*, literally "you haven't yet been tied up," that is, by the marriage bond. It is clear that in this section he is addressing a different case, that of the man who is not yet married, or the widower.

20. Again, emending *devictus* to *devinctus*.

21. *Ipso officio pietatis*, an almost impossible phrase to translate. *Pietas* is essentially the mutual loving kindness of members of a family. Here it indicates the concern of the patriarchs and "saints of the Old Testament" for the continuation of God's chosen people, their own kin.

22. Emending the text's *diligantur*, "may be loved," to *deligantur*.

23. See Nm 15:40; 1 Pt 2:9-10.

24. A non-scriptural text quoted by the Manichee Faustus, and then taken up by Augustine in his response to him and in other works, like *The Excellence of Marriage* and *The Excellence of Widowhood*. But see Dt 25:5.10 for the scriptural basis of the saying.

25. This is where the extract begins which Bede took for his anthology, Sermon 354A (III, 10). For this whole theme see also Sermons 160, 7 (III, 5) and 283, 2-3 (III, 8).

26. See Lk 11:9-10. See also Sermons 315, 8 (III, 9) and 389,2 (III, 10).

27. Emending the text's *jam*, "what you are not now demanding," to *etiam*.

Dolbeau 2
SERMON 359B
Mainz 5

SERMON OF SAINT AUGUSTINE ON OBEDIENCE

Date: 404[1]

Only the love Bishop Aurelius has for him brings Augustine to Carthage

1. Yesterday's disturbance,[2] for which I was as much to blame as you, more in fact because of my responsibility to you, would properly, I admit, be calling for silence today. But because charity, whose slave one has of necessity to be, has brought an order from our master and brother[3]—though there is also evident in you a positive lust for hearing something, which we confidently hope God will be good enough to make fruitful in your good behavior and your obedience—I am going to be your slave in the name of Christ, since I am the slave of Christ whose members you are.

This however I will confess in God's sight, personally appearing before you and before him, in whose ears my thoughts speak as loudly as words; he it is whom I summon to bear witness upon my soul,[4] that absolutely the only thing which brings me to this city, in order to say something to you as the Lord enables me, is the charity of your bishop—and I don't mean the charity with which I love him, but that rather with which I am aware of being loved by him without the slightest pretense. While it's true, I mean, that you know both of us, you cannot possibly know us in the way we know each other, we who are your slaves to serve you in the love of Christ, because of course we also love you too, God knows, as[5] you can see. Nonetheless, dearly beloved, you ought to know—I say this in the presence of Christ himself—that if you longed to have me here more than anything else that you long for, and perceived in your bishop's mind even the slightest disapproval of me, you would never see me here.

How Aurelius overruled the primate of Numidia

2. You see, he thought fit to send me a letter recently, in which he actually said that if I imagined my arrival should be put off for a while, or thought I should weigh the pros and cons of coming or not coming, then I would be

offending against the very charity which God is called.[6] Just think of my feebleness, launched upon such a long journey in the middle of winter! And here's something else for your graces to bear in mind. The blessed and venerable old man, Xanthippus, Primate of Numidia, had summoned a council to meet at Constantine on the 28th of January.[7] A council was summoned by the Primate of Numidia for the bishops of Numidia, where I too am a bishop.

In that city of Constantine, what's more, as I rather think your graces know, the bishop is one who is very close to me.[8] That is to say, he was brought up in the word of God and held the office of presbyter in the town of Thagaste;[9] from there he was given to Constantine as its bishop. I can't tell you with what sort of letters he tried to induce me to visit Constantine; when the council was also summoned to meet there, he overcame all my delays and hesitations. And yet, my dearest friends, such a letter then came to little, lowly me from my lord and brother Aurelius, your bishop, that it quite overruled by the weight and seriousness of its contents any previous arrangements I had made, and didn't so much bring me as haul me here, putting all else aside.

I reckoned, after all, that if he had seen fit to give me these orders, not merely with such assurance but with such dire threats coming not from himself but from God, then I could say to myself that if I came here and yielded to his will—or rather through him to God's—then I could quote his letter in excusing myself to my lord the old man Xanthippus for my withdrawal from that other engagement. Otherwise he might well be very indignant at my leaving the council of the Numidian bishops, where my presence was required by virtue of my very rank as one of them, and my choosing to come here instead.

A brief account of yesterday's disturbance

3. But where's it leading to, all this that I've been saying? Yesterday my own eyes could see that there was a space which wasn't fully occupied by brothers and sisters, close enough both for their ears[10] and my tongue. I wasn't responsible for the decision that the preaching should rather be done from that place;[11] it was just that we could see that those people should give way and come up to where the bishops were, rather than the bishops give way and go to that other place, which would involve a huge disturbance of the bigger crowd which had already surged round the apse to make sure of being able to hear. Was a much bigger group to be moved from this place to that?[12]

But fine, perhaps it would be all right to ignore the men; what about the weaker sex? Can there be any doubt that when the women began to press forward in their eagerness to get close, they would have made a greater din and raised voices which above all, according to all the rules of decency, should not be heard in church?[13] So the only thing we were asking was that those few people who were pressing on the altar railings would have the goodness to move up to the spaces next to the place where we were speaking. Was that a very big thing to ask? But that's just what they refused to listen to, and the disturbance followed, and great sadness for me, which God has just now been good enough to relieve by means of the sermon from your venerable bishop. For the rest, though, brothers and sisters, I must urge you not to think it was he who did not give me leave to preach from the place which some people were so obstinately asking for with their rowdy demands. There you are then, that's why I've said all this; because if I were to become aware of the slightest little reserve toward me in the heart of my most saintly brother,[14] I would not come to this city, especially with all my other responsibilities weighing heavily upon me.

None of it the responsibility of Aurelius

4. What's the case, after all? Can't your graces recall that I held forth against the party of Donatus from that place inside the altar railings for four days running?[15] Did we wait for you to ask for that? Was it even suggested by me? He of his own accord saw that it should be done, and he did it; this time he saw it shouldn't be done, and he didn't do it. But perhaps you're saying, "What's so great or difficult about what we were asking for?" Even if what you were asking for was trifling enough, there's nothing trifling about the obedience we require of you. That, you see, is what I would prefer to speak about.

Because I heard that some brothers were saying, "Look, he preached himself on the duty of serving the weaker brethren.[16] He preached on it one day, he failed to do it the next. So we should have been served. Why did he come down from the pulpit?" I will tell your holinesses why I came down. He,[17] after all, is the one I should really have to be forgiven by, seeing that I came down without his instructing me to. In fact, I deliberately came down without even consulting him, in case he should forbid me to do so. And of course if I had consulted him and he had forbidden me, I wouldn't have been able to do anything now but obey. I would have been obliged not to come down. So I preferred to ask his pardon afterward for coming down from the pulpit without consulting him or his instructing me to, rather than not do what I thought should be done.

The reforms of Aurelius carried out thanks to the people's obedience

5. Now let me tell you why I thought this should be done. Not only do I know how the people here have always obeyed their bishop when he was present, the whole of Africa knows it, and very possibly the whole world, wherever they have heard of the Church of this city. We all know, after all, what dissolute and disorderly goings on there used to be here betweeen males and females in days gone by, because I myself was part of that blot on the escutcheon. The Lord brought it about through his servant[18] that there should be no mixing of the sexes at vigils. I as a lad used to attend vigils when I was a student in this city, and I kept vigil like that, all mixed up together with women, who were subjected to the impudent advances of men, which no doubt on many occasions put the virtue of even chaste people at risk.[19]

How honorably now are vigils kept, with what chastity, what holiness! Not even those against whom these careful precautions were directed will be able to vote against them.²⁰ Those cheeky fellows themselves, impudently waylaying the chastity of others, can wring their hands over these measures, they cannot possibly fault them. But was this the only measure taken, so that maybe this is the only thing for us to rejoice at now? What about the separate passages and entrances? What care was taken, with what foresight was a way found, with what firmness was it carried out, to ensure that those who would be allotted separate places when they had come in should also come in through separate entrances! This, to prevent those cheeky, impudent slaves from beginning, as they entered through the narrow passage ways, what they would later do their best to finish: from making the remarks with which they are in the habit of embarrassing the ladies as they pass. With what a watchful eye were these things noted, how energetically put a stop to!

If we remember the things that used to go on in the church at Mappalia²¹ at the shrine of the blessed bishop and martyr Cyprian, we will still perhaps be wringing our hands over them, while if we forget them, we are proving less than grateful to God. Would your graces please join me in calling those things to mind, brothers and sisters; what I am reminding you of is the benefits God has conferred on you through your bishop. Where in those days the din of dirty songs was heard, nowadays it is the singing of hymns that lifts the roof off; where vigils used to be kept in pursuit of licentious gratification, now they are kept in pursuit of holiness; in a word, where God used to be offended, God is now being propitiated. I beg your graces not to forget these things; they are recent and can be compared with the present; they were happening yesterday, today they are not.

When, though, could your bishop ever have brought all this about, if he hadn't had charge of an obedient people? To say something too, and no small something it is, about your virtue of obedience, if you had not eagerly consented to your bishop as he strove to introduce these reforms, he would never have been able to implement them at all. So God's mercy was evident both in the bishop's diligence and in your obedience. So then, knowing all this, how submissive you always used to be, I used to hold you up as an example for others to imitate, and used to say to the tiniest little congregations in the countryside, when they were clamoring against their bishops and opposing them, "Go and take a look at the people of Carthage." So then, since I used to find your good example such an abundant source of joy, imagine how saddened I must have been yesterday, brothers and sisters, by your disobedience, as though my coming here so assiduously were teaching you how to be disobedient!

The disturbance an act of sheer disobedience

6. So would your graces please listen carefully! What made me come down from the pulpit was painful disappointment at the wretched effect of my ministry. You were insisting on being able to hear. What could the speaker build up, when the listener was threatening to reduce it to ruins?

"What do you mean, ruins?" you say. "What was so big, after all, in what we were asking? What was so bad about what we were requesting?"

I'll tell you what I mean by ruins; I'll tell you, to put the fear of God in you, not to make you fall. Don't you know that a blazing fire can spring from a mere spark? Don't you know that the tiniest drops fill rivers, and sweep away whole farms?[22] Don't let disobedience seem to you just a slight sin.

Certainly, I'll tell you straight out. It would have made not the slightest difference whether you listened from here or from there; that there was space enough near us for a crowd to fill, both I knew and you also knew. What did your opposition spring from, your refusal to come over here, but solely and simply from your obstinacy? "Either just this happens that we want, or else what you want won't happen." We, I mean to say, wanted you to be able to hear, and what we wanted would benefit everybody. There were some people though, who were just lounging against the altar rails, and when we didn't agree to their unreasonable wishes, they even shouted out, "Time for dismissals."[23] Look how far away you are, and how calmly I said, "Time for dismissals"; and there you are, you all heard me, because you were patiently keeping quiet; what if I was wishing to test your obedience now?[24] "But how could you test it," says someone or other, "in such a slight matter?"

If you don't obey in a slight matter, are you going to obey in a greater one? Haven't you read what the Lord said, *Whoever is faithful in a small matter is also faithful in a great one; and whoever is unfaithful in a small matter is also unfaithful in a great one* (Lk 16:10)?

The prohibition imposed on Adam in paradise a test of obedience

7. Do you really want to know what's so bad about disobedience, because I said, "The listener was threatening ruin"? Everything God planted in his paradise was good. If everything he made in the whole world was good, with scripture saying. *And God saw everything that he had made, and behold it was very good* (Gn 1:31), if everything, how much more the things too which he set, as being even more delightful, in paradise? So where everything he had planted was good, what can be the meaning of *Do not touch this tree* (Gn 3:3; 2:17)? Don't you realize that this is invariably made into a problem by people who cannot see either how good a thing obedience is, or how bad a thing disobedience? Look, everything had been planted good; "Don't touch," says God.

Why shouldn't I touch? Did you put something bad here? If you did put something bad here, take it away, and stop forbidding me to touch.

"Don't touch," he repeats, "this tree," which of course wouldn't be in paradise unless it were good.

Or is this perhaps what you are thinking, that outside paradise God had filled the earth with things that were all good, and in paradise had planted one that was bad? In the rest of the earth too, of course, they were all good, but undoubtedly better in paradise. And yet, because among all the good things put in paradise obedience was better still, God slapped a prohibition order on one of them, or else by not forbidding anything he might have ceased to be master.

Really? Someone will probably assume that it was out of haughtiness that

God wanted to be master. God's being master is of benefit to those he's the master of, not to God himself. Our ignoring him doesn't make him any smaller, nor our serving him make him any greater. That we are under such a Lord and master is to our advantage, not to his. In wanting to be our master he is wanting it for our benefit, not his own. He stands in no need of any good of ours; we are in need of all his good things, and above all of God himself, our supreme good. God himself, you see, is our supreme and best good, than which there can be nothing better. Notice his servant admitting this, listen to him out of the psalm: *I said to the Lord: It is you who are my God, because you have no need of my good things* (Ps 16:2).[25]

So God forbade something, in order to impose a commandment, so that he might be served as master, so that obedience might be distinguished from disobedience as virtue from vice. And that tree was called *the tree of the knowledge of good and evil* (Gn 2:9), not because apples were hanging from it, so to say, of good and evil; but the reason it was called the tree of the knowledge of good and evil was that if the man were to touch it against the commandment, he would experience in that tree what the difference was between the good of obedience and the evil of disobedience. From that tree, after all, once the commandment was ignored, came death as a consequence. Had the commandment been observed, immortality would have followed. So you can see just precisely how bad a thing disobedience is, my brothers and sisters. It was the first ruin of mankind.

Christ's example of obedience; Phil 2:6-8

8. Surely we all wish to recover from this lapse; why repeat what caused us to fall? Let Adam suffice, Christ has come. *In Adam all die, in Christ shall all be made alive* (1 Cor 15:22). From Adam the human race learns disobedience, the root of evil; in Christ it finds obedience, the root of immortality. Thus Adam was for us the author and model of disobedience, Christ of obedience. And how is Christ the model of obedience? Though he is equal to the Father, he says he is the slave of the Father. Surely you join me, you Catholics, in acknowledging the Catholic faith. You acknowledge *I and the Father are one* (Jn 10:30); you acknowledge *Whoever sees me sees the Father* (Jn 14:9); you acknowledge *And the Word was with God, and the Word was God* (Jn 1:1); you acknowledge *Since he was in the form of God, he did not think it robbery to be equal to God* (Phil 2:6). For Christ, you see, equality is not robbery, but nature. The one for whom it was robbery stood up and fell; the one for whom it was nature stayed on his feet even as he stooped down.

Let the same apostle Paul, though, spell out the full extent of the obedience of our Lord and savior Jesus Christ. It's worth the trouble to hear and remind ourselves of the whole passage. Here we are; observe the Son equal to the Father in the form of God, but read what follows: *Since he was in the form of God, he did not think it robbery to be equal to God.*

"But what did he do?"

But he emptied himself.

"In what way, emptied? I'm afraid he must have lost his equality."

Don't get that idea; listen to what follows, listen to how he emptied himself, hear how he didn't empty himself by losing what he was, but by taking on what he was not.

He emptied himself, he says.

"In what way? I implore you, tell me at once."

Taking the form of a slave.

"Who took the form of a slave?"

The one who, *since he was in the form of God*; there, "was in the form," here, "taking the form." *Taking the form of a slave, being made in the likeness of men*—made of course in the mother whom he had made—*made in the likeness of men, and found in condition as a man.*

"But we were talking about obedience. You've already said a lot,[26] and we haven't heard the word 'obedience.' I've heard *emptied himself,* I've heard *taking the form of a slave,* I've heard *being made in the likeness of men.* But prove, if you please, that he did this out of obedience."

Listen finally: *being made in the likeness of men, and found in condition as a man, he humbled himself, becoming obedient to the death* (Phil 2:6-8).

We must be each other's slaves, as Christ was ours

9. Let us take a look, we slaves, at the Lord and master; does the master listen attentively, the slave take no notice? I hope none of you are saying to yourselves, "But he did this, because he's the Lord." What did he do because he's the Lord? Did I myself say this sort of thing to you: "Kindle the sun, make the moon run its monthly course of waning and waxing; cause the stars to shine from the sky, the springs to well up from the earth, the animals to walk, the birds to fly, the fishes to swim"? Finally, did I even say this: "Open the eyes of the blind, crack open the ears of the deaf, drive off the fevers of the sick, raise up the flesh of the dead"? I'm not saying any of these things. These are the things he did as God; what I'm demanding of you is the obedience which he rendered before you as a slave.

Obedience, I repeat, is what I am demanding. By immortality you will be like him; by obedience he became like you. He will give you his life, because he accepted your death. But you're saying, "He, though, obeyed God the Father."

Well, who is it you are being instructed to obey? He, after all, obeyed God the Father as his equal. Or do you think it makes any difference that he made himself the slave of God the Father, and you are being told, "Obey your bishop"? I mean, who put your bishop over you, for you to obey him? Or has the gospel slipped your mind: *Whoever hears you hears me; whoever receives you receives me, and whoever receives me receives the one who sent me* (Lk 10:16; Mt 10:40)?

Finally, you're saying, "He made himself the slave of the Father." What if he also made himself yours? Are you too his father and his mother? Because he was prepared to have a mother here, and not a father, to show that both his "generations" were wonderful,[27] both the divine and the human: the divine one without a mother, the human one without a father. And yet as a boy *he submitted to his parents* (Lk 2:51)—read the gospel; in boyhood minority submissive to his parents, in divine majesty the Lord and master of his parents. You, though, are not his mother, and yet he also made himself your slave.[28]

I mean, he taught us to serve, not only by his words but by his example. It was little enough for the Lord to say to his disciples, *Serve one another* (Gal 5:13). The Lord, after all, is ordering it to be done; it should, of course, have been sufficient that it was ordered by the Lord. Or was it to be expected that he would demonstrate what he was ordering? Indeed, indeed, would any of us have the audacity to insist that our Lord should first carry out himself what he was commanding? And yet, without any of us having the audacity to insist on it, of his own accord he gave his disciples an example of serving one another: *Whoever wishes*, he said, *to be the greater among you shall be your slave* (Mk 10:43-44). And straightaway, in case the disciples should be upset by the word "slave," and say to him, "So, Lord, we are to be slaves, are we, we whom you have redeemed? Slaves, are we, for whom you shed your blood? Can't we recognize our right to freedom in the price paid for us, your blood?"; he soothed what was perhaps pride that was upset, not yet cured: *Shall be*, he said, *your slave, just as the Son of man came, not to be served, but to serve* (Mk 10:44-45). There you are, he even became our servant, and we aren't his mother. Or perhaps we are his mother too? *These are my brothers and my mother, who do my will* (Mk 3:34-35).[29]

Christ serves precisely by giving orders

10. "But look here," somebody will say; "my bishop should follow my Lord's example, and serve me as my slave." I'm telling your graces—let those get the point who can—if he wasn't serving you as your slave, he wouldn't be giving you orders. You see, the one who gives useful orders is serving you, serving you by watching over you, serving you by taking care of you, serving you by worrying over you, serving you, finally, by loving you. I mean, even the one who in that text made himself a servant, a waiter, certainly gave orders to his disciples. Do you want to hear him giving orders and them serving him? *Where would you like us to get the passover ready for you?* (Mk 14:12). And he sends those he wishes to, instructs them to get what he wishes ready for him; what he was giving orders about was done where he wished it, and yet it was he more than they who was doing the serving. He wasn't lying, after all, when he said, *Just as the Son of man came, not to be served, but to serve.*

"How did he not come to be served but to serve? Here you are, I see the disciples running around preparing the passover, arranging the supper; how did he not come to be served but to serve?"

But to serve them with what? He continues, *and to lay down his life for his friends* (Mk 10:45; Jn 15:13). Do you really want to know what he served up to us? What he then served up is what we are living on today, what we are being fed with today at his table.

Be the foal on which Christ rides into Jerusalem

11. *Go,* he said, *into the village which is over against you; there you will find a donkey's foal tied up on which nobody has ever sat. Fetch it, and if they say to you, "What are you doing? Where are you taking the foal?" answer, "The Lord needs it," and they will let you have it* (Mt 21:2-3).[30] They heard, they went, they did it. Was there anyone objecting, anyone saying, "Why does he want a foal fetched for him? The man, surely, who has raised the dead can't have worn himself out walking." Listen then, slave; do what you're ordered to by the one who certainly wants you in good health, by the one who is taking care of your salvation. Asking why he gave the order amounts to discussing it, not to complying with it. First comply with it promptly, so that you can then discuss it properly.

Wash yourselves, be clean; they are words of command. *Take away the vile deeds from your souls and from the sight of my eyes*; they're words of command. *Learn to do good, take the orphan's part, stand up for the widow*—have you done what he told you to?—*and come, let us discuss things, says the Lord* (Is 1:16-18). The foal was untied and led from the village which was over against them. What's the village over against the disciples, if not this world? *Go to the village which is over against you.* This world is against the disciples, falsehood is against truth, lechery against chastity, disobedience against obedience. In this village which is the world a foal was tied up, on which nobody had ever sat. What is this foal, tied up in the village over against them, on which nobody had ever sat, what can it be but the people of the nations tied up in the devil's chains, and nobody had ever sat on it because it had never carried any prophet? It's untied, it's fetched, it carries God, it's ridden by the Lord, it's directed by the Lord along the way, it's admonished by the Lord with a whip. Both by those who complied and fetched the foal was obedience displayed, and by those who let the foal go the moment they heard the Lord needed it, was obedience displayed. I would like you to understand who those people are. Perhaps, you see, it is the powers over against us that have tied up the foal; perhaps those people who had tied up the foal represent the devil and his angels, by whom the people of the nations had been tied up in knots of destructive superstition; so great, all the same, is the authority of the one giving the orders, that even they don't dare hold on to what the Lord says he needs.

Which are you, my brothers and sisters? Which do you want to be, the ones untying the foal, or the foal? Perish the thought, I mean, that you should be the ones who had tied up the foal; and yet even they didn't raise any objection. So which do you want to be, my brothers and sisters; those who untied the foal or the foal itself? You daren't claim for yourselves the role of those the foal was untied by; it was apostles who did this. This is the role of men in charge, the role we ourselves have to sustain with whatever strength the Lord is pleased to grant us, with total, anxious vigilance; it's in this role that I am speaking to you. You are the foal;[31] be obedient to those who are leading you off to carry the Lord. Of course, my dearest friends, you must reflect on the manner in which the disciples untied the foal and led it along to the Lord. They were leading it, and it was following them; I mean, they weren't dragging it, while it was digging in its heels. And yet, because we are talking about our service, our being your slaves, when the disciples were leading the foal to the Lord, they were really, in fact, being the slaves of the foal. That's how we too act as your slaves, when we lead you to the Lord, when we teach you obedience and admonish you. If your weakness wasn't being served in this way, you wouldn't have come to listen to us today.

NOTES

1. To be a little more precise, 23 January 404, the day after the feast of the popular Spanish martyr, Saint Vincent. Augustine tells us this himself in the course of the sermon, sections 13 and 14. Dolbeau concludes to the year 404 from a complex series of indications in the sermon itself, some of which will be pointed out in the notes.

2. The disturbance had occurred the day before, when Augustine had got up and gone to the pulpit to preach, the pulpit being, it seems, a movable stand. He will describe the disturbance in section 3. The upshot had been that he had come down from the pulpit without preaching at all, and now feels rather guilty about the way in which he had reacted to the disturbance.

3. Aurelius, the bishop of Carthage, one of Augustine's oldest friends, as well as the senior bishop of the African provinces.

4. That is, if I am lying in what I say.

5. Reading *ut videtis* instead of the text's *et videtis*, "and you can see." Throughout this passage Augustine is freely using the first person plural, "we, us," in the most ambiguous manner; sometimes meaning "I, me," sometimes "I and Aurelius," once quite possibly "you and me," "us all." As we have happily discarded this trick of style in English, of using the plural for the singular—except in what we call "the editorial we," we are sometimes at a loss how to interpret it when we find it in a more florid tongue.

6. See 1 Jn 4:8.16. He is surely getting in a little side swipe at Aurelius here!

7. Literally, "on the 5th of the Kalends of February." Xanthippus was "the old man," *senex,* that is to say, the senior by ordination of the Numidian bishops, and hence primate. Numidia was, roughly, the eastern part of modern Algeria. Xanthippus was bishop of Thagora, modern Taoura, and was primate from 401 until his death in 410 or 411. Thus these dates set the limits, still fairly wide ones, to the date of this sermon.

8. *De latere nostro,* literally, "from our side."

9. Augustine's home town. The implication is that he belonged to the community which Augustine set up there on his return from Milan, while still a layman. From other of Augustine's works, for example Letter 176, we gather that his name was Fortunatus.

10. Reading *et auribus eorum,* following a suggestion by one of Dolbeau's colleagues, instead of the text's simple *et auribus,* "for ears."

11. *Ut inde potius disputaretur.* Here I am sure *disputo* must be understood in the sense of discussing—hence preaching—rather than of disputing. He is not immediately referring to the dis-

pute, or rather disturbance which arose, but to the issue over which it had arisen, whether the preaching should be done from the apse, where the movable pulpit has first been placed, or from the altar rails. We have to understand that the altar was right in the nave of the basilica, with railings, *cancelli*, all round it, and that the congregation stood on all sides of it during the mass, from the offertory onward. I think Augustine is implying that the placing of the pulpit by the apse was simply the proper, customary practice, one justified too by the actual situation.

12. In the text this is punctuated as a statement, not a question. As a statement it merely looks absurd; he is surely referring to the bigger crowd which had surged round the apse.

13. See 1 Cor 13:44. It rather looks as if at this period Augustine had a kind of running feud with some of the ladies of Carthage. See Sermon 32, 23.25 (III, 2) and notes 29 and 37 to that sermon. It would have been preached, perhaps, some six months before this one.

14. Aurelius. The phrase, "the slightest little reserve . . . heart," is my rendering of *vel modicam contractiunculam in corde. Contractiuncula*, it need hardly be said, is a very rare word. Lewis & Short record its use by Cicero in the phrase *contractiuncula animi*, which they say means dejection, a drooping of spirits. While Augustine's use of it here no doubt echoes the master's employment of it, he doesn't here say *contractiuncula cordis*, but *in corde*. So I think I am justified in understanding something like affection to be the sentiment which might suffer some little contraction.

15. Dolbeau suggests that he had done this in August or September 403.

16. Possibly referring, so Dolbeau suggests, to *Expositions of the Psalms* 103 (104), Sermons 3, 9.

17. Aurelius again. Augustine had come down from the pulpit without preaching a sermon in protest against the disturbance, and had not asked Aurelius' permission to do so.

18. Aurelius again.

19. A slightly cumbersome spelling out of the more succinct—and abstract—*ubi forte et casti- tatem temptabat occasio.*

20. I take it that Aurelius' first measure was simply to arrange for the segregation of the sexes in different areas in his churches. Augustine goes on to mention what was clearly a subsidiary or secondary measure, the allotting of separate entrances to men and women. "Will be able to vote against them" is my rendering of *poterit displicere*; literally, "this diligence will not be able to displease" these people. But clearly it will displease them intensely. So I take *displicere* to have here the particular sense of saying *non placet* to a measure, of formally manifesting one's "displeasure."

21. A suburb of Carthage. See Sermon 62, 17 (III, 3) and note 32 there.

22. For these comparisons see Sermons 9, 17 (III, 1); 56, 12; 58, 10 (III, 3); 261, 10 (III, 7).

23. *Missa fiant*; see Sermon 49, 8 (III, 2), note 11, *missa* meaning the dismissal of the catechumens. The only peculiarity of our text here is that it is treated as a neuter plural noun, not a feminine singular. It will be the same in sections 20 and 23 below.

24. I think he is implying that they pricked up their ears when he said *Missa fiant*, in case he really meant it, to see whether they would obey.

25. For this whole theme see Sermons 335B, 1 (III, 9); 341, 19 (III, 11); 374, 20 (III, 11)—both these (III, 11).

26. Emending the text's *Multa jam diximus*, "we've already said a lot," to . . . *dixisti*. For this whole theme see Sermons 92, 23 (III, 3); 183, 5 (III, 5); 265E, 2 (III, 7).

27. There is an allusion here to Is 53:8, which according to the Septuagint and Vulgate reads, "who shall declare his generation"—that is, his begetting. So I have to keep the word "generation," odd though it sounds in English in this "active" sense. For this whole theme of Christ's two generations, see Sermons 140, 2 (III, 4); 189, 4; 190, 2; l96, 1 (III, 6); 380, 2 (III, 10).

28. See Sermon 51, 19 (III, 3).

29. Mk's complete text also mentions "sisters," unlike the parallels in Mt and Lk. For this whole section on service see also Sermons 51, 19 (III, 3); 340A, 3 (III, 9).

30. Here it really does look as if he is quoting from a translation of Tatian's *Diatessaron*, or some other harmony of the gospels. Neither Mk nor Lk says that the foal was a donkey's, while Mt has the disciples find a donkey and its foal, and bring them both to Jesus, and very oddly has him

sit on them both. The transition in the sermon from sending disciples to prepare the passover, in section 10, to sending them here to fetch the foal, is exceedingly abrupt. I wonder if something has not disappeared from the text in between.

31. See Sermon 189, 4 (III, 6).

Dolbeau 2
SERMON 359B
Mainz 5

SERMON OF SAINT AUGUSTINE ON OBEDIENCE

Date: 404

The authority of the bishops puts them under the feet of their people;
obedience is the daughter of charity

12. Of course, dearly beloved, *we also are human beings* (Acts 14:15), and as being weak we bishops too are carrying the Lord. You caused us grave disquiet yesterday, and in our very disquiet we feared all the more for you, in case you should be grieving in us the Spirit of God,[32] through whom we try to serve you. Imagine, brothers and sisters, imagine how deeply disquieted I could have been, already standing there and ready to address you, well knowing (as I have already reminded you) how obedient you normally are—and in my very presence you showed yourselves so disobedient, as though it were I who was teaching you disobedience, as if I wasn't in my small way holding your reins, in order to lead you to the Lord!

And yet, dearly beloved, however deeply I care about you or for you—which you heard from his own lips[33]—can it be more than he does himself, seeing that he is in a very special way at your service, set over you in such a manner that he is in fact under you? This higher place where we sit gives the impression that we bishops are set over you; yet so heavy is the burden of anxious solicitude and care for you that it presses us down under your feet. Well then, stamp on us and live![34]

What, my brothers and sisters, what is any virtue at all in a servant of God without obedience? What is obedience, after all? You all love charity; she's her daughter, obedience is the daughter of charity. Now it's impossible for charity to be barren. Accordingly, let nobody take you in, nobody say, "I don't have obedience, but I do have charity."

Charity is precisely what you don't have. Wherever this mother may be, she gives birth. If she's there she has given birth; if she hasn't given birth, she's not there. The root is hidden, brothers and sisters, the fruit is out in the open. I don't trust what's stuck in the soil, unless I can see what's hanging from the branches.

You have charity, do you? Show me its fruit. Let me see obedience, let me rejoice over obedience, let me have the child to hug, so that I can recognize the mother.

The right order of authority and obedience

13. Look how great are the good things which even bogus heroes[35] seem to have. Yesterday we heard the praises of a true martyr: what torments he endured, how hideous they were, how various, how continuous! Let charity be lacking, that would all be sheer madness. What do we sing his praises for, what should we rejoice with him for, if not because we can see in which Church, for which faith he suffered, and what the ruler he refused to obey was ordering him to do? It's not, you see, because he refused to obey orders, but because they were orders to do what it would be a sin to comply with, because it shouldn't even be called obedience, where what is being commanded is something pernicious and sacrilegious. Just as it isn't faith, after all, when something false is believed, so it isn't obedience when something injurious is commanded.

How, I mean to say, could I call anybody obedient who gives in to a man,[36] while ignoring God? Authorities in this world *have been set in order* (Rom 13:1), and over all authorities is the authority of God. You wouldn't be obedient if, by attending perhaps as a slave to your father, you paid no attention to your master. What I'm saying is this:[37] just supposing you were a slave, and your father and your fellow slave gave you one command, contrary to what your master had commanded you, and you obeyed your father rather than your master, wouldn't I have to say you were disobedient and a disturber of right order? The one to be listened to first, surely, is the one with the greater, the one with legitimate authority. So I wouldn't say you were obedient if you complied with the city manager's wishes against those of the governor,[38] or with those of the governor against those of the emperor. In the same way, I don't call anyone obedient who complies with the emperor's wishes against those of God.

Vincent obedient, in putting God's commandment
above the emperor's decree

14. So what is it that made Vincent obedient, made him holy, made him the winner of a true crown, made him victor over so many sufferings, and thus true to his name?[39] What is it? Look at who was giving the orders, to whom he was giving them, what the orders were. The emperor was giving the orders,[40] he was giving them to a Christian, he was ordering him to offer incense to idols. If you pay attention to the ranks of the one giving and the one receiving the orders,[41] the emperor gave orders to a provincial.

"So it looks as if there's a place for obedience here, when I hear who gave the orders, and to whom he gave them."

But wait; notice what orders he gave: to offer incense to idols: "Let anyone who does not offer incense to idols be punished." Let the provincial now comply,[42] if no higher authority gives orders to the contrary. But prick up your ears, ready to hear two voices; hear one from the bench, hear the other from heaven. What did you hear from the bench? "Whoever has not sacrificed to the gods shall be punished." What from heaven? *Whoever sacrifices to the gods shall be rooted out* (Ex 22:20).

Here let your obedience be truly tested, dear martyr. Distinguish the voices, weigh the authorities against one another. You can see the one who's giving the orders, fear rather the one who is countermanding them. Here's the crown of martyrdom, here's the triumph, with the devil routed and trampled underfoot, whose wheedling the martyr feared, whose wrath he ignored. He expressed this himself, as we heard when the account was being read, he expressed it in his own words; when the one who was savaging him appeared to be willing to take pity on him, that's when the martyr had supremely to be on his guard.[43] Some crafty pity, you see, could do him much more harm than open savagery. The roaring of the angry lion didn't terrify him; he didn't deny that he feared the wheedling of the dragon's pity. He's both lion and dragon, you see, the one with respect to whom it is said, *You will trample on the lion and the dragon* (Ps 91:13).

The devil more to be feared as serpent than as lion

15. So let none of you say, dearest brothers and sisters, let none of you say—because you are just deceiving yourselves if you do say it—that the Church doesn't suffer persecution nowadays, because the emperors are Catholics, because since they are going to give God an account of their rule, they give all their orders on behalf of the Church, they are intent upon its progress. Let none of you make that a reason for saying that the Church doesn't suffer persecution; it doesn't suffer from the lion, but the dragon doesn't sleep. Listen to Peter warning us about him as a lion in the manifest sufferings of the saints, and encouraging the martyrs to conquer him triumphantly: *Your adversary the devil,* he says, *is prowling around like a roaring lion, seeking whom he may devour* (1 Pt 5:8). In those days, you see, the nations were making horrifying threats and showing savage ferocity against the saints of God, in those days hostile edicts were being hurled at them, and the authorities were furiously thundering against them; the lion was roaring, but the dragon wasn't keeping quiet either.

You've heard Peter encouraging them in the face of the lion; listen too to Paul putting them on their guard against the dragon: *I have betrothed you,* he says, *to one husband.*[44] There were many, you see, who wanted to become the husbands of one woman. Now just think a moment, brothers and sisters, just think what many husbands make one woman into. They make her into what has to be thought about, for us to detest it, but not spoken out loud for us to be shocked by it. So then there were many who wanted to be husbands to the one woman.[45] But that man who was a *friend of the bridegroom* (Jn 3:29), and jealous for the bridegroom, not for himself—*I have betrothed you,* he said, *to one husband, to present you as a chaste virgin to Christ. But I am afraid that just as the serpent seduced Eve, so your minds too may be corrupted from the chastity of God, which is in Christ* (2 Cor 11:2)—he was afraid she would be corrupted, not by the savagery of the lion, but by the wheedling of the dragon. Peter warned you that for God's sake you shouldn't worry about the lion; Paul is warning you that for God's sake you should be on the watch against the dragon, and in God should *trample on the lion and the dragon* (Ps 91:13).

Having previously made false gods, the devil now makes false martyrs

16. Because you want to know, don't you, what this dragon is like, how totally to be avoided are his snares, how great is the cunning of the enemy? Here you are, for almost six thousand years[46] now he has been flexing his muscles tempting the saints, and has made many false gods against the one true God. But then there came the one and only Son of God, as foretold by his heralds sent ahead of him; there came the Son of God, he undid the works of the devil like the tie-rope of that foal,[47] he taught by word, he gave support by example; he showed that the one true God is to be worshiped, he alone to be adored and not any angels in his place—though of course the angels too, because they love God, because among them charity reigns supreme, wish God to be loved together with them, not themselves in his stead.[48]

So after teaching these things he also taught this: that the saints have to die, if necessary, for this teaching.

"For which teaching?"

The one which has *charity from a pure heart and a good conscience and a faith unfeigned* (1 Tm 1:5). It was to die for this that he taught God's saints, and then commended them to the veneration of the Church.

"To be venerated on what grounds?"

Precious in the sight of the Lord is the death of his just ones (Ps 116:15). That's what makes Peter's death precious, what makes Paul's death precious, what makes the death of Vincent precious, what makes the death of Cyprian precious.

"Well, what makes them precious?"

Their coming from pure charity and a good conscience and a faith unfeigned. Now that snake in the grass saw this, that ancient serpent saw this—martyrs honored, temples deserted; because that cunning and venomous watchfulness against us could no longer make false gods for Christians, it made false martyrs. But as for you, sprigs of the Catholic Church,[49] I appeal to you, spend a little time with me comparing these false martyrs with the true martyrs, and turn your loyal and godly faith[50] to distinguishing what the devil is making every effort with his venomous deceitfulness to confuse.

It's the cause, not the penalty that makes martyrs

17. That one wants to obscure for us the distinction between true martyrs and false ones, he wants to put out the eyes of the heart in order to stop us distinguishing them. He wanted to do this against them through something similar in form; but let us, against the devil, pay attention to the apostle, where

he says about some people, *Having the form of godliness, but denying its power* (2 Tm 3:5). What is the power of godliness? Charity;[51] that mother, remember, of obedience. Accordingly, take a look at the form under which the devil attempts to link false martyrs with true martyrs.

"Look," he says; "they too suffer persecution."

You're still, you enemy of ours, still confusing the issue. They suffer persecution, you say. Go on, bring on bandits, murderers, parricides, adulterers, sorcerers; don't these too all suffer persecution?

Didn't my Lord foresee your wiles and warn us? My Lord whom I accept, and yours too, like it or not, because he would also be mine even if I didn't like it; but his being my Lord is the making of me, because I accept him and like it, and it would be my undoing if I didn't like it. Weren't you foreseen, ancient enemy, by the one who, in encouraging his disciples to see the glory of suffering,[52] said, *Blessed are those who suffer persecution for the sake of justice* (Mt 5:10)? Against all your poisons, against your two-tongued or three-tongued or multi-tongued[53] attempts he was on the watch with one word: "for the sake of *justice.*" Because of this word, murderers suffer persecution and are not martyrs, adulterers suffer and are not martyrs. Now you just show me your martyrs; you boast that they suffered, I ask why they suffered. You're praising the punishment, I'm examining the cause. I'm examining the cause, I repeat, I'm asking about the cause. Tell me why he suffers, the one whose suffering you're bragging about. Is it for the sake of justice? Tell me that; that, after all, is the cause of the martyrs. It isn't, you see, the penalty that crowns the martyrs, but the cause.[54]

18. Oh, you enemy of ours and cunning seducer, against your false martyrs the true martyrs cried out in the psalm, *Judge me, O God, and distinguish my cause from an unholy nation* (Ps 43:1). *Judge me,* he says, *and distinguish my cause.* You can see, dearly beloved, how many things he passed over; it was his cause he wanted distinguished. It's precisely the cause, after all, that distinguishes him. The true martyr didn't say, "Distinguish my fasts"; I mean, they also fast in the same way. He didn't say, "Distinguish my good works, which I do for the poor"; they also do them, you see. He didn't say, "Distinguish my baptism"; they too have the same one as we do.[55] He didn't say, "Distinguish my creed"; they too confess the same one as we do. In all these things he found he was like them; it was only his cause he prayed to have distinguished.

Distinguish my cause. I fast and he fasts. But why do I, why does he? I do it for Christ.

"But so do I," he says, "do it for Christ."

Really for Christ? If it's for Christ, I think, then of course it's also for the words of Christ. If it's against Christ's words, clearly it's against Christ.

"And what," he says, "are the words of Christ against which I suffer?"

Are you really so raving mad in your false suffering that your heart has forgotten the true preaching? Take a close look at our common Lord, whom you confess together with me, even when you don't believe him.

*To confess Christ, the bridegroom, you must also confess
the Church, his bride*

19. Just see if Christ didn't wish to show us both himself and his Church, in such a way that those invited to the wedding and wearing a wedding garment[56] would not be mistaken about either of them, neither about the bridegroom nor about the bride. How did the bridegroom show himself? *It was necessary for the Christ to suffer and to rise again on the third day* (Lk 24:46). I recognize the bridegroom; that is what the prophets too had said, what the servants had said who had been sent out in advance to invite people to the wedding. *It was necessary for the Christ to suffer and to rise again on the third day.* That's how he was showing himself to them, that's what he was demonstrating to the doubters as fulfilled in himself in accordance with the prophets.

What about the bride? Surely he didn't keep quiet about her, did he? He went on immediately to show us her too. After all, he could see that she[57] was already being desired in consequence. *It was necessary,* he said, *for the Christ to suffer and to rise again on the third day.*

"Fine, I can see the bridegroom, fine, I recognize the bridegroom. What about the bride?"

And for repentance and forgiveness to be preached in his name throughout all the nations, with you beginning from Jerusalem (Lk 24:46). This is the Church you must acknowledge if you are a martyr, the Church expressly named by Christ's own lips, foretold by the prophets, his heralds, this the one you must hold onto; shed your blood in this Church and for this Church, pay back what has been previously paid out to you.

Listen to the apostle John: *That's why,* he says, *Christ laid down his life for us, because we too ought to lay down our lives for the brethren* (1 Jn 3:16). Wake up! For the brethren, not against the brethren. What's the use of your confessing the bridegroom, of your honoring the master of the household, and I don't say neglecting his wife, but inveighing against her with false accusations? You, man, have a wife whom you didn't redeem with your blood; but still you love her in such a way that if someone were to pay his court to you, attending at your house every day, throwing himself down at your feet, lauding your name to the skies, never and nowhere ceasing to sing your praises, and were to bring a single accusation against your wife, all his services would go for nothing.

True and false martyrs compared

20. Accordingly, let the confessions of the true and of the false martyrs be produced and compared; let us set before our eyes the spectacle we were watching yesterday. We saw, I mean to say, a certain most delightful spectacle;[58] the martyr contending against the ruthless force of ungodliness, true faith not overwhelmed by any pain or penalty, Vincent everywhere victorious. We saw it all, we were actually present. That account of his passion spoke to our hearts; we were enthralled. That ancient serpent, jealous of the martyrs, that snake in the grass whose blandishments Vincent was on his guard against, being unable

to find fault with that martyrdom, stirred us up to be quarrelsome; let them admit it and be sorry for it, those who lent him the use of their tongues. What else, after all, was the meaning of those shouts, "Announce the dismissal; the dismissal, announce the dismissal,"[59] if not that the praises of the martyr should not continue any longer?

So let us compare them, compare the confession of the true martyrs and the false martyrs. The reason I'm calling you a martyr[60] is that you are standing up to authority. To authority ordering you to do what? Look, I can hear what the true martyrs were ordered to do; let me also hear what you were being ordered to do. I can see how glorious their refusal was, because I can see what it was they refused to do; now it's your turn to show me what you refuse to do. Let me compare your words, your refusals, let me see which I ought to imitate, which to follow.

"Offer incense to the gods."

"I refuse."

We've heard the glorious voice of the true martyr, now let us also hear it from that side:

"Make peace with your brother."

Oh what an abominable reply, and one rightly to be condemned not only by God above, but also by human authorities!

"Make peace with your brother."

"I refuse."

Certainly, you are suffering punishment against Christ.[61]

Appeal to the Donatists to be reconciled with their brothers

21. Open the gospel, read it: *If you have been offering your gift at the altar and there have remembered that your brother has something against you, leave your gift there and go first to be reconciled with your brother, and then come and offer your gift* (Mt 5:23-24). *If*, he says, *you have remembered that your brother has something against you.* What's the meaning of "has something against you"? You've wronged him, you've carried out something unfairly against him. "*Go to be reconciled with your brother*; I accept a gift from those at peace with one another." What kind of gift are you offering at God's altar, when your heart has in it the devil's throne? Who sowed discord there, who planted it, who finally is dwelling there? Isn't that one always the sower of discord, the author of divisions, the source of all quarrels?

If Christ said this about two individuals, inculcated such care, such fear, required concord so seriously that it's as if he said, "You're offering one thing, I'm indicating another; I will also take what you've offered, if you bring along what I've indicated"—if all this for two individuals, how much more for two large groups?[62] If it's dangerous and deadly to be involved in such a case against one individual, how much more so against the whole world, how much more so against that whole bride of Christ, spread *throughout all the nations, with you beginning from Jerusalem* (Lk 24:47)?

22. Or perhaps you have a case against me? The Lord, after all, did say this: *If you have remembered that your brother has something against you* (Mt 5:23). So you will be saying to me, "Your brother, he says, has something against you; well, I on my side have something against you, because you on yours have nothing against me."

So let's inquire, then; if the fault is found in me, it's I that must put it right; if it's found in you, you then put it right. Explain to me the case you have against me; I on my side can tell you what I have against you in next to no time. What I have against you is what my Lord has against you. You are leveling accusations against his lady,[63] and his lady is the whole wide world in his holy and faithful followers; this is the one you are bringing a charge against. Or have you conducted an inquiry, have you given judgment? In what court were you sitting, when did the whole wide world stand before you to be tried? You don't even take cognizance of your neighbor's case;[64] have you definitively passed judgment on the whole wide world?

I can cite the records, I can show who the real betrayers were; I read that the very ones who sat in judgment on the innocent Caecilian had confessed to their own crimes; the public archives declare that it was your predecessors who were the first to transfer the case of Caecilian, bishop of this city, to the emperor Constantine. However I am not imputing to you the villainy of your predecessors.[65] As far as I'm concerned, the whole matter is closed, and I won't blame you for someone else's misdeeds. You, however, don't bring forward anything by which to convict my predecessors, and yet you accuse me, though I was born so many years later.

"So then," he says, "if you don't impute to me the deeds of my predecessors, why impute to me your own deeds?"

Which deeds of mine?

"That you are not with me."

And why is it bad for you that I am not with you? Didn't I tell you that the case I have against you is the one my Lord has against you? Listen to him talking: *Whoever is not with me is against me* (Lk 11:23).

Concluding assurance of their bishop's love for them,
and appeal for their obedience

23. And so, dearly beloved, to the best of my ability, and perhaps a little beyond it, with your eagerness forcing me on, so that we might together make up for yesterday's unpleasantness, I have perhaps been rather more talkative than was called for, keeping us all standing for longer than our feebleness, whether yours or mine, could really take. But I shall make this my main plea to you, and with this I prefer to conclude the sermon; since I have just reminded you of that saying of our Lord's which we should certainly not be careless in heeding: *If you are offering your gift at the altar, go first to be reconciled with your brother* (Mt 5:23-24), let us be reconciled with each other from the heart.

First and foremost you must never suppose that your bishop, either yesterday or at any other time at all, gets angry with you out of hatred; no, no, it's out of love. Never can what he owes you for Christ's sake be shaken out of his heart. Let the clouds of yesterday give way to clear skies. Let us call back, not merely charity which has never departed, but also the old cheerful spirit, so that all of us together, as we have often encouraged you in Christ, may take care to be of service to the weaker brethren to their advantage, not just to do what they want even when it's harmful. After all, dearly beloved, you certainly have to be at the service of sick patients in such a way that when perhaps they ask for food, or when they refuse it, you have to make yourself something of a nuisance to them, and worry them and insist, and force them to take it in case they die; but that doesn't mean that you must put yourself at their service in such a way that even if they ask for poison, you give it to them.

So then, please, please don't get into the habit of this great evil of disobedience. And don't let any of you ever say again, "Well what's the fuss? Were we, please, asking for poison, because we wanted the pulpit moved from one place to another?" It's disobedience that's the poison, that's what slew the first man. Is this what I'm objecting to, brothers and sisters, that you asked for this? No, truly I can assure your graces, that even if you had continued asking for it a little longer, all the same you couldn't have displeased me by asking, as you did displease me by getting angry and saying, "Time for dismissals." That's what I really want you to be sorry for.

When you ask for something, if it seems right, then it's granted you; if it doesn't seem right, then please change over from making the request to showing compliance. If, however, it's into anger that you are determined to burst out, into confrontation and provocation of those who serve you in Christ with such thoughtful care, then that is already poison, if indeed it isn't death itself. Don't do it, brothers and sisters, I beg you, I implore you; you must distinguish the church of God from the theaters.[66] It's here in church that it's customary for all those bad things which are done in theaters to be punished, customary for them to be healed, customary for them to be brought back to confession and to repentance, not for them to be brought in and done here. To surge forward here, to shout back here, to dominate the scene here—may God remove such ideas from your hearts and from our sorrow; and may we always find joy in your obedience.

NOTES

32. See Eph 4:30. For this whole theme of the bishops being the servants of their people, and so to say under their feet, see Sermons 23, 1 (III, 2); 134, 1; 146, 1, note 3 (III, 4).

33. Aurelius' lips.

34. *Postremo, calcate et vivite.* Either savage irony, or else meaning, "Stamp on us, exact the service we owe you, which is to govern and direct you."

35. The text just says, *habere videntur et ficti*; "even the bogus seem to have." Dolbeau suggests we should understand *martyres* after *ficti* (I put "heroes" to give a wider reference), and he suspects that something has dropped out of the text, perhaps a few dismissive remarks about Donatist martyrs or circumcellions. The good things they appear to have are of course "virtues" like courage and constancy. The true martyr they celebrated yesterday was Saint Vincent of Saragossa, who was actually put to death in Valencia.

36. Emending the text's *qui credit homini*, "who believes a man," to *qui cedit homini*.

37. I suspect murmurs of disagreement were heard here from the congregation, or rather of shocked surprise, "piety" toward parents being one of the most sacred of duties.

38. He is contrasting the authority of a *curator* with that of the *proconsul*.

39. *Vincentius*, deriving from *vinco*, "I overcome, conquer"; hence meaning the same as *Victor*.

40. Actually the emperor's representative, Dacian, the governor of Spain. The emperor was Diocletian, and the date of Vincent's martyrdom 304. See Sermon 274, note 1 (III, 8). In general, see all the sermons on Saint Vincent in that volume, 274—277A, though Sermon 277 is not really about the saint's martyrdom, but about the resurrection.

41. The Latin just says, perhaps Augustine just said, "the ranks of the one giving the orders," *gradus jubentis*. I have supplied "and the one receiving." Augustine could not very well have said *jubentis et jussi*, as that would have meant "of the one giving the orders and the orders given."

42. Reading *obtemperet*, instead of the text's *obtemperat*, "the provincial now complies."

43. Vincent's words, according to the account of his martyrdom, his *passio*, were: "I don't fear your punishments, whatever you may command in your rage; what I dread much more is your pretending that you want to show mercy."

44. For this theme see also Sermons 213, 8 (III, 6) and 299, 12 (III, 8).

45. By these Augustine would be thinking, quite happily anachronistic, of the various heresies of his time.

46. The generally accepted age of the world at that time. See Sermon 93, 8 (III, 3); also *The City of God* XII, 12.

47. See Lk 19:30.

48. See Rv 19:10; 22:8-9. See also Sermon 198, 16, 24, 46 (III, II).

49. Emending *catholica germina*, "Catholic sprigs," to *catholicae germina*. He used this word, *germina*, in Sermon 34, 6 (III, 2), where it is translated "seedlings," when he was addressing, it seems clear, the newly baptized *infantes*, "infant" Christians. It also occurs in Sermon 146, 1 (III, 4), where he is addressing, as here, the long-standing faithful; so I there translate it "sprigs," as here. In both cases it is *germina catholicae*; and it would surely have been the same expression here.

50. *Pia fide*; that impossible word, *pius*. Immediately in the next sentence we have the noun, *pietas*, with references in the next note to sermons in which it is translated, for want of a better word, "godliness," since that is quite a good translation for the Greek word lying behind it, *eusebeia*.

51. See Sermons 229U; 229V (III, 6); 269, 3 (III, 7). For charity the mother of obedience, see section 12, above.

52. See 1 Pt 4:14.

53. *Multilingues*, a word possibly invented by Augustine, so Dolbeau suggests, for the occasion.

54. See Sermons 53A, 13 (III, 3); 94A, 1 (III, 4); 327, 1; 328, 4; 331, 2; 335C, 12 (III, 9).

55. This makes it crystal clear that the false martyrs he has in mind throughout are those of the Donatists. While they denied the reality of Catholic baptism, the Catholics accepted the validity of Donatist baptism, and of all their sacraments.

56. See Mt 22:2-14.

57. Reading *eam jam consequenter desiderari*, instead of the text's *eum . . . desiderari*, "that he was being desired." But if Augustine had wanted to say that (which seems highly unlikely, it being a thoroughly inconsequential thing to say), and had said *eum*, he would have been making a bad grammatical mistake. No, he would have used the reflexive pronoun, and said *se . . . desiderari*. For this use of this text against the Donatists see Sermons 116, 6 (III, 4); 162A, 10; 183, 11 (III, 5); 238, 3 (III, 7).

58. That is, the account of Saint Vincent's martyrdom.

59. *Missa fac; missa, missa fac.* See section 6 above, note 23.

60. He seems to be addressing his congregation as an individual, as a "false martyr," for standing up against the true authority of the bishop. But in fact it will emerge that he is addressing a representative Donatist (some were no doubt present). The confusion, the ambivalence was possibly deliberate, to shame his Catholic congregation.

61. And not for his sake. Dolbeau says that this appeal, "Make peace with your brother," fits the policy launched by the Council of African bishops held in August 403, while it would be almost unthinkable after the imperial edict of union issued in February 405—unless of course the final sentence of this section refers to the penalties imposed on the Donatists by that edict.

62. Literally "for two peoples," *in duobus populis.*

63. His *matrona.*

64. That is, the case of the Catholic Church in Africa. The Donatists condemned the rest of the Catholic Church in other countries simply as being guilty by association.

65. See Sermons 47, 17 and notes 26 & 30 (III, 2); 164, 12, note 11 (III, 5); 340A, 12, note 20 (III, 9); 358, 5, 6, notes 9, 17, 18; 359, 5-6 (III, 10).

66. See Sermon 252, 4, note 14 (III, 7).

Dolbeau 24
SERMON 360A
Mainz 60

TREATISE OF SAINT AUGUSTINE THE BISHOP ON THE TESTIMONIES OF
SCRIPTURE AGAINST THE DONATISTS AND AGAINST THE PAGANS

Date: 403[1]

Hear, daughter, and see; the Church being addressed in Ps 45:10

1. God's promises were the foundation of faith for our ancestors, and God's gifts are the fulfillment of faith for us. In them the promise was made to us, in us it has also been kept for them. There are two senses of the body through which faith enters: hearing and sight. They heard, we see. But they too see in us, and we too heard in them. That's why God also addresses the Church itself in this way: *Hear, daughter, and see. Hear*, he says, *and see, and forget your own people and your father's house, since the king has desired your beauty.* Which king? He goes on to say: *because he it is who is your God* (Ps 45:10-11). What then must be the dignity, the grandeur of the woman for whom God is her king, and for whom her husband is God! *Hear*, he says, *and see, and forget your own people and your father's house.*

He fixes something in her memory, to remove something else from her memory. She used to be, you see, under the authority of another father, and in another people. The Lord, in fact, once said to those who were still unbelievers, and still darkness,[2] *You people are from your father, the devil* (Jn 8:44). It's the people, though, of the ungodly who are the devil's son and his gang, belonging like parts of his body to a head that is doomed. She is commanded to forget this father's house and this people by hearing and seeing, listening and looking, so that she too might reply from another psalm in the persons of her faithful members, *As we have heard, so too we have seen* (Ps 48:8).

What was heard by our ancestors is seen by us

2. What our ancestors heard was, *In your seed shall all the nations be blessed* (Gn 22:18). This is seen by us, because it is being fulfilled in us.[3] What they heard was, *There will be a root of Jesse, and one who will arise to reign among*

354

the nations; in him shall the nations hope (Is 11:10 LXX; Rom 15:12). From Jesse David, from David the lineage of Christ. The root of Jesse, Christ, is now reigning among the nations, in him the nations now hope. They place their hopes in their king as provincial subjects of their king, and slaves of their lord and master, and fellow heirs of their brother. All this, just as it is woven into the many colors of the queen's gown, so is it plainly evident to our eyes and to our faith. You see, about this queen it was said, *The queen has taken her stand at your right hand, in a garment of cloth of gold, and robed in many colors* (Ps 45:13-14). What are the many colors of her gown? The great number of languages. Latin speakers talk in one way, Greeks in another, Punic speakers in another, in another Hebrews, in another Syrians, in another Indians, in another Cappadocians, in another Egyptians. Variety in color, unity in weave. Many colors, I mean to say, all included in the one woven cloth, embroider it, they don't tear it. Variety of speech, but unity of charity.

And how could the apostle say, *This is our boast, the testimony of our conscience* (2 Cor 1:12), which the eyes of God are turned to, which is open to the sight of the one we have become pleasing to, unless because[4] he forgave us, while we were sinners, what made us displeasing to him, and endowed us with the means of pleasing him? So because it has come about that by his gift, not by our own merit, we can say with the apostle and from the apostle, *This is our boast, the testimony of our conscience*, it is therefore also said of that queen, *All the loveliness of the king's daughter is within* (Ps 45:14 LXX). She is being outwardly adorned with fine clothes to be visible, while being inwardly formed by faith to be saved. By what means, if not by hearing and seeing, as she was told, *Hear, daughter, and see* (Ps 45:10), so that she might reply, as we said, and sing in harmony with, and somehow be echoed by, all her members, *As we have heard, so too we have seen* (Ps 48:8)?

The sign of Gideon's fleece

3. The whole world was bare of Christians, and dry for lack of grace. There was one people worshiping God, sprung from the fleshly stock of Abraham by descent through the generations. In this people were many saints, prophets, just men, patriarchs, our ancestors; in it grace was to be found in the worship of God, and the merit that deserved and the hope that looked forward to receiving a reward. And this was one nation among all the nations, with the whole world otherwise being devoid of this grace. Come now to our times; that nation alone has remained in drought for lack of this grace, and the rest of the world has been well watered.

Now let me tell you how a sign of this was given in advance in the time of the ancestors. It's after its solution that I am putting the problem, which is normally solved after being put. So please forgive me when I put it, after this little introduction. In the book of Judges it's written how Gideon, going off to battle, to fight for his country against the foreigners, asked for a sign.[5] He was apparently asking for a sign with reference to the matter in hand; but that particular sign wasn't really suited to that particular matter which he had in hand. He was asking for something there and then, he was foretelling something in the future.

What is he asking for, after all? Listen; here it is. He is asking God for a woolen fleece to be placed on the threshing floor, and he wanted rain to be found on the fleece, so that the fleece should be wet, the whole threshing floor dry. He asks for a second sign and says to God, *Lord, let not your wrath be angry with me; I would ask for yet a second sign, and make trial yet again with the fleece. This is what I am asking; that the whole threshing floor may be wet, the fleece dry* (Jgs 6:39). He got his sign; the next day he found the fleece dry, the threshing floor soaked.

The threshing floor is the world, in the fleece is the Jewish people. The whole world was devoid of this grace, so the threshing floor was dry. This grace was to be found with the Jewish people, but "in the fleece." What does "in the fleece" mean? Not in a manifest faith, but it was hidden in a kind of cloud of wool, it wasn't out in the open. It wasn't there to be shown in a public demonstration but rather to be wrung out in a trickle. *The fleece was wrung out, and filled a basin with water* (Jgs 6:38). And not for nothing a "basin," a *pelvis*; a *pelvis*, you see, is so called from *pedibus luendis*, from washing feet.[6] So the very wringing out of the fleece dripped Christ. Christ, you see, as an example of humility, washed the feet of the disciples in a basin.[7]

So the fleece is dry now, Christ has been wrung out of it. He has indeed been wrung or pressed out, because he was thrown out through oppression. *The tenants said*, you see, *This is the heir; come, let us kill him, and the inheritance will be ours. And they killed him*, it says, *and threw him outside the city* (Mk 12:7-8).[8] Having wrung out the fleece, they tossed the water away outside. From it, however, to spread further afield the humility of the one who had been wrung out, he took whom he would[9] and went to the nations, to fulfill the second sign; the fleece being now dry, he watered the threshing floor. And this faith is not concealed in the woolly cloud of the fleece, but is openly manifest; it is proclaimed to all, it is known by all. It celebrates its sacrament in secret,[10] its word in public. All these things are to be seen now, exactly as they were foretold; exactly as promised has payment now been made. *As we have heard, so too have we seen* (Ps 48:8), because it was we who in the unity of the Church[11] were told, *Hear, daughter, and see* (Ps 45:10).

The Donatists betray the scriptures by not following them

4. But now the heretics on the other hand, having cut themselves off from any links with this global reality,[12] neither wish to hear what they read nor to see what they know. We have been invited to the wedding, we have been praising the bride, and presenting her divine testimonials from the scriptures. We have been presenting our own testimonials to ourselves, or rather it is the Lord who gives us a testimonial. Let them open their eyes and see what they have heard.

You hear with me, you there, so see to it you see with me. Or rather, the case is much worse; you both hear with me and see with me, and you are not together with me.[13]

So why be surprised, brothers and sisters, if the pagans refuse to hold onto what they scorn, when the Donatists refuse to believe what they read? The pagan wanted to consign this volume of mine to the flames, he detested the scriptures themselves, he persecuted them. Small wonder, wouldn't you say, if it pains him to live according to what he wanted to burn?

You, however, you heretic, say that you saved this volume from the flames. As you didn't want it burnt, acknowledge it when it's produced, listen to it when it's read. This volume certainly contains these words: *In your seed shall all the nations be blessed* (Gn 22:18). You certainly didn't want these words to go up in flames. Why have you gone up in flames yourself over them, in your lust for dissension? Why, I beg you, if not because you're lying, because you say that you saved what you have in fact handed over and betrayed?

Don't let's go into what happened a long time ago;[14] let the volume itself be produced, let the one that has been preserved from the flames judge between us. Let's see who it is that belongs to the eternal flames, who it is that has handed this volume over to temporal flames. Both the one who had the audacity to burn the scriptures[15] and the one who was shameless enough to hand them over wanted them destroyed, but they weren't destroyed. They were preserved, they're safe, let them be produced. You ask by whom they were handed over, by whom they were preserved. Let them be produced, let them be read; anyone who believes them didn't hand them over and hasn't betrayed them.

Do you want to see how dear to me that scripture is? It's read, and I follow it. Do you want to see how hateful it is to you? It's read, and you fight back, you resist, you turn a deaf ear.[16] Since you haven't any ears in your mind, you have closed your mind; the scripture you say you have preserved is knocking, and you don't open. If you really have preserved this volume, your bookcase is better than your mind. But perish the thought I should believe that you saved, when it was being searched for, what I see you rejecting when it is being read. From the volume that has been saved you want to fit me up with a crime; from the volume that has been read I can show the crime is yours.

The pagan, if he doesn't believe, hates what I read out; you, though you don't want to appear to have been led by a pagan into committing an impious act, have surpassed the pagan in impiety. He hates this object and chucks it away; you hold on to it and deny it. You say that I burnt the will and testament, while you can see that I hold the inheritance; you say that you preserved the will and testament, though you have disinherited yourself. I produce the will, I read the will; you don't want me to produce it, produce it yourself. Yes, you should bring into court what lends my case support.[17] Bring it in yourself, hold it yourself, open it yourself, read, see. Your hands as you hold it, your eyes as they see it, your tongue as it speaks the words, are all on my side. It's from your side that I'm pleading my case against you. The one who chants from the volume in your congregation, yes, he's your reader, he's my witness.

But these ones[18] hear and see, while those others neither hear nor see. Let us pass on from these, and leave them, if it can be done without persistent animosity, to reflect on their impiety by themselves.

He turns to the pagans, who are less to blame than the heretics
for not believing the prophecies

5. Now the pagans that are left are still left for this reason, so that our faith may still have those who reject it, in order to have God to protect it. May he address them,[19] and let them know that what is happening was written down before it happened, and that its future happening was foretold; and they shouldn't be appalled because things are happening which they don't like, but should rather believe that they are happening because God promised they would. However much they would have liked their will to be done, God preferred his promises to be kept. They mustn't be angry with him; he, I rather think, is better than they are, he is more powerful. However superior they may be, God is greater.

So I have selected a few instances from the holy scriptures, as many as I could for want of time, of how the prophets foretold that sooner or later the time would come when idols would be done away with, and this has been fulfilled, just as they foretold that the time would come when the Church would spread through the whole world, and this too has been fulfilled in the same way. So we shouldn't be too indignant with the pagans because they refuse to believe this about the idols, when the heretics refuse to believe it about the Church. They both see the facts, they both fail to believe, but the former pay no attention, the latter are attentive readers.[20] The pagan's crime of not believing what he pays no attention to is not as great as the heretic's of not believing what he reads so attentively. But all the same, insofar as the things that have been foretold are being fulfilled, the pagans too ought to recognize and acknowledge who the foreteller is and the fulfiller. So then, let me give you some of the things that have been said on this point.

A text from the book of Wisdom

6. Here's what's written in the book of Wisdom: *Therefore notice will also be taken of the idols of the nations.*[21] It's as if, you see, God used to take no notice of the idols worshiped for so long, of the sacrifices so long offered to idols. The time came when the one who always sees also takes notice; he saw and put up with it; he took notice and put a stop to it. *Notice will be taken,* it says, *of the idols of the nations, since creatures of God were made hateful* (Wis 14:11). You see, they vex God by means of God's own creatures. How do they vex God by means of his creatures? Well, a carpenter made a god, but God the wood. A goldsmith made an idol, but God the gold. Why, from his material, do you make something he's bound to hate, out of God's creation fashion wrongly what he's bound to hate? See to it that you are well fashioned into what he's

bound to love. You want to put your image on a piece of wood; receive God's image in yourself.

What are you erasing inside, and what are you engraving outside? *Creatures of God*, it says, *were made hateful, and into temptations for the souls of men, and into a mousetrap for the feet of fools. For the beginning of fornication is the devising of idols.* If a woman can be praised who has many men, let the soul too be praised which worships many gods. If a woman becomes an adulteress through real men, how much more does the soul through false, unreal gods? *For the beginning of fornication is the devising of idols, and the invention of them the corruption of life.* There you have what he convicted them of; now let's see what he predicted for them: *For neither were they there from the beginning, nor will they be there forever* (Wis 14:11-13).

Another from the prophet Zechariah

7. Zechariah the prophet also says something similar:[22] *On that day.* Notice what he means by "that," and recognize what day it is. He puts "day" for "time," by the way, like the apostle: *Behold, now is the acceptable time, behold now is the day of salvation* (2 Cor 6:2). So what is Zechariah saying? *On that day there will be an open place for the house of David.* That's the thing I was saying was closed up in the fleece, open on the threshing floor.[23] *There will be an open place*; there will be a publicly manifest Church. What's the meaning of "there will be an open place"? *A city set on a mountain cannot be hidden* (Mt 5:14). *There will be an open place for the house of David. And it shall come to pass on that day, the Lord will banish the names of the idols from the earth, and no mention will be made of them at all* (Zec 13:1-2).

Let the pagans listen to these words. Let them observe that what was foretold is all happening. If they love divination, let them recognize divinity. Why do they make such a big thing of going to one crazy astrologer to consult him about one single person—and his words are likely to be more often false than true, as it's through false ones he likes to make mischief?[24] So why does he want to listen to what an astrologer is going to say about one single person? Let him listen to God making forecasts about the whole human race. The names of the idols are being wiped off the face of the earth, the names of Christians are being written in heaven.

Another from Isaiah

8. Let Isaiah also say, *And the wrongdoing[25] of men shall be humbled and fall, and the Lord alone shall be exalted on that day, and they will hide all things made by their hands, taking them into the dens and caverns of the rocks* (Is 2:17-19). Just see if that's not now the case, just see if it isn't happening, just see if scripture is lying. As though we for our part were looking for idols, and not rather wishing to make the worshipers of idols into worshipers of God, they hide them in the earth, hide them in some den, hide them in some rocky cavern.

Wherever they hide one, it's dragged out of there when it's overthrown in their hearts.

How many there are who hid their gods when they were going wrong, and brought them out[26] when they put themselves right! Because, to generalize, we can see two sorts of people in the Church, or rather one sort of them in the Church, the other in the neighborhood of the Church, both the sort who hide the idols and the sort who reject them and bring them out. Each sort was foretold by God. You have heard about the sort who hide them; now in the same chapter, in the one single testimony of Isaiah, hear about the sort who bring them out and toss them aside: *The Lord*, he says, *shall be exalted on that day, and they will hide all things made by their hands, taking them*[27] *into the dens and into the caverns of the rocks, and the crevasses of the earth, from the face of the fear of the Lord, from the splendor of his might, when he rises up to crush the earth* (Is 2:17-19). What does "crush the earth" mean? To terrify the earthy. That's why we say of any bold, pushful characters, when they turn fearful, that they've been crushed by fear. It's not surprising that the earth is afraid, because heaven is thundering; the thunder comes from the prophetic scriptures.

So people of that sort will hide them; what about the other sort? They too *from fear*, but from a better kind. The first sort of people hide the idols out of fear of the laws;[28] this second sort, out of fear of the divine law, bring them out and toss them aside. It's fear that prompts each sort, but some show a profit from fear, others a deficit. We've heard about the hiders of idols, now let's hear about the other sort: *For on that day men will throw away their abominations of silver and gold which they have made* (Is 2:20). It's rather wonderful that gold and silver should be thrown away; piety is throwing away what impiety loves. They are throwing away their abominations, but aren't they also throwing away their wooden ones, also throwing away their earthenware ones, also throwing away their abominations made of stone? Still, to impress upon us the example of a more total commitment and devotion, "they throw away," he says, "their gold and silver ones." What do people love, who no longer love gold? What losses are they afraid of, when they no longer fear the loss of gold and silver?[29]

They throw away their abominations of silver and gold, which they have made to adore. The former sort hide these *vain and noxious things,*[30] the latter throw them away. In either case, the abomination is done away with. Yes, let it be done away with—and if only it could be done away with from the hearts of earthly men, as it has been from these earthly places! May God do away with these things from places through the hands of his servants, through his own hands from people's hearts!

Others from Jeremiah

9. Let's also listen to Jeremiah. Although I also mentioned this yesterday,[31] it's such a lovely text, and can do with repeating today as well—after all, we can't possibly be sick of it yet: *Lord, my strength, and my help and refuge in the day of evils* (Jer 16:19). My refuge is no longer stone and wood, no longer do I

find refuge in *gold and silver, the work of men's hands.* I don't, he is saying, run for refuge to those who can't run away themselves; *they have feet and cannot walk* (Ps 115:4.7). *Lord, my refuge in the day of evils,* in the day of trials and temptations, in the day of this heavy labor, in the day of sickly life, in the day of sighing with longing for the *Jerusalem that is above* (Gal 4:26). As long, after all, as we are not where we are eager to be, it is a day of evils. We are *rejoicing in hope* (Rom 12:12), not yet in the real thing.[32] Thus we also have in another psalm, *You have led me along, because you have become my hope.* Our hope along the road, when he is leading; and how is he our refuge? *A tower of strength in the face of the foe* (Ps 61:2-3).

So what about the idols, what was going to happen to them? *To you,* he says, *the nations shall come from the ends of the earth and shall say: How our fathers did gain possession of lies!* That "how" is expressing the astonishment of the children at the error of their fathers, as if they were saying, "Oh how sensible our ancestors were, how they worshiped these objects, how they bent their upright posture double before wood and stones,[33] how they forsook the one by whom they had been made, and took possession of vain things which they made themselves!" *How our fathers did gain possession of lies!* What were those lies? *Idols, and they are of no use at all* (Jer 16:19). There are some money-grubbers, no doubt, to whom lies sometimes seem to be of use; and the businessman will swear falsely in order to sell at a dearer price, he will swear by Lucre in order to make money, will tell a lie by Lucre in order to make money,[34] will tell a lie by an idol in order to perish.

Not that these lies are of any real use, if we reflect on what is of genuine and salutary use. But at least that's how it seems to men, that's what ignorant people think.[35] In this case, though, to conclude, what are you spending to hire a craftsman, spending to feed him, spending to adorn the idol, spending to set it up, spending to sacrifice to it? You're spending all that to make no money out of it, to lose a great deal, and to perish yourself.

10. Jeremiah again: *Do not walk in the way of the nations.* Hey there, my brothers and sisters, let none of you spring to the defense of idols. Every defender of idols is next door to being a worshiper of idols. *Do not walk in the way of the nations, and do not shrink in dread from the signs of the heavens, since their countenances fear these things* (Jer 10:2), since it's customary with the nations to be afraid of the signs of the heavens, that is, to pick days when you can travel, when a wife may be married, when a piece of cloth may be woven, when another may be torn up[36]—*since their customs are vain.* And now hear what he says about idols: *It is wood cut from the forest, the work of a smith, and a casting of silver.* He seems to be talking about a familiar object, but the one he's talking to is excessively deaf. He's trying to rouse him from a kind of sleep, so that he may see with his mind what he already sees with his eyes. *The work of a smith and his casting,[37] they are adorned with silver and gold, they fix them firm with hammers and nails, and they will not be toppled* (Jer 10:3-4).

It is beaten, chased silver; and he adds, *they will not walk. From Tharsis will come gold of Ophaz*—precious gold and plenty of it—*and the hands of crafts-*

men (it is all the work of craftsmen) will clothe them with blue and purple. They are picked up and taken away, since they cannot walk. Do not fear them, since they can do no harm, and there is no good in them. Thus shall you say to them. What shall we say to them? *Gods which did not make heaven and earth, let them vanish from the earth and from under heaven* (Jer 10:9.5.11; the LXX order). What's the meaning of "Thus shall you say to them"? You're Christians, listen to the prophet; thus shall you say to them, don't keep quiet: *Gods which did not make heaven and earth, let them vanish from the earth and from under heaven.* Not from heaven, surely, where they never were?

Let those idol-worshipers too[38] observe how these things were foretold; let them observe it and believe. Let these gods vanish from under heaven, let those people be *written in heaven* (Lk 10:20). Yes, certainly, thus shall you say to them. Don't be led astray by those who say, "Don't either worship or mock at idols." Take the advice, rather, Mr. and Mrs. Christian, of the prophet; listen to God, rather, through the prophet: *Thus shall you say to them: gods which did not make heaven and earth, let them vanish from the earth and from under heaven.* And as though he were to ask, "Whom shall I worship, when these have vanished?" *God made heaven and earth by his power* (Jer 10:12). Why do you want to worship earth, with earth and on earth and you yourself made from the earth? You have God founding the earth;[39] he hasn't withdrawn from you in his work; let him not either be a stranger to your mind.[40] It's he that made what you tread on, he that made what you look up at; let him be the one in whom you believe.[41]

God made the earth by his power, he founded the globe of the earth by his wisdom (Jer 10:12). Listen to the apostle Paul: *Christ the power of God and the wisdom of God* (1 Cor 1:24). *He stretched out the heavens and the multitude of waters in the heavens, and he has brought out the clouds from the ends of the earth, he made lightning into thundershowers, and brought out light from his treasury. Every man has turned foolish from his knowledge, and every craftsman has been confounded over his sculptures, since they have cast lies, there is no breath in them. They are vain, works to be made fun of; they shall vanish at the time of their visitation* (Jer 10:12-15). The false gods disappear; you, though, have not remained without the true God, provided you are Jacob the younger son, whom the elder serves.[42] Let the false gods vanish; as for you, hold on to the true one. I mean, listen to what comes next: *Not of this kind is the portion of Jacob.* These vanities, these false gods shall vanish, but the portion of Jacob does not vanish. "The portion of Jacob," the inheritance of Jacob. The inheritance of Jacob which God gives him, or which is God himself? I make bold to say that it is God himself. I accept the psalm, the statement is plain: *Lord, the portion of my inheritance* (Ps 16:5). *Not of this kind is the portion of Jacob, since the one who fashioned all things, he is his inheritance, the Lord is his name* (Jer 10:16).

11. We have heard the predictions, what was going to happen to the idols; now let us hear the precepts, what is to be done with the idols. Nobody should say, ". . . are going to vanish."[43] Certainly it was said that the idols were going to vanish; may he abolish them; as for you, what are you breaking?[44] But God wished to abolish them by means of people whom he did not wish to see perishing. *And he will lead you in,* he says, *to the Amorite and the Hittite and the Perizzite and the Canaanite and the Girgashite and the Hivite and the Jebusite, and I will rub them out. You shall not adore their gods or serve them. You shall not act according to their works, but overthrowing you shall overthrow them and smashing you shall smash their idols* (Ex 23:23-24). And, *Behold, I myself will cast out before your face Amorite, Canaanite and Hittite and Perizzite and Hivite and Girgashite and Jebusite. You shall not make a covenant with those occupying the land into which you will enter to them, lest it become a trip-wire for you among you all. You shall overthrow their altars and smash their monuments and cut down their groves. For you shall not worship foreign gods. For the Lord is a jealous God, his name is God the Jealous* (Ex 34:11-14). Listen, brothers and sisters; you're shaken to the core because it said, "the Lord is jealous." O soul of the Church, O that wife of his, you're afraid of your husband's jealousy; guard and preserve your chastity.[45]

NOTES

1. By comparing the text of the sermon with other of Augustine's works whose dates are fairly certain, and with certain external events, namely the enactment of imperial laws against pagans and Donatists, which are likewise securely dated, Dolbeau concludes that it was preached between 401 and 405—I just take the mean—and most probably on 30 June; this because Augustine, in quoting at length Jer 16:19 (section 9 below), remarks that he had also referred to it the day before; and the only other sermon in which, to our knowledge, he does quote it is 299A (Mz 9), preached on the feast of Saints Peter and Paul.

2. See Eph 5:8. For a parallel to this line of thought, see Sermon 110, 4 (III, 4).

3. See also Gn 12:3; 28:14. See Sermons 22, 4 (III, 2); 113A, 10 (III, 4); 159B (III, 11).

4. Following a suggestion of Dolbeau's, who at the beginning of the sentence suggests reading "how," *quomodo,* instead of the text's "since," *quoniam,* and here reading *nisi quia* instead of the text's simple *quia,* "because." Left unemended the text is both incoherent in itself and at odds with the context.

5. Jgs 6:36-40.

6. Here, where I put the English of his far-fetched Latin etymology, he explains the probably archaic word *luendis* by adding, *id est a pedibus lavandis.* Then comes an almost impossible little phrase, *tanquam pelvis quod pedes luat.* That *quod* cannot be the relative "which," with *pelvis* its antecedent, because this is a feminine noun, while *quod* is a neuter pronoun. I omit it, treating it as a marginal gloss, explaining how Christ can be signified by a basin—which Augustine does not in fact say, anyhow, and as a gloss could be translated, "as a basin, because he washes feet."

7. See Jn 13:5.

8. A curious variation on the text. It could be an echo of Lk 4:29, where the inhabitants of Nazareth "cast Jesus out of the city," intending to push him over a cliff. But see also Acts 7:58, where Stephen is "cast outside the city" to be stoned, and Rv 14:20, where the winepress of God's wrath is trodden "outside the city."

9. The apostles and first disciples, and the converts at Pentecost.

10. A reference to the "discipline of the secret." Although in Augustine's time most non-Christians would know about the eucharist, it was still only celebrated with the baptized faithful present, after all others, most of them catechumens, were dismissed at the end of "the mass of the catechumens," shortly after the homily. But when he says, literally, "it has the sacrament in secret," I think he is also suggesting that this practice is somehow represented by the water "hidden" in the fleece. That Old Testament sign was, in Augustine's language, also a sacrament.

11. He simply says, "in the unity." I feel I have to add "of the Church" to make his meaning clear; "the unity" was one of his names for the Church. He is about to turn his attention to the heretics (the Donatists) who were outside that unity, and its enemies.

12. Literally, "with this *orbis*," this "orb." The word usually occurs in the phrase *orbis terrarum*, the round world. Here he clearly means the worldwide Catholic Church.

13. An imaginary Donatist is being berated.

14. That is, the question of who really handed over the sacred books to the authorities during the great persecution launched by Diocletian in 303. In the previous sentence Augustine did insinuate that it was in fact the leaders of the Donatist schism, not the Catholic bishops, who had done this. But what he wants to discuss now is their present betrayal of the scriptures by their disregard for what they say.

15. He just said "it," *illam*. But this is the feminine pronoun, and *codex* (the volume) is masculine. So in his mind, it seems, he has turned *codex* into *scriptura*. I put them in the plural, as being our more customary usage in English.

16. Literally, "you estrange your hearing," *alienas auditum*.

17. *A te proferatur quod pro me legatur*; literally, "let that be produced by you which is read for me," but spoken, I suspect, purely for the sake of the easy-to-remember rhyming jingle.

18. The Donatists; he is now going to turn to the pagans again.

19. Through the scriptures which he is going to quote. The singular here, *Adloquatur*, is Dolbeau's emendation of the text's plural *Adloquantur*. Reasonable enough; but it is just possible that Augustine did use the plural, of which the antecedent would be either "our faith and God" or "the scriptures."

20. His contrast in Latin is a more effective word-play: *alii neglegunt, alii legunt*; literally, "the former ignore, the latter read."

21. See Sermons 113A, 9 (III, 4), and 299A, 7 (longer text, III, 11).

22. Reading *simile* for the text's *Zacharias similis propheta*, "Zechariah a similar prophet also says." Dolbeau remarks that the word *similis* is scarcely legible in the manuscript. In the next sentence the edited text lacks "that" (*illo*, quoting the quotation); but it is inserted by one of the correctors of the text, who may well, Dolbeau thinks, be right.

23. Back in section 3.

24. An almost impossible parenthesis to translate—put in, I suspect, purely for the sake of the play on words, and to suggest that astrologers were frequently actuated by malice: *et plura falsa quam vera dicat per casum, qui in falsis facit occasum*.

25. *Injuria*; a curious reading, entirely unsupported by the Greek Septuagint, which has "the highness (grandeur) of men."

26. To be smashed.

27. The Latin here omits "taking them in," *inferentes*, which occurred in the previous quotation of the text. This is presumably by an oversight of a copyist; Dolbeau does not remark on it.

28. Imperial laws, in particular a law of 399 against pagan cults.

29. For the same treatment of idols see Sermon 23B, 8 (III, 11).

30. *Vana et noxia*, possibly the Old Latin rendering of "the moles and bats" of the Hebrew, which the Greek Septuagint also partly follows.

31. It would seem, in Sermon 299A, 7 (III, 11), preached for the feast of Saints Peter and Paul. See note 1 above.

32. The familiar *spes/res* jingle, though here rather subdued: *in spe gaudemus, nondum in re.*

33. I think there is an allusion here to the woman in the gospel who had been bent double for eighteen years, bound by Satan, Jesus says (Lk 13:11.16). Augustine would certainly have taken her to be a type of the Gentiles in Old Testament times.

34. I am assuming that he is personifying *lucrum* here; *in lucro jurat ut acquirat, in lucro mentitur ut acquirat.* It's hard to make sense of the remark otherwise.

35. Dolbeau, for some reason, treats this statement as a question; but in the Latin manuscript text, as he tells us in the apparatus, it is a statement. And such, surely, the whole drift of the passage requires it to be.

36. Caesarius of Arles in a sermon (52, 2) mentions "wretched women who in honor of Jove refuse either to weave or to spin on a Thursday" (the day of the god Thor for us, of Jove for the Latins: French *Jeudi*).

37. He seems to have misquoted the first time, reading out *conflatio argenti*, "a casting of silver." Now he phrases the passage correctly: *Opus fabri et conflatio, argento et auro adornata.*

38. In addition to the Christians who in practice "defend idols" by observing various pagan superstitions.

39. Dolbeau puts the question mark here, instead of after the previous "earth," where I put it. But that, so he informs us in his apparatus, is where the Mainz manuscript also puts it. With his reading, the whole joint sentence would run: *Quid vis colere terram, cum terra et in terra et tu, factus ex terra, habes deum fundantem terram?* "Why do you want to worship earth, when earth and on/in earth and you yourself, made from earth, have God founding the earth?" But this makes the grammar of the central section most peculiar, as my literal translation indicates. And to treat *cum* as the conjunction "when," which his punctuation requires, instead of as the preposition "with," when it is followed immediately by *et in terra et . . . ex terra*, is to strain language and credibility to breaking point.

40. Emending the text's *non est alienuset a corde*, "he is not either a stranger to your mind," to *non sit alienus . . .*

41. Again, a similar emendation of *ipse est in quem credis*, "it's he in whom you believe," to *ipse sit in quem credis.*

42. See Gn 25:23. The reason this allusion is made will become clear in a moment. For extensive treatment of the Jacob/Esau theme, see Sermon 4 (III, 1).

43. The gap in the Latin text is indicated as coming after *Peritura*, "are going to vanish." Dolbeau then himself suggests repeating *Peritura* as the beginning of the next sentence, thus filling in part of the lacuna.

44. This could be translated, "As for you, why are you breaking them?" In that case he would be discouraging his congregation from going round smashing idols, in line with the policy of Aurelius and the other bishops, because they didn't want their people taking the law into their own hands, and very possibly provoking riots. See Sermon 24 (III, 2), especially note 1. But the text he goes on to quote at length positively enjoins the smashing of pagan idols; so he is perhaps more likely to be suggesting that his hearers are being too slow in smashing their domestic idols, or in giving up their pagan superstitions.

45. From the supreme kind of fornication, which was idolatry and the worship of alien gods.

Dolbeau 25
SERMON 360B
Mainz 61

SERMON OF SAINT AUGUSTINE PREACHED AT BOSETH
WHEN THE PAGANS WERE ALLOWED IN

Date: 404[1]

God is to be both loved and feared

1. The word of God never ceases to admonish and to encourage us with trustworthy promises and salutary threats. It's not good for us, after all, either to stop loving or to stop being afraid. Now just as we have to love God the maker of promises, so we have to be afraid of God the utterer of threats. In neither role does he deceive the hearer, in neither does he disappoint the believer. None of you should be saying to yourselves, "What he promises us is real, but what he threatens us with is make-believe." Each is real. Love him, and fear him. Without the slightest doubt the one who has already come is going to come again. Now he came in order to teach you patient endurance, he is going to come again to award you the prize for patient endurance. When he comes, he will assuredly award the prize to what he taught when he came; and what he threatened when he came, he will carry out when he comes.

Now there are these two prospects: God's promise, eternal life; God's threat, eternal punishment. If you don't yet know how to love what he promises, at least start being afraid of what he threatens. That, you see, is also what scripture says: *The fear of the Lord is the beginning of wisdom* (Ps 111:10), while the apostle John says, *There is no fear in charity, but perfect charity turns fear out of doors* (1 Jn 4:18). So as soon as we hear, *The fear of the Lord is the beginning of wisdom*, let us start being afraid. But because fear brings torment to the heart, you won't be long in torment if charity grows in you and is perfected. It cannot, however, get started in you, unless you make your heart ready with fear to receive the seeds of charity. Once charity takes root, though, the more it grows the more fear diminishes. And if it diminishes to the extent that charity grows, when charity is at its peak fear withers away altogether.

We can form no proper idea of the good things God has prepared
for those who love him

2. You see, dearly beloved, it's not only impossible for our words to express what God promises us, it's beyond the powers of any human thought to conceive it. I mean this is how it is also presented to us: *What eye has not seen nor ear heard, nor has it come up into the heart of man, what things God has prepared for those who love him* (1 Cor 2:9). If it were some sort of color or light such as the eyes in our heads are acquainted with, it wouldn't say, *Neither has eye seen*; if it were some sweet sound such as human ears usually delight in, like organ music, or that of other musical instruments, it wouldn't say, *nor has ear heard.* And because the only good things human beings can mull over in their thoughts are what they have perceived through the senses of the body, it adds, *nor has it come up into the heart of man.* After all, Mr. & Mrs. Man, you can't think about any good thing, except such as you have been in the habit of seeing or hearing or encountering with some such sense, nor can anything that hasn't entered through a sense of your body be the subject of your thoughts.[2]

The inner eye of the heart needs to be cleansed
in order to see the light of God

3. And so when we're told that we are going to be in paradise, we think of some pleasant garden.[3] And if we think of something on a grander scale than we are accustomed to see, we are still only amplifying the same kind of thing. If, for example, we are accustomed to seeing small trees, we think of them as big, and if we are used to this or that kind of apples or fruits, we think of them as larger. If we're used to seeing meadows of a certain size, we can unroll them in our minds to a limitless immensity, but we're still only increasing in our thoughts the same things as we have got to know with our eyes. Again, when we hear that God *dwells in light inaccessible* (1 Tm 6:16), we measure that light from this kind that we perceive with our eyes, and amplify it to an infinite degree, but we still do it by increasing this that we know, whereas in fact that light is of a totally different kind; it is the light, after all, not of eyes but of minds.[4]

Now our fleshly eyes need to be cleansed if they are to bear this bodily light, which shines from the sky above and gleams from lamps at night; and if the eyes have been hurt and disturbed by some internal secretion or something getting into them from outside, they will feel the light they have usually been nourished by to be painful, and will be tormented by what they have usually rejoiced in. In the same way too, to be capable of bearing that intelligible and immortal light, it is not the eye of flesh but the eye of the mind and heart that needs to be cleansed. Because just as the eye of flesh is disturbed in its functioning by that gummy secretion which causes inflammation, so is this other one by iniquity. So just as this eye of the body needs to be cleansed in order to see its bodily light, in the same way that inner eye too needs to be cleansed in order to see that light which *neither eye has seen nor ear heard, nor has it come up into the heart of man* (1 Cor 2:9).

4. Why has it not come up into the heart of man? After all, it's by the heart or mind that it is perceived, when and if it is perceived. But why has it not come up into the heart of man? Because it's "of man." Why because it's "of man"? Those of you who know the scriptures will understand, and will be running ahead in thought to what I'm going to say. "Men" is what our scriptures, by a certain twist of meaning, call those who are still fleshly-minded. They are, after all, "men," that is, they are Adam.[5] Now you know that Adam sinned, and that from that source all who are born into this mortal life derive the origin of fleshly desire. So they carry with them that wound of the inner eye, and are each and every one of them "man" as long as[6] they have in them what was damaged and disturbed in its functioning by the first sin.

That's why someone cries out in the psalms, and says to God, sighing and groaning, *And the light of my eyes is not with me* (Ps 38:10). So as long as "men" have fleshly-minded sentiments like that, they cannot reflect upon that other light, nor grasp it with their minds, and that's why it says, *What eye has not seen nor ear heard, nor has it come up into the heart of man* (1 Cor 2:9). What does it mean, "of man"? Of one still carrying Adam. So then, those who were men, what did he want to make them into,[7] those for whom it was a disgrace that they were "men"? He says to them, you see, *For since each of you is saying, I am Paul's man, I though am Apollo's, I though am Cephas'* (1 Cor 1:12; 3:4). You see, they had been sharing out God's ministers among themselves, and making themselves parties out of the Church of Christ, thus initiating the evil of schisms, which were later on made permanent by the errors of men. They were saying these things because they were entertaining fleshly-minded sentiments, and pinning their hopes not on God but on man,[8] not singing from the heart what we were singing a few moments ago: *In you our fathers hoped* (Ps 22:4).

5. So the apostle says, upbraiding them for talking like that, *Are you not men,[9] and walking according to men?* (1 Cor 3:3). Again it says in a psalm, speaking in the person of God, *I myself said: You are gods, and all of you sons of the Most High. You, however, shall die like men, and fall like one of the princes* (Ps 82:6-7). As you know, by one of the princes he means the one who has been the devil from of old. For though he was an angel, he fell away through pride and became the devil. So the one who fell away at that time and was jealous of the man still standing upright, he is the same as the one who now at this time is jealous of man returning to grace.[10]

The reason men were reduced to being mortal[11] was to train them up to humility by punishing them with affliction, so that being scourged, after a fashion, by their own mortality, and reflecting that they cannot live here very much longer, and that even if they did live much longer they would still not live here always, and that some time or other this life would have to come to an end, they would humble themselves before God and strive to lay hold of the future life, while the present life is fleeing away.

After all, you cannot hold onto something that is fleeting or slipping away. Or can any of us now, either I myself as I stand here and talk, or you as you all stand and listen, can any of us hold onto our age, so that children won't grow up and young adults won't grow old? You can see that time has passed since I started to speak; and if time has passed since I started to speak, and it is the case that by length of time we decline toward old age, already in this time I've been speaking we've all aged a little. Now these changes in our condition can be grasped by reason, but cannot be observed with the eyes. Because you can't even see your hair growing, and yet if it wasn't continually growing, you wouldn't go looking for a barber every few days; after all, what the barber is going to cut off tomorrow doesn't all just grow in a night. Well, just as our hair is growing now, but cannot be seen to be, so too at this very moment we are all getting nearer to old age, yet this fact cannot be grasped with the eyes.

The shortness and uncertainty of life; the need for humility

6. So men love the present life, which fleeting as it is they cannot hold on to, and which slips away equally while they grow up and during their declining years. So how much better for them to hold onto something firm, to which they are going to come when this life is at an end! Add to this that while the life of man is short, it is also uncertain, because even if every man could be certain of old age, he still ought to reflect how short life is, even if all were allowed to reach the finishing post. What, after all, is really long if it comes to an end? So add to this that death is the constant companion of your mortality, and that as she steps along beside you on the road, you haven't the slightest idea of when she may take possession of you.[12]

Since then life is not only short, but quite uncertain with death looming at any age, men ought as they reflect on this to behave humbly before God, to entreat their creator, to confess their sins and groan over them, to tell their doctor of their sickness so that they may be inwardly cured, and have that inner eye cleansed, with which alone that light may be seen that never can be seen as long as a man's inner eye is still that of "man."

So they should wake up when they hear God saying, *I myself have said, You are gods and all of you sons of the Most High* (Ps 82:6). What's the meaning of "I myself said"? It's I who am calling you to this, I who want to make you into this. Listen to the gospel: *He gave them the right to become children of God* (Jn 1:12). So then, "While I myself say, You are gods and all of you sons of the Most High, *you however shall die like men*, and not even your mortality is any use to you in prompting you to straighten yourselves out; but no, you insist on being to all intents and purposes immortal. Very well, in that case *you shall fall like one of the princes* (Ps 82:7); that is, you are behaving just as proudly as that angel had the audacity to behave." But if pride was able to cast down an angel, what is it going to do with mere man? So you will be gods; and if you don't worship false gods, you yourselves will be gods. And how will you yourselves be this? By him making you into gods who also made you into men. The one, you see, who made us men wants to make us gods, not gods to be worshiped instead of him, but gods in whom he himself may be worshiped.[13]

Be God's throne by being humble

7. So there is then, as I started to say, dearly beloved, an inner eye which is wounded and disturbed by sins, by fleshly lusts and earthly desires, to such effect that the man himself who sinned heard the words, *Earth you are and into earth shall you go* (Gn 3:19). So if the proud, unruly man deserved to hear the words "Earth you are and into earth shall you go," why should not the humble, God-fearing man hear, "Heaven you are and into heaven shall you go"? It's by being humble, in fact, and God-fearing that he becomes God's throne. And when he has become God's throne, isn't he already heaven? It says in the scriptures, *Heaven is my throne, while the earth is the stool for my feet* (Is 66:1). So if heaven is God's throne, be heaven, in order to carry God. When you start carrying God, you will be heaven.[14]

But in order for you to carry him totally, he himself will clean you up when he starts living in you, until he brings that eye of the heart and mind to such a state of cleanliness that it can actually see the face of him in whom it believed while it couldn't see him. So then, believe before you actually see, in order that with your heart *cleansed by faith* (Acts 15:9), you may deserve to see what you have believed. A light, after all, is being promised you, which *neither has eye seen*, because it isn't a color, *nor ear heard*, because it isn't a sound, *nor has it come up into the heart of man* (1 Cor 2:9), because man who is properly called "man," fleshly, feeble, merely animated,[15] can only think about what he has taken in through the senses of the body. Not of such a kind is that light. The soul must not presume to form any idea about God as fancy may suggest. It must first learn to "unfind" the one it wishes to find.

The importance of "unknowing" God

8. What's this I've just said: it must first learn to "unfind"? That when it's reflecting on God, and something occurs to it that it has seen, perhaps the beauty of the earth occurs to it, it must clear it out of its mind.[16] The loveliness of the waters occurs to it, the tranquillity of fine clear weather occurs to it, all this too must be cleared out of its reflections. It must say to itself, "This is not my God, it's the work of my God." This is not, I repeat, my God, it's the work of my God; you're reflecting on what has been made.

O my mind and heart,[17] look for the one who made these things. When, though, your reflections reach the heavenly bodies, don't let even that heavenly light seduce you, not even in its supreme form. What I mean is, the supreme form of heavenly light is to be found in the sun. The primacy of brightness among the heavenly bodies is accorded to the sun, which suffices to light up the day. Don't even think of your God as being anything like that, not even by increasing that brightness to something greater, and wandering off by yourself into the spaces of your imagination. That isn't God either, which your mind represents to itself as of the same kind of light as normally shines for the eyes of the body. God is not this.

God is not even like the human soul, great though that is

9. Come now to the soul itself, because it too cannot be seen. The soul cannot be seen, and it is a great force of a non-bodily nature. I mean, the soul is not a body, it is something invisible and it is something great; it cannot be seen, but from its works stand amazed at what you cannot see. What is it that delights you about everyday human affairs? Look round at the order imposed on things, at the beauty of cultivated fields, of thickets uprooted, of fruit trees planted and grafted, all the things we see and love in the countryside; look at the very order of the state, at the noble piles of buildings, at the variety of arts and crafts, at the number of languages, at the depths of memory, at the ripeness of eloquence. All these things are works of the soul. How many and how great are the works of the soul, all of which you can see, and you can't see the soul itself!

So when some nature of that sort starts occurring to you, is it now at last your God whom you were seeking? It can't be seen, already it's something non-bodily, it's something spiritual, something great, which quickens even mortal bodies, which restrains and holds in check the body's flux, so to put it, of putrescence. But this is something that an animal's soul can do too. The soul of an animal, indeed, is also something great, it too is something invisible. But pass beyond it to the soul of man; observe where man is made to the image of God.[18] He is, of course, not made to the image of God in his body but in his mind, in that element by which a person directs and regulates all these activities, in that part by which a person surpasses the great beasts. How many beasts, after all, are superior to us both in strength of body and in acuteness of the senses of the flesh! Both in speed of movement and in all our bodily endowments we are outdone by many beasts. What is it that makes us better than the beasts, if not our having understanding, if not our having the power of reason which enables us to tame even wild animals. We on the other hand cannot be tamed by any wild animal. Now just as man is capable of taming beasts, so the only one capable of taming man is God.

So when something like that occurs to you, and you think of the human mind as being free at least of bodily ties, don't you dare to imagine that God is any such thing as that. You will already, indeed, be having a closer sight of him, but still at a great distance. Closer, in that there is nothing above the human mind nearer to God; but all the same, between your mind and God who created your mind, there is the greatest difference. It's not that some nature or place lies between, but it's dissimilarity that puts the distance between them, in that the mind has been made, and God made it, and what has been made cannot in any way be compared to the maker. Nonetheless in your mind there is to some extent the image of your God.

The inner eye requires an inner light to see by

10. Pass beyond even your mind, if you can—provided, of course, you have reached a genuine conception of your mind. Take a good look, brothers and sisters, at what I'm saying. It may be, after all, that when you think about your

mind, being habituated to the senses of the flesh you think of something bodily, so that your mind seems to you to be air or fire, or this light which you can perceive. You're thinking of something like that when you're thinking of your mind. Well, don't think of anything like that. The moment it strikes you that you understand something, say to yourself, "What is this sheer fact that I understand things?" Obviously, I mean, unless there were some sort of light there, you wouldn't understand. You can discern, you see, an inner light in the same kind of way as you discern the outer light. The light of your body, after all, is your eye.[19] But when there's no light, what's the use of opening your eyes? You have your own lights, indeed, whole and entire; but it's only with the help of another light that you can see.

In the same way too, when you understand something, there's a similar I don't quite know what that is able to enjoy an inner light, which is not this kind that you see with your eyes. Think of your mind as being that sort of thing, if you can; but if you can't, what kind of thing is that being above your mind, who terrifies your mind, who encourages your mind, who fashions your mind? You cannot think worthy thoughts about that being above the mind—how could you?[20]—whom you are going to see with a mind that has been cleansed. So then, if you can't even do this, and your God cannot rightly be said to be earth, or heaven, or air, or this starry light, or that so marvelous force and nature of the rational soul itself, you are bound in every case to say, "This is not my God."[21]

God promises us what has not come up into the heart of man

11. So then, you cannot know what he is unless you first learn what he is not. So first reflect on what he is not, in order to discover what he is. This is what I said a short while ago: Learn to be ignorant of God, in order to be worthy to find him.[22] You learn, you see, to be ignorant of him with an ignorance that is better than false knowledge. Ignorance that is not going astray, after all, is better than what is called knowledge and isn't really so.

You will be saying to me, you see, "I know God." I inquire what God is. You start wanting to explain, and straightaway you show your ignorance, by thinking you can explain what you are unable to reflect upon. So you are going to tell me your ideas, you're going to tell me the things "that have come up into your heart." But notice that you are "man," that what you're going to tell me "has come up into the heart of man." The being, however, who promised himself to his lovers to be enjoyed by them, certainly didn't promise what eye has seen, or what ear has heard, or what has come up into the heart of man. How, on the other hand, can they love one whom they cannot see, unless it's by believing before they see? So what is he promising to his lovers? *What eye has not seen, nor ear heard.* Perhaps he can be reflected on? Don't kid yourself; *nor has it come up into the heart of man* (1 Cor 2:9).

12. Well, what then? How can you prepare yourself? Say, "I want to see my God." Tell him, "I want to see"; tell the one who says, *Ask and you will receive, knock and and it will be opened to you* (Lk 11:9). Knock as you stand in front of the door, knock insistently. The one who is keeping it shut is not turning you away; he just wishes to train and exercise the one who's knocking. So knock then, go on knocking, not with your bodily hand, but with your eager heart. Tell your Lord what you sing in the psalms: *To you has my heart said: I have sought your face, your face will I search for* (Ps 27:8). Say also what it says in another psalm: *One thing have I asked for from the Lord, this will I seek: that I may dwell in the house of the Lord for all the days of my life, that I may contemplate the delight of the Lord* (Ps 27:4). You must be filled with longing for this contemplation, you must say to him, "I want to see you."

But what shall I see you with? If with the eyes of flesh, it follows that you are bodily light. Right now my good sense[23] is already informing me that you, my God, are not bodily light. So what are you? I have passed beyond all these things, I have come to my own mind, and that isn't my God either. And yet the nature of mind surpasses all bodily things, whether of earth or of heaven, but that is not yet my God. My mind, after all, is changeable, while my God is unchangeable; I'm looking for something unchangeable when I'm looking for my God. How, though, do I tell that my mind is changeable? Now it remembers, now it forgets, now it's wise, now it's foolish, now it wishes, now it doesn't, now it gets angry, now it calms down. I'm looking for something unchangeable when I'm looking for my God. That's how my God has spoken to me in the scriptures, so that I might be able at least somehow or other to reflect upon what I can believe, though not yet to have what I can see. I am looking for something which always remains unchangeable.[24]

13. But what shall I see with?

The gospel will give you your answer: *Blessed are the heart-pure, because it is they who shall see God* (Mt 5:8).

"So if *blessed are the heart-pure, because it is they who shall see God*, while we are carrying around hearts made impure by the load of our sins, what are we to do? How shall we purify that inner eye of ours, with which alone the face of our God can be seen?"

How shall we purify it? You will find this too in scripture: *Purifying their hearts by faith* (Acts 15:9).

So let us hold onto these two testimonies, one from the gospel, the other from the Acts of the Apostles. What's the one from the gospel? *Blessed are the heart-pure, because it is they who shall see God*. You have taken a good look at yourself, you've found some impurity of heart in yourself. Longing to see God, and hearing that he can only be seen by pure hearts, being on fire with longing to see him, you naturally seek to purify your heart. So how shall you purify it? Pay attention to the one who says in Acts, *Purifying their hearts by faith.* Hold onto these two one as a promise, the other as action. What as a promise? *Blessed are the heart-pure, because it is they who will see God.* What as action? *Purifying their hearts by faith.* So then, believe before you see, in order to be able, when you do see, to rejoice.

The absurdity of wanting to see before believing

14. Don't let the vacuous thought come up into your heart: "What's this that the Christians keep on saying: Believe, believe?" It's the doctor who says it, who knows what's to be done with your eye.

Now just push the doctor's hands away, and say, "I won't believe, unless you show me."

The doctor will answer you, "There's nobody there for me to show it to. What I wish to heal in you is something to enable you to see what you want me to show you now."

Imagine a person blinded by some misting up of the eyes,[25] and perhaps from the very beginning of his life, so that now he doesn't even know what is being seen by those who can see; and the doctor says to him, "There's something I'd like to show you. Here you are then; you have some perception of being blind, while others can see; at the very least because you need a guide which they don't need, there is clearly some difference between you and them. So they can see something which you can't; but if you could, you would enjoy it very much." He arouses a desire in him to see what he doesn't know, wishing to cure him so that he may be able to see what he can't see now.

But if the other were so absurd and averse to all reason and truth as to say to the doctor, "You won't cure me, unless you first show me what I am going to see," what do you suppose the doctor will answer? "The right thing is for you to be cured in order to see not for you to see in order to be cured. You've got it all wrong, you're putting the cart before the horse. First let that be done which you don't want, so that you may be able to get to what you do want. If you had eyes to which I could show what I've mentioned, there would be no need for you to be cured."

The other, maybe, will reply, "And what am I to do? Prescribe whatever treatment you like."

Now the doctor: "I'm going to apply some rather strong ointments,[26] which will wipe away the mistiness from your eyes, but their strength means you are going to feel some pain. But you've just got to put up patiently with the salutary pain, and not be so intolerant of it that you nervously push away my hands. After all, I know what to do to your eyes, so that what now can't even be called eyes may really be eyes. I know what I'm doing, and that's why I'm telling you beforehand that you're going to suffer some discomfort, which will result in your being able to see the light."

The other, terrified of being stung by those remedies the doctor is going to apply, perhaps goes back to that attempt to fend it off and keep it at bay: "Do you think I'm going to endure such agonies as you're going to put me through? Unless I can first see what you are going to show me, I won't allow it."

The doctor retorts, "You can't. This is what I'm aiming at; I beg you, let yourself be cured. You will be able to see, the mistiness will be eliminated, that light which you hear mentioned by people who can see, and which you can't see, will dazzle you with its brilliance. I mean, you hear about light, color, lightning flashes; you hear these words. These words signify certain things, the things themselves you can't see. Those who can see them are better off than you. So then, put up with a little pain as the price of great joys."

If he agrees, he will be cured and will be able to see. If he doesn't agree, wishing to see before being cured and thus getting the means to see with, he will prove the most ridiculous of men and the enemy of his own health as he turns his back on the doctor.[27]

Faith first, then sight

15. Now turn your attention to the salvation doctor who has come to us, our Lord Jesus Christ. He found us blind of heart, he promised us a light which *eye has not seen nor ear heard, nor has it come up into the heart of man* (1 Cor 2:9). This is what the angels see, what they enjoy. I mean, just as healthy people see what the blind don't see, so angels see what man doesn't see. Why doesn't man see it? Because he still wants to be "man." So let man himself start getting cured, so that from being "man" he may be numbered among the sons of God,[28] because *he gave them the right to become children of God* (Jn 1:12), that is, "he gave them the right to be cured, to have the mistiness of heart wiped away," because *blessed are the heart-pure, because it is they who shall see God* (Mt 5:8).

And listen how you will also find in the gospel what is said elsewhere, *purifying their hearts by faith* (Acts 15:9). After saying *he gave them the right to become children of God*, the Lord immediately addded, *to those who believe in his name* (Jn 1:12). So if he gave those who believe in his name the right to become children of God—now it is the children of God who will be able to see what has not come up into the heart of man—then it's by faith that he purifies their hearts so that they can be *heart-pure, because it is they who shall see God.*

It's painful, living according to the faith

16. So then, blessed are you, brothers and sisters, who believe; pray for those who don't believe, that they too may earn the right to see. Blessed are you that believe; you don't see, but you believe; you aren't yet perfectly healthy, but you are still being cured. Your health, your salvation,[29] lies in hope, not yet in reality. Persevere under the doctor's treatment, put up with his orders as with strong ointments; keep yourselves from the destructive pleasures of the world; don't let the illicit doings of the nations lead you on, the trifling nonsense of the theaters, the self-indulgence of drunkenness, the poison of unlawful curiosity.[30] Keep yourselves from all these things.

But you have got into the habit of finding enjoyment in these things, and when you start giving them up, the hunger caused by a habit broken off will cause you pain. But that's the harshness of the strong ointments with which eyes are cured. Accept the doctor's orders. Whatever he imposes on you to be endured, he first underwent himself. And in him, indeed, there was nothing to be cured, because he was in no way ill, but in carrying out his duty of healing, he endured what he was proposing to the patient. He was giving a special bitter potion to a patient swollen and blown up with pride; he himself came in humility, and suffered every conceivable humiliation from proud individuals.

Christ's humility the remedy for our pride

17. Christ's humility is the remedy for your pride. Don't sneer at what can bring you health. Be so good as to be humble, you on whose account God was good enough to humble himself. That this would be the medicine for restoring your health was the considered judgment, you see, of the one who really knows both what is making you ill and how you should be restored to health. As regards all parts of the body, good[31] doctors look for the root cause from which come[32] all the ills that are most difficult to tolerate. And that's why many unskilled practitioners, taking care of superficial causes and not bothering about the basic ones, appear to have remedied the trouble for a time; but with the fountain head, so to say, of the diseases still flowing, the trouble that persists in the source bursts out again in streams of distress.

So just listen to what is making man ill, to why he has no health, not just in his eyes but in any part of his body at all. Listen to what makes him ill, accept it from the scriptures in which the art of the doctor has been written down. I mean, the man who diagnoses your illness for you from Hippocrates[33] is not more to be relied on by you than the one who demonstrates to you from the divine scripture how you are internally ill. So listen to scripture saying, *The beginning of every sin is pride* (Sir 10:13)—and yet there you go, running off about the health of your body; about your soul you remain indifferent. A bit of straw has blown into your eye, there's no delay in your getting it out. Iniquity is pressing down on the eye of your heart, you don't hurry off to the doctor.

Though, while you were unable to run off to the doctor, the doctor himself came to you—and what is much more serious, the very fact of his coming to you is something you sneer at, you treat his mercy and compassion as worthless.[34] He came, he wants to help, he knows what treatment to apply. That's why God came in lowliness, otherwise he would be beyond man's imitation. I mean, how would you imitate him high up there? Without imitating him, how would you be restored to health? So he came in lowliness down below, because he knew what sort of potion he should give you. Somewhat bitter, indeed, but wholesome. You, though, are still sneering at him as he brings you the potion, and you're saying to yourself, "What sort of God am I going to have? One who was born, suffered, was smeared with spittle, crowned with thorns, hung up on a cross?" Wretched soul! You see the lowly humility of the doctor, you don't notice the tumor of your own pride. That's why this humble one is displeasing to you; he's displeasing to your pride, the remedy the doctor is giving you is displeasing to your disease.[35]

Our doctor makes a remedy for our sins from his death

18. If you still go on sneering, it means you are in a frenzy.[36] Frenzied or frantic patients often beat up the doctors, and yet they in their kindheartedness not only don't get angry with them for beating them up, they even go on seeking their health. Sometimes, however, they are so extraordinarily strong that they are able even to kill the doctor. He, though, makes very, very sure of not being killed, because he cannot rise again and heal the frenzied patient. That doctor of ours, on the other hand, wasn't afraid even of being killed by his frenzied patients, and from his very death he prepared a remedy for their frenzy. He died, you see, and rose again.

And notice how the true doctor does not get angry with the frenzied people who are beating him up, but feels more sorry for them than ever, and by means of what he is suffering he wants to heal them as they rage against him. Listen to the doctor as he hangs on the cross; looking round at the frenzied crowd raving and raging against him, he said, *Father, forgive them, because they do not know what they are doing* (Lk 23:24). Nor were his words in vain. Because after he had risen again, and been glorified in the eyes of his disciples, in such a way that he could show them even the scars of the same flesh that had been restored to life—and he didn't only present himself to be seen but also to be touched and felt—he ascended into heaven, sent the Holy Spirit; miracles started happening in the name of the one slain, in the name of the crucified, and the consciences of those who killed him pricked them more painfully then than when they had seen him hanging on the cross. They were reflecting, you see, that such great things were happening in the name of one who they assumed had been killed at their own hands. They sensed that he was alive, the one they had mocked as he was dying.

They were cut to the heart (Acts 2:37), as it says in the Acts of the Apostles; many of the very Jews who had been crucifiers of the Lord sought the advice of the apostles; what's more they accepted their advice, because it had not been for nothing that he said as he hung there, *Father, forgive them, because they do not know what they are doing.* An apostle said to them, *Repent, and be baptized every one of you in the name of our Lord Jesus Christ, and your sins are forgiven you* (Acts 2:38). It happened; they were baptized and they believed[37] in him whom they had crucified. That's what I said, brothers and sisters: that from his very death he was making remedies for their frenzied condition.

Christ's resurrection eliminates the fear of death in his disciples

19. From there they went to the Gentiles; the apostles were sent to the nations. They found the whole wide world given over to idols. They themselves began,

the disciples of that doctor, among whom the selfsame doctor was presiding, because they had become heaven and were carrying God around,[38] so they began to preach the one who had been crucified and had died *for our transgressions and risen again for our justification* (Rom 4:25). With so many signs and miracles also bearing witness to the message, the whole wide world began to be filled with it. And first, in order for it to be filled, the disciples too of the doctor were being killed, just as the doctor himself had been done to death. But when would these ever be afraid of being killed, having observed even the flesh[39] rising again in their head? Could they be afraid for any soul that was never going to die, when as regards the body they had already risen in the Lord? Now he has made all believers into a body as for the head, so that he himself is their head, while all those who believe and trust him would be joined together with him and with each other as parts of the body.

Now from the beginning of the world to its end there has been and will be belief in Christ, because even before he was born of Mary the virgin, there were many who believed he was going to come, just as now they believe in him who has already come. And it is through this very faith that all are restored to health, nor is there any other ointment for that clouding of the spiritual eye, except as it's written, *Purifying their hearts by faith* (Acts 15:9).

So he has made all the saints into a body for himself, a body of which he himself is the head. Nor would he be head of this body, unless he had received something from the body itself. Where, after all, did he take flesh from, which was able to die in him? I mean, if the human soul cannot die, when would the divinity of the Word ever be able to die? So thousands of martyrs have also been killed, and the crops of the Church, sown as it were in their blood, have sprung up all over the world.

Faith made easy by the fulfillment of the ancient prophecies

20. So then, brothers and sisters, these things were foretold thousands of years beforehand, and just as they were foretold, so can they be seen to have been carried out and put into effect. Only a few are left which we read of and still have to believe, because there are more which we read of and can already see fulfilled. Now from the ones which we read of and see fulfilled, it isn't a great thing to believe in the few enough that remain to be fulfilled. For those who never saw any of the things which we see, it was a great thing to believe; nowadays it's no longer particularly praiseworthy to believe, but it's damnation-worthy not to believe. Let them wake up and get cured, those who still refuse to be cured. Let them believe; then they will see.

They mustn't be so perverse as to say to us. "Let me see first, and then I will believe." What can that mean, "Let me see, and then I will believe"? If you see something, after all, you don't strictly speaking believe it, do you? You believe if you don't see; believing is one thing, seeing another. Believe because you don't see, in order that by believing what you cannot see, you may deserve to see what you believe. What earns sight is faith; what rewards faith is sight. Why look for the reward before the work? So believe then, and walk in faith; your salvation lies in hope. The best of doctors, after all, has begun to cure you, and for him no disease is incurable. Don't be afraid for your past misdeeds, however frightful, however unbelievable the things you have perhaps committed. They are grave diseases, but the doctor has mastered them. So don't worry about past sins; in one moment of the sacrament they will be forgiven, and absolutely all of them will be totally forgiven.[40]

Nothing of past sins will remain, to vex you with care and anxiety. You will be without a single care, secure though, not in your own strength, but in the hands of the doctor. So let yourself be carefree under him, because he will heal even what remains—that weakness of our mortality, from which sins, lesser ones indeed, continue to creep in as long as we live. He will heal everything, purify everything. All that cloudy mistiness will be removed—but may you be given such an eye of mind and heart that you may be blessed when you see, because you believed when you heard, *Blessed are the heart-pure, because it is they who shall see God* (Mt 5:8).

Let those who have not yet believed observe, O my dear brothers and sisters, let them observe how many are the things that God has put into effect. Everything that we can see is being done in the name of Christ throughout the whole wide world was foreseen, foretold, written down beforehand. The volumes[41] are in our hands, the facts before our eyes.

Justifying the godless more difficult for God
than making the godly like the angels

21. And come to think of it, brothers and sisters, he has done something more difficult than what he is going to do. What do I mean, "He has done something more difficult"? He has justified the godless, from the idolater he has made a believer, from the drunkard a model of sobriety, from the self-indulgent an austere person, from the miser one who donates his possessions, not making donations to hunters[42] with the devil cheering him on, but making them to the poor with Christ awarding him the prize, and in this way amassing a fortune for himself which cannot pass away. What God has done was more difficult; after all, he has made a godly person out of an ungodly one, and will he not more easily reward the godly?

Consider, my dear brothers and sisters: which is harder to believe, the making of a godly person out of the godless, or the making of an angel out of the godly? Godless and godly are opposites to each other; godly and angel are not opposites. He has changed you from your opposite, and will he not complete you in your kind? I mean, now that you have begun to be godly, you are beginning to imitate the life of an angel; but when you were godless you were far removed from the choir of angels. Faith, however, came and justified you. You now humble yourself before God, where you once used to blaspheme God; and where you once turned all your attention to creatures, you now desire the creator.

Just look at what he has heaped upon you; he has displayed his Church to the whole world; he has displayed it just as he promised. It was foretold that idolatry would some time or other be slain and done away with; our ancestors read about it and did not see it, while we both read about it and see it.[43] Heresies were foretold, schisms were foretold; there they are also, which is why Christians are not unduly upset when they see heresies and schisms. This gives them all the more assurance in hoping that everything they have been promised is going to come about, since what has been foretold is coming about now.[44]

The folly of Christians consulting astrologers

22. So then, shun the misdeeds of all heresies and schisms, shun the sacrilegious practices of the Gentiles, the conjuring of demons out of curiosity,[45] the various cults of idols, the sacrilege of heathen remedies,[46] the consultation of astrologers. Shun these things, brothers and sisters. Whatever you may hope for from them, you don't get it. They have never made any promises concerning the life to come; if they say anything concerning this present life, they are lying to you. Just stand up, anyone who can really say, "To me, I know for sure, an astrologer did tell the truth, and to me. I know for sure that a soothsayer[47] did tell the truth, and I got that remedy, and it worked."

The only thing your graces should know for sure is something that can be seen easily enough. The good fortune and misfortune of the present time, which are neither true good fortune nor total misfortune, are scattered higgledy-piggledy among all human beings. If those people alone who do these things were fortunate in this time, you, brothers and sisters who have believed, ought to set at nought present good fortune for the sake of the good fortune to come. But since you can see that people who do these things and people who don't are mixed higgledy-piggledy in being healthy; people who do them and people who don't are mixed higgledy-piggledy in dying; mixed higgledy-piggledy in being rich and poor are those who do them and those who don't; mixed higgledy-piggledy in being held in honor and in being of no account are those who do them and those who don't; so since you can see temporal good fortune and misfortune mixed higgledy-piggledy in the human race, why not rather be on your guard against the eternal misfortune that will follow on being told, *Go into eternal fire*; and why not make sure of obtaining the true good fortune that will follow on being told, *Receive the kingdom* (Mt 25:41.34)?

The folly of worshiping pagan gods for temporal benefits

23. "Juno," he says, "takes care of women in labor, and Mercury of hunters or literary men, and Neptune of those at sea."[48] It's all simply untrue. I mean if it were true, women who blaspheme Juno would not give birth easily. What's so terrific, my brothers and sisters, about opening your eyes to see these facts? Did the prophets foretell these things too? Just ask yourselves; let the human race reply. Must all those who don't worship Neptune be shipwrecked? Must all merchants and trader who deride Mercury suffer financial loss? But if all this

is untrue, and they never promised you the life to come, they are worth nothing for the present life.

Why are they worshiped, if not to tie up the feet of those going along the way of the Lord, to stop them seeking immortality and some rest after the labors and difficulties of this life? That devil, you see, with his angels[49] sets himself in opposition, and makes himself seem necessary in order to reduce you all to slavery. Make use rather of your freedom; the one who has redeemed you from slavery is greater than that one who is assailing you. Whoever has consented to that one will be judged with him; whoever has believed in Christ will sit with him in judgment. These are things that are still in the future; but from the things which have already come about, draw your conclusions about those that remain.

*Why Christ gained emperors through fishermen,
not fishermen through emperors*

24. The persecutions were foretold that would be raised against Christians by the kings who ruled the world; they came about, there was a wholesale slaughter of martyrs, and those who were doing this thought they could finish off Christians by killing them. The Church grew from its own blood, the persecutors were overcome, those who were suffering persecution overcame. We also find in the holy scriptures that the kings themselves would submit their necks to the yoke of Christ, though at first it seemed that the Church had to beware of persecution at their hands. This too happened, brothers and sisters. Now the cross of Christ is on the foreheads of kings;[50] kings venerate what the Jews subjected to mockery.

And because we find something like this written: *God chose the weak things of this world to disconcert the strong, and the low-born things of this world he chose, and the things that are not like those that are, that the things that are might be brought to nothing* (1 Cor 1:27-28); we have to remind ourselves[51] that our Lord Jesus Christ came not only for the salvation of the poor but also of the rich, not only of commoners, but also of kings. He refused, all the same, to choose kings for his disciples, refused rich people, refused the nobly born, refused the learned; but instead he chose poor, uneducated, low-born fishermen, in whom his grace would shine through more clearly. He came, you see, to give the potion of humility and to cure pride. And if he had first called a king, the king would have said that it was his rank that was chosen; if he had first called a learned man, he would have said it was his teaching that was chosen. Those who were being called to lowliness and humility would have to be called by lowly and humble people. And so it is that Christ did not gain a fisherman through an emperor, but an emperor through a fisherman.[52]

The scriptures fulfilled in the conversion of the world

25. Kings, lately, are coming to Rome.[53] It's terrific, brothers and sisters, how it was all fulfilled. When it was being uttered, when it was being written, none

of these things were happening. It's marvelous. Take note of it and see, rejoice. May those who refuse to take note of the event just be a little curious; about these things we want them to be curious. Let them leave aside the vicious trifles of their vain curiosity,[54] let them occasionally at least be curious about the divine scriptures, let them find there so many things foretold which they can now see happening.

They're astonished, you see, at the way the human race is converging on the name of the crucified and streaming together, from kings to ragamuffins. No age passed over, no manner of life, no school of thought. It's not the case, you see, that the unlearned have believed and the learned haven't, or that the low-born have believed and the high-born haven't, or that women have believed and men haven't, or that children have believed and old people haven't, or that slaves have believed and free persons haven't. Every age has been called to salvation, every age has already come, every degree, every human level of wealth and property. It's high time for all and sundry to be inside. Now just a few have remained outside, and they still go on arguing; if only they would wake up some time or other, at least at the din the world is making! The whole world is shouting at them.

The emperor Honorius kneels at the tomb of Peter,
not in the temple of Hadrian

26. As I had begun to say, kings are coming to Rome. That's where the temples of emperors are to be found, who in their pride required divine honors to be paid them by men, and because they had the power—they were kings, after all, and absolute rulers—they extorted rather than earned such honors. From whom could a fisherman extort any such thing? There in Rome is to be found the tomb of a fisherman, there the temple of an emperor. Peter is there in a tomb, Hadrian is there in a temple. A temple for Hadrian, a memorial chapel for Peter. The emperor comes. Let us see where he hurried off to, where he wished to kneel: in the emperor's temple or in the fisherman's memorial chapel? Laying aside his diadem, he beat his breast where the fisherman's body lies; it's on *his* merits that he reflects, in the crown *he* received that he believes, through *him* that he is eager to reach God, by *his* prayers that he feels and discovers he is assisted.[55]

There you are, that's the achievement of the one who was crucified and scorned on the cross, there you have what he mowed down the nations with, not with ferocious steel, but with a scorned piece of wood. So then, let the proud drink the potion of humility, seeing that Christ has let himself be humiliated. Let them condescend to be humble, let them now recognize their medicine, let them come and believe.

The folly of putting conversion off till tomorrow

27. Encourage them, brothers and sisters, and urge them not only in words but also with your way of life, and I too am urging them not to put it off any

longer. Some of them, you see, are perhaps thinking and saying, "Tomorrow I'll become a Christian." If it's a good thing tomorrow, it's a good thing today. After all, to become a Christian he isn't going to be seeking an auspicious day from an astrologer. God made every day. That day is a good one for you on which you accomplish anything good. So if it's good to believe in Christ, so that *the heart may be purified by faith* (Acts 15:9), and that that eye may be healed which is going to see such a great light, why put it off, why has the crow's caw remained so popular with human beings? "*Cras, cras*, tomorrow, tomorrow," says the crow, who didn't return to the ark after being sent out; it was the dove that returned.[56] The crow caws "*cras*, tomorrow," the dove moans every day. So don't make your own the cawing of procrastination, but the moaning of confession.

Would those who are tired out by listening please excuse those who are eager for more. Would those who still want to hear more please excuse those who are tired out, because time too is pressing us to bring the sermon to an end. Because such, I can see, is your greediness in Christ, that you could easily listen to more; but we cannot afford the time. Any who are here that have not yet come to believe, well, here are we, here is the church; if they wish, they can become believers. If they think it's to be put off, which in my opinion they ought not to be thinking any longer, let them give up their places to those who are about to celebrate the divine mysteries.[57]

Postscript

(And after the pagans had gone out:)

28. I've already said to you yesterday,[58] brothers and sisters, and I say it again now and am always begging you to win over those who haven't yet believed, by leading good lives—otherwise you too, I fear, will have believed to no purpose. I beseech you all, in the same way as you take pleasure in the word of God, so to express that pleasure in the lives you lead. Let God's word please you not only in your ears but in your hearts too; not only in your hearts but also in your lives, so that you may be God's household, acceptable in his eyes and *fit for every good work* (2 Tm 2:21). I haven't the slightest doubt, brothers and sisters, that if you all live in a manner worthy of God, the time will very soon come when none of those who have not yet believed will remain in unbelief.

NOTES

1. Three short extracts from this sermon have already appeared in Sermon 97A (III, 4), which is thus shown to be not a sermon in itself but a catena of extracts from other sermons, this one included. The fairly precise date 404 is deduced from the mention of an imperial visit to Rome in sections 25 and 26. This almost certainly refers to a visit to the city, staged as a triumph, by the

Emperor Honorius in January of that year; his usual residence was in Ravenna. The notice in one manuscript from Lorsch that it was preached at Boseth, almost certainly a small town between Carthage and Thagaste, and the fact that Augustine visited several towns along that route in June of that year, as he tells us in his *Answer to Cresconius*, written in 405, confirm this date fairly conclusively. Possidius refers to this sermon in his *Index*, and it is from there and from the Lorsch manuscript that I take the title. Dolbeau gives the shorter title from the Mainz manuscript: "When the pagans were allowed in." This. incidentally, is my slightly amplified rendering of *Cum pagani ingrederentur*. As Dolbeau says, it is clear that what is meant is not "when the pagans were entering the Church (by being converted)," but "when the pagans were entering the church building, the basilica"—which at the end of section 27 they are required to leave.

2. For a more sustained reflection on this text of Saint Paul see Sermon 127 (III, 4), especially sections 1, 3, 5, and 11.

3. See Lk 23:43.

4. See Sermon 159B, 5 (III, 11).

5. And he didn't think his congregation needed to be told that the name "Adam" means "man."

6. Reading *tamdiu . . . quamdiu* for the text's *quamdiu . . . quamdiu*, which was no doubt just a slip on the part of a copyist.

7. The answer is "gods," but he will just touch on it at the beginning of the next section; it is not until section 6 that he spells it out.

8. See Ps 78:7; Jer 17:5.

9. The apostle actually says, "Are you not of the flesh, *carnales*?" I suspect that that is also what was written in Augustine's text, and that it was he who changed it to "men," though not perhaps deliberately.

10. I have added the words "to grace," to make the over-succinct Latin clear.

11. See Gn 3:19.

12. Death, *mors*, is feminine in Latin—as also is life; but life hasn't yet been personified.

13. For another sermon on this psalm see Sermon 23B (III, 11). But it only deals with the opening verses.

14. For this idea see also Sermon 53, 14 (III, 3).

15. In the Latin, *animalis*—one of many untranslatable words. It is in fact usually treated as synonymous with *carnalis*, and always opposed to *spiritalis*. However, to translate it here as "animal" would be to downgrade it too far. By "merely animated" I wish to imply that he is not (yet) "inspirited"—by the Holy Spirit, which is what is really meant as a rule by the adjective *spiritualis*.

16. Out of its *animus*—the *anima* must rid its *animus* of false notions.

17. Now addressing his *animus*, which at the end of the paragraph will be found in its turn to have an *animus*! It all amounts to what in English we can term "the self."

18. See Gn 1:26-28.

19. See Lk 11:34. For the eyes being called lights see Sermon 4, 6 (III, 1). He calls them windows (which we call lights!) in Sermon 241, 2 (III, 7). For the general comparison of the outer and inner eye, the outer and inner light, see also Sermon 159, 3 (III, 5).

20. The Latin text has *illud unde potes, quem pura mente visurus es?* Dolbeau emends the *illud* to *illum*, thus giving the sense, "how can you [think worthy thoughts about] him whom you are going to see?" But I don't think this really makes sense. So I myself emend by omitting *illud* and repunctuating; I treat *unde potes* simply as an interjection, and find the antecedent of the relative *quem* in "that being," *ille*, mentioned before the interjection.

21. A non-sentence in the Latin too. There seems to be a certain lack of coherence in the way he expresses himself throughout these sections.

22. See the end of section 7 and the beginning of section 8.

23. Literally "my heart"—but the heart as the organ of intelligence, especially practical intelligence.

24. For other treatments of this whole theme see Sermons 223A, 3 (III, 6); 241, 2 (III, 7); and 159B, 6 (III, 11).

25. Literally "by some fog," *aliqua caligine*. But the word was used medically for unspecified eye disorders, most commonly, perhaps, for cataracts. I like to preserve the underlying metaphor.

26. See Rv 3:18.

27. For parallel treatment of the theme see Sermon 374, 8 (III, 11).

28. Readers must please tolerate a little apparently sexist language here. There are a number of allusions to texts in which one simply has to use the word "sons." We must just allow it in English, as it does in many other languages, sometimes to include "daughters." Augustine is here, I presume, immediately thinking of texts where the angels are called sons of God—for example 1:6; 2:1, 38:7—but coming to them, I suspect, through Wis 5:5, where the allusion is clearly to the angels.

29. A single word in the Latin: *salus*. The whole sentence runs, *Salus vestra in spe est, nondum in re*.

30. Indulged in by superstitious practices of all sorts, chiefly consulting astrologers.

31. A short gap in the text, which Dolbeau suggests filling with the word *boni*.

32. Another short gap, at the end of which appear the two letters *la: unde . . . la omnia quae difficillime tolerantur*. I suggest supplying *sunt ma*.

33. The semi-legendary "father of Greek medicine," who lived on the island of Cos in the middle of the fifth century BC. A whole collection of medical writings was attributed to him.

34. He is here, evidently, addressing the pagans, the unbelievers present in the congregation.

35. For this theme of Christ's humility being the remedy for man's pride see Sermon 159B, 11, 12 (III, 11).

36. For the frenzied or frantic patient (often contrasted with the lethargic) see Sermons 16A, 8 (III, 1); 87, 14; 111, 2 (III, 3); 359, 8 (III, 10).

37. The first of the extracts from this sermon to be found in Sermon 97A (III, 4); this one appears there in section 2.

38. See section 7 above.

39. "Even" the flesh, because flesh is the least noble element constitutive of the complete human being. The pure Platonist was satisfied with the immortality of the soul, and was in fact rather distressed by the notion of the resurrection of the flesh, while the Christian Platonist, which Augustine had certainly been since his conversion, tended to be almost exclusively interested in "the resurrection of the soul," that is, its restoration to the life of grace from the death which is sin. But Augustine progressively allowed the Christian doctrine of the resurrection of the flesh to qualify, indeed to a large extent to displace, his Platonist preconceptions. Here he goes on in a very interesting if somewhat puzzling way to associate the resurrection of the body (our bodies) with the doctrine of the Church being Christ's body—because it is assured of this, so it seems, through his bodily resurrection. The background texts to his thought are from Ephesians (1:22-23; 4:4-13) and Colossians (1:18) and Romans (12:4-5), rather than the usually more prominent text from 1 Cor 12:12-28.

40. This section has appeared in Sermon 97A, 2 (III, 4) just before the previous quotation there from this sermon. That one (end of section 18 above) follows on the heels of this one after one short introductory half-sentence. The sacrament Augustine is referring to here is of course baptism.

41. The scriptures in those days were never, or scarcely ever, bound in a single volume or codex (the word used here), like our bibles today. For the theme of this section see Sermons 43, 1 (III, 2); 113A, 4-6 (III, 4).

42. Hunters of wild beasts in the arena, who seem to have replaced the gladiators of more pagan times.

43. These three paragraphs are to be found in Sermon 97A (III, 2) in sections 1 and 2, where they precede the other two passages culled from this sermon.

44. For this whole section see Sermons 22, 4 (III, 2); 77B, 6 (III, 3); 114B, 6 (III, 11); 159B, 15 (III, 11).

45. He just says *curiositates daemonum*, literally "the curiosities of demons." But he is certainly alluding to the practice of what was called "theurgy ("working" the gods), magical rites for communicating with the gods encouraged by neo-Platonists like Porphyry.

46. Just "of remedies" in the text. He is referring, I think, to such things as protective amulets.

47. For astrologers, soothsayers, heathen remedies etc., see Sermons 4, 36; 9, 17; 15A, 4 (III, 1); 63A, 3 (III, 3); 335D, 3 (III, 9); 198, 58 (III, 11).

48. See Sermon 198, 63 (III, II).

49. Who were for the most part simply identified by Christian preachers with the pagan gods.

50. Put there in the sacrament of confirmation, which was then the concluding rite of the whole baptismal liturgy. The "prophecies" of this which he had in mind would have been, for example, Ps 72:10-11, Ps 110:1.5 etc. See Sermons 22, 4 (III, 2); 113A, 5, 9, (III, 4); 114B, 6 (III, 11); 299A, 7 (III, 11). The "christianizing" of the Roman emperors was a slow and uncertain process—it hadn't just happened instantaneously and forever with the "conversion" of Constantine; the cross was not marked on his forehead, anyway, until he was dying. His successor Constantius favored the Arians; he was followed by Julian, called the Apostate, who reverted to "traditional, civilized" paganism, and made things rather difficult for the Church; and it was not until Theodosius became emperor in 379 that the "kings" may be said to have become definitively Catholic Christians. I think all that is what Augustine is alluding to, when he qualifies his statement about their submitting to the yoke of Christ, by saying that at first it seemed as if the Church had to be on its guard against persecutions at their hands.

51. I have added "we have to remind ourselves," since what he goes on to say is by no means an inference to be obviously drawn from what Paul says!

52. See Sermons 43, 6 (III, 2); 198, 60 (III, 11); 341, 4 (III, 11).

53. This general statement will be given particular reference, at the beginning of the next section, to the visit of the Emperor Honorius to Rome in January 404. See note 1 above.

54. Consulting astrologers and so forth. "Curiosity" is for Augustine normally a vice, of which he often accused himself, and which, fortunately for the effectiveness of his preaching, he never entirely overcame—not that he went on consulting astrologers after his conversion, but that he never stopped being insatiably curious about everything going on around him and about the world at large. But as a vice he paired it against the virtue of *studiositas*, eager interest in serious study, which really amounts, in his view, to the "curiosity about the scriptures" of which he goes on to speak.

55. For another treatment of this occasion see Sermon 341, 4 (III, 11), and note 15 to that sermon.

56. See Gn 8:6-12. See also Sermons 82, 14 (III, 3) and note 19 there; 224, 3 (III, 6), and note 21 there.

57. And then would come the *missa*, the dismissal of the catechumens and pagans, by the deacon.

58. This sermon seems to have been lost.

SERMON 360C

SERMON OF SAINT AUGUSTINE ABOUT THOSE WHO COMPLAIN
THEY ARE BEING FORCED INTO UNITY: AGAINST THE PARTY OF DONATUS

Date: 406[1]

Opening appeal for quiet in the congregation

1. Nothing, after all, is more gratifying than the eagerness of you brothers and sisters; but nothing is more dangerous than disagreements in congregations and communities.[2] In the sound, indeed, coming from our mouths and tongues, the words *caro* and *caritas* (flesh and charity) seem very close to each other; they are close as spoken sounds. I mean, what could sound more alike than *caro* and *caritas*? But for all that, they differ vastly from each other even at this time. How different these two are, which sound so alike, will be obvious enough to you when you consider that where there is charity, the heart is expanded, the flesh is squashed and squeezed tight.[3] But because even our very charity is toiling away in the flesh, and we haven't yet been received into the spacious demesne of divinity as long as we are being held here by the chains of infirmity—but all the same, dearly beloved, just consider what ample space is provided by this great building! Do you suppose that those at the back find it more difficult to hear? Your stillness will let my voice find a way through to them.[4] Look how easily, when you keep still, you hear even what isn't being said in a loud voice! So then, have some consideration for one another, and as it is written, *bear one another's burdens* (Gal 6:2), so that you may all receive together what is being given to you all.

Why Augustine had not come to Thagaste sooner;
he has come with the ex-Donatist bishop, Maximinus

2. It is after desiring it long and continuously that I now see your graces present in the body; in spirit we have never parted, neither you from me nor I from you. When we all have our "hearts lifted up," you are dwelling with me in that place where we none of us are squashed up against each other. Still,

brothers and sisters, I ask your pardon if in the opinion of some of you I seem to have come to you later than both you and I would have wished. I was detained throughout the summer by the most pressing needs, and those needs certainly did not escape your notice,[5] because we were all certainly helped by your prayers, so that what had been painful necessities found the most satisfying solutions. In the city of Hippo, where I serve my children, your brothers and sisters, I was for a long time in labor, and finally saw unity realized. Again and again I beg you, please go on helping us with your good wishes and prayers, that *the Lord may confirm what he has wrought for us* (Ps 68:28).

Now however, although we were still involved in this business there in the city, even in the country districts of Hippo little congregations were beginning to be converted, which are much slower at laying hold of unity, in that the rustic mind finds it harder to understand the issue. So your desire has not so much drawn me here now as dragged me away from there, so that I may go back to them again, where my presence is also desired.[6] And so please grant my request, and excuse my lateness in coming.

It was then, you see, that my right reverend brother and colleague Maximinus[7] was also converted to the Catholic Church. So it was impossible at that time, and would have been most improper, for me to abandon him at his fresh start in the Catholic Church by which he was breaking with the harsh domination of stale old habits; nor would it have been right for him to leave that place straightaway.[8] So when the Lord judged it opportune, he allowed us both to come here together. So I reckon you will find it easy to excuse my slowness in coming, because I did come later on with the man on whose account I did not come sooner.

Christ is our bread, our peace, our way and our goal

3. And so now, dearly beloved, let's get down to the business in hand. We heard all about the rough times you had, though we weren't here with you; you heard all about ours, though you weren't there with us. You cherish unity, you love peace, you maintain peace, you are hungry for peace. We all welcome and rejoice over the soundness of your taste-buds, so that *you taste how sweet the Lord is* (Ps 34:8; 1 Pt 2:3). Good bread, you see, is good for a healthy person, while a sick person cannot eat the bread he is offered, though he can praise it as good when he sees it.

What, after all, is our bread, if not the one who said, *I myself am the living bread, who have come down from heaven* (Jn 6:51)? Can he possibly be bread and not be peace? Let me prove that he is also peace, because I have proved that he is bread by his own clearest possible testimony: *I myself am the living bread, who have come down from heaven.* Let the apostle also have his say: *For he himself is our peace* (Eph 2:14). So about the one who says, *I myself am the living bread, who have come down from heaven,* it is also said, *he himself is our peace.* So the bread we have is peace[9]—but only if we are healthy; let's eat it.

4. You heard the bread speaking himself, just now in the gospel. The disciples

were seeking the first and the highest place, and there was competition for glory among the children of charity. They were arguing about *who was the greater among them* (Lk 22:24). Infirmity was seeking the higher place, which certainly goes to charity. They weren't yet aware of the way they were going, even if they realized where they were going. It's by way of humility that one reaches the heights. Christ is the way.[10] He is bread, he is peace, again he is also the way. Ask him where it is you want to go, he answers, "To me"; ask the way to go where you want, he has given you the answer: "By me." He both remained the goal we were to go to,[11] and came as the way we were to go by.

So then, dearly beloved, *children of peace* (Lk 10:8), *children of light* (Jn 12:36; Eph 5:8), children of charity, sprigs of the Catholic Church,[12] if we are strong, let us serve the weak and infirm; if we are in good health, let us make ourselves the slaves of the sick. You observe that our Lord made himself a slave; the sick person is a slave, whom his Lord and master serves as a slave. Come on, let us praise our bread with all the powers we can muster: *Behold, how good and how delightful, brothers dwelling together as one!* (Ps 133:1). *Take delight, you just, in the Lord* (Ps 33:1).

> *Even Donatists have to admit that unity is a good thing;*
> *forcing it on them by law is like forcibly feeding the sick*

5. Plainly a good thing, *brothers dwelling together as one*. Everyone agrees that it's good; not everyone accepts that it is delightful. Ask anyone you like, whether he's still a heretic, or now putting on a front, hiding his real mind; ask him, question him when he's turning up his nose at unity, rejecting it, pushing away the hand of the person serving him and wishing to feed him in his sickness. Stick to him all the same, go on asking him, "Is unity a good thing?" Let him say if he can, "It's a bad thing."

I'm not letting you off, I insist on the question: Is unity a good thing?

He answers, "Yes, a good thing." Willy-nilly, that's what he answers, "Unity is a good thing."

Or do you just keep quiet? Even if you keep quiet, the reason you do so is that you cannot say, "It isn't a good thing." Iniquity won't let you say it's a good thing, but truth won't allow you to deny that it's a good thing.

Still, I insist on extracting a word from you; I won't give up, I won't go away, you won't get rid of me unless you say something. At long, long last I've found your ears.[13] If I can't hold onto you through your love, I'm at least holding onto you through your fear.[14] Speak, answer me. It's perfectly easy, what I'm asking for, a short answer is all I require. Is unity a good thing?

What's he to do? In no way at all is he going to say, "It isn't a good thing." So at least to get rid of me, he's going to say, "Yes, it's a good thing."

And I reply: If what you're praising like that is a possession, possess it together with me; if it's a garment, wear it together with me;[15] if it's bread, eat it together with me.

"It's a good thing," he says, "I don't deny it. But because I'm being forced into it, that's why I'm refusing it."

So it's a good thing, but just because you are being forced into the good thing, that's why you don't want the good thing, as though, forsooth, I on my side would be making a nuisance of myself in forcing you into it, if you on yours were eagerly and avidly seeking it! If it's a good thing, and you don't want it, that's why I'm using force.

Since you admit, after all, that it's a good thing, it isn't out of a concern for truth that you decline it, but because you're ill. I'm at your service in your illness; you're sick, I'm ministering to you. I'm offering you nourishment, accept the food which you praise as being good. Or surely you're not going to be like sick people, are you, when they refuse the food set before them, and find fault with it as being badly cooked? You won't be able to say anything like that against the food I'm offering you. This bread is Christ, this peace is Christ. This food was kneaded and molded in the virgin's womb, it was baked in the fire of Christ's passion. Accept it, brother; take it, brother, take something, or you will die. You undoubtedly praise unity as a good thing; it's your illness that is opposing me, not your judgment. I'm offering you food, food not only to strengthen the sick, but also to support the sick.[16] I'm making a nuisance of myself when I forcibly feed you with it, but I will be inhumanly cruel if I take it away from you.

"All right," he says, "I'll accept it."

The maternal solicitude of God and of the Church

6. What sort of sick people we have to put up with, brothers and sisters! "All right," he says, "I'll accept it." Some have come along, giving in to the nagging of us their servants, to the importunity, unseasonable if you like, but still of their parents showing a truly maternal love and charity. What do I mean by parents, brothers and sisters? Not me, I don't mean any human being. Our parents, feeding the healthy, restoring the sick, are God our Father, and our mother the Church. And so it's this doting mother, conceiving and giving birth to her children when their lives are in danger, who hasn't ignored the sickness of her offspring. Even if she makes a nuisance of herself, even if she is unseasonably importunate, she has come up to their bedsides; she has forcibly fed those who were refusing food. They hate her taking care of them; they should rather be afraid[17] of experiencing her mourning them. She takes care of the sick; she mourns the dead. May she go on being a nuisance in . . .[18]

NOTES

1. Dolbeau dates it more precisely to the autumn of 406, September to November. The sermon follows and refers to an imperial edict of February 405, which imposed union on the Donatists. For such legislation against the Donatists, see also Sermon 46, 41 (III, 2). This sermon came also after a busy and exhausting summer (section 2), which Augustine endured in 406, but not in 405.

The Mainz manuscript is damaged, and the last part of the sermon is missing, the actual text ending in mid-sentence. It also seems to me, though Dolbeau does not mention the point, that the beginning too may well have been lost. At least, to begin a sermon with the conjunction *enim* (*Nihil est enim dulcius*) would surely be an odd thing to do. But possibly all that had preceded the sermon was a stentorian shout of "Quiet, please!" from deacon or verger.

2. The reference is ultimately, no doubt, to the "disagreement" (*dissensio*) of Donatists with Catholics. But immediately, so I infer, it was most likely to bickering, within the actual congregation present, between some groups who were being rather noisy and those at the back of the basilica who couldn't hear the preacher.

3. By the hard labor imposed on it by charity.

4. See Sermon 380, 1 (III, 10).

5. The *magnae necessitates* were, according to Dolbeau, the need to get the edict of February 405 enforced, and the troubles, often violent, that accompanied its enforcement. It called for the confiscation of all church property of the Donatists and the transfer of it to the Catholics, and probably imposed exile on Donatist bishops who refused to conform. The trouble would have been at its height in the summer of 406 rather than of 405, Dolbeau thinks, because it appears, from Augustine's Letter 86, that the authorities in Hippo Regius were very slow in enforcing the edict, and Augustine had to lean on them to do so.

6. A very condensed sentence, not easy to make sense of. I think the clause "so that . . ." is explaining why he says he has been dragged away from Hippo Regius (*rapti*, snatched away, seized). Normally he would have been delighted to come; Dolbeau argues plausibly that he was preaching this sermon in his home town of Thagaste, where his bosom friend Alypius was the bishop.

7. A Donatist bishop, most probably of the little town or large village of Siniti, which seems not to have had a Catholic bishop, but to have been a district of Augustine's own diocese of Hippo Regius. Maximinus had very recently joined the Catholic Church, in which the validity of his orders as a bishop was acknowledged; and so he had become Augustine's colleague, and doubtless they had been going round the area together, encouraging other still reluctant Donatists to follow the good bishop's example. In Siniti itself, according to Letter 105, 2 and 4, his action had in fact provoked a violent reaction. He seems to have died about 408, or a little before, which makes that year the latest possible for the date of this sermon.

8. Either Siniti itself, or Hippo Regius.

9. A little play with assonance—*Panem ergo pacem habemus*—not quite so forced as his earlier play with *caro* and *caritas*.

10. See Jn 14:6.

11. Augustine means that Christ remained the eternal divine Word. He always interprets Jesus' saying, *I am the way, the truth and the life*, as meaning that he is in his humanity our way to him as divine truth and divine life.

12. See Sermon 359B, 16 (this volume), note 49, and the other sermons there referred to: 34, 6 (III, 2) and 146, 1 (III, 4).

13. That is, he has found the reluctant ex-Donatists, those who are complaining about being forced into unity, as a captive audience in his Catholic congregation.

14. Fear of the penalties imposed by the imperial edict of unity.

15. The allusion is to the "seamless robe" of Christ (Jn 19:23), always treated in the patristic tradition as a symbol of the Church's unity.

16. What distinction, if any, he sees between strengthening (*confirmet*) and supporting (*sustinet*, which should be *sustineat*) I cannot tell. Dolbeau qualifies the passage as "scarcely sound"; whether because of its intrinsic lack of sense or some defect in the manuscript, I cannot tell either.

17. Reading *timeant*, subjunctive, as Dolbeau suggests, rather than the text's indicative, *timent*, "they are afraid . . ."

18. Here the Mainz text breaks off, after the words, *Sit molesta in eo . . .*

Dolbeau 23
SERMON 374
Mainz 59

SERMON OF SAINT AUGUSTINE PREACHED ON THE EPIPHANY

Date: 409[1]

The reward God has promised us is to see him face to face

1. The annual celebration of this day exacts an annual sermon from me, a debt owed to your ears and minds[2] and, if you listen devoutly and dutifully, owed also to your consciences.[3] Justice, you see, is the whole product of our lives, and eternal life is the payment it earns, and justice begins with faith. We have not, after all, been called to what we can now see, and we do not yet possess what we have been promised. But because the one who made the promise is true to his word, we first have to live in hope, in order to earn the life that is the real thing.[4] God is undoubtedly going to give us what he has promised; but because what he is going to give us is so great, by putting it off he is stretching our desire for it, in order to make us capacious enough to take such a gift.

He is not, after all, going to give us what passes as good things in this world, perishable, changeable, fragile things, which fill us with fears of all sorts when we have them in plenty, while when they are withdrawn they fill us with grief. But he's going to give us—what do you suppose? Something of this earth? Perish the thought! Something of the heavens, such as we can see with our bodily eyes? This too is utterly paltry, compared with the promised gift, to take hold of which hearts are purified.[5] I mean, if God were going to give you something now which belongs to the present time, he would ask you to open your eyes to see what he was giving you. But because he is going to give *what eye has not seen nor has ear heard nor has it come up into the heart of man* (1 Cor 2:9), as the apostle says, what is he preparing for you as one to whom he can give it?[6] *Blessed*, he says, *are the pure-hearted, because it is they who will see God* (Mt 5:8).

So then, our total reward will consist in seeing God. Or is it a paltry reward, to see the one you were made by? Yes, by all means stretch wide the lap of your greed, be avid and grasping in desiring what such a great one has promised; he still cannot give you anything better than himself.[7] Whatever God has made, after all, is inferior to and worth less than its maker.

392

The good things of creation are not enough

2. And where does God's creation begin? With the angels. And where does God's creation leave off? With the mortal things of earth. The created order has an upward limit, beyond which is God; the created order has a downward limit, beyond which is nothing. So begin meanwhile to count the gifts which you have, not yet having received those you have been called to. Start away. Observe the good things of earth—the light, the sort of nourishment given by the air, without which we cannot exist for a moment; next the fruits of the earth, the springs, the very health of our bodies, and any other such things you can make a list of, which had to be touched on briefly. They are gifts of God, they are the divine bounty.

But don't long for these things, as though they were of the first importance, from the one in whose image you were made.[8] You can see, after all, that these are things you are still sharing with animals, and you won't find anyone you can get them from besides that true God, the creator and bestower of all things. But for all that, you mustn't now be content with these things, just because he is the one who gives them too; he's keeping something special for his image which he doesn't give to animals. So let us inquire what it might be, and once it has been identified let us set our hearts on it, and having set our hearts on it let us wait for it, and in order that we may obtain it, let us do what the one who has promised it tells us to.

The heavenly reward must be worked for on earth

3. There the payment, here the work.[9] The one who has promised payment has also given instructions; while telling you beforehand what you are to receive, he is also telling you what you are to do. If you love the reward of faith, you shouldn't run away from the toilsome work it involves. He will give the reward; God, after all, is true to his word. Someone who promises something and doesn't give it fails to give it in two ways: either because he's false, or because he's unable to give it. What things of that sort can we possibly say about God? Can Truth be false? Is there anything the Almighty cannot do? So if he's both true to his word and has the means of giving, why should he deceive you? Take heart, have no anxiety about your hopes; the one who made the promise is powerful, he's eternal.

Or are you afraid that when you've done what you're told, before you get what you've been promised, something may happen to the maker of the promise?[10] So let's rather look at what has been promised. Let us rise above these good things we share with animals; let us see what human beings have more than animals, which you already possess: speech, intelligence, the ability to distinguish the true from the false, the just from the iniquitous, to desire, finally,[11] the one by whom we were made.

It is not anything shared with the unjust that is promised us

4. It's a supreme work to seek the one whom it is supremely rewarding to find. So then, what sets a man apart from animals is his speech-making capacity; or rather, he differs from animals in his capacity for speech, from some other human beings in his capacity for making eloquent speeches.[12] It's a great thing, this gift of eloquence, a great good; but bad people also possess it. It isn't shared with animals, but it *is* shared with the unjust. Many people are endowed with eloquence, and are bad, and they make use of this very eloquence in running rings round many others and defrauding them, and in seeking secular power for themselves. All such people are to be condemned, but still they are human beings.

Seek something from God which, as well as not sharing with animals, you don't even share with a bad man. If I mentioned eloquence just now, take the same thing as applying to riches. You see, he didn't give riches to animals, but to human beings. It belongs to human beings, after all, to direct, to rule, to govern. But still, many bad people also possess riches. This is still an earthly good, which both good people possess and bad people possess, and which both good people lack and bad people lack. Look for something nobler. Why be afraid that when you have found something choice which cannot be given either to animals or to bad men, the Almighty won't be able to give it to you, after calling you to the performance of the work and the reception of the bounty?

"I've found something."

What are you going to find? Bad people too have talents, bad people too have good memories, bad people too, as I said, have riches, bad people too have honors and power in the world. What are you going to find?[13]

The good with which we can do good, and the good that makes us good

5. Oh, if only you would listen to me, don't look for anything from God except God. Certainly, anyone he gives this to, it also makes that person good. It cannot be shared with bad people, seeing that when received it is what distinguishes you from bad people. There is, you see, one kind of good thing with which you can do some good, and there's another kind of good thing by which you can become good.[14] You've got gold; it's good, but to do good with. You're eloquent, you've the gift of gab; it's good, but to achieve good ends with. You enjoy health of body; use it well. Many people, after all, have been much improved by a bout of illness and ruined by good health. Many have caught an illness for their good, been restored to health for their undoing. So even actual bodily health, which is the poor man's patrimony,[15] can also be harmful unless it is turned to good use.

A sharp mind is a great good, but still the sort that the good can use well and the bad badly; it's not yet a good by which you can become good. All the perversities of all errors, all sects preaching deviant morals and ungodliness,[16] have had as their authors men of great brilliance. They weren't the brain-children of any sort of men, they were started by men of the sharpest intelligence.

All the trifling tricks of the theater—it was only by men of great ingenuity that they were thought up for the corruption of the human race.

"They all do great harm, they are certainly disgraceful."

They're disgraceful, you say. So then, how can it be honorable to watch what it is disgraceful to act? You admit it's disgraceful, and your favor makes it possible to put it on. I don't know whom I should call worse, the seller of disgraceful performances or the buyer.[17] And yet these things were thought up and started by very sharp minds.

So then, intellectual brilliance is a good thing, but only if you use it well. Up to now I have been listing those goods with which you can do good, not by which you can become good. If that good by which you can become good comes upon you, you make good use of the other goods, while if that good by which you can be made good does not come upon you, how will you, bad as you are, be able to make good use of the other goods? What is the good by which you become good? It is God himself.

Spirit better than body; it can see things invisible to bodily eyes

6. There is a kind of thing which can be descried by the mind. It is not, surely, the case that the eyes have something they can see and the mind does not. Which is better, body or spirit? I think that even lifeless bodies, if they could, would answer that spirit is better.[18] But he doesn't want to tell me that spirit is better than body. So I put the question like this: "Which is better, the one who controls or the one who is controlled?" Now here I rather think that not even the animals would hesitate to answer that the one in control is the better. So which is in control? The spirit, of course, which is thus better than the body.

If the spirit goes missing, the windows of the body, even if the shutters are open, have no one who can see through them. The eyes are open, the ears are open; if the occupier is absent, what's the use of the shutters being drawn back? So it's the spirit that perceives certain things through the eyes—light, colors, shapes; the spirit that perceives certain things through the ears—voices, words and sounds; the spirit that perceives certain things with the sense of smell—all odors; the spirit that perceives all flavors with the sense of taste, the spirit that perceives with the whole body what is hard and soft, rough and smooth, cold and hot, light and heavy. The eye doesn't hear, and the ear doesn't see, while the spirit both sees through the eye and hears through the ear. It can't do both through each, but still it alone can do what it can do through each.[19]

Can the spirit do nothing by itself? It can do things even through the body, can't do anything by itself? It sees white and black through the body, can't see just and unjust by itself? And yet there are many people who think the only things that exist are what can be seen through the body, thus doing injustice to their own minds and showing themselves ungrateful to God, by whom they have been made in his own image. The occupier is inside, he has other eyes of his own.

7. If I wanted to display jewels, if I wanted to display things of silver and gold, hand-made vessels, precious garments and any other things that are

counted as very precious and beautiful among human treasures, if finally I wished to point to the sky and what is the star-studded, not the paneled, bed-chamber of the poor, what should I look for in you? Your eyes. When I want to show what is just and what is unjust, what do I look for, to what do I show it?

But perhaps in this case I don't have anything to show. Because this too is what some people have thought—that there is no such thing as justice by nature, but that it is constituted by opinion; that is to say, that only that is just—or rather is called just—which men have decided is just by a kind of agreement of human society, not by any objective nature of justice. Is there really, when all's said and done, no nature of justice? We toil away at demonstrating—and yet what we know by the spirit alone is what we ought to know most definitely—we toil away at demonstrating what the nature of justice is, and we don't have to toil away at demonstrating that there is such a thing as gold, as the earth, as the sky. Do I have to toil away to point these things out? Everyone cries out that what can be seen through the body exists, and many deny that what can only be seen by the spirit exists.

Faith the indispensable cure for blindness of spirit

8. This spirit,[20] if I'm not mistaken, is sick, its eyes, if I'm not mistaken, have been damaged or even put out. How are they to be restored, how are they to be healed? The door to a cure is faith. In order to see, after all, what it doesn't see, it will have to believe that what it is to see exists, but that it is not itself yet such a one as is fit to see it.

"Perhaps I can see it; point it out to me."

But to whom shall I point it out? As a matter of fact, not even I can do this, but he alone can, who also pointed it out to me, if I do see anything on this score. The doctor has come to the sick patient whose eyes have been damaged, or perhaps already lost—he has forgotten he could ever see, or possibly he has never been able to see from birth. But still the doctor is so skilled that he is able to rid the patient of this ancient blindness by an operation. He promises that there is something he can point out and show, if the patient will suffer himself to be cured. As for him, of course, how will he ever be cured if he doesn't believe the doctor before he is actually able to see?

"There is," he says, "something for you to see; but you will only see it when your eyes are in good health."

And the patient answers: "Unless I, though, can first see, I will not be cured."

What an absurd and perverse answer! Wanting first to see in order to be cured, when of course if he could see, there would be no reason for him to be cured. So believe the doctor who is going to show you, and don't oppose him when he's going to cure you.

"Show me," he says.

What shall I show you?

"God."

To whom?

"To me, if you want me to believe, because I only believe what I can see."

Whom are you seeking to have shown, to whom are you seeking to have him shown, by whom are you seeking to have him shown? It is God who is to be shown, a human being to whom he is to be shown, by a human being that he cannot be shown. Only he himself can show himself. All I here can do is advise you what to do, so that you may earn the right to see.

As the soul can be seen through its works, so too can God through his

9. "There most certainly isn't," he says, "no, there isn't any God." Everybody is horrified. Who can have said this? And yet the psalm didn't keep quiet about it: *The fool has said in his heart: There is no God* (Ps 14:1; 53:1). Because it's the kind of saying that horrifies everybody, he said it in his heart, he didn't commit it to tongue and voice.

However, I too have a request to make. "Show me God," he says. Brother, let us look for him together. All the same, even if I attempt to show him to you and don't succeed—I mean, perhaps time too is needed, some study is needed, some rules are needed—still, I too have a question to ask. You say, "Show me God"; I say, "Show me your soul." You for your part are looking for the most exalted of things from me, I on the other hand for just a lowly one; you for the one from whom you are absent, I for the one which is present; you for the one to be looked for, I for the one doing the looking.

Look here, if I say you haven't got a soul, what will you do? I mean, if it's only our eyes that we must believe, then you haven't got a soul. Unless I can see your soul, I won't believe there is such a thing.

You're going to say, "Indeed my soul can't be seen with the eyes, but it can be demonstrated through its actions. You see me walking, hear me talking; you speak, I answer, and can you doubt I have a soul?"[21]

So we've got to the point that I haven't seen your soul, but I have seen the actions of your soul. If I acknowledge the existence of your soul through the actions of your soul, you just acknowledge the existence of God through the actions of God. The soul must exist, because it moves the flesh; and doesn't God exist, who moves the world?

Doesn't the very ordering of things fill you with awe: earthly affairs governed by heavenly bodies, the alternations of night and day, the arrangement of the seasons, the shining of the sun filling the day with brightness, of the moon and the stars moderating the darkness of the night, the crops and fruits growing from the earth, the springs flowing? The very animals which are born on the earth are born with life; what is made is alive, and does the one who makes have no life? So there is a God, God does exist, far be it from us to doubt it. But even so, there may be doubters still seeking, but they should seek in such a way that they begin by believing, or else they will not earn the right by believing to find what they are seeking.[22]

10. So there is a God, and the question really is how he is to be worshiped, rather than whether he exists. So what now, then? On this point too I would like

to speak. Well, it's easy enough for me, I think, to speak about it to Christians; God is to be worshiped in the way he said he was to be worshiped. I mean, if Christians ask me how God said he was to be worshiped, I don't put out my own words, I just read out the book which they undoubtedly submit to in virtue of their faith; they are not permitted, after all, to have doubts about the divine scriptures. God also wished to have written down how he wished to be worshiped; what he wished to be written down, he wished to be read out, and he gave such a peak and pitch of authority to this writing that he placed all authors of any other books under its feet.

There have been people, after all, who wrote whatever they liked as they liked; have any of their books been placed on such a peak of authority that the world responds to them by saying "Amen"?[23] When I have to deal, perhaps, with someone who hasn't submitted to the authority of our books, and who argues with me and says, "It was human beings who wrote these things for themselves," what am I to do? How are we to prove that these writings are divine?

*New Testament miracles not really more wonderful than the miracles
performed every day by God in nature*

11. Apart from the orderly workings of nature by which the world is governed, people have not felt any awe at most of God's works, unless they have been deeds and words that were miracles.[24] Nature indeed is full of marvelous miracles, but all these marvelous things have grown cheap by their regular frequency. Thus, let one man who already existed among men rise from the dead, it's a divine work acclaimed by everyone; so many who didn't exist are born every day, and nobody marvels at it. Christ turned water into wine, a great miracle![25] Who else does the same thing every year in the vine? You don't think it's particularly wonderful that moisture is drawn from the earth, converted into the quality of that kind of wood, passes through the branches, opens out the leaves, also produces the swelling clusters of grapes, makes them grow while they are unripe, gives them color when they ripen? To find out how all this happens, question the roots. What numbers there, what measures must there be, what skillful activity in such a minute and insignificant appearance![26]

I'm still admiring the work that goes on in the root, and the original seed turns out more wonderful still. How small it is, how almost nothing, and yet in it are all the numbers of the root that is to come, of the tree trunk and the branches, of the fruit, of the leaves, all the busy working numbers drawing up the sap and turning it into such a lovely and delightful work. Such are the stupendous works of the creator. You haven't yet gone up to heaven to see him actually present, and you already find him forging and fashioning everything on earth. These things all demand an appreciative observer, because what could be more wonderful than such works?

And yet because they are of daily occurrence, as I said, they have become commonplace and cheap. That's why God, wanting to stir up people's imaginations, kept back some things for himself which are not greater but are certainly rarer. Making a human being, after all, is certainly something more than resuscitating one. But because nobody was moved to wonder at his making them every day, he showed himself on occasion resuscitating them.[27] He granted sight to the blind, hearing to the deaf, speech to the dumb.[28] He does these things in seeds without causing any surprise; he did them in human beings to everybody's utter amazement.

The miracle of prophetic prediction

12. These things have been written down, these things are read out. "But nowadays," he says, "they don't happen, and I rather fear that these stories were written by men, and didn't happen in fact." We sometimes experience such questioners—not indeed that you here ought to be like that, but that you should be capable of answering people like that. I know that what I'm saying is almost totally unnecessary for believers, but let me be, for the moment, like one trying to convince unbelievers, so that you for your part can be well equipped against unbelievers. There are people who say, only a few such nowadays, but still there are some: "These stories were written down, but they didn't really happen."

So how am I going to prove that they did happen? Clearly, every miracle is either one that is done or that's spoken. Miracles that are done are things that are done outside the ordinary course and order of nature, while ones that are spoken are those by which the future is foretold. Accordingly, if you don't want to believe the miracles that were done, which have been written down in order to be read out, at least believe the spoken miracles which are shown to be true by the event itself. It's here, you see, that the one who has told you the story of past marvels proves his trustworthiness, when you see the future things he foretold actually present before your eyes. Or perhaps divination is not divine, though that's how it gets its very name, divination which has such a grip on human curiosity that the reason many people today decline to be Christians is that they want to be allowed to consult mediums, astrologers, soothsayers and—what else can I say?—magicians, magi? But the works too of this art are being brought to nothing by the same power of Christ which led the magi from such a far distant nation to come and worship him.[29]

The magi offered Christ what they had hitherto offered to their false gods

13. They came to worship an infant, the Word of God.[30] Why did they come? Because they had seen an unusual star. And how did they know it was Christ's star? I mean, they could see a star; could it speak to them and say, "I am the star of Christ"? There can be no doubt that they were shown this by some other means, by some revelation. Still, a king had been born in unusual circumstances, one who was also to be worshiped by foreigners. Hadn't kings been born before in Judea, or throughout the whole earth in different nations? Why was this one to be worshiped, and worshiped by foreigners, with no army to cow them, but in the poverty of the flesh, concealing the majesty of his power?

When he was born, he was worshiped by Israelite shepherds, to whom angels had proclaimed him.[31] But the magi were not from Israel; they worshiped idols, or the gods of the nations, that is to say, demons, whose deceptive powers were constantly leading them astray. So they saw some unusual star, they were astonished; they undoubtedly inquired whose sign it might be, this new and unprecedented thing they had seen, and of course they heard the answer.

But you're going to say, "From whom did they hear it?" Surely from angels, from some revealing suggestion.

You will ask, perhaps, "From good angels, or bad ones? Bad angels too, that is to say, demons, confessed that Christ was the son of God."[32]

But why shouldn't they have also heard it from good angels, seeing that it was their salvation that was already being sought through their worshiping Christ, and not iniquity that was controling them?[33] So it could have been angels saying to them, "The star you saw is the Christ's; go and worship him where he was born," and at the same time indicating precisely who and what it was that had been born. When they heard this, they came and worshiped him. They offered gold, frankincense and myrrh[34] as gifts, according to their custom. Such were the things, you see, that they were in the habit of offering to their gods.

Why the magi had to ask the Jews where the Christ was born

14. Before they did this, of course, before they found him in the city where he had been born, they came with their inquiry, *Where has the king of the Jews been born?* (Mt 2:2). Couldn't they have also come to know this by revelation, just as they had come to know that that star was the star of the king of the Jews, who was to be worshiped by foreigners as well? Couldn't the same star have led them to that city, just as later on it led them to the place where the infant Christ was to be found with his mother? Of course it could have, but still that didn't happen, so that they would have to make this inquiry from the Jews. Why did God want to have this inquiry made of the Jews? So that while they point out the way to the one in whom they don't believe, they might be condemned by their very action in doing so.

Notice that this is also happening now. The magi, the first-fruits of the nations, give all the greater glory to their deliverer, the greater the godlessness they are delivered by.[35] They inquire, *Where is the one who has been born king of the Jews?* When Herod hears the name "king," he trembles as at the threat of a rival.[36] He summons the learned lawyers, he asks them to indicate according to the scriptures where the Christ would be born. They answer, *In Bethlehem of Judah* (Mt 2:3-5). The magi went on and worshiped him; the Jews stayed behind, though they had shown where he was.

15. What a significant dispensation![37] Today it's from the volumes of the Jews that we convince unbelievers they should become believers; through their volumes that we demonstrate to pagans what they are unwilling to believe. Sometimes, you see, pagans put this sort of question to us, when they see that what has been written in the scriptures has been fulfilled in such a way that they

can't possibly deny that things are presently happening through the name of Christ among all nations which have been foretold in the holy books—kings coming to believe, idols overthrown, a revolution in human affairs. And sometimes they are so upset that they say, "You saw all these things happening, and you wrote them up as though they had been foretold."

This is what one of their own poets did; those who have read it will catch the reference. He told the story of someone going down to the underworld, and coming to the region of the blessed, where he was shown the leading men of the Romans that were going to be born, though the writer knew all about them since they had already been born.[38] He was in fact, you see, telling the story of past events, but he wrote of them as though they were future events being foretold. "In the same way you people too," the pagans say to us, "have seen all these things happening, and you have written volumes for yourselves in which these things can be read about as having been foretold."

Oh the glory of our king! How appropriate that the Jews were conquered by the Romans, and yet not wiped out! All the other nations subjugated by the Romans went over to the laws of the Romans; this nation was both conquered and yet remained with its own law. As far as the worship of God is concerned, it preserved its ancestral customs and rites. Even though their temple had been demolished and their ancient priesthood extinguished, as foretold by the prophets,[39] they still keep circumcision and a certain way of life which distinguishes them from other nations. For what other purpose but for bearing witness to the truth? The Jews have been dispersed everywhere, carrying the volumes in which the pagans can be shown how Christ was foretold, and then can be presented with him being precisely as he was foretold. I bring out a volume, I read a prophet, I point out how the prophecy has been fulfilled. The pagan has his doubts, he wonders whether I have perhaps fabricated it all myself. My opponent has this same volume, handed down to him from of old by his forebears. From this I convince them both: the Jew, because I know that what was there prophesied has been fulfilled; the pagan, because it certainly wasn't fabricated by me.

The old sacrifices now give way to the one true sacrifice

16. So don't let the demons, with their specious divination, lead astray the careless and those who are idly curious about temporal affairs, nor deceive the godless with their proud disdain, and exact from them the honor of being offered sacrifices. The foretelling of divine truths belongs to the one true God. The true sacrifice[40] is owed to the one true God; various models of it were sketched beforehand in incense and victims. Thus divine providence, by foretelling in many ways what was going to be accomplished in one way, would show how great this true sacrifice would be. Because among the other things that were foretold as going to come about in Christian times,[41] this too was prophesied, that all the things that were previously offered to God in various sacrifices were to be totally changed.

"So why were they laid down," you say, "if they were due to be changed?"

O my dear sick man, don't start giving the doctor advice about how you are to be cured. One man, Adam, has filled the whole wide world with his progeny. The human race, as if it were a single individual, is lying like a great big sick patient from the furthest east as far as the extreme west, and in need of a cure. A great big patient, but a greater and bigger doctor. So let's now take a comparison from the actual human profession of medicine.[42]

The doctor visits the patient, and says, "Take this one in the morning,and that one in the afternoon."

And the patient comes back to the doctor with, "Why not the same one in the afternoon as in the morning?"

Doesn't the doctor rightly reply, "You can get sick, you can't cure yourself; allow the profession to advise on your health."

"So," retorts the patient, "the profession is inconsistent, prescribing one thing to begin with, another one later on."

"Just lie back and rest, if you don't mind, and let yourself be restored to health. The profession is consistent, it knows what to apply in the morning, what in the afternoon. It's not the profession that has changed, but your sickness is changeable. The profession knows what is suitable when; it copes with variable diseases as changes in time require."

So in the same sort of way, then, some things were good for the benefit of the human race in earlier times, other things are good in later times. You ask why? Be friendly with the doctor, and perhaps you will come to understand, or else perhaps even today you may not think that we ought by rights to go off and sacrifice to God except with a bull, with a ram, with incense.

Proof from Jeremiah that there would be a new covenant

17. "Show me," somebody says, "that he gave these orders and foretold that these things were to be changed, and I will believe, in case you are maybe telling me this on your own, not on divine authority." So listen to God's words, just a few out of many. *Behold the days will come, says the Lord.* It's a prophet speaking. If you think this has been made up by Christians, let the Jew bring out the volume. So how can it be me who made up what my opponent has been carrying around from long ago? So let the volume be produced from the library of the Jews, and let us read out from that.

What are we going to read out? *Behold the days will come, says the Lord, and I will draw up for the house of Israel and the house of Judah a new covenant* (Jer 31:31).

"But perhaps he's talking about that covenant which the Jews received, and he says that it was new when our forebears[43] received what had been given through Moses on Mount Sinai, because it hadn't been previously in the history of the human race."

You've prepared your case well;[44] but wait a bit. I'm insisting on patience until I read out the rest. Listen to this about the new covenant: *Behold the days will come, says the Lord, and I will draw up for the house of Israel and the house of Judah a new covenant.* I'm still not giving the rest of it. Who is it that's speaking? Jeremiah. When did Jeremiah prophesy? Long after Moses, through whom the first covenant was given. So if it's Jeremiah who is saying, *Behold the days will come*—he's talking about the future—*and I will draw up for the house of Israel and the house of Judah a new covenant,* there is no reason for saying that the covenant meant was the one given through Moses. So he's calling another covenant the new one. But still, listen also to the rest of it: *Behold the days will come, says the Lord, and I will draw up for the house of Israel and the house of Judah a new covenant, not according to the covenant which I arranged with their fathers, on the day when I took hold of their hand to lead them out of the land of Egypt* (Jer 31:31-32). What could be clearer? That, you see, is when the first covenant, which is called the old one, was given through Moses.

18. Come now, brothers and sisters, pay attention to the divine utterances. We read the prediction, we observe the fulfillment, and do we still have doubts about the divine authority of these books? So nobody should now go on saying, "Look, the magi gave incense to Christ; why don't we too burn incense to Christ?"

Note first of all that the magi gave incense, they hadn't burnt it.

"But why," you say, "did he accept this gift?"

As if, forsooth, these magi are going to be forbidden from offering anything created to the creator! God, not demons, made incense, God made myrrh, God made gold. The magi, and magicians in general,[45] sin by giving them to demons and thereby showing them honor, thus using creatures to wrong the creator.

Today, however, you must get used to the idea[46] that these magi gave the same sort of things as they had been accustomed to give to their gods. Still, it wasn't to no purpose that Christ allowed them to give him such things; they were signs rather more than gifts. He accepted incense as God, gold as king, myrrh as one due to die, for his burial. At that time, though, it was not only incense but also animal victims that were offered both by pagans and by Jews, that is, by those who were worshipers of many false gods and by those who were worshipers of the one true God. These things, I repeat, used to be offered to God according to the old covenant, but he changed it under the new covenant. *Behold, he says, the days will come, says the Lord, and I will draw up for the house of Israel and the house of Judah a new covenant, not according to the covenant which I arranged with their fathers, on the day when I took hold of their hand to lead them out of the land of Egypt* (Jer 31:31-32).

The same point proved from Isaiah about sacrifices in particular

19. "But," someone says, "he didn't say this about sacrifices." So do you want to hear something about sacrifices? That God foretold that it would come to pass that all those sacrifices would be done away with, and that one sacrifice would be given, the body of Christ purging away sins, is something the faithful know.[47] And what I am saying will not, I realize, be understood by everybody; but those who do understand should rejoice and live in a manner worthy of such

a great sacrament, while as for those who don't yet understand, it's in their power to change their way of life, to receive the sacrament of change,[48] and to know what is offered by the faithful, what is received by them.

It's there, you see, that you find what was foretold: *You are a priest forever according to the order of Melchizedek* (Ps 110:4). The first priesthood, you see, was according to the order of Aaron, but later our high priest was told, and this through a prophet long before he came in the flesh, *You are a priest for ever according to the order of Melchizedek*. So the order of Aaron was changed, and in its place came the order of Melchizedek. According to the order of Aaron it was animal victims, according to Melchizedek the body of Christ.

"But you still haven't said," someone insists, "whether God foretold that those sacrifices were going to cease."

Look, I'll read it to you, in case something should by chance escape my memory. I, after all, brothers and sisters, didn't study this literature from my youth, while other pointless texts I can still recite by heart which makes it much worse. These, on the other hand, to which I didn't apply myself from boyhood on, I am unable to recite unless I look at the texts.[49] Or perhaps it's more useful for you that you should hear from a divine book what it is salutary for you to know, and not from my mouth. Listen now, and stop being surprised that we don't anymore come to Christ with incense, not since he instituted this other sacrifice of which all previous ones were mere shadows.[50]

20. Among many other things the prophet Isaiah, whose volume I have in my hand, says—what does Isaiah say? *There is no cause for you to be mindful of ancient things or to call old things to mind*. There you are, brothers and sisters, already the abolition of the old ways is evident.

"But still," you say, "he hasn't said anything about sacrifices. Perhaps he changed other things, didn't change these."

Although it's a general statement, "not to call old things to mind," even there let me understand what the apostle's teaching coming later taught me, what I am to offer, what I am no longer to offer—I do have an expounder of this obscurity, I do have a master who tells me in what respect to take it. Still, not even the prophet himself allows a man to guess what he likes; he says openly, I mean, what you are going to hear. So listen.

There is no cause for you to be mindful of ancient things or to call old things to mind. For I will do new things which will spring up now, and you will understand (Is 43:18-19). What's this, *For I will do new things which will spring up now, and you will understand*? It means, "I will do new things which were not there before, so that you can understand the things that were there before." An animal used to be slaughtered, blood poured out, and by means of the blood God was being placated. But was God really being placated by means of the blood, and does God really hanker after blood, and does God really take delight in the smoke of sacrifices, or does the one who created all things, who gives you all things, really have a craving for the smell of incense or other aromatic spices? Far be it from you to believe that! It's your devotion that he feeds on, and that indeed for your benefit, not for that of the one you are serving as his slave.

Every human slave of a human lord and master serves his master for his master's benefit, and again the master takes care of his slave for his slave's benefit. It's not like that with God. Those who serve him serve him for their own benefit, not for his. And am I perhaps saying this from myself? Listen to the prophet: *I said to the Lord*—what? *It is you who are my Lord*—why? *Since you have no need*, he says, *of my good things* (Ps 16:2). There you have an unconditional statement, there's nothing you can have any hesitation about; God has no need of your good things. So stop believing that your God is in need of such sacrifices, but ask yourself what lesson they are teaching, what they mean.

Previously blood used to be shed by animal victims, because the blood was being foretold that was to be shed by the one true victim, the blood of your Lord, the blood that is the price paid for you, the blood by which the bond of your debt would be cancelled, by which, that is, the old staleness of your sin would be eliminated.[51] It has happened, it has been shed, he himself is being offered. *Let the day now breathe, and the shadows withdraw* (Sg 2:17; 4:6). *There is no cause for you to be mindful of ancient things or to call old things to mind. For I will do new things which will spring up now, and you will understand.* Now at last we can understand why those things came before which were foretelling things to come. They all point to Christ, they all have their end in Christ. *I will do*, he says, *new things which will spring up now, and you will understand.* Before all these new things came about, the old ones were being practiced and not being understood.

21. What comes next? *I will make a way in the wilderness.* In which wilderness? That of the nations, of course, where there was no worship of the true God. *I will make a way in the wilderness, and streams in the dry places.* Nowhere among the nations were the prophets ever read, now their writings are flooding all the nations. You can see the *streams in dry places. The beasts of the field shall bless me.* What's "the beasts of the field," if it isn't to be understood as the Tentiles? *The beasts of the field shall bless me and the siren daughters of ostriches*[52] (Is 43:19-20). Some godless souls, daughters of demons, shall bless me. How, if not by forsaking the devil and being converted to Christ?

"But the whole passage is still obscure, and needs to be explained more plainly in a way suited to our capacity. Tell us where it is demonstrated that God was displeased with the sacrifice of animal victims."

I certainly, if I couldn't read out anything plainer, would never have dared take this volume in my hands. So would your graces please listen patiently. *The beasts of the field shall bless me and the siren daughters of ostriches.* Why shall they bless me? Listen to what follows: *Since I will give water to the desert, and streams in the place where there was no water, that I may give my chosen race to drink.* Which chosen race? *My people which I have acquired for myself. It is not just now that I have called you, Jacob, nor did I make you that you should toil, Israel. What use to me sheep for holocausts?* (Is 43:20-23).

Come now, brothers and sisters. I don't know if there's anybody who would say to me, "I don't understand. You're saying what you like, you're interpreting it as you like." Just now I became a reader, not a debater. Think back to where we began, where he says, *There is no cause for you to be mindful of ancient things or to call old things to mind* (Is 43:18). This surely is evident, I mean, that God gave orders for these things to be done before for the sake of a particular sacrifice, foretelling the just blood that was to be shed, and adumbrating it in the similar form of animal victims. After all, what's he saying now? *What use to me sheep for holocausts? For you have not honored* [53] *me with sacrifices, indeed neither have you served me with your sacrifices. For it was not for this that I made you, that you should toil with incense*—in case someone might just possibly say that he had forbidden animal sacrifices, but permitted incense. *For it was not for this that I made you*, he says, *that you should toil with incense, or that you should trade incense for me with silver, nor have I craved the fat of your sacrifices* (Is 43:23-24).

Why God changed the covenant and the sacrifices

22. Are we to have the nerve to say to the Lord our God, "And why did you previously institute these things?" On this point too we are now seeking understanding, because through these sacrifices was to be found not the abolition but the attestation of sins. Yes, I know what I've said is obscure and in need of some clarification. But I'll put it briefly, because I've said so much already. If perhaps I'm not able to explain it fully because of shortage of time, the Lord will be at hand to enable me to do it some other time. Still, I'll put it like this: that people was so constituted that it had some wise persons in it, holy and just; it also had a fleshly minded crowd, ignorant of why these things were ordered, doing them rather than understanding them. But now he showed in a few words through this prophet why he ordered them.

After saying, *Nor have I craved the fat of your sacrifices*, and more to that effect, he straightaway added something, as though he were being asked why he ordered them at that time, and said, *But in your sins and iniquities you will stand before me* (Is 43:24). All these things, you see, were effective as bearing witness against sinners. What was the point of this, if not to put down the stiff neck of pride? What was the meaning of this, if not that the Christ was going to come with grace, erasing the charge sheet of sins,[54] and the Jews were going to say, "We, though, are just"? But what does the apostle say to them? *For all have sinned and are in need of the glory of God* (Rom 3:23).

"How," he says, "do you prove that we have sinned?"

The sacrifices you used to offer for sins[55] bear witness against you. This is what God says: *Nor have I craved the fat of your sacrifices, but in your sins and iniquities you will stand before me.* Thus the sacrifices which you used to offer were convicting, not purifying you. So now then let the guilty people, its pride smashed, confess its sickness, seek restoration to health, and say to itself, "So what am I to do? If my sins have not been purified by those sacrifices, how shall I be purified?"

A commendation of divine grace

23. Listen to what follows: *I am, I am the one who blots out your iniquities, that you may be justified* (Is 43:25.26). "I am, I am the one; it's not a bull, not a ram, not a goat, not any aromatic spices, not incense, but *I am, I am the one who blots out your iniquities, that you may be justified.*" How he did commend his grace! In case anyone should should start boasting about the merits of his works, or the abundance of his sacrificial victims, it wasn't enough for him to say *I am* just once, but he doubled it, to make a more vehement commendation: *I am, I am the one.* He himself is the doctor, the medico, he himself the medicine; the medico because he's the Word, the medicine because *the Word became flesh* (Jn 1:14). He himself the priest, himself the sacrifice. *I am, I am the one who blots out your iniquities, that you may be justified*, in case, because he says "I blot out your iniquities," you should be tempted to go on sinning all the time, his aim in blotting them out is *that you may be justified*, that is, that with your previous iniquities blotted out you may then proceed to live an upright life, in order to receive what he has promised.

How right it was that those magi too, the first-fruits of the nations, in whom, to the extent that *sin had abounded in them, grace abounded all the more* (Rom 5:20), should be warned by God *not to go back to Herod*, and that *they returned by another way* (Mt 2:12)! The one who then changed the way of the magi, he it is who also now changes the lives of the wicked. It is his manifestation in the flesh, which in Greek is called Epiphany, that the nations who have been justified in the Spirit[56] are all celebrating together in today's solemnity. Let us hope that our solemn celebration may refresh our memories, our piety may be invigorated by our devotion, charity may grow more fervent in our congregation, truth may shine on the ill-disposed.[57]

NOTES

1. Dolbeau infers 6 January 409 as the date of this sermon, by fairly exhaustive arguments, too complex to summarize here. Sermon 374 (III, l0) of this series represents a radical abbreviation of the sermon by the compilers of medieval lectionaries. Dolbeau compares the length of this sermon with the average length of all the Epiphany sermons published by the Maurists (of which 374 [III, 10] is typical), and as a result he fears that the others too are the remains of similar drastic mutilations, and that most of the complete originals are irretrievably lost—unless another such goldmine as the Stadtbibliotek in Mainz should be discovered.

2. This is how Sermon 374 begins; it proceeds immediately to the next extract from this sermon, Mainz 59, at the end of section 12.

3. Literally, to your morals, to your way of life, *moribus vestris.*

4. The familiar *in spe/in re* jingle.

5. See Acts 15:9.

6. An almost impossibly succinct expression: *quid tibi parat cui det.* It refers not only to what God is preparing for you, but also to how he is preparing you to be capable of being given it.

7. See Sermons 105A, 2; 142, 8 (III, 4).

8. See Gn 1:26-28.

9. See Sermon 213, 5 (III, 6).

10. Perhaps this should be rendered, "that . . . your promiser may have a successor," that is, may die, and his heir not feel bound by his promises. *Succedo* used impersonally and idiomtically, here in the passive, always according to Lewis & Short has the positive meaning of something good happening, something successful. Obviously that cannot be the case here, so it could here be used non-idiomatically to mean succeeded, superseded. But I suspect that in common African Latin speech its idiomatic use had come to mean just something happening to you, something befalling you, usually bad.

11. The Latin text just reads, "the one, finally, by whom we were made"; *ipsum denique a quo factus est* (the subject of *factus* being *homo*, earlier on in the sentence); the verb governing *ipsum* must then be *dignoscere*, "to distinguish." But I suspect, on comparing this text with a parallel passage from *Expositions of the Psalms* 36 (37), given by Dolbeau, that the word *desiderare* has dropped out, omitted by a common copyist's error, as it begins with the same syllable as the next word, *denique*. So I emend the text to *ipsum desiderare denique a quo factus est*.

12. The distinction in the Latin is between *loquendo* and *eloquendo*.

13. For this section see also Sermons 18, 1 (III, 1); 38, 2 (III, 2); 317, 1 (III, 9).

14. See Sermons 61, 2-3 (III, 3); 105A, 2 (III, 4).

15. Dolbeau suggests that this was a proverbial saying; see Sermons 41, 4 (III, 2); 306, 4 (III, 9); 359A, 6 (III, 10). Perhaps it should rather be called a comfortable cliché of the more affluent classes. See note 4 to Sermon 41.

16. *Omnes sectae praevaricationis et impietatis*; by the former sort, preaching deviant morals, he is likely to have had pagan philosophical schools in mind like those of the Epicureans and Cynics; by the latter, teaching ungodliness, impiety, Christian heresies.

17. See Sermon 313A, 3 (III, 9). Nearly all theatrical performances verged on the pornographic.

18. The reason is more immediately obvious in the Latin; lifeless, *exanimia*, bodies would answer that *animus* is better. The same thing is said in a rather different context in Sermon 88, 3 (III, 3).

19. For this whole theme see Sermons 52, 18; 65, 5 (III, 3); 126, 3 (III, 4); 241, 2 (III, 7).

20. That is, I think, the spirit that denies the existence of things which only the spirit can see. For a similar treatment of the theme of this section see Sermons 88, 5-7 (III, 3); 360B, 14 (III, 11).

21. That is, an *anima* animating me. It's a pity the English word "soul" lacks this connotation. For a similar treatment of the topic see Sermons 223A, 4 (III, 6); 198, 31 (III, 11).

22. The text behind this idea is one of his favorite quotations; Is 7:9, LXX: "Unless you believe, you shall not understand."

23. See Neh 8:6, where all the people answer "Amen" to Ezra's reading of the law.

24. He will explain at the beginning of section 12 what he means by "spoken miracles," or "miraculous words."

25. See Jn 2:1-11. For parallels to this topic see Sermons 126, 4 (III, 4); 242, 1; 247, 2 (III, 7).

26. Numbers, *numeri*, measures, *modi*, and finally appearances, *species*; there is an allusion here to another of Augustine's favorite texts, Wis 11:20: "You have arranged all things by measure and number and weight." See *The Trinity* III, 16 for a passage not unlike what we have here in the sermon; and XI, 17-18 for a more general reflection on these elusive concepts. Elsewhere, especially in *The Literal Meaning of Genesis*, he will call them *rationes seminales*, the seminal ideas with which God has "programmed" his creation.

27. Rather than Christ's own resurrection he has in mind here, I think, Christ raising the dead to life—Jairus' daughter, Mk 5:22-34; the son of the widow at Naim, Lk 7:11-15; and Lazarus, Jn 11:38-44.

28. See Mk 7:32-37; 8:22-26.

29. See Mt 2:1-12. Here, with slight variations, Sermon 374 (III, 10) resumes its extracts from this sermon, immediately after its opening sentence.

30. The paradox here, much more obvious to the ears of Latin speakers, is that *infans* means, literally, "not speaking," "speechless"; the Word of God is wordless!

31. See Lk 2:9-13.

32. See Mk 5:7.

33. Here I follow the same reading as is found in Sermon 374, (III, 10): *non iniquitas dominabatur*. The text here of Mz 59 has *non iniquitas damnabatur*, "and not iniquity that was being condemned," which in the context makes much less sense, but could easily have been the correction of a not very bright copyist—or simply a matter of misreading those tiresome abbreviations.

34. See Mt 2:11.

35. The text and punctuation in Sermon 374, (III, 10) differed here slightly, and yielded a rather different sense; in particular, the last phrase seemed to have the more natural meaning—"the greater the godlessness they were delivered from"—that is, their heathen religion and magical, astrological practices. But here he is suggesting that they were delivered, not *from* but *by* greater godlessness—namely that of Herod and the Jews directing them to their deliverer. This paradoxical idea is much more likely to be what Augustine was putting forward.

36. Reading *tanquam aemulum contremiscit*, instead of the text's *tanquam aemulus . . .* , "like a rival."

37. His most characteristic exclamation, *O magnum sacramentum!* The next sentence varies in several details from the text of Sermon 374, (III, 10).

38. Virgil, *Aeneid*, 6, lines 752-887, writing about Aeneas being guided through the realms of the dead, or more accurately of disembodied souls, by his late father, Anchises.

39. See Ps 110:4; Heb 7:11-12. For the Jews as witnesses see Sermons 5, 5 (III, 1); 200, 3; 201, 3 (III, 6); 373, 4 (III, 10).

40. That is, the sacrifice of Christ himself. See Sermon 275, 4 (III, 8).

41. Christian times, *Christiana tempora*, were what the pagans were constantly reproaching Christians with, saying, "Look what dreadful things keep on happening in Christian times"; and they would take up this taunt more vigorously than ever after the sack of Rome in 410, a few years after this sermon was preached. See *Saeculum*, by R.A. Markus (C.U.P, 1970; 2nd edition 1988), chapter 2, "*Tempora Christiana*, Augustine's historical experience."

42. For this whole medical analogy see also Sermons 80, 2 (III, 3); 175, 1 (III, 5); 286, 5 (III, 8); 340A, 5 (III, 9); 360B, 20 (III, 11).

43. Meaning the first Gentile Christians.

44. The Latin has *Bene te monuit*, "He has advised you well"; but as Dolbeau says, the passage can hardly be right. He suggests emending it to *Bene te movi*, "I have moved you well"; but that does not seem much better. I am suggesting *Bene te monuisti*, literally "You have advised yourself well."

45. I have amplified the Latin *magi* by adding this phrase, because the Latin word here has a general as well as a particular reference, meaning in fact "magicians," whereas in English this Latin word is restricted to these particular wise men from the east in Matthew's gospel. The exception, which proves the rule, is that we usually call the character who appears in Acts 8:9-11 Simon Magus.

46. The Latin with commendable brevity just has *disce*, "learn!"

47. A reference to the eucharist, under the "discipline of the secret." Those who don't understand, in the next two sentences, are the catechumens and other non-baptized persons present.

48. That is, baptism and confirmation, seen as one total sacrament of initiation, sacrament indeed of a most radical change.

49. If he really means what he says here (and perhaps he's just being modest), the thought occurs to me that it may indicate a somewhat earlier date for this sermon than 409. For the inescapable impression one gets from reading his sermons is that he did, fairly soon, come to know practically the whole of scripture by heart. But here what he is all the time insisting on is the authority of the divine writings, and so he really wants to read the text out from a volume in his hand.

50. See Col 2:17; 2 Cor 5:17; Heb 10:1. These are presumably some of the texts he has in mind in the next section, when he says he relies on the apostle to be his expositor of prophecies.

51. See Col 2:14; 1 Cor 5:7-8.

52. The sirens were the mythical birds, with women's faces, who sang beautifully on either side of the straits of Messina, luring sailors to destruction either on the rocks of Scylla or in the whirlpool

of Charybdis; see Homer's *Odyssey* 12, line 39. The daughters of ostriches here in the Latin are *filiae passerum*, and *passer* normally means a sparrow—which is surely ridiculous. But a *passer marinus* was Plautus' phrase for an ostrich, presumably because ostriches in Rome were imported from overseas, from Africa, and the Greek Septuagint here has *struthon*, "of ostriches." But this Greek word too primarily means "sparrow," and is applied to the ostrich either with the adjective "big," or else in the compound *strutho-kamelos*, "camel bird." So the African Latin translator was within his rights, translating with *passerum*. He certainly wouldn't add the word *marinorum*, as they didn't reach his part of the world from overseas.

53. Reading *non honorasti*, instead of the text's *non ornasti*, "you have not adorned." This emendation is tentatively suggested by Dolbeau.

54. See Col 2:14.

55. See, for example, Lv 5—7.

56. See 1 Tm 3:16; 1 Cor 6:11.

57. The sermon ends with a very forced piece of rhetoric—four phrases ending respectively with the words *solemnitas*, *pietas*, *caritas* and *veritas*, rather reminiscent of Augustine in his earlier days. Perhaps another slight indication that the sermon was preached possibly ten years or more before 409. See note 49 above.

INDEX OF SCRIPTURE

(prepared by Michael T. Dolan)

(The numbers after the scriptural reference refer to the particular sermon and its section)

Old Testament

Genesis

1:3-31	110A, 5
1:24	198, 19
1:26	159B, 5; 159B, 6; 198, 26
1:26-28	90A, 6
1:31	72, 18; 359B, 7
2:2	110A, 5
2:9	359B, 7
2:17	341, 13; 359B, 7
2:24	159A, 9; 341, 20; 341, 22
3:3	359B, 7
3:4	341, 13
3:19	360B, 7
6:11-7:23	114B, 1
12:3	114B, 6
14:18-19	198, 38
22:18	114B, 6; 159B, 16; 299A, 9; 360A, 2; 360A, 4
25:23	341, 23
27:29	341, 23
30:37	341, 25
49:9	218, 12

Exodus

3:14	162C, 6
3:14-16	341, 17
20:12	159A, 6
20:13-17	159B, 14
20:17	130A, 11; 283, 2
21:24	110A, 8
22:20	359B, 14
23:23-24	360A, 11
34:11-14	360A, 11

Leviticus

24:20	110A, 8

Deuteronomy

5:16	159A, 6
6:13	159A, 8; 198, 46
6:16	159A, 8
8:3	159A, 8
10:20	198, 46
13:3	341, 7
25:4	29, 9
32:9	341, 23
33:9	159A, 6

Judges

6:38	360A, 3
6:39	360A, 3

1 Samuel

21:6	198, 50

Tobit

4:15	130A, 7
12:12	198, 48

Job

1:21	114B, 11

Psalms

1:1	198, 43
2:6	218, 5
2:7-8	218, 6
3:9	20B, 9
4:2	72, 18
4:3	72, 12; 198, 8
4:4	72, 8
4:5-6	72, 10
4:6	72, 9; 72, 16
4:7	72, 12

Luke

John

Acts of the Apostles

INDEX

(prepared by Joseph Sprug)

A

Aaron, 198:50; 374:19
abandonment: fear of, 130A:5,7
Abel, 341:19
Abraham, 114B:6; 130A:10; 218:7;
    360A:3,4
    Christ revealed to, 198:32
    In your seed. . . , 159B:16
    parable of Lazarus, 142(appendix):3
accidents:
    temptations (Pelagian view)), 348A:11
actions:
    words and, 306E:11
Adam and Eve, 114B:12; 198:38,43
    disobedience learned from, 359B:8
    do not touch . . . test of obedience,
        359B:7
    earthly; heavenly, 159B:2
    Eve and the serpent, 341:12
    Eve as serpent's agent, 159A:7
    Eve fashioned from side of Adam,
        218:14
    Eve's creation (terminology), 162C:6
    fleshly desire, 360B:4
    tempted, 159A:7
adoption (theology), 162C:6
    children of God, 341:18
    deification of man, 23B:2
    redemption of our bodies, 198:44
adultery, 90A:13; 283:7
    conjugal rights, 354A:6
affection, 159A:2,7,13
    fast hold on humans, 198:62
    if anyone does not hate . . . ,
        159A:2,6,7,13
    limit the claims of, 159A:13
affliction:
    close, 159A:4
    deliverance from, 306E:10

prayer for relief from, 20B:9
    sin and, 306E:1
aging: passing of time, 360B:5
air: 374:2
    Juno, 198:21,22
    parts, 341:8
    ruler of the power of, 198:26
    transcended, 198:27
    vain powers, 198:37,62
airy spirits, 198:38
almsgiving, 198:56; 360B:21
    fasting and prayer, 198:8
    good luck presents and, 198:2,4
Amen (the word), 348A:13
amputation, 159A:7
angels, 90A:5; 110A:6; 130A:3,10;
    142(appendix):3; 162C:15;
    198:24,25,44; 293A:12; 306E:8;
    341:5,14,19
    abiding in the South (Apocalypse),
        198:14,16,46
    association with, 23B:9
    birth of Christ, 374:13
    Christ tempted by devil, 159A:8
    demanding special worship, 198:48
    fellow slave, 198:16
    godliness and, 360B:21
    holy, as sons, 198:15
    humans will become like, 159B:15
    imitating the life of, 360B:21
    intellectual life, 198:26
    messengers; attendants, 198:48
    models for humble, or proud, people,
        198:15
    right way of honoring, 198:46
    see what man does not see, 360B:15
    singing Alleluia, 159B:15
    veneration of, 198:47
    wish God to be loved, not selves,
        359B:16

devotion; burning, 198:7
earth yielding its fruit, 130A:8
expanded by charity, 360C:1
fear and love in, 360B:1,11
fire of love, 198:8
grown cold, 198:27
haughty rich, 114B:12
highest good found in, 72:13
humble, 198:33
iniquity in eye of, 360B:17
Jesus: gentle and humble . . . ,
142(appendix):4
lift up your hearts, 159B:18
lifted up, 110A:6
purification of, 360B:13,15,19,27
raised, 299A:5
sacrifice, 114B:2
silence as voice of, 341:16
temple of prayer, 198:11
unclean desires of, 198:33,34
weighed down, 198:9
where God's spirit rests, 198:11
heaven, 110A:6; 198:26,53; 283:1
See also eternal life
come, you blessed of my Father . . . ,
341:6
drunks and heretics in the kingdom,
293A:16
eye of a needle . . . , 114B:9-10; 341:3
heavenly bodies, 360B:8
people written in, 360A:10
reward must be worked for on earth,
374:3
rich people entering, 114B:9-10;
341:3
shut against the proud and greedy,
114B:11
suffering in, 341:20
throne, 360B:7
Hebrew language, 218:6
hell, 283:1
Hera (Juno), 198:21
heresy:
foretold, 360B:21,22
persistence in, 293A:16
Son is less than the Father, 341:13
spreads, when ignored, 348A:8
heretics, 198:15
entering heaven, 293A:16
savaging the sheep, 299A:3
seeing, they fail to believe, 360A:5
universal Church and, 299A:9
Herod, King, 110A:2,3; 374:14

Hippo, 348A:7; 360C:2
Hippocrates, 360B:17
hired servants (in Church), 198:12
holiness, 359B:5
grace from God, 162C:1
loving God's glory, 198:15
holy of holies, 198:53
Holy Spirit, 94A:4,5; 110A:7; 360B:18
bishops; obedience, 359B:12
buying, for money (Simon), 198:15
canonical scriptures, 162C:15
council at Jerusalem, 162C:9
desires hearts of lovers, 341:7
figure: seven loaves, 198:51
human discernment; judging, 23B:6
love poured into our hearts,
130A:8,11; 283:2
received from God, 283:8
rod of the plane tree (Jacob's), 341:25
seven operations (gifts) of, 198:51
Spirit gives life; letter kills, 283:2
home country, 198:59,61
honor, 159A:4
private, personal honor (pride),
198:46
risk to the one doing the honors,
198:15
Honorius, Emperor, 360B:26
hope, 72:9,10,11; 198:53; 283:5; 348A:4;
360A:3,9
belief and, 130A:3
Donatists, 198:45
dwelling singly in, 72:16,18
Gentile vs Christian, 198:3,4
God's promises, 159B:16
goodness, 94A:5
humility; hope in God, 198:44
last days, 114B:14
misplaced; danger, 94A:7
perishing out of, 94A:6
riches, 114B:12
salvation, 360B:16
sentiment of the soul, 198:2
strength and firmness of purpose,
159A:12
wrong way, 94A:9
hospitality:
sharing Christ's suffering, 28A:4
human acts:
we too have a part to do, 348A:14
human beings (humans; humankind):
See also image of God
angels to be, 159B:15